Women and Justice

It's a Crime

Fifth Edition

❖

ROSLYN MURASKIN
Long Island University

Prentice Hall

Boston   Columbus   Indianapolis   New York   San Francisco   Upper Saddle River
Amsterdam   Cape Town   Dubai   London   Madrid   Milan   Munich   Paris   Montreal   Toronto
Delhi   Mexico City   São Paulo   Sydney   Hong Kong   Seoul   Singapore   Taipei   Tokyo

Editorial Director: Vernon Anthony
Senior Acquisitions Editor: Eric Krassow
Editorial Assistant: Lynda Cramer
Media Project Manager: Karen Bretz
Director of Marketing: David Gesell
Marketing Manager: Adam Kloza
Senior Marketing Coordinator: Alicia Wozniak
Production Manager: Laura Messerly
Creative Director: Jayne Conte
Cover Design: Suzanne Duda
Cover Illustration/Photo: Fotolia
Full-Service Project Management/Composition: Chitra Ganesan/PreMediaGlobal
Printer/Binder: R. R. Donnelley & Sons

Library of Congress Cataloging-in-Publication Data
Women and Justice: It's a Crime / [edited by] Roslyn Muraskin. — 5th ed.
    p. cm.
Includes bibliographical references and index.
ISBN-13: 978-0-13-512089-7 (alk. paper)
ISBN-10: 0-13-512089-6 (alk. paper)
1. Female offenders. 2. Women criminal justice personnel. I. Muraskin, Roslyn.
HV6046.I86 2011
364.3'740973—dc22

                                        2010042143

10 9 8 7 6 5 4 3 2 1

Dedication

This fifth edition is dedicated to those persons who continue to persevere to bring equality to all, regardless of race, gender, or creed.

And this fifth edition is dedicated as well to my six grandchildren, Lindsay, Nickia, Benjamin, Zachary, Sloane, and Sydney, the delight of our lives, with the hope that they will follow my compassion to ensuring that there be equality for all persons.

And a special dedication to my husband, Matthew, who has always been there with an encouraging word and understanding as he shares me with my love for writing and researching.

A special THANK YOU to all the contributors for their dedication in making the fifth edition of *Women and Justice: It's a Crime* a work of love.

—*Roslyn Muraskin*

Prentice Hall
is an imprint of

www.pearsonhighered.com

ISBN 10: 0-135-12089-6
ISBN 13: 978-0-135-12089-7

Contents

❖

Contents

Preface

--- ❖ ---

This is the fifth edition of *Women and Justice: It's a Crime*—an all-inclusive work on the issues of women and justice. "Never doubt that a small group of thoughtful, committed citizens can change the world. Indeed, it's the only thing that ever has" (Margaret Mead). Over these many generations, dramatic social and legal changes have been accomplished on behalf of women's equality. Women have made these changes happen. They have not been passive, but rather have worked together to make such changes, to create a better world where there are few constrictions. When America gained a new democracy, women had yet to gain the freedom they deserved as human beings. There continue to be women throughout today's world in the twenty-first century who strive for their own betterment and the betterment of society.

We are told that, a decade into the twenty-first century, for every dollar a man makes, a woman makes seventy-seven cents. Have we reached the time when women can be considered the equals of men?

The words of the late Reverend Martin Luther King sums it up well:

We ain't what we oughta be
We ain't what we wanta be
We ain't what we gonna be
But thank God, we ain't what we was.

When we talk about women, we need to understand that women's rights are human rights.

Many "experts" are out there who have spoken about women and what they were put on earth for. It was Napoleon Bonaparte who indicated that "nature intended women to be our slaves. They are our property, we are not theirs. They belong to us just as a tree belongs to a gardener. What a mad idea to demand equality for women! Women are nothing but machines for producing children." Lord Alfred Tennyson stated: "Man for the field, and woman for the hearth. Man for the sword and for the needle she. Man with the head and woman with the heart. Man to command and woman to obey. All else confusion." Sexist thinking has been embedded in the English language. As an example do the words *handyman*, *foreman*, or *freshman* preclude women? Today, we think not.

According to Catherine MacKinnon, "equality in human societies is commonly affirmed but rarely practiced. As a principle, it can be fiercely loved, passionately sought, highly vaunted, sentimentally assumed, complacently taken for granted, and legally guaranteed. Its open detractors are few. Yet despite general consensus on equality as a value, no society is organized on equality principles. Few lives are lived in equality, even in democracies. . . . social equality is hard to find anywhere" (2001, p. 2).

At the Seneca Falls Conference in 1848, women gathered together to declare that "we hold these truths to be self-evident that all *men and women* [emphasis mine] are created equal." In the *Declaration of Sentiments*, Elizabeth Stanton pointed out that the "history of mankind is a history of repeated injuries and usurpations on the part of men toward women, having in direct object the establishment of an absolute tyranny over her. To prove this, let facts be submitted to a candid world." It went into specifics:

- Married women were legally dead in the eyes of the law.
- Women were not allowed to vote.
- Women had to submit to laws when they had no voice in their formation.
- Married women had no property rights.
- Husbands had legal power over and responsibility for their wives to the extent that they could imprison or beat them with impunity.
- Divorce and child custody laws favored men.
- Women had to pay property taxes although they had no representation in the levying of these taxes.
- Most occupations were closed to women; even when did women gain entry, they were paid only a fraction of what men earned.
- Women were not allowed to enter professions such as medicine or law.
- Women had no means to gain an education since no college or university would accept women students.
- With only a few exceptions, women were not allowed to participate in church affairs.
- Women were robbed of their self-confidence and self-respect and were made to feel totally dependent on men.

These were strong words. This was the status quo for women in the United States in 1848. In the words of Elizabeth Stanton: "Now in view of this entire disenfranchisement of one-half the people in this country, their social and religious degradation—in view of the unjust laws . . . and because women feel themselves aggrieved, oppressed and fraudulently deprived of their most sacred rights, we insist that they have immediate admission to the rights and privileges which belong to them as citizens of these United States." That was then. The movement produced few results. Women did not receive the right to vote until the passage of the Nineteenth Amendment to the Constitution early in the twentieth century.

"Equal legal treatment for women, in their capacity as members of their gender, was not originally envisioned under either section of the Fourteenth Amendment. The ratification debates in Congress to the extent they considered women as such centered on whether the Amendment would mandate women's suffrage" (MacKinnon, p. 15).

It was not until the early 1970s that the case of *Reed v. Reed*, 404 U.S. 71 (1971), which guarantees equal protection, would be interpreted to stop different rights for different genders. In the words of Supreme Court Justice Ruth Bader Ginsburg: "I think about how much we owe to the women who went before us—legions of women, some known but many unknown. I applaud the bravery and resilience of those who helped all of us—you and me—to be here today" (1998).

The potential for progress in the realm of women's issues and the criminal justice system is possible because of the unremitting battles that women have continued to fight in striving for something called *equality* or *parity of treatment.* The legal history of women indicates that gender should not be a factor in determining the legal rights of women and men. Dating back to 1776, when the United States was being formed and laws were being written by men, it was Abigail Adams, in a letter to her husband, John, who insisted that if in the new American Constitution "care and attention are not paid to the ladies," they will foment a revolution. Women been fomenting that rebellion ever since. The reader of this work will find that the struggle is yet to be won, even though women may have a voice and are being heard, though they were not always listened to.

This new edition is an up-to-date text on those issues still out there. We present the history, the theories, the issues concerning women and the law, women who are victims of violence, women and their health problems within the criminal justice system, issues of gender and race, women and prison issues, and women in criminal justice professions—but we go deeper than before. We show systemic gendered racism and the role of parenting for women who are incarcerated, we try to understand why women kill their children, we look at trafficking in women, we look at women incarcerated and "hear" their voices, and most importantly we look at the challenges of a new century already finishing its first decade. The material and topics provide the best there is, as they concern the gender-based problems facing us in the twenty-first century.

The chapters in this work continue to be written by the *who's who of scholars in justice issues and women.* Traditional literature continues to ignore the role of women in criminal justice. There are those who still deprecate and/or ignore a woman's point of view entirely. For women, public denigration is not socially acceptable. Personal attacks should be a thing of the past, but are they?

"Sex equality as a principle has become firmly, if incompletely, entrenched in U.S. constitutional jurisprudence. At the same time, the solidity, meaning, vitality, and reach of sex equality as a constitutional principle are far from settled, its direction far from certain, its development far from over" (MacKinnon, p. 16).

Today, women and girls live the legacy of women's rights. It continues to be my fervent hope that this work will result in more meaningful and thought-provoking dialogue concerning the major tribulations women face in the criminal justice system. Indeed, *it's a crime,* if we do not realize the significance of the role that women play. Basic human rights are fundamental to all, women and men alike. Women are simply persons as much as men are. The new material is presented in this text—hopefully, you will make it come alive.

Roslyn Muraskin
Long Island University

REFERENCE

MACKINNON, C. A. (2001). *Sex equality*. New York: Foundation Press.

Acknowledgments

Tremendous thanks to all the contributors to the fifth edition of *Women and Justice: It's a Crime*. This is a work of love and a work dedicated to all women who throughout history have made it happen. All of us know that women are deserving of the same rights as all men and are now considered persons. The fact that this is a topic studied in most colleges and universities as part of the curriculum is a tribute to how far women have come in being identified as worthy of study.

All the contributors have dedicated a great deal of time and research in writing their chapters, and it shows. And the people at Prentice Hall are to be complimented for allowing this work to go into its fifth edition, a work that is read throughout the United States and beyond, giving us a clearer understanding of all that women have had to go through to reach the point of recognition, if not equality.

To Eric Krassow, Lynda Cramer, and Jessica Sykes, as always it is a pleasure to work with you and to know that you are always there when needed. And to Tiffany Bitzel and Chitra Ganesan, new to the team but a delight to know and work with, a big thank you.

And of course I cannot leave out the C.W. Post Campus of Long Island University, where I have worked for close to 30 years (it seems like only yesterday), and to have their continued support and encouragement as I continue to write and research. They are to be continuously commended for their continued support.

Thank you as well to all my students and to all students of women and justice. They have come to understand the plight of women and how important it is to study this topic and to appreciate all that women have had to go through to get where they are today.

And to my husband, Matthew, thank you for tolerating my busy evenings and weekends as I continue to write and work. Without his understanding, I could not do this. Love always.

Roslyn Muraskin

Contributors

---　❖　---

Alana Van Gundy, Ph.D., is an assistant professor as well as criminal justice program coordinator at Miami University, Hamilton.

Amanda Redd is at Hampton University in Virginia.

Ann Janette Alejano Steele, Ph.D., is a professor in the departments of women's studies and Psychology at Metropolitan State College of Denver.

Barbara H. Zaitzow, Ph.D., is a faculty member in the Department of Political Science and Criminal Justice at Appalachian State University.

Brenda Geiger, Ph.D., is a senior lecturer of educational psychology at the Western Galilee Academic College of Bar Ilan University.

Brittany Kirkland is at Hampton University in Virginia.

Cara Rabe-Hemp, Ph.D., is a faculty member at Illinois State University.

Cheryl L. Meyer, Ph.D., J.D., is a faculty member at Wright State University in the School of Professional Psychology.

Christine E. Rasche, Ph.D., is professor emeritus at the University of North Florida.

Cindy E. Weisbart, *with Cheryl, Chapter 7.*

Corina Schulze is a faculty member at the University of Alabama.

Courtney A. Waid, Ph.D., is in the Department of Criminal Justice and Political Science at North Dakota State University.

David Baker, Ph.D., J.D., is an associate professor of sociology in the Behavioral Sciences Department at Riverside Community College.

Erika Duncan, director and founder of Herstory, a Woman's Writers Workshop.

Etta Morgan, Ph.D., is the interim coordinator of criminal justice and an associate professor of criminal justice and sociology at Jackson State University.

Helen Eigenberg, Ph.D., is a professor of criminal justice at the University of Tennessee at Chattanooga.

Hoan N. Bui, Ph.D., is a faculty member at the University of Tennessee, Department of Sociology.

Janice Joseph, Ph.D., is a professor of criminal justice at the Richard Stockton College of Criminal Justice.

Jennifer McMahon-Howard is in the Department of Sociology and Criminal Justice at Kennesaw State University.

Jody Clay-Warner, Ph.D., is an associate professor of sociology at the University of Georgia.

Jonathan C. Odo is an associate professor of criminal justice at the University of Maryland Eastern Shore.

Katie James is in the Department of Sociology at the University of Georgia.

Kdari Taylor-Watson is at Hampton University in Virginia.

Kim M. Lersch, Ph.D., is an associate professor in the Department of Criminology at the University of South Florida Polytechnic.

Lanette Dalley, Ph.D., is a faculty member at the Indiana University of Pennsylvania.

Laura Moriarty, Ph.D., is an associate professor in the Department of Criminal Justice and assistant dean of the College of Humanities and Sciences at Virginia Commonwealth University.

Liying Li, Ph.D., is chair and professor in the Department of Criminal Justice and Criminology at Metropolitan State College of Denver.

Mark M. Lanier, Ph.D., is professor and chair of criminal justice at the University of Alabama.

Martin L. O'Connor, J.D., is an associate professor of criminal justice at the C.W. Post Campus of Long Island University, Department of Criminal Justice.

Mary Ellen Hughes is a behavioral health specialist II.

Michael Fischer, Ph.D., is an associate professor of criminal justice in the Applied Sociology Program at Norfolk State University.

Mona J. E. Danner, Ph.D., is an associate professor of sociology and criminal justice at Old Dominion University.

Peter C. Ezekwenna is an assistant professor in the Department of Mathematics and Computer Science at the University of Maryland Eastern Shore.

Ramona Brockett

Rhonda R. Dobbs, Ph.D., is in the Department of Criminology and Criminal Justice at the University of Texas at Arlington.

Rosemary Guido, Ph.D., is an associate professor of criminology at the Indiana University of Pennsylvania.

Stacey L. Shipley, Psy.D., is the chief forensic psychologist at the Social Learning Rehabilitation and Extended Treatment Program at North Texas State Hospital.

Stacy L. Mallicoat, Ph.D., is an associate professor in the Division of Politics, Administration of Justice at California State University, Fullerton.

Suzanne Faries Lowe, *with Laura, Chapter 18.*

Tara C. Proano-Raps, Ph.D., *with Cheryl, Chapter 6.*

Tara O'Connor Shelly, Ph.D., is at the Center for the Study of Crime and Justice at Colorado State University.

Thomas Bazley, Ph.D., is a faculty member at the University of South Florida.

Thozama Mandisa Lutya, M.S., has done gender studies and lectures undergraduate and postgraduate degree courses in the Criminology Programme of the Department of Social Work and Criminology at the University of Pretoria.

Tiffany Hampton

Venezia Michalesen, *Chapter 4.*

Whytnee Foriest is at Hampton University at Virginia.

Zina T. McGee, Ph.D., is an endowed university professor of sociology at Hampton University, Virginia, where she also serves as codirector of the Behavioral Science Research Center.

SECTION I

Historical Development
of Women's Issues

1

"Ain't I a Woman?"

Roslyn Muraskin

❖

What is a woman? This is a question that has been asked over the many decades since the founding of this country. Women were never considered bright; rather they were emotional beings who were not logical. According to Schopenhauer, "[woman is] in every respect backward, lacking in reason and true morality . . . a kind of middle step between the child and the man who is the true human being."

We are well into the second decade of the twenty-first century. Over the past several hundred years, women have struggled for equality—struggling to make changes occur. Today, we are still advocating change. Change in the criminal justice system is part of the change needed. What is equality? No society exists that can actually boast about the principles of equality being present. According to Catherine MacKinnon, "the second-class status of women as a group is widely documented to be socially and legally instituitionalized, cumulatively and systematically shaping access to life chances on the basis of sex" (2001, p. 2). Using the words of Richard Rorty, a philosopher, a woman "is not yet the name of the way of being human" (MacKinnon, p. 3).[1]

Controversy still abounds even in the twenty-first century. Although women are involved in professions where once they were not allowed, the classification by gender, although slowly eroding, still does not give equality where equality is due. The women's movement has been the most integrated and populist force in the United States. More than 200 years have passed since the Declaration of Independence declared that *all men are equal* (emphasis mine). We still wait for the day when both women and men will be defined as persons; then equality will abound for all.

Justice David Bower stated in 1908 that "the two sexes differ in the structure of the body, in the functions to be performed by each, in the amount of physical strength, in the capacity for long continuing labor. . . . " The physical structure of women and their ability to be mothers, and mothers only, as was always thought to be the case, had positioned them at such a disadvantage that any and all decisions of legislators were focused on *their* protection (Kerhber & De Hart, 2004, pp. 8–9).

Sojourner Truth gave her famous "Ain't I a Woman" speech at the Women's Rights Convention in 1815 in Akron, Ohio. Sojourner Truth, a Negro slave, stood at the podium and began to talk: "Well, children, where there is so much racket, there must be something out of kilter, I think between the Negroes of the South and the women of the North—all talking about rights—the white men will be in a fix pretty soon. But what's all this talking about?"

At this point Sojourner pointed to one of the ministers and stated: "That man over there says that women need to be helped into carriages, and lifted over ditches, and to have the best place everywhere. Nobody helps me any best place. And ain't I a woman?" She then raised herself to her full height, about six feet tall, and stated: "Look at me! Look at my arm. I have plowed, I have planted and I have gathered into barns. And no man could head me. And ain't I a woman? I could work as much, and eat as much as a man—when I could get it—and bear the lashes as well! And ain't I a woman? I have borne children and seen most of them sold into slavery, and when I cried out with a mother's grief, none but Jesus heard me. And ain't I a woman?"

The women in the audience cheered. Sojourner then pointed to another minister and stated: "He talks about this thing in his head. What's that they call it?" "Intellect," some women whispered. "That's it, honey. What's intellect got to do with a woman's rights or black folks' rights? If my cup won't hold but a pint and yours holds a quart, wouldn't you be mean not to let me have my little half-measure full? That little man in black there! He says women can't have as much rights as men. 'Cause Christ wasn't a woman.' "

At this point she stood with outstretched arms and with eyes lit like fire: "Where did your Christ come from? From God and a Woman! Man had nothing to do with Him!" It is believed that there was deafening applause at that moment. "If the first woman God ever made was strong enough to turn the world upside down all alone, these women together ought to be able to turn it back and get it right-side up again. And now that they are asking to do it men better let them."

HISTORICAL OVERVIEW

Women's search for equality is not a recent phenomenon. Earlier, in 1776, Abigail Adams admonished her husband, John, to "remember the ladies" in the drafting of the Constitution. She insisted that

> in the new code of laws which I suppose it will be necessary for you to make, I desire you would remember the ladies and be more generous and favorable to them than your ancestors. Do not put such unlimited power into the hands of the husbands. Remember, all men would be tyrants, if they could. If particular care and attention is not paid to the ladies, we are determined to foment a rebellion, and will not hold ourselves bound by any laws in which we have no voice or representation.

Adams replied to his wife:

> As to your extraordinary code of laws, I cannot but laugh. We have been told that our struggle
> has loosened the bonds of government everywhere; that children and apprentices were dis-
> obedient; that schools and colleges were grown turbulent; that Indians slighted their guardians
> and Negroes grew insolent to their masters. But your letter was the first intimation that an-
> other tribe, more numerous and powerful than all the rest, were grown discontented.

The wife, Abigail, responded:

> I cannot say that I think you are very generous to the ladies; for, whilst you are proclaiming
> power and good-will to men, emancipating all nations, you insist upon retaining an absolute
> power over wives. But you must remember that arbitrary power is like most other things
> which are very hard, very liable to be broken; and not withstanding all your wise laws and
> maxims, we have it in our power, not only to free ourselves, but to subdue our masters, and,
> without violence, throw both your natural and legal authority at our feet.

 Nowhere in the Constitution of the United States is the word *woman* used. The battle had
begun.

The Declaration of Independence as signed in 1776 stated that all men are created
equal and that the government derives its power from the consent of the governed. Women
were not included in either concept. The only time the word *sex* is referred to is in the Nineteenth Amendment to the Constitution, signed in 1920, giving women the right to vote.

The original American Constitution of 1787 was founded on English law; it did not
recognize women as citizens or as individuals with legal rights. A woman was expected to
obey her husband or nearest male kin, and the power of the ballot had been denied to her.
Women were not considered persons under the Fourteenth Amendment to the Constitution, which guaranteed that no state shall deny to "any person within its jurisdiction the
equal protection of the laws." Women have historically been victimized by policies
designed to protect them (Muraskin & Alleman, 1993).

SENECA FALLS

Constitutionally, no obligation existed for the government to provide any benefits beyond
women's basic requirements. In 1848, a convention was held in Seneca Falls, New York,
to mark the beginnings of the first organized feminist movement of the nineteenth century.
The convention, attended by nearly 300 women, demonstrated a collective effort to
achieve equal rights for women. Their focus was property and suffrage. They went so far
as to adopt their own Declaration of Independence:

> We hold these truths to be self-evident; that all men and women are created equal; that they
> are endowed by their creator with certain inalienable rights; that among these are life, liberty
> and the pursuit of happiness; that to secure these rights governments are instituted, deriving
> their just powers from the consent of the governed. Whenever any form of government be-
> comes destructive of these ends, it is the right of those who suffer from it to refuse allegiance
> to it, and to insist upon the institution of new government. . . . The history of mankind is a
> history of repeated injuries and usurpation on the part of men toward women, having in direct

object the establishment of an absolute tyranny over her. To prove this let the facts be submitted to a candid world.

> He has never permitted her to exercise her inalienable right to the elective franchise.
>
> He has compelled her to submit to laws in the formation of which she has no voice.
>
> He has withheld from her rights which are given to the most ignorant and degraded men—both natives and foreigners.
>
> Having deprived her of this first right of a citizen, the elective franchise, thereby leaving her without representation in the halls of legislation, he has oppressed her on all sides.
>
> He has made her, if married, in the eyes of the law civilly dead.
>
> He has taken from her all rights in property, even to the wages she earns.
>
> He has made her, morally, an irresponsible being, as she can commit crimes with impunity, provided they be done in the presence of her husband, he becoming to all intents and purposes, her master—the law giving him power to deprive her of her liberty, and to administer chastisement.
>
> After depriving her of all rights as a married woman, if single, and the owner of property, he has taxed her to support a government which recognizes her only when her property can be made profitable to it.
>
> He has denied her the facilities for obtaining a thorough education, all colleges being closed against her.
>
> He allows her in church, as well as State, but in a subordinate position.
>
> He has endeavored, in every way that he could, to destroy her confidence in her own powers to lessen her self-respect, and make her willing to lead a dependent and abject life. (Schneir, 1972, pp. 77–82)

So 300 women declared. They therefore resolved the following at Seneca Falls:

> That all laws which prevent women from occupying such a station in society as her conscience shall dictate, or which place her in a position to that of men, are contrary to the great precept of nature, and therefore of no force or authority.
>
> That the women of this country ought to be enlightened in regard to laws under which they live, that they may no longer publish their degradation by declaring themselves satisfied with their present position. . . .
>
> That the same amount of virtue, delicacy, and refinement of behavior that is required of women in the social state, should be required of men, and the same transgression should be visited with equal severity on both man and woman. . . .

And that it be further resolved "[t]hat the speedy success of our cause depends upon the zealous and untiring efforts of both men and women, for the overthrow of the monopoly of the pulpit, and for the security to women an equal participation with men in the various trades, professions, and commerce" (Schneir, 1972).

THE LEGAL SYSTEM

According to Catherine MacKinnon (2001), "[e]quality in human societies is commonly affirmed but rarely practiced. As a principle, it can be fiercely loved, passionately sought, highly vaunted, sentimentally assumed, complacently taken for granted, and legally guaranteed. Its open detractors are few. Yet despite general consensus on equality as a value, no society is organized on equality principles. Few lives are lived in equality, even in democracies" (p. 2).

Seneca Falls took place in 1848. The property rights of U.S. women in the nineteenth century as truly reflected in the declaration at Seneca Falls were set forth earlier by the legal scholar Blackstone, who wrote that by marriage, the husband and wife are one person in law. The very being of all women at this time was suspended during marriage. Laws were passed that gave the husband the right to give his wife "moderate correction"; he could hit her to restrain her but with nothing wider than his thumb.

A federal equal rights amendment was first introduced to Congress in 1923 and was submitted to the states continuously over a period of time for ratification until it finally failed in 1972. Stated simply:

- *Section 1*. Equality of rights under the law shall not be denied or abridged by the United States or by any other State on account of sex.
- *Section 2*. The Congress shall have the power to enforce, by appropriate legislation, the provisions of this Article.
- *Section 3*. This Amendment shall take effect two years after the date of ratification.

It never happened.

Jean-Jacques Rousseau, an eighteenth-century French philosopher, wrote in his work *Émile*:

> Men and women are made for each other then, but their mutual dependence is not equal. . . . We could survive without them better than they could without us. . . . Thus women's entire education should be planned in relation to men. To please men, to be useful to them, to win their love and respect, to raise them as children, care for them as adults, counsel and console them, make their lives sweet and pleasant; these are women's duties in all ages and these are what they should be taught from childhood. (Deckard, 1979, p. 217)

Oberlin College was the first college to admit women, in 1833. Until 1841, women could take only a shortened literary course, on the theory that the education of women had a different purpose from that of men. For many years women were not permitted to speak in class and were required to wait on male students. It was believed that women's highest calling was to be the mothers of the race and that they should stay within that special sphere in order that future generations should not suffer from want of devoted and undistracted mother care. If women were to enter the areas of law, religion, medicine, academics, government, or any sort of public character, the home would suffer from neglect. Washing men's clothes, caring for their rooms, serving the men at dining tables, and remaining respectfully silent in public assemblages, the Oberlin coeds were being prepared for motherhood and to serve their men.

Elizabeth Blackwell was the first woman in the United States to get a medical degree, in 1849. She applied to 29 medical schools until one finally accepted her. She had to fight for the right to be present at the dissection of human organs, part of the training for any doctor.

In 1873, the U.S. Supreme Court upheld an Illinois state law prohibiting female lawyers from practicing in state courts (*Bradwell v. Illinois*, 1872). The Court in its *wisdom* (emphasis mine) noted that

> the civil war as well as nature herself, has always recognized a wide difference in the respective spheres and destinies of man and woman. Man is or should be women's protector and

defender. The natural and proper timidity and delicacy which belong to the female sex evidently unfits it for many of the occupations of civil life. The constitution of the family organization, which is founded in the divine ordinance, as well as in the nature of things indicates the domestic sphere as that which belongs to the domain and functions of womanhood. The harmony of interests and views which belong or should belong to the family institutions, is repugnant to the idea of a woman adopting a distinct and independent career from that of her husband.

The Court continued by declaring that "[t]he paramount destiny and mission of woman are to fulfill the noble and benign offices of wife and mother. This is the law of the Creator. And the rules of civil society must be adopted to the general constitution of things, and cannot be based upon exception cases."

Justice Miller summed it up when he stated: "I am not prepared to say that it is one of her fundamental rights and privileges to be admitted into every office and position, including those which require highly special qualifications and demanding social responsibilities. In the nature of things it is not every citizen of every age, sex, and condition that is qualified for every calling and position." This decision demonstrated that law reflected society as it was meant to be since the founding of the United States.

It took until 1860 in New York to pass the Married Women's Property Act, an attempt to give to women property that she owned as her sole and private property. Until this time a married woman was not entitled to own or keep property after marriage. This act stated "that which a woman married in this state owns at the time of her marriage, and the rents, issues and proceeds of all such property, shall not withstanding marriage, be and remain her sole and separate property."

The right to vote, which was not won until 1920 with the passage of the Nineteenth Amendment to the Constitution, was a struggle for women. In the case of *Minor v. Happersett* (1874), the U.S. Supreme Court denied women the right to vote. The argument then was "that as a woman born or naturalized in the United States is a citizen of the United States and of the State in which she resides, she has therefore the right to vote." The Court stated further that there is no doubt that women may be citizens. The direct question as presented was whether all citizens are necessarily qualified to be voters. "The Constitution has not added the right of suffrage to the privileges and immunities of citizenship as they existed at the time it was adopted" (Minor). In no state constitution was suffrage conferred upon women. It took the Nineteenth Amendment to the Constitution to grant women the right to vote. Neither John Adams nor those following him were willing to "remember the ladies." "Federal and state legislation prohibiting sex discrimination in selected areas does not fill the absence of a constitutional prohibition of discrimination on the basis of sex. Under the federal Constitution and most state constitutions, women have not yet been raised to the status of constitutional protections enjoyed by males" (Thomas, 1991, p. 95). The Nineteenth Amendment did not automatically mean an end to women's oppression. It did not "negate the term 'male' in Section 2 of the Fourteenth Amendment. The lack of an explicit guarantee of sex equality has limited the U.S. Constitution as a vehicle for securing women's rights and social advancement" (MacKinnon, 2001, p. 16).

Even the language of the law referred to such terms as a *reasonable man*, *he*, and *his*. When a question about this issue is raised, the answer given is usually that the male terms used generally include females. As Justice Scalia has stated: "The word 'gender' has acquired the new and useful connotation of cultural or attitudinal characteristics (as opposed to physical characteristics) distinct to the sexes. That is to say, gender is to sex as feminine is to female and masculine is to male" (MacKinnon, 2001, p. 210).

Gender-neutral language does not solve the problem. Such gender-neutral language "serves only to reward the employers ingenious enough to cloak their acts of discrimination in a facially neutral guise, identical though the effects of [a facially neutral seniority] system may be to those of a facially discriminatory one" (Thomas, 1991).

RIGHT TO WORK   1908

During the nineteenth century, differential treatment of women and men was challenged. A most striking incident was the enactment of the protective state labor laws. In the early twentieth century, protective labor laws were allegedly enacted to protect both men and women from inhuman conditions. However, it was women who suffered. In the case of *Muller v. Oregon* (1908), a challenge was made to the Oregon statute prohibiting the employment of women in mechanical establishments, factories, or laundries for more than 10 hours a day. This law was upheld by the U.S. Supreme Court using a reasoning that was to haunt the advocates of women's rights for years to come.

Justice Brenner delivered the majority opinion of the Court:

[W]omen's physical structure and the performance of maternal functions places her at a disadvantage in the struggle for subsistence. . . . This is especially true when the burdens of motherhood are upon her. [And] even when they are not, by abundant testimony of the medical fraternity continuance for a long time on her feet at work, repeating this from day to day, tends to injurious effects upon the body. . . . the physical well-being of woman becomes an object of public interest and care in order to preserve the strength and vigor of the race. [As dictated by history] woman has always been dependent upon man. He established his *control at the outset by superior physical strength* [emphasis mine], and this control in various forms, with diminishing intensity has continued to the present. . . . She is properly placed in a class by herself, and legislation designed for her protection may be sustained, even when legislation is not necessary for men, and could be sustained.

THE RIGHT TO SERVE ON JURIES   ~~1961~~ 1975

And so it continued. Struggles ensued, with women bringing to court their case to serve on juries. In the case of *Hoyt v. Florida* (1961), Justice Harlan delivered the opinion of the Supreme Court. The issue was whether exclusion of women from jury service discriminated against a defendant's right to a fair trial. Justice Harlan stated:

Manifestly, Florida's [law] does not purport to exclude women from state jury service. Rather the statute "gives to women the privilege to serve but does not impose service as a duty." It accords women an absolute exemption from jury service unless they expressly waive that privilege.

It has given women an absolute exemption from jury based solely on their sex, no similar exemption obtaining as to men.

Despite the enlightened emancipation of women from the restrictions and protections of bygone years, and their entry into many parts of community life formerly considered to be reserved to men, *woman is still regarded as the center of home and family* life.

In 1975, in *Taylor v. Louisiana* (1975), a male criminal defendant challenged his conviction on the ground that his jury had not been drawn from a fair cross section of the community. Women had systematically been excluded from jury lists. Using statistics to demonstrate that 54.2 percent of all women between 18 and 64 years of age were in the labor force, that 45.7 percent of women with children under the age of 18 were working, that 67.3 percent of the mothers who were widowed, divorced, or separated were in the workforce, and that 51.2 percent of the mothers whose husbands were gainfully employed were also working, the Court declared: "[I]f it was ever the case that women were unqualified to sit on juries or were so situated that none of them should be required to perform jury services that time has long past." A victory had been achieved.

GENDER AS A SUSPECT CLASSIFICATION

What has not been declared is that gender is a suspect classification. It was not until 1971 that the U.S. Supreme Court considered that many of the laws and official practices at all levels of government as practiced were in violation of the equal protection clause. The Fourteenth Amendment states that "[n]o state shall deny equal protection of the laws to any person." But what does that mean?

A rational relationship test was developed indicating that any classification "must be reasonable, not arbitrary, and must rest upon some ground of difference having a fair and substantial relation to the object of the legislation, so that all persons similarly situated shall be treated alike" (*Reed v. Reed*, 1971). No discrimination can exist against women unless it is demonstrated that reasonable grounds exist for such discrimination.

Throughout the history of the courts, several classifications, including gender, religion, and national origin, have been labeled suspect classifications. This means that any time a law is passed that discriminates in its language or is found to have a discriminatory effect on a suspect class of persons, the state has the burden not simply of showing that the law is rational, but of proving additionally that such a law serves a compelling governmental interest and that no other discriminatory law could accomplish the same or similar purpose. This is the principle referred to as a compelling state interest. We came close with the case of *Frontiero v. Richardson* (1973), but because there was a 4–4 plurality vote of the justices of the Supreme Court, such a decision of gender as a suspect classification never came about. With gender not being labeled a suspect classification, the government has the power to justify any type of discrimination as not being arbitrary and irrational. In the words of Justice Brennan: "There can be no doubt that our Nation has had a long and unfortunate history of sex discrimination. Traditionally, such discrimination was rationalized by an attitude of 'romantic paternalism' which in practical effect, put women, not on a pedestal, but in a cage."

If there had been just one more vote, the courts would have been obliged to treat gender classifications as they do race classifications. It was not to be. The rational basis for classifications is still based on the factor of women being dependent on their spouses, girls being dependent on parents for support, and men having more and better business experience than women. If the courts can determine that discrimination serves the purpose of the rational relationship test, it can and will stand. To this day confusion remains regarding the standard of review in cases of gender discrimination. The issue remains whether gender and race classifications are ever constitutionally permissible. Are there instances in which it is proper to afford preferential treatment to one group over another? Clear answers do not exist. Each case is considered on an individual basis and on individual merit.

Even the Equal Rights Amendment (ERA) could not be passed. Concerns about family law, protective labor laws, the military, and the establishment of unisex bathrooms were enough to vote down the ERA. If ever there were stereotypical attitudes about women, they are found in the wisdom of many of the justices of the Supreme Court.

GENDER NEUTRAL

Admittedly, progress has been demonstrated, as, for example, the changing roles of women and men have led to gender-neutral, functional family laws. Today, the obligation of supporting a spouse is predicated on who can afford it, not simply on who needs it.

Women are not inferior to men. Nevertheless, in the twenty-first century, there remains evidence of sexual discrimination, even with all the history and struggles to gain equality and similar treatment under the law. According to MacKinnon (2001), "[u]nless something is done, even if recent rates of measurable progress for elite women continue, no American now alive will live in a society of sex equality, nor will their children or their children's children" (p. 2).

In the 1970s, there were feminists who challenged both the institutions and laws of the land that continued to deny women equality. There was a "barrage of test cases in state and federal courts challenging practices" denying women benefits, as noted earlier, as well as unequal age requirements with regard to marrying and drinking (Kerber & DeHart, pp. 17–18). What was won were equal pay for equal work and equal employment benefits, as well as the ability to obtain credit but "building on the tactics and achievements of the civil rights movement . . . [women] discovered that guarantees of equality in a system structured with men's needs as the norm does not always produce a gender-neutral result" (Kerber & DeHart, p. 18).

We have yet to reach the day when we can say honestly that women have been raised to the status of full constitutional protections as men have always enjoyed. We must remember the words of Sojourner Truth: "Ain't I a woman?" We are constantly reminded of her statement and that of Abigail Adams, "remember the ladies"; yet we are constantly reminded of the statement in the case of *Glover v. Johnson* (1975): "Keep it simple, they are only women."

REFERENCES

DECKARD, B. S. (1979). *The women's movement: Political, socioeconomic, and psychological issues.* New York: Harper & Row.

KERHBER, L., & DE HART, J. S. (2004). *Women's America: Refocusing the past.* New York: Oxford University Press.

MACKINNON, C. (2001). *Sex equality.* New York: Foundation Press.

MURASKIN, R., & ALLEMAN, T. (1993). *It's a crime: Women and justice.* Englewood Cliffs, NJ: Regents/Prentice Hall.

SCHNEIR, M. (ED.). (1972). *Feminism: The essential historical writings.* New York: Vintage Press.

THOMAS, C. S. (1991). *Sex discrimination.* St. Paul, MN: West Publishing.

ENDNOTE

1. This paragraph is taken from *Visions for change: Crime and justice in the twenty first century* (fifth edition), Englewood Cliffs, NJ: Prentice Hall.

CASES

Bradwell v. Illinois, 83 U.S. 130 (1872).
Frontiero v. Richardson, 411 U.S. 677 (1973).
Glover v. Johnson, 478 F. Supp. 1075 (1975).
Hoyt v. Florida, 368 U.S. 57 (1961).
Minor v. Happersett, 88 U.S. 162 (1874).
Muller v. Oregon, 208 U.S. 412 (1908).
Reed v. Reed, 404 U.S. 71 (1971).
Taylor v. Louisiana, 419 U.S. 522 (1975).

2

Feminist Theories

Are They Needed?

Roslyn Muraskin

Historically, most criminological theories have been developed by and for men. It appears that "the extent of female crime is consistently obscured relative to the incidence, severity, and awareness of male criminality" (Shipley & Arrigo, 2004). As female crime increases, there exists the need to understand why. Are women as gentle as they have been described to be or are they capable of becoming hard-core criminals? The latter appears to be the answer. Feminism has challenged the overall *masculinized* nature of criminology by pointing to the repeated omission and misrepresentation of women in criminological inquiry. This chapter explores the thoughts of the theorists and how and if their theories apply to women.

According to Meda Chesney-Lind (2010),

> the feminist criminology of the 20th century clearly challenged the overall masculinist nature of theories of crime, deviance, and social control by calling attention to the repeated omission and misrepresentation of women in criminological theory and research. Turning back the clock, one can recall that prior to path-breaking feminist works on sexual assault, sexual harassment and wife abuse, these forms of gender violence were ignored, minimized, and trivialized. . . . girls and women in conflict with the law were overlooked or excluded in mainstream works. . . . The impact on the field of criminology and particularly criminological theory was mixed, however, in part because these offenses did not initially seem to challenge androcentric criminology per se. Instead, the concepts of "domestic violence" and "victimology" although pivotal in the development of feminist criminology also supplied mainstream criminologists and some criminal justice practitioners with a new area in which to publish, "new" crimes to study. . . . More recently, the field of domestic violence has even been home to a number of scholars who have argued that women are as violent as men. . . . (Chesney-Lind, 2010, pp. 564–565)

According to Meda Chesney-Lind, "feminist criminology in the 21st century, particularly in the United States, finds itself in a political and social milieu that is heavily affected by the backlash politics of a sophisticated and energized right wing. . . . The centrality of both crime and gender in the current backlash politics means that feminist criminology is uniquely positioned to challenge right-wing initiatives" (p. 566). We should no longer think in terms of a patriarchal system, where men dominate women, rather we should "theorize patriarchy [which means] that we have done cutting-edge research on the interface between patriarchal and criminal justice systems of control . . ." (p. 567).

> When the United States embarked on a policy that might well be described as mass incarceration, few considered the impact that this correctional course change would have on women. Yet the number of women in jail and prison [as demonstrated throughout this text] continues to soar (outstripping male increases for most of the past decade), completely untethered from women's crime rate, which has not increased by nearly the same amount. . . . At the turn of the new century [twenty-first century] we now have more than 100,000 women doing time in U.S prisons. (Chesney-Lind, 2010, p. 573)

If we look at the case of Andrea Yates who killed her five children and attempted unsuccessfully to present the defense of postpartum syndrome, do we conclude that she was/is mentally ill or a cold-blooded murderer who got up one day and set out to kill? "[W]hen women deviate substantially from their status as wife or mother, adopting instead a life of violent crime, they are deemed especially corrupt or evil" (Shipley & Arrigo, 2004). Of course in the case of Andrea Yates the decision was overturned because the prosecution's psychologist failed to give a truthful statement regarding the show *Law and Order*, where it was stated that a similar case was presented, and that Yates was an ardent fan. The decision of the trial court was overturned by the appellate court, which found that the psychiatrist's testimony was untrue. Yates was retried and found not guilty by reason of insanity, and today she is being treated in a psychiatric hospital.

According to Belknap (1996), criminology is concerned with the development of theories that show the cause and effect of crime. The field of criminal justice focuses on workers "in the criminal justice system and how decisions are made about victims and offenders" (p. xi). Belknap refers to invisibility as a universal criteria of women as offenders as well as victims.

When we review criminological theory regarding women we look at biological influences, whereas with men we have traditionally looked at economic and sociological factors. If we look at crime statistics, we tend to believe that black offenders are more likely to be sex offenders. When we talk about sexual victimization, we conclude that women need protection for their own good, and therefore they are not to work in those jobs that have physical demands considered dangerous, such as policing.

James Messerschmidt (1993), in his work *Masculinities and Crime*, rethinks feminist theories by addressing the impact of gender not merely on the criminality of women but on that of men as well. His definition of social structure is "regular patterned forms of interaction over time that constrain and channel behavior in specific ways" (p. 378). In their research of both male and female offenders, Kathleen Daly and Meda Chesney-Lind (1988) spotlight women's individual pathways to breaking the law: street women, harmed and harming women, battered women, drug-connected women, and what they refer to as "other."

According to Sarri (1979), women's prior victimization places the human race at risk for offending as our prisons appear to be disproportionately populated with women of color. It appears that we as a society permit women to drift into the field of crime in order for them to survive and thereby ending up in correctional facilities that take better care of them than any welfare agency.

It is no secret who commits the majority of crime: men. It appears from all the research and the statistics provided that men and boys do perpetuate the more conventional crimes and the more serious of these crimes than women and girls, or so it appears historically. Gender has always been used by criminologists as the strongest indicator of who commits what crime. Theoretical works appear to have been gender blind, believing that men and boys should be the norm to be studied, not women and girls.

Traditionally, as men and boys have continued to be the "normal" subject studied, the gender content of women's legitimate and illegitimate behavior has been virtually ignored. The question often asked is "why is it that women do not offend?" Of course, they have and do. All these assumptions have resulted in an arrogant, biological-based misrepresentation of women. The fact that the study of women and girls has attracted the attention of criminologists as a special category explains the gendered nature of crime.

Feminism has challenged the overall masculinized nature of criminology by pointing to the repeated omission and misrepresentation of women in criminological inquiry.

Robert Merton's (1938) theory of anomie suggests that there is a lack of it in U.S. society because of the culturally defined goals (economic success as measured by monetary rewards) and the socially structured legitimate means (education and paid work) to achieve these goals. It is the "American Dream" to strive for economic success, while distributing unequally the legitimate opportunities to succeed. Though Merton's theory of anomie has attracted many to explain the class differences in crime, and it has been seen as "perhaps the consummate male theory of deviant behavior," anomie theory is clearly inadequate for comprehending the high gender ratio and gendered character of crime. Assuming that economic opportunities have been less available to women than men, and that women appear to strive for the same or similar goals as men, if we were to pursue the logic of Merton's argument in reality there should be more crime by women and less by men.

If we turn to the control theory of Travis Hirschi (1969), we find here, too, that the theory is incapable of deciphering the gendered nature of crime. A majority of criminological theories use conformity as the norm and concentrate on explaining criminal behavior. Such theorists generally inquire as to why people offend, and then proceed to use men and boys as the norm to be studied. Hirschi's control theory makes the assumption that crime is normal and that it is conformity that becomes problematic. He differs from traditional criminology by asking why people conform. Society, according to Hirschi, has developed ways of controlling its members by inhibiting their "drive" to deviate.

Hirschi has identified four factors as being critical to the control of deviation: (1) *attachment* to parents, schools, and peers; (2) *commitment* to conventional lines of action; (3) *involvement* in conventional activities; and (4) *belief* in conventional values. In order to address the gendered nature of crime then, control theory would have to show that women and girls maintain higher levels of commitment to conventional activities, values, and people than do men and boys. As a result of such commitment, women and girls would engage in higher levels of legitimate behavior. But Hirschi presented no such data. It is curious that Hirschi started out by studying both boys and girls, but for some unexplained reason he concentrated his studies on boys and men. As the obvious substantially more law-abiding gender, especially considering Hirschi's "own argument that criminologists should reorient their thinking by making conformity, rather than criminality, the central object of study" (Hirschi, 1969), his theory as conceptualized becomes incapable of explaining why men and boys engage in more crime than do women and girls.

Next is labeling theory. Because of continuous labeling, primary deviants eventually accept their labeled identity as deviant, thereby acting in accordance with the societal reaction. This means that they are well on their way to a career in secondary deviation.

For labeling theorists, to acquire a deviant self-image from labeling is determined by one's own power to counteract potential labeling contacts. According to Edwin Schur (1965), "those with the least power are most susceptible to deviating," while those with social power of sorts are the ones who will be much more able to "avoid initial identification as a deviator, and to avoid or reduce stigma even after being so identified," and to "influence the outcome in the course of official 'processing.'" Given the fact that men exercise greater power in society than women, and following the logic of labeling theory, men should therefore have increased opportunity to counteract official labeling, thus resulting in a lower rate of crime than for women.

It was the work of Caesar Lombroso (1895) that set the stage for asking why it is that women do not offend. Lombroso is well known for his strict biological determinism, and thus his conception of the *born criminal* or individuals whose atavistic qualities indicated a throwback to earlier evolutionary periods. It was Lombroso who collected data on a sample of men who were incarcerated and then compared them to a control group of soldiers. According to Lombroso, since the group of prisoners had more atavistic characteristics than did the soldiers—enormous jaws, high cheekbones, prominent superciliary arches, and handle-shaped ears—criminals could thus be identified and categorized simply from observing and counting their "degenerate physical stigmata" (Smart, 1976, p. 33).

Lombroso and Lombroso-Ferrero (1972) stated that "all statistics show that women are much less criminal than men." In the *Female Offender*, Lombroso and his son-in-law, William Ferrero (1895), concluded that women's lesser criminality is explained by their "piety, maternity, want of passion, sexual coldness, weakness and an undeveloped intelligence." It shows that when women do commit crime, it is significantly different from those of men, primarily because of women's biological makeup:

> That women are less often engaged in highway robbery, murder, homicide, and assault is due to the very nature of the feminine constitution. To conceive an assassination, to make ready for it, to put it into execution demands a certain energy and a certain combination of intellectual functions. In this sort of development women almost always fall short of men. It seems on the other hand that the crimes that are habitual to them are those which require a smaller degree of physically and intellectual force, and such especially are receipt of stolen goods, poisoning, abortion and infanticide. (Smart, 1976)[1]

What Lombroso did was similar to all other criminological theorists: He constructed a general theory of crime based on men. Eventually he was to understand that such a theory could not be applied to both men and women. Lombroso maintained that "the born female criminal makes up for what she lacks in relative numbers by the excess vileness and cruelty of her crimes" (Smart, 1976, p. 3).

It was Sigmund Freud, a psychiatrist, whose theories based on the unconsciousness were a great influence on female criminality. He claimed that women were biologically inferior to their male counterparts. "In particular, he asserted that female offenders were passive, narcissistic, and masochistic as a result of a masculinity complex or as a consequence of penis envy" (Freud, 1963). It was Freud's belief that "women were unable to resolve the oedipal conflict, leaving them less in control over their impulses." As such, they were motivated by anatomical deficiencies (e.g., relative size, strength, dexterity), [which] predisposed women to immorality (Shipley & Arrigo, 2004).

It was William I. Thomas (1969) who linked "the social environment to a woman's proclivity for criminality." His belief was that many of the gender differences were a direct result of "social and cultural influences rather than biological differences, although biology was seen as playing an important role. . . . [Thomas] argued that female criminality was a socially induced pathology, steeped in instinctive processes rather than biologically predetermined states. . . . the wish or desire for new experiences significantly impacted female criminality" (Pollock, 1999). "More specifically, he maintained that wishes, as derived from biological instincts, could be socialized to achieve appropriate goals. . . . [Thomas] alleged that the intense need to give and feel love frequently led women to adopt criminal patterns of behavior, especially in relation to sexual offenses (e.g., prostitution)" (Shipley & Arrigo, 2004, p. 5).

The socialists were the first to introduce the idea that crime under capitalism is, in part, correlated to economic conditions. It was in their eagerness to identify the economic forces that encouraged such crimes as prostitution, that socialist theorists denied women any role other than that of a passive victim. The assumption of the socialist movement, as well as other criminologists of the time, was that any sex outside of marriage was both improper and degrading, and that no right woman would or could choose prostitution. Socialists focused on how a capitalist economic system could turn "good" women into "bad" women, thus damaging their prospects for marriage and their ability to raise children.

Bonger (1969), who was considered a socialist criminologist, proposed an explanation of why women commit less crime than men. In his discussion on strength and courage, he concluded that the average woman of our time has less strength and courage than the average man and, consequently, commits on the average fewer crimes than a man. He also held the belief that women are not involved in what were typically sexual crimes because of their nature and very being. He believed that when it came to sex, women were more passive while men were more active. Bonger failed to offer any reason for this theory other than to imply an inherent quality. This also became apparent in his portrayal of women as lacking in courage, and therefore engaging in less property crime. Women would engage in prostitution because of its profitability. Bonger felt that because working-class women work outside the home in the paid labor market, their children became demoralized.

> The development of capitalism has led to the paid labor of married women, and consequently to one of the most important causes of the working class. When there is no one to watch a child, when he is left to himself, he becomes demoralized.

He concluded that if women were home, where they were supposed to be, children would not become demoralized, and young girls would not become prostitutes. Bonger did not regard men's wage labor and the onset of the dissolution of the family as the agency of child socialization. He objected to the removal of women from the family to work, but accepted men and husbands having to go out to work, and therefore not the cause of any failures of the family.

Otto Pollack (1950) addressed the high gender ratio of crimes in a manner that was significantly different from that of both Lombroso and Bonger. Lombroso and Bonger argued that women's biology created a "weaker sex," resulting in less crime being committed by women. Pollack argued that women's crime most likely equaled men's, but because of the biology of women interacting with certain social conditions, "the criminality of women is largely masked criminality" (Smart, 1976, p. 47). Pollack believed that women were addicted to crimes that were easily concealed (e.g., shoplifting, thefts by prostitutes, domestic thefts, abortion, and perjury). Accordingly, the crimes that women commit would be underreported. Also, because of the nature of women's biology, women were more prone than men to be deceitful. In Pollack's mind this criminal concealment on the part of women was a result of the biological fact that a man "must achieve an erection in order to perform the sex act and will not be able to hide his failure," yet for the woman:

> Lack of orgasm does not prevent her ability to participate in the sex act. It cannot be denied that this basic psychological difference may well have a great influence on the degree of confidence which the two sexes have in the possible success of concealment and thus on their character pattern in this respect. (Smart, 1976)

Additionally, Pollack felt that as women conceal their menstruation, the biology of women and its impact on sexuality make the factor of concealment and misrepresentation in the eyes of women a socially required and commendable act, and must condition them to a different attitude toward sincerity than men. It was because of women's social position in society that they more often than not were accomplices than perpetrators of crime. Pollack argued further that the division of labor placed women in the primary role of homemaker and mother, which furnished them the many occasions to commit crimes in ways and by means not available to men, thus lessening the public character of many crimes. It was this social position that helped keep women's crimes hidden from public view.

Another factor that entered into the picture was that of chivalry:

> One of the outstanding concomitants of the existing general protective attitude of man toward women . . . [is that] men hate to accuse women and thus indirectly to send them to their punishment. Police officers dislike to arrest them, district attorneys to prosecute them, judges and juries to find them guilty, and so on. (Pollack, 1950)

It was John Hagan's (1989) power-control theory that integrated some feminist insights into a framework for understanding young girls' crimes and developing a criminological theory that was to take gender seriously as an explanatory variable. Hagan asserted that working in a position of authority within the paid labor market would automatically translate into power and authority within the home. Though economic independence for women was a first step toward equality with men, it did not guarantee a reduction in gender power and authority for them within the home. The conclusion drawn was that the power-control theory and mother's liberation caused daughters to go out and commit crimes. Those women who defy traditional femininity by working outside the home in the paid labor market increase the chance that their daughters will become delinquent. In spite of the increasing women's labor force participation rate, it appears that the increase in the rate of crime has not been evident.

If we compare Hirschi's control theory with Hagan's power-control theory, the covert masculine nature of criminological theory becomes evident. In Hirschi's mind, his conforming boy is depicted as an admirable character who is energetic and intelligent and denotes a rational being. But when we review the conforming girl in Hagan's theory we discover

> a grey and lifeless creature. She is passive, compliant and dependent. Gone is Hirschi's rational and responsible agent, intelligently evaluating the risks and costs of crime. Conformity is now described as "compliance." The law abiding female is biddable rather than responsible. Hagan's female seems unable to construct complex and caring relationships even with her mother who subjects her to her control. She is merely the "object" of her mother's instrumental training to be compliant. Hagan is explicit about the status of the female as a manipulated thing. (Hagan, 1989, pp. 788–816)

Summing up, both Hirschi and Hagan perpetuate what criminology has continuously done, and that is to devalue women and girls and place a higher value on men and boys, even when both exhibit the same social behavior.

Others believe that women have not only been misrepresented in criminology's efforts to understand the gendered nature of crime, but for the most part, have been omitted entirely from criminological discourse as well. Understanding that theoretical criminology has been developed by and for men, the theories are not up to the analytical task of explaining female crime, if in fact we need separate theories. The theories as developed are reflective not of all human behavior but of male behavior alone. Regardless, it does not mean that those theories explain fully why men commit crimes.

Edwin Sutherland (1939) argued that using interaction and communication within certain intimate personal groups, individuals learn the techniques, motives, needed drives, as well as rationalizations and attitudes necessary to commit crime. Sutherland believed that criminal behavior is learned in the same manner as conforming behavior is learned. A particular person engages in criminal behavior "because of an excess of definitions favorable to violations of law over definitions unfavorable to violations of law." Therefore, individuals become criminals because their associations with criminal behavioral patterns far outweigh their associations with noncriminal behavioral patterns in terms of frequency, duration, priority, and intensity. Around 1947 Sutherland attempted to explain why boys engage more frequently in criminal acts than girls. It was his argument that boys engaged in more crime than girls due to the differences in supervision of each. He asserted that as boys and girls live in the same poverty-ridden neighborhoods, social environment does not

> explain the relatively high rate of boy delinquency and relatively low rate of girl delinquency. The significant difference is that girls are supervised more carefully and the behavior in accordance with social codes taught them with greater care and consistency than is the case with boys. From infancy girls are taught that they must be nice, while boys are taught that they must be rough and tough; a boy who approaches the behavior of girls is regarded as a "sissy." This difference in care and supervision presumably rested originally on the fact that the female sex is the one which becomes pregnant. (p. 21)

Thus, Sutherland's work asserted that whether a boy turns to a life of delinquency rests on the assumption that socialization is grounded ultimately in the biological differences between men and women and between boys and girls.

According to the works of Parsons (1964), "dichotomous sex roles structure the family," meaning that the instrumental role involves goal attainment, focusing on the relationship between family and society taken as a whole, whereas the expressive role involves the integration on both the internal structure and the functions of the family. The family unit prepares children for their adequate participation in society by teaching them the appropriate gender roles (i.e., masculine or instrumental and feminine or expressive). Therefore when children are socialized into their proper gender roles, society remains stable over generations.

Parsons used this functionalist perspective in the early 1940s to explain why boys turn to acts of delinquency. His thesis was that in the family, girls are more apt to be relatively docile, to conform in general according to adult expectations to be good, whereas boys are more apt to be recalcitrant to discipline and defiant of adult authority and expectations. When a girl is physically able, she begins a direct apprenticeship as a female adult, forming a feminine identification with the mother. It was Parsons's contention that women were inferior to men, and therefore to grow up like a woman was shameful for any man. It is this reaction formation and resulting compulsive masculinity that creates a strong "tendency for boyish behavior to run in anti-social if not directly destructive directions, in striking contrast to that of . . . girls." Parsons's work was flawed as he was the first to attempt to connect masculinity with the gendered nature of crime.

In Albert Cohen's (1955) work *Delinquent Boys*, he argued that a working-class delinquent subculture comes to pass in answer to discriminatory middle-class standards. According to Cohen's theory, teachers characteristically evaluate children entering school according to how their behavior approximates middle-class standards. Boys traditionally socialized in working-class families are relatively unprepared for the challenges set forth in the classroom. As individuals who constitute the working class and have internalized middle-class standards as they see in others, their status becomes unclear and they look for other means to adjust. "The obvious solution is the collective repudiation of middle class standards and adoption of their very antithesis—the public display of non-utilitarian, malicious, and negativistic delinquent behavior" (my notes).

According to Cohen, who used himself and his wife as examples, "my skin has nothing of the quality of down or silk there is nothing limp or flute-like about my voice. I am at a total loss with needle and thread, my posture and carriage are wholly lacking in grace . . . my wife on the other hand is not greatly embarrassed by her inability to tinker with or talk about the internal organs of a car, by her modest attainment in arithmetic or by her inability to lift heavy objects" (my notes).

Continuing, Cohen points out that because of the structure of the modern family and the nature of our occupational system, children of both genders tend to form early feminine identification. The boy, however, unlike the girl, comes later under strong social pressure to establish his masculinity and his difference from female figures. Because his mother is the object of the feminine identification that he feels is the threat to his status as a male, he tends to react negatively to the conduct norms that have been associated with mother and therefore have acquired feminine significance. Since mother has been the principal agent of indoctrinating good, respectable behavior, goodness comes to symbolize femininity, and engaging in bad behavior requires denying his femininity and therefore asserting his masculinity. This is the motivation to juvenile delinquency, according to Cohen.

The conclusion reached is that when the nature of male gender-role socialization does not run efficiently, the problem associated with male anxiety within the home is solved by the boy becoming a member of a street gang. The delinquent subculture is a tailor-made answer to the problems of the male role, but is an unsuitable solution to correct problems of the female (Cohen). We understand how the delinquent subculture applies to men but not to women.

The conclusion reached is that when looking at middle-class-boy delinquency, it becomes an attempt to muddle through with a basic apprehension in the area of gender-role identification, whereas the incentive for working-class-boy delinquency is bending to evils created by his class position.

If we look at the theories of liberal feminism, we discover that women are discriminated against on the basis of gender and therefore are deprived of the same opportunities as men and kept outside the mainstream of society (e.g., politics, business, finance, medicine, law—all of which are fields now open to women). It is the very goal of liberal feminism to remove all sexist stereotypes that are promoted through gender-role socialization within the family, at school, and by the media and government, clearing the road for women's rapid integration into what has traditionally been regarded as the world of men.

It was the works of Freda Adler and Rita Simon that were credited with the "female emancipation theory of female criminality. This theory postulates that the rise in female crime is a result of the Women's Liberation Movement or increased opportunities" (Edwards in Shipley & Arrigo, 2004, p. 5). In a keynote address by Adler (1975) in Washington, DC, at the National Conference on Women and Crime, she implied that "although males will commit by far the greater number of absolute offenses, females are surpassing them in rates of increase for almost every major crime." She continued, "it is apparent, that [women] are no longer willing to be second-class criminals, limited to 'feminine' crimes of shoplifting and prostitution, but that they are making their gains noticeable across the offense board." This factor becomes evident in the proceeding chapters on women and crime.

Adler's work was important at the time, as she argued that a correlation existed between the Women's Liberation Movement and technology, signifying that such a combination provided the capacity for women to commit violent crimes comparable to those committed by men (Adler, 1975, p. 6).

Other scholars have taken exception to the idea of female emancipation as causing women to go out and commit crimes. At the meeting of the American Association for the Advancement of Science in the 1970s, Denmark declared:

> The female offender, whether acting by herself or with others, is not typically the emancipated intellectual striving for civil liberties. Her crime is rarely an assertion of civil rights, or an unconscious attempt at achieving her own or others' rights. She may feel dominated by men or even wish to imitate men or obtain male approval for her actions. (as cited in Shipley & Arrigo, 2004, p. 6)

It was Simon (1975) who looked at female criminality as being analogous to male offenders. Simon suggested that "women have no greater store of morality than do men. Their propensities to commit crimes do not differ, but in the past, their opportunities have been much more limited" (Shipley & Arrigo, p. 6). Simon made a case that the increase in female crime had more to do with property offenses than their ability to commit crimes of violence.

Many feminists became outraged by Adler's and Simon's correlation between women's liberation and crime. Their frustration came about with the masculinization theory of Adler and the opportunity theory of Simon, which challenged the myth that the equalization of the sexes diminishes crime. The critics "contended that many female offenders represented minority, poor, undereducated, and unemployed groups—constituencies that did not benefit from the increased opportunities afforded to women by the Liberation Movement" (Shipley & Arrigo, 2004, p. 6). Their contention was that the liberation movement had no connection to the rates of criminality of disenfranchised women.

A number of radical inspired feminist theories "have challenged the liberal position and the social structure within which the liberal-feminist viewpoint operates. . . . radical feminists look at the function of patriarchy in society and the subservient roles that women play in relation to it. . . . They contend that individuals are socialized within 'core gender identities.' [It is the] Marxist feminists [who] tie the patriarchy of society to the economic structure of capitalism. Men are thought to control the economy and, as such, many of the property crimes committed by women are related to the unequal distribution of resources" (Shipley & Arrigo, pp. 6–7).

Meda Chesney-Lind (1998) has pointed out that factors such as economic marginalization and victimization lead women to crime. To illustrate, she indicates that a disproportionate number of female criminals have histories that include drug-using parents, violent partners, childhood sexual abuse, and rape. Criminal roles represent caretaking, which is demonstrated when a mother sells or prostitutes herself to feed her children, and no other options exist. Chesney-Lind argues that in most cases women offenders are socialized into exploitation. With no marketable skills and little education, these women find themselves structurally dislocated. Given the abusive and victimizing experiences that women endure, she questions "not why women murder but why so few murder" (p. 98).

In reviewing female violence and aggression studies, Shipley and Arrigo have found that "many theories about women's roles in crime relative to those of men stem from the notion that men are biologically more aggressive and more prone to violence." Commenting on the phenomenon of aggression, Berkowitz (1964, p. 104) defines it as "the emotional state resulting from a frustration, presumably creating a readiness for aggressive acts" (p. 7). Closer study is needed to understand female violence and aggression.

As an example, again cited in Shipley and Arrigo's work,

> Eagley and Steffen (1986) undertook a meta-analytic review of sex differences in relation to aggression, finding that differences were inconsistent across studies. For example, whereas men were more likely to aggress in situations that produced pain or physical injury, the differences were less pronounced when it came to social or psychological harm. (p. 8)

Interestingly, women were more prone to guilt than men. Other researchers, such as Campbell, Muncer, and Gorman (1992), felt that aggression on the part of women "was more appropriately attributable to an expressive act or a cathartic discharge of anger" (p. 8). Others have speculated on what the true meaning of aggression denotes as applied to men and women. As an example, according to Fry and Gabriel (1994, p. 165), "a reluctance to focus on female aggression may be a reluctance to consider similarities between women and men." It is further suggested that "aggressive and violent behavior in men is valorized, whereas in women it is pathologized." They concluded that "aggression was a malegendered category; one that was not amenable to understanding feminine identity and the existence of woman as synonymous with motherhood and pacifism."

There are other factors besides criminological theories that lead to criminality. According to Shipley and Arrigo (p. 9), "female deviance or criminality is frequently associated with broken homes." Researchers have found a strong correlation between women felons who are convicted and those coming from broken homes. The U.S. Department of Justice, Bureau of Justice Statistics (1992), found that more women living in jail or prison in 1989 lived with only one or neither parent as they were growing up. Flowers (1994) and others have found that a relationship exists between female runaways, prostitution, and sexual abuse.

As summarized by Baskin and Sommers (1993),

> typically, then, the chain of events leading to criminalization is described as beginning with child physical or sexual abuse; this produces a vicious cycle that includes running away, institutionalization, return to the dysfunctional family, and ultimately street deviance, for example, prostitution and drug use. (p. 561)

Another factor of women turning to crime is that they are abused by others. There are approximately 2.0 million husbands who abuse close to 1.8 million wives. Recurring sexual and physical violence causes women to kill their significant others, whereas other researchers have found that women who abuse drugs wind up committing crimes as well. Research shows that minority women have more contact with law enforcement than white women, so the issues of race and gender have a causal effect on women and crime. As we will see in later chapters, specific gender defenses that have been used, such as postpartum syndrome, battered women's syndrome, premenstrual and postmenstrual syndrome, are noted as effective causes of women committing crimes. One other factor is that of mental illness. "Historically, women who commit offenses, particularly those considered violent, are viewed as more pathological than their male counterparts. Women who resort to violence are frequently considered *sick* rather than willful. . . . [W]omen who commit crimes are viewed as psychiatrically disordered as a result of gender typescripts. In other words, the stereotypes for women and the stereotypes for criminals do not produce a combined stereotype of the female criminal" (Shipley & Arrigo, 2004, p. 11). Other violent crimes and child maltreatment also bear some relationship.

According to the late Ted Alleman (Muraskin & Alleman, 1993),

> the oppression of women becomes of secondary concern in traditional Marxism since women are seen as merely another class who would benefit from a socialist transformation of society. When analyzing the traditional Marxist literature from a broader socialist perspective it is clear that: (1) Marx and Engels as theorists, like everyone else, were products of their environment and cannot have been expected to totally transcend their time and place in history . . . and (2) the essence of Marxism is really its analytic method and not the attitudes of Marx and Engels concerning women and their social conditions. (p. 29)

[B]y identifying the essence of female oppression to be the control men have over female sexuality, crime of and against women comes clearly into focus. Marx . . . saw prostitution as merely another example of the "universal prostitution of the worker." By not seeing women as an oppressed class in their own right, Marx . . . found no reason to pay special attention to women and crime. [However,] with a new sensitivity to the importance of gender as a causal variable, socialists are now able to trace the origin of crimes such as prostitution (male pimps manipulating and controlling the bodies of women) back to the rape and sexual abuse experienced in childhood by many prostitutes. (p. 31)

When we look at radical feminists we find that in the arenas of crime and criminal justice "radical feminists are successfully formulating into the law what were previously considered by many to be outlandish claims. By extricating themselves from their dependence on men, radical feminists have managed to expose the roots of female oppression" (Muraskin & Alleman, p. 33). Those thoughts allied with the word *feminist* result from the actions and efforts of radical feminism. The position of radical feminists has been that men are the problem and men's dominance has to be removed.

The fact is that female participation in crime is on the rise and has been for some time. However, women do not act in a vacuum. All theories presented can be attributed to women and crime. Is there a need for a specific feminist theory of crime? We can only conclude "no!" Women commit crimes like men today.

As summed up nicely by Adler (1975):

Women are no longer indentured to the kitchens, baby carriages, or bedrooms of America. . . . Allowed their freedom for the first time, women—by the tens of thousands—have chosen to desert those kitchens and plunge exuberantly into the formerly all-male quarters of the working world.

There are now female admirals, longshorewomen, stevedores, and seagoing sailors[2] (tattoos and all); there are police women patrolling in one-person cars, women FBI agents and female sky marshals. Women can now be found clinging to telephone poles as installers and line workers; peering from behind acetylene welding torches and seated behind the wheels of over-the-road tractor-trailer trucks. They can be found at work as forklift drivers and crane operators, pipe fitters and carpenters, mail carriers, and morticians, commercial airline pilots and jet-engine mechanics. Women now serve as Congressional pages[3] and have run for, and won, a substantial number of powerful positions throughout the American political system; an ever-increasing numbers of women continue to become judges, lawyers, and high level executives in industry and government.

In the same way that women are demanding equal opportunity in fields of legitimate endeavor, a similar number are forcing their way into the world of major crimes. . . . Like her sisters in legitimate fields, the female criminal is fighting for her niche in the hierarchy. . . . The mob, like other successful organizations, reacts to competition and accomplishment. They are not likely to ignore the increasing numbers of women who are using guns, knives, and wits to establish themselves as full human beings, as capable of violence and aggression as any man. (p. 3)

"For feminist criminology to remain true to its progressive origins in very difficult times, we must seek ways to blend activism with our scholarship . . ." (Chesney-Lind, 2010, p. 576). And according to Liz Kelly (who was quoted by Heidenshohn, in 1995), "feminist research investigates aspects of women's oppression while seeing at the same time to be part of the struggle against it" (Chesney-Lind, 2010, p. 576).

According to Tibbetts and Hemmens (2010, p. 2), " few theories in criminology will ever meet the strict criteria required to prove that key factors actually cause criminal behavior." The whole realm of social existence is affected today by women's involvement in crime.

REFERENCES

ADLER, F. (1975). *Sisters in crime: The rise of the new female criminal.* New York: McGraw-Hill.

BASKIN, D. R., & SOMMERS, I. (1993). Females' initiation into violent street crime. *Justice Quarterly, 10,* 559–581.

BELKNAP, J. (1996). *The invisible woman.* Belmont, CA: Wadsworth.

BONGER, W. (1969). *Criminality and economic conditions.* Bloomington, IN: Indiana University Press.

CAMPBELL, A., MUNCER, S., & GORMAN, B. (1992). Sex and social representation of aggression: A communal-agentic analysis. *Aggressive Behavior, 19,* 125–135.

CHESNEY-LIND, M. (1998). *The female offender: Girls, women and crime.* Thousand Oaks, CA: Sage.

CHESNEY-LIND, M. (2010). Patriarchy, crime, and justice: Feminist criminology in an era of backlash. In Stephen G. Tibbets & Craig Hemmens (Eds.), *Criminological theory.* Thousand Oaks, CA: Sage.

COHEN, A. (1955). *Delinquent boys: The culture of the gang.* New York: Free Press.

DALY, K., & CHESNEY-LIND, M. (1988). Feminism and criminology. *Justice Quarterly, 5,* 497–538.

DEPARTMENT OF JUSTICE REPORT (1992).

EAGLEY, A. H., & STEFFEN, V. J. (1986). Gender and aggressive behavior: A meta-analytic review of the social psychological literature. *Psychological Bulletin, 100,* 309–330.

EDWARDS, S. S. M. (1986). Neither bad nor mad: The female violent offender reassessed. *Women's Studies International Forum, 9,* 79–87.

FERRERO, W. (1895). *The female offender.* Littleton, CO: Fred Rothman. (Original work published in 1895.)

FLOWERS, R. B. (1994). *Female criminals, crimes, and cellmates.* Westport, CT: Greenwood Press.

FREUD, S. (1963). Some psychical consequences of the anatomical distinction between the sexes. In S. Freud (Ed.), *Sexuality and the psychology of love.* New York: Collier Books.

FRY, D. P., & GABRIEL, A. H. (1994). On aggression in women and girls: Cross-cultural perspectives. *Sex Roles, 30,* 165–170.

HAGAN, J. (1989). *Structural criminology.* Cambridge: Polity Press and Newark, NJ: Rutgers University.

HIRSCHI, T. (1969). *Causes of delinquency.* Berkeley, CA: University of California Press.

LOMBROSO, C., & LOMBROSO-FERRERO, G. (1972). *Criminal man, according to the classification of Cesare Lombroso.* Montclair, NJ: Patterson Smith. (Original work published in 1911.)

MERTON, R. (1938). Social structure and anomie. *American Sociological Review, 3,* 672–682.

MESSERSCHIMIDT, J. (1993). *Masculinities and crime.* Lanham, MD: Rowman & Littlefield.

MURASKIN, R., & ALLEMAN, T. (1993). *It's a crime: Women and justice* (1st ed.). Upper Saddle River, NJ: Prentice Hall.

PARSONS, T. (1964). *The social system.* New York: Free Press.

POLLACK, O. (1950). *The criminality of women.* Philadelphia, PA: University of Philadelphia Press.

POLLACK, J. M. (1999). *Criminal women.* Cincinnati, OH: Anderson.

SARRI, R. (1979). Crime and the female offender. In Edith S. Gomberg and Violet Frank (Eds.), *Gender and disordered behavior: Sex differences in psychopathology.* New York: Brunner/Mazel.

SCHUR, E. (1965). Crimes without victims: Our criminal society—*Deviant behavior and public policy.* New York: Random House.

SHIPLEY, S. L., & ARRIGO, B. A. (2004). *The female homicide offender: Serial murder and the case of Aileen Wuornos.* Upper Saddle River, NJ: Prentice Hall.

SIMON, R. (1975). *The contemporary woman and crime.* Washington, DC: U.S. Government Printing Office.

SMART, C. (1976). *Women, crime, and criminology*. London: Routledge.

SUTHERLAND, E. (1939). *Principles of criminology*. Philadelphia, PA: Lippincott.

THOMAS, W. I. (1969). *The unadjusted girl*. Montclair, NJ: Patterson Smith. (Original work published in 1923.)

TIBBETTS, S. F., & HEMMENS, C. (2010). *Criminological theory*. Thousand Oaks, CA: Sage Publications.

ENDNOTES

1. One could only wonder what these theorists would think of women who are suicide bombers today.
2. And of course women fighting in wars.
3. And of course women are serving in Congress as well as holding other major positions in government.

3

A Contextual History of Black Women Executions

Resistance to Systemic Gendered Racism

David V. Baker

This review chronicles the systemic oppression of executed black women since the earliest periods of American history. The historical record on black women executions reveals that challenging the gendered and racist exploitation of white men is the most consistent factor giving rise to black women executions throughout U.S. history. Colonial and antebellum slavery institutionalized the persecution of slave women who often retaliated against their oppressive brutality by killing white masters. White lynch mobs effectively augmented the legal killing of black women in postbellum society and lowered black female execution rates. Reduced to a peonage state in the apartheid of Jim Crow, black women's crimes of resistance against white brutality paralleled those of slave women decades earlier. And despite the delusional expansion of civil rights and the sovereignty of black people over the confines of segregation in the modern era, the gendered racism of American criminal justice has rendered black women ever more vulnerable to the death penalty.

INTRODUCTION

Criminal justice researchers have afforded scant attention to gendered racism in capital sentencing,[1] and what little research investigators have done on gender issues in capital sentencing is limited largely to the modern era.[2] Few scholars have linked the atrocities committed against black women by contemporary justice practitioners to comparable forms of maltreatment experienced by black women to the centuries of black oppression preceding the modern era in capital punishment.[3] As bell hooks makes clear, "sexism looms as large as racism as an oppressive force in the lives of black women."[4] Surprisingly, although

27

death penalty jurisdictions put to death the vast majority of black women executed in the United States before the end of slavery, criminal justice researchers have failed to study the historical context of black female executions during that period, as well as during Reconstruction, Jim Crow, and the civil rights period, beyond simply constructing descriptive profiles of dubious historical data.[5] As a result, criminal justice researchers do not account for black women executions as corresponding to the U.S. justice system's historical legacy of devaluing black women.

This chapter furthers understanding of the intersection between gendered racism and capital punishment in the U.S. criminal justice system by examining the contextual peculiarities giving rise to black women executions. The historical record makes clear that challenging the racist and sexist exploitation of whites largely accents black women executions during slavery, when black women retaliated violently against white oppressive brutality. Lynch mob violence toward black women was so pervasive in the postbellum period that black women execution rates actually decreased over their numbers in colonial and antebellum slavery. In the apartheid of Jim Crow, black women's crimes of resistance against white brutality paralleled those of slave women decades earlier. And the racialized sexism of mostly white judicial officers in the modern era has rendered black women vulnerable to the death penalty even supposing a national civil rights agenda diminishing the gendered racism troubling the lives of black women.

AFRICAN WOMEN AND THE SLAVE TRADE

The gendered racism accenting the lives of black women in the United States began when European slavers transported some 650,000 Africans from West African coastal nations to colonial enterprises in British North America. The experiences of slave women were significantly different from those of enslaved men.[6] For one, traders limited the number of female captives because most disliked purchasing women and young girls since young males garnered much higher market prices. One captain's directive, for instance, was to "buy no girls, and few women." Consequently, females comprised less than 40 percent of slave imports to mainland British colonies.[7] But once planters learned that slave women could produce high work yields, traders began transporting far more women.[8] For another, traders did not place female slaves in ship holds with shackled males, thus rendering them particularly susceptible to the vicious maltreatment of white slavers. Slave traders usually positioned female slaves on quarterdecks where they could move freely and were far more accessible to the sexual perversions of officers who "were permitted to indulge their passions."[9] Rape was a common torture for captured, disobedient slave women. This is true even of very young slave girls. Captain David Wilson of the *Eagle*, for instance, delighted at raping female slaves as young as 8 and 9 years old.[10] Traders often branded slaves once aboard ship and would ruthlessly beat slave women who resisted stripping naked for the practice. Crewmembers particularly "ridiculed, mocked, and treated contemptuously" slave women with children.[11] Slavers sadistically abused slave children just to watch the mothers' anguish, and if a child died from the cruelty, slavers forced mothers to throw their child overboard or suffer even more brutality. Slavers were no less barbaric in their treatment of captured pregnant slave women. Aboard the American ship *Pongas* carrying some 250 mostly pregnant slave women, for instance, females "who survived the initial stages of pregnancy gave birth aboard ship with their bodies exposed to either the scorching sun or the freezing cold."[12] Even if a newborn survived the ordeal, captured mothers often smothered to death their babies fearing the child would grow up in slavery.[13] And despite obvious danger to their lives, slave women regularly participated in slave ship insurrections as resistance against their white slavers.[14]

The historical record is clear—in the earliest periods of initial contact with Africans, American slave traders viciously mistreated their female captives. African women suffered excessively from the "brutalization and terrorization" of the slave trade with slavers commonly subjecting black women to such unique forms of abuse as rape, sexual assault, and vicious attacks against their pregnancies and motherhood.[15] Yet, historians have largely excluded black women from studies on slave resistance.[16] One scholar examined the gendered nature of slave conflict using ex-slave oral interviews conducted during the 1930s to illustrate the myriad of ways in which slave women directly challenged institutional slavery.[17] Largely defending their needs as slaves, "slave women resisted sex assaults, feigned illness, were insolent, participated in work slow downs and overt rebellions, murdered their masters, performed acts of sabotage, joined maroon colonies, and fled North to freedom."[18] In response to slave women's resistance to the gendered oppression of slavery, jurisdictions all along the eastern seaboard put to death hundreds of slave women and domestic black servants during slavery. Most jurisdictions hanged or burned to death black women for murder and infanticide, while others executed black women convicted of burglary, arson, poisoning, theft crimes, and slave revolts. Slave women mostly committed these offenses in resistance to the oppression of white masters, their families, and overseers. Examining the contextual peculiarities giving rise to black slave women executions since the earliest periods of American history furthers understanding of the intersection between gendered racism and capital punishment. The historical record reveals that challenging the racist and sexist exploitation of white masters accents black women executions in slavery.

SLAVE WOMEN EXECUTIONS IN COLONIAL AND ANTEBELLUM SLAVERY

Slavery was a societal system of domination, degradation, and subordination, with an especially rigid legal structure allowing privileged, landowning whites to manage African women as chattel property.[19] The concerted efforts of colonial legislatures, judicial officers, regional sheriffs, and local constables formed the justice system of slavery.[20] Slave historians distinguish *colonial* slavery from *antebellum* slavery to acknowledge the variant forms of slavery that developed in discrete regions of the United States at differing times and for separate reasons.[21] Despite this delineation of slave history and its resulting regionalization, scholars find it difficult to develop much understanding of the legal frameworks in which slave women lived out their lives in the early colonial period because not much exists in the historical record about the treatment of slave women.[22] There is so little in the record on slave women in early colonial history that one legal historian refers to the period as "the dark ages of American law."[23] As one distinguished slave historian explains, "[r]ecords of offenses by slaves are scant because on the one hand they were commonly tried by somewhat informal courts whose records are scattered and often lost, and on the other hand they were generally given sentences of whipping, death or deportation, which kept their names out of the penitentiary lists."[24] Still, existing records reveal that women accounted for substantial numbers of slaves convicted of capital crimes.

Slavery was horrible for men but it was far more dreadful for women—"superadded to the burden common to all, [slave women had] wrongs, and sufferings, and mortifications peculiarly their own."[25] The racist and sexist oppression of black women remained unabated once in the British colonies, and the severity of the punishments increased for slave women as the institution expanded throughout the colonies. Limited historical death penalty data show that jurisdictions executed roughly twice as many slave women in antebellum slavery than in colonial slavery.[26] Beginning with Massachusetts' execution of young slave woman Marja in September 1681 for arson-murder, officials executed 68 slave women before 1790 and 146 slave women from 1790 to emancipation. Undoubtedly, authorities executed far more slave women than what the historical record reveals. In his analysis of county court proceedings in colonial Virginia, for instance, Schwarz verifies 152 actual hangings of 567 cases where officials sentenced slaves to death, but the state may have condemned as many as 945 slaves and actually hanged some 400 to 800 slaves. Schwarz also shows that Virginia hanged 635 slaves in the antebellum period.[27] Surely female slaves comprised a significant proportion of these executions. In antebellum South Carolina, women were roughly 10 percent of the 296 slave executions.[28]

Jurisdictions put to death nearly 40 percent of all executed slave women during colonial slavery for murder, accessory to murder, and arson-murder, but in antebellum slavery murder crimes committed by slave women increased to nearly 70 percent.[29] Slave women mostly strangled, clubbed, stabbed, burned, shot, poisoned, or hacked to death their white masters, mistresses, overseers, and even their owner's children.[30] Streib claims that of the 109 slave women executed for murder where historical records sufficiently identify victims, 67 murdered a member of their master's family and 35 murdered unrelated victims.[31] Schwarz claims that whites were nearly 92 percent of the victims of slaves condemned to hang in colonial Virginia, and officials convicted 241 slaves for the violent killing of whites in antebellum Virginia. Of these homicides, slaves murdered 119 of their masters or members of their masters' families and 122 other whites including persons of authority, overseers, hirers, and constables. Regrettably, the historical record does not distinguish between male and female slaves involved in these killings.[32]

There was little regional variation in slave women executions in the colonial and antebellum slave periods. Mostly southern states hanged and burned to death capital offending female slaves. One reason for southern dominance in slave women executions is that slavery mostly flourished in the South after 1790; Virginia alone accounted for 35 percent of all female slave executions. The jurisdictional authority for women slave executions lied mostly with British military officials in the early colonial period and almost exclusively with state authorities in the antebellum period. Slave women executions took place in county facilities, mostly in jail courtyards. Black women suffered uniquely under the institutional confines of colonial and antebellum slavery. The historical record makes clear that slave women fought back viciously against the sexualized brutality of white masters by killing their owners, members of their owners' families, and destroying their owners' property. Slave women responded to the violence of white masters by intentionally aborting pregnancies and at times killing their own children. The retort of the state to such defiant undertakings of brutalized slave women was judicial murder.

Mostly, it was slave women's reaction to white oppression that accented their murder of white owners.[33] Early colonial governments used *burning to death* as an execution method almost exclusively against slave women for killing white masters or destruction of a master's property. In one of the earliest confirmed cases, New York authorities put to death a slave woman in February 1708 by roasting her alive "over a slow fire for several hours with a vessel of cool water held near her mouth. When she finally expired, her body was burnt to ashes."[34] The slave woman had participated along with three others in axing to death her owner William Hallett, his wife, and five children while they slept. The slave woman appears to have been the "catalyst of the whole affair." The reason for the slaves murdering Hallet and his family was their resentment for not being allowed to move about freely on Sundays—a cherished activity among slaves.[35] Albany officials in New York roasted to death an unidentified slave woman over a slow fire for her connection in the murder of a white man named Trucax in January 1717, most likely the slave woman's master.[36] In other cases, Virginia burned to death an unknown slave woman belonging to Prudden in February 1737 who confessed to axing Prudden's wife to death. Remarking on the case, Schwarz explains, "If voluntary, her confession suggests either that she would rather die than tolerate her mistress any longer or perhaps that she subsequently regretted a moment of explosive passion."[37]

Maryland is the only colonial government that gibbeted to death slave women for murdering white masters. In May 1723, officials gibbeted to death an unnamed slave woman for the murder of her master in Annapolis, and in July 1755 authorities executed slave woman Jenny by gibbeting her to death for killing her master in Port Tobacco. Most states hanged slave women for murdering white masters, however. Slave woman Esther belonging to Wise in Virginia hanged for the murder of her master in May 1767. In early 1818, slave woman Caty belonging to the Vaughan household hanged for murdering her former owner Linah Harwell who had once referred to Caty as "a bitch and a strumpet [prostitute]."[38] Slave woman Susan hanged in November 1844 in Missouri for axing to death her mistress, Rosa Ann King, while she napped. Susan killed King because she wanted to return to her previous owner.[39] Slave woman Pauline of the Rabbeneck household hanged in March 1846 at the "parish prison for cruelty to her mistress."[40] In March 1848, slave woman Lucy belonging to Mrs. Maria Dougherty hanged for beating to death her owner. In retaliation for punishment from Dougherty for some minor infraction, Lucy set fire to the Columbia Hotel where she lived with Dougherty and who owned the "ramshackle wooden structure." Dougherty punished Lucy severely for setting the small fire, and Lucy swore vengeance against her. Lucy made good on her threat; authorities found Dougherty's body floating in an underground brick cistern with her head crushed from repeated blows from a club. Lucy admitted killing Dougherty and vowed she would do it again. Indicted for murder, Judge Peter Gray assigned counsel to defend Lucy, but a jury found her guilty and Judge Gray sentenced Lucy to death by hanging. Sheriff Westerlage hanged Lucy shortly after noon; Lucy was the first woman hanged in Texas and the only woman hanged in Galveston County.[41]

Slave women often acted in concert with slave counterparts in response to white oppression. Roughly half of the slave women executed during colonial and antebellum slavery involved multiple executions. Slave women confederates were usually one or two slave men. Virginia hanged Winney and her accomplice Phill for murdering their master John Knox "most barbarously" near Fredericksburg in July 1769.[42] In several multiple execution cases, slave women acted with one or two other slave women to commit murder or poisoning in retaliation for their mistreatment from white owners. Officials in Virginia hanged Creasy and Sall for killing their mistress Mrs. Morrisett who had been repeatedly violent toward Creasy. Both women slaves earned reprieves from execution due to pregnancies in April and hanged in May 1806.[43] Slave woman Sarah and five male confederates hanged in Virginia in 1818 after they beat their slave owner Dr. Robert Berkeley to death, burned his body in a cabin fireplace, and then buried the remains. Shortly before Berkeley's murder, one of the killers confessed to a friend "his master was a bad master and he would sooner die than serve him."[44] Slave woman Melvaine belonging to Florentine Frivaz, and Melvaine's slave brother named Mango belonging to William Elien Kinair, hanged in February 1855 in the St. Charles Parish, Louisiana, jail yard for killing young Wesley Latham, the son of the overseer of the plantation of Mr. Lanfear.

Jurisdictions often imposed harsher punishment on slave women than did their male co-conspirators; slave women frequently *burned to death* for their crimes while their co-conspirators *hanged* for the same offense. The Salem County sheriff in New Jersey dragged slave woman Hagar and her accomplice Ben (a slave) on a wooden sledge through town to their executions after a Special Court of Magistrates and Freeholders had convicted them of murdering their master, lawyer James Sherron. Another accomplice was a white servant named John Hunt. The three had conspired to kill Sherron and, in April 1717, while inspecting his fields and distracted by Hagar's purposeful small talk, Hunt hacked Sherron to death with a hatchet after Ben had retrieved the murder weapon from a tool shed. At their execution site, "Hagar was chained to a stake and burned to ashes—probably while still alive and conscious." Ben hanged by his neck until dead. After that, his body was dipped in tar and set in a wrought iron frame [a gibbet].[45] Hunt hanged a month later. Slave woman Dolly, belonging to Charlestown merchant James Sands and her accomplice Liverpool owned by Price, burned alive in 1769 for poisoning Sands, his wife, and child.[46] In December 1770, North Carolina authorities across five counties hanged nineteen persons for murder and unspecified felonies, including three whites, three slave women, and thirteen slave men. The white participants were indentured servants with unidentified masters, but the three slave women were Annis and Phyllis belonging to Henry Ormond and slave woman Lucy belonging to Wyriot Ormond (brother to Henry Ormond). Along with two slave male confederates, the slave women killed Henry Ormond earlier that summer. A slave court found the slave women and their accomplices guilty of Ormond's murder and sentenced Annis to burn at the stake and for Mary and Phyllis to hang on the gallows.[47] Their male confederates also hanged. Henry Ormond's estate received £70 compensation for Annis and £20 for Phyllis, while North Carolina paid Wyriot Ormond £65 for the loss of Lucy. Henry Ormond was excessively abusive toward his slaves and garnered no mercy when the slave women sought revenge for his cruelty.

Slave women were often vicious in killing their white oppressors. Officials in New Jersey hanged young Jane Huff, a slave girl belonging to Sarah Hight in May 1837. Sarah "nagged and scolded Jane about almost everything" and at times "struck Jane with household objects." Jane was often indifferent to Sarah's concerns and disobeyed her orders prohibiting Jane to see her young boyfriend. One night after Sarah had fallen asleep in a chair, Jane hit Sarah between the eyes with a fire poker severely stunning her. Jane then dragged Sarah over to a fireplace where meat was boiling in a kettle, removed the meat, and then thrust Sarah's head into the boiling water—"Jane did not release her grip until Sarah

Hight's head was cooked like a lobster."[48] In later cases, Texas officials tried, convicted, and sentenced to death slave woman Jane Elkins for killing her owner Mr. Wisdom in 1853. Scholars know little of the events surrounding Elkins' crime, but on the night of her hanging, members of a medical fraternity exhumed Elkins' body "for the grisly purpose of serving as a medical cadaver."[49] In another case, Joseph Dougharty requested that the Texas state legislature pay him $460 in reimbursement for the execution of his property, slave woman Lucy, in March 1858 that the state tried, convicted, and hanged for the murder of his wife Maria Dougharty. There is nothing in the historical record explaining why Lucy murdered Mrs. Dougharty.[50]

Besides white masters, slave women frequently killed their abusive overseers. In May 1793, Virginia slave women Daphne and Nelly belonging to Edward Champion attacked and killed their overseer Joel Gathright who apparently had accused pregnant Nelly of leaving a gate open that allowed sheep to get into a cornfield. Nelly denied it most disrespectfully, and for her brazenness Gathright beat Nelly severely until Daphne went to her defense and the two women thrashed Gathright with their fists, sticks, and rocks, leaving him dead from a crushed skull. The county court tried the two slave women separately, denying both the benefit of legal counsel. The court convicted Daphne and Nelly of Gathright's murder and sentenced them to hang. Daphne hanged on July 19, but authorities reprieved Nelly's hanging until October 4 after she had delivered her baby.[51] In 1820, Celia, along with Abel, axed to death Mr. and Mrs. James Powell and then set their house on fire with them in it, although they managed to save the couple's infant child. Celia and Abel's owner, a man named Daughtry, hired out Abel to James Powell who repeatedly whipped Abel. Southampton County officials hanged the two for the murders in August 1821.[52] Also, in March 1844, Judge Henry Goldthwaite sentenced slave woman Nancy to hang in Alabama for assaulting with intent to kill Mary Beasley, a white woman.[53]

Young slave women murdered their masters' children to bring the wretchedness of slavery to their masters' doorstep. Young slave woman Chloe hanged in Pennsylvania in July 1801 for murdering the two young daughters of her owners Andrew and Mary Carothers. On a Saturday afternoon in January of that year, Chloe drowned 4-year-old Lucetta Carothers in a nearby creek, and on the next Saturday, she drowned 6-year-old Polly Carothers in the same creek. Some suspect that Chloe was mentally retarded and emotionally unstable, whereas others suppose that the young woman was so maltreated as a child that she was unmanageable; Chloe had several different masters over the years. Authorities tried Chloe for the two murders and found her guilty and sentenced her to death by hanging. Chloe confessed to the killings to Reverend James Smith who visited Chloe in jail just days before her scheduled execution. The court most likely ignored Chloe's cognitive disabilities, Mrs. Carothers' daily beatings of Chloe with a cowhide whip while stripped naked, or that Chloe had no legal counsel present during her trial.

New York executed young Dayon belonging to Abraham Bruyn in July 1803 for killing her master's infant child because she was angry over having to care for the child.[54] Missouri hanged young Mary when she confessed to beating and drowning Vienna Jane Brinker, one of her owner's children, in 1838, because she did not want to be sold.[55] Virginia executed Jane Williams in September 1852 for slashing to death with a hatchet the wife and infant of her master Joseph P. Winston while they slept. The Winstons badly mistreated Jane and had threatened to sell Jane without also selling her child. A newspaper at the time characterized Jane as "a fiend" and "a wretched murderess" and that she would die "without the smallest particle of sympathy from any human being possessed of the ordinary feelings of justice."[56]An estimated 6,000 people watched Jane's hanging. Jane's husband John died alongside her for the same crime. The state paid Winston $500 compensation for taking his property by execution. In still another case in 1839, a Lincoln Circuit Court in Missouri found slave woman Fanny belonging to William Prewitt guilty of murdering William Florence, a 10-year-old white boy found dead in Prewitt's peach orchard. The evidence showed that Fanny had killed the boy although authorities garnered the testimony of slave witnesses under the threat of death. There is nothing in the record showing that Fanny hanged for the murder (she most likely did) since an appeals court reversed and remanded the case to the trial court for a new hearing.[57] In still another case, Richmond authorities in Virginia hanged slave woman Margaret belonging to Mary M. Butt in January 1863 for killing a white infant. Another slave woman testified against Margaret, but Margaret denied the accusation and blamed the child's death on the woman who testified against her.[58] Still further, Joseph and Anne Wynn pleaded to the General Assembly of North Carolina for reimbursement of slave woman Vina, and her two slave male accomplices Charles and Jack, that authorities tried, convicted, and executed for the murder of their young daughter Mary the day after Christmas in 1822. All three slaves hanged in September 1823.[59]

In September 1731, slave woman Hannah belonging to Moses Atwater in Connecticut hanged for murdering a teenage white girl, Jemima Beecher (a servant to the Atwater household), and seriously injuring Hannah Merriman (a niece to Mr. Atwater) residing at Atwater's house. For some unexplained reason, the slave woman crept into the girls' bedroom and stabbed Jemima in the throat with a large butcher knife killing her instantly and then stabbed Hannah in the chest where one of her ribs deflected the knife surviving the attack. Tried in New Haven and found guilty of murdering the Atwater servant, the county sheriff dragged the slave murderess to the gallows through the street, hanged her, and then buried her beneath the gallows. In November 1737, officials in Rhode Island hanged young slave woman Ann for killing an 11-year-old white servant girl named Alice Allen indentured to John Easton and then throwing the body into a well.[60] Authorities in Boston hanged young slave woman Phillis belonging to John Greenleaf in 1752 for the arsenic poisoning of Greenleaf's one-year-old son. Phillis had mixed the poison in the child's milk and the boy died two days later. Phillis hoped the death would free her from caring for the child. On the day Phillis hanged, her mother collapsed from a nervous breakdown and died.[61] Slave woman Dolly belonging to James Sands burned to death on a workhouse green in South Carolina in 1769 for poisoning her master's infant.[62] In 1773, South Carolina authorities tried, convicted, and executed slave woman Bess and her male slave accomplice Charlie, both owned by Joseph Warnock, for poisoning Warnock's entire family including him and his wife and six children. Two of Warnock's six young children died as a result of the poisoning. Warnock petitioned the Court of Justices and Freeholders for compensation for the executions of Bess and Charlie.[63] In April 1820, Wyat Smith sought compensation for his female slave Cela, executed for killing one of his children.[64]

Authorities executed black slave women for killing white persons other than their masters, mistresses, their masters' children, and overseers. Slave woman Lucy belonging to Richard Randolph of Virginia hanged for killing a white man named John Lee in 1742. In September 1795, the Court of Common Pleas for South Carolina affirmed the conviction of a black woman named Arden for the murder of a Spanish seaman named Jewets.

A county court had tried Arden separately from her accomplice, Campbell, and found that she was guilty of murder for stabbing Jewets in the throat and chest with a pair of scissors. A jury found Campbell guilty of manslaughter for severely beating the victim with a club or stick. The court postponed Arden's hanging after she claimed to be pregnant. A matron of twelve women found Arden was not pregnant and officials immediately executed the defendant.[65] In some black female execution cases, slave women had white servant accomplices; Esther Foster (a black convict) and James Clark (a white male confederate) hanged in Ohio in February 1844 for murder.

Jurisdictions *convicted* slave women of infanticide disproportionately to white women accused of the crime—"a rate one and a half times the rate of white women."[66] Even so, during the early colonial period there were relatively few slave women executed for infanticide. Slave women's resistance to their oppression included controlling reproductive and maternal functions such as inducing abortions and committing infanticide.[67] One Tennessee physician confirmed that slave women used medicines, violent exercise, and external and internal manipulations as rudimentary birth control or to effect miscarriages.[68] Jurisdictions executed a relatively low number of black women for infanticide compared to white free women. In many cases, slave women "killed their children because they did not want them be slaves."[69] Of some 118 female slave executions identified by Streib, seven slave women murdered their own children.[70] Schwarz identified three slave women sentenced to death for infanticide during the antebellum period but none during the colonial period. Records show that Annice drowned five slave children belonging to her owner Jeremiah Prior. The county court found Annice guilty of pushing "one Ann a negro child slave . . . into a certain collection of water of the depth of five feet and there choked, suffocated, and drowned of which . . . the said Ann [Phebe, Nancy, Bill, and Nelly] instantly died." Five-year-old Bill and 2-year-old Nelly were Annice's children. Annice hanged in August 1828. Undoubtedly, Annice wanted to deprive her master the value of the children.[71] Annice was the only slave woman put to death in Missouri for infanticide.

Southern states executed most black women put to death for infanticide. Sussex County officials in Virginia hanged slave woman Poll belonging to Bobbitt for infanticide in January 1779. A Virginia court also found a young slave woman guilty of murdering her newborn infant and sentenced her to hang in 1818.[72] Slave woman Milley to Hanley hanged in Virginia for infanticide in 1826. Kentucky hanged an unknown slave woman to Rumsey for infanticide in 1812. Slave woman Hannah Miller hanged in Pennsylvania in 1805 for infanticide; she is the only confirmed black woman hanged after 1700 in a northern state for infanticide. Some 2,000 spectators watched her execution.[73] Servant woman Elizabeth Moore, "a mulatto," hanged in May 1809 in York County for poisoning to death her 9-year-old son, whom she reportedly wanted in Heaven with his younger sister whom she murdered years earlier. Elizabeth was born a slave but ran away to Maryland where she became a free domestic. "She had a son by another man whom she had placed in an almshouse and for whom she seemed to have had a distorted feeling of affection and concern." While in jail awaiting execution, Elizabeth became pregnant and delivered the child before her execution.[74]

White recounts several cases where slave women committed infanticide out of concern for the well-being of their children.[75] In many infanticide cases, masters or their sons fathered the illegitimate newborns; yet the identity of the baby's father was not part of the official record.[76] In one case, an Alabama slave woman killed her baby because her master was the father; her mistress knew it and treated the child callously. The slave mother confessed to killing her baby claiming that she wanted to save the child from further cruelty. One slave woman killed her newborn to keep her master from selling the child as he had her other three children. Records of the General Assembly for South Carolina reveal that in 1824 Ellis Palmer solicited for reimbursement for the execution of slave woman Anaca for the murder of her two children.[77] Many whites interpreted these events as evidence that slave women lacked maternal feelings. Infanticide was mostly an uncharacteristic behavior of slave mothers, and in many cases, infant deaths were accidental with mothers inadvertently overlaying and suffocating infants while sleeping. Smothering accounted for more than 60,000 slave infant deaths during the antebellum period. Yet this explanation troubles slave historians as well as contemporary medical practitioners.[78] Johnson suggests that most reported cases of slave mothers suffocating their children might actually have been "crib deaths," or what the medical community today refers to as Sudden Infant Death Syndrome (SIDS).[79] Malnutrition and planters overworking pregnant slave women surely contributed to infant deaths. In some cases, slave women rendered psychotic raised reasonable doubts as to the culpability of women for killing their children.[80] A Powhatan County Court in Virginia sentenced Jenny to death, for instance, for drowning her three young children even though the judge found her insane. Lucy, a slave woman belonging to Thomas Balton, believed to have killed her mulatto child, actually abandoned the child or it was born dead and not intentionally killed. Frantic about running away from her abusive master, one Virginia slave woman killed her 4-year-old child. Clearly, as Schwarz points out, "slavery played a crucial role in the paternity, birth, or death of these unfortunate children. Slavery was like an unindicted co-conspirator or a perpetrator in many infanticides committed by slave women."[81]

Slave rebellion was a major concern among white planters as early as 1642 and a crucial component of slave codes was to deter insurrections by imposing harsh punishments. Most female slave insurrection amounted to day-to-day resistance that took on a variety of forms, including "malingering; self mutilation; suicide; destruction of owner's crops, tools, and livestock; running away; or criminal activity like stealing and violent insurrection."[82] Slave women also manifested resistance to bondage by assaulting or poisoning overseers and owners, breaking tools, pilfering, and burning barns.[83] Jurisdictions put to death hundreds of slave men but few slave women for insurrection. Execution figures on slave revolts remain circumspect since Aptheker speaks of hundreds of slave executions for uprisings that are largely unaccounted for in death penalty inventories.[84] Slave women executions for revolt took place exclusively during colonial slavery. New Orleans hanged the first black women for insurrection in June 1731. She remains nameless, but she was one of eight slaves executed after officials in colonial Louisiana uncovered a widespread conspiracy to kill slaveholders. It seems that an intoxicated French soldier demanded a slave woman retrieve needed wood for his fire but refused to do so because she was too weary and wanted only to eat her lunch. It was then that the soldier gave the slave woman a violent slap across the face. Angry, the insolent slave woman shouted to the French soldier he would not slap blacks for much longer.[85] Suspicious of her comment, bystanders seized her and took her before the governor who imprisoned her and launched an inquiry into the possibility of a slave conspiracy to insurrection. Officials soon learned that a plot was indeed in the making wherein "[t]he *nègres* planned to get rid of all the French and establish themselves in their place, taking over the Capital and all we owned."[86] Eight conspirators eventually confessed, "After which the eight negroes were condemned to be broke on the wheel, and the woman to be hanged before their eyes; which was accordingly done, and prevented the conspiracy from taking effect."[87] In other cases, jurisdictions executed slave women for crimes where the historical record remains silent. Charleston in South Carolina suffered a rage of rebellious slave activity in 1740 and 1741 with devastating fires destroying hundreds of buildings. In July of the later year, an unknown slave woman died by an unknown execution method for her participation in the activities.

Slave women accounted for all female executions in the United States for arson, assault, attempted arson, and petty treason.[88] Poisoning and arson, however, were the most prevalent methods slave women used to kill their white oppressors and destroy property unjustly acquired through slave labor. Some alleged poisonings and related attempted murders by slave women resulted from unintentional acts, however, even if poisoning was "well-suited to women's resistance because of their duties as cooks and nurses on the plantation."[89] Cases of poisoning typically involved an accusation of poisoning food prepared by slave women for the owner's family that mostly resulted from a lack of safe food preparation methods than intentional acts of harm.[90] Other cases involved slaves unknowingly administering poisonous medicine or unlawfully administering medicines. Jenny hanged in chains for poisoning to death her master in Maryland in 1770—"a horrible punishment that amounted to slow starvation" beyond the state's law.[91] Charleston authorities in South Carolina hanged a slave woman belonging to Fickling in January 1761 for poisoning her master. The unidentified slave woman hanged alongside Abraham, a male accomplice owned by Gibbons. Virginia authorities also burned to death slave woman Eve for poisoning her master Peter Montague with a glass of milk. Eve's executioner afterwards quartered her burned body and displayed it publicly. There is nothing in the historical record as to why Eve killed her master, but to Schwarz, "Eve died because of common law, her status as a slave, and her identity as a woman."[92] In 1793, Sheriff Archibald Griffin petitioned the North Carolina legislature for fees he incurred in hanging slave woman Beck belonging to Sarah Taylor for poisoning her husband and two sons.[93] Even an *attempted poisoning* of a slave master warrants execution. In June 1764, for instance, Calvert County officials in Maryland executed slave woman Betty along with two accomplices named Sambo and Toby for attempting to murder their owner Mr. Smith and his wife by poisoning. Interestingly, the court gave the slave owners in this case a choice to either export the slaves out of the province (a common practice in colonial America called *transportation*) or for the state to execute them—the owners chose to execute.[94]

Slave jurisdictions executed *juvenile* female slaves for poisoning as well. Authorities in Boston hanged a 17-year-old in 1751 for the arsenic poisoning of her master's one-year-old son. Phillis had mixed the poison in the child's milk. Virginia Beach hanged 16-year-old Chastity, along with male slave accomplice George, both belonging to Lawson, for poisoning in October 1803. Missouri hanged 16-year-old Rosanne Keen for poisoning her owner, Enos Seeley, a former clerk for Cumberland County. Young Keen reportedly poisoned both Mr. and Mrs. Seeley with arsenic borrowed from a neighbor that she mixed with butter and served to the couple. Both victims became seriously ill but only Mr. Seeley succumbed to the poison. Authorities believed Seeley died of natural causes, but when a neighbor told authorities that she had given the poison to young Keen, suspicions escalated and officials exhumed Seeley's body. A laboratory analysis confirmed Seeley had died from arsenic poisoning, and officials tried, convicted, and sentenced Keen to death for the murder. Local authorities hanged Keen in the jail yard in April 1844. Keen apparently was motivated to kill the Seeleys so that she could steal jewelry and possessions. Some argued that Keen was "deficient in intellect."[95]

Arson convictions brought severe penalties for slave women as well. Arson was a crime appealing to slave women since they often "did not have the physical strength to confront their white enemies," and arson was a "powerful way to deprive whites of their property and injure their economic well-being."[96] Slave women burned their master's houses, jails, shops, wheat stacks, and agricultural buildings such as mills and barns. In colonial Virginia, slave women were 30 percent of slaves convicted of arson.[97] Accordingly, these figures "give some perspective on the method these women employed to counter the power of their masters."[98] Charleston in South Carolina suffered a wrath of devastating fires that authorities attributed to insurgent slaves, and in July 1641 put to death an unknown slave woman "as punishment for having set fire to a house with the evil intent of burning down the remaining Part of the Town."[99] In another early case, Sarah belonging to the Curtis household in Virginia hanged for arson in 1705. Officials in neighboring Maryland executed Jenny and Grace, two slave women belonging to Joseph Galloway, for arson in 1751.[100] Charleston County officials in South Carolina burned to death two unidentified slave women belonging to Childermas Croft in June 1754 "for setting fire to their master's dwelling house and the outbuildings, all of which were destroyed."[101] Slave woman Rose belonging to the Rabour household hanged in North Carolina for arson in November 1766.[102]

New York burned to death an unidentified slave woman belonging to Nathaniel Smith for arson resulting in a murder sometime in 1771. Slave woman Sitty belonging to Johannes Hellis burned at the stake in March 1774 after confessing that the devil possessed her to set fire to her owner's barn.[103] Authorities executed a slave woman to William Crafts for arson of Mr. Craft's house in November 1774. Maryland executed a slave woman in 1776 "for destroying by fire her master's house, his outhouses, and tobacco house."[104] Pennsylvania hanged slave woman Sucky for arson of her master's property in July 1780. Virginia hanged Violet of Sawyer in 1780 for burning her master's house; the county court that convicted Violet demanded that her "severed head was to remain on display on a pole near Staunton."[105] Dinah, a slave woman to Peter Damon, hanged in New Jersey in October 1788 for poisoning Damon's wife and burning down his barn. New York hanged Nelly belonging to Daniel Braine for burning Jeremiah Vanderbilt's house in October 1790. Slave woman Creese belonging to the Fisher household hanged in Virginia in March 1789 for arson.

Fires in Albany, New York, destroyed 26 houses and did more than $200,000 in damage in 1793. Three slaves were involved in setting the fires including two female slave teenagers: 12-year-old Bett belonging to Philip Van Rensselaer and 14-year-old Dean belonging to Vokert A. Douw. Both hanged in March 1784 and their accomplice, a male slave named Pompey belonging to Mathew Visscher, hanged a month later.[106] West Virginia hanged slave woman Millay belonging to the Robe household in September 1798 for arson. In 1805, St. Louis hanged an unidentified slave woman belonging to Pierre Chouteau, the patriarch of the most prominent French family in Missouri at that time, for "wilfully and maliciously burning her owner's dwelling, barn, or stable."[107] Scott County officials hanged slave woman Nancy belonging to Rhodes for arson in September 1808. Young black servant woman Rose Butler hanged before some 10,000 spectators in July

1819 in New York for an attempted arson of her mistress's house. Butler was employed by William Morris. Actually, Rose had scattered hot coals on three steps of the stairwell, but the court was more concerned with her intent to burn the house than the amount of actual damage.[108] In December 1829, Richmond County hanged slave woman Jenny belonging to Jones for arson, and six months later in June 1830, the same county officials hanged slave woman Cinda belonging to Lubbock for arson. Caroline County authorities in Virginia hanged slave woman Malina in 1861 along with her confederate Andrew for burning their master's barn, stable, corn house, and tobacco house.[109]

Slave women often reacted violently to sexualized brutality. White sexual violence toward slave women was so pervasive that today "at least three-quarters of black Americans have at least one white ancestry."[110] Thomas Jefferson may have written eloquently about *equity* and *liberty* in forming the federal government, but he is one slave owner who "coerced the enslaved teenager Sally Hemming into his bed" and fathered several children.[111] Celia's hanging in Missouri further illustrates the perversion in such cases. Seventy-year-old Robert Newsome bought 14-year-old Celia and forced sexual relations upon her immediately and repeatedly. One night when Newsome went to Celia's cabin to abuse her, she struck him with a stick and killed him instantly. Celia was pregnant for the third time by Newsome and was very ill when he last approached her. At her trial, the court was concerned only with whether Celia had a right to defend herself against her master's assault. The trial judge made it clear that Celia did not have that right. To the court, Celia had no sexual rights over her own body because she was Newsome's property and she ought to have submitted to Newsome's demands. Celia was guilty of murder and hanged four days before Christmas in 1855.[112] In an earlier Florida case, incestual victimization provoked mulatto slave woman Celia to kill her master, Jacob Bryan, a North Florida white planter. Bryan cohabitated with a freed slave woman named Susan whom he could not marry given Florida's constitutional prohibition against interracial marriages. Celia was the oldest of the couple's six illegitimate children. What's more, Bryan was the father of Celia's four children, daughter Mary Jane, and sons William, Darius, and Francis. The events that transpired between Bryan and Celia are not entirely clear since the records are mostly missing. The case reportedly began on a morning in December 1847 with Bryan attempting to discipline Celia. As one newspaper put it, "It appears that he attempted to punish her, and being at the time engaged in making a hoe-handle with a drawing knife, she at first resisted him with the hoe-handle, and then used the drawing knife, with which she cut open his skull so as to produce instant death." A jury of Florida's Eastern Circuit Court comprising only white males tried and convicted Celia of manslaughter and recommended clemency and mercy. Trial judge Thomas Douglas, however, sentenced Celia to death fearing that Celia's hanging would exemplify the consequences of slaves that lash out against their white owners. The state's governor, William D. Moseley, commuted Celia's hanging for three months while he reviewed the case but eventually denied clemency and Celia hanged on September 22, 1848. At the gallows, Celia blamed her mother for her death. Her body remained on the gallows for an hour before being cut down and interned. Celia is the first confirmed woman execution in Florida.[113]

Slave woman resistance in the early colonial period also entailed theft-stealing crimes, burglary, larceny, and other rebellious activity for which authorities put some slave women to death. Slave woman Phoebe belonging to Joseph Richardson hanged in Pennsylvania in 1764 for "burglariously entering the house of Thomas Barnard and stealing divers goods."[114] Richardson received £55 for the loss of his chattel property. New York authorities hanged young slave woman Venus belonging to Catherine Ball in February 1767 for burglary and stealing "several articles from the house of Mr. Forbes, a resident of New York City."[115] In still another burglary case, slave woman Mary "pled guilty to a charge of masterminding a sizable theft of goods" and hanged in September 1706 while authorities whipped her confederate Tom (race unknown) for his participation in the crime.[116] New York officials hanged slave woman Bett belonging to Wilhelmus Houghtaling for burglary in July 1748. There are no details of the crime, but Hearn claims Bett hanged with a male accomplice.[117] As late as March 1865, South Carolina hanged young Amy Spain in part for stealing "linens, sheets, pillow cases, flour, sugar, lard, and some furniture" from her master Major A.C. Spain.[118] In August 1829, while traders led some one hundred slave men, women, and children from Maryland to points South for sale, two of the slave men abruptly dropped their shackles that had been filed through and began fighting as a pretense to attacking and killing the traders. Upon recapturing the entire group of slaves, the circuit court tried, convicted, and sentenced six of the leaders of the uprising to hang for the murder of the traders. Among them was a slave woman named Dinah who was "pregnant and quick with child." The court delayed her execution until the delivery of her child, and on May 25, 1830, Dinah hanged in the courthouse yard at Greensup, Kentucky.[119]

Slave women also hanged for unknown crimes. Officials in Virginia hanged an unidentified slave woman for an unspecified felony some time in 1751. An unidentified slave woman belonging to Derek Day in New Jersey burned at the stake in May 1755 for an unknown crime. At least four Virginia slave women hanged for unspecified felonies. Charles City hanged slave woman Penelope to the Copeland household for an unspecified felony committed against an unknown person in April 1781. Dinwiddie County hanged slave woman Molly to the Clark household sometime in 1783 for an unspecified felony also committed against an unknown person. Fauquier County officials hanged slave woman Molly belonging to the Marshall household in July 1791 for an unspecified felony against a white person. In addition, King George County hanged slave woman Nan belonging to Smith in April 1801 for an unspecified felony against an unknown person.

Slave women's executions were often gruesome events. Mary Glass, a free black (*quadroon*) woman of property, tortured to death a young white indentured servant girl named Emilia Davis belonging to William Walker. The witnesses against Mary included whites, free negroes, slaves, and three Choctaw Indians who testified that Mary viciously whipped young Emilia to death. Three slave men helped Mary bury Emilia. A Baton Rouge judge sentenced Mary to a gruesome death in July 1781: "to have her right hand cut off under the Gallows, then immediately to be hanged . . . And when cut down, her head to be severed and stuck up upon a pole at her former residence . . . and her right hand to be nailed to the same Post."[120]

 There is only one confirmed black woman execution for spousal murder throughout all of slavery. In that case, Elizabeth Freeman killed her husband David. Elizabeth was a free black woman. No record indicates any reason for Elizabeth slitting David's throat with a razor, although both suffered from acute alcoholism. Elizabeth admitted her guilt on the gallows and hanged in July 1832 in New Jersey.[121]

BLACK WOMEN EXECUTIONS IN RECONSTRUCTION

Jurisdictions executed far fewer black women in the immediate postbellum period than in the previous decades of colonial and antebellum slavery. Jurisdictional authorities in southern states put to death three black women for murder, two for spousal murder, and one for infanticide. The dramatic decrease in black women executions during Reconstruction surely resulted from what some scholars insist was a period of positive social relations and a growing complacency in criminal justice policy toward "dangerous classes."[122] But there is little historical evidence to support this proposition; in fact, emancipation ushered in one of the most chaotic and turbulent periods in U.S. history. While the demise of slavery brought about critical developments in black *political rights*, blacks found improving their *social rights* a far more formidable task.[123] In effect, legal emancipation did not move southern society appreciably toward racial equality during Reconstruction; the South remained as segregated and racially unequal as it had during slavery. The Reconstruction Amendments had introduced an ambiguity into black–white race relations, and keeping "blacks in their place" had become more difficult to enforce and often resulted in chaotic and unpredictable forms of racial domination over blacks. To white planters, the loss of nearly 4 million bonded workers profoundly threatened the South's economic and political viability, and immediately after emancipation, southern states limited black rights by adopting laws similar to those used to regulate blacks in slavery. Poor whites viewed the gains made by blacks during Reconstruction as rebellious and launched violent retaliations against blacks.[124] By 1866, all southern states had enacted *black codes* to regulate black lives with Mississippi and South Carolina enacting the first and harshest codes.[125] Southern states sought to keep blacks subordinated to whites by imposing these discriminatory measures precluding blacks from voting, serving on juries, and testifying in court cases involving whites.[126]

One result of the continued subjugation of blacks in this period was the loss of their labor value after emancipation. But southern justice systems quickly recognized the pecuniary benefit of black prisoners as lessees to private and public enterprises. Black prisoners comprised large numbers of leased prison work gangs for mining and railroad interests and on prison farms that was unprecedented in slavery. Fewer black female executions during the period resulted from the dramatic increase in black women prison populations in southern states immediately following the Civil War. Before emancipation, southern states rarely incarcerated slaves since planters' production needs made few slaves eligible for public punishment. After 1865, however, newly freed black women swelled the ranks of southern prison populations with black females comprising between 40 and 70 percent of females committed to southern penitentiaries. Black female incarceration rates increased because many black women had significant contact with whites as domestic servants and housemaids, thus rendering them especially prone to crime accusations. Although imprisoned black women committed mostly property crimes, violent crimes were still common among black females.

Also attributable to reducing executions of black women in the immediate aftermath of the Civil War was an increase in white violence directed toward black people as a related means of imposing capital punishment.[127] Black female lynchings became commonplace during this period. Racial violence was an insidious and a pervasive feature of everyday life for black women with southern whites employing the selective and deliberate strategies of such vigilante groups as the Ku Klux Klan, the Red Shirts, and the Knights of the White Camellias to terrorize blacks. Assaulting, murdering, lynching, politically repressing, and executing black women continued throughout postbellum period.[128] The vulnerability of black women to white male sexual violence was greater in the postbellum period than it had been during slavery.[129] Regarding some 160 confirmed black female lynchings of both adults and children across fifteen states in the South and West, one scholar notes that rape of black women and the lynching of victims became one and the same in the postbellum period.[130] The sexual brutalization of black women continued with white men raping, shooting, scalping, and cutting off the ears of black women who resisted their sexual advances.[131] In his chronicle on the hidden history of racial cleansing in the United States, Pulitzer Prize–winning author Elliot Jaspin tells that when Mary Turner threatened to swear out arrest warrants against a mob that, the day before, had lynched her husband Hayes Turner and left his body hanging for two days, "[t]he mob grabbed Mary, eight months pregnant, hung her upside down from a tree, doused her with gasoline, set her on fire, then disemboweled her and tore out her fetus. The baby made a feeble cry before a member of the mob stomped it to death."[132] In Texas, some 1,524 acts of violence against blacks took place between 1865 and 1868. Nearly 200 of these incidents involved the victimization of black women. White employers beat black women for "using insolent language," for refusing to call her employer "master," and "for crying because he whipped my mother."[133] White mobs even whipped, flogged, beat, assaulted, castrated, and murdered black children.[134] Whites killed 295 blacks in Caddo Parish in Louisiana between 1865 and 1876, and in 1865 alone whites killed more than 2,000 blacks including women and children near Shreveport, Louisiana.[135] Whites set fire to an entire black settlement in 1866 and lynched 24 blacks including women and children. Rioting white mobs in cities in Tennessee and Mississippi "raped black women as they went on an antiblack rampage."[136] In an 1864 Mississippi case, the owners of two slave women named Mary and Tena sought compensation for their lynchings. Apparently, the two slave women "plotted to murder several 'helpless' white families and to destroy the property of their masters by setting fire to a store, warehouse and several dwelling houses. The two women were captured as they sought to flee to their friends—the Yankees—for protection. The petitioners assert that due to the virtual suspension of the courts and the insecurity of the jails, the two women were hanged without due process of law."[137] From 1884 to 1900, white mobsters in the black belt states lynched 1,678 blacks including 51 women that white men raped before their lynchings.[138] Mississippi, Alabama, Louisiana, and Georgia—the black belt states—had the worst records.[139]

Southern states put to death six black women during Reconstruction: one for murder, three for child murder, and two for spousal murder. Black women executions attest to the systemic racist and sexist brutality suffered by black women during the period. It was in this era that state authorities executed one of the youngest black females put to death in U.S. history. Kentucky officials hanged 12-year-old servant girl Susan in February 1868 for killing Walter Graves, a 2-year-old white child under her care as a babysitter. Susan confessed to the killing after white neighbors of the Graves's threatened her with lynching. Officials arrested and tried Susan for Walter's murder. Though the trial judge rendered her confession involuntary and inadmissible given the lynching intimidation, a jury nevertheless convicted Susan for the white boy's death.[140] Susan reportedly "writhed and twisted and jerked many times" during her hanging. Many witnesses to Susan's hanging acquired pieces of the hanging rope.[141] In another case, Maryland hanged domestic servant Mary Wallis in the jail yard in Marlboro in February 1871 for poisoning the nine-month-old infant child of the Read family—Albert M. Read was a clerk in the U.S. Treasury Department in Washington, D.C. Mary was born into slavery and belonged to Richard D. Hall, and after the Civil War she worked as a house servant for several families and eventually the Reeds. One newspaper report explains that Mary reportedly had stolen some clothes from the Reeds' child's nurse "and being charged with the theft became very sullen and threatening in her manner." Mary had difficulties with the nurse that became intensified when she discovered Mary's theft of the nurse's clothes. Mary poisoned the infant's milk with strychnine, killing the child and hoping to blame the murder on the baby's nurse. Mary confessed to her misdeeds. A trial jury found Mary guilty of first-degree murder, but because Mary was mentally challenged and, because of her age and mental deficiency, the jury recommended leniency in sentencing Mary. But as many white trial judges did at the time, the judge overruled the jury's suggestion and sentenced Mary to death.[142] There is no public information concerning the December 1869 hanging of Sarah Jane Bradley in Sussex County, Delaware, for killing a white child.

There are also a few cases of black women killing their spouses in retaliation for *domestic maltreatment*. A simple footnote to history shows that Lucy Parnell hanged in Maryland in February 1868 for the confessed murder of a black man named Hanson Robbins with whom she and her two young daughters lived. Apparently, one night Robbins aggressively demanded sex from Lucy or he would throw her out of the house. Lucy refused and after another try at seducing Lucy she hit Robbins in the head with a nearby tool. Lucy dragged Robbins to the side of a road, dug a whole, and buried Robbins while he was still alive.[143]

Little is known also about the facts in most of spousal murder cases during the period, but in one case, in May 1874, authorities in Elberton, Georgia, hanged Ann Hunt for an interracial murder. Ann and a white man named John R. Fortson lived together and had five children. John apparently had a romantic interest in Elizabeth Brawner against whom Ann conspired with a friend, America Burden, to murder Brawner. Burden gave Brawner a flask of whiskey laced with strychnine from which Brawner died soon thereafter. Authorities arrested Ann and Burden and indicted John as a co-conspirator but he had left the country. The punishment dealt to Burden is unclear, but Ann hanged for involvement in Brawner's murder. In another case, Ouachita County authorities in Louisiana hanged Alcee Harris in November 1875 for her part in the killing of her husband Henry Harris. Alcee and Henry had been arguing, and afraid Henry was going to kill her, she convinced Toney Nellum to kill Henry with an axe. Alcee and Toney confessed to their respective parts in the killing of Henry and hanged together before some 5,000 spectators. Alcee died immediately, but Toney strangled to death because the drop was too short. Virginia hanged Lucinda Fowlkes in April 1881 for murdering her husband with an axe because he was mean to her and consistently beat and abused her.[144]

These cases of black female violence most likely result from what one scholar explains as higher levels of violence accenting the gendered racism of southern society that rendered black women more likely to murder. These black women were most likely responding to the brutalization of whites accenting much of slavery. The violent reaction of black women to killing white children may have been individual responses to "the stress generated by their dislocation, isolation, and economic marginality."[145]

BLACK WOMEN EXECUTIONS IN JIM CROW

Whites in postbellum society harbored a gross intolerance toward marginalized persons, and the legal system was the most effective apparatus to ensure their social, political, and economic supremacy. Jim Crow segregation took hold as an institutional means of subordinating blacks with the collapse of Reconstruction, and by 1890 southern society had fully established the legal separation of blacks.[146] Segregationist polices were not limited to the Jim Crow South and governed northern black as well.[147] Congress and the U.S. Supreme Court were complicit in sanctioning this institutionalization of white supremacy in the post–Reconstruction era. Beginning with the *Civil Rights Cases* (1893) striking down the provisions of the Civil Rights Act of 1875, a series of U.S. Supreme Court decisions effectively dismantled the federal civil rights protections put in place during Reconstruction and which ushered in a constitutionalization of white hegemony in the United States.[148] These judicial mandates effectively replaced laissez-faire segregation and brought about the complete legal domination of black people. As a result, whites had the full force of law behind them in their social, political, and economic dominion of black people.

The social instability of Jim Crow ushered in yet another killing period for black people. Legal and extralegal forms of the death penalty killed more than 8,100 black persons during the period; death penalty jurisdictions killed 4,912 black prisoners and lynch mobs killed 3,445 black victims.[149] Lynching victims often included black women, of whom many were pregnant.[150] White terrorists often lynched black women alongside their children and other family members: An Arkansas mob lynched Mary Briscoe with her husband in 1891; the daughter of John Hastings died by a lynch mob with her brother in Calahousla, Louisiana, the same year; a Kentucky mob lynched a black woman with her daughter and granddaughter in Bardstown in 1893; Mrs. Sam Padgett suffered a lynching in Tatnall County, Georgia, with her son in 1904; in 1908, Mrs. David Wallace died at the hands of a lynch mob with her husband and five children in Hickory Grove, Kentucky; a mob in Okemah, Oklahoma, lynched Laura Nelson and her son in 1911; and the list goes on.[151] Black women were 3 percent of the 2,364 black lynching victims identified in ten southern states between 1882 and 1930.[152] The killing of black women was particularly heinous; white mobs lynched few white females and there is no confirmation that white female lynching victims suffered the savagery inflicted on black women.[153]

The execution of black women from the end of Reconstruction to the early days of the civil rights movement accents the brutality and violence suffered by black women during Jim Crow. Most southern jurisdictions executed black women for crimes of murder. Because white society excluded black women "with little or no formal education and few technical skills from the urban industrial workplace," most black women executed during the period were domestic servants and housemaids whose offenses,[154] one can reasonably conclude, involved horrid crimes of resistance against violent white aggression similarly experienced by slave women. Such is the case with young Margaret Harris bound over as an indentured servant since she was a child to widow Nancy Barnwell in Fairmount, Georgia. In an attempt to relieve herself of her indenture, Margaret poisoned Barnwell and her two grandchildren at a dinner meal and one of the children (Lela Lewis) died from the poisoning. A court tried and convicted Margaret for the child's death and sentenced her hanged in October 1883 before some 5,000 onlookers. As was usually the case with newspapers referencing executed black females, a *New York Times* article gave an unsavory description

Media

M 1

of Margaret as "coal black, five feet two inches in height, heavily built, and weighted 150 pounds. She had only one eye, the right one being put out, and altogether her face was not pleasant to look upon. Added to this she had very large hands and feet, which made her appearance even worse looking."[155]

There were several other child murder cases in the Jim Crow south. Alabama hanged young Pauline McCoy in January 1888 for murdering Annie Jordan, a 14-year-old white girl, for her shoes. There was significant speculation that Pauline could not have committed the murder. Annie Jordan was mentally retarded ("half-witted" and "demented" to use the language of the day) and had wandered away from home. Days later, authorities found her unclothed body in a pine thicket and discovered that someone had strangled the young girl to death. Officials questioned Pauline when they found her with the dead girl's shoes. Pauline immediately accused her father of killing young Annie; it was highly plausible that Pauline's father had sexually assaulted Annie and then killed her. Some speculate that Pauline lacked the upper body strength to kill Annie. Nevertheless, a trial court convicted Pauline of the murder and sentenced her to death. In another case in October 1892, South Carolina hanged 14-year-old Milbry Brown for poisoning a white infant. The mentally retarded Brown worked as a domestic servant for W.C. Carpenter of Gaffney, South Carolina. Mrs. Carpenter regularly badgered Brown about her work habits, and on one occasion Brown became incensed by Mrs. Carpenter's criticism that she was sweeping too slowly. Ostensibly in retaliation for her mistreatment, Brown poured carbolic acid down the throat of the Carpenter's infant that died hours later. The state hanged Brown in the jail yard at Spartanburg.[156]

Jurisdictions put to death black women in the postbellum period for infanticide and child murder. In the first instance, there is little public information concerning the hanging of a black woman named Henrietta Murrell in September 1891 at Smithville in Charlotte County, Virginia, for confessing to the drowning death of her 8-year-old child.[157] Murrell claimed that she killed her child because she could not obtain work and support herself and the child.[158] Regional newspapers gave considerably more attention to the case of Caroline Shipp, a poor, illiterate black girl no more than 20 years old, and her hanging in front of some 3,000 spectators. Caroline's parents treated her badly as a young child, and both died when Caroline was in her early teens. Caroline had two children by different men at a young age; her first child died from injuries suffered in a fall. The Gaston County sheriff in North Carolina hanged Caroline Shipp in January 1892 for poisoning to death her 11-month-old son. A jury found her guilty of the crime but Shipp always denied killing her child claiming that her boyfriend Mack Farrar was responsible for poisoning the child. Jurors acquitted Farrar based on an alibi but convicted Caroline. That her defence lawyers believed Caroline was guilty as an accomplice undoubtedly influenced their ability to adequately defend her against the murder charge; there was no appeal. There are conflicting reports that authorities actually tried Caroline Shipp for the poisoning murder of her husband James Shipp.[159] In any event, once on the gallows Caroline held a white handkerchief that she dropped once she was asked if the Sheriff was ready. Shipp's hanging was a particularly perverse execution; not only did state authorities present very weak evidence of her culpability at her trial, but officials botched her hanging with too short of a drop to kill instantaneously, two spectators had to pull on Shipp's legs to break her neck. Reports also revealed that Shipp may have miscarried an unborn child at the gallows—once again, the state executed an innocent child. The execution was so ghastly that newspaper reporters had to look away. What's more, Sheriff officials did not immediately take away Shipp's body for burial but left the body hanging all day.[160]

In another case, although Anna Tribble proclaimed her innocence, the young unmarried woman hanged at Newberry in South Carolina in October 1892 after a trial, conviction, and death sentence for murdering her illegitimate newborn son. There was no appeal. Conflicting reports show that Anna either deserted the child in a field or threw the infant into a stream next to which she had given birth. Anna did not go to the gallows willingly; the county sheriff had to hold her while he fastened the knot and adjusted the rope around her neck.[161] At least one black female hanged for killing her stepchild during this period. In a territorial hanging, federal authorities in Oklahoma executed Dora Wright in July 1903 for the murder and whipping mutilation of her young stepdaughter named Alice Williams. Evidence revealed that Dora had beaten little Alice on several occasions and that scaring revealed torture with a red-hot poker. Dora had mutilated Alice's corpse after death. The jury took twenty minutes to render its verdict with no mercy. Wright was a domestic servant, and the reason for the killing remains unknown. Hundreds of people in McAlester viewed the execution after President Roosevelt denied clemency remarking, "A woman mean enough to do that ought to have nerve enough to meet her punishment."[162]

In still other cases, jurisdictions put to death black women convicted of spousal murder. Farm worker Matilda Carter, along with two black male accomplices, named Eldridge Scales and Joe Hayes, hanged in Rockingham County in North Carolina before a crowd of 5,000 people in January 1882 for the murder of her husband Nash Carter.[163] South Carolina hanged Lucinda Teasdale in June 1882 along with her half sister's husband, Anderson Singleton, for the murder of Lucinda's sister and Singleton's wife, Phoebe Teasdale.[164] Sheriff Southward of Henrico County in Virginia hanged Barbara Miller in September 1883 for conspiring with her paramour, Charles Henry Lee, to kill her husband. Barbara was born a slave to a well-known planter in the county and in due course married Daniel Miller, a man 20 years her senior. Charles killed Daniel with an axe and then left the body on the railroad tracks where a train so mutilated the body that it was almost unrecognizable. Barbara confessed to the killing when arrested with Charles. The county court tried Charles first, found him guilty, and sentenced him to hang a month before Barbara hanged; Barbara's confession went far toward the conviction of Charles. Barbara hanged before several thousand people surrounding the jail yard; the Sheriff bungled the hanging by providing too long of a drop and Barbara strangled to death. One testament to Barbara's level of impoverishment was that after her hanging, Barbara's mother had to solicit donations from the crowd to pay funeral expenses.[165] Virginia hanged Margaret Lashley in January 1892 as an accessory to murder for her role in the killing of Margaret's husband by James Lyles, her boyfriend, in October 1890. Lyles confessed his crime and declared that he acted alone. Lashley protested her innocence and died proclaiming that she had no hand in the murder.[166] Georgia hanged Amanda Cody with her male lover, Florence English, for the murder of Amanda's husband Cicero in November 1895.[167] Mississippi hanged Ann Knight along with Will Gray in October 1922 for killing Knight's husband John. News reports of the day explain little more than details of the hangings. An appeal to the Mississippi Supreme Court reveals nothing about the crime other than she committed "a foul murder of her husband."[168] Gray appealed his conviction where the same court noted that he had confessed to the murder; he appealed the voluntariness of his confession.[169]

Scholars know little of the first predatory murderer hanged in the later part of the postbellum period. In the case of Ellen Osgood's hanging in Liberty County in Georgia in December 1878, all that one can learn stems from an appeal of her conviction and newspaper reports. Apparently, Samuel Gauldin went to the home of Simon Osgood to inquire about a debt that he owed Osgood but which he had already turned over to a constable for collection. An argument ensued, and Simon Osgood's sons and grown daughter (Ellen) beat Gauldin to death with sticks, fence rails, and a hoe. A jury convicted Raymond and Ellen of Gauldin's murder and sentenced them to death, while the court sentenced James Osgood to a year in prison for involuntary manslaughter. Ellen and Raymond hanged the same day.[170]

More revealing is the hanging death of black woman Ella Moore who hanged along with four black men (Kiddick Powell, Simon O. Guinn, Joseph King, and Robert Donaldson) in the jail yard in October 1882 for the shooting and beating death of James Harwood, a white man.[171] It was unusual for blacks to attack whites in the South; the South was in turmoil in the 1880s and 1890s when political and economic instability often resulted in open conflict between whites and blacks when whites mostly attacked blacks. But in the Eastman Race Riot in late summer 1892 in Dodge County, Georgia, blacks violently confronted whites. Accounts from the period explain that thousands of blacks had gathered in Eastman for a religious revival (often referred to as a camp meeting) with many of those attending openly drinking and gambling. An argument between two black men (one named Jake Tarrapin) ensued when one of the men who had wagered his watch in a gambling game demanded its return. When Tarrapin refused to give the watch back to its owner, the man reported his loss to Marshall Pete Harrell (white) who quickly arrested Tarrapin. While escorting Tarrapin to jail, Harrell ended up in a nearby ditch and Tarrapin ran off, but the man who had complained to Harrell shot and killed Tarrapin. Blacks attending the revival became violent over the killing and mistakenly believed that Harrell had killed Tarrapin. A mob attacked Harrell and one of his deputies but they escaped unscathed. The mob became frenzied and yelled out for killing whites and burning their houses. The mob killed James Harwood who was not involved in the melee. Police eventually quieted the mob and began making arrests. Authorities arrested, indicted, and in a thirty-day trial convicted Ella Moore and the four men with whom she hanged, as well as seventeen other black men sent to prison with life sentences. Ella Moore had no appeal.[172]

In another southern case, Franklin County, Louisiana, officials hanged in July 1885 black servant woman Matilda Jones for her role in the robbery-murder of her employer, an elderly white widow named Mrs. Henrietta Cole. One commentator reported that Jones' part in the murder was to lead three black accomplices (George Wilson, Charles Davis, and Sol Price) to the house, "showing them how to enter, and revealing where Cole kept her money, jewelry, and other valuables hidden." All the accomplices made confessions after their trial.[173] In another case, there is little information about the hanging of Ada Hires for murder in July 1893. At least one source contends that Ada was a lynching victim for killing a white.[174] As late as 1892, Louisiana hanged an unidentified 15-year-old black child for poisoning, but there are no facts about the case in the historical record.

Virginia Christian's killing of her white employer Ida Virginia Belote represents an all-too-familiar story of black females in southern society. As Streib and Sametz characterize the killing, "The social position and popularity of the victim stood in stark contrast to Christian's family background, unkempt appearance, and rude manner in describing the crime."[175] Young Christian was a poor, mentally retarded black girl whose family were sharecroppers on Belote's farm and for whom Christian was a laundress. She was one of eight children, and her father's meager wages could not adequately support the family. Christian's mother was an invalid who had a reputation for dishonesty, and some argue that Christian had "adopted her mother's habits of immorality, dishonesty, and thievery,"[176] but Christian was not a hardened criminal.[177] In contrast, Ida Virginia Belote was an older white woman and one of the town's "white aristocracy by way of her father's prominence as the owner of a large grocery."[178] Belote frequently mistreated Christian, and in mid-March 1912, a violent argument ensued between the two in which Belote accused Christian of stealing a locket and a skirt. Belote hit Christian with a cuspidor—commonly called a "spittoon"—which sent Christian into a violent frenzy. The altercation escalated when Christian and Belote ran for two broom handles Belote used to prop up her bedroom windows. Christian grabbed one of the broom handles and struck Belote on the forehead. In an attempt to stifle Belote's screams, Christian stuffed a towel down Belote's throat and died by suffocation. When Christian left the house, she stole Belote's purse with some money and a ring. One newspaper reported that police found Belote's body "laying face down in a pool of blood, and her head was horribly mutilated and a towel was stuffed into her mouth and throat."[179] The police soon arrested Christian, and during questioning, she admitted hitting Belote but was shocked that Belote was dead. Christian claimed she had no intent in killing Belote. With a lynch mob looming in the background, an Elizabeth City County Court tried and convicted Christian for murder and the trial judge sentenced her to death in the state's electric chair. One day after her 17th birthday in August 1912, a short five months after the crime, Virginia authorities executed Christian at the state penitentiary in Richmond. The state's medical school took possession of Christian's body since her parents were too poor to transport the body home.

The 1940s saw poor young black girls from North Philadelphia often standing on street corners in prominent neighborhoods waiting for affluent housewives to hire them as housemaids.[180] In one such case, Mrs. Freda Wodlinger, an older public school teacher and housewife from a prominent white family in West Oak Lane, hired young Corrine Sykes. Corrine was shy and petite, had low intelligence, and was illiterate and inclined to hysteria. A psychiatrist who examined Corrine before her trial claimed "her to be a constitutional psychopathic inferior, and, according to her school records, she had a mental age of about 8 years old at a time when she was in fact nearly 13 years old."[181] Three days after Corrine's hire, police found Wodlinger dead from multiple stab wounds; there was a terrific struggle with the killer hacking Wodlinger to death with a heavy kitchen knife. Missing from the house was $50 in cash, $2,000 in jewelry, and a sable fur piece. Suspicion immediately turned to Corrine, whom police arrested after an extensive search. Corrine gave conflicting stories but in the end signed a written confession despite her illiteracy. A jury convicted Corrine of first-degree murder, and the trial judge sentenced her to death by electrocution. Pennsylvania executed Corrine Sykes in October 1946. Troubled by doubts that Corrine was Wodlinger's killer, some believe Corrine's judicial killing was a wrongful execution. For one, immediately upon her arrest Corrine implicated her boyfriend, J. C. Kelly, saying that he had threatened to kill her and her mother if she did not steal the valuables for him.[182] Others find it strange that when Corrine's boyfriend learned of her arrest, "he raced to his boarding house, burned the sable, and dumped the diamonds."[183] Another point is that Corrine was far too small to have inflicted the severity of the knife wounds that killed

Scapegoat

Community of Reaction

Wodlinger. There is also speculation that years after Corrine's execution, Wodlinger's husband made a deathbed confession that he had killed his wife. Whatever happened, Corrine's execution had a poignant impact on North Philadelphia's black community. Some 10,000 people attended Corrine's viewing although it was open only to family members and close friends. On the day of her execution, most housemaids in the city went home early from their jobs. According to a woman whose grandmother worked as a housemaid in North Philadelphia at the time, city buses were full of black housemaids going home early on that day and an uncanny quite settled over the city. What's more, employers would no longer allow housemaids' boyfriends or husbands in their houses; an increasing mistrust accented the relations between white employers and black housemaids.[184]

Like many other cases of black female executions during the period, the case of Rosana Lightner Phillips more than illustrates "the manner in which gender, race, and status operated dialectically to shape the historical social construction of the southern Negro female offender."[185] Rosana was a black female born into rural southern poverty. She was illegitimate and born to a mother who dropped out of school in the sixth grade to give birth to Rosana. Her mother gave Rosana to her grandmother and a sister to raise. After her grandmother's death, Rosana moved back to live with her mother at the age of six. Rosana became sexually promiscuous at an early age and by the time she was 14 years old, Rosana had become pregnant, dropped out of school, and gave birth to the first of two illegitimate children. As a young teenager, Rosana worked as a nurse and house cleaner earning $2 a week. Rosana developed a criminal record during this time that included arrests for drunkenness and violent assault on a police officer; by the time she was 17 years old, Rosana faced a 2-year prison sentence for larceny. After leaving prison in 1937, she met her husband Daniel Phillips who was a farmer and textile worker with a fifth-grade education earning $60 a month. At that time she gave birth to her second illegitimate child that was not Daniel's. They had a tumultuous relationship accented by persistent violence. In early 1942, Rosana and Daniel went to work as domestics for Harry F. Watkins and moved into a tenant dwelling on Watkins' property. In September of that year, authorities found Watkins' decomposed body at the bottom of a well with a wound on the back of his head and another wound through the front of the neck that nearly severed the head. Suspicion immediately focused on the Phillips who had recently abandoned Watkins property for a nearby town. Officials arrested Rosana and Daniel and the state's prosecutor filed felony murder charges against the two with robbery as the underlying cause of the murder. Their Orange County trial lasted 13 hours and it took an all-white male jury less than an hour to render a unanimous guilty verdict against the "Negro farm tenants." The North Carolina Supreme Court affirmed the trial court's judgment and dismissed the appeal.[186] Both admitted complicity in the murder yet implicated the other as the actual killer. There is nothing in the historical record indicating why the Phillips killed Watkins other than stealing Watkins' wallet. But if one were to believe Rosana, she had nothing to do Watkins' killing and watched Daniel commit the murder from the kitchen window where she stood washing the morning dishes. North Carolina executed Rosana and Daniel Phillips by lethal gas on the same day in November 1942.[187] Rosana was the first woman put to death in the state's gas chamber.[188]

The historical record is silent on several early black women executions in this period of female executions in the United States. Scholars know little, for instance, of Carrie McCarty's execution by an unknown method for murder in Mississippi in April 1921; an appeal to the Mississippi Supreme Court simply affirmed McCarty's conviction without comment.[189] Hattie Perdue hanged along with Leon Viverett in Wayne County in Mississippi for the robbery and murder of a white man named Alton Page in August 1921. Newspaper reports of the period reveal that a fight broke out between Viverett and Page in Perdue's house in which Viverett killed Page. Perdue and Viverette apparently dismembered Page's body, burned the body in a stove, and then buried the remains in a "negro cemetery." Perdue proclaimed her innocence on the gallows. There is nothing in the historical record explaining why Perdue and her male companion murdered the victim other than possibly involving a robbery.[190]

Alabama electrocuted Selina Gilmore at Kirby Prison in January 1930 for the shotgun killing of Horace Johnson, a white waiter who quarreled with Gilmore over a food order. After several hours of drinking corn whiskey, Gilmore apparently went to a restaurant and ordered takeout. Gilmore ordered sandwiches and brains with eggs, but only got the sandwiches since kitchen help had yet to cook the remainder of the order. Gilmore became uncooperative when Johnson told her she would have to wait for her order but then asked her to leave the restaurant. It was then that Gilmore went home, retrieved her loaded shotgun, returned to the restaurant, cornered Johnson, and shot and killed him.[191]

Mary Holmes was the last woman hanged in the United States. Mississippi hanged the black woman in April 1937 along with her black male accomplice Selmon Brooks for the robbery and murder of E. W. Cook, a prominent planter in Sharkey County for whom Holmes worked as a cook. While Cook was preparing the payroll, Holmes and Brooks brutally beat Cook, partially scalped him, and dismembered the body. Afterwards they burglarized the house and then set fire to it to conceal the crime.[192] There is little in the historical record accounting for why Holmes and Brooks burglarized the home and murdered Cook, but a local newspaper doubtlessly overstated Cook's relationship with Holmes when it claimed Holmes deserved to hang because she had betrayed a *friendship*.[193] It is cynical to believe that Cook and Holmes had such familiarity given Cook's status as a wealthy white southern planter and that of Holmes' as a poor black cook. There is no record that Mary Holmes appealed her conviction and death sentence, but the Supreme Court of Mississippi affirmed Brooks' conviction and death sentence stating the Brooks' confession to the murder should stand.[194] Holmes hanged shortly before Brooks.

Mississippi executed Mildred Louise Johnson in the electric chair in May 1944 for murdering Annie Laura Conklin, her elderly white landlady who lived alone in Vicksburg. Mildred savagely beat Conklin to death with a stick, a fireplace poker, and a pair of tongs.[195] The motive for the crime was robbery.[196] Before her trial and conviction, Mildred confessed to the killing and implicated Jessie James, Mildred's common law husband, and Charles H. Barley, Mildred's father-in-law, accountable for Conklin's killing. At her arraignment, however, she denied that the two had anything to do with the killing. The trial court granted severance and tried James and Barley separately. The Mississippi Supreme Court affirmed the trial court's judgment and death sentence.[197] There is no record, however, that either James or Barley appealed any conviction, nor is there any record of their executions. Jim Crow southerners needed not much more justification than the murder of an elderly white woman to execute a poor black woman. Officials executed Mildred in the Warren County jail using the state's portable electric chair.

Helen Ray Fowler was a black woman who by the age of thirty-seven had married several times and had five children and a grandchild. She supported herself, her children, and a nephew by prostitution. In fact, Helen lived in a neighborhood known as one of the nation's most notorious red-light districts. She was poor and uneducated. Conflicting testimony revealed no clear picture of the crime at her trial. Even the state's attorney, David Marsh, failed to identify or produce a murder weapon, had no clear theory of the facts surrounding the case, and after 30 witnesses produced no evidence that Helen actually committed the killing of William Fowler (no relation), a gas station owner. But her defense lawyer, Earl W. Brudges, did little more than call two witnesses. In early summer 1943, with cash and several uncashed checks totaling about $1,000 in hand, William and his cousin, Lee Clark, patronized several local gin mills and William somehow ended up at Helen's house. In December of that year, William's bloated and badly decomposed body washed up on the shore of the Niagara River. Most likely, George Knight, a black man who lived with Helen, killed William during a brawl in Helen's house. Knight admitted as much to police after his arrest; he claimed that he beat Williams after robbing him, hit him in the back of the head with a hammer, and then he and Helen dumped the body. Helen's defense counsel claimed that Helen was guilty of many number of crimes, none of which had state prosecuted her, but she was not liable for first-degree murder. Even so, an all-white jury convicted her and George Knight of killing William Fowler. New York electrocuted Helen and George on the same day in November 1944. Jon Getz, a New York attorney, provides some idea why the state executed Helen Fowler, "I think race may have played a strong factor—you've got two black people killing a white guy. [Helen] was a disposable person in [the jury's] mind. I think they threw her in for good measure, so to speak. She certainly didn't get her fair day in court, and so she died an early death. The system is supposed to be about fairness."[198] Without comment, the Court of Appeals of New York affirmed the convictions of Fowler and Knight.[199]

Bessie Mae Williams was 19 years old when North Carolina executed her and her 18-year-old accomplice Ralph Thompson by lethal gas in December 1944. Along with Cleve Bryant Johnson and 14-year-old Annie Mae Allison, the defendants robbed and stabbed to death Charlotte taxi driver Mack Minyard. The defendants admitted being in Minyard's taxi and gave police details as to what happened. Officials arraigned the defendants and entered pleas of not guilty; Johnson plead guilty to second-degree murder and received a prison sentence. After her arrest, an intake worker at the detention center described Bessie Mae as economically destitute, of low mentality, and a grouchy nature. The clerk also noted that Bessie Mae was illiterate and moronic.[200] A Mecklenburg County trial court found Williams, Thompson, and Allison guilty of murder and sentenced them to death in the state's gas chamber. On appeal, the Supreme Court of North Carolina found that the trial judge and the attorneys appointed by the court to represent the defendants were extremely careful to safeguard the rights of the defendants and found no trial errors.[201] The state's governor refused to intervene in the executions of Williams and Thompson, but commuted Allison's death sentence because of her age who was fourteen at the time of the murder.[202]

Authorities rarely exonerate black women of capital crimes and execute black women despite doubts of guilt or legal culpability. In the case of Lena Baker, for instance, a black woman wrongfully convicted of murder by an all-white male jury and executed in Georgia in March 1945 that some have called a "legal lynching." Testimony from the one-day trial reveals that Lena shot and killed 67-year-old gristmill owner Ernest B. Knight with a pistol she pulled from him when Knight threatened her with a metal pipe. Baker, a domestic servant and mother of three, apparently had an intimate relationship with Knight and the two often drank together. There is no record of an appeal, but 60 years after her execution in the state's electric chair, the Georgia Board of Pardons and Paroles pardoned Lena Baker for the murder claiming that her execution was "a grievous error." While the pardon does not declare Baker innocent, the Board suggested, "She could have been charged with voluntary manslaughter, rather than murder" and received 15-year prison term and not death. But given the racial hostility of the Jim Crow South, a black woman killing a white man demanded execution.[203]

Rose Marie Stinette died in South Carolina's electric chair in January 1947 for the contract murder of her husband for an insurance policy. Roy Singletary and two other men had bludgeoned Stinette's husband to death; authorities found his mutilated body beside a railroad track. The trial judge, L.D. Lide, sentenced Stinette and Singletary to death even though eleven of the twelve jurors in the case sought clemency for the two. Judge Lide sentenced the other two accomplices to life sentences. The day before Stinette and Singletary's execution, however, the state's governor granted Singletary a reprieve leaving only Rose Stinette to answer for the killing by execution *although it was the three men who actually did the killing*. There is no record of an appeal. During her electrocution, a fuse blew from the surge of electricity required for the execution. One newspaper reported, "Witnesses then saw sparks from the woman's head and arms dimly illuminating the death scene."[204] Prison officials buried poor executed black women in a Potter's Field whose families could not afford to claim prisoners' bodies, such was the case with Rose Marie Stinette.

Betty Butler was the last black woman executed in the apartheid of Jim Crow. Butler reportedly strangled and drowned Evelyn Clark with whom Butler had had a brief lesbian relationship. Butler had left her husband and her two young children and moved to Cincinnati to start a new life. She met Clark, had a sexual relationship, and then became repulsed by the lesbian affair and apparently tried to break off the relationship. Apparently, Clark propositioned Butler by offering her money for sex. Butler became so irate that she tried to strangle Clark but was unsuccessful. Later in the day, she pulled Evelyn's body to the edge of the water where they had been fishing and drowned her in the lake. Other evidence suggests that Betty was bisexual and killed Clark in rage over her attention to another woman. In any event, a Hamilton County court convicted Butler of first-degree murder and sentenced her to death. Ohio electrocuted her in June 1954.[205] Butler's execution was yet another in a long line of death penalty cases in the period where female status, race, and poverty bolstered convictions and executions. Unquestionably, much of the poor black female violence for which they suffered execution resulted mostly from the gendered racism of an apartheid society accenting their daily existence.[206]

BLACK WOMEN EXECUTIONS IN THE MODERN ERA

White violence against black Americans remains pervasive in U.S. society: "From lynching to cross-burning and church-burning, anti-black violence has been and still remains the prototypical hate crime—an action intended not only to injure individuals but to intimidate an entire group of people."[207] Though black resistance to racial inequality in the early civil rights period succeeded in effecting legislative and legal reforms, these developments have had little enduring impact on the burden of blackness in U.S. society.[208] As critical sociologist Joe R. Feagin explains: "Civil rights laws and desegregation decisions have been overwhelmed by the massiveness of racial discrimination."[209] The lower socioeconomic status of most black women today reflects the failure of government reforms in the modern era. Black women remain far below national averages in levels of educational attainment, placement in the occupational structure, and income.[210] The continued marginalization of black women in American society undoubtedly has placed them at disproportionate risk of contact with the criminal justice system. The effect of public policy reforms producing such draconian measures as mandatory minimum sentences, three strikes laws, and reductions in the availability of parole and early release programs have had a perverted impact on black women and their communities. The human cost of these measures on "weakened lives, wrecked families, troubled children are incalculable, as are the adverse social, economic, and political consequences of weakened communities, diminished opportunities for economic mobility, and extensive disenfranchisement."[211] The racialized sexism of mostly white judicial officers in the modern era renders black women ever more vulnerable to the death penalty even supposing a national civil rights agenda ostensibly diminishing the gendered racism troubling the lives of black women.

Modern jurisdictions have executed two black women, Wanda Jean Allen and Francis Elaine Newton. But it is Allen's execution for murdering her black lesbian lover that most notably accents the legal problems facing condemned black women today. Allen is a contentious figure in the imposition of capital punishment because her case symbolizes how poverty, mental health, race, and sexuality distinctively accent capital sentencing of black lesbian women.[212] These social characteristics distinguished Allen as executable to the sentencing jury because state prosecutors successfully portrayed Allen erroneously, yet decisively, as "disobedient, dangerous, a threat to society, immoral, manly, and sexually deviant."[213] The evidence in Allen's case overwhelmingly reveals that state judicial authorities should have never permitted the execution to take place.

Allen was the second of eight children born to a mother who suffered from alcoholism and mental retardation, and who drank excessively during her pregnancy with Wanda. Acting as a surrogate mother to her younger siblings after her father abandoned the family, Wanda regularly stole food and clothing for the children that led to several juvenile arrests. Allen performed poorly in school, and at the age of 15 officials diagnosed her as mentally retarded. Years later, while serving a prison term for a manslaughter conviction—a case so dubious that she was able to plead guilty and receive a minimum sentence—Allen met Gloria Leathers with whom she began a lesbian relationship. After their release from prison, Allen and Leathers lived together and had a tumultuous relationship. In late 1988, the two women argued at a grocery store over a welfare check. A police officer escorted the women to their house and watched as Leathers collected her belongings and moved out. Afterwards, Leathers went to the police station to file a complaint against Allen who followed her hoping to talk to Leathers. One account has it that Allen shot Leathers in the abdomen with a handgun as she exited the car she drove to the police station. Allen's account is that she shot Leathers in self-defense after Leathers attacked Allen with a rake. During an argument earlier the same day, Leathers had attacked Allen and slashed her face with a garden rake. Allen also feared Leathers because Leathers had killed a woman ten years earlier in Tulsa, Oklahoma.[214] Leathers died two hours after police arrested Allen. Oklahoma tried Allen and after a short deliberation, a jury convicted her of capital murder and recommended the death penalty. At most, Allen's crime was a heat-of-passion manslaughter that did not warrant a death sentence.

The state prosecutor successfully convinced the jury that Allen posed a significant societal danger because she was a lesbian killer. One contemptible feature of gendered racism in the criminal justice system today is that white prosecutors consistently marginalize black female lesbian defendants by using their sexuality to malign and disparage them to juries.[215] Allen's lesbianism and her alleged "dangerousness" overwhelmed the state's case. The state prosecutor freely, yet erroneously, asserted that Allen dominated her lover when factually she and Leathers largely mistreated each other. The state prosecutor won the trial court's rejection of defense motions outlining Leathers' violent nature.[216] The prosecution inaccurately, yet purposefully, portrayed Wanda as wearing "the pants in the family" and that she was the masculine one in the relationship. The state's attorney even solicited testimony from Allen's mother that Allen used the male spelling of her middle name (Gene). Wanda's sexuality played a prominent role in her trial and "evidences, again, that when a woman acts out from society's gender expectations, she faces harsher penalties."[217] Even Oklahoma's black churches rebuffed efforts for leniency for Allen from the state's governor because she was a lesbian.

Allen's case also provides a particularly egregious illustration of how prosecutorial gendered racism taints capital cases involving black women. During closing arguments the prosecutor depicted Allen as a black monster deserving of the death penalty by comparing Allen to a gorilla. The prosecutor produced a greeting card belonging to Allen with the picture of a gorilla on the cover with a caption that read, "Patience my ass, I'm going to kill something." While showing the card to the jury, the prosecutor said, "That's Wanda Allen in a nutshell." The sole purpose of the prosecutor showing the picture to the jury was to portray Allen as an aggressive beast. An appeals court, however, found no prejudicial error in the prosecutor's racist tactic. The racist scheme employed by the prosecutor to denigrate Allen was especially effective since "the definition of Allen as a brutal beast undeserving of mercy persisted long after her trial;"[218] at her clemency hearing Allen was mostly concerned with dispelling the way the racist prosecutor had characterized her during the trial.[219]

In Allen's case the prosecutor engaged in seven separate instances of misconduct including withholding evidence at trial, making false statements to the Parole and Pardon Board, biased behavior, and outright lying to the jury.[220] Common forms of prosecutorial misconduct in capital cases involving black female defendants include suppressing exculpatory evidence, ignoring circumstances that may mitigate a death sentence, subornation of perjury, intimidation of witnesses, fabrication of incriminating evidence, rendering improper argumentation, and providing false information to juries.[221] What's more, state attorneys use peremptory challenges in capital cases to discriminate openly against black women in jury selection. Prosecutors use peremptory challenges as a procedural devise to remove potential jurors during voir dire for unexplained reasons. While prosecutors must give a reason when challenging jurors for cause, the peremptory challenge requires no justification and is "exercised without a reason stated, without impunity, and without being subject to the court's control."[222] It is the capricious nature of the peremptory challenge, however, that effectively masks race and sex discrimination in jury selection by allowing prosecutors to discriminate intentionally against black female jurors.[223] Jurists often hold that striking black women as jurors does not amount to racist exclusion. In one case, a trial judge responded to a defense lawyer's objection to the prosecutor's striking of black women: "You have got women on the jury. What function does a Black woman fulfill that the White woman doesn't?"[224] Prosecutors prefer white jurors in capital cases because they are more punitive and more prone to convict black defendants.[225] It is difficult to make the case for gendered race discrimination when prosecutors abuse peremptory challenges since courts allow "almost any conceivable justification for peremptory challenges, however arbitrary or irrational, while ignoring evidence that such challenges were exercised in a racially discriminatory manner."[226]

Allen's indigence was a significant factor leading to her execution because poor black women accused of capital crimes cannot afford private attorneys and rely on court-appointed lawyers or public defenders who are largely ineffective in mitigating capital cases.[227] As a poor black woman, Allen relied on a court-appointed lawyer (Robert Carpenter) who denied Allen her Sixth Amendment right to competent counsel and an adequate defense. Carpenter, who had never tried a capital case, sought to recuse himself or to have assistance from the state's public defenders office, or at least the assistance of an experienced investigator.[228] The court rejected these requests. Carpenter's most severe errors were failing to introduce well-documented evidence of Allen's mental retardation and mental disability. Had he adequately investigated Allen's troubled and delinquent childhood, he would have discovered that she had an IQ of 69 (within the range of low-functioning, mild mental retardation) resulting from brain damage incurred from a head injury suffered in an automobile accident when she was 12 years old.[229] She had also endured a stab wound to the temple as a teenager that certainly exacerbated her problem. Allen never completed high school and it is doubtful she functioned intellectually even at an eighth-grade level. Carpenter's incompetence precluded the trial court from fully litigating Allen's mental retardation; her mental impediments surely would have kept Allen from execution since the U.S. Supreme Court ruled shortly after her judicial killing that executing mentally retarded defendants is unconstitutional.[230]

In September 2005, Texas executed Frances Elaine Newton after a Harris County jury convicted Newton of killing her husband, a drug addict and dealer, and her two young children allegedly for $100,000 in insurance proceeds in April 1987. Newton always maintained her innocence and claimed that drug dealers killed her husband and children.[231] More than for any other reason, Texas succeeded in executing Newton because her court-appointed trial lawyer was incompetent. Newton repeatedly requested that the court dismiss her lawyer, but without a hearing on the issue, the trial court summarily rejected her pleas. Her appellate attorneys maintained that her trial lawyer failed to competently investigate the case, to include reasonable allegations that the murders were committed by someone else, to interview witnesses, to challenge the state's mishandling of evidence, and to introduce mitigating circumstances. The attorneys further determined that Newton's defense lawyer had a dubious history and an official record of professional incompetence.[232] Commentators assert, "There is no doubt that Newton was prejudiced by [her trial lawyer's] ineffectiveness: no reasonable juror would have found her guilty beyond a reasonable doubt had she received competent counsel."[233]

CONCLUDING REMARKS

A substantive conclusion that one can make from a historical-contextual analysis of the racialized, sexist oppression of executed black females in the United States is that criminal justice investigators must recognize black women as a group worthy of study.

Although much of the discussion in this chapter attempts to isolate the racist and sexist conduct of justice practitioners directed toward black women and the imposition of capital punishment, often systemic oppression accenting executions is blurred between black women and black men. Indeed, the predominantly white judiciary and its agents of social control have directed much of their racial violence and brutalization to black people without much regard to gender. Yet, as this chapter shows, there is much about the racist and sexist context of criminal justice history that is specific to the execution of black women in this country. Scholars must move more deliberately to employ substantive theoretical frameworks that more appropriately explain the sociological, political, and economic forces effecting highly predictable criminal justice outcomes for black women.

One historically consistent factor giving rise to black female executions is that justice authorities have executed black women for challenging their racist and sexist exploitation by whites. Although colonial and antebellum slavery fully institutionalized the sexualized persecution of slave women, the perversion of sexual violence against black women continued throughout Reconstruction and Jim Crow. Today, as in the past, white violence remains manifested in the indifference of criminal justice officials to black females as victims of white male violence. The transparency of the racialized, sexist oppression experienced by black women in the U.S. criminal justice system today is the disregard justice officials have toward safeguarding the most fundamental rights of black women accused of capital crimes. Gendered racism toward black female capital defendants is systemic to the prosecutorial selection of capital cases, the deliberate abuse of peremptory challenges in gaining advantage of white jurors, the racist judges overriding jury recommendations of leniency, the racist (and often criminal) misconduct of prosecutors in failing to meet *Brady* safeguards, and the ineffectiveness and often racist disregard of defense lawyers.[234]

The historical-contextual analysis furthers our understanding of black female executions occurring in a societal system of white domination and black subordination. The analysis illustrates, in a graphic sense, the brutality of black female executions rooted in our society's racist and sexist social fabric, and shows that these roots are so deeply buried in our racist and sexist relations that they prevent change. The death penalty has proven to be an effective means of subjugating black females to white interests, even if it is often beyond social scientists and legal scholars to prove purposeful and deliberate discrimination. As one scholar explains, for the most part, contemporary racism "is not manifested in a straightforward and overt manner to allow for such showing. Indeed, what we know about why race still matters and will likely always matter in our system of capital punishment suggests a covert, subtle, and diffuse process whereby an easily identified racist action or utterance performed by a biased judge, juror, witness, or prosecutor is not likely to be found."[235] Even so, the structural influences of gendered racism in capital sentencing persist and are highly predictable outcomes of intentional and calculated discriminatory motives. The racially oppressive outcomes accenting the capital sentencing of black females are systemic and multifaceted.

ENDNOTES

1. Clarice Feinman, *Women in the Criminal Justice System* (Westport: Greenwood, 1994).
2. Robert M. Bohm, *Deathquest II: An Introduction to the Theory and Practice of Capital Punishment in the United States* (Cincinnati: Anderson, 2003); Phyllis L. Crocker, "Is the Death

Penalty Good for Women?" *Buffalo Criminal Law Review*, 4 (2001): 917–965; Joan W. Howarth, "Executing White Masculinities: Learning from Karla Faye Tucker," *Oregon Law Review*, 81 (2002): 183–229; Joan W. Howarth, "Deciding to Kill: Revealing the Gender in the Task Handed to Capital Jurors," *Wisconsin Law Review*, 1994 (1994): 1345–1424; Elizabeth Rapaport, "Staying Alive: Executive Clemency, Equal Protection, and the Politics of Gender in Women's Capital Cases," *Buffalo Criminal Law Review*, 4 (2001): 967–1007; Elizabeth Rapaport, "Equality of the Damned: The Execution of Women on the Cusp of the 21st Century," *Ohio Northern University Law Review*, 26 (2000): 581–600; David E. Schulberg, "Dying to Get Out: The Execution of Females in the Post-*Furman* Era of the Death Penalty in the United States," in Roslyn Muraskin (ed.) *It's A Crime: Women and Justice*, pp. 273–288 (Upper Saddle River: Prentice Hall, 2003); David E. Schulberg, "The Execution of Females," *Orange County Lawyer*, 42 (2000): 25–32; Etta F. Morgan, "Women on Death Row," in Roslyn Muraskin (ed.) *It's A Crime: Women and Justice*, pp. 289–304 (Upper Saddle River: Prentice Hall, 2003); Thad Rueter, "Why Women Aren't Executed: Gender Bias and the Death Penalty," *Human Rights*, 23 (1996): 10–11; Loraine Schmall, "Forgiving Guin Garcia: Women, the Death Penalty and Commutation," *Wisconsin Women's Law Journal*, 11 (1996): 283–326; Victor L. Streib, "Executing Women, Juveniles, and the Mentally Retarded: Second Class Citizens in Capital Punishment," in James R. Acker, Robert M. Bohm & Charles S. Lanier (eds.), *America's Experiment with Capital Punishment: Reflections on the Past, Present and Future of the Ultimate Penal Sanction*, pp. 301–324 (Durham: Carolina Academic Press, 2003); Andrea Shapiro, "Unequal Before the Law: Men, Women and the Death Penalty," *American University Journal of Gender, Social Policy and the Law*, 8 (2000): 427–470.

3. Melinda E. O'Neil is misguided when she cites Victor L. Strieb's work and argues, "Since colonial times there have been numerous studies developed which focus on the execution of women." While some scholarship has outlined the historical evolution of capital punishment in the United States, there are no publications specifically exploring the execution of black females in the United States with emphasis on the historical context in which jurisdictions have executed black women. See Malinda E. O'Neil, "The Gender Gap Argument: Exploring the Disparity of Sentencing Women to Death," *New England Journal on Criminal and Civil Confinement*, 25 (1999): 213–244; see also Victor L. Strieb, "Death Penalty for Female Offenders," *University of Cincinnati Law Review*, 58 (1990): 845–880. Compare Ann Jones, *Women Who Kill* (Boston : Beacon Press, 1996); David V. Baker, "A Descriptive Profile and Socio-Historical Analysis of Female Executions in the United States: 1632–1997," *Women & Criminal Justice*, 10 (1999): 57–93; Keith Harries, "Gender, Execution, and Geography in the United States," *Geografiska Annaler, Series B, Human Geography*, 74 (1992): 21–29; Paula C. Johnson, "At the Intersection of Injustice: Experiences of African American Women in Crime and Sentencing," *American University Journal of Gender and Law*, 4 (1995): 1–76; Trina N. Seitz, "The Wounds of Savagery: Negro Primitivism, Gender Parity, and the Execution of Rosanna Lightner Phillips," *Women & Criminal Justice*, 16 (2005): 29–64; Victor L. Strieb, "Death Penalty for Female Offenders," *University of Cincinnati Law Review*, 58 (1990): 845–880; Victor L. Strieb & Linda Sametz, "Executing Female Juveniles," *Connecticut Law Review*, 22 (1989): 3–16.

4. bell hooks, *Ain't I a Woman: Black Women and Feminism* (Boston: South End Press, 1981), p 15.

5. Streib, "Death Penalty for Female Offenders."

6. Deborah Gray White, *Ar'n't I a Woman? Female Slaves in the Plantation South* (New York: Norton, 1998).

7. Robert William Fogel & Stanley L. Engerman, *Time on the Cross: The Economics of American Negro Slavery* (Boston: Little, Brown and Company, 1974); see also David Eltis & Stanley L. Engerman, "Was the Slave Trade Dominated by Men?" *Journal of Interdisciplinary History*, 23 (1992): 237–257.

8. G. Ugo Nwokeji, "African Conceptions of Gender and the Slave Traffic," William and Mary Quarterly, 58 (2001): 47–68.

9. Paula Johnson, "At the Intersection of Injustice: Experience of African American Women in Crime and Sentencing," *The American University Journal of Gender, Race and Justice*, 4 (1995): 1–76, at 15 note 84.

10. Marcus Rediker, *The Slave Ship: A Human History* (New York: Viking, 2007), p. 152.

11. hooks, *Ain't I a Woman*, at 19.

12. Ibid., at 18–19.

13. Lerone Bennett, *Before the Mayflower: A History of Black America* (New York: Penguin, 1982).

14. David Richardson, "Shipboard Revolts, African Authority, and the Atlantic Slave Trade," *William and Mary Quarterly*, 58 (2001): 69–92; Harvey Wish, "American Slave Insurrections Before 1861," *Journal of Negro History*, 22 (1937): 299–320.

15. See hooks, *Ain't I A Woman*; Emma Christopher, *Slave Ship Sailors and Their Captive Cargoes, 1730–1807* (New York: Cambridge University Press, 2006).

16. Amrita Chakrabarti Myers, "'Sisters in Arms': Slave Women's Resistance to Slavery in the United States," *Past Imperfect*, 5 (1996): 141–174 (1996); Betty Wood, "Some Aspects of Female Resistance to Chattel Slavery in Low Country Georgia, 1763–1815," *The History Journal*, 30 (1987): 603–622.

17. Myers, "Sisters in Arms."

18. Ibid., p. 142.

19. William Weicek, "The Origins of the Law of Slavery in British North America," *Cardozo Law Review*, 17 (1996): 1711–1792, at 1714.

20. Thomas D. Morris, *Southern Slavery and the Law: 1619–1860* (Chapel Hill: University of North Carolina, 1996).

21. Ira Berlin, "Time, Space, and the Evolution of Afro-American Society in British Mainland North America," *American History Review*, 85 (1980): 44–78; Ira Berlin, *Many Thousands Gone: The First Two Centuries of Slavery in North America* (Cambridge: Harvard University Press, 1998); Donald R. Wright, *African Americans in the colonial era: From African origins through the American Revolution* (Arlington Heights: Harlan Davidson, 1991).

22. Jonathan A. Bush, "The First Slave (And Why He Matters)," *Cordozo Law Review*, 35 (1996): 599-629.

23. Lawrence M. Friedman, *A History of American Law* (New York: Simon & Schuster, 1985), p. 33; see also Douglas Greenberg, "Crime, Law Enforcement, and Social Control in Colonial America," *The American Journal of Legal History*, 26 (1982): 293–325.

24. Ulrich Bonnell Phillips, *American Negro Slavery: A Survey of Supply, Employment, Control of Negro Labor as Determined by the Plantation Regime* (New York: D. Appleton and Company, 1918), p. 454.

25. White, *Ar'n't I a Woman?*, p. 62.

26. M. Watt Espy & John Ortiz Smykla, *Executions in the United States, 1608–2002: The Espy File* [Computer file]. 4th ICPS ed. Compiled by M. Watt Espy and John Ortiz Smykla, University of Alabama. Ann Arbor, MI: Inter-University Consortium for Political and Social Research [Producer and distributor]. 2004.

27. Phillip J. Schwarz, *Slave laws in Virginia* (Athens: University of Georgia Press, 1996); Phillip J. Schwarz, *Twice condemned: Slaves and the Criminal Laws of Virginia, 1705–1865* (Union, NJ: Lawbook Exchange, 1998).

28. Michael Stephen Hindus, "Black Justice Under White Law: Criminal Prosecutions of Blacks in Antebellum South Carolina," *Journal of American History*, 63 (1976): 575–599.

29. Espy & Smykla, *Executions in the United States.*

30. Jordan, *White Over Black.*

31. Streib, "Death Penalty for Female Offenders."
32. Schwarz, *Slave Laws in Virginia*; see also Phillips, *American Negro Slavery.*
33. Schwarz, *Twice Condemned.*
34. Hearn, *Legal Executions in New York State*, p. 6.
35. Ibid., p. 6.
36. Ibid., pp. 7–8; Sellin, "The Philadelphia Gibbet Iron," p. 18.
37. Schwarz, *Twice Condemned*, p. 81.
38. Ibid.
39. Harriet C. Frazier, *Slavery and Crime in Missouri, 1773–1865* (Jefferson: McFarland, 2001), p. 184.
40. "The Execution of Pauline," *The Daily Picayune* (March 29, 1846), p. 2.
41. W.T. Block, "Myth of Texas Executions Debunked: Slave Lucy Was First Woman to Die," *Beaumont Enterprise* (September 13, 1978), p. 9C.
42. Schwarz, *Twice Condemned*, p. 147.
43. Todd Lee Savitt, *Medicine and Slavery: The Diseases and Health Care of Black in Antebellum Virginia* (University of Illinois Press, 2002), p. 116.
44. Schwarz, *Twice Condemned*, p. 237.
45. Hearn, *Legal Executions in New Jersey*, p. 5.
46. Spruill, *Women's Life and Work in the Southern Colonies*, p. 335.
47. Milton Ready, *The Tar Heel State: A History of North Carolina* (Columbia: University of South Carolina Press, 2005), p. 80; Marvin L. Michael Kay & Lorin Lee Cary, *Slavery in North Carolina, 1748–1775* (Chapel Hill: The University of North Carolina Press, 1995), p. 115.
48. Hearn, *Legal Executions in New Jersey*, p. 80–81.
49. James Michael Davidson, *Mediating Race and Class Through the Death Experience: Power Relations and Resistance Strategies of an African-American Community, Dallas Texas (1869–1907)*, University of Texas at Austin (Unpublished doctoral dissertation, 2004), p. 49.
50. Digital Library on American Slavery, University of North Carolina at Greensboro, PAR Number 11585901.
51. Martha W. McCartney, *A Study of the Africans and African Americans on Jamestown Island and at Green Spring, 1619–1803* (Williamsburg: Colonial Williamsburg Foundation, 2003), pp. 167–168.
52. Schwarz, *Twice Condemned*, p. 237.
53. Morris, *Southern Slavery and the Law*, p. 295.
54. Hearn, *Legal Executions in New York State*, p. 29.
55. Frazier, *Death Sentences in Missouri*; Frazier, *Slavery and Crime in Missouri*, pp. 170–174; Streib & Sametz, "Executing Female Juveniles."
56. Marlin Shipman, *The Penalty of Death: U.S. Newspaper Coverage of Women's Executions* (Columbia: University of Missouri Press, 2002), p. 149.
57. *Fanny (a slave) v. State* (1839).
58. Ervin L. Jordan, Jr., *Black Confederates and Afro-Yankees in Civil War Virginia* (Charlottesville: University Press of Virginia, 1995), p. 171.
59. Digital Library on American Slavery, University of North Carolina at Greensboro, PAR Number 11282304.
60. Hearn, *Legal Executions in New York State*, p. 128.
61. Ibid., p. 140.
62. George C. Rogers, *Charleston in the Age of Pinckneys* 23 (1980).
63. Digital Library on American Slavery, University of North Carolina at Greensboro, PAR Number 11378503.
64. Ibid.
65. M. Leigh Harrison, "A Study of the Earliest Reported Decisions of the South Carolina Courts of Law," *American Journal of Legal History*, 16 (1972) 65; see also *State v. Arden*, 1 Bay 487, 1 S.C.L. 487, 1795 WL 395 (S.C.Com.Pl.Gen.Sess.) (1795).

66. Peter Charles Hoffer & N.E.H. Hull, *Murdering Mothers: Infanticide in England and New England, 1558–1803*, (New York University Press, 1981), p. 48.

67. Pamela D. Bridgewater, "Un/Re/Discovering Slave Breeding in Thirteenth Amendment Jurisprudence," *Washington and Lee Race and Ethnic Ancestry Law Journal*, 7 (2001), pp. 11–43.

68. White, *Ar'n't I A Woman?*, p. 85; Herbert G. Gutman, *The Black Family in Slavery and Freedom, 1750–1925* (New York: Vintage Books, 1976), pp. 80–82.

69. Morris, *Southern Slavery and the Law*, p. 301.

70. Streib, "Death Penalty for Female Offenders."

71. Frazier, *Slavery and Crime in Missouri*, pp. 168–169.

72. Schwarz, *Twice Condemned*, p. 252, note 33.

73. Jensen, *Loosening the Bonds*, p. 69.

74. Teeters, "Public Executions in Pennsylvania 1682 to 1834," p. 107.

75. White, *Ar'n't I a Woman?*

76. Hearn, *Legal Executions in New York State*, p. 135.

77. Digital Library on American Slavery, University of North Carolina at Greensboro, PAR Number 11382407.

78. Todd Lee Savitt, *Medicine and Slavery: The Diseases and Health Care of Blacks in Antebellum Virginia* (Urbana: University of Illinois Press, 1978), pp. 122–129.

79. Michael P. Johnson, "Smothered Slave Infants: Were Slave Mothers At Fault?," *The Journal of Southern History*, 47 (1981): 493–520; Richard H. Steckel, "A Dreadful Childhood: The Excess Mortality of American Slaves," *Social Science History*, 10 (1986): 427–465.

80. Margaret G. Spinelli, "Maternal Infanticide Associated with Mental Illness: Prevention and the Promise of Saved Lives," *American Journal of Psychiatry*, 161 (2004): 1548–1557.

81. Schwarz, *Twice Condemned*, pp. 253–254; see also Halimah Abdullah, "Researchers Link Black Infant Deaths to Stress of Racism," *McClatchy Newspapers* (October 10, 2007).

82. Oliver Reiss, *Blacks in Colonial America* (Jefferson, NC: McFarland, 1997), p. 198.

83. Reich, *Colonial America*.

84. Herbert Aptheker, *American Negro Slave Revolts* (New York: International Publishers, 1993); see also Espy & Smykla, *Executions in the United States*.

85. Gwendolyn Midlo Hall, *Africans in Colonial Louisiana: The Development of Afro-Creole Culture in the Eighteenth Century* (Baton Rouge: Louisiana State University Press), pp. 107.

86. Ibid., p. 108.

87. Aptheker, *American Negro Slave Revolts*, p. 182.

88. Streib, "Death Penalty for Female Offenders."

89. Johnson, "At the Intersection of Injustice," p. 22.

90. Streib, "Death Penalty for Female Offenders."

91. Morris, *Southern Slavery and the Law*, p. 277.

92. Ibid., p. 92.

93. Digital Library on American Slavery, University of North Carolina at Greensboro, PAR Number 11279304.

94. Helen Tunnicliff Catterall (ed.), *Judicial Cases Concerning American Slavery and the Negro*, Volume 4 (Washington, D.C.: Carnegie Institution of Washington, 1926–1937), p. 43.

95. Streib & Sametz, "Executing Female Juveniles," pp. 17–18.

96. Schwarz, *Twice Condemned*, p. 115–116.

97. Schwarz, *Slave laws in Virginia*, p. 116.

98. Harriet C. Frazier, *Slavery and Crime in Missouri, 1773–1865* (Jefferson: McFarland, 2001), p. 168.

99. Aptheker, *American Negro Slave Revolts*, p. 190.

100. Morris, *Southern Slavery and the Law: 1619–1860*, p. 331.

101. Gabriele Gottlieb, *Theater of Death: Capital Punishment in Early America, 1750–1800*. Unpublished doctoral dissertation (University of Pittsburgh, 2005), p. 30.

102. Kay & Cary, *Slavery in North Carolina,* p. 115.

103. Hearn, *Legal Executions in New York State,* p. 18.

104. Aptheker, *American Negro Slave Revolts,* p. 145.

105. Schwarz, *Twice Condemned,* p. 115.

106. Don R. Gerlach, "Black Arson in Albany, New York: November 1793," *Journal of Black Studies,* 7 (1977): 301–312.

107. Frazier, *Slavery and Crime in Missouri,* p. 168.

108. Elisa Ann Everson, *A Little Labor of Love: The Extraordinary Career of Dorothy Ripley, Female Evangelist in Early America,* Georgia State University (Unpublished doctoral dissertation), 2007.

109. Morris, *Southern Slavery and the Law,* p. 334.

110. Joe R. Feagin, *Racist America: Roots, Current Realities, and Future Aspirations* (New York: Routledge, 2001), p. 46.

111. Ibid., p. 47.

112. Melton A. McLaurin, *Celia, A Slave: A True Story* (New York: Avon Books, 1991).

113. Lori Rozsa, "Woman on Death Row: Echoes of a Slave's Hanging in 1848," *The Miami Herald* (March 29, 1998), p. 1A; Daniel L. Schafer, "'A Class of People Neither Freemen Nor Slaves': From Spanish to American Race Relations in Florida, 1821–1861," *Journal of Social History,* 26 (1993): 587–609, pp. 598–599.

114. A Leon Higginbotham, *In the matter of color: Race and the American legal process. [Vol. 1], The colonial period,* (Oxford University Press, 1978), p. 289.

115. Streib & Sametz, "Executing Female Juveniles," p. 11.

116. Hearn, *Legal Executions in New York State,* p. 5.

117. Hearn, *Legal Executions in New York State.*

118. Streib & Sametz, "Executing Female Juveniles," p. 19.

119. Anita P. Wholuba, *A Generation of Witnesses: Neo-Testimonial Practices in Flight to Canada, Dessa Rose, Beloved, Kindred, and the Chaneysville Incident,* Flordia State University, unpublished doctoral dissertation (2007), p. 26; see also Aptheker, *American Negro Slavery,* p. 287.

120. Helen Tunnicliff Catterall, *Judicial Cases Concerning American Slavery and the Negro,* Volume 4, Washington, D.C.: Carnegie Institution of Washington, pp. 442–443; see also Harris Downey, "The Hand and Head of Molly Glass," The Kenyon Review, 23 (1961), pp. 229–254, at p. 248.

121. Hearn, *Legal Executions in New Jersey,* p. 76.

122. David E. Barlow, Melissa Hickman Barlow & Theodore G. Chiricos, "Long Economic Cycles and the Criminal Justice System in the U.S.," *Crime, Law and Social Change,* 19 (1993): 143–169; Jonathan H. Turner, Royce Singleton & David Musick, *Oppression: A Socio-History of Black-White Relations in America* (New York: Nelson Hall, 1984).

123. Reva Siegel, "Why Equal Protection No Longer Protects: The Evolving Forms of Status-Enforcing State Action," *Stanford Law Review,* 49 (1997): 1111–1148.

124. James McPherson, "Comparing the Two Reconstructions," *Princeton Alumni Weekly,* 16 (1999): 18–19.

125. A. Leon Higginbotham, *Shades of Freedom: Racial Politics and Presumptions of the American Legal Process* (New York: Oxford University Press, 1996).

126. Eric Foner, *Reconstruction: America's Unfinished Revolution* (New York: Harper & Row, 1988).

127. Adalberto Aguirre, Jr. & David V. Baker, *Race, Racism and the Death Penalty in the United States* (Berrien Springs: Vande Vere, 1991); James W. Clarke, "Without Fear or Shame: Lynching, Capital Punishment and the Subculture of Violence in the American South," *British Journal of Political Science,* 28 (1998): 269–289; Emma Coleman Jordan, "Crossing the River of Blood Between Us: Lynching, Violence, Beauty, and the Paradox of Feminist History," *Journal of Gender, Race and Justice,* 3 (2000): 545–580; Charles J. Ogletree, Jr., "Black Man's Burden:

Race and the Death Penalty in America," *Oregon Law Review,* 81 (2002): 15–38; Stewart E. Tolnay & E.M. Beck, *A Festival of Violence: An Analysis of Southern Lynchings, 1882–1930* (Urbana: University of Illinois Press, 1995); Margaret Vandiver, *Lethal Punishment: Lynchings and Legal Executions in the South* (New Brunswick: Rutgers University Press, 2006); Charles David Phillips, "Exploring Relations Among Forms of Social Control: The Lynching and Execution of Blacks in North Carolina, 1889–1918," *Law and Society Review*, 21 (1987): 361–374.

128. For discussions on black female lynchings, see Maria DeLongoria, " 'Stranger Fruit': The Lynching of Black Women, The Cases of Rosa Jefferson and Marie Scott," Unpublished doctoral dissertation, Department of Philosophy, University of Missouri-Columbia (December 2006); Crystal Nicole Femister, "Ladies and Lynching: The Gendered Discourse of Mob Violence in the New South, 1880–1930," Unpublished doctoral dissertation, Princeton University (2000).

129. White, *Ar'n't I a Woman?*

130. DeLongoria, "Stranger Fruit," p. vii.

131. Wyn Craig Wade, *The Fiery Cross: The Ku Klux Klan in America* (New York: Oxford University Press, 1987), p. 18.

132. Elliot Jaspin, *Buried in the Bitter Water: The Hidden History of Racial Cleansing in America* (New York: Basic Books, 2007), p. 61.

133. Foner, *Reconstruction*, p. 120.

134. William D. Carrigan, *The Making of a Lynching Culture: Violence and Vigilantism in Central Texas, 1836–1916* (Urbana: University of Illinois Press, 2005).

135. Foner, *Reconstruction*, p. 119.

136. Feagin, *Racist America*, p. 58.

137. Digital Library on American Slavery, University of North Carolina at Greensboro, PAR Number 11086402.

138. Ray Stanard Baker, "Following the Color Line," *American Magazine* (1908), available at http://www.spartacus.schoolnet.co.uk/USAlynching.htm; Alisa Bierria, *An historical perspective on anti-rape organizing.* Communities Against Rape and Abuse (2003), available at http://cara-seattle.org/w_historical.html.

139. Davis, *Women, Race, and Class*, 89-90.

140. Victor Streib & Linda Sametz, Executing female juveniles, *Connecticut Law Review,* 22 (1989), pp. 3–16, at pp. 21–22. Streib and Sametz refer to the slave girl as "Eliza" but her name was actually Susan belonging to a slave owners named Eliza.

141. *Female Hangings 1632 to 1900.*

142. "Execution of Mary Wallis," *The New York Herald* (February 11, 1871), p. 6; "Execution of Mary Wallis—State of the Culprit for Some Time Before The Execution," *New York Times* (February 11, 1871).

143. Kerry Segrave, *Women and Capital Punishment in America, 1840–1899: Death Sentences and Executions in the United States and Canada* (Jefferson: McFarland, 2008), pp. 69–70.

144. Shipman, *The Penalty Is Death*, p. 154; Segrave, *Women and Capital Punishment in America*, pp. 113–115.

145. Nicole Hahn Rafter, *Partial Justice: Women, Prisons, and Social Control* (New Brunswick, NJ: Transaction, 2004), p. 145.

146. Howard Sitkoff, *The Struggle for Black Equality, 1954–1980* (New York: Hill & Wang, 1981).

147. Leon F. Litwack, *North of Slavery: The Negro in the Free States, 1790–1860* (Chicago: University of Chicago Press, 1961).

148. *Civil Rights Cases*, 109 U.S. 3 (1883); *Plessey v. Ferguson*, 163 U.S. 537 (1896); *Williams v. Mississippi*, 170 U.S. 213 (1898); *Giles v. Harris*, 189 U.S. 475 (1903).

149. Espy & Smykla, *Executions in the United States*; Robert L. Zangrando, *The NAACP Crusade Against Lynching, 1909–1950* (Philadelphia: Temple University Press, 1980).

150. Manning Marable, *How Capitalism Underdeveloped Black America* (Boston: South End Press, 1985).

151. O'Shea, *Women and the Death Penalty in the United States.*

152. Tolnay & Beck, *A Festival of Violence.*

153. Walter White, *Rope and Faggot: Biography of Judge Lynch* (New York: Arno Press, 1969).

154. Trina N. Seitz, "The Wounds of Savagery," p. 41; see also Rafter, *Partial Justice.*

155. Segrave, *Women and Capital Punishment in America*, p. 125.

156. Ibid., p. 162; see also Streib & Sametz, "Executing Female Juveniles;" "Three of a Kind: Two Women and One Man Hung in South Carolina," *Sandusky Daily Register* (October 8, 1892), p. 1

157. USA—*Female Hangings 1632 to 1937*, available at http://www.capitalpunishmentuk.org/amfemhang.html.

158. *Waterloo Daily Courier* (September 30, 1891), p. 2.

159. See "Last Public Hanging," *Gastonia Daily Gazette* (October 5, 1946), p. 53; Bill Williams, "Residents of Dallas Recall Hanging of Caroline Shipp," *Gastonia Gazette* (November 7, 1953), p. 20.

160. "Colored Woman Hanged in Gaston County," *The Landmark* (December 24, 1891), p. 2; Daniel Jackson, "Last Woman Hanged in North Carolina Executed in Dallas," *The Gaston Gazette* (August 1, 2008); Megan Ward, "Choked To Death By Law: Gastonia Gazette Story From Jan. 28, 1892," *The Gaston Gazette* (August 1, 2008).

161. Segrave, *Women and Capital Punishment in America*, pp. 161–162; see also "Anna Tribble Hanged for the Murder of Her New Born Babe," *The State* (October 8, 1892).

162. "Double Hanging," *The Emporia Gazette* (July 17, 1903), p. 1.

163. *The Landmark* (January 20, 1882), p. 1; Segrave, *Women and Capital Punishment in America*, p. 117.

164. "Wholesale Hanging," *Fort Wayne Daily Gazette* (June 24, 1882), p. 2; see also Segrave, *Women and Capital Punishment in America*, p. 118.

165. "Barbara Miller Hanged," *New York Times* (September 15, 1883); "Barbara Miller's Last Day Among the Living," *Boston Daily Globe* (September 14, 1883), "Barbara Miller Goes to the Scaffold Chanting Negro Hymns," *The Washington Post* (September 15, 1883); see also Ann Field Alexander, *Race Man: The Rise and Fall of the "Fighting Editor" John Mitchell, Jr.* (University of Virginia Press, 2002), p. 24.

166. "A Double Hanging," *Logansport Journal* (January 23, 1892), p. 1; see also Segrave, *Women and Capital Punishment in America*, p. 161.

167. Segrave, *Women and Capital Punishment in America*, p. 187.

168. *Knight v. State*, 92 So. 559 (1922).

169. *Gray v. State*, 92 So. 559 (1922).

170. See *Osgood et al. v. The State of Georgia*, 63 Ga. 791; 1879 Ga. LEXIS 338 (1879); *Petersburg Index Appeal* (December 25, 1878), p. 3.

171. Segrave, *Women and Capital Punishment in America*, p. 117.

172. "Finis For Five! The End of Eastman Rioters," *The Atlanta Constitution* (October 21, 1882), p. 1.

173. "Triple Execution," *The Galveston Daily News* (August 1, 1885), p. 5; Segrave, *Women and Capital Punishment in America*, pp. 140–141.

174. John Edgar Wideman, *My Soul Has Grown Deep: Classic of Early African-American Literature* (Philadelphia: Running Press, 2001), p. 802.

175. Streib & Sametz, "Executing Female Juveniles," p. 26.

176. Ibid., p. 25.

177. Rick Halperin, *Death Penalty News—Virginia* (August 15, 1999), available at http://venus.soci.niu.edu/~archives?ABOLISH/rick-halperin/oct99/0103.html.

178. Streib & Sametz, "Executing Female Juveniles," p. 25.

179. Ibid.; see also Derryn Eroll Moten, *A Gruesome Warning to Black Girls: The August 16, 1912, Execution of Virginia Christian*, University of Iowa (unpublished doctoral dissertation, 1997).

180. Kia Gregory, "Soul Searching," *Philadelphia Weekly* (June 2, 2004).

181. *Commonwealth v. Sykes*, 353 Pa. 392, 45 A.2d 43 (1946).

182. Vertamae Grosvenor, *Remembering Corrine Sykes*. National Public Radio (NPR) All Things Considered (April 3, 1998). Transcript No. 98040320-212. Linda Wertheimer, Reporting.

183. Ibid.

184. Ibid.; see also Death Row Divas, *Corrine Sykes* (2005), available at http://www.geocities.com/as_k13/corrine.html; Moten, "A Gruesome Warning to Black Girls."

185. Seitz, "The Wounds of Savagery," p. 56.

186. *State v. Phillips et al.*, 222 N.C. 440, 23 S.E.2d 342 (1942).

187. Seitz, "The Wounds of Savagery," p. 56.

188. Gillespie, *Dancehall Ladies*, p. xxi.

189. *McCarty v. State*, 83 So. 753 (1920).

190. "Special Term Is Ordered for Trial of Two Negroes," *The Anniston Star* (August 30, 1921), p. 1; see also Shipman, *The Penalty Is Death*, p. 167.

191. O'Shea, *Women and the death penalty in the United States*, pp. 210–211; Shipman, *The Penalty Is Death*, pp. 168–169; Seitz, "The Wounds of Savagery."

192. Seitz, "The Wounds of Savagery;" O'Shea, *Women and the Death Penalty in the United States.*

193. Shipman, *The Penalty Is Death*, p. 168.

194. *Brooks v. State*, 178 Miss. 575, 173 So. 409 (1937).

195. Seitz, "The Wounds of Savagery"; O'Shea, *Women and the Death Penalty in the United States.*

196. *Johnson v. State*, 196 Miss. 402, 17 So.2d 446 (1944); "Man, Woman Die in Chair at Vicksburg," *The Delta Democrat Times* (May 19, 1944), p. 1.

197. *Johnson v. State*, 196 Miss. 402, 17 So.2d 446 (1944).

198. David Staba, "Falls Murder Case Presents Contrast to Northrup Verdict," *Niagara Falls Reporter* (December 4, 2001).

199. *People v. Helen Fowler and George F. Knight*, 293 N.Y. 721, 56 N.E.2d 733 (1944).

200. Gillespie, *Dancehall Ladies*, pp. xvii–xviii.

201. *State v. Ralph Thompson, Cleve Bryant Johnson, Bessie Mae Williams, and Annie Mae Allision*, 224 N.C. 661; 32 S.E.2d 24; 1944 N.C. LEXIS 449 (1944).

202. Shipman, *The Penalty is Death*, pp. 162–163; see also "Negress, Two Negro Men Go To Death in Gas Chamber; Two Confess, Third Denies," *The Daily Times News* (December 29, 1944), p. 1.

203. Carlos Campos & Bill Torpy, "Post-Execution Pardon; One-Day Trial in 1945 Sent Georgia Woman to Electric Chair," *The Atlanta Journal Constitution* (August 16, 2005), p. A1; Gary Younge, "Pardon for Maid Executed in 1945: Campaigners Celebrate Clemency for Woman Who Killed Employer," *The Guardian* (August 17, 2005), p. 14; Lela Bond Phillips, "Execution in a Small Town—The Lena Baker Story," *Justice Denied: The Magazine for the Wrongfully Convicted*, 29 (2005), p. 8.

204. Shipman, *The Penalty Is Death*, p. 165.

205. Ibid., pp. 183–185.

206. Sally S. Simpson, "Caste, Class, and Violent Crime: Explaining Differences in Female Offending," *Criminology*, 29: 115–135.

207. Leadership Conference on Civil Rights, Leadership Conference Education Fund, *The Bush Administration Takes Aim: Civil Rights Under Attack* (2004), p. 13, available at http://www.civilrights.org/publications/reports/taking_aim/bush_takes_aim.pdf.

208. Sheryll Cashin, *The Failures of Integration: How Race and Class Are Undermining the American Dream* (New York: Public Affairs, 2004).

209. Feagin, *Racist America,* p. 242.

210. Carmen DeNavas-Walt, Bernadette D. Proctor, Jessica Smith, *Income, Poverty, and Health Insurance Coverage in the United States: 2006*, U.S. Bureau of the Census, Current Population Reports (2007), available at http://www.census.gov/prod/2007pubs/p60-233.pdf.

211. Human Rights Watch, *Incarcerated America* (2003), available at http://hrw.org/backgrounder/usa/incarceration.

212. Shipman, *The Penalty Is Death*; Michele B. Goodwin, "Gender, Race, and Mental Illness: The Case of Wanda Jean Allen," in Adriene Katherine Wing (ed.) *Critical Race Feminism: A Reader* (New York: New York University Press, 2003), pp. 228–237.

213. Goodwin, "Gender, Race, and Mental Illness," p. 229.

214. Joey L. Mogul, "The Dykier, The Butcher, The Better: The State's Use of Homophobia and Sexism to Execute Women in the United States," *New York City Law Review*, 8 (2005), pp. 473–493.

215. David Kirby, "Was Justice Served? The Execution of a Lesbian Raises Tough Questions About the Death Penalty," *The Advocate* (February 27, 2001).

216. American Civil Liberties Union, *The Forgotten Population: A Look at Death Row in the United States Through the Experience of Women* (2004), available at http://www.aclu.org/capital/women/10627pub20041129.html.

217. Janice L. Kopec, "Avoiding a Death Sentence in the American Legal System: Get a Woman to Do It," *Capital Defense Journal,* 15 (2003): 353–382, at p. 362.

218. Ryan Patrick Alford, "Appellate Review of Racist Summations: Redeeming the Promise of Searching Analysis," *Michigan Journal of Race and Law*, 11 (2006): 325–365; see also Chana Barron, "The Evil Woman: The Impact of Gender Roles and Expectations on Appellate Outcomes in Women's Capital Convictions" (September 14, 2008), paper presented at the annual meeting of the The Law and Society, J.W. Marriott Resort, Las Vegas, Nevada; Chana Barron, "Gendered Definitions and Expectations: Their Influence on Outcomes in Women's Death Penalty Appeals" (November 15, 2005), paper presented at the annual meeting of the American Society of Criminology, Royal York, Toronto.

219. Goodwin, "Gender, Race, and Mental Illness," p. 234.

220. *Allen v. Massie*, 2000 U.S. App. LEXIS 316 (2000); Goodwin, "Gender, Race, and Mental Illness"; Shortnacy, "Guilty and Gay."

221. Ken Armstrong & Maurice Possley, "Trial and Error: How Prosecutors Sacrifice Justice to Win" (Series: Tribune Investigative Report: The Failure of the Death Penalty in Illinois. Parts I–V), *Chicago Tribune* (1999); Stephen B. Bright, "Discrimination, Death and Denial: The Tolerance of Racial Discrimination in Infliction of the Death Penalty," *Santa Clara Law Review,* 35 (1995): 433–483; Andrea Elliot & Benjamin Weiser, "When Prosecutors Err, Others Pay The Price," *New York Times* (March 21, 2004), pp. 25, 30; Michael Kroll, *Killing Justice: Government Misconduct and the Death Penalty*" (1992), available at http://www.deathpenaltyinfo.org/article.php?scid=45&did=529; Texas Defender Service, *A State of Denial: Texas Justice and the Death Penalty* (2000), available at http://www.texasdefender.org/publications.asp; Penny J. White, "Errors and Ethnics: Dilemmas in Death,"*Hofstra Law Review,* 29 (2001): 1265–1299.

222. Arielle Siebert, "*Batson v. Kentucky*: Application to Whites and the Effect on the Peremptory Challenge System," *Columbia Journal of Law and Social Problems,* 32 (1999): 307–330, at p. 308.

223. Raymond J. Broderick, "Why the Peremptory Challenge Should Be Abolished," *Temple Law Review,* 65 (1992): 369–423; Patricia J. Griffin, "Jumping on the Ban Wagon: *Minetos v. City University of New York* and the Future of the Peremptory Challenge," *Minnesota Law Review,* 81 (1997): 1237–1270.

224. Barbara Allen Babcock, "A Place in the Palladium: Women's Rights and Jury Service," *University of Cincinnati Law Review,* 61 (1993): 1139–1180.

225. David C. Baldus, George Woodworth, David Zuckerman, Neil Allan Weiner & Barbara Broffitt, "Use of Peremptory Challenges in Capital Murder Trials: A Legal and Empirical Analysis,"

University of Pennsylvania Journal of Constitutional Law, 3 (2001): 3–170; Broderick, "Why the Peremptory Challenge Should Be Abolished"; William J. Bowers, Benjamin D. Steiner & Marla Sandys, "Death Sentencing in Black and White: An Empirical Analysis of the Role of Jurors' Race and Racial Jury Composition," *University of Pennsylvania Journal of Constitutional Law,* 3 (2001): 171–274; Douglas L. Colbert, "Challenging the Challenge: Thirteenth Amendment as a Prohibition Against Racial Use of Peremptory Challenge," *Cornell Law Review* 76 (1990): 1–128; Richard C. Dieter, *The Death Penalty in Black and White: Who Lives, Who Dies, Who Decides* (1998), Death Penalty Information Center, available at http://www.death penaltyinfo.org/article.php?scid=45&did=539; Griffin, "Jumping on the Ban Wagon; Sheri Lynn Johnson, "Black Innocence and the White Jury," *Michigan Law Review,* 83 (1985): 1611–1708; Barbara D. Underwood, "Ending Race Discrimination in Jury Selection: Whose Right Is It Anyway?" *Columbia Law Review,* 92 (1992): 725–774.

226. Charles Conrad, *Jury Nullification: The Evolution of a Doctrine* (Durham: Carolina Academic Press, 1998), p. 190; see also Jonathan B. Mintz, "Note: *Batson v. Kentucky*: A Half Step in the Right Direction (Racial Discrimination and Peremptory Challenges Under the Heavier Confines of Equal Protection)," *Cornell Law Review,* 72 (1987): 1026–1046; David Savage, "Justices Weight State's Jury Selection Law," *Los Angeles Times* (April 19, 2005), p. A12.

227. Stephen B. Bright & Patrick J. Keenan, "Judges and the Politics of Death: Deciding Between the Bill of Rights and the Next Election in Capital Cases," *Boston University Law Review,* 75 (1995): 760–835; Adriene Katherine Wing, "Examining the Correlation Between Disability and Poverty: A Comment from a Critical Race Feminist Perspective—Helping the Joneses to Keep Up!" *Journal of Gender, Race and Justice,* 8 (2005): 655–666; William S. Lofquist, "Putting Them There, Keeping Them There, and Killing Them: An Analysis of State-Level Variations in Death Penalty Intensity," *Iowa Law Review,* 87 (2002): 1505–1557.

228. Kelly Reissmann, "Our System Is Broken: A Study of the Crisis Facing the Death-Eligible Defendant," *Northern Illinois University Law Review,* 23 (2002): 43–79.

229. *Allen v. State,* 871 P.2d 79 (1994).

230. *Atkins v. Virginia,* 536 U.S. 304 (2002).

231. Amnesty International, *Francis Elaine Newton* (November 19, 2004), available at http://www .amnesty.org/en/library/asset/AMR51/163/2004/en/dom-AMR511632004en.pdf; National Coalition to Abolish the Death Penalty, *Do Not Execute Francis Newton* (September 14, 2005), available at http://www.demaction.org/dia/organizations/ncadp/campaign.jsp?campaign_ KEY=1132; "Frances Elaine Newton . . . Coming Texas Execution," *The New Criminologist,* available at http://www.newcriminologist.co.uk/news.asp?id=230585759; Texas Department of Criminal Justice, *Death Row Information: Scheduled Executions,* available at http://www.tdcj .state.tx.us/statistics/deathrow/drowlist/newton.jpg; Allan Turner & Cynthia Leonor Garza, "Newton Is Executed For Slaying Her Family. She Is The First Black Woman Put To Death In Texas Since Civil War," *The Houston Chronicle* (September 15, 1005), p. A1; "New Evidence of Frances Newton's Innocence Ignored By Courts And TX Governor," *Justice Denied: The Magazine for the Wrongfully Convicted,* 29 (2005), p. 4, 5.

232. *Newton v. Dretke,* 371 F.3d 250 (2004); Texas Defender Service, *A State of Denial.*

233. David R. Dow & Jered Tyler, *Ex parte Francis Elaine Newton.* Application for Postconviction Writ of Habeas Corpus and Motion for Stay of Execution. In the 263rd Judicial District, Texas, and In the Court of Criminal Appeals of Texas, p. 8.

234. *Brady v. Maryland,* 373 U.S. 83 (1963).

235. Mona Lynch, "Stereotypes, Prejudice, and Life-and-Death Decision Making: Lessons from Laypersons in an Experimental Setting," in Charles J. Ogletree, Jr., & Austin Sarat (eds.) *From Lynch Mobs to the Killing State: Race and the Death Penalty in America,* pp. 182–207 (New York: New York University Press, 2006), p. 182.

SECTION II

Women and the Law

4

Mothers, Children, and Crime

The Role of Parenting in Women's Desistance after Incarceration

Venezia Michalsen

There are over 100,000 women incarcerated in American prisons today; most of them are mothers, and almost all of them will be released into the community within five years. As a society, we must examine the place where these two facts intersect: How do mothering and successful reentry into the community come together for formerly incarcerated mothers? The process by which individuals end, or desist from, criminal behavior is an emerging focus of theoretical and research inquiry. While previous research has shown that for men social bonds to prosocial institutions such as marriage and employment encourage desistance, there have been far fewer studies of women's desistance. In this chapter, we will look at what research has shown about incarcerated and formerly incarcerated mothers and their relationships with their children. This chapter pays specific attention to recent research findings about the role (and lack thereof) of relationships with children in their mothers' desistance. It also discusses policy implications and directions for future research.

INTRODUCTION

There are almost 2.5 million people incarcerated in American prisons and jails today (Sabol, West, & Cooper, 2009), a number that dwarfs the incarcerated population of any other country in the world (Walmsley, 2009). Over 800,000 of these people are parents to approximately 1.7 million minor children (Glaze & Maruschak, 2009). Because most of the people in our prisons are male (93 percent), most of these parents are likewise male. However, the increase of women incarcerated since 1977 (almost 1,000 percent) has dwarfed the rate of increase for men over the same time period (Frost, 2006; Sabol, West, & Cooper, 2009), which has meant that the number of children affected by a mother's absence has also increased dramatically. Adding to the effects of this dramatic population explosion, women prisoners are more likely to report being a parent (62 percent) than their male counterparts (51 percent). Perhaps even more significantly, these women are more likely than incarcerated men to have been single custodial parents of their children just before their arrest, and intend to resume that parenting after their release (Bruns, 2006; Bloom, 1993; Harm & Phillips, 2001; Glaze & Maruschak, 2008; Greenfeld & Snell, 1999; Richie, 2001; Robbins, Martin, & Surratt, 2009). It has been argued, therefore, that the incarceration of women can have disproportionately negative effects on families and communities.

The intersection of parenting and incarceration, however, is not only important for the ways in which children are affected by a mother's absence. Though limited, some research suggests that children may play a prosocial role in promoting women's desistance from crime after incarceration. In this chapter, we will discuss mothers' relationships with their children during and after incarceration, and the effects of reunification with children (or lack thereof) on women after incarceration.[1]

WOMEN'S CRIME

Although some criminologists in the 1970s and 1980s suggested that women's increased social standing in society would mean that women would make up a larger proportion of criminals (e.g., Adler, 1975), criminologists today attribute much of this increase to enforcement practices, particularly the war on drugs, rather than to increases in women's criminal behaviors (Mauer & Chesney-Lind, 2002). About a third of women incarcerated are incarcerated for drug offenses (28 percent of women in prison), which is almost as often as they are incarcerated for violent (32 percent) and property (29 percent) offenses[2] (Sabol, West, & Cooper, 2009). In addition, many non-drug-related convictions are reported by women themselves to be associated with their efforts to support their addictions (Belknap, 2001; Bloom, Owen, & Covington, 2004). Increases in the number of women incarcerated, however, do not reflect increases in women's crime: imprisonment rates have been increasing disproportionately to arrest rates (Women's Prison Association, 2004). The policies of the war on drugs increased mandatory and longer sentences for drug-related crimes in a way that brought more lower-level offenders, disproportionately female, into the system for longer periods of time. This punitive policy shift against drug-involved women and their families, disproportionately poor and African-American or Latina, has meant that the community sanctions of the past have been replaced by prison sentences (Bloom, Owen, & Covington, 2004).

MOTHERING AND INCARCERATION

The incarceration of fathers, without a doubt, can have devastating effects on the children they leave behind (Clopton & East, 2008). However, research suggests that the incarceration of mothers can have a far more profound effect on children in the community for a number of reasons (Greene, Haney, & Hurtado, 2000; Michalsen, Krupat, & Flavin, 2010). To begin, more than half of incarcerated mothers and approximately one-third of incarcerated fathers report that they lived with their children in the month before their arrest. Mothers are particularly likely to report that they lived alone with their children as the sole caretaker before their arrest (Glaze & Maruschak, 2008). Likewise, the level of disruption in children's and families' lives is affected by the gender of the parent who has been arrested: When a father is incarcerated, children are most likely (88 percent) to remain in the care of their own mother, and experience little disruption of their living situation (Dallaire, 2007; Glaze & Maruschak, 2008). When a mother is incarcerated, however, children are far more rarely (37 percent) cared for by their fathers (Glaze & Maruschak, 2008) and are often broken up, both from family members and from siblings (Johnston, 1995). Research, though limited, indicates that children's outcomes, from risk for school failure and aggression to attachment and incarceration themselves, are more severe for children with incarcerated mothers than for children of incarcerated fathers (Dallaire, 2007).

Despite extensive research, which shows the negative effects of enforced parental absence on the outcomes for both children and parents, correctional policies fail to facilitate family contact in service to security. For both men and women, maintaining contact with family during incarceration has been shown to increase the likelihood that people will complete their parole without incident, or have lower recidivism overall (Casey-Acevedo & Bakken, 2002; Petersilia, 2003). In practice, however, almost 60 percent of women incarcerated in state prisons report never having had a visit with their children. One in five women receive monthly visits with their children, and less than half reported monthly phone contact. Twenty-two percent reported that they had never had contact with their children via the mail, and 41 percent that they had never had phone contact with their children (Glaze & Marushak, 2008; Johnson & Waldfogel, 2002). However, visits, phone calls, and letters are difficult to maintain across prison bars for a number of reasons, from literacy and embarrassment to distance and cost (Michalsen, Krupat, & Flavin, 2010). There are fewer prison facilities for women than there are for men, which has meant that women's prisons are often particularly distant from families. Children of incarcerated mothers are most likely to be in the care of grandparents, for whom the combination of distance, expense, and hardship often means that visits are difficult and infrequent. Furthermore, the experience of visiting a prison can be a traumatic experience for children, who may have to go through lengthy wait times, humiliating screening procedures, and time in inhospitable visiting rooms.

Aside from the disruption inherent in changing children's caretakers and homes, the additional involvement of the child welfare system, used when a family member or friend is unavailable to care for a child, brings with it additional risks. When children are cared for by foster care families or agencies, mothers are at risk for having their parental rights to those children terminated (Genty, 1995; Mauer & Chesney-Lind, 2002; Raimon, 2001). The Adoption and Safe Families Act of 1997 (ASFA; P.L. 105-89) mandates termination of parental rights once a child has been in foster care for at least 15 of the past 22 months. As Jacobs (2001) points out, ASFA requirements are difficult enough to meet for single mothers with substance abuse problems in the community. Their incarcerated counterparts, serving an average of 18 months, are even more handicapped in their pursuit of reunification (Beckerman, 1989, 1991, 1998; Genty, 1995, 1998). Services for women in prison are often narrow in focus, teaching parenting skills while neglecting broader family system issues, or practical applications that aid them in their reunification efforts are also often limited (Cecil, McHale, Strozier, & Pietsch, 2008; Craig, 2009). Any lack of communication with and support from social and foster care workers, therefore, affects access to visits, referrals, and assistance with placement in correctional or reentry programs (Beckerman, 1994; Johnson & Waldfogel, 2002; Johnston, 1995).

Although the legal routes to reunification after incarceration are often fraught with difficulties, incarcerated mothers usually report that regaining custody of their children is one of their highest priorities for their reentry into the community (Baker & Carson, 1999; Grella & Greenwell, 2006; Michalsen, 2007; Richie, 2001). And so we are left with an equation: the desire to reunify with children who are likely in unstable living situations and the practical realities of women's reentry, which usually involve homelessness, unemployment, domestic violence, and physical and mental health problems (such as sobriety). The research into women's desistance, though limited, seeks to discover the answer to this problem: What is the role of children in women's desistance, and how can policy and practice intervene (or not) to promote better outcomes for these women and their families?

MOTHERS' DESISTANCE FROM CRIME: WHAT IS THE ROLE OF CHILDREN?

The traditional approach to criminal behavior (or the lack thereof) in reentry is to focus on the likelihood that individuals commit more crime after being released, also known as recidivism. More recently, researchers have focused on the concept of *desistance*, or the process by which individuals stop criminal behavior. Further still, some researchers refer to the concept of *social reintegration*, not just the absence of recidivism, but also the presence of vital family and community ties (Arditti & Few, 2008; Travis, Solomon, & Waul, 2001).

The punishment of imprisonment may motivate women to avoid criminal behavior (and, as a potential result, re-imprisonment), but the lack of programming, particularly present in women's facilities, usually means that women leave incarceration much as they came in: with limited educational and work experience, unstable housing, health and mental health problems, addictions, and poverty (Bloom, 1999; Freudenberg, Daniels, Crum, Perkins, & Richie, 2005). In that women were the primary caretakers before incarceration, and want to reunify, all of these issues must be dealt with simultaneously. Unfortunately, this is very difficult, and women often fail, leading to recidivism and re-incarceration (Brown & Bloom, 2009; Richie, 2001).

Recent theoretical and research focus has shifted from investigation of *recidivism* (why people get in trouble again) to desistance (what keeps people out of trouble). So far, most of the research on desistance has been about men because they make up the vast majority of people with criminal justice system involvement. This research shows that attachments to prosocial institutions of social control, such as employment, the military, and marriage, are effective at keeping men out of trouble. For example, substantial quantitative research confirms that men's desistance from crime is correlated with a number of events, including obtaining stable employment (Glaser, 1964; Mischkowitz, 1994; Sampson & Laub, 1993; Shover, 1985), getting married (Farrington & West, 1995; Gibbens, 1984; Irwin, 1970; Mischkowitz, 1994; Sampson & Laub, 1993; Zoccolillo, Pickles, Quinton, & Rutter, 1992), and completing education (Farrington, Gallagher, Morley, St. Ledger, & West, 1986; Rand, 1987). There has not been much research, however, about the effects of children on men's desistance. This may be because most men are not primary caretakers of children, or because men's roles as fathers are not as much of a cultural focus as are women's roles as mothers. The majority of research on the effects of fatherhood on desistance has focused on whether becoming a new father acts as a turning point, encouraging desistance—and findings from this research have so far been mixed (see Moloney, MacKenzie, Hunt, & Joe-Laidler, 2009, for a review)—but has not focused on the role of reunification with children after incarceration in desistance.

Research into what works for women shows some differences. For example, because of women's increased rates of domestic violence, marriage is not as protective as it is for men. Likewise, in that women have lower education and less work experience, employment does not appear to be as protective as it is for men (Michalsen, 2007). In fact, much research into women's reentry focuses on the impact of multiple stressors on women's health, well-being, and desistance. In particular, mothers' stress about parenting (and the related economic, relational, and emotional responsibilities) is related to negative outcomes such as emotional distress, health challenges, and dysfunctional intimate relationships (Arditti & Few, 2008).

The fact that women are far more likely than men to plan for and achieve reunification with children after their incarceration, however, has meant that a small and growing body of research has focused on the role of children and reunification in desistance. This investigation follows in the footsteps of research on successful substance abuse treatment, which has shown that children can be effective motivators for women pursuing sobriety, particularly in the correctional setting (see Robbins, Martin, & Surratt, 2009, for a review).

Research has shown that there is a complicated relationship between reunification with children and desistance. In one study (Michalsen, 2007), women's desistance was related less to the legal fact of reunification than it was to the amount of time women spent with their children in reentry. This may be due to the fact that the practical challenges facing women in reentry made reunification difficult or impossible. Specifically, mothers spoke about being faced with the realities of raising children affected by poverty and parental absence and with difficulties ranging from mental and physical health problems (including substance abuse problems) to strong emotional reactions to perceived abandonment. Regardless of a desire to reunify, mothers often indicated that their children might be better off in the care of others for the sake of continuity and resources. This finding is consistent with the findings of Brown and Bloom (2009), who found that women with criminal justice system involvement often blame themselves and their failure to conform to the conventional motherhood "script" for their children's outcomes. In fact, in the Michalsen (2007) study, mothers' desire to be role models for their children seemed to encourage desistance.

CONCLUSION AND IMPLICATIONS

Although research so far is limited on the relationship between children and mothers' desistance, findings so far indicate that children may play an important role in mothers' behavior. Moving forward, there are a number of policy and program implications, and future research directions, that can be made in light of this research.

On the broadest level, it is clear that our nation's "war on drugs" has been counterproductive, particularly for communities of color, who have been disproportionately affected by the destabilizing effects of the removal and return of citizens (Rose & Clear, 2002). Alternatives to incarceration, which allow individuals to remain in the community, preserving ties to family and employment, are more effective at reducing recidivism and are less expensive than traditional correctional solutions (Jacobson, 2005). Because so many incarcerated women were convicted of low-level drug offenses (and property offenses related to drug use), the de-carceration of people convicted of these offenses would affect women, in particular, and their children in the community. While de-carceration is important, it must not happen in a vacuum: If women are released as they were when they entered prison, with lower employment and educational experience, substance abuse problems, and homelessness, for example, they are likely to re-offend no matter their intentions. Support in the form of job programs, substance abuse treatment, and housing must be provided if women are to be successful in reentry. Recent efforts at "justice reinvestment" have been successful at taking costs saved from reducing correctional populations and subsequently reinvesting them in other programs shown to be effective at preventing violence and decreasing recidivism. Further, Flavin (2004) suggests that women coming out of incarceration should be supported not only with connections to "state capital" resources, such as housing and employment assistance, but also with the "social capital" inherent in strengthened families and communities.

While women's relationships with their children are clearly very important to them and to their children, it is important not to essentialize women so that their identities are limited to their roles as mothers. Indeed, in the same way as their non-criminal-justice-system-involved counterparts, formerly incarcerated mothers view themselves as more than just parents, and their desistance is also related to their desire to achieve sobriety, to avoid future involvement in the traumatic and debasing criminal justice system, and to become productive members of society. Much like their male counterparts in reentry (Maruna, 2001), women are often eager to renew their focus on themselves and on their own needs, including their spirituality and on being good people and productive citizens (Michalsen, 2007).

REFERENCES

ADLER, F. (1975). *Sisters in crime.* New York: McGraw Hill.

ARDITTI, J., & FEW, A. (2008). Maternal distress and women's reentry into family and community life. *Family Process, 47*(3), 303–321.

BAKER, P. L., & CARSON, A. (1999). "I take care of my kids": Mothering practices of substance-abusing women. *Gender & Society*, *13*(3), 347–363.

BECKERMAN, A. (1989). Incarcerated mothers and their children in foster care: The dilemma of visitation. *Children and Youth Services Review, 11*, 175–183.

BECKERMAN, A. (1991). Women in prison: The conflict between confinement and parental rights. *Social Justice, 18*, 171–183.

BECKERMAN, A. (1994). Mothers in prison: Meeting the prerequisite conditions for permanency planning. *Social Work, 39*(1), 9–14.

BECKERMAN, A. (1998). Charting a course: Meeting the challenge of permanency planning for children with incarcerated mothers. *Child Welfare*, 77(5), 513–529.

BELKNAP, J. (2001). *The invisible woman: Gender, crime and justice.* Belmont, CA: Wadsworth Publishing Co.

BLOOM, B. (1993). Incarcerated mothers and their children: Maintaining family ties. In American Correctional Association (Ed.), *Female offenders: Meeting the needs of a neglected population* (pp. 60–68). Laurel, MD: American Correctional Association.

BLOOM, B. (1999). Gender-responsive programming for women offenders: Guiding principles and practices. *Forum in Corrections Research, 11,* 22–27.

BLOOM, B. E. (2003). A new vision: Gender-responsive principles, policy, and practice. In B. Bloom (Ed.), *Gendered justice: Addressing female offenders* (pp. 267–288). Durham: Carolina Academic Press.

BLOOM, B., OWEN, B., & COVINGTON, S. (2004). Women offenders and the gendered effects of public policy. *Review of Policy Research, 21*(1), 31–48.

BROWN, M., & BLOOM, B. (2009). Reentry and renegotiating motherhood: Maternal identity and success on parole. *Crime & Delinquency, 55*(2), 313–336.

BROWNE, A., MILLER, B., & MAGUIN, E. (1999). Prevalence and severity of lifetime physical abuse and sexual victimization among incarcerated women. *International Journal of Law and Psychiatry, 22*, 301–322.

BRUNS, D. A. (2006). Promoting mother-child relationships for incarcerated women and their children. *Infants & Young Children: An Interdisciplinary Journal of Special Care Practices, 19*(4), 308–322.

CASEY-ACEVEDO, K., & BAKKEN, T. (2002). Visiting women in prison: Who visits and who cares? *Journal of Offender Rehabilitation, 34*(3), 67–83.

CECIL, D. K., MCHALE, J., STROZIER, A., & PIETSCH, J. (2008). "Female inmates, family caregivers, and young children's adjustment: A research agenda and implications for corrections programming." *Journal of Criminal Justice, 36*(6), 513–521.

CHESNEY-LIND, M. (1997). *The female offender*. Thousand Oaks, CA: Sage.

CLOPTON, K. L., & EAST, K. K. (2008). 'Are there other kids like me?' Children with a parent in prison. *Early Childhood Education Journal, 36*, 195–198.

CRAIG, S. C. (2009). A historical review of mother and child programs for incarcerated women. *The Prison Journal, 89*(1), 35S–53S.

DALLAIRE, D. H. (2007). Incarcerated mothers and fathers: A comparison of risks for children and families. *Family Relations, 56,* 440–453.

FARRINGTON, D. P., GALLAGHER, B., MORLEY, L., ST. LEDGER, R. J., & WEST, D. J. (1986). Unemployment, school leaving and crime. *British Journal of Criminology, 26*, 335–356.

FARRINGTON, D. P., & WEST, D. J. (1995). Effect of marriage, separation and children on offending by adult males. In Z. S. Blau & J. Hagan (Eds.), *Current perspectives on aging and the life cycle, Volume 4: delinquency and disrepute in the life course* (pp. 249–281). Greenwich, CT: JAI Press.

FLAVIN, J. (2004). Employment counseling, housing assistance. . . . And Aunt Yolanda? How strengthening families' social capital can reduce recidivism. *Criminology and Public Policy, 3*(2), 209–216.

FREUDENBERG, N., DANIELS, J., CRUM, M., PERKINS, T., & RICHIE, B. E. (2005). Coming home from jail: The social and health consequences of community reentry for women, male adolescents, and their families and communities. *American Journal of Public Health, 95,* 1725–1736.

FROST, N. A. (2006). *Hard Hit: The growth in the imprisonment of women, 1977–2004*. New York: Women's Prison Association.

GENTY, P. M. (1995). Termination of parental rights among prisoners: A national perspective. In K. Gabel & D. Johnston (Eds.), *Children of incarcerated parents* (pp. 167–182). New York: Lexington Books.

GENTY, P. M. (1998). Permanency planning in the context of parental incarceration: Legal issues and recommendations. *Child Welfare, 77*(5), 543–559.

GIBBENS, T. C. (1984). Borstal boys after 25 years. *British Journal of Criminology, 24*, 46–59.

GLASER, D. (1964). *Effectiveness of a prison and parole system*. Indianapolis: Bobbs-Merrill.

GLAZE, L. E., & MARUSCHAK, L. M. (2008). *Parents in prison and their minor children*. Washington, D.C.: U.S. Department of Justice, Bureau of Justice Statistics.

GREENE, S., HANEY, C., & HURTADO, A. (2000). Cycles of pain: Risk factors in the lives of incarcerated mothers and their children. *Prison Journal, 80*, 3–23.

GREENFELD, L. A., & SNELL, T. L. (1999). *Women offenders*. Washington, D.C.: U.S. Department of Justice, Bureau of Justice Statistics.

GRELLA, C. E., & GREENWELL, L. (2006). Correlates of parental status and attitudes toward parenting among substance-abusing women offenders. *Prison Journal, 86*(1), 89–113.

HARM, N. J., & PHILLIPS, S. D. (2001). You can't go home again: Women and criminal recidivism. *Journal of Offender Rehabilitation, 32*(3), 3–21.

HARRISON, P. M., & BECK, A. (2005). *Prisoners in 2004*. Washington, D.C.: Bureau of Justice Statistics.

IRWIN, J. (1970). *The Felon*. Englewood Cliffs, NJ: Prentice Hall.

JACOBS, A. L. (2001). Give 'em a fighting chance: Women offenders reenter society. *Criminal Justice, 16*(1), 45–46.

JACOBSON, M. (2005). *Downsizing prisons: How to reduce crime and end mass incarceration*. New York: New York University Press.

JAMES, D., & GLAZE, L. (2006). *Mental health problems of prison and jail inmates*. Washington, D.C.: Bureau of Justice Statistics.

JOHNSON, E. I., & WALDFOGEL, J. (2002). Parental incarceration: Recent trends and implications for child welfare. *Social Service Review, 76*(3), 460–479.

JOHNSTON, D. (1995). Effects of parental incarceration. In K. Gabel & D. Johnston, (Eds.), *Children of incarcerated parents* (pp. 59–88). New York: Lexington Books.

MARUNA, S. (2001). *Making good: How ex-convicts reform and rebuild their lives*. Washington, D.C.: The American Psychological Association.

MAUER, M., & CHESNEY-LIND, M. (2002). Introduction. In M. Mauer & M. Chesney-Lind (Eds.), *Invisible punishment: The collateral consequences of mass imprisonment*. New York: The New Press.

MICHALSEN, V. (2007). *Going straight for her children? Mothers' desistance after incarceration*. Doctoral Dissertation.

MICHALSEN, V., FLAVIN J., & KRUPAT, T. (2010). More than visiting hours: Ties between incarcerated mothers and their children. *Sociological Compass, 4*(8): 576–591.

MISCHKOWITZ, R. (1994). Desistance from a delinquent way of life? In E. G. M. Weitekamp & H. J. Kerner (Eds.), *Crossnational longitudinal research on human development and criminal behavior* (pp. 303–327). London: Kluwer Academic.

MOLONEY, M., MACKENZIE, K., HUNT, G., & JOE-LAIDLER, K. (2009). The path and promise of fatherhood for gang members. *British Journal of Criminology, 49*, 305–325.

MUMOLA, C. (2000). *Incarcerated parents and their children*. Washington, D.C.: U.S. Department of Justice, Bureau of Justice Statistics.

PETERSILIA, J. (2003). *When prisoners come home*. Oxford: Oxford University Press.

RAIMON, M. L. (2001). Barriers to achieving justice for incarcerated parents. *Fordham Law Review, 70*, 421–426.

RAND, A. (1987). Transitional life events and desistance from delinquency and crime. In M. Wolfgang, T. P. Thornberry, & R. M. Figlio (Eds.), *From boy to man: From delinquency to crime* (pp. 134–162). Chicago: University of Chicago Press.

RICHIE, B. E. (2001). Challenges incarcerated women face as they return to their communities: Findings from life history interviews. *Crime & Delinquency, 47*(3), 368–389.

ROBBINS, C. A., MARTIN, S. S., & SURRATT, H. L. (2009). Substance abuse treatment, anticipated maternal roles, and reentry success of drug-involved women prisoners. *Crime and Delinquency, 55*, 388–411.

ROSE, D., & CLEAR, T. R. (2002). *Incarceration, reentry and social capital: Social networks in the balance*. Paper prepared for the "From Prison to Home" Conference, New York.

SABOL, W. J., WEST, H. C. & COOPER, M. (2009). *Prisoners in 2008*. Washington, D.C.: U.S. Department of Justice, Bureau of Justice Statistics.

SAMPSON, R. J., & LAUB, J. H. (1993). *Crime in the making: Pathways and turning points through life*. Cambridge, MA: Harvard University Press.

SHOVER, N. (1985). *Aging criminals*. Beverly Hills, CA: Sage Publications.

TRAVIS, J., SOLOMON, A., & WAUL, M. (2001). *From prison to home: The dimensions and consequences of prisoner reentry*. Retrieved January 2, 2010, from http://urbaninstitute.org/UploadedPDF/from_prison_to_home.pdf.

WALMSLEY, R. (2009). *World prison population list* (8th ed.). London: King's College London. Retrieved January 2, 2010, from http://www.kcl.ac.uk/depsta/law/research/icps/downloads/wppl-8th_41.pdf.

WOMEN'S PRISON ASSOCIATION. (2004). *Focus on women & justice: Trends in arrests and sentencing*. New York: Women's Prison Association.

ZOCCOLILLO, M., PICKLES, A., QUINTON, D., & RUTTER, M. (1992). The outcome of childhood conduct disorder: Implications for defining adult personality disorder and conduct disorder. *Psychological Medicine, 22,* 971–986.

ENDNOTES

1. While the effects of mothers' incarceration on children are widespread and may be profound, these effects are beyond the scope of this chapter.
2. Public order (7 percent) and other/unspecified (5 percent) offenses make up the remaining conviction reasons. Rounding accounts for the fact that the numbers do not add up to exactly 100 percent.

5

Perpetrators and Victims

Maternal Filicide and Mental Illness

Stacey L. Shipley

> I t may seem paradoxical, but it is not vice that leads to the death of the infant,
> rather it is morbid and mistaken maternal solitude. (Baker, 1902, p. 16)

This chapter will address maternal filicide resulting from postpartum depression; postpartum psychosis; other forms of psychotic illness, such as schizophrenia, delusional disorder, and bipolar disorder; or severe depression. This chapter elucidates the nomenclature of child murder such as neonaticide, infanticide, and filicide, with the focus remaining on maternal filicide. It discusses a classification system, prevalence, motives, methods, victims, and the disposition of offenders. Specifically, altruistic filicide and acute psychotic filicide will be explored using the case example of Andrea Yates to illustrate how unidentified and untreated or undertreated mental illness can culminate in the occurrence of these tragic acts. Maternal filicide is in direct contradiction to society's firmly held notion that all mothers instinctually and unconditionally love, nurture, and protect their children. Women who kill their children as a result of an acute psychosis do not generally kill for the motives that are typically associated with murder such as punishment, revenge, and secondary gain. They often believe that they are being instructed by God or are in some way saving their children from unspeakable torment or disease, and they are driven by delusions and other perceptual disturbances. What are the legal implications for this type of crime? Whether or not these women belong in prison or a forensic psychiatric hospital and to what extent the media and public opinion influence their disposition will be examined in this chapter. This chapter also discusses treatment implications for mental health professionals who will provide services to these women in a forensic setting (e.g., in a jail or in a maximum-security forensic hospital). Women who kill their children due to psychosis often become very depressed and potentially suicidal after receiving psychiatric treatment in jail or forensic hospital. Additionally, these women face unique issues such as grieving the loss of their children by their own hands, likely divorce, alienation from loved ones, and coming to terms with their mental illness under the harshest of circumstances. When their psychosis remits, these mothers are left asking, "How could I have done such a thing?" This chapter will discuss risk factors and will explore the importance of identifying those women who are most vulnerable to maternal filicide in order to provide successful treatment and prevention programs.

Child murder is so tragic and evokes such a strong response from the media and our communities that the women who commit these heinous acts are often demonized with little understanding of their actual plight. Women who murder their children vary in their motives, and a rush to judgment and punishment often further exacerbates a horrible tragedy. The nation was horrified in June of 2001 at the news that Andrea Yates had drowned her five children in the bathtub of her Houston home. A collective reaction of "What kind of monster could have done such a thing?" and that someone had to pay for such brutal and senseless murders was heard across the country. As more information about the history of Ms. Yates's mental illness, as well as her seemingly altruistic, albeit, delusional motives, became apparent, it was impossible to compare her actions to the cold, calculated murder of one's children for personal or material gain or, in some instances, revenge.

In October 1994, Susan Smith and her husband stood in front of media cameras and pled for the return of their two sons who had reportedly been kidnapped by an African-American man with a gun. For nine days the country prayed for the safe return of the Smiths' children. It was later discovered that it was the tearful mother the public had seen on the news who was the actual killer. It was hard to imagine that a mother could drive her car into a lake with her two young boys strapped into their seats and watch as the car took several minutes to sink. When one thinks of murder for secondary gain, think of Susan Smith sending her car with her boys strapped inside deep into a lake. It was later revealed that Susan Smith had disposed of her sons in an attempt to further a romantic relationship with a man who did not want children. She viewed her children as a liability, and she callously murdered them for her own personal gain. While it is clear that there is something deeply wrong with her character, she was not out of touch with reality due to mental illness. She knew the difference between right and wrong but was indifferent to the fate of her children in an effort to advance her own interests. She went to great lengths to hide her crime, which is not typical of severely mentally ill women, depressed or psychotic, who kill their children. The various categorizations of child murder based on age, motive, and impulse to kill will be discussed in this chapter. However, this chapter seeks to increase the understanding of mentally ill mothers who kill their children from delusionally misguided altruistic motives. Consider the Andrea Yates case.

On June 20, 2001, in Clearwater, Texas, Andrea Yates drowned all five of her children in the family bathtub after her husband Rusty left for work. Ms. Yates had a longstanding history of mental illness including four hospitalizations, since 1999, and two attempted suicides, and she had had an outpatient prescription for Haldol, an antipsychotic medication used to help control hallucinations and other symptoms of psychosis (Gesalman, 2002; Manchester, 2003). She was suffering from a severe postpartum psychosis with numerous delusions and hallucinations.

Andrea Yates was the valedictorian of her high school class and a champion swimmer, and she went on to become an excellent nurse. She was an intelligent and gentle woman who by all accounts was a devoted mother who homeschooled her children, as well as providing them with Bible studies. She had been pregnant or breastfeeding almost continually for the seven years prior to the murder of her children (Spinelli, 2004). In addition to caring for Noah (age seven), John (age five), Paul (age three), Luke (age two), and Mary (six months), she was also caring for her beloved father, who was slipping away from Alzheimer's disease. He passed away six weeks after the birth of Mary, which was also a significant stressor for her. She was caring for her frail mother and her newborn, mourning the loss of her father, and homeschooling her three elder children all while suffering from postpartum psychosis (Oberman, 2003). She had a family history of diagnosed and treated bipolar disorder and major depression (O'Malley, 2004; Spinelli, 2004). Each time she gave birth, she experienced a postpartum depression, and her mental illness worsened with each subsequent birth.

Her first reported psychotic episode occurred after the birth of Noah in 1994. At that time, she refused to tell anyone of her experience because she had delusions that Satan would hear her and harm her children. With subsequent deliveries she became more depressed, psychotic, overwhelmed, and impaired. "Mood states of high energy and a hyperreligious focus on Satan and religious doctrine switched to documented worsening depression, psychosis, and suicide attempts. After her last two children were born, she had a total of four psychiatric hospitalizations. . . . After hospital discharge, a catatonic, psychotic Andrea Yates appeared to her friends and family like a 'caged animal,' staring for hours and scratching bald spots into her head. Discussions about Satan's presence were not uncommon in the Yates home, where a rigid religious belief system dominated the family's life" (Spinelli, 2004, p. 1554). She attempted suicide on two occasions after her fourth delivery because she was trying to resist demonic voices or command hallucinations instructing her to kill her infant (Spinelli, 2004).

Each time she was discharged from the hospital, there was no family intervention. Mr. Yates indicated that she would begin to feel better and agree to have more children (Denno, 2003; Spinelli, 2004). She would frequently refuse medication because she was pregnant or lactating. According to Spinelli (2004), professional perinatal support and education were not available to teach her and her husband about the risks and benefits of pharmacotherapy and the use of psychotropic medications for prevention of postpartum psychosis during pregnancy and lactation. Ms. Yates's psychiatrist discontinued her Haldol two weeks prior to the event, resulting in her becoming floridly psychotic. She reported that Satan commanded her to kill her children to save them from the fires and torment of hell. She had delusional beliefs that she was influenced by the devil and that she had irreversibly damaged her children and the only way to protect their innocence and ensure their entrance to heaven was that she must kill them. It appears that everyone around her failed to appreciate the severity of her illness.

Andrea Yates was charged with capital murder with a maximum possible penalty of death, which the prosecution aggressively sought. While in jail, she requested a razor to shave her head and reveal the "mark of the beast-666" and reported "I am Satan" (Spinelli, 2004, p. 1549). The jury returned after three and a half hours with a verdict of guilty. During the sentencing phase, it took the jury only 35 minutes to decide on a sentence of life in prison. During her first trial, the Texas jury rejected her insanity defense despite the overwhelming psychiatric evidence. Manchester (2003) writes:

In the United States, courts continue to evaluate postpartum depression defenses and other mental illnesses under the existing insanity defense [*M'Naghten test*]. The prevailing insanity defense test applied across United States jurisdictions is extremely narrow and makes proving legal insanity exceptionally difficult for even the most severely postpartum psychotic women. Therefore, the Yates case is most significant because it demonstrates the pressing need for insanity defense reform to address the realities of postpartum psychosis and other mental illnesses. (p. 715)

In January of 2005, after Andrea had already been incarcerated for four years with deteriorating mental health, a Texas appeals court overturned her conviction based on the misleading and prejudicial information provided by an expert witness for the prosecution, Dr. Park Dietz. She was granted a new trial with a much different outcome. The second trial resulted in a Texas jury finding her not guilty by reason of insanity (NGRI). As much new information has come to light regarding Ms. Yates's mental illness and its impact on her ability to appreciate the wrongfulness of her actions, there seems to have been an appreciable shift in public opinion that the justice rendered for someone like Susan Smith is not justice for Andrea Yates. She was a woman in deep torment due to her illness and the loss of her children, who was in need of intensive psychiatric treatment and therapy, not the harshest of punishments handed down to the most violent of offenders.

DEFINING CHILD MURDER

The killing of children by their parents is an almost unthinkable crime, particularly when the mother is the perpetrator. It is so antithetical to what it means to be mother, nurturer, and the ultimate protector of her children. Fifty-seven percent of the murders of children under the age of 12 have been committed by the victims' parents (Dawson & Langan, 1994). According to the U.S. Department of Justice, Bureau of Justice Statistics (2002), out of all of the children under age five who were murdered between 1976 and 2000, 31 percent were killed by fathers; 30 percent were killed by mothers; 23 percent were killed by male acquaintances of the mother; 7 percent were killed by other relatives; and 3 percent were killed by strangers. The statistics on adult murder show that male perpetrators and victims outnumber females by a ratio of 5:1 or 6:1 (Jason, 1983; Marks & Kumar, 1993; Stanton & Simpson, 2002). Men predominate as perpetrators of family homicides, involving both spouses and children (Liem & Koenraadt, 2008). When infants are killed within the first 24 hours, it is almost always by their mothers, with equal number of male and female victims. For babies and children killed after one year, studies demonstrate that slightly more of the perpetrators are male or the numbers are almost even between male and female perpetrators and children are most frequently killed by one of their parents (Stanton & Simpson, 2002). Remarkably, infanticide and neonaticide are common causes of childhood deaths (Dawson & Langan, 1994).

"Filicide" is often used as a generic term to describe the killing of children by their parents or stepparents and can include neonaticide, infanticide, and filicide (Stanton & Simpson, 2002). Dr. Philip Resnick, a forensic psychiatrist, was the first to categorize filicides based on the age of the children, when they were killed (1969, 1970). He categorized neonaticide as the killing of a child directly after birth or within the first 24 hours after birth. The perpetrators are typically young women who deny they are pregnant to themselves and others, and fear, not psychotic illness, motivates the crime (Oberman, 2003). Infanticide is the killing of a child up to one year, by the mother who has not fully recovered from pregnancy and who typically suffers from some degree of mental disturbance often associated with postpartum mental illness (Bourget & Labelle, 1992). Filicide is the killing of a child older than one year and is very frequently associated with psychosis in the female perpetrator (Manchester, 2003). Filicide is often associated with mental illness and suicide of the parent. Although filicide is a form of homicide, rates of infanticide are more congruent with suicide rates rather than murder rates (Putkonen, Weizmann-Henelius, Lindberg, Eronen, & Hakkanen, 2009). Pitt and Bale (1995) highlighted the characteristic differences between parents who commit infanticide as opposed to those who commit neonaticide. The results indicated that mothers in the neonaticide group were significantly younger than the mothers in the infanticide or filicide group. The mothers in the infanticide or filicide group were more likely to suffer from depression or psychoses and have histories of attempted suicide. "Eighty-eight percent of the infanticide mothers were married, while eighty-one percent of the neonaticide mothers were unwed" (Pitt & Bale, 1995, p. 378). Resnick (1970) found that the mothers involved in neonaticide are younger, often unmarried, and less frequently psychotic than mothers who commit filicide. He indicated that most neonaticides are carried out because the child is not wanted due to illegitimacy, rape, or social stigma, rather than altruistic reasons.

"Studies have documented that neonaticide offenders are often single young women who deny the pregnancy and kill their newborn infants in an effort to avoid the social and parental pressure against an illegitimate child" (Manchester, 2003, p. 724). These young women may feel unable or unwilling to pursue alternatives such as adoption or abortion rather than murdering their newborns due to religion, culture, money, ambivalence, fear, denial, and immaturity (Oberman, 2003). It is fairly common for these women to make no plans for labor and often labor on the toilet and in silence. According to Oberman (2003), they may have a history of disassociative states related to a history of early abuse and chaotic family life and are frequently emotionally isolated from adults in their lives. The lack of mental illness in most perpetrators of neonaticide could be due to the possibility that newborns are more easily seen as objects as compared to older children, who are viewed as more valuable based on a more developed relationship (Gold, 2001). This also helps to explain why the murders of older children by their mothers are typically related to psychosis. Some researchers contend that the very young women who usually commit neonaticide are amenable to treatment, are not typically repeat offenders, and do not pose a threat to public safety, requiring rehabilitative services rather than prolonged prison sentences (Fazio & Comito, 1999; Schwartz & Isser, 2001). According to Schwartz and Isser (2001), "In the case of neonaticide, a delicate balancing act is needed to educate, rehabilitate, correct, and punish the woman who has killed her newborn" (p. 713).

Researchers have developed organized classification systems for child murder to improve mental health professionals' understanding of events leading up to these tragedies in the hope of intervening and educating to prevent future offenses (Pitt & Bale, 1995). These classifications have been based on interpretations of the perpetrator's motive, psychiatric history, psychosocial stressors, or source of impulse to kill (Lewis & Bunce, 2003). Resnick's (1969) seminal work reviewed 131 (88 mothers, 43 fathers) child murder cases from the international literature from 1751 to 1967 and proposed a classification system for filicide. He devised five categories based on motives for murder. They are (1) altruistic filicide, (2) acutely psychotic filicide, (3) unwanted child filicide, (4) accidental filicide, and (5) spouse revenge filicide. He also introduced or coined "neonaticide" as a separate phenomenon and operationally defined it at that time.

1. Altruistic filicide can be separated into two subgroups, but is ultimately committed out of love or what is perceived by the parent as in the child's best interest. The first would involve an offense committed by a parent who believes he or she must relieve the child from some real or imagined (often delusional) condition—unbearable, inescapable torment or disease—or from the anticipated suffering from the parent's suicide (McKee & Shea, 1998). The second is more typically associated with a major depression of the parent and involves a murder suicide, which was the most common (56 percent of maternal filicide reports). The parent believes that due to his or her deep love and devotion to the child, the child would be better off dead or that the child would experience the same tortured existence as the parent or not be able to go on without the parent. Resnick indicated that the most dangerous period for the victim is the first six months, and that when a mother commits suicide due to a postpartum depression, she typically sees the child as an extension of herself (Palermo, 2002). Scott (1973) separated this category into "primary" altruistic killings, which have also been termed as "mercy killings" where there is a real state of suffering (e.g., mental retardation or disease) and no evidence of secondary gain for the perpetrator. Wilczynski (1995, p. 368) states: "The much more common 'secondary' altruistic killings involve no real degree of suffering in the child, and typically occur in the context of depression in the parent (virtually always the mother). These women expressed acute feelings of failure to measure up to society's standards of 'good' mothers or wives, such as one woman who regarded herself as a bad mother and wife, worried that the child was abnormal in some way, and felt that she did everything but it was never enough."

2. Acutely psychotic filicide would typically include parents who kill their children as a direct result of the delusions, hallucinations, or other forms of psychosis they experience, as well as epilepsy or delirium but does not include all psychotic child murders (24 percent of maternal filicide reports). This category includes those cases without a clear or discernable reality-based motive and the parent kills a child while under the pressure and effects of severe mental illness. The motives are typically tied closely to delusional beliefs or command hallucinations. Resnick (1972) found that three-quarters of the parents who killed their children presented with psychiatric symptoms prior to the homicide. Forty percent of these parents (almost always mothers) were seen by a physician shortly before committing the homicides.

3. Unwanted child filicide is carried out because the infant was never wanted or is no longer wanted by the parents unrelated to any mental illness or psychosis (11 percent of maternal filicide reports). Child murder for these reasons is frequently associated with extramarital affairs or illegitimacy (Resnick, 1969). It has been postulated that murder for this motive has decreased due to society's increasing acceptance and the growing commonness of unwed or single mothers in the United States, as well as women's increased presence in the workforce.

4. Accidental filicide is usually a result of an unintended homicide resulting from abuse that went too far or a "battered child syndrome" (7 percent of maternal filicide reports). The parent usually has a long history of abusing the child and

in a rage strikes a fatal blow. It is most common for episodes of violent abuse to occur at mealtimes and bedtimes, as these are the times most associated with stress, arguments, and the need to discipline the child (Oberman, 2003).

5. Spouse revenge filicide is indicative of child murder that is perpetrated to retaliate against perceived rejection or wrongdoing by a spouse (Pitt & Bale, 1995). This has been referred to as the "Medea Complex" based on Greek mythology (Stern, 1948). After discovering her husband's betrayal through infidelity, she killed their two sons for revenge. The Medea Complex refers to maternal hatred for a child that can involve anything from rejection to murder (Simpson & Stanton, 2000). Resnick (1969) found that this group comprised only 2 percent of the maternal filicide reports.

Resnick (1969) found that the most common methods used by mothers committing filicide (infanticide) included strangulation, drowning, or gassing and that fathers typically used striking, squeezing, and stabbing. Head trauma was also a frequent cause. He reported that the most frequently diagnosed mental illnesses at the time of the offense, particularly for mothers, included schizophrenia, melancholia and manic-depressive disorders, and character disorders. An absence of psychosis was typical for the paternal offenders. The child's risk of murder was thought to be decreased as they aged. In 1999, out of the children who were killed by their parents, 42 percent were younger than one year and only 6 percent were older than four years (Gold, 2001). Resnick maintained that they were particularly vulnerable when bonding and maternal attachment had not yet been established (Palermo, 2002).

Approximately 30 years after Dr. Resnick began his research on parents who kill their children, he served as an expert witness for the defense in *Texas v. Andrea Pia Yates* and attempted to define "rationality within irrationality." To illustrate his aforementioned categories within the context of this case example, consider the following (as cited in O'Malley, 2004):

> According to Resnick, there are five classifications of parents who harm their children. This was not a case of spousal revenge: Andrea Yates believed Rusty Yates was a good husband. It was not a case of battered child syndrome: the Yates children weren't abused. It was certainly not an example of the children's being unwanted: Andrea Yates was a determined Supermom. Three of the five classifications did not apply, in Resnick's opinion. Yates, he said, did fit into the two remaining categories: "acutely psychotic" (no logical motive to do what she did—say, for insurance money) and "altruistic" (killing because she thought it was in the children's best interests). He classified Yates children's killings as "altruistic."
>
> "Mrs. Yates," he said, "had a choice to make: to allow her children to end up burning in hell for eternity or to take their lives on earth." By taking their earthly lives she achieved two good things: the children were happy through all eternity, and Satan was "eliminated for humankind. . . . She would give up her life on earth . . . *and her afterlife* for the purpose of eliminating Satan and protecting her children from the fate of eternal damnation." (p. 157)

To further elucidate the contrast between Andrea Yates, a mentally ill mother who killed for altruistic reasons, and Susan Smith, who appeared to kill for selfish ones, Dr. Resnick had been consulted by the defense team of Susan Smith, but concluded that he could not "be helpful to the defense with regard to an insanity defense in that case of child killing" (as cited in O'Malley, 2004, p. 157).

Scott (1973) developed a classification system with a sample of 39 maternal filicides that was more focused on the source of the impulse to commit filicide and included the following categories: (1) battering mothers, (2) mentally ill mothers, (3) retaliating mothers, (4) unwanted children, and (5) mercy killing. Scott (1973) found that the diagnoses of the women who killed their children included personality disorders (43 percent), reactive depression (21 percent), or psychotic illness (16 percent). The psychotic illness group included postpartum psychosis, schizoid paranoid psychosis, and depressive psychosis. Regarding psychosocial stressors, he identified stress in the family, such as severe marital problems, housing problems, and financial difficulties, and social issues such as being a young mother as risk factors (Palermo, 2002).

D'Orban's (1979) classification of maternal filicide was developed from her review of 89 cases of all English and Welsh women incarcerated at Holloway Prison over a six-year period convicted of murdering or attempting to murder their children. Information was available from psychiatric assessments, case records, and direct interviewing by the author in approximately half of all the cases. Her model is a modification of Scott's 1973 system and incorporated neonaticide basing classification on the source of the impulse to kill (e.g., parent, child, or situation). She had six categories which included: (1) battering mothers (36 cases, 40.4 percent), where the killing was an impulsive act triggered by the victim's behavior; (2) mentally ill mothers (42 cases, 27 percent), which included all psychotic, depressed, or suicidal women; (3) neonaticides (11 cases, 12.4 percent), which included newborns killed within 24 hours of birth; (4) retaliating women (9 cases, 10.1 percent), who took out aggression toward the spouse onto the child with the stimulus being revenge; (5) mothers of unwanted children (8 cases, 9 percent), "whose children died from passive neglect or active aggression" (p. 680); and (6) mercy killings (1 case, 1.1 percent), where the mother murders her child to end her child's suffering from a real illness without apparent secondary gain (McKee & Shea, 1998). Battering mothers and mentally ill mothers were the most common classifications in D'Orban's (1979) sample. The mentally ill mothers were most commonly married with the least marital stress, were older, attacked older children, and more commonly had multiple victims (Stanton & Simpson, 2002). D'Orban (1979) found that 60 percent of the sample was in contact with health workers or social workers, and 17 percent of the mentally ill sample was specifically in contact with psychiatric services. The retaliatory groups were related to chaotic personalities, with high rates of suicide attempts and marital conflict but also were typically older, more frequently married, and were more likely to kill older children (Stanton & Simpson, 2002). Finally, Oberman (2003) indicated that the mentally ill mothers often murdered their children not only due to the mental illness, but their relative isolation in caring for the child also played a role. Once again, Andrea Yates was cited as exemplifying the case of a severely mentally ill mother left to care for five children with virtually no outside support. She was under the incredible stress of attending to the emotional and physical demands of her children, while experiencing a significant depressive and psychotic episode that would have inhibited her ability to meet those needs (Oberman, 2003).

Although the categories are similar to Resnick's (1969), these categories do not include paternal filicides and attempt to reduce misclassification from filicides that could fall into more than one category. "For example, her category of mentally ill mothers incorporates all psychiatrically impaired women and is distinguished from mercy filicides in that the child's suffering was from a real, not delusionally based illness. In Resnick's (1969) classification, a parent might be placed in either category depending on which motive seemed to the clinician to be more prominent" (McKee & Shea, 1998, p. 680). Both D'Orban's (1979) and Scott's (1973) classification systems are based on characteristics of the female parent as a result of most filicides being perpetrated by mothers of children who are under the age of 12 (McKee & Shea, 1998).

Studies have shown that homicidal parents have high rates of suicide attempts; mothers are more likely to commit suicide after the act than fathers, and that suicide attempts by homicidal parents are often highly lethal and successful (Bourget & Gagne, 2002; Myers, 1970; Rodenburg, 1971; West, 1965). Bourget and Gagne (2002) identified a psychiatric motive for greater than 85 percent of the mothers in their study and a majority of the mothers had prior psychiatric treatment for a depressive or psychotic disorder. Numerous researchers have identified major depression with psychotic features as the most common diagnosis in maternal offenders (Bourget & Gagne, 2002; Bourget, Grace, & Whitehurst, 2007; Hatters-Friedman & Resnick, 2007; Myers, 1970; Putkonen et al., 2009; Rodenburg, 1971; West, 1965).

In a study comparing parental and nonparental homicide, Bourget and Bradford (1990) determined that 30.8 percent of parents who commited filicide had a diagnosis of major depression compared with none of the nonparental perpetrators. Of the nine maternal filicides, five of the mothers were in a postpartum period of less than five weeks from delivery, at the time of the offense. Greater than 46 percent of the parental offenders had a personality disorder, 23 percent had a substance abuse disorder, and 15.4 percent had an adjustment disorder. Most nonparental offenders had a personality disorder (53.2 percent), substance abuse disorders (25.5 percent), and adjustment disorders (8.5 percent). When examining groups of both male and female filicide offenders, personality disorders, particularly borderline personality disorder, are frequently found, although not in the altruistic motive group (Bourget et al., 2007; Putkonen et al., 2009).

MENTAL ILLNESS AND MURDER

There are a variety of reasons for which parents kill their children. Explanations range from postpartum depression or psychosis to schizophrenia. Postpartum depression is a mental disorder that occurs with new mothers shortly after they give birth. Postpartum mental illness is vastly underdiagnosed and can have devastating consequences for the mother, child, and parental relationship (Born, Zinga, & Steiner, 2004). According to the American Psychiatric Association's *Diagnostic and Statistical Manual of Mental Disorders,* Fourth Edition, Text Revision (*DSM-IV-TR*) (American Psychiatric Association [APA], 2000), the severest form of postpartum depression, postpartum psychosis, often presents with episodes of delusions in which the mother feels that the infant is possessed or the mother has hallucinations that tell her to kill the child. Most incidents of postpartum depression do not include delusions or hallucinations, but there are suicidal ideation, obsessional thoughts of violence toward the child, and psychomotor agitation. Whereas the postpartum blues are very common (up to 80 percent), only about 0.2 percent of childbearing women will experience postpartum psychosis, which typically emerges within two weeks of the childbirth and frequently requires hospitalization (Dobson & Sales, 2000; Manchester, 2003). Postpartum blues peak three to five days after birth and involve a period of emotional lability with frequent crying, irritability, confusion, and anxiety that is transient and does not typically require treatment.

Postpartum depression has gained the acknowledgment of many in the mental health field. Some have hypothesized that environmental stressors associated with becoming a parent, along with the immediate demands required of the parent, can overwhelm and cause this disorder in even the most psychologically sound mother (Ewing, 1997). Hormonal changes have also been reported to be a major factor in explaining the incidence of severe depression and unusual actions by some mothers after the birth of their children (Ewing, 1997). According to Pruett (2002, p. 353), "The postpartum depression that often precedes an infanticide is a distinct, transitory illness that should be designated as such. Identifying mothers with postpartum depression who commit infanticide may not be easy . . ., but the possibility of early intervention and the potential role for hospitals and pediatricians to play in screening and intervention, render these mothers an important subgroup to identify."

Postpartum affective disorders are due in part to sensitivity to large changes in hormones such as progesterone, estrogen, and cortisol that occur near the end of pregnancy or after delivery of the child (Glover & Kammerer, 2004). Postpartum depression is more likely to occur in women who have experienced it with previous children and have a familial history of affective disorders. It usually begins in the first 6 to 12 weeks after delivery, although the onset can be later following a period of well-being (Born et al., 2004). The symptoms are similar to that of a major depressive episode but additional symptoms "include feelings of guilt or inadequacy about the new mother's ability to care for the infant, and a preoccupation with the infant's well-being or safety severe enough to be considered obsessional" (p. 31). Both anxiety and depression are as common during pregnancy as after childbirth (Glover & Kammerer, 2004). The prevalence of depressive symptoms in the first few weeks following childbirth is between 10 percent and 20 percent (Born et al., 2004). Fortunately, postpartum depression rarely results in maternal filicide (Gold, 2001). These women are more likely to seek help from their primary care physicians or their obstetricians than from mental health professionals. "While severe depression and psychoses are easily recognized, milder or more insidious forms of depressive or other psychiatric illness are frequently missed" (Born et al., 2004, p. 29). The conditions can progress to the point of requiring hospitalization. Schwartz and Isser (2001) contend that postpartum depression and postpartum psychosis do not occur until several days to weeks after delivery and cannot account for neonaticide.

In a study ($n = 100$) evaluating new mothers' experiences of intrusive thoughts of harm related to the newborn, Fairbrother and Woody (2008) found that postpartum intrusive thoughts of accidental harm to the infant were universal. Close to half of their sample reported unwanted thoughts of intentionally harming their infant. Accidental harm thoughts were more frequent and time consuming, but less distressing. Researchers found that high parenting stress and low social support were predictive of thoughts of intentional harm; however, there was little evidence that these thoughts typically translate to aggressive parenting (Fairbrother & Woody, 2008).

There is a strong genetic component to postpartum psychosis and there is a joint vulnerability with bipolar disorder. In other words, a family history of bipolar disorder is a strong risk factor for postpartum psychosis, and research also indicates that this creates vulnerability to a puerperal trigger (Kim, Choi, & Ha, 2008; Glover & Kammerer, 2004; Payne, MacKinnon, Mondimore, et al., 2008). Women with a genetic predisposition for a mental illness or a personal history of mental illness, a mood disorder in particular, are far more vulnerable to the flood of hormones associated with the postpartum period. Having symptoms of depression during pregnancy has been correlated with a reoccurrence of a bipolar depressive episode after delivery, and approximately one in two women with bipolar disorder will have a relapse postpartum (Born et al., 2004; Chaudron & Pies, 2003). Early screening, identification, and intervention with those women at risk or who are already experiencing symptoms are imperative. In addition to the psychosis that is biologically driven, a woman with postpartum psychosis also experiences mood lability consistent with bipolar disorder.

According to Papapietro and Barbo (2005), the onset of a filicidal mother's symptoms is subtle and often overlooked until there is a rapid decompensation to florid mood symptoms, typically with psychotic symptoms and violent acts. In a study that reviewed the cases of ten mothers who committed filicide, it was found that the mother's conditions deteriorated rapidly, and the filicide was committed when the mother was left alone with the baby despite her apprehension or reluctance (Kauppi, Kumpulainen, Vanamo, et al.). It was further noted that the babies were well taken care of, not neglected or abused. Seeking or receiving the appropriate help is often delayed due to shame, stigma, or judgment that has been severely impaired by mental illness.

Manic symptoms rather than depressive symptoms can result from a postpartum period as the primary symptoms in approximately 40 percent of cases (Huysman, 2003). These women typically have a genetic predisposition to mania, based on their family history. Mania is typically characterized by elation, a decreased need for sleep, irritability, agitation, poor, impulsive judgment, and severe hyperactivity. This period of mania or hypomania can last for hours, days, or weeks and can be followed by a period of depression. Often, these women find their increased productivity and extreme feelings of well-being as a positive, not alarming, experience and fail to immediately recognize it as symptoms of mental illness. Stanton et al. (2000) found that the women who were manic prior to killing their children demonstrated no premeditation and developed delusions within a day before the offense as compared to women who commit filicide due to depression, who ruminate about the death of their children days or weeks in advance of the filicide.

Hypomanic symptoms are common after childbirth with studies indicating between 9 percent and 20 percent (Sharma et al., 2009). It is expected that women who have just had a child should be experiencing the happiest moments of their lives. While women who are suffering feelings of depression and anxiety often feel alienated and ashamed, women who are experiencing hypomanic symptoms as a manifestation of bipolar disorder can be overlooked. Symptoms that are related to postpartum hypomania include racing thoughts, decreased need for sleep, over talkativeness, increase in goal-directed activity, distractibility, and irritability. As opposed to baby blues, the peak prevalence of hypomanic symptoms is immediately after childbirth, although the risk remains increased for several weeks and is of most concern as it relates to bipolar depression later in the postpartum period (Sharma et al., 2009).

As indicated above, research on postpartum mood disorders has focused primarily on major depression, bipolar I disorder, and puerperal psychosis with little mention of bipolar II disorder (Sharma et al., 2009). Although hypomania is common after childbirth, it is often overlooked. While bipolar I disorder is distinguished by recurrent episodes of mania and depression, bipolar II disorder is defined by recurrent episodes of depression and hypomania. According to Brockington et al. (1998), unipolar postpartum depression can be differentiated from postpartum bipolar depression in that postpartum bipolar depression has an earlier onset (within two weeks of delivery) and a typical clinical profile including: less anger, less self-rated emotion, and more animation. Likely due to the less significant or debilitating impairment of hypomania versus mania, it is often missed in bipolar II disorder and a later severe depression is characterized as only a depression. The consequences of this misdiagnosis can have serious implications when the correct treatment is withheld or delayed. If there is an inappropriate prescription of antidepressants for someone with bipolar depression, it may bring on mania, a mixed state (e.g., depression and mania), rapid cycling, and suicide risk, therefore increasing the risk of psychiatric hospitalization (Sharma et al., 2009; Yerevanian, Koek, Mintz, et al., 2007). One study (Payne et al., 2007) found that 20 percent of women diagnosed with bipolar disorder retrospectively reported that they had postpartum mood episodes with the majority being the depressed type. Compared to women with major depressive disorder, those diagnosed with bipolar disorder are more likely to have episodes of postpartum depression. Sharma et al. (2009) report that misdiagnosis of bipolar depression as a major depressive disorder during the postpartum period appears to be common.

Postpartum psychosis occurs in only 1 in 500 to 1,000 childbirths, but the risk of reoccurrence is very high (Glover & Kammerer, 2004). It typically begins within the first 48 to 72 hours after delivery but the risk of onset is high for up to four months. Typically, the individual presents with lability of mood, rambling speech, disorganized behavior, and hallucinations or delusions. According to Born et al. (2004, p. 32), symptoms characteristic of this disorder include:

- Delusional beliefs, often related to the baby (e.g., infant death, denial of birth, belief that infant is possessed or has special powers)
- Hypervigilance about the baby
- Exhilaration and sleeplessness
- Psychomotor hyperkinesias and akinesia affecting expressive and reactive emotions
- Hypersensitivity to neutral comments
- Visual, tactile, olfactory, or auditory hallucinations
- Feelings of being perplexed, confused, or disoriented (organic-like presentation)
- Impaired cognition
- Delirium-like symptoms
- Poor appetite
- Stupor
- Waxing and waning course with lucid periods

Women who experience postpartum psychosis also have more unusual psychotic symptoms, such as tactile, olfactory (e.g., smelling sulfur), and visual hallucinations consistent with an organic psychotic presentation (Wisner, Gracious, Piontek, Peindl, & Perel, 2002). The waxing and waning course of the illness would be consistent with a woman who looks stable one minute and can be floridly psychotic the next. When she appears confused or is in a "zombielike" state or a lucid state that is different from her episodes of florid psychosis, the credibility of her psychosis may be called into question, particularly by individuals who are not aware of the unpredictable nature of the psychosis (Spinelli, 2004). This unpredictability necessitates that mothers be separated from their children while experiencing these symptoms and until thoroughly treated and mentally stable. She may be compelled, particularly by delusions or command hallucinations, to commit violent acts despite reasoned behavior in other contexts. "For example, in the case of Andrea Yates, the prosecutors concluded that she could not have been psychotic when she murdered her children because she was later lucid enough to call for help and to report her actions to the police" (Spinelli, 2004, p. 1551).

Postpartum psychosis severely impacts daily living and the risk for infanticide or suicide is high, frequently requiring inpatient hospitalization (Born et al., 2004; Chaudron & Pies, 2003). "Hospitalization is mandatory when parents express concern over harming their children and are overconcerned about their children's health" (Pitt & Bale, 1995, p. 384). The average length of hospitalization is approximately two months but a full recovery may necessitate more than a year (Born et al., 2004). It has been estimated that between 39 percent and 81 percent of these women may endure a relapse of illness not during a postpartum period. Specifically, the relapse rate for postpartum psychosis is 80 percent or greater (Altshuler, Hendrick, & Cohen, 1998; Gold, 2001; Stowe et al., 2001). The postpartum psychosis may also reoccur with each subsequent delivery (Spinelli, 2004). Some contend that a progressive postpartum depression can extend for months or even years after the postpartum period if not identified or treated (Huysman, 2003; Spinelli, 2004). Rates of infanticide that resulted from untreated postpartum psychosis have been estimated to be as high as 4 percent (Altshuler et al., 1998; D'Orban, 1979; Gold, 2001). Huysman (2003) describes the devastating effects of this phenomenon:

> We expect that a simple and time-limited postpartum depression will abate on its own or be treated in a timely fashion. The mother with *progressive* postpartum depression (PPPD), however, does NOT recover without treatment. She merely experiences a hiatus until her next episode. Subsequent episodes are very often triggered by rejections, separations, and losses, and recur throughout the woman's life. Usually the next episode is worse than the last. If this pattern goes unchecked, the mother will spiral into a cycle of illness that can destroy her life and her family. (p. 43)

Psychopharmacological interventions before or after delivery can dramatically prevent the reoccurrence of postpartum mental illnesses, which occurs in 20 percent to 50 percent of the cases (Spinelli, 2004). Research has demonstrated the efficacy of administering an appropriate antipsychotic, mood stabilizer, or antidepressant in the immediate postpartum period in preventing a relapse of postpartum psychosis, mania, or depression (Austin, 1992; Spinelli, 2004; Wisner & Wheeler, 1994). As compared to women with nonpostpartum psychosis, women with postpartum depression take longer to respond to psychotropic medication for depression and necessitate more antidepressant medications to gain a response (Gold, 2001). An increasing number of studies indicate that the use of antidepressant medication during the end of a pregnancy and after delivery produces minimal risk to the mother or baby (Altshuler et al., 1998; Gold, 2001; Wisner, Perel, & Findling, 1996). "The relatively low risk of the use of psychotropic medication during breast-feeding, must be weighed against the risk of untreated postpartum disorder and the benefits of improvement in maternal mood" (Gold, 2001, p. 345). A family or personal history of mood disorder is the most important risk factor in determining the need for early medication management of postpartum depression (Spinelli, 2004). These women may also be unwilling to admit to having inappropriate and unnatural thoughts about harming their children, believing they have failed as mother and women (Gold, 2001). Their unwillingness to seek help and signs missed by medical or mental health professional who have contact with some of these women too often result in tragic consequences for the children.

SYMPTOMS AND MOTIVES

It is uncommon for women to kill their children as a result of coldhearted, callous disregard, revenge, or some other self-serving motive. It is far more common that maternal filicide results from severe mental illness. Sadoff (1995) indicated that there is little evidence that these mothers kill in a callous, calculated manner but rather as a result of depression, psychosis, or in a disassociative state, or state of fear or panic. When women kill children who are over one year of age, depression and psychosis are often factors in the extreme emotional and impaired reality orientation that leads to this tragic event. Certainly, psychosis is more common in filicide as compared to any other form of child murder. Resnick (1970) found that psychosis was the primary factor in two-thirds of the women in his sample who committed filicide. These women kill their children based on altruistic beliefs of being merciful or ending real or imagined (delusional) suffering. Mood-congruent delusions or hallucinations may also result in a mother believing that she has irreversibly hurt or damaged her child or children in some way (Gold, 2001). Andrea Yates has reported that she believed she was possessed and was a "Jezebel" and that her poor mothering threatened her children's ability to go to heaven. She saw only two choices: either kill her children while some innocence remained, therefore, allowing them entrance in heaven, or continue to damage them and ensure their eternal damnation. In her delusional state, her love for her children and her belief that she was saving them from eternal suffering led her to follow through on the grotesque act of drowning all five of her children. A severely depressed and suicidal mother will murder her child in order to prevent the child from the suffering associated with growing up motherless in a harsh, cruel world that will only cause them the same pain as what she endured.

In some instances, a woman experiencing ongoing grandiose delusions and a strong religious background may believe that she is being commanded by God to kill her children as a testament to her faith and to ensure entrance into heaven for both her and her children. She may, in her delusional state and within the context of her strong religious upbringing, believe that she should not only do God's bidding without questioning, but that she has done a good thing that is in the best interest of her child. Certainly, the story of Abraham being instructed by God to kill his son has been referenced and may even serve as a model for this type of delusional belief. Consider many evangelical religions that encourage speaking in tongues, being filled by the Holy Spirit, and directly communicating with God. While these religions are in no way responsible for the actions or mental illness of these women, the norms of the church may make her perceptual disturbances more difficult to identify. If a woman casually described receiving instructions or directly communicating with God, she would likely not be challenged or questioned further and this could be missed as a sign of mental illness. Let us be clear, strong religious convictions or experiences do not equal mental illness; however, a woman who is predisposed to mental illness and begins to become symptomatic might be completely overlooked if her delusions and hallucinatory experiences occur in this manner. The psychotic woman with grandiose delusions of a religious nature may believe that otherwise meaningless things in her environment symbolize messages or are signs from God that require her action. Implications of this type of psychotic presentation will be further explored later in this chapter. In each of the aforementioned examples, these women's beliefs are not reality based and are directly resulting from their mental illness. The very act of the murders is so heinous that society immediately reacts to punish the monsters who could have committed such acts. Little is understood about the tragic, tortured, and often very psychotic motives that underlie these deaths.

Women with schizophrenia have been found guilty of infanticide. Depending on the defense team's strategy, many of these women will plead insanity due to their disorder. Most likely, these women would not be considered the victims of postpartum depression considering their past or current history of schizophrenia, although the symptoms are similar. However, women with chronic mental illness (e.g., schizophrenia) are more likely to commit infanticide due to postpartum stressors or symptom exacerbation at a time when they have discontinued their medication (Spinelli, 2004). Researchers have found that there exists increased risk for mental illness among mothers who kill their children, with major depression with psychotic features being diagnosed most frequently (Pruett, 2002). It is also very common for mentally ill mothers who kill based on altruistic, depressive, and psychotic motives to not conceal their crimes. In fact, it is not uncommon for these women to confess and to request punishment (Brockington, 1995; Gold, 2001). While they might understand that according to the strict letter of the law it was wrong, they may believe that they had no other choice, were acting in the best interest of their children, or were morally justified in answering to a higher power. In some cases, the mother may be so psychotically disorganized at the time of the crime that she could not appreciate the wrongfulness of her actions in any legal or moral context. Legal alternatives and ramifications will be further discussed later.

Krischer, Stone, Sevecke, and Steinmeyer (2007) conducted a study based on data gathered through a retrospective chart review of all filicidal women admitted to the Mid-Hudson Forensic Psychiatric Hospital in New York State between 1976 and 2000 ($n = 57$). Their sample excluded filicidal mothers who went directly to prison without any prior forensic hospitalizations. The sample did include women found as NGRI, women incompetent to stand trial, or convicted offenders who were seriously mentally ill and were not sent to prison. Fourteen percent committed neonaticide, 21 percent committed infanticide, and 65 percent committed filicide by murdering a child older than one year. The motivational profiles of these women differed. The filicidal women were characterized as severely depressed, with a history of self-injurious behavior and a high rate of suicide attempts following the filicide. These women tended to kill an older child by stabbing, and psychosocial factors (e.g., poverty, marital status, substance abuse) played less of a role than psychological ones. These researchers found that the mothers in this group had a history of being abused as a child along with a history of depression (Krischer et al., 2007).

Myers (1970) noted that the psychotically depressed mother will kill her child in an attempt to "save" the child from a hostile, punitive world. Myers also noted that the schizophrenic mother may view the child as being defective, much as her own sense of self or her own body image is distorted. He indicated that the mother may repeatedly seek out a family physician or pediatrician with the unrelenting conviction that something is physically wrong with her child. Some mothers may seek psychiatric consultation due to being obsessed with fears of harming their children or are distressed by homicidal impulses toward them. Andrea Yates attempted suicide on one occasion because she was so distressed about her ongoing thoughts of harming her children.

When considering the mental state of these mothers, consider the following (as cited in Stanton & Simpson, 2002):

> Altruism has been seen as central as described by Baker (1902), "It may seem paradoxical, but it is not vice that leads to the death of the infant, rather is it morbid and mistaken maternal solitude" (p. 16). McGrath (1992) cited several examples of offenders' initial statements as recorded in police reports, several of which exemplify this perspective, e.g. "I have given her peace. . . . I loved him so" (p. 284). Resnick (1969) classified more than half his series as "altruistic filicide" or murders committed out of love. In this view, the murder would be seen as a rational act in the context of the mother's delusional perception of the world. (p. 10)

There are some women, while in the grips of psychosis to include paranoid delusions, who act violently toward their children out of fear. Some women have been known to kill an infant that they delusionally believed to be possessed by demons or to accidentally kill a child, while attempting to extricate an evil force within the child, without any other person's involvement and only based on their psychosis. Harder (1967) explained altruistic filicides as part of a gender role stereotype, whereby we view all women as nurturing caregivers devoted to protecting their children at all costs and must incorporate mothers killing their children into this schema (Stanton & Simpson, 2002). He further described the extreme of the maternal attentiveness as an example of reaction formation, in which the hostility toward the child is defended against by attempting to overnurture or care for the child (Stanton & Simpson, 2002). Additionally, the psychoanalytic viewpoint of mothers who kill their children as an extension of themselves involves her overidentifying with the child and that the aggression was actually directed toward herself (Stanton & Simpson, 2002). Tuteur and Glotzer (1959) described suicide-murder situations as an effort to erase the "total-all" or to completely annihilate the self due to a deep sense of rejection (as cited in Stanton & Simpson, 2002, p. 10).

Stanton, Simpson, and Wouldes (2000) undertook a qualitative study of filicide by mentally ill mothers. Six women were identified and interviewed and each described an intense investment in mothering her child or children. There were not significant external stressors, but rather the experience of their mental illness was described as extremely stressful. The motivations were described as altruistic or as an extension of their own suicides. These women, once stabilized with psychiatric and psychological interventions, further described feeling deep regret about the murders and feeling responsible, despite their awareness of their mental illness at the time of the offense. This study sought to explain the experience of these women from their own frame of reference. Each of the women in the study suffered from a major mental illness to include severe mood or psychotic disorders, which had required active, ongoing, inpatient and outpatient treatment for a year or longer. The *DSM-IV* diagnoses given included major depressive disorder, schizoaffective disorder (in either a manic or depressed phase prior to the killing), and schizophrenia. It was noted that the women who described being manic prior to the filicide described mood incongruent delusions at the time of the filicide. Each described her experience of mothering as changed with the onset of their mental illness, although she continued to love and care for her children to the best of her ability. While they were so depressed, even minor events could be experienced as extreme stressors.

Stanton et al. (2000, p. 1454) noted that being a good mother was important to all in their study. One of the mothers stated, "You know, I've always sort of wanted to be the perfect Mother." It is not uncommon for mothers who commit maternal filicide to feel that they must be perfect and see themselves as fatally flawed and perhaps their children by extension. So many high-profile cases involve women who were caring for their children at home full time with little support, as well as homeschooling them, and the like. Mentally ill mothers have the precarious balance of often trying to hide mental illness and nurture their sense of belonging through their ability to address the needs of their children (Montgomery, Tompkins, Forchuk, & French, 2006). The identity of 'mother' symbolizes possibilities of normalcy, security, and responsibility that they feel slipping away due to their severe mental illness. These women may also feel that they are inadequate in their marriages or that nothing they do can match up to what is expected of them. In the study by Stanton et al. (2000, p. 1454), one mother stated, "I expected so much of myself but when I look back now. . . . I mean I was looking out the window and seeing, you know, the neighbors and everything doing really well, but, and feeling that I wasn't, but I actually was. I was actually just doing so well and I couldn't see it." Some of the women in the study described living with delusions of persecution, which caused ongoing, severe stress. One mother stated, "I thought people were following me or vehicles were following me, or people were listening into where I was staying or spying on me. It was terrible, yeah" (p. 1454). Another extremely difficult manifestation of their psychosis was seeing signs and messages in otherwise benign things around them. They described the challenge of psychotic reality where nothing was what it seemed. One mother stated, "One of the things I used to do was like watch cars go past, each color meant something different and each number plate meant something different and they used to tell me things. The plates used to tell me things. I did that a lot. I hated it."

Stanton et al. (2000) found that the descriptions from women who were manic before they killed their children were artificially positive. One woman reported, "Everything was so good and wonderful. Well, I felt I had it under control, really, I didn't realize." A woman with this experience is unlikely to view her more euphoric feelings, a sense of well-being, or increased productiveness as problematic or a sign of mental illness. The researchers indicated that self-monitoring would have been impossible for the women who experienced mania before the filicide due to symptoms such as grandiosity and euphoria. Finally, some of the depressed women in the study described thinking about the deaths for a few days or a few weeks prior to the event. Some of these women described feeling very worried about their children while depressed but with hindsight were clear that the concerns were not reality based. "The psychotic women described no warning at all and were adamant that if they had been asked about ideas of killing their children before the event they would have had no indication that it was likely or even possible" (p. 1455).

The methods of murder used by the six women in this study included stabbing ($n = 3$), jumping with her child from a high place, setting fire to the house, attempted drowning, and suffocation. There were multiple victims in some cases. These women did not express hostile or negative perceptions of their children, which are often seen in unwanted or abused child killings. Their perceptions were favorable or unremarkable. There was also a lack of significant premeditation or planning. A majority of the women were not able to give well-organized accounts of what motivated them to kill, but altruism was prominent in the discernable accounts of motivation offered. Some of the women offered delusionally based mercy killings, "killing to protect or rescue the children from some awful fate that was indicated by their delusional system. They were clear about acting in the interest of their child(ren)" (p. 1456). Consider one of the participant's accounts:

A. I thought that they [people in the mother's delusional world] were going to use my daughter as well, I don't know, and um . . .

B. So you were kind of scared for her?

A. Yeah, I thought she was going to go through what I had been through. I just thought that the devil was going to take [the baby] in a cot death, that I had to save her and return her to the angels because if he took her, she'd go to Purgatory, she'd be stuck there forever. (p. 1456)

Stanton et al. (2000) found that all of the women bitterly regretted the deaths of their children, grieved their loss, and desperately wanted what was done to be undone. They stated that the filicide was ego-syntonic as a result of their delusions, but was undoubtedly ego-dystonic once the woman stabilized or recovered from her illness. All of the women in the study were found NGRI and were, therefore, not legally responsible, but still carried a tremendous burden despite their illness at the time of the crime. They questioned why it had to happen, and indicated it was something they would have to live with for the rest of their lives. When reflecting on what had happened at the time, the women in this study described having the intention to kill and not being out of control, although their actions were not reality based. None of these women attempted to avoid detection and had went to the police, family, or neighbors to let them know what had happened. A woman stated, "Even though that is what I have been diagnosed as, and, I can't just say, Oh, I wasn't in my right mind, everything is fine. You know, I still blame myself and feel a lot of guilt. I really hate myself that I didn't get the right sort of help" (Stanton et al., 2000, p. 1457).

Finally, Stanton et al. (2000) concluded that impaired reality, disorganized thinking, and the instability of the women's mental states, not abuse or other psychosocial stressors, were the main factors for the mentally ill filicidal mother. "One might postulate that the intensity of the suffering perceived in a delusional state is of such a magnitude as to explain the filicide rationally. However, other features of the illness such as impaired impulse control, affective dysregulation, lack of cognitive flexibility, and unbalanced judgment are likely to contribute" (p. 1459).

Lewis and Bunce (2003) conducted a study to examine a sample ($n = 55$) of filicidal mothers and compared those with and without psychotic symptoms at the time of the filicide. The mothers with psychosis more frequently confessed immediately after the homicide, used weapons, attempted suicide at the time of the crime, killed multiple children, and expressed homicidal thoughts or concerns regarding their children to psychiatrists and family before the filicide. Psychotic and nonpsychotic mothers were equally likely to have used alcohol or illegal drugs at the time of the offense. As one might expect, psychotic women were more likely to be adjudicated as incompetent to stand trial and to be found NGRI than nonpsychotic women. Lewis and Bunce (2003) found that filicidal mothers were more likely to be psychotic if they had expressed homicidal ideation toward their children at least two weeks before killing them, and voiced concerns to their family about their children within two weeks of the filicide. Neither the gender of the victim nor the age of the victim was significantly associated with maternal psychosis. Lewis and Bunce concluded that maternal filicide was an extremely difficult event to predict and prevent.

Another explanation for why a mother would kill her child is Munchausen's syndrome by proxy (MSBP) and has not been addressed elsewhere in this discussion. Munchausen's is a disorder found in the *DSM-IV-TR* as an appendix to factitious disorder. It differs from factitious disorder in that persons with Munchausen's syndrome have a psychological need to feign certain illnesses but for no external purpose, as is found with factitious disorder. In other words, they feel compelled to play the sick role and to acquire the likely attention that accompanies that state. Patients with this syndrome have been known to inject themselves with poisons, urine, and feces so that they will become ill and be admitted to a hospital or otherwise receive medical attention. MSBP occurs when parents cause illness in their children through these means, requiring constant medical attention. In a very distorted and damaging way, they are meeting some type of psychological need with little evidence of direct external incentive. Although the incidences of MSBP are rare, there have been enough cases to support its existence (O'Shea, 2003). In most of the known cases, death is the ultimate fate of the children because the parents will stop at nothing to fulfill their own needs (Pitt & Bale, 1995). Sheridan (2003) found that mothers were the perpetrators in 76.5 percent of 451 cases reviewed. Lasher (2003) states that there is an underidentification of MSBP due to a lack of public awareness and professional expertise and that overall awareness must increase in order to protect victims. These women do not fit into the model of mentally ill mothers and would be more likely to fall into the abuse filicide category. Usually their goal is to make the child sick but not to intentionally kill them; however, they take the ruse too far or for too prolonged a period.

MODE OF KILLING OR WEAPONS USE

Numerous researchers have discussed the very act of killing one's own child as offending our deepest level of humanity (Pruett, 2002). Considering the mode of killing and viewing crime scene photos or videos can traumatize and horrify even the most seasoned law enforcement, legal, and mental health professionals. A collective sense of outrage can create a rush to retribution without consideration of the myriad factors that led to these devastating crimes. No one in their rational mind could fathom that any mother could consider such carnage and death as being in the best interest of her children, yet, as previously described this is often the motive for the mentally ill filicidal mother. Oberman (2003, p. 493) states, "the thought of a mother killing her child evokes a deep sense of horror and outrage, as it represents a betrayal of the presumption of maternal love and altruism upon which civilization rests." It is not uncommon for the most shocking crime scenes to be a result of the most mentally ill or psychotic mothers. There are many factors involved in the prevalence and type of weapon use in maternal filicide and there are different patterns that emerge with psychotic mothers as compared to nonpsychotic mothers. As compared to murder in general, the typical means by which children are killed are less violent (Stanton & Simpson, 2002). Female offenders rarely use weapons and will typically use less violent means like drowning, suffocation, banging, hitting, or throwing. It is common for psychotic women to use more violent means than nonpsychotic women. Statistics show that in countries other than the United States, firearms are rarely if ever used as a means for maternal filicide (Stanton & Simpson, 2002). This should not be surprising as firearms are used more frequently in violent crimes in the United States, overall.

Unlike other types of maternal filicide, the psychotic mother intends to kill her child, albeit for delusional reasons, and takes some specific action to this end (Lewis & Bunce, 2003). She is driven by overwhelming feelings, impulses, or delusional ideas that make her impervious to actual reality as she is overtaken by her illness-driven reality. Lewis, Baranoski, Buchanan, and Benedek (1998) conducted a study to identify the factors associated with weapon use in a group of filicidal women ($n = 60$) who were evaluated at Michigan's Center for Forensic Psychiatry or through Connecticut's Psychiatric Security Review Board from 1970 to 1996. They defined weapon use as either with a gun or with a knife and found that one in four women used a weapon. Thirteen percent of filicidal women used guns and 12 percent used knives. Psychosis was present in every woman who used a knife to murder her child and in seven out of eight of the women who killed their children with a gun. Women experiencing psychosis were 11 times more likely to kill their children with a weapon than a nonpsychotic woman. Weapons were used almost exclusively with older children and were used infrequently in the deaths of infants or very young children. Weapons are typically used with children who are older than one year. Victims of filicide have been killed by diverse and sometimes bizarre methods (e.g., biting a child to death; forcing a child to eat pepper; overdosing the child on morphine rubbed on the nipples of the mother) (Lewis et al., 1998). When comparing filicidal mothers to filicidal fathers, Resnick (1969) noted that mothers tended to use more passive means of killing (e.g., smothering, drowning, gassing) than men (e.g., stabbing, striking, squeezing). Yet, other studies have also shown high rates of battering deaths for the victims of maternal filicide (Lewis et al., 1998).

Neonaticides are typically committed by drowning, beating, or strangling, without any weapon use (Lewis et al., 1998). Certainly the helplessness of the child would suggest that a weapon would not be needed to commit the murder. Psychotic women who used weapons were almost as likely to pick a knife as a gun, which is in contrast to statistics for murders of juveniles or children outside the home. Certainly, knives are more readily available in the home and could be considered as weapons of opportunity even for disorganized killers. Lewis et al. (1998) found that in a majority of cases where a child under ten years was killed with a weapon, the mother had psychotic symptoms. They stated:

> In the majority of cases, there were delusions specifically about the victims which the mother described as terrifying. For example, one woman stabbed her infant 45 times because she had become convinced that the baby was possessed by the devil. It is not surprising that a mother, when confronted with a force which she believes is overpowering, uses a weapon rather than her own strength to confront it. Our study shows that the women who killed the youngest children with weapons were uniformly psychotic and a majority had command hallucinations and paranoid delusions. (p. 617)

Lewis et al. (1998) identified 36 percent of the filicides by psychotic women in their study involved a knife or gun, regardless of the age of the victims, while only 5 percent of the nonpsychotic women used a weapon to commit filicide. They noted that nonpsychotic women will kill by way of extreme and sometimes heinous forms of normal punishment or out of rage or frustration (e.g., a 25-year-old that beat her child to death after much prior abuse by "accident" because the child wet its pants). Weapon use by psychotic mothers is uncommonly related to punishment or anger, but rather it is typically related to delusions involving the child being in some type of suffering or danger or the child being dangerous (Resnick, 1969). Lewis et al. (1998) found that approximately 25 percent of filicidal women used weapons in the commission of their crime. However, a majority of women who had used weapons had a past history of mental illness (e.g., hallucinations and delusions) and about 75 percent were receiving treatment at the time of the filicides. Greater than half had expressed fears about their children to family members or clinicians and about an eighth had contacted the police to express their concerns. Stanton et al. (2000) found that mentally ill mothers were more likely to use violent methods of killing, have older victims, and kill multiple children as compared to nonmentally ill mothers.

A MOTHER'S BURDEN

"Hell awaits them when restored to reality" (Gold, 2001, p. 346). Mentally ill mothers who have killed because they believed they had no choice and that what they were doing was in the child(ren)'s best interest are dealt a crushing blow, when they become stabilized and realize the gravity of what they have done. Their experience of remorse, disbelief, and horror is often the most severe punishment inflicted upon them. While still in their psychotic, manic, or depressed state, they often do not appreciate the wrongfulness or senselessness of what has happened. For example, a woman who believes she has been instructed by God to commit such an act feels certain that it is God's will or a good thing and that she will be reunited with them in heaven or due to their resurrection. This type of delusion would prevent a mentally ill mother from appreciating what has happened. Lewis and Bunce (2003) found that it was not uncommon for the women in their sample to express sorrow, fear, or regret about what they had done, while at the same time maintaining that their children had died for the best at the time or shortly after the incident. She likely believes at the time that there was an unavoidable purpose for the death(s). Now, imagine the cold reality when you realize that all you believed (e.g., painful terminal illness, eternal torment in hell, demonic possession, a test by God) that led to the killing(s) was only a product of your mental illness. A biochemical or psychological mistake has cost you your child(ren), your freedom, likely your marriage, and much, much more. Again, imagine a woman who has defined herself as a "mother" and values this role above all others that define her. Now sit with the knowledge that your body and mind have betrayed you and what you believed were self-sacrificing or altruistic actions were actually the senseless murder of your children by your very own hands. It is an unfathomable pain and suffering the enormity of which most other persons will not have to contend with in a lifetime.

Stanton and Simpson (2006) explored recovery experiences derived from a semi-structured interview study of six women who committed filicide in the context of major mental illness. The women described incomplete but horrific memories they avoided thinking about. Most of the women expressed some relief about having either no memory or hazy memory of the event. Intense self-hate and punishment feelings were common. These women were tormented about the perception that they might be an ongoing danger to other children. Better understanding their mental illness and how it could have so completely impaired their thinking and judgment is critical in helping them to make some sense out of what has happened.

Another realization is the confusion, fear, and betrayal the child must have felt and having no tangible way of explaining or taking back what you have done. There is a domino effect of pain and confusion that leaves family members in shock and disbelief, wondering what they missed or how such a devoted mother could have taken the lives of her children. Stanton et al. (2000, p. 1458) state, "Having to live with having killed one's own child is a considerable burden for someone already struggling with a major mental illness." Study after study suggests that these women display significant remorse, even when their mental illness is only partially stabilized (Stanton et al., 2000; Schwartz & Isser, 2001).

Psychotic women who kill their children from motives such as saving or relieving their children from spiritual and other physical torture, suffering, and doom, or the belief that God instructed it are qualitatively much different from coldblooded murderers. A system of delusions leaves them believing that there are no other alternatives and they must act out of love for their children. Some argue that these women have lost their children and do not pose a significant threat to others as long as they are maintained on their medication and have a firm understanding of their mental illness and are committed to ongoing management of their mental illness. No measure of punishment such as extended incarceration or death will compare to the guilt they feel for what they have done. This way of thinking would not apply to the psychopathic killer who kills for personal or material gain. The psychopathic killer has only remorse for being caught and has no regard for the victim who has been objectified, murdered, and thrown away. The mentally ill maternal filicide offender who was devoted to her child does not demand the same type of justice as the quite different psychopathic or even revenge- or anger-motivated offenders. The mentally ill filicidal mother will punish herself extensively with her guilt. Ford (1996) asks the following difficult questions (as cited in Schwartz & Isser, 2001):

> If a mother is stunned and genuinely horrified by her own actions, is it necessary for the state to impose the longest or most severe penalties when she, herself, is her own worst punishing agent? . . . Generally, society considers random, repeated, and cold-blooded killers as the most dangerous to society. How much does a murdering mother's profile conform to this description? (p. 714)

RISK FACTORS

Due to the infrequency of child murder, accurate prediction is unlikely. Child murder is a rare and difficult event to predict but successful treatment and intervention programs are contingent upon identifying potential perpetrators. There are risk factors that make some women more vulnerable than others to maternal filicide. Wilczynski (1995, p. 365) found that numerous background stress factors to include: "financial, housing, marital problems, social isolation, psychiatric disorder, children who were regarded as particularly difficult to care for in some way, and the use of illegal or legal substances such as alcohol and prescription drugs were among the most common features of the cases" of child killing by parents in England in the 1980s and 1990s. Putkonen et al. (2009) contend that psychopathy is not a risk factor for filicide as the two are not significantly related.

Research has shown that depression or anxiety during pregnancy, a family history of mental illness, an unwanted pregnancy, sleep deprivation, and significant psychosocial stressors, such as marital discord, are all risk factors for postpartum mental illness (Born et al.,

2004). Warning signs for new mothers that might indicate the onset of a postpartum illness include the mother becoming quite unkempt while the child is excessively well groomed and dressed or the mother becomes hypersexual in a way that was uncommon for her previously (Huysman, 2003). Risk factors associated with mood disorders should be queried by obstetricians during their initial visit with an expectant mother regarding her experience and her family background. She should be queried, for example, about any substance abuse history, hypersexual behavior, unstable relationship history, unstable employment history, periods of depression, suicidal ideation, suicide attempts, violent acting out or aggression, grandiosity, family history of mental illness, and the like. The family might complain to the physician that the mother is not sleeping or that she is obsessively worried about the baby. The mother may be unable to involve her husband or significant other into the new family dynamic with the infant (Huysman, 2003). Conversely, family members might report that the mother is unable to care for the child as a result of fearing she will harm the child or because she is always sleeping and unable to get out of bed. Huysman (2003, p. 102) reported that the families will often make excuses for the erratic behavior such as: "She must be jealous of the baby" or "She's too tired to have sex or even be affectionate." A woman who is suffering from postpartum depression can be overly preoccupied with her baby, abnormally angry, sad, or detached. Regarding infanticide that results from postpartum depression or psychosis, Huysman (2003, p. 103) stated, "it . . . crosses racial, cultural, and socioeconomic lines. It's not black, Hispanic, Asian, Native-American, or white; it's not rich or poor. PPD (postpartum depression), PPPD (progressive postpartum depression), and the infanticide cases that sometimes occur as a consequence of the illness when it is left untreated, does not discriminate."

Other signs of postpartum depression include panic attacks, severe anxiety, insomnia, disinterest in the child, spontaneous crying, trance-like states, vague comments to others about "not being well" (Huysman, 2003, p. 39), chronic irritability, and episodes of hyperactivity that include insomnia and increased energy. While postpartum psychosis is far more rare than postpartum depression, it is far more dangerous with approximately 4 percent of women who develop this disorder killing their children (Huysman, 2003). Maternal filicides that involve children older than one year reach beyond the postpartum period; however, researchers have found that progressive postpartum depression involves a chemical imbalance that is triggered by the birth event that sets in motion a longstanding, serious mental illness that will likely wax and wane in its course if left untreated. As the mental illness progresses, an episode can be triggered by a psychosocial stressor such as a loss. Certainly, a genetically vulnerable woman would be at continued risk with each subsequent birth, particularly if untreated. In most cases, this mental illness is controllable if identified and effectively treated, especially on the front end.

The risk of postpartum illness is greater in women over 25 years of age who have a history of mood instability with 30 percent to 40 percent of these women having a postpartum episode (Huysman, 2003). Women with a family history of mood instability are also more vulnerable to progressive postpartum depression. The medical and psychological history of the woman's biological family will provide critical information about her level of risk for mental illness in general and her risk for postpartum illness. While the more severe manifestations often result in hospitalizations or, perhaps, some contact with the criminal justice system, this is not the case for more moderate symptoms or expressions of mood instability. Familial traits that could indicate a predisposition to psychotic or affective episodes of postpartum illness include "addiction to alcohol and/or drugs, family history of multiple marriages, compulsive gambling, poor judgment, indiscreet financial or sexual behaviors, impulsive or violent behavior, aggression, and inflated self-esteem or grandiosity. . . . At risk are mothers from families that displayed one or more of the following: unstable or chaotic lifestyles . . . too much dependence on one another or too much independence from one another, extreme rigidity, compulsive behavior, and frequent bouts of rage" (p. 55). Bear in mind, this list is not exhaustive and actually targets the more severe and overt signs of a family history of mood disorders or other mental illness.

Of those with clinical depression, individuals with marked anxiety and a hypochondriacal pattern or overconcern or exaggeration of somatic symptoms are more likely to attempt suicide (Huysman, 2003). A preexisting psychotic depression would make a woman extremely vulnerable to a progressive postpartum depression that would be more enduring and dangerous. Medical professionals are more likely to initially encounter these women than mental health professionals and should be well educated on this literature.

Command hallucinations and paranoid delusions correlate with a higher risk of violence in general; but delusions and paranoia about the child are very significant risk factors for maternal filicide. Certainly psychosis as a component of a postpartum illness, affective disorder, or a psychotic illness greatly increases the likelihood that child murder will occur in these women. A severe delusional depression, where the children are a key focus of the delusional system, is a serious red flag. According to Laporte, Poulin, Marleau, and Roy (2003), evaluating the dangerousness of filicidal women who are facing disposition includes whether or not delusions about the children exist, the age and number of children, availability of weapons, and the support available by having another responsible adult take care of the children until a mental health crisis or postpartum crisis is resolved. Due to the high lethality of firearms, women with a history of depression or postpartum mental illness should not have guns in the home.

Stanton et al. (2000) indicate that it is very difficult to predict risk and to prevent mentally ill filicide in mothers who are described being devoted and are observed as very caring toward their children, providing little to no warning of filicidal urges. For these types of filicidal mothers, those at risk include mothers who have psychological significance or importance to the perpetrator, due to the nature of their motives (Bowden, 1990).

A majority of these women have a major mental illness that they are often trying to manage without treatment and are attempting to appear normal. They may be experiencing depression and psychosis, and they might be suicidal. These symptoms can lead to homicidal impulses even if for altruistic reasons or rationale. Certain women have a biological vulnerability based on a family history of mental illness, especially affective disorders. If a woman is experiencing postpartum mental illness, it is likely to become worse with each subsequent pregnancy and can extend far beyond the postpartum period. If a woman already has a genetic predisposition to mental illness, she may be particularly vulnerable to the huge influx of hormones, and the biochemical imbalance of an emerging mental illness may be set in motion.

When considering other categories of filicidal women such as battering mothers or fatal child abuse or retaliating women, threats to the husband–wife pair bond may end in violence toward the children by mothers (Stanton & Simpson, 2000). The loss of the father would certainly be a destabilizing event. Vulnerability factors include psychiatric history, social supports, and the nature and stability of significant or central interpersonal relationships.

THE RESPONSE OF THE CRIMINAL JUSTICE SYSTEM

The response of the courts to maternal filicide has a history of vacillating between leniency and retribution. What is the appropriate degree of culpability to attach to mentally ill mothers who kill their children for what they believe are altruistic reasons? The current response of society, the media, and the criminal justice system is punitive with mentally ill mothers often tried and convicted with the fervor given to any other coldblooded murder case. Certainly, the overzealous prosecution, conviction, and subsequent sentence of life imprisonment of Andrea Yates after her first trial, despite her well-documented history of mental illness and devotion to her children, illustrate this. It was only on a legal error that her conviction was overturned. Sentences are often very inconsistent ranging from probation with counseling for some neonaticide offenders to commitment in a maximum-security forensic hospital as NGRI or life in prison with a guilty verdict. Prosecutors sought the death penalty for Andrea Yates, although the jury rejected it. Community outrage and public opinion during a time when it seems that everything is politicized have a tremendous impact on jurors' verdicts and the severity of sentences. Jurors arrive at trials with preconceived notions about what type of woman could commit such a crime and what would constitute justice for such a seemingly heinous crime—child murder. Some might be able to set aside these ideas and some might not. Finkel, Burke, and Chavez (2000) indicate that public opinion changes over time based on cultural, legal, moral, historical, and psychological trends, as well as the cogent influence of media saturation of high-profile cases. Additionally, mandatory sentencing has become more common for the most serious offenses. Judges have much less discretion to include taking into consideration mitigating factors, particularly the severe mental illness of mothers who are found guilty of murder. While the victims of such crimes deserve justice, it should be a humane, well-informed justice.

The media can influence the leniency or severity of society and our criminal justice system, when conclusions are presented from outlier cases that give the impression that infanticide or filicide defendants are "getting away with murder," or "getting off light" (Finkel et al., 2000, p. 1115). With the 24-hour coverage on various cable news channels of high-profile cases, the offenders are tried in the media before even stepping foot in the courtroom. This type of presentation can cause the public to believe that the outlier cases are more common than what they are, creating outrage and a push for more punitive sentences. Public opinion or their constituents' views likely heavily influence our legislature that pass bills regarding sentencing laws. People are very suspicious of insanity defenses, and successful NGRI verdicts are rare and frequently result in lengthy incarceration in maximum-security forensic hospitals (Finkel et al., 2000). Fathers who commit filicide and are tried for their crimes are more frequently incarcerated than hospitalized (West, Hatters-Friedman, & Resnick, 2009).

McKee and Shea (1998) found that 75 percent of filicidal parents had exhibited psychotic symptoms prior to their child's homicide and that 40 percent had been seen by a psychiatrist shortly before the event. Twenty percent of the women in their study had a finding of legal insanity. Similar percentages have been found in other studies; for example, 27 percent in D'Orban's (1979) study, and 15 percent in Bourget's and Bradford's (1990) study. This is much greater than the rate of 0.1 percent for insanity acquittees in other criminal cases where the insanity plea was raised (McKee & Shea, 1998).

Regarding factors that work against mitigating infanticide, Finkel et al. (2000, p. 1121) state, "If manslaughter is a low probability verdict, and if exculpation to madness is low as well, then murder might be the default option." Finkel et al. (2000) found that neither depression alone nor childbirth, which may be associated with postpartum illness, has a mitigating effect on verdicts like NGRI or guilty but mentally ill (GBMI). Expert testimony on either of the aforementioned issues also does not have much of an impact, unless jurors are provided with evidence of psychosis at the time of the crime. In general, sentencing and treatment decisions are decided by the courts with little or no involvement from psychology or psychiatry. The courts and individuals who sit on juries are almost invariably undereducated about this devastating phenomenon. While it is still far more likely that an NGRI or GBMI verdict will not be reached, the chances are greater when psychosis is present, particularly when the act is seen as bizarre. Research has also shown that prospective female jurors are not more forgiving or lenient toward maternal infanticide offenders (Finkel et al., 2000). It is possible that the crime is so gender incongruent that some female jurors might judge more harshly.

The United States has extremely restrictive laws that govern infanticide or filicide cases the same as any other homicide. The United States does not have an infanticide statute. Traditionally, the older the child, the more likely the conviction rate. British law has specific infanticide laws that govern infanticide, which some view as overly lenient that take into consideration the very enormous possible impact of childbirth, depression, and other issues relating to the postpartum period. Britain's law more closely equates infanticide to manslaughter with regard to penalties, rather than murder, which is much more common in the United States. In Great Britain, the Infanticide Act of 1922 and 1938 both maintained that postpartum psychosis was an appropriate cause to reduce charges for neonaticide and infanticide from murder to manslaughter. The diminished responsibility defense utilized in New South Wales allows for probation or for an individual to be sent to a psychiatric facility for treatment rather than to prison (Schwartz & Isser, 2001). Finland has legislation comparable to that of the British Infanticide Act of 1922, proposing that women who are vulnerable in the postpartum period often receive no sentence and are referred for mental health treatment (Kauppi et al., 2008).

In approximately 30 countries throughout the world, to include Britain, Canada, and Australia, murder charges are ruled out for a lesser charge for women who kill their children within the first year after giving birth. This legislation implies that childbirth may have had a destabilizing effect on mothers, and that the infant homicide may have happened due to the resulting unstable psychological conditions, presenting a case for diminished responsibility for the crime (Marks, 2001). Their stance does not promote devaluing the lives of the infants, but rather reflects a greater understanding and mitigation for postpartum illnesses. Clearly, this should not take the place of prevention and education. Insanity defenses based on postpartum depression are not often successful. According to Gold (2001, p. 346), "This is, in no small part, because altruistic homicide, even in a psychotically disorganized individual, is voluntary, often premeditated, planned logically, and accomplished methodically, always in full consciousness, and perfectly remembered."

Laporte et al. (2003, pp. 96–97) stated that the most cogent arguments against sentencing women with postpartum depression to terms of incarceration are as follows: "1) an illness beyond their control caused these women's homicidal acts, 2) they have already suffered enough, 3) they have lost their offspring and have to live with the guilt related to their behaviour, and 4) they do not represent a threat to others as long as they do not have other children" (Ewing, 1997; Pitt & Bale, 1995).

Women who do not commit suicide following a depressive, typically psychotic filicide for altruistic reasons normally will make no attempt to hide the crime, will readily confess, and will often request punishment (Brockington, 1995; Gold, 2001; Lewis & Bunce, 2003). The actions of a mentally ill mother around the filicide may be quite confusing, particularly to a layperson who does not understand her mental illness. What may initially appear as a rational behavior that would suggest appreciation of wrongfulness (e.g., calling the police or 911) might actually be a product of psychotic illness. "For example, one might suggest that when a woman confesses or expresses regret that she killed her child, she recognizes that what she did was wrong. Instead some confessions may be representative of underlying psychotic illness that interferes with full appreciation of wrongfulness" (Lewis & Bunce, 2003, p. 467). This type of maternal filicide offender at or shortly after her arrest will believe her actions were justified or she may have had no choice. Sometimes, her affect is even unusually jovial or elated based on her illness and belief that she just did a good thing for the child, God, or the world. Lewis and Bunce (2003, p. 467) found that the delusional thinking of the women in their sample could be based on "factors such as believing that their children were dangerous, inherently flawed, or at risk; that they, the mothers, were unfit in some way; or that they had helped the world or remaining family members by killing their children."

ISSUES FOR TREATMENT AS THE CURTAIN LIFTS

The treatment considerations discussed in this section will be specifically targeted for mentally ill mothers who have committed filicide or infanticide for altruistic reasons, rather than neonaticide or other categories of filicide. Suicide risk is high even at the time of the filicide or directly after. Yet, for those women who believe that they had to kill their children for some greater good, the reality of the senselessness of what they have done becomes apparent only when their mental illness has been stabilized. These women are at high risk of experiencing suicidal ideation or attempting suicide at that time. It is very common for these women to be placed on suicide watch in the jails or if they are in a psychiatric hospital setting to be placed on one-to-one observation status. In addition to medication management for their mood and psychotic symptoms, receiving support and having a mental health professional to talk to about what they are experiencing are important. Obviously, when such a woman is on pretrial, what she should or would be advised or able to discuss about her situation is extremely limited. It would not be unexpected for a treatment provider in a jail or forensic hospital setting to be called as a fact witness at the criminal trial or competency hearing. Sometimes the woman believes she should be punished by death or desires suicide by capital punishment, and this deep sense of hopelessness and despair may contribute to an ongoing state of incompetency to stand trial until her mood stabilizes.

If a mentally ill maternal filicide offender is found NGRI and is likely committed to a maximum-security forensic hospital, treatment concerns and relevant issues can be more effectively observed and addressed. Grief is another cogent ongoing issue. As the curtain of psychosis, depression, or mania lifts and the mother is left with the realization that her offspring are dead and she is responsible, the grief is usually unbearable. The loss of a child brings a void beyond compare under any circumstances. These women must face bereavement as a result of murder, and therapists can be overwhelmed by the enormity of their suffering (Stanton & Simpson, 2006). Maternal filicide offenders are aware and negatively impacted when they believe mental health professionals are uncomfortable or want to avoid the horror of their crimes. This will undoubtedly increase the likelihood that they will not express what they are experiencing and leave the patient with important issues unresolved (Stanton & Simpson, 2006).

The maternal filicide offender will need to be informed about the emotions associated with grief, its nonlinear process, and the expectation that she will likely encounter head-on the grief of others associated with the children or family. Those women who had planned or attempted their own suicide in conjunction with the filicide but failed are likely to have survivor's guilt. Mental health professionals must be aware of the range of reactions from surviving family and friends including anger, fear, sadness, confusion, and the like and how their emotions and actions will impact the mental health of the mother/patient. These women may be extremely isolated from the remaining family who are torn apart and in conflict about what has occurred. The shock, disbelief, and horror of what she has done are likely to give way to a deep, overwhelming remorse and sadness. Every woman is different, but for those who respond to treatment and emerge from their delusions and other symptoms, this type of reaction can likely be anticipated. She will not be able to grieve her children at the graveside but from a prison cell or hospital ward. She must grieve in a vacuum until and if she is eventually released to the community.

Mental health education is absolutely essential. Helping her to understand all of the signs, symptoms, and triggers of her illness, particularly those that led to the offense, is mandatory to get her mentally well, to reduce risk for relapse, and to protect society. She will need to understand and follow up with her treatment for the rest of her life to ever have an opportunity to safely reintegrate into society. These women struggle desperately with the question, "Why did this have to happen?" The whys and the what ifs are brutal and can lead to much depression and anguish. Depending on the nature of their mental illness, some women will respond much better than others to treatment. While many will respond very well to medication management, psychosocial rehabilitation, and psychotherapy, there may be some whose illness is treatment refractory and must remain in an institutional setting to prevent harm to self or others. The former is much more common, and with ongoing treatment and a healthy support system, she can likely be safely reintroduced into the community at some point in the future.

For those women who had a strong religious component to their delusions that may have led to the crime itself, there often remains an anger and distrust of God or their previous faith. If at the time of the crime they believed they were serving the will of God or were instructed to not question the action of killing their children, they may fear any strong relationship with God or trust themselves to unquestioning faith in whatever they may have believed before. Certainly, due to their vulnerabilities for mental illness and the way their symptoms were previously demonstrated, they will have to be much more cautious and prudent in their involvement and expression of spirituality. For example, if a woman who had previously been raised in a faith that believed and encouraged speaking in tongues, she may have been less inclined to interpret auditory hallucinations or hearing voices as a sign of mental illness, when it began. She may have viewed her experience of

God having actually spoken to her and commanded her to do certain things as a wonderful blessing. To be clear, religion does NOT cause mental illness, but for those women who are susceptible or who are mentally ill, it is quite possible that their religious ideation will mask or become intertwined with their delusional system. This is a very personal and complicated issue but a reality for those women whose delusions that led to the deaths of their children had strong religious meaning or components. This also has implications for educating church officials and congregations about signs of mental illness, including postpartum illnesses.

Many women who committed filicide were married at the time of the offense. This action almost invariably leads to divorce. While this may not come as a shock, it can still be traumatic for the recovering woman who is coming to terms with what she has done, the loss of her children, and now the loss of her marriage. She will often feel deep guilt and remorse about what she had done to their children, but cannot help also feeling a sense of abandonment at her darkest hour. She may no longer feel that she is the same woman or in the same frame of mind as she was when the filicides occurred and desperately long for some sense of normalcy or security in the face of such tragedy and chaos. Even when the spouse forgives his wife and understands the role of her mental illness, it is quite understandable that his feelings for her have changed in addition to the reality of a lengthy hospitalization or incarceration. In other instances, there may be only anger and confusion about what has happened or, perhaps, even some self-blame that he was unable to see, stop, or intervene in what has transpired. The families may be strongly divided about whether or not to support or shun the woman in question. If the woman is an insanity acquittee, there is also the question of the division of marital property and assets. As long as they remain married, he can also be responsible for her costly psychiatric care. While these issues pale in comparison to the loss of the children, there exists a harsh reality of the rest of the story long after the glare of unwanted media attention and public interest wanes.

Mentally ill women who killed for altruistic motives were typically devoted mothers prior to their emerging illness and subsequent filicides. If they primarily defined themselves or their role as wife and mother, how do they pick up the pieces and what kind of future might they have? It can be painful for these mothers to have the realization that they are likely going to be unable to participate in regular family contact or parental roles with surviving children. If they remain delusional or unstable, they will be kept safely in the confines of a maximum-security hospital. Insanity acquittees who respond to treatment, at some point, could and likely will be returned to the community. Facing the prospect that they are no longer mothers and wives, or that they may not be able to return to their communities or churches, what happens next? She may wonder if once returned home, nieces and nephews will fear her or if she will be a burden to those family members willing to accept her. Helping these women make realistic plans for the future and helping prepare them for the many changes they will encounter is yet another function of treating clinicians. A majority of these women were very vulnerable to their mental illness as a result of pregnancy and childbirth. Many infanticide offenders were experiencing postpartum illnesses and future childbirth would put them at high risk. So, the reality of never being a mother again is prudent but is often difficult to accept.

Whether the female offender is in prison or a psychiatric hospital, there is an inescapable stigma attached to killing children and she may suffer harsh reactions or treatment, particularly in a prison setting. This type of treatment, shame, and deep sadness are often rekindled when a story reemerges in the media, through television or in print. It is common for graphic details, pictures, and the names of all involved to be widely publicized. Coping with the reality of media coverage, including when and if they are ever released to the community, is another reality for which to prepare. Encouraging these women to find meaning in their tragedies and to have some hope for the future is a difficult but important role for mental health professionals involved in their treatment.

IMPLICATIONS

Early identification of signs of depression and psychosis is imperative in the prevention of maternal filicide (Sharma et al., 2009; Myers, 1970). When a physician or a mental health professional has contact with a mother who is presenting with symptoms of severe depression or schizophrenia, he or she should not ignore the possibility of maternal filicide and inquire appropriately. Whether or not psychosis is present and the severity of the symptoms both have implications for the treatment, prognosis, and prevention efforts for potentially filicidal women (Lewis & Bunce, 2003). Preemptive action in these cases serves the best interest of the child and the mother. Identifying those women at risk, and providing early and appropriate treatment and ongoing management of the mental illness is critical. Education should be provided for mental health professionals, family members, general practitioners, emergency room doctors and nurses, pediatricians, obstetricians, police, child-protective services personnel, members of the clergy, and social workers. A number of women who commit maternal filicide will come into contact with mental health professionals before the event, and the possibility of homicidal impulses or ideation should never be overlooked in depressed individuals, particularly mothers (Bourget & Labelle, 1992).

Screening for bipolarity in addition to depression in pregnant women will assist in identifying those at risk and allow for a formalized risk assessment and management plan that will allow an opportunity to address avoidable risk factors in late pregnancy and in the early postpartum period (Sharma et al., 2009). Regarding risk for postpartum mental illness, Spinelli (2004, p. 1554) states, "Since antepartum screening is the best strategy for identifying women at risk, the prenatal clinic is the optimum environment in which to use simple screening tools and objective mood scales. . . . Although these tools do not replace a diagnostic interview, they facilitate collection of focused information to identify women at risk in time for intervention." Physicians who treat women planning families should receive and offer education about risk for postpartum depression and available treatment routinely as part of their primary care. Physicians should also explain the risk versus the benefits of utilizing medication while pregnant or postpartum, based on the severity of the illness. Family members of these women should be given emotional support in addition to education.

If a woman has a severe depression, or has any history of severe mood instability to include depression or mania with associated psychosis, or schizophrenia, the severity of the illness would require psychotropic medications, and ideally therapy when stabilized. If pregnant, the stage of the pregnancy would have implications that the physician should advise her about. The more severe forms of the illness would not likely remit without pharmacotherapy. "Treatment during lactation requires minimizing infant exposure and adverse effects while maintaining optimum maternal mental health" (Sharma et al., 2009,

p. 1219). According to these researchers, "Despite the lack of efficacy and safety data, antidepressants are regularly used as first-line pharmacotherapy in the management of bipolar postpartum depression" (p. 1218). Additionally it was noted that treatment with antidepressants can result in a highly unstable treatment course with bipolar postpartum depression and discontinuation of antidepressants and initiation of mood stabilizers and atypical antipsychotics can result in sustained improvement. For women who appear to have serious bipolar illness during the postpartum period, Sharma et al. (2009) also recommend continued mood stabilizing medication after the first postpartum year. If medication is discontinued, these women should be psychiatrically monitored to ensure ongoing maternal emotional stability. Additional pregnancies and postpartum periods should also be closely monitored.

Mental health and medical professionals should be particularly vigilant to hypochondriacal or psychosomatic concerns from the mother about her or her children's health. It is not uncommon for the mother to make numerous doctors' visits, often seeking second or third opinions because of her unshakable belief that she and her children are suffering from an incurable disease. It is critical that the aforementioned professionals be well educated that this is a risk factor for maternal filicide and to conduct the appropriate inquiries and risk assessments to prevent such a tragedy. For example, if a primary care physician notes that this is likely a psychiatric problem, he or she should not only suggest to the spouse that his wife be evaluated by a psychiatrist, but the medical professional should speak candidly about the correlation with maternal filicide and possible suicide risk. Many individuals do not trust mental health professionals and will balk at the idea of seeking mental health care. The contact with the medical personnel may be the solitary interface with a woman at high risk for maternal filicide. It is imperative that medical professionals are well aware of this literature and properly educate the women and families involved, as well as referring them to a mental health profession or seek immediate civil commitment if the mother is actually expressing homicidal impulses toward her children. The mother who is experiencing a major mental illness will likely have significant difficulty monitoring her parenting effectiveness and level of risk (Stanton et al., 2000).

Oberman (2003) suggests that in order to eliminate maternal filicide, we must first understand the individuals who commit the crime and the larger societal context in which it takes place. Women who experience postpartum illness should be approached as individuals, and all possible causes for their illness should be explored. Medical professionals should not assume that a new mother's behavior, questions, or complaints are just related to her insecurities, fatigue, or hysteria (Huysman, 2003); but rather they should be able to ask the right questions and make appropriate referrals to mental health professionals if warranted. In addition to medication management and psychotherapy, those women need to have a strong emotional support system through their families, friends, communities, and churches. The lack of general education of mental illness by these individuals and institutions leaves a void in the prevention chain. Support groups and educational counseling have proven to be beneficial, particularly during pregnancy (Huysman, 2003). Those women who are at-risk or who are identified as having a mental illness should be provided with help if possible with nocturnal infant care to minimize sleep disruption that could trigger or exacerbate their symptoms. Close follow-up should be undertaken during the most critical periods of risk.

Stanton et al. (2000) contend that psychotic forms of child abuse or murder should be explained separately from typical forms of abuse or murder. The unique and complex motives and the driving force of mental illness behind these tragedies make them qualitatively much different from murders resulting from anger, revenge, or some form of secondary gain. Lewis et al. (1998) indicate that most women who kill their children do not have a history of abusing them, and, as such, programs focused on preventing child abuse will not be meeting the needs or effectively addressing the issues for these women that may lead to maternal filicide. A better understanding of motivating factors causing a woman to kill a newborn, a toddler, or an older child could better facilitate finding appropriate interventions for whatever stage the mother is in (Krischer et al., 2007). Additionally, for women who are raising a child while suffering from a severe depressive episode, it is recommended that both intensive marriage counseling and therapy are recommended.

Those in contact with at-risk women should not be lulled into believing that a mother's devotion to her children would automatically preclude her from harming her baby or child. Research has demonstrated that a number of these women kill for motives that they believe are in their child's best interest; therefore, their apparent love and nurturance of their child does not reduce their risk. In fact, the risk may be increased due to the emotional investment in the child (Stanton et al., 2000). "Evident devotion to the child and parenting is not likely to be a protective factor" (p. 1459). These mothers often place undue pressure on themselves to be good or better mothers, further complicating their increased risk with additional stress. Aggressive treatment of psychotic symptoms and ensuring medication compliance in the mentally ill mother are critical in reducing the risk of weapon-related filicide deaths (Lewis et al., 1998).

The seemingly unthinkable act of a mother killing her child may prevent an otherwise prudent clinician from exploring the possibility of a female client committing filicide. Clinicians are trained to inquire about suicidal and homicidal ideation, but rarely do they inquire specifically about a mother's homicidal ideation toward her children (McKee & Shea, 1998). Resnick (as cited in McKee & Shea, 1998, p. 685) suggested that when a mother presents with suicidal ideation, the evaluating professional should always ask, "What are your plans for the children?" Lewis et al. (1998) describe using structured methods of assessing maternal feelings toward children. For example, clinicians could ask a mother at risk if she ever has feelings of fearing her child or being fearful for her child in order to identify children at risk. Structured interviews should be designed to assess the mother's feelings about her children, her ability to care for them, and any fears she may have related to her children. For those women who are identified as being at risk, home visits, which provide the opportunity to observe the mother interacting with her children, and clinical observations of the mother are recommended as methods of creating greater awareness of children at risk for maternal filicide (Lewis et al., 1998). Most parents with psychiatric vulnerabilities or mental illness do not harm their children. However, as children are increasingly suffering at the hands of their parents, it is crucial that we identify children who need protection from parents, who cannot manage their aggressive or homicidal impulses and take action (Pruett, 2002).

Frequently women who were grossly psychotic at the time of the offense, at the time of arrest, and when first housed in the jail are stabilized and appear quite "sane" at their criminal trials. What impact does this have on the ability of jurors to imagine a woman so ravaged by mental illness that she would take the life of her own child? Particularly if there is a significant mood component to her illness, many of these women respond very well to appropriate pharmacological treatment and present a completely different and often stable picture at their criminal trial or other court hearings. Is it in the best interest of the client to remain unmedicated? If left untreated, these women will often not be restored to competency to even proceed to their trials. Clearly, it is a double-edged sword and raises many complex and ethical questions.

It is important that judges and the legal community be educated about the mental health issues surrounding postpartum depression or psychosis and other types of mental illness associated with filicide. Attorneys and judges should be educated about the potential altruistic motives for the crime that impact appreciation of wrongfulness, motivation for confessing, and the premeditation involved in the crimes committed by mentally ill mothers. A "delicate balance is needed to educate, rehabilitate, correct, and punish the woman who has killed" her child(ren) (Schwartz & Isser, 2001, p 713). Spinelli (2004) warns that postpartum depression or psychosis is severely minimized in the judicial process and is inadequately explained to jurors with devastating consequences for the mothers. Educating the legal communities and participants in the courtroom, including juries, is of critical importance. Professionals should be utilized and well trained to explain the biological and psychological factors to jurors and to use the courtroom as a classroom to help facilitate verdicts based on accurate understanding of the facts (Spinelli, 2004).

When considering the disposition and sentencing of mentally ill mothers, it is critical that juries and judges recognize the impact of incarceration or other options would have on the mental health of the defendant. These women are unlikely to receive adequate treatment and rehabilitation in the prison system. Unlike other Western countries that have infanticide laws that recognize the unique plight of mentally ill mothers and the potential impact of postpartum illnesses, the United States has no such law and sentencing and verdicts have recently been harsh. Severe punishment is meant to be a deterrent but the mentally ill maternal filicide offender is acting with impaired reality testing and often under the influence of severe depression, command hallucinations, delusions, and other types of perceptual disturbances. It is very unlikely that if they are ill enough to harm their children as a result of psychotic process or severe mental illness, the threat of severe punishment would have any impact on their decision making at the time of the offense. After the benefits of effective treatment, the mother is likely to agonize about how she could have believed what she did and committed the filicide as a result. To further illustrate the problematic nature of using punishment as retribution, Spinelli (2004, p. 1553) wrote, "In cases of infanticide, it often seems difficult to blame a single individual. Inevitably, clues and obvious signs were ignored, leaving one with a sense that there might be more than one blameworthy party."

The disparity between clinical insanity and legal insanity differs and the definition of legal insanity also differs based on the relevant country, state, jurisdiction, or judge. Filicidal mothers who are deemed to be NGRI are almost invariably treated within institutions due to the severity of their crimes if not found guilty and sentenced to a term of incarceration. Therefore, they are typically not involved in community-based programming to help facilitate family reintegration upon their release (McKee & Shea, 1998). More attention is needed in incorporating their families into mental health education efforts and plans for the offender's safe reintegration into the family and community.

While the media can be used to villainize or convict mentally ill women, it could also be used as a powerful vehicle to educate the public about the role of mental illness and postpartum illnesses in some cases of child murder. This knowledge would be extremely important in preventing future tragedies. Rather than sensationalizing tragedies and further victimizing remaining family members, this medium could be used as a vehicle for an increased understanding, awareness, and prevention. Far too many people believe that mental illness and crime are things that happen to someone else. Most of the families who have endured the tragedy of maternal filicide would have never believed it could have happened to their daughter, sister, aunt, or cousin.

FUTURE RESEARCH

Future research on larger samples of filicidal women would facilitate a more robust and reliable set of predictive criteria to identify those women at higher risk for maternal filicide (Lewis & Bunce, 2003). They also suggest that research on women who do not kill children or have those impulses, but are mentally ill and are exposed to similar psychosocial stressors, would also be important in this endeavor. In order to achieve larger samples, international cooperation could facilitate a large-scale database.

There is a lack of screening instruments that are created specifically for use before and/or after child birth in women with diagnosed or suspected bipolar depression. The most commonly used screening instruments (e.g., Edinburgh Postnatal Depression Scale) have not been validated in women with bipolar disorder. Additional research is needed to distinguish the best course of treatment and other distinguishing characteristics between unipolar and bipolar depression.

McKee and Shea (1998) found from their sample of 20 women who had been charged with killing their children and been referred to a forensic psychiatric hospital for pretrial evaluation that 78 percent of the multichild families had sibling survivors who would likely require treatment for issues like posttraumatic stress disorder or major depression. They noted the complete absence of research on sibling survivors of filicidal parents and clearly this is a cogent area for future research. Further research on the impact of psychosis on weapon use, as well as factors that impact the method of maternal filicide, should be explored in order to find avenues for prevention.

CONCLUSIONS

Although paradoxical, the motivation of mentally ill mothers who kill for altruistic reasons is compassion. As these women become stabilized through aggressive mental health treatment, they are often shocked and bewildered that they could have so dangerously miscalculated their situation or believed so fully their delusions. This chapter explored the definition of child murder specifically, discussing the different categories of filicide. The focus was then narrowed to mentally ill filicide offenders, and the impact of their symptoms on their motives and methods was described. These mentally ill mothers are dealt a crushing blow when they become stabilized and realize the gravity of what they have done. Their experience of remorse, disbelief, and horror is often the most severe punishment inflicted upon them and this burden was described. Next, the risk factors associated with maternal filicide were discussed to help inform strategies for prevention and intervention. The response of the criminal justice system to include charges, pleas, verdicts, sentencing, punishment, and treatment was presented. Specific areas of concern that are prominent in the treatment of these women while awaiting trial in jail, or more commonly after having been found NGRI and while hospitalized in a maximum-security forensic psychiatric setting, were examined. Implications for treatment, education, prevention, intervention, the legal system, sentencing, verdicts, and the disposition of these women were discussed. Finally, suggestions for future research were offered. This chapter provided a comprehensive overview of the many issues and controversies that surround maternal filicide with the goal of education and prevention of these tragedies.

ACKNOWLEDGMENT

I deeply appreciate John St. Clair's ongoing encouragement and support for all of my professional endeavors.

REFERENCES

ALTSHULER, L. L., HENDRICK, V., COHEN, L. S. (1998). Course of mood and anxiety disorders during pregnancy and the postpartum period. *Journal of Clinical Psychiatry, 59,* 29–33.

AMERICAN PSYCHIATRIC ASSOCIATION (APA). (2000). *Diagnostic and statistical manual of mental disorders* (4th ed.), *Text Revision.* Washington, DC: Author.

AUSTIN, M. P. (1992). Puerperal affective psychosis: Is there a case for lithium prophylaxis? *British Journal of Psychiatry, 161,* 692–694.

BAKER, J. (1902). Female criminal lunatics. *Journal of Mental Science, 48,* 13–28.

BORN, L., ZINGA, D., & STEINE, M. (2004). Challenges in identifying and diagnosing postpartum disorders. *Primary Psychiatry, 11*(3), 29–36.

BOURGET, D., & BRADFORD, J. (1987). Affective disorder and homicide: A case of familial filicide theoretical and clinical considerations. *Canadian Journal of Psychiatry, 32,* 222–225.

BOURGET, D., & BRADFORD, J. (1990). Homicidal parents. *Canadian Journal of Psychiatry, 35,* 233–238.

BOURGET, D., & GAGNE, P. (2002). Maternal filicide in Quebec. *Journal of the American Academy of Psychiatry and the Law, 30,* 345–351.

BOURGET, D., GRACE, J., & WHITEHURST, L. (2007). A review of maternal and paternal filicide. *Journal of American Academy of Psychiatry and the Law, 35,* 74–82.

BOURGET, D., & LABELLE, A. (1992). Homicide, infanticide, and filicide. *Psychiatric Clinics of North America, 15*(3), 661–673.

BOWDEN, P. (1990). Homicide. In R. Bluglass & P. Bowden (Eds.), *Principles and practice of forensic psychiatry* (pp. 507–522). London: Churchill Livingstone.

BROCKINGTON, I. F. (1995). *Motherhood and mental health.* Oxford: Oxford University Press.

BROCKINGTON, I. F., MARGISON, F., SCHOFIELD, E., & KNIGHT, R. (1998). The clinical picture of the depressed form of puerperal psychosis. *Journal of Affective Disorders, 15,* 29–37.

CHAUDRON, L. H., & PIES, R. W. (2003). The relationship between postpartum psychosis and bipolar disorder: A review. *Journal of Clinical Psychiatry, 64*(11), 1284–1292.

DAWSON, J. M., & LANGAN, P. A. (1994). Murder and families. *Bureau of Justice Statistics Special Report.* July 1994. Washington, DC: Bureau of Justice Statistics.

DENNO, D. (2003). Who is Andrea Yates? A short story about insanity. *Duke Journal of Gender Law and Policy, 10,* 61–75.

DOBSON, V., & SALES, B. (2000). The science of infanticide and mental illness. *Psychology, Public Policy, & Law, 6*, 1098–1112.

D'ORBAN, P. (1979). Women who kill their children. *British Journal of Psychiatry, 134*, 560–571.

EWING, C. P. (1997). *The dynamics of intrafamilial homicide.* Thousand Oaks, CA: Sage.

FAIRBROTHER, N., & WOODY, S. R. (2008). New mothers' thoughts of harm related to the newborn. *Archives Womens Mental Health, 11*, 221–229.

FAZIO, C., & COMITO, J. L. (1999). Note: Rethinking the tough sentencing of teenage neonaticide in the United States. *Fordham Law Review, 67*, 3109.

FINKEL, N. J., BURKE, & CHAVEZ, L. J. (2000). Commonsense judgments of infanticide: Murder, manslaughter, madness, and miscellaneous. *Psychology, Public Policy, and Law, 6*(4), 1113–1137.

FORD, J. (1996). Note: Susan Smith and other homicidal mothers—in search of the punishment that fits the crime. *Cardoza Women's Law Journal, 3*, 521–549.

FRIEDMAN, S. H., HORWITZ, S. M., & RESNICK, P. J. (2005). Child murder by mothers: a critical analysis of the current state of knowledge and a research agenda. *American Journal of Psychiatry, 162*(9), 1578–1587.

GESALMAN, A. B. (2002). Signs of a family feud: The trial of Andrea Yates tests the insanity defense as relatives try to cope with an "unspeakable" crime. *Newsweek,* January, 21, 2002.

GLOVER, V., & KAMMERER, M. (2004). The biology and pathophysiology of peripartum psychiatric disorders. *Primary Psychiatry, 11*(3), 37–41.

GOLD, L. H. (2001). Clinical and forensic aspects of postpartum disorders. *Journal of the American Academy of Psychiatry and the Law, 29*, 344–347.

HARDER, T. (1967). The psychopathology of infanticide. *Acta Psychiatrica Scandinavica, 43*, 196–245.

HATTERS-FRIEDMAN, S., & RESNICK, P. J. (2007). Child murder by mothers: Patterns and prevention. *World Psychiatry, 6*, 137–141.

HUYSMAN, A. M. (2003). *The postpartum effect: Deadly depression in mothers.* New York: Seven Stories Press.

JASON, J. (1983). Child homicide spectrum. *American Journal of Disease of Childhood, 137*, 578–581.

KAUPPI, A., KUMPULAINEN, K., VANAMO, T., MERIKANTO, J., & KARKOLA, K. (2008). Maternal depression and filicide—case study of ten mothers. *Archives of Women's Mental Health, 11*, 201–206.

KIM, J. H., CHOI, S. S., & HA, K. (2008). A closer look at depression in mothers who kill their children: Is it unipolar or bipolar depression? *Journal of Clinical Psychiatry, 69*(10), 1625–1631.

KRISCHER, M. K., STONE, M. H., SEVECKE, K., & STEINMEYER, E. M. (2007). Motives for maternal filicide: Results from a study with female forensic patients. *International Journal of Law and Psychiatry, 30*, 191–200.

LAPORTE, L., POULIN, B., MARLEAU, J., & ROY, R. (2003). Filicidal women: Jail or psychiatric ward? *Canadian Journal of Psychiatry, 48*(2), 94–98.

LASHER, L. (2003, April). Munchausen by proxy (MBP) maltreatment: An international educational challenge. *Child Abuse Neglect, 27*(4), 409–411.

LEWIS, C. F., & BUNCE, S. C. (2003). Filicidal mothers and the impact of psychosis on maternal filicide. *Journal of the American Academy of Psychiatry and the Law, 31*, 459–470.

LEWIS, C. F., BARANOSKI, M. V., BUCHANAN, J. A., & BENEDEK, E. P. (1998). Factors associated with weapon use in maternal filicide. *Journal of Forensic Sciences, 43*(3), 613–618.

LIEM, M., & KOENRAADT, F. (2008). Filicide: A comparative study of maternal versus paternal child homicide. *Criminal Behaviour and Mental Health, 18*, 166–176.

MANCHESTER, J. (2003). Beyond accommodation: Reconstructing the insanity defense to provide an adequate remedy for postpartum psychotic women. *The Journal of Criminal Law & Criminology, 93*(2–3), 713–752.

MARKS, M. (2001). Parents at risk of filicide. In G. F. Pinard (Ed.), *Clinical assessment of dangerousness: Empirical contributions* (pp. 158–180). New York: Cambridge University Press.

MARKS, M. N., & KUMAR, R. (1993). Infanticide in England and Wales. *Medicine, Science and Law, 33,* 329–339.

MCGRATH, P. (1992). Maternal filicide in Broadmoor Hospital. *Journal of Forensic Psychiatry, 3,* 271–297.

MCKEE, G. R., & SHEA, S. J. (1998). Maternal filicide: A cross-national comparison. *Journal of Clinical Psychology, 54*(5), 679–687.

MONTGOMERY, P., TOMPKINS, C., FORCHUK, C., & FRENCH, S. (2006). Keeping close: mothering with serious mental illness. *Journal of Advanced Nursing, 54*(1), 20–28.

MYERS, S. A. (1970). Maternal filicide. *American Journal of Disorders of Childhood, 120,* 534–536.

OBERMAN, M. (2003). Mothers who kill: Cross-cultural patterns in and perspectives on contemporary maternal filicide. *International Journal of Law and Psychiatry, 26,* 493–514.

O'MALLEY, S. (2004). *"Are you there alone?": The unspeakable crime of Andrea Yates.* New York: Simon & Schuster.

O'SHEA, B. (2003, March). Factitious disorders: The Baron's legacy. *International Journal of Psychiatry in Clinical Practice, 7*(1), 33–39.

PALERMO, G. B. (2002). Murderous parents. *International Journal of Offender Therapy and Comparative Criminology, 46*(2), 123–143.

PAYNE, J. L., MACKINNON, D. F., MONDIMORE, F. M., et al. (2008). Familial aggregation of postpartum mood symptoms in bipolar disorder pedigrees. *Bipolar Disorders, 10,* 38–44.

PAYNE, J. L., ROY, P. S., MURPHY-EBERENZ, K., WEISMANN, M. M., et al. (2007). Reproductive cycle-associated mood symptoms in women with major depression and bipolar disorder. *Journal of Affective Disorders, 99,* 221–229.

PITT, S. E., & BALE, E. M. (1995). Neonaticide, infanticide, and filicide: A review of the literature. *Bulletin of the American Academy of Psychiatry and the Law, 23,* 375–386.

PRUETT, M. K. (2002). Commentary: Pushing a new classification schema for perpetrators of maternal filicide one step further. *Journal of the American Academy of Psychiatry and the Law, 30,* 352–354.

PUTKONEN, H., WEIZMANN-HENELIUS, G., LINDBERG, N., ERONEN, M., & HAKKANEN, H. (2009). Differences between homicide and filicide offenders; results of a nationwide register-based case-control study. *BioMed Central Psychiatry,* 9,27. Available at http://www.biomedcentral.com.

RESNICK, P. J. (1969). Child murder by parents: A psychiatric view of filicide. *American Journal of Psychiatry, 126,* 73–82.

RESNICK, P. J. (1970). Murder of the newborn: A psychiatric review of neonaticide. *American Journal of Psychiatry, 126,* 1414–1420.

RESNICK, P. J. (1972). Infanticide. In J. G. Howells (Ed.), *Modern perspectives in psycho-obstetrics* (pp. 410–431). Edinburgh: Oliver & Boyd.

RODENBURG, M. (1971). Child murder by depressed parents. *Canadian Psychiatric Association Journal, 16,* 41–48.

SADOFF, R. L. (1995). Mothers who kill their children. *Psychiatric Annals, 25,* 601–605.

SCHWARTZ, L. L., & ISSER, N. K. (2001). Neonaticide: An appropriate application for therapeutic jurisprudence? *Behavioral Sciences and the Law, 19,* 703–718.

SCOTT, F. (1973). Parents who kill their children. *British Journal of Psychiatry, 13,* 120–126.

SHARMA, V., BURT, V. K., & RITCHIE, H. L. (2009). Bipolar II postpartum depression: Detection, diagnosis, and treatment. *American Journal of Psychiatry, 166*(11), 1217–1221.

SHERIDAN, M. (2003, April). The deceit continues: An updated literature review of Munchausen syndrome by proxy. *Child Abuse & Neglect, 27*(4), 431–451.

SIMPSON, A., & STANTON, J. (2000). Maternal filicide: A reformulation of factors relevant to risk. *Criminal Behaviour and Mental Health, 10,* 136–147.

SPINELLI, M. G. (2004). Maternal infanticide associated with mental illness: Prevention and the promise of saved lives. *American Journal of Psychiatry, 161*(9), 1548–1557.

SPINELLI, M. G. (2005). Infanticide: contrasting views. *Archives of Women's Mental Health, 8*, 15–24.

STANTON, J., & SIMPSON, A. (2002). Filicide: A review. *International Journal of Law and Psychiatry, 25,* 1–14.

STANTON, J., & SIMPSON, A. (2006). The aftermath: aspects of recovery described by perpetrators of maternal filicide committed in the context of severe mental illness. *Behavioral Science and the Law, 24,* 103–112.

STANTON, J., SIMPSON, A., & WOULDES, T. (2000). A qualitative study of filicide by mentally ill mothers. *Child Abuse & Neglect, 24*(11), 1451–1460.

STERN, E. S. (1948). The Medea complex: The mother's homicidal wishes to her child. *Journal of Mental Science, 94,* 321–331.

STOWE, Z. N., CALHOUN, K., RAMSEY, C., SADEK, N., & NEWPORT, D. J. (2001). Mood disorders during pregnancy and lactation: Defining issues of exposure and treatment. *CNS Spectrums, 6,* 150–166.

TUTEUR, W., & GLOTZER, J. (1959). Murdering mothers. *American Journal of Psychiatry, 116,* 447–452.

U.S. DEPARTMENT OF JUSTICE, BUREAU OF JUSTICE STATISTICS. (2002) Homicide trends in the U.S.: Intimate homicide. Available at: http://www.ojp.usdoj.gov/bjs/homicide/intimates.htm.

WEST, D. J. (1965). *Murder followed by suicide.* London: Heinemann.

WEST, S. G., HATTERS-FRIEDMAN, S., & RESNICK, P. J. (2009). Fathers who kill their children: An analysis of the literature. *Journal of Forensic Science, March, 54*(2), 463–468.

WILCZYNSKI, A. (1995). Child killing by parents: A motivational model. *Child Abuse Review, 4,* 365–370.

WISNER, K. L., GRACIOUS, B. L., PIONTEK, C. M., PEINDL, K., & PEREL, J. M. (2002). Postpartum disorders: Phenomenology, treatment approaches, and relationship to infanticide. In M. G. Spinelli (Ed.), *Psychosocial and legal perspectives on mothers who kill* (pp. 36–60). Washington, DC: American Psychiatric Publishing.

WISNER, K. L., PEREL, J. M., & FINDLING, R. L. (1996). Antidepressant treatment during breastfeeding. *American Journal of Psychiatry, 153,* 1132–1137.

WISNER, K. L., & WHEELER, S. B. (1994). Prevention of recurrent postpartum major depression. *Hospital Community Psychiatry, 45,* 1191–1196.

YEREVANIAN, B. I., KOEK, R. J., MINTZ, J., et al. (2007). Bipolar pharmacotherapy and suicidal behavior part 2: The impact of antidepressants. *Journal of Affective Disorders, 103,* 13–21.

6

Postpartum Syndromes and the Legal System

Cheryl L. Meyer and Tara C. Proano-Raps

Postpartum syndromes are inconsistently acknowledged by the psychological and medical communities, resulting in lack of definitive criteria for diagnosis. This lack of clarity can affect legal processes, particularly in criminal courts. In this chapter the current and historical statuses of postpartum syndromes are examined, particularly as they relate to the admission of postpartum syndromes into evidence in criminal and civil courts. The authors of this chapter assert that gender inequality and cultural expectations of "good" women and mothers impact the use and success of postpartum syndromes in court processes.

On November 22, 1965, in Hawaii, Maggie Young drowned her five children, ages 8 months to 8 years, one by one in the bathtub. She then laid the bodies out on twin beds, four girls on one bed and the only boy on the other bed. Young was reportedly despondent over her perceived inability to care for her children. Earlier that year, she had been hospitalized for two months as a result of a "mental breakdown." Young immediately confessed to the killings and was committed to a state hospital. Approximately six months later, she escaped while on a pass and hung herself (Shapiro, 2001). When this tragedy occurred, Andrea Yates was just over a year old.

Thirty-six years later, on June 20, 2001, Andrea Yates drowned her five children ages 6 months to 7 years, in their home in a Houston, Texas, suburb. Like Young, she reportedly held them under the bath water, one by one, first Luke, 2, then Paul, 3, and John, 5. Noah, age 7, walked in while his mother was drowning 6-month-old Mary. He asked his mother, "What's wrong with Mary?" According to Ms. Yates, she told Noah to get into the bathtub. He ran but she caught him and forced him under the water. She then called 911 and her husband Rusty, a NASA computer engineer, who had left for work approximately an hour earlier. When police arrived, they found the four youngest children wrapped in sheets on a bed and the oldest child still in the bathtub. All were dead.

116

Ms. Yates reportedly told police that she had thought about killing the children for months because she believed that they had been permanently damaged as a result of her bad mothering (Thomas, 2001).

By all accounts, Ms. Yates was a compassionate, generous person and a loving mother. She was valedictorian of her high school class and was described as a "perfect" child. As both a child and an adult, she was eager to please. Previously a nurse, Ms. Yates quit her job to stay home with her children. She took care of her father when he was ill with Alzheimer's and home-schooled the children. However, at the time of the murders, Ms. Yates was suffering from severe postpartum depression, her second episode. She experienced her first episode in 1999, after the birth of her fourth child. She attempted suicide and was subsequently hospitalized. Through the use of psychotropic medications, Ms. Yates recovered, but in November 2000 the Yates had a fifth child and the postpartum depression returned. In March 2001, Ms. Yates's father died and she became even more withdrawn and robotic. The psychotropic medications were not as successful this time. Just prior to the killings, Ms. Yates's medications were changed and she was taken off her antipsychotic medication (suggesting that she may have had postpartum psychosis). A private person, she had been reluctant to seek counseling, although she told a friend that she was considering it (Thomas, 2001).

James Young, Maggie Young's husband, had the following to say about the Yates tragedy: "Medical science needs to recognize this condition earlier and help the mother before it develops into paranoid schizophrenia, as it did in the case of Maggie. . . . This ill woman [Yates] does not need to be sentenced to prison; certainly not charged with first-degree murder. . . . My wife was charged with first-degree murder. But Hawaii justice recognized her illness and gave her the medical help she needed. Unfortunately, she did not survive the cure" (Shapiro, 2001).

Like James Young, some people responded to Andrea Yates with compassion. Others reacted with anger. Many felt shocked and confused and asked themselves: "How could a mother do this to her children?" For them, the diagnosis of postpartum depression did not sufficiently explain the behavior of Andrea Yates. They wanted more details, a clearer understanding of how an apparently loving family could experience such tragedy.

Andrea Yates was tried but she was not successful in pleading insanity. She was sentenced to 40 years to life in a prison facility. The prosecutor sought the death penalty, but at sentencing, the jury recommended prison. Subsequently her conviction was overturned because false testimony was provided during her trial by the psychiatrist for the defense, Dr. Park Dietz. Dietz indicated that Yates had been influenced by an episode of the television show *Law and Order*, where a mother who drowned her children was found not guilty by reason of insanity. However, that episode had never been produced or aired so Yates could not have seen it. The appeals court felt Dietz's testimony could have influenced the jury's decision and ordered a retrial. Yates was found not guilty by reason of insanity and committed to a state mental hospital. Her husband has divorced her and is remarried.

In this chapter, we discuss why postpartum syndromes are regarded with such suspicion by both professionals and laypersons and, in particular, how this can result in unjust legal outcomes for women with a postpartum syndrome. Initially, a brief history and description of postpartum syndromes is presented. Then we focus on the level of recognition and acceptance of postpartum syndromes by scientific communities and the resulting difficulty this can create in admitting postpartum syndromes into evidence in criminal courts. This is contrasted with the relative ease with which postpartum syndromes can be admitted into evidence in civil courts. An additional focus of this chapter is the politics of gender and the social construction of motherhood, which is used to explain why disparities in the legal system can continue to exist.

DESCRIPTION OF POSTPARTUM SYNDROMES

Three separate postpartum syndromes have reached some consensus in professional communities. From the mild to the moderate to the severe end of the continuum, the syndromes are termed postpartum or baby blues, postpartum depression, and postpartum psychosis, respectively (Lee, 1997).

Postpartum or baby blues is the least severe of the syndromes and occurs quite commonly, in 50 to 80 percent of all mothers (Mauthner, 1998). Baby blues is described as a transient condition that typically occurs within the first week postpartum and usually lasts no more than 10 days. Symptoms include tearfulness, irritability, and mood swings (Lee, 1997). This condition could be the result of changing hormonal levels, medical procedures, or a reaction to the physical strains of childbirth (Lee, 1997).

Postpartum depression is often used as a catchall term for all three syndromes. In actuality, postpartum depression is a more severe form of postpartum blues, more reflective of the *DSM-IV-TR* diagnostic criteria for a major depressive episode. Symptoms may include depression, insomnia, crying, irritability, subtle changes of personality, diminished initiative, and difficulty coping, especially with the baby (Baran, 1989; Hamilton, 1989; Jebali, 1993). Anxiety regarding how to cope with the baby is often present in postpartum depression. The depression may be related to medical issues or to sociocultural issues such as the conflict between women's expectations of motherhood and their actual experiences of motherhood. These women are often discouraged by their perceived weaknesses as a mother, with regard to issues such as childbirth, caregiving, and bonding with the child (Mauthner, 1998).

Postpartum depression develops slowly throughout the weeks following delivery (Hamilton, 1989), with the highest frequency of new cases occurring between the third and ninth months postpartum (Steiner, 1990). Most investigators estimate that the syndrome affects 10 to 20 percent of new mothers (Hamilton, 1989; Harding, 1989; Stern & Kruckman, 1983).

The most serious of all the syndromes is postpartum psychosis. In one such case, Angela Thompson went from being an honor society member, her school's first female senior class president, and an athletic and sociable person to a mother who drowned her second child, a 9-month-old son, in a bathtub after hearing voices telling her that her child was the devil (Japenga, 1987). After Thompson gave birth to her first child, she also suffered hallucinations, panic, and obsessions. She even attempted suicide by jumping out of a moving vehicle and then jumping from a bridge 30 feet high, which led to psychiatric hospitalization. Unfortunately, when she became pregnant with her second child, her doctors told her to forget about her previous psychosis, saying that it would not happen again (Brusca, 1990).

In another case, Bethe Feltman, a Sunday school teacher and former grade-school teacher, murdered her two young children. She drugged both children and then strangled

3-year-old Ben and suffocated 3-month-old Moriah. When her husband arrived home that day, both children were dead and Mrs. Feltman was "incoherent." Mrs. Feltman had suffered from postpartum depression since the birth of her second child and had been hospitalized three times. She was released from the hospital on the last occasion just three days prior to the killings. She was scheduled to see a doctor the day after her children's deaths. In July 1998, Mrs. Feltman was declared insane and sent to a state psychiatric hospital. A psychiatrist testified that she was having auditory hallucinations and was almost catatonic at times. Mrs. Feltman was released from a psychiatric hospital in December 2002 (Blevins, 1998; "Colorado Man," 2001; Oulton, 1998).

Postpartum psychosis symptoms usually begin to appear within three weeks after delivery (Baran, 1989). Symptoms of postpartum psychosis include hallucinations, delusions, confusion, irritability, emotional lability, mania, obsessional thinking, feelings of hopelessness, insomnia, headache, agitation, violence, and early signs of depressive illness. Hamilton calls postpartum psychosis mercurial because of the rapidity with which moods and symptoms change (Hamilton, 1989). However, "the principal hazard of puerperal psychosis is violent, impulsive self-destruction. Infanticide is also a hazard, when the syndrome is unrecognized or disregarded and the [mother] is left alone with her child" (Hamilton, p. 94). However, instances of infanticide are rare in proportion to the number of women who suffer symptoms of postpartum psychosis.

PROPOSED CAUSES OF POSTPARTUM SYNDROMES

The cause of postpartum syndromes is unknown. There are, however, several theories as to why a woman develops postpartum syndromes. The medical model focuses on hormonal shifts that occur during and around the birthing process and on a woman's predisposition to mental illness. Certain hormonal levels, such as those of estrogen and progesterone, drop dramatically in the days after birth (Gitlin & Pasnau, 1989). Although all women normally experience these severe changes in body chemistry, women who have previously experienced a mental illness or have a history of mental illness in their family may be at greater risk of developing a postpartum disorder (Harding, 1989).

Medical explanations provide one perspective on the cause of postpartum syndromes. However, when studying postpartum syndromes, women's accounts and subjective perspectives have often been ignored (Mauthner, 1998). Mauthner argues that the devaluing of women's experiences accounts for part of the "mixed" and "inconclusive" results produced by postpartum syndrome studies. Since mothers' viewpoints are often excluded, and since most medical diagnoses, descriptions, and explanations have been developed by men, it is likely that the medical model of postpartum syndromes has largely been constructed by men. This is problematic since important issues for women may be neglected. For example, medications are the treatment of choice according to the medical model. However, medications would not cure postpartum symptoms but rather control the symptoms. This could create dependence issues, with women reluctant to discontinue medications lest the symptoms return. If the woman is breastfeeding, medications could actually increase her anxiety, as she may be concerned about the quality of her breast milk. Most important, the issue of social support is ignored with a purely medical treatment.

The medical model views postpartum syndromes as an illness, or, more specifically, a pathological condition relating to the individual mother's personality or inherent characteristics. Although having a medical label attached to their condition is comforting for some women who believe that it relieves them of blame (i.e., the postpartum condition is something happening to them), other women feel helpless, as though their condition is beyond their control (Mauthner, 1998).

In contrast, other explanations for postpartum syndromes focus on sociological factors (Thurtle, 1995). For example, rather than identifying individual or personality factors related to the development of postpartum syndromes, feminist perspectives believe that postpartum syndromes are related to social and cultural issues. Many feminists believe that postpartum syndromes are related to women's inferior status in society and to "structural conditions and constraints such as the medicalization of childbirth, poor provision of state-funded child care, current labour market structures and policies, inadequate parental leave options, the loss of occupational status and identity, isolation and gendered divisions of household labor" (p. 329). Based on these conditions, feminists argue that it is normal for mothers to become depressed.

Also in contrast to the medical model, feminist sociologists and social psychologists emphasize mothers' accounts and experiences of postpartum syndromes. They have found that certain sociocultural factors such as single motherhood, low socioeconomic status, lack of social support, and other stressful life events appear to increase women's risk for developing a postpartum syndrome (Abrams & Curran, 2009; Harding, 1989; Lee, 1997; Thurtle, 1995). Fox and Worts (1999) conducted interviews with 40 women who had just given birth for the first time and report that women with strong support from their partners were less likely to develop a postpartum syndrome. Further, women in their study identified that the development of postpartum symptoms was related to a lack of social support and feeling overwhelmed by the responsibilities of motherhood. In a meta-analysis of qualitative studies on postpartum depression, Knudson-Martin and Silverstein (2009) found that mothers feeling that they had not lived up to the cultural standard of a "good mother" was central to the experience of postpartum depression. In addition, increasing social support and decreasing isolation promoted recovery. This suggests that, at best, the medical model may only partially explain the experience of postpartum depression.

Sociological factors are given greater examination in a later section of this chapter. It is shortsighted to consider either approach independently, when it may be the unique interaction of medical and sociocultural factors that contribute to or precipitate postpartum syndromes.

HISTORY OF POSTPARTUM SYNDROMES

Despite the heightened attention recently given to postpartum syndromes, they are not a new phenomenon. Hippocrates recorded the first known reports of postpartum syndromes over 2,000 years ago (Baran, 1989). In describing postpartum psychosis, he wrote that it was "a kind of 'madness,' caused by excessive blood flow to the brain" (Lynch-Fraser, 1983). Since that time, physicians have struggled with the etiology of the syndromes. For example, an eleventh-century gynecologist, Trotula of Salerno, provided an interesting explanation for postpartum syndromes, suggesting that postpartum blues resulted from the womb being too moist, causing the brain to fill with water, which was then involuntarily shed as tears (Steiner, 1990). However, it was not until the nineteenth century that physicians described the symptoms of postpartum syndromes in detail and formally began to theorize about a connection between physiological events and the mind (Hamilton, 1989). Marce termed this connection morbid sympathy and provided the first clear description of the syndromes (Hamilton, 1989). However, physicians were unable to agree upon a classification system or even a pattern of symptoms.

Once psychologists began to study postpartum syndromes, they too struggled with classifying them. Similar to physicians, psychologists found that postpartum syndromes defied easy definition and were too elusive, diverse, and inconsistent to classify (Hamilton, 1989). In the early twentieth century, when it was suggested that there was no connection between psychiatric disorders and childbirth, the argument persuaded the medical and psychological communities. Therefore, when physicians began the task of creating a comprehensive list of all medical disorders, now known as the *International Classification of Diseases (ICD),* they excluded the postpartum syndromes. Similarly, when professionals in the mental health field created their own comprehensive list, now called the *Diagnostic and Statistical Manual of Mental Disorders (DSM),* they too excluded the postpartum syndromes. These exclusions were particularly damaging since these manuals are a means by which professionals within the two fields communicate, produce research, and develop treatments.

Subsequent revisions to both the *ICD* and *DSM* ultimately began to mention postpartum syndromes. The *ICD-10,* the latest version of the *ICD,* lists three specific levels of mental and behavioral disorders associated with the puerperium, or childbirth, ranging from mild to severe: postnatal depression, postpartum depression, and puerperal psychosis. However, physicians may use these diagnoses only for patients whose symptoms do not meet criteria for other disorders, such as depression (World Health Organization, 1992).

The *DSM-IV-TR* (2000), the latest version of the *DSM,* has increased the recognition of postpartum syndromes slightly. With regard to postpartum depression, the *DSM-IV-TR* indicates that the onset of a mood disorder can be triggered by a birth, but postpartum depression is not a separate diagnosis. It can be used only to specify what triggered the onset of a mood disorder. This postpartum onset specifier in the *DSM-IV* can be applied if the onset of the depression is within four weeks after the birth of a child. However, postpartum depression may not become severe until several months after the birth of a child.

Postpartum psychosis is listed under the catchall category "Psychotic Disorder Not Otherwise Specified" but not described or explained (APA, 2000). This "category includes psychotic symptomatology (i.e., delusions, hallucinations, disorganized speech, grossly disorganized or catatonic behavior) about which there is inadequate information to make a specific diagnosis or about which there is contradictory information, or disorders with psychotic symptoms that do not meet the criteria for any specific Psychotic Disorder." Neither postpartum depression nor postpartum psychosis is a specific diagnosis, but they are relegated to a more general status. This lack of *DSM-IV-TR* categorization fosters the idea that postpartum syndromes are elusive and difficult to define, despite research that suggests that postpartum syndromes have identifiable patterns of symptoms.

This lack of clarity trickles down to popular literature impacting public knowledge of the postpartum syndromes. In a content analysis of popular press articles (primarily magazines) about postpartum affective disturbance from 1980 to 1998, Martinez, Johnston-Robledo, Ulsh, and Chrisler (2000) found a surprising shortage of articles on postpartum depression or "baby blues." Moreover, the information in those articles was "often confusing and contradictory, and that the dominance of medical etiologies and treatments suggests that the postpartum period, like menstruation, menopause and childbirth, is another example of the medicalization of women's experience" (p. 49). Perhaps most disconcerting were their observations regarding the content of the articles.

> The popular press pathologizes and sensationalizes women's postpartum affective disturbances. The purpose of 32% of the PPD articles appeared to be to warn or scare readers, and three of the articles were written in reaction to recent cases of infanticide for which PPD was named as the defense. . . . Stories of women who have killed their children are attention grabbing and newsworthy, but infanticide is more likely a consequence of postpartum psychosis than of PPD. Articles that build stories around images of postpartum women as murderers may lead readers to believe that only "crazy" women experience postpartum blues and irritability or cause readers to link PPD and the baby blues to infanticide rather than to feelings of loss and anger. Furthermore, the stories about infanticide would not be problematic if the authors of the articles were careful to define and differentiate postpartum psychosis from PPD and the baby blues. Instead, the three are often discussed together in a way that blurs their definitions. This makes it difficult for readers to see the difference between feelings and experiences that are normal and common and those that are abnormal and infrequent. (pp. 51–52)

The case of Andrea Yates certainly reflects the confusion and inconsistency frequently seen in the media. Unfortunately, although the Yates case presented an opportunity to help educate the public about postpartum syndromes, many from the popular press attempted to sensationalize the situation. This sensationalism did not help the public to distinguish between different types of postpartum syndromes or to develop empathy for women who suffer from postpartum syndromes.

Martinez, Johnston-Robledo, Ulsh, and Chrisler's research was recently replicated using popular press articles from 1998 to 2006 (Schanie, Pinto-Foltz, & Logsdon, 2008). Since Andrea Yates killed her children in 2001, it would be expected that there would be an increase in the number of articles published in the popular press and the clarity of those articles. Schanie et al. did not find that there was a substantial increase in the number of articles published. Moreover, they still found that many of the articles that were published contained inaccurate and contradictory information about postpartum syndromes. Like Martinez et al., Schanie et al. also found that some articles targeted the fears of new mothers. These findings are particularly disturbing given that the popular press is often a resource for new mothers and is considered to provide accurate information. It is not surprising then that Sealy, Fraser, Simpson, Evans, and Hartford (2009) found that despite exposure to information about postpartum depression, many community members were not aware of the symptomatology of postpartum depression or the community resources that were available to mothers suffering from it.

Not surprisingly, this lack of clarity is also responsible for conflicting research findings (Thurtle, 1995). Additionally, the tendency of the *DSM* series to understate the importance and distinction of postpartum syndromes has probably been a significant cause of the lack of research because resources and funding are generally not available unless there is a definite diagnosis. Since research provides a foundation for recognition, the paucity of research relating to postpartum syndromes has also probably contributed to their lack of recognition. This vicious cycle is especially problematic because treatment and prognosis for postpartum depression and psychosis may vary from other mood or psychotic disorders, so it is particularly important that research be conducted.

The use of *DSM* diagnoses in trials involving other reproductive health issues of women, such as menopause, illustrates the importance of clarity within the *DSM* (Bookspan & Kline, 1999). Although there was no *DSM* diagnosis of menopause, symptoms of menopause became associated with the *DSM* diagnosis involutional melancholia, or agitated depression in a person of menopausal age. From this, a "menopause defense" was created. The first reported case citing the menopause defense occurred in 1900. In that case, a San Antonio gas company claimed that injuries a woman received when she fell into an uncovered trench were due to menstrual difficulties, not her physical injuries from the fall. The gas company was unsuccessful in their claim.

The menopause defense was used to persuade juries that menopausal plaintiffs were damaged people entitled to little or no recovery. In one case an insurer denied life insurance benefits to a common-law wife since, they argued, a menopausal woman could not be a wife. In another case, a woman injured in an auto accident spent 31 days in a hospital, yet when she sued the driver for negligence, the defendant attempted to deny liability, claiming her injuries were due to menopause. Interestingly, some of the women were not even menopausal. The defense was used primarily in civil cases such as divorce, workers' compensation, and negligence/personal injury cases. Bookspan and Kline (1999) indicate that the menopause defense was "a creation of a civil defense bar that seized upon a cultural stereotype of aging women and prevailing sexist norms. The defense predominantly was asserted by men, in male dominated courtrooms, to devalue female plaintiffs, cast blame upon them, and attempt to deny women compensation or other remedies. . . . The essential premise of this defense was that a woman approaching mid-life was either mentally ill, physically ill or both."

Bookspan and Kline (1999) found over 50 appellate decisions between 1900 and the 1980s, using the menopause defense. This is likely an underestimate of the actual frequency with which the defense was used, since very few cases are appealed. Some defendants were successful in reducing damages, others were not. Use of the defense waxed and waned until it finally disappeared in the 1980s. Bookspan and Kline indicate that the success of the defense was largely dependent on experts who applied the *DSM* diagnosis of involutional melancholia to plaintiffs. Coincidentally, involutional melancholia was dropped from the *DSM* in 1980, about the same time that the menopause defense disappeared from court records. The authors discuss how *DSM* recognition and social influences affected the use and success of the defense. Although there was no diagnosis of menopause, it was admitted into evidence at trials, generally at the expense of women. The lack of *DSM* clarity allowed for broad judicial discretion in the use of the menopause defense. The same lack of *DSM* clarity also allows for broad judicial discretion in the use of postpartum syndromes.

THE LEGAL SYSTEM AND POSTPARTUM SYNDROMES

Postpartum syndromes have been admitted into evidence in both criminal and civil courts. Clearly, the use of postpartum syndromes in criminal cases has become more infamous. This could be due to the nature of the crime, usually infanticide (killing a child during the first year of life), or to the media frenzy that surrounds any criminal cases that involve the mental health of the defendant. The fact patterns of these cases are chillingly similar (see, e.g., Gardner, 1990). Generally, the defendant had no prior history of criminal activity and often went to great lengths, including using reproductive technologies, to become pregnant. In other words, often these were planned pregnancies or wanted children. In many cases, the women became psychotic, often perceiving the child as a source of evil, such as the devil. The murders are particularly gruesome, including running over the child with the car, throwing the child in an icy river, and strangulation. Afterward, the mother either purportedly has no recollection of the event and reports the child missing or kidnapped or, like Andrea Yates, may call the police and report the murders.

It is difficult to estimate the frequency of infanticide in the United States. However, children under one year of age are at great risk of death from homicide, and they are more likely to die at the hands of their mothers than anyone else (Oberman, 1996). Still, very few infanticide cases are tried, as many defendants plea bargain. Of those tried, few raise postpartum syndromes as a defense. Relatively speaking, only a small percentage of women who kill their children seem to involve postpartum syndromes (less than 5 percent; Meyer & Oberman, 2001).

In colonial times, women who killed their infants were often executed (Gardner, 1990). In the eighteenth century, juries became reluctant to impose such a harsh penalty, especially if women had committed infanticide due to social and economic hardship. This resulted in an increasing number of acquittals. In the twentieth century, postpartum syndromes became formally linked to infanticide under British law. The Infanticide Act of 1922 provided for a reduction in charge from murder to manslaughter for mothers who killed their newborns while suffering from the effects of childbirth. This act was amended in 1938 to include children up to 12 months of age and the effect of lactation (Infanticide, 1938). The Infanticide Act served as a model for similar codes in numerous other countries, such as the Canadian Criminal Code provision that was enacted in 1948 (Canadian, 1970). There is no similar statute in the United States.

In the United States postpartum syndromes can enter into the criminal proceedings at a variety of phases, including competency issues, pleading, or sentencing. At the outset, the competency of the woman to stand trial could be at issue. Competency refers to a defendant's ability to assist in her defense, including the ability to understand the charges against her and the rules of the court. Competency to stand trial is not an issue in most instances of postpartum syndromes since the majority of women are not continuing to experience postpartum effects at the trial. Since the statute on murder never runs out, the defendant would have to remain in a treatment facility until competency could be achieved in order for a trial to take place. A treatment facility would be an inappropriate place for most defendants who previously had a postpartum syndrome, as postpartum syndromes are often transitory conditions and the women are no longer suffering from them by the time they go to trial.

More commonly, postpartum syndromes are used in an attempt to exculpate a defendant. At issue is whether the defendant could have had the requisite mental state (mens rea) to commit murder. One way to challenge the mental state requirement would be through use of an insanity defense. Since most of these cases are not federal cases, the jurisdictional or state definitional test for legal insanity would be used. However, state definitions are incredibly inconsistent regarding insanity. In fact, some states do not have insanity statutes. The remaining states have adopted tests (criteria) to determine insanity. There are numerous tests used in the United States but at least half of the states use a variation of the M'Naghten test (Melton, Petrila, Poythress, & Slobogin, 1997).

The M'Naghten test is a cognitive test that primarily addresses the question of whether the defendant knew that her actions were wrong at the time that she committed the crime. This is a relatively strict test of insanity, as even very debilitated persons generally know that their actions are wrong. Under the M'Naghten test, it is difficult to wage a successful insanity defense for mothers suffering postpartum syndromes. For example, in *People v. Massip* (1990), the defendant threw her colicky baby into the path of an oncoming car after voices told her to do so. When the car swerved and missed the infant, the defendant put the infant under the front tire of her own car and ran over him, disposing of his body in the trash. Under M'Naghten, the jury found her guilty of second-degree murder. However, the judge rendered a judgment notwithstanding the verdict and found Massip not guilty by reason of insanity. The prosecution then appealed this judgment, but their appeals were eventually dismissed. Andrea Yates was also tried under a M'Naghten type of insanity defense and was found guilty. She knew what she did was wrong. After all, she called the police to report what she had done.

Other states have different tests for insanity. These can take various forms but generally they focus on whether the defendant could appreciate the wrongfulness of her conduct or could control her conduct rather than on whether she knew the act was wrong. Such tests have a tendency to be more liberal than M'Naghten. For example, Angela Thompson, a nurse, claimed that voices told her to drown her 9-month-old son and she did so. The defendant was found not guilty of voluntary manslaughter and felony child abuse by reason of insanity but would probably have been deemed guilty by the M'Naghten test. A not guilty by reason of insanity (NGRI) verdict means that the defendant is not guilty of the crime but may be sentenced to a treatment facility until she is deemed safe to be released. Thompson was committed to an inpatient facility for 90 days. She was also required to meet other conditions placed on her by the court, such as receive outpatient follow-up with a psychiatrist for six years (Japenga, 1987).

Alternatively, the defendant may be found guilty but mentally ill (GBMI). In general, a GBMI verdict holds the defendant responsible for the murder but the mitigating role of illness is usually recognized in sentencing. The defendant may serve the same sentence length as if she were found guilty but may stay in a treatment facility until she has recovered enough to be transferred to a prison. In *Commonwealth v. Comitz* (1987), Sharon Comitz pled GBMI to dropping her 1-month-old into the icy waters of a stream and then reporting the child's disappearance to police as a kidnapping. Only under hypnosis did she recall the killing. Under M'Naghten she would have been found guilty of murder, especially given the fabricated kidnapping. Comitz received an 8- to 20-year sentence. Less than half of the states have GBMI provisions, and support is dwindling. In any case, this may not be a very functional strategy for women suffering from postpartum syndromes, as they are generally recovered by the time of the trial.

As these verdicts indicate, the criminal cases involving postpartum syndromes as a defense are very similar, but the outcomes are quite disparate (see Brusca, 1990). Brusca indicates that these defendants must overcome skepticism about the diagnosis, which may stem from the public's lack of clear and consistent information (Martinez et al., 2000). In addition, "another obstacle faced by defendants who plead the postpartum psychosis

defense is that the illness lacks the full acceptance of the medical and psychiatric communities. Postpartum psychosis is not accepted as a distinct and separate form of mental illness, and therefore is not listed in the psychiatric community's bible of disorders, the
DSM III-R" (p. 1167). Brusca discussed these obstacles in 1990, before the most recent
revision of the *DSM*, which provides more recognition of postpartum syndromes than the
DSM III-R. Still, the present lack of precise definition perpetuates such obstacles and creates a situation where experts are left to do definitional battle in the courtroom. Brusca indicates that "this problem of the lack of medical acceptance will arise when defense
attorneys try to establish proof of insanity, for which they must bring in a psychiatrist.
Most psychiatrists are either not familiar with the illness, or are split down the middle on
its diagnosis. Prosecutors are, therefore, likely to impeach any psychiatrist offering a postpartum psychosis diagnosis on the grounds that the psychiatrist is going against the weight
of the psychiatric community" (p. 1167). The reality is that if there is debate over coverage of postpartum syndromes in the *DSM*, their validity and admissibility, it will almost
always occur in criminal cases, not in civil cases.

THE USE OF POSTPARTUM SYNDROMES IN CIVIL CASES

The standard of proof and rules of evidence are not the same in criminal and civil cases, as
illustrated in the well-publicized criminal and civil trials of O. J. Simpson. In criminal
cases, the standard of proof is that the prosecution must prove each element of the crime
"beyond a reasonable doubt." In contrast, in civil cases the plaintiff can be successful if
the "preponderance of the evidence" is in her favor. These standards can have a significant
impact on what evidence is admitted into criminal and civil trials. In addition, admissibility of scientific evidence is determined by the Frye rule (*Frye v. United States,* 1923). Frye
held that scientific evidence should not be admitted unless it has gained general acceptance in the field to which it belongs. Therefore, the medical or psychological community
should generally accept a disorder before it can be admitted into evidence. Federal and numerous state courts have now shifted from Frye to the Daubert standard of admissibility
(*Daubert v. Merrell Dow Pharmaceuticals*, 1993). Daubert usually requires a pretrial hearing regarding the degree of professional acceptance and recognition of evidence, such as a
disorder, before it can be admitted into evidence. The judge then determines admissibility.
Given the level of *DSM* recognition and acceptance for postpartum syndromes, coupled
with the strict standard of proof in criminal courts, postpartum syndromes are less likely
to be a part of criminal proceedings than civil proceedings.

In civil courts, the rules of evidence are much less stringent, as is the standard of
proof. Although Frye may apply, the civil court has broader discretion. Recall that the
menopause defense, which was used in civil cases, was admitted into evidence despite
Frye. In custody matters, the trial court can allow in evidence regarding the mental health
of parents. Mental health can be considered and weighed in relation to other factors in
custody decisions. Postpartum syndromes have been raised as a health consideration
in custody cases. It is difficult to estimate how frequently the issue is raised because
undoubtedly many mothers abandon their pursuit of custody after the father indicates that
he intends to make mental health an issue. In addition, it is impossible to determine
how heavily postpartum syndromes weigh in the decision because trial court transcripts

are often inaccessible. If custody awards are appealed, the court's opinion becomes more accessible. However, custody awards are infrequently appealed.

In custody disputes involving postpartum syndromes, the father generally asserts that the mother is an unfit parent, due to her history of postpartum mental illness, even though the mother may not be currently mentally ill and may have no other history of mental illness or unfit parenting. For example, in one of the first recorded cases (*Pfeifer v. Pfeifer,* 1955), the father appealed an order that gave care, custody, and control of the child to the mother, based solely on the potential threat to the child due to her history of postpartum psychosis. When the couple separated, Kent, their child, went to live with Mr. Pfeifer and the paternal grandparents. Ms. Pfeifer was recently recovered from postpartum psychosis, was trying to rebuild her life, and had no home to offer Kent. The paternal grandmother became Kent's primary caretaker. Mr. Pfeifer remarried and relocated, but Kent continued to live with his paternal grandparents. Ms. Pfeifer, who had also remarried, sued and eventually won custody of Kent. Mr. Pfeifer appealed the custody award, citing the mental instability of Ms. Pfeifer. At the time of the custody hearing the mother had been asymptomatic for five years and had no intention of having more children.

On appeal, the father claimed there had been no change in circumstances warranting modification of the original custody award. The court held that "the mother has remained in good mental health for more than two years without relapse; she has remarried, can offer the child a good home, and is willing to give up her profession to take care of him and her household. This change in the circumstance of the mother could in itself justify the change of custody ordered. Moreover, the father has also remarried and has moved out of the home of his parents to another neighborhood. The grandparents, with whom the child remained, have reached an age, which, notwithstanding their love and devotion, must make them less fit to educate a child of the age of Kent, and compared to them, the mother has, if she is not unfit to have custody, certainly a prior claim to the child" (*Pfeifer v. Pfeifer,* 1955, p. 56). Mr. Pfeifer's appeal was denied. However, several aspects of this opinion bear nothing.

This case was appealed solely on the issue of postpartum psychosis. There was no other reason for Ms. Pfeifer not to be awarded custody. First, it was not Mr. Pfeifer who would have retained custody but the paternal grandparents. Had Mr. Pfeifer chosen to fight for custody, it is quite possible that the court would have reached a different opinion. Second, Mr. Pfeifer had led Kent to believe that his stepmother was his biological mother. The court felt that this posed a danger that Kent would never learn the identity of his real biological mother. This may have swayed the court's opinion. Third, Ms. Pfeifer's marriage was important to the court. It is questionable whether the court would have reached the same decision if Ms. Pfeifer had not been remarried. Fourth, the paternal grandparents were becoming too elderly to care for the child. Fifth, Ms. Pfeifer had no intention of bearing another child. Sixth, Ms. Pfeifer had been asymptomatic for five years. It would have been difficult to deny Ms. Pfeifer custody under these circumstances. In contrast, consider the following case.

Susan and Gary Grimm were married for 13 years and parented three children (*In re the Marriage of Grimm,* 1989). Gary's occupation is unclear, but Susan was a licensed practical nurse. After the birth of each child, Susan suffered from postpartum depression and was hospitalized for treatment. During these hospitalizations, Susan phoned home daily to speak with her children and had personal visits with them. Following the last hospitalization in 1985, the Grimms separated. During the separation the children resided with their father, while the mother lived nearby and visited daily. Susan organized, washed dishes, laundered and mended clothes, cooked for the children, and stayed with the children at night whenever Gary was working.

Eventually, the Grimms petitioned for dissolution and each sought sole custody of the children. The custody evaluation submitted to the court indicated that both Grimms were evaluated as excellent parents. Susan's treating psychiatrist testified that the depression was resolved and it had been two years since Susan's last postpartum hospitalization. However, the court placed custody with Gary. Susan appealed. The court affirmed the custody award.

It is clear that Susan Grimm's postpartum depression was an important factor in this custody award. Her treating psychiatrist was called to testify regarding her stability. Similar to *Pfeifer v. Pfeifer* (1955), Susan Grimm had not been hospitalized for a long period prior to the custody hearing. In addition, Susan had been and wanted to continue to be actively involved with the children's lives. Interestingly, Ms. Peifer, who had been diagnosed with postpartum psychosis, fared better in court than Susan Grimm who had been diagnosed with postpartum depression.

A recent but unique custody dispute involving postpartum depression occurred in Wisconsin (*In the Matter of Guardianship*, 2009). Kristine O. gave birth to a son in September 2007 and was shortly thereafter diagnosed with postpartum depression. Although she was able to care for the baby, her husband described her as a "wreck." On the advice of Kristine's obstetrician, Kristine and her husband asked a family member to provide respite for her. Since they did not have family members near where they lived in Oregon, Kristine's mother came from Wisconsin to help out. When she had to return to Wisconsin, Kristine's mother offered to take the baby with her. Eventually, Kristine's mother sued for custody. Both parents sought to retain custody. As with most cases that go to trial, there are complicated facts in this case. However, in its opinion the court stated that Kristine's postpartum depression had "pivotal relevance to the events leading up to this case." The court did not find Kristine was an unfit parent because she had struggled with postpartum depression. Still, postpartum depression was a key factor in the case and was easily admitted into evidence. It is impossible to tell how the court would have ruled if Kristine was fighting for custody without the support of her husband.

Despite the fact that postpartum syndromes have been a key factor in custody cases, courts have refused to allow testimony regarding postpartum depression to be persuasive in other civil matters. For example, in a 1997 adoption appeal, a biological mother who had given her child up for adoption asserted that postpartum depression rendered her incompetent to consent to the adoption. The Tennessee Appellate Court stated: "We do not dispute that [the mother] was probably depressed or emotionally distraught following this rather traumatic experience, but it is not unusual for there to be depression and distress following the birth of a child, even under the best of circumstances. If emotional distress meant that a parent was always incompetent to consent to an adoption, we would rarely have adoptions in this state" (*Croslin v. Croslin*, 1997, p. 10).

Similarly, the court did not find that postpartum depression nullified a woman's competency to consent to a postnuptial agreement. Kim and Anthony Latina had a 1-year-old son when Kim gave birth to a daughter, Jill, who was premature and had to be returned to the hospital daily for a short time after her birth. Kim was caring for both children and preparing to return to work while suffering from postpartum depression. Approximately three weeks after Jill was born, Kim had to be rushed to the hospital for severe hemorrhaging. Although she was not admitted to the hospital, the court acknowledged, "it was obviously a very frightening and traumatic experience" (*Latina v. Latina,* 1995, p. 19). A few days after Kim was rushed to the hospital, approximately one month postpartum, Anthony presented her with a postnuptial agreement to sign. Less than three months postpartum, Anthony presented Kim with a separation, child custody, and support agreement to sign. Kim signed both but later filed a motion to rescind the agreements based on a number of factors, including the impact of postpartum depression on her consent. Regarding the effect of postpartum depression on Kim's capacity to consent, the Delaware Family Court indicated:

> The break-up of a marriage never comes at a good time, and, as noted in many earlier opinions, usually separation agreements are signed in a highly charged atmosphere, thereby necessitating the precautions taken by the Delaware courts to ensure the agreements' fairness. However, if the courts could set aside agreements based upon their being signed during the emotional turmoil of a marriage splitting up, no separation agreement would ever be permitted to stand. Although the court recognizes Wife was extremely distraught and probably feeling somewhat vulnerable when she signed the agreement, the Court finds that Wife signed more because she did not understand the implications of the agreement than because she was coerced. It should be noted that the second agreement was signed by Wife approximately six weeks after the first agreement, by which time Wife's postpartum depression and concern for Jill's health should have lessened. (*Latina v. Latina,* 1995, p. 19)

All of these cases demonstrate lack of a clear understanding of postpartum syndromes and are patronizing and paternalistic. For example, the opinion in *Latina* indicates the court did not understand the etiology of postpartum depression, as it often begins weeks after a birth and can last for a year. Moreover, it is difficult to find other cases in which the court admitted in its opinion that a party was exposed to a recent trauma and yet proceeded to validate capacity to consent. In *Latina,* the court treats postpartum depression as if it is an emotional issue not a medical one. Yet in a recent employment discrimination case (*Reilly v. Revlon,* 2009) the court determined that it was unclear whether postpartum depression was covered under the Americans with Disabilities Act. These inconsistencies simply amount to disparate treatment. How can a disorder be a key factor in one civil case but be easily dismissed in another? This is particularly confusing since court cases in which postpartum syndromes were given extensive consideration involved women who had been asymptomatic for several years. Conversely, the cases in which postpartum syndromes were easily dismissed involved women who made decisions in the midst of experiencing postpartum syndromes. Even more disconcerting is the fact that this disparate treatment generally results in hardships for women.

THE LEGAL DILEMMA

The current status of postpartum syndromes in the medical and psychological communities affects legal decisions. However, they are compounded by legal discrepancies that foster subjectivity in criminal and civil cases. This can even be seen in cases that involve disorders that are recognized by the psychological/medical community, such as posttraumatic stress disorder (PTSD). When asserted in court, the validity of these recognized disorders, including their exculpatory capability, often becomes the subject of dispute between experts. This dispute may be problematic for experts, whose credibility and authority in the courtroom are already under scrutiny (see, e.g., Hagen, 1997). Experts are in an even more difficult situation when disorders are ambiguous, as in the case of postpartum syndromes.

One argument against routine recognition of postpartum syndromes in criminal courts is the even greater vagaries that could be created in the already ambiguous area of mental health defenses. Courts strive for bright lines, or clear criteria, on which to base decisions. Bright lines are rare but are desirable because they reduce disparate treatment that results from subjectivity. Recognizing postpartum syndromes in the legal system could create relatively fine lines and slippery slopes. For example, would a woman accused of child abuse now be able to assert postpartum syndromes as an exculpatory defense? Would the defense be available for other crimes, such as assault or shoplifting?

Although at first glance it appears that recognition of postpartum syndromes could lead to such unwieldy outcomes, it is unlikely. First, this has not been the case in England, where the defense is available but rarely used. Second, and more important, perpetrators with postpartum psychosis have very specific crimes and victims—harm to themselves or to their children. Additionally, the trigger does not have multiple origins as with PTSD, but is clearly due to one cause, pregnancy, and this cause is not likely to reoccur with any frequency in a defendant's lifetime and can be monitored. Third, the dangerousness is temporary. If anything, postpartum syndromes seem to have more specificity than already recognized defenses (such as PTSD) and represent much less threat to the integrity of the legal system.

Overall, recognition of postpartum syndromes in criminal cases would constitute a gender defense (Denno, 1994) and, in general, the court has not been responsive to recognizing or ameliorating gender biases against women in defenses. Criminal defenses, particularly with regard to murder, have generally been more applicable to men than those committed by women. For example, who is more likely to offer a defense of "irresistible impulse," a man or a woman? Who do you think is more likely to be successful using such a defense? More men than women murder, but the fact that women represent a minority of murder defendants should not preclude their equal treatment under the law.

Courts could facilitate preventive action and clarification by the medical community if they acknowledged the importance of postpartum syndromes in their opinions. The courts have been able to address this issue directly in cases involving insurance and disability claims for postpartum syndromes. As far back as 1964, the court was asked to determine whether postpartum syndromes represented a sickness or mental illness (*Price v. State Capital Insurance Company,* 1964). If postpartum syndromes represent a sickness, the level of coverage under insurance and disability is generally expanded. Conversely, if they represent a mental illness, the coverage is generally restricted. The courts have held that the cause of postpartum syndromes has not been proven to be physical and the treatment is generally psychological; therefore, postpartum syndromes are excluded from coverage (see, e.g., *Blake v. Unionmutual Stock Life Insurance Company,* 1990). This is reinforced in court decisions regarding pregnancy. In pregnancy discrimination, "the cases define pregnancy in terms of a biological process that begins with conception and ends with delivery" (Greenberg, 1998, p. 227). The impact on consideration of postpartum syndromes is clear, since "by using a narrow, medicalized definition of pregnancy, they [the court] have excluded the time that women take to care for young children from the statute's protection" (p. 226).

The idea that legal institutions influence the medical processes, and vice versa, is discussed at length in a thought-provoking law review by Noah (1999). He suggests "just as social forces have shaped medical practice, legal institutions influence both nosology and diagnosis. Law and medicine are not autonomous domains, fully insulated from one another in spite of numerous points of intersection concerning the definition and identification of disease. Instead, at these junctures, law and medicine are mutually constitutive or perhaps co-dependent" (p. 257). Noah outlines the dangers to both professions inherent in such co-dependence. For women, the danger is reflected repeatedly in court decisions regarding reproductive issues from contraception to postpartum and beyond.

THE MEDICAL AND PSYCHOLOGICAL DILEMMA

The lack of a clear definition of postpartum syndromes and inconsistencies in the medical and psychological literature probably becomes self-perpetuating by leading to the inaccurate education of health professionals. Small, Epid, Johnston, and Orr (1997) found that fourth- and sixth-year medical students had inaccurate or incomplete knowledge of postpartum syndromes. Medical students had a narrower view of the factors that contribute to postpartum depression than did women who had experienced the disorder. For example, students selected hormonal or biological factors and a "tendency to depression" as most influential in the development of postpartum depression. The women, however, identified social and experiential factors, such as lack of support, as contributing the most significantly to postpartum depression. The biological focus endorsed by the students suggests a likelihood to overlook the wide range of social, physical health, and life-event factors in diagnosis and treatment (Small et al., 1997). Indeed, Mauthner (1998) indicates that "the majority of research in the area of postpartum depression has disregarded mothers as a source of knowledge or understanding about their experiences" (p. 143).

If health professionals are unaware that factors such as lack of social support are common for women with postpartum depression, they will not realize that these factors place women at greater risk for postpartum syndromes. Moreover, they will probably prescribe treatments that are not consistent with the woman's needs: for example, medications instead of counseling. As a result, women are disadvantaged on multiple levels: health professionals recognize only biological contributors to postpartum syndromes, reducing treatment effectiveness, while the court denies these biological components, preventing women from receiving disability or insurance coverage for postpartum syndromes.

SOCIOCULTURAL CONTEXT

Fortunately, in recent years there has been an increase in the recognition of sociocultural factors that influence the development of postpartum syndromes by some professionals, such as sociologists and psychologists and by feminists. As stated previously, feminist researchers and practitioners believe that postpartum syndromes are a natural response to a patriarchal society that devalues motherhood (Lee, 1997; Mauthner, 1998).

Examining the sociocultural context of postpartum syndromes involves considering the tremendous pressures that mothers face. For instance, gender roles in the United States dictate that women understand and love everything about motherhood (Cox, 1988; Mauthner, 1993). This value can be overwhelming to new mothers, who may be feeling unsure of their caregiving abilities. Women may feel inept and inadequate if they do not instinctively know how to care for their children (Thurtle, 1995).

Further, motherhood can be a stressful time for women because it entails the adoption of new roles and perhaps the loss of others. Despite the happiness that motherhood often brings, many new mothers experience grief due to their loss of freedom (Hopkins, Marcus, & Campbell, 1984). Activities of interest and important projects may need to be put on hold or may have less time allotted to them. Lee (1997) states that women's satisfaction with their new role of mother, and the quality of their relationship with their partner, both decline with the arrival of a child. She reports that the research results have unequivocally found that this decline in satisfaction is due to the "unexpected and inequitable division of household labour" (p. 101). In fact, Lee provides strong evidence to support the sociocultural underpinnings of postpartum syndromes.

Motherhood can also be a difficult time, as many women feel societal pressure to make motherhood their primary role (Miles, 1988). This may have been true in the case of Andrea Yates who not only quit her nursing job to stay home with her children but also home-schooled the oldest children (Thomas, 2001). Although Ms. Yates's feelings about her role as a stay-at-home mother are unknown, for many mothers, choosing whether to work outside the home is a no-win situation. Although U.S. society gives lip service to mothers who stay at home with their children, motherhood continues to be underappreciated. We often hear the question "Do you work or do you stay at home?" as if staying at home is not work. Therefore, working outside the home may be the only opportunity to receive respect and recognition. However, mothers are then faced with stress related to juggling multiple roles and finding adequate childcare and may experience guilt about not staying at home with their children (Thurtle, 1995).

Mothers who decide to stop working outside the home may experience a decrease in self-esteem related to loss of roles and the lack of importance given to a mother's work. Additionally, these women may experience a further decrease in self-esteem, due to isolation and work that is repetitive and frustrating (Gove, 1972). As wonderful and exciting as children are, one can only imagine the time-consuming and monotonous work required of Andrea Yates to raise five children under age 7. Multiply this by the weight of the isolation that can easily occur for stay-at-home mothers, particularly those who home-school their children.

The pressure to be a perfect mother makes many women reluctant to disclose symptoms of postpartum depression. This, in turn, makes early detection difficult and may result in the increased severity of their symptoms, especially since lack of social support has been shown to contribute to depression (Inwood, 1985; Jebali, 1993; Lee, 1997). Mauthner (1999) interviewed 40 women with postpartum syndromes and found that many of them attributed at least a part of their condition to a conflict between their expectations (i.e., the mother they wanted to be) and their perceptions of themselves as mothers. Mauthner reports that the women's unrealistic expectations for themselves appeared to stem from the cultural context in which they lived as well as their interpersonal relationships. The women generally felt that admitting their needs and feelings was an indication of weakness or failure as a mother. This hesitancy to disclose symptoms of a postpartum syndrome is particularly evident in the case of Andrea Yates, who did not want to talk with a therapist and reportedly said that she felt "OK," even when family members began to notice serious symptoms (Thomas, 2001).

One of the strongest pieces of evidence in support of the influence of sociocultural factors is the decreased incidence of postpartum syndromes in non-Western cultures (Hayes, Roberts, & Davare, 2000). There are cultural differences in the structure and organization of the family and in role expectations for the new mother and significant others. For instance, in some non-Western cultures, women are considered quite vulnerable after pregnancy and are allowed a period of rest. Relatives support this rest period by fulfilling the new mother's normal duties. Additionally, while in the United States attention is typically paid to the newborn child, in some non-Western cultures much attention and importance is also lavished on the new mother. As with other major changes in the life cycle (i.e., puberty, death), pregnancy and childbirth are considered rites of passage and are marked by special ceremonies (Stern & Kruckman, 1983). The postpartum period of rest and support and clear recognition of the important status of motherhood may make women less likely to develop a postpartum disorder.

Stern and Kruckman (1983) believe that the development of postpartum syndromes in the United States results from the lack of several practices that are present in non-Western cultures: (1) social structuring of a distinct postpartum time period; (2) protective activities and rituals resulting from the presumed vulnerability of new mothers; (3) social seclusion; (4) a mandated period of rest; (5) instrumental assistance to the new mother; and (6) social recognition of the new social status of the mother (i.e., rituals, gifts). Even between cultures within the United States the impact of sociocultural factors is evident. Abrams and Curran (2009) found that mothers who have a low income level were more likely to experience postpartum depression but less likely to seek help for it than mothers who had a middle income level. Moreover, McGarry, Kim, Sheng, Egger, and Baksh (2009) found mothers who were not White were less likely to seek help than mothers who were White. Still, although sociocultural factors may play an important role in the progression of postpartum syndromes, the onset is generally a medical event, birth.

THE IMPACT OF INCREASED RECOGNITION OF POSTPARTUM SYNDROMES

Recognition of a condition that affects women solely or primarily creates the risk of pathologizing women with that condition. This phenomenon is seen with conditions such as premenstrual syndrome (PMS). Although the aim of increased recognition of PMS has been to provide more effective prevention and treatment for women, some argue that increased recognition has pathologized a normal life event so that it is seen as a defect in a woman's character (Rome, 1986). This viewpoint may then be used to patronize or discriminate against women in situations involving education or career, since women can be seen as incapable of handling these challenging situations. Additionally, some argue that increasing the role of the medical, psychological, and legal communities with regard to PMS has taken power away from women as diagnosis and treatment of this condition has come under the control of these professions.

Beaman (1998) discusses criticisms of "women's defenses," such as battered woman's syndrome, premenstrual syndrome, and postpartum depression, which recognize, within the legal system, women's unique biology and socialization. For instance, arguments against using battered woman's syndrome as a defense include the "tendency for the experiences of the abused women to be overshadowed by expert testimony; the negative ramifications of syndromization; and the boundaries imposed by creating the 'ideal' abused women" (Beaman, 1998, p. 88). Increasing the recognition of postpartum syndromes could potentially have the same medical, psychological, and legal consequences as increased recognition of other conditions affecting women.

Thus there are significant risks associated with increased recognition of postpartum syndromes. However, deciding to keep the status quo in an effort to avoid pathologizing women has its own risks: namely, the status quo involves no opportunities for the improvement of treatment or legal options for women. Further, the status quo already involves the pathologizing and paternalization of women.

Males control the medical, psychological, and legal systems in this country. Males have the power to invent and deny disorders, and they do so based on societal standards of male health. For instance, research has shown that the concept of a healthy male differs from the concept of a healthy female. In one classic study, mental health professionals were asked to select traits characteristic of either a healthy male, healthy female, or healthy adult person. Results showed that the participants' concepts of a healthy mature adult were similar to the concepts of a healthy male, but different from concepts of a healthy female (Broverman, Broverman, Clarkson, Rosenkrantz, & Vogel, 1981). Although this study was conducted two decades ago, in many respects men continue to be the standard against which women are compared.

As the Broverman et al. (1981) study demonstrates, women are already pathologized and have little control over the treatment of their bodies. The idea that recognition of postpartum syndromes will provide an excuse for the sexist practices happening in this society seems unfounded since sexism is already occurring. With regard to postpartum syndromes, sexism is seen in the medical and psychological communities. Health professionals indoctrinated in patriarchal practice choose conditions to which they want to devote resources. Thus, certain medical or psychological states receive more funding than others for research, education, or treatment. Because postpartum syndromes are conditions affecting women, there are no male norms with which to compare them. Not surprisingly, there appears to be less interest in the male-dominated health fields for these conditions. Sexism is also found in the legal arena, where postpartum syndromes are not dealt with in any uniform fashion.

We must increase recognition of postpartum syndromes if women are to receive the medical, psychological, and legal help that they need. Beaman (1998) states that women have different biologies, psychologies, and socialization than men and thus need different or new legal strategies. Some feminist scholars hesitate to use women's legal defenses because "different" has traditionally been seen as "inferior and in need of protection" (p. 89). They worry that these defenses would be seen as evidence of women's biological inferiority to men. However, Beaman (1998) argues that women's legal defenses should be designed carefully rather than discarded because if these women's conditions are minimized, researchers will continue to ignore them and women will continue to have inadequate treatment.

Some pathologizing might actually be necessary for women to receive treatment and recognition for medical and psychological conditions. Without pathologizing, health providers minimize women's syndromes, causing women to feel "crazy" for believing that something is wrong with them and leading to further problems as women's conditions go untreated. Indeed, Mauthner (1998) explored postpartum depression from the mothers' point of view and found that many women preferred that the severity of their depression be recognized, regardless of the pathology associated with this recognition. When others took their symptoms seriously rather than minimizing or trivializing them, the women said that their experience felt less "terrifying and abnormal" (Mauthner, 1998, p. 331).

Therefore, pathologizing may help normalize the experience of women suffering from postpartum syndromes. Additionally, pathologizing some types of postpartum syndromes and not others may decrease the overall level of pathology assigned collectively to these conditions. For example, pathologizing postpartum psychosis, which is a rare and serious disorder, may increase the distinction between this condition and less severe types of postpartum syndromes, which would then be able to be normalized.

Some may argue that even pathologizing one type of postpartum syndrome does an injustice to women. In response to this argument, it is important to remember that women with postpartum syndromes are already being pathologized. One has only to consider the negative comments made toward Andrea Yates (i.e., "monster," "bad mother") to recognize this. Increased recognition may pathologize postpartum psychosis by pointing out the danger of the condition but also increases awareness of the context in which these conditions develop—biological, psychological, and societal stressors, rather than "evilness" or "bad mothering." It would also allow greater opportunity for education and awareness.

CONCLUSIONS

Encouraging women to become active with decisions affecting their bodies and their lives does not negate the influence and responsibility that men as well as medical, psychological, and legal professionals have with regard to postpartum syndromes. Women do not exist in a vacuum; therefore, a condition that affects women affects their families, friends, work, and, eventually, the larger society. The impact of one woman's behavior on society and the importance of societal response to her future is illustrated by Andrea Yates. People and institutions influence the fate of women with postpartum syndromes; thus each is instrumental in helping to ameliorate the disparate treatment experienced by these women.

Simple interventions could alter tragic outcomes. After Andrea Yates killed her children, James Young, Maggie Young's husband, indicated that he hoped that increased awareness of postpartum depression would result in better screening of expectant and new mothers (Shapiro, 2001). He stated: "Why not train obstetricians to screen mothers-to-be for their potential to suffer [postpartum mood disorders]? How about a simple interview?" Young suggested that pregnant women could be asked how they felt following earlier births. Perhaps even more important, their partners should be interviewed. After all, when someone is suffering from postpartum syndromes or some mental illnesses, it is often best to solicit additional viewpoints regarding the person's health. As Young suggested, earlier intervention could lead to more effective treatment.

In fact, efforts at intervention have been successful. Zlotnick, Johnson, Miller, Pearlstein, and Howard (2001) provided four sessions of interpersonal-therapy-oriented group intervention to pregnant women receiving public assistance who had at least one risk factor for postpartum depression. Three months postpartum, 33 percent of a control group of women had developed postpartum depression, whereas none of the women receiving treatment had developed postpartum depression. The treatment consisted of four 60-minute group sessions that focused on education regarding postpartum syndromes, issues, and concerns. Despite the fact that even relatively brief cost-effective interventions, such as the four-session therapy group in the Zlotnick et al. study, have been shown to be effective, they are rarely used. Wisner, Logsdon, and Shanahan (2008) indicated training on the recognition and treatment of postpartum depression is generally not a part of education in medical school or even continuing education after medical school. They designed a website for health care providers and the general public to increase awareness and education of postpartum depression (http://www.mededppd.org/). The site has attracted a large number of professionals and consumers and has received positive evaluations. Other grassroots efforts toward education also provide valuable information (see http://postpartumprogress.typepad.com/weblog/ or http://www.postpartum.net/).

EPILOGUE

Andrea Yates's crime has begun to fade from memory. Although some people still remember her actions few remember her name or the outcome of her case. For a brief moment, postpartum syndromes were the focus of attention. On August 27, 2001, a coalition of activist groups, including the National Organization for Women and anti–death penalty groups, formed a coalition and voiced support for Andrea Yates. Beatrice Fowler of the American Civil Liberties Union was quoted as saying: "This case has touched a nerve. Every single woman I have spoken to has had the same reaction I had: What could she have possibly been going through for her to take that kind of action? It's not real" (Parker, 2001). The Andrea Yates case focused attention on postpartum syndromes and their use in the legal system. However, the momentum has faded and the country has other issues of concern such as conflicts and the economy.

In 2001, shortly after the Andrea Yates tragedy, a bill was introduced into congress to expand research on and services for postpartum syndromes. The bill was named after Melanie Blocker Stokes who suffered from postpartum psychosis and jumped to her death from the twelfth story of a Chicago hotel (H.R. 20-Melanie Blocker Stokes Postpartum Depression Research and Care Act). The bill eventually passed the House in 2009 and was introduced into the Senate and referred to the Committee on Health, Education, Labor, and Pensions. However, the act is not without critics who suggest it may make screening mandatory for mothers and increase prescriptions that are unsafe for mothers. The fate of the bill may hinge on the fate of overall health care reform.

For those fortunate enough not to have had their lives touched by postpartum syndromes, perhaps the best model for their attitudes and sentiments should be those who have lived with postpartum syndromes: either themselves or a loved one. Rusty Yates, who presumably knew his wife better than anyone, has described the changes she experienced as a result of her postpartum depression and has stated unequivocally that his wife, as he knew her, "is not the woman who killed my children . . . she wasn't in her right frame of mind" (Thomas, 2001). Mr. Yates is not alone in his feelings. James Young is supportive of both his late wife and Andrea Yates, stating: "I feel compelled to do what I can to help this woman who is a victim of postpartum depression and the terrible feelings of inadequacy she must have felt—the same feelings my late wife must have felt. Behavioral signs we all recognized in hindsight" (Shapiro, 2001). Additionally, Jeff Thompson, Angela Thompson's husband, supported his wife after the murder and stated: "Doctors are literally ignoring mothers to death on this thing" (Japenga, 1987). Further, Glenn Comitz, husband of Sharon Comitz, said that if they had understood his wife could have a second episode of postpartum psychosis: "We would have thought twice about having a second child, or have taken precautionary measures to control the situation" (Japenga, 1987). In fact, most of the husbands whose wives killed their child or children as the result of a postpartum syndrome were extremely supportive. If these men, who have lost more than most of us can even imagine, are able to look past their shock and sadness and recognize the need to help rather than blame women with postpartum syndromes, perhaps it is time for the rest of us to do the same.

REFERENCES

ABRAMS, L. S., & CURRAN, L. (2009). "And you're telling me not to stress?" A grounded theory study of postpartum depression symptoms among low income mothers. *Psychology of Women Quarterly, 33*, 351–362.

AMERICAN PSYCHIATRIC ASSOCIATION. (2000). *Diagnostic and statistical manual of mental disorders-IV-TR*. Washington, DC: Author.

BARAN, M. (1989). Postpartum illness: A psychiatric illness, a legal defense to murder, or both? *Hamlin Journal of Public Law and Policy, 10*, 121–139.

BEAMAN, L. G. (1998). Women's defenses: Contextualizing dilemmas of difference and power. *Women and Criminal Justice, 9*(3), 87–115.

BLEVINS, J. (1998, April 12). Mom not queried in deaths of kids. *Denver Post*, p. B-02.

BOOKSPAN, P. T., & KLINE, M. (1999). On mirrors and gavels: A chronicle of how menopause was used as a legal defense against women. *Indiana Law Review, 32*, 1267.

BROVERMAN, I. K., BROVERMAN, D. M., CLARKSON, F. E., ROSENKRANTZ, P. S., & VOGEL, S. R. (1981). Sex-role stereotypes and clinical judgments of mental health. In E. Howell & M. Bayes (Eds.), *Women and mental health* (pp. 86–97). New York: Basic Books.

BRUSCA, A. (1990). Postpartum psychosis: A way out for murderous moms? *Hofstra Law Review, 18*, 1133–1170.

CANADIAN CRIMINAL CODE. (1970). 2 R.S.C. 216.

COLORADO MAN KNOWS PAIN OF CHILDREN'S DEATH. (2001, June 21). Associated Press.

COX, J. (1988). The life event of childbirth: Sociocultural aspects of postnatal depression. In R. Kumar & I. F. Brockington (Eds.), *Motherhood and mental illness: Vol. 2. Causes and consequences* (pp. 64–77). London: Butterworth.

DENNO, D. W. (1994). Gender issues and criminal law: Gender crime and the criminal law defenses. *Journal of Criminal Law and Criminology, 85*, 80–173.

FOX, B., & WORTS, D. (1999). Revisiting the critique of medicalized childbirth: A contribution to the sociology of birth. *Gender and Society, 13*, 326–346.

GARDNER, C. A. (1990). Postpartum depression defense: Are mothers getting away with murder? *New England Law Review, 24*, 953–989.

GITLIN, M. J., & PASNAU, R. O. (1989). Psychiatric syndromes linked to reproductive functions in women: A review of current knowledge. *American Journal of Psychiatry, 146*, 1413–1422.

GOVE, W. R. (1972). The relationship between sex roles, marital status, and mental illness. *Social Forces, 51*, 34–44.

GREENBERG, J. G. (1998). The pregnancy discrimination act: Legitimating discrimination against pregnant women in the workplace. *Maine Law Review, 50,* 225.

HAGEN, M. A. (1997). *Whores of the court: The fraud of psychiatric testimony and the rape of American justice.* New York: Regan Books.

HAMILTON, J. A. (1989). Postpartum psychiatric syndromes. *Psychiatric Clinics of North America, 12,* 89–103.

HARDING, J. J. (1989). Postpartum psychiatric disorders: A review. *Comprehensive Psychiatry, 30,* 109–112.

HAYES, M. J., ROBERTS, S., & DAVARE, A. (2000). Transactional conflict between psychobiology and culture in the etiology of postpartum depression. *Medical Hypotheses, 55*(3), 266–276.

HOPKINS, J., MARCUS, M., & CAMPBELL, S. (1984). Postpartum depression: A critical review. *Psychological Bulletin, 95,* 498–515.

INFANTICIDE ACT OF 1938. (1938). 1 & 2 Geo. 6, Ch. 26, § 1.

INWOOD, D. G. (1985). The spectrum of postpartum psychiatric disorders. In D. G. Inwood (Ed.), *Recent advances in postpartum psychiatric disorders.* Washington, DC: American Psychiatric Press.

JAPENGA, A. (1987, February 1). Ordeal of postpartum psychosis: Illness can have tragic consequences for new mothers. *Los Angeles Times,* p. 1.

JEBALI, C. (1993). A feminist perspective on postnatal depression. *Health Visitor, 66*(2), 59–60.

KNUDSON-MARTIN, C., & SILVERSTEIN, R. (2009). Suffering in silence: A qualitative meta-data-analysis of postpartum depression. *Journal of Marital and Family Therapy, 35*(2), 145–158.

LEE, C. (1997). Social context, depression and the transition to motherhood. *British Journal of Health Psychology, 2,* 93–108.

LYNCH-FRASER, D. (1983). *The complete postpartum guide: Everything you need to know about taking care of yourself after you've had a baby.* New York: Harper & Row.

MARTINEZ, R., JOHNSTON-ROBLEDO, I., ULSH, H. M., & CHRISLER, J. C. (2000). Singing "the baby blues": A content analysis of popular press articles about postpartum affective disturbance. *Women and Health, 31*(2–3), 37–55.

MAUTHNER, N. (1993). Towards a feminist understanding of "postnatal depression." *Feminism and Psychology, 3,* 350–355.

MAUTHNER, N. S. (1998). "It's a woman's cry for help": A relational perspective on postnatal depression. *Feminism and Psychology, 8*(3), 325–355.

MAUTHNER, N. S. (1999). "Feeling low and feeling really bad about feeling low": Women's experiences of motherhood and postpartum depression. *Canadian Psychology, 40*(2), 143–161.

MCGARRY, J., KIM, H., SHENG, X., EGGER, M., & BAKSH, L. (2009). Postpartum depression and help-seeking behavior. *Journal of Midwifery and Women's Health, 54*(1), 50–56.

MELTON, G. B., PETRILA, J., POYTHRESS, N. G., & SLOBOGIN, C. (1997). *Psychological evaluations for the courts: A handbook for mental health professionals and lawyers.* New York: Guilford Press.

MEYER, C. L., & OBERMAN, M. (2001). *Mother who kill their children: Understanding the acts of moms from Susan Smith to the "prom mom."* New York: New York University Press.

MILES, A. (1988). *The neurotic woman.* New York: New York University Press.

NOAH, L. (1999). Pigeonholing illness: Medical diagnosis as a legal construct. *Hastings Law Journal, 50,* 241.

OBERMAN, M. (1996). Mothers who kill: Coming to terms with modern American infanticide. *American Criminal Law Review, 34,* 1–110.

OULTON, S. (1998, September 2). A tragedy is retold on Web site Internet page dedicated to wife, dead children. *Denver Post,* p. B-01.

PARKER, L. (2001, August 28). Coalition supports Houston woman. *USA Today,* p. 1A.

ROME, E. (1986). Premenstrual syndrome (PMS) examined through a feminist lens. In V. L. Olesen & N. F. Woods (Eds.), *Culture, society, and menstruation* (pp. 145–151). Washington, DC: Hemisphere Publishing.

SCHANIE, C. L., PINTO-FOLTZ, M. D., LOGSTON, M. C. (2008). Analysis of popular press articles concerning postpartum depression: 1998–2006. *Issues in Mental Health Nursing, 29,* 1200–1216.

SEALY, P. A., FRASER, J., SIMPSON, J. P., EVANS, M., & HARTFORD, A. (2009). Community awareness of postpartum depression. *Journal of Obstetric, Gynecologic and Neonatal Nursing, 38,* 121–133.

SHAPIRO, T. (2001, June 26). Father whose wife killed their five kids in Aiea in 1965 urges compassion. *Honolulu Star-Bulletin.*

SMALL, R., EPID, G. D., JOHNSTON, V., & ORR, A. (1997). Depression after childbirth: The views of medical students and women compared. *Birth, 24,* 109–115.

STEINER, M. (1990). Postpartum psychiatric disorders. *Canadian Journal of Psychiatry, 35,* 89–95.

STERN, G., & KRUCKMAN, L. (1983). Multi-disciplinary perspectives on post-partum depression: An anthropological critique. *Social Science and Medicine, 17*(15), 1027–1041.

THOMAS, E. (2001, July 2). Motherhood and murder. *Newsweek, 138*(1), 20–25.

THURTLE, V. (1995). Post-natal depression: The relevance of sociological approaches. *Journal of Advanced Nursing, 22,* 416–424.

WISNER, K. L., LOGSDON, M. C., & SHANAHAN, B. R. (2008). Web -based education for postpartum depression: Conceptual development and impact. *Archives of Women's Mental Health, 11*(5–6), 377–385.

WORLD HEALTH ORGANIZATION. (1992). *The ICD-10 classification of mental and behavioral disorders: Clinical descriptions and diagnostic guidelines.* Geneva: Author.

ZLOTNICK, C., JOHNSON, S. L., MILLER, I. W., PEARLSTEIN, T., & HOWARD, M. (2001). Postpartum depression in women receiving public assistance: Pilot study of an interpersonal-therapy-oriented group intervention. *American Journal of Psychiatry, 158*(4), 638–640.

ENDNOTE

1. The statute Greenberg refers to is the Pregnancy Discrimination Act.

CASES AND BILLS

Blake v. Unionmutual Stock Life Insurance Company, 906 F.2d 1525 (1990).

Commonwealth v. Comitz, 530 A.2d 473 (Pa. Super. 1987).

Croslin v. Croslin, 1997 Tenn. App. LEXIS 84.

Daubert v. Merrell Dow Pharmaceuticals, 509 U.S. 579 (1993).

Frye v. United States, 392 F. 1013 (D.C. Cir. 1923).

In re the Marriage of Grimm, 1989 Minn. App. LEXIS 143.

In the Matter of the Guardianship of Clive R.O.: Cynthia H., Petitioner-Appellant, v. Joshua O. and Kristine O., Respondents, 2009 Wi. App. 176; 2009 Wisc. App. LEXIS 856.

Latina v. Latina, 1995 Del. Fam. Ct. LEXIS 48.

Melanie-Blocker Stokes Postpartum Depression Research and Care Act, H.R. 20.

People v. Massip, 271 Cal. Rptr. 868 (Cal. App. 1990).

Pfeifer v. Pfeifer, 280 P.2d 54 (Cal. App. 1955).

Price v. State Capital Insurance Company, 134 S.E. 2d 171 (Super. Ct. 1964).

Reilly v. Revlon, 620 F.Supp.2d 524 (D.C. 2009).

7

Listening to Women's Voices

Considering Why Mothers Kill Their Children

Cheryl L. Meyer and Cindy E. Weisbart

There is a morbid curiosity related to mothers who kill their children. One need only observe the fascination of the cases of such women as Andrea Yates, Susan Smith, and Melissa Drexler (aka. the "prom Mom") to view the level of public interest. Not only does the topic fascinate us, but it produces strong reactions that range from sympathy, to disgust, to horror. These reactions often become the basis of vehement opinions regarding the women involved and what should happen to them.

However, it is not as if mothers killing their children is a new phenomenon. In fact, "there is every reason to believe that infanticide is as old as human society itself, and that no culture has been immune. Throughout history, the crime of infanticide has reflected specific cultural norms and imperatives. Historians of infanticide cite a host of factors associated with the incidence of this crime: poverty, over-population, laws governing inheritance, customs relating to non-marital children, religious and/or superstitious beliefs regarding disability, eugenics, and maternal madness" (Meyer & Oberman, 2001; p. 1).

Given the pervasiveness and longevity of the crime of filicide, the killing of one's own child, there is scant research. Mothers who kill their children are often referred to as a single entity with little differentiation among the women. However, even in a cursory review of cases it is clear there are at least two types that can quickly be distinguished from each other, mothers who kill their newborns and mothers who commit other forms of filicide. For example, Melissa Drexler, a teenage mother who disposed of her newborn baby in a restroom at her high school prom, is very different from Susan Smith, who drowned her 14-month-old and 2-year-old children by submerging her car in a lake. In obvious ways, their actions, demographics, and reactions were very different. Prevention and intervention strategies should also differ.

Meyer and Oberman (2001) developed a typology to aid in understanding why mothers kill their children. They have five categories of mothers who kill their children: filicide related to an ignored pregnancy, abuse-related filicide, filicide due to neglect, assisted or coerced filicide, and purposeful filicide and the mother acted alone. Their typology addresses the unique interaction of social, environmental, cultural and individual variables within each of these categories of filicidal mothers, in order to provide some insight into the factors that come together and result in these acts. Although other typologies have been formulated, prior to 2001, only one included any U.S. cases (for an extensive discussion of other typologies, see Meyer & Oberman, pp. 20–31. For another example of a recent typology, see McKee, 2006). Meyer and Oberman's typology is based solely on U.S. cases and is current. In this chapter, we discuss Meyer and Oberman's types and provide an illustrative case study for each one. The case studies we include were generated through our interviews with mothers who were convicted of killing their children.

In order to create their typology, Meyer and Oberman searched NEXIS, a news database, which provides full text articles and publications from newsmagazines, regional and national newspapers, newsletters, trade magazines and abstracts, for cases of filicide from January 1990 through December 1999. Three independent reviewers from their research team read every case. The cases were assigned to one of the categories based on the reviews. When the cases had been separated into categories, the researcher for that category then followed up all their cases in regional databases. For example, if a case occurred in Florida, the researcher for that case would access the NEXIS regional databases and local news resources (e.g., *The Miami Herald*) for the years following the initial report in order to determine the disposition of the case and access further details. We also searched LEXIS for legal documents related to the case such as appeals. Cases that could not be followed up extensively through further searching were deleted from the sample. These included cases where the mother was never located or the name of the mother was not released because she was a juvenile. More details regarding case selection and exclusion are included in Meyer and Oberman (p. 33). Meyer and Oberman's data set included 219 cases.

In order to determine patterns, Meyer and Oberman recorded available information for each case including the age of the mother, age and gender of child, method of death, marital status, number of children in the family and in the home, geographical location, date of crime, charge/conviction, mother's behavioral response after death, history of domestic violence, mental health and substance abuse history, socioeconomic status, children's protective service involvement, frequency of weapon use, any motive mentioned, and birth order of child. Furthermore, the researcher for each category also tracked characteristics that were specific to the category.

As previously noted, the case studies included in this chapter were generated from individual interviews conducted with mothers convicted of killing their children as part of the second author's dissertation (Weisbart, 2002) and Oberman and Meyer's subsequent interviews (2008). The interviewer was always accompanied by a trained note-taker since audio or video recording is ill-advised within the prison setting (given the previous negative association that taping has for these women with the courts, media, etc.). Care was taken to train each note-taker to provide as much word-for-word transcription of each interview as possible, thus preserving the verbalized meaning that each woman gave to her story. The interviews were guided by several semi-structured questions that were driven by the overall research question: What is it like to be a woman who has killed her children? Each woman who was interviewed could answer any or all of the following eight questions:

1. Tell me about what your life has been like, growing up as a youngster, up until now?
2. What was going on in your life at the time your child died (precipitating events, increased stress)?
3. Did anyone know you were going through a difficult time? Who were the people you confided in and what help did they offer?
4. In your own words, tell me about what happened.
5. How do you think this could have been prevented?
6. How do you feel you have been treated by the system (the police, the courts, etc.)?
7. What changes would you make to the "system" in general?
8. If you had three wishes for the future, what would they be?

Each interview lasted approximately two hours. Forty interviews were conducted. Five years after the initial interviews, Oberman and Meyer returned and re-interviewed nine women (2009). The case studies provided in this chapter *paraphrase* portions of the interviews. The essence of the interview remains the same but the mother's words and/or details of the crime have been changed to protect confidentiality. Some cases represent an amalgam of two cases.

THE TYPOLOGY

Meyer and Oberman (2001) provide five main types.

Filicide Related to an Ignored Pregnancy

At the time of her crime, Mary was a young woman in her early 20s with three young children. Mary was living with relatives and became pregnant with her fourth child. This pregnancy was the result of a rape by a "friend" of the family. Mary gave birth to her baby alone in the bathroom of her house. She describes feeling terrible pain and believed that she was physically ill. Instead, she was undergoing labor and when she realized this, she became very scared and describes blacking out and then later burying her daughter in the backyard. Mary is not sure how the baby died. According to the coroner's report, Mary's newborn died from suffocation. Mary was convicted of first-degree murder and received a sentence of 15 years to life.

Mary was obviously very young when she had her first three children. As Mary looks back at the time of the death of her fourth child, she notes that she had support from her family. However, Mary concealed her pregnancy by wearing over-sized clothes and by denying she was pregnant to anyone who asked. Despite desperately wanting to share the burden of her secret with close family members, she did not disclose her pregnancy or seek medical attention.

Mary states:

"After my daughter died, it's like a piece of my life died. Several times I have thought to myself . . . you should have died instead of your daughter. I hid the pregnancy from everyone . . . that was the hardest part—ignoring my pregnancy. It was so hard to deny and hide knowing that

there is a life inside you. I had no medical care. . . . I didn't even see a doctor. I kept thinking, 'it can't be true . . . this isn't happening to you.' Several times I wanted to talk with my family but I was too scared . . . several times I wanted to sit down and tell them but I thought 'they'll think less of you or that it was your fault.' It was not that way at all. Now they tell me 'you should have come to us and we would have helped you any way we could. . . .'

It's hard being in here [prison] knowing that I am convicted of killing my child—the hardest thing is knowing that I am convicted of killing my child. People turn up their nose at you and treat you differently. Some don't care and treat you human but a lot don't. I don't even talk to people about my case. I just want to be treated like a human. We are all here and we all made mistakes."

Meyer and Oberman (2001) found mothers in this category committed neonaticide after either denying or concealing their pregnancy. Resnick (1969) created the term neonaticide to refer to killing a child within the first 24 hours of life.

Meyer and Oberman analyzed 37 cases of neonaticide. Mary's story is very typical of the patterns they found in other cases. The mothers in their sample ranged in age from 15 to 39, but the average age was 19.3 years. Clearly these women were young. It appears most of these women did not receive prenatal care, which is consistent with the fact that they were denying or concealing their pregnancy. All but one of the women was single. Sometimes the fathers were not aware of the pregnancy, other times they were but rejected the mother and her pregnancy or, as in Mary's case, the pregnancy was the result of a rape. Approximately one-third of these women had other children prior to committing the neonaticide.

Whether it was self-imposed or real, most of these women felt they would receive little or no support related to the pregnancy, and in fact might be ostracized or physically punished. In general, they were overwhelmed by feelings of shame, guilt, and/or fear. Due to this fact, some actively concealed their pregnancy, like Mary, while others denied it even to themselves. This was not difficult to do given some of these women continued to menstruate and gained minimal weight. When they began to experience the abdominal cramps and indigestion that often comes with labor, many thought they needed to defecate and some, like Mary, completely dissociated with what happened during the birth. They were later horrified to learn what had become of their infants. Approximately 80 percent of the women were at home when labor began with 38 percent of those women giving birth in the bathroom. In 70 percent of the cases, the child died from lack of oxygen, generally from being smothered.

The reaction of the criminal justice system to mothers who commit neonaticide is quite varied. Like Mary, a very few women are charged with first-degree murder. Compounding this is the question of whether the women should be tried as adults if they are minors. Ultimately, the charges vary as does the outcome of the case. Some women receive relatively light sentences, such as public service, while others receive life imprisonment.

There is some societal recognition that neonaticide is becoming a widespread problem. Individual citizens and communities have begun to create initiatives such as anonymous drop-off ordinances or "safe havens." These ordinances allow mothers to drop-off their newborns at designated locations with no legal repercussions. However, dropping off a newborn at a safe location such as a church or hospital is not a new option. Moreover, these initiatives fail to take into account that neonaticide is rarely a premeditated act so it is unlikely a young woman will consider these options since she is, and has been, concealing or denying her pregnancy. In addition, for a young woman to use the drop-off initiative she would often have to physically sneak out of the house with her newborn in order to drop the child off at a center. This would be difficult to do without alerting her family when she has worked so hard to hide the pregnancy from them. Finally, these laws have become subject to ridicule as some parents have "abused" them. For example, in 2008 in Nebraska, a widower legally abandoned 9 of his 10 children at a medical center indicating he was financially and emotionally unable to deal with them.

It may be more successful to place emphasis on intervention and prevention. This could be accomplished by educating the women themselves, and those who often spend the most time with teens, their peers. It would be relatively inexpensive to place information and resources related to neonaticide into high school sex education curriculums. In addition, teachers and school counselors could also be provided with seminars to aid them in assisting girls who may be struggling with an unplanned pregnancy.

Greater emphasis on education could assist physicians as well. Although most of the women did not seek prenatal care, when they did, physicians failed to detect the pregnancy or asked the teen about her sexual activity with her mother present. If a teen is concealing a pregnancy, it is unlikely she will admit her sexual activity in front of her mother. These neonaticides may have been prevented if the physician was better educated on the topic; increased awareness by the physician might lead to more direct examination and an understanding of the importance of an interview without the young woman's caregiver present.

Abuse-Related Filicide

Felicia is a young woman who was incarcerated in her early 20's for involuntary manslaughter and child endangerment. She was sentenced to up to 25 years for hitting her four year-old child so hard she died. Felicia readily admitted that she had a history of abusing her daughter and that she herself was the victim of extensive and severe physical and psychological abuse and neglect by her stepfather. She also observed incessant violence against her mother by her stepfather which, she noted, led to her mother abusing drugs heavily. In addition to abuse she experienced and witnessed at home, Felicia was later assaulted by her baby's father, who beat and raped her. This rape resulted in the conception of her daughter.

Felicia has spent much of her time behind bars thinking about why she hurt her daughter and has finally concluded that she learned her behaviors from her parents' modeling.

Felecia states:

"My mother and stepfather are both recovering addicts. The abuse came at the hand of my stepfather. I recall my stepfather hitting me . . . and he also hit my mother. He threatened me with a knife several times if I didn't do exactly what he said. I tried to commit suicide three times when I was a kid. I was tired of being hit on—you know what I mean?

When I finally saw a counselor, she told me about the cycle of abuse and the 'generational curse.' I feel like the system failed me until I was sent to her. She really helped me to understand myself. In my case, my daughter was just doing something she knew she wasn't supposed to do. . . . I never had any patience and I slapped her real hard in the face. She fell, hitting the corner of the wall and she died two days later in the hospital.

My whole thing is to get to the core of it and try to prevent it. I feel like in my situation had that been done, I wouldn't be here."

Mothers who abuse their children or who kill their children through abuse have received scant research attention. In part, this may be due to definitional issues. For example, a fine line often distinguishes abuse from neglect. In addition, there are clear ethnic and cultural variations in what constitutes acceptable discipline practices and what is abusive. Generally only extreme cases come to the attention of the public.

Meyer and Oberman's (2001) abuse-related filicide category is comprised of mothers whose purposeful physical assault unintentionally led to the child's death. Like Felicia, most of these women had previously assaulted their child or children. However, none of these mothers purposely killed their child and even the courts recognized this fact since many were charged with involuntary manslaughter instead of voluntary manslaughter or murder.

Meyer and Oberman researched 15 cases in this category but there was very little information available on three of those cases. The children killed ranged in age from six weeks to six years. The women had an average of four children but ten of the women had four or more children. All of the children but one, who was drowned, died as a result of beatings. Almost half of the fatal assaults involved a blow to the head. Although the mothers seemed to abuse all their children, several cases mentioned that the victim seemed to be a target of violence more often than the other children.

Child welfare had previously been involved with 12 of the women and was likely involved with two more although that was not clear. In two-thirds of the cases the mother had previously lost custody and killed the child after reunification. Although it was unclear how long the mother and child had been reunited, in at least five cases it had been less than six months. No one in our sample of mothers was an adolescent, although many were adolescents when they first bore a child. The average age was 27 with a range of 21–39 years. Substance use was clearly a factor in eight of the cases and at least a third of the victims had been born addicted to substances, but information was not available on the other cases. At least two of the women were pregnant at the time of the killing. Information about the mother's childhood could only be found on two women and they had both been exposed to childhood violence. What was also glaringly absent from most of the cases was any discussion of the fathers and their level of involvement with the children. Most of the fathers did not appear to reside with the mother.

A few factors have been identified which may indicate a mother is at risk for abusing her child. Clearly the factor that has received the most attention, as it relates to both parents, is the Intergenerational Transmission Hypothesis (Milner, Robertson, & Rogers, 1990). Quite simply, this theory suggests that being abused as a child, or observing abuse as a child, is related to abusing as a parent. Felicia referred to this theory when she talked about the "generational curse" and the cycle of abuse. The transactional model (Cicchetti, 1989) suggests that the actual occurrence of abuse depends on a host of mitigating and aggravating circumstances. Aggravating factors include poverty, adolescent parenting, drug use, lack of emotional support, poor social skills, domestic violence, and depression. Mitigating factors would reflect the opposite of these.

When examining these findings, several issues emerge as potential areas of reform to assist in prevention and intervention. Given that most of Meyer and Oberman's sample had previous contact with the child welfare system that would be one place to begin.

In general, there are both procedural and policy criticisms leveled at many child welfare systems. The procedural criticisms include the following: (1) the caseloads are too high and there is lack of supervision; (2) the record-keeping systems are outdated and records are lost or destroyed; (3) case workers are not adequately trained; (4) services are not provided or not provided long enough; and (5) case workers are not adequately paid resulting in high turnover. All of these stem from inadequate funding. After a particularly tragic death in New York, funding was increased which resulted in numerous reforms in the child welfare system. As New York increased funding, their child welfare system became more efficient and less criticized. However, it is difficult to convince legislators to address economic needs until such tragedies occur. Although most people would likely agree those who abuse their children need services, they may not want to fund such services.

In addition to procedural concerns, policies have also been recently challenged. For example, child welfare systems have been accused of placing too much emphasis on family reunification/preservation and that parents' rights should be terminated more quickly (for a full discussion of this issue, see Meyer & Oberman, 2001). However, calling for a quick termination of parental rights is short sighted. The majority of children (up to 90 percent) are not removed from parental homes because of abuse but neglect. The neglect is usually the result of poverty. Terminating parental rights more quickly would adversely affect these families without addressing the real problem, poverty. Since a disproportionate number of families involved with the child welfare system are families of color, terminating parental rights more quickly would result in destabilizing homes that are already impacted by racism on other levels. In addition, some families of color likely became involved in the child welfare system because of discriminatory practices. This could be due to racial biases of child welfare workers and/or the difficulties and ambiguities inherent in defining abuse and neglect. This is further exacerbated by a general lack of ethnocultural understanding and training on the part of child welfare workers.

Further compounding these concerns with the child welfare system are abuses within the foster care system. In November 2000, the lead article on the cover of *Time* magazine was entitled "The Shame of Foster Care." The article began with numerous stories of child abuse in the foster care system, generally by *foster* parents or families. The authors argued the foster care system is in a crisis nationwide with lawyers threatening class action suits in 20 states. They reported the number of children in foster care doubled from 1995–2000 from approximately one quarter of a million to half a million. Agencies are plagued with poor and outdated record-keeping, inadequate case monitoring, bad decisions, high turnover, poorly trained staff, low accountability, and unwieldy bureaucracies, which are often created when agencies contract with private facilities to aid them in providing services.

Perhaps the best prevention and intervention for mothers who abuse their children will come from grassroots community involvement. These would include neighborhood-based services such as citizen watches or volunteer advocates. Certainly schools could hire a counselor or redefine the responsibilities of a counselor to act as more of a liaison with child protective services. The goal of all of these programs is to allocate more responsibilities to inner systems including schools, families, and communities, making the village more responsible for raising the child. However, in the end it is not the innovativeness of the program as much as the commitment of the community and individuals within the community that insures programs are implemented and monitored thus facilitating success.

Filicide Due to Neglect

Linda was the victim of physical and sexual abuse at the hands of her uncle from age 2 to age 11. At the age of 13, she was raped. As an adolescent, she received some counseling because she was acting out in school but Linda doesn't feel this was very helpful for her. At the age of 18, she became pregnant as a result of a relationship with a man she eventually married. They had another child together. However, Linda describes the relationship as troubled. They eventually divorced and

Linda moved into her own apartment in the same neighborhood. Her ex-husband began stalking her and making threatening phone calls to her. She was forced to move to a different town in order to get away from him. The apartment into which she moved was where the incident occurred in which both of her children were killed.

Linda had been living at the new apartment for over a year and had begun dating a young man who lived in a nearby house. On the evening of the incident, Linda put her two children to sleep and decided to go visit her new boyfriend, ostensibly for just a short time. She left her apartment, leaving a space heater on in the master bedroom where her children were asleep. While she was gone, the space heater somehow caught the bedding on fire and both children died. Linda was charged with 2 counts of involuntary manslaughter and received a prison term of 10 years.

Linda talks about her circumstances in the following excerpts:

"A lot of people here call me "baby-killer" and it bothers me. People say I'm a violent killer. It's not that I purposefully did anything to them. . . . I am not a violent person. When they call me baby-killer, it is really painful. I don't think I killed my children . . . its hard to deal with being in here and its hard to understand how my family can stick by me . . . because I have a lot of guilt and I started hating myself and I am thinking, 'how can they not hate me'?"

Meyer and Oberman (2001) found that, like Linda, mothers in this category did not purposely kill their child but either failed to attend to the child's basic needs or were irresponsible in their reaction to the child's behavior. Therefore, they subdivided their cases into neglect-omission and neglect-commission cases, respectively. Neglect-omission cases included instances where the mother did not attend to health, nutrition or safety needs of the child, often by not providing adequate supervision. There were six predominant ways children died: fire, automobile suffocation, bathtub drowning, layover suffocation, poor or lack of nutrition, and inattention to safety needs. Some fires were the result of children playing with matches, while others were the result of structural issues such as faulty wiring. However, as in the case of Linda, the children were generally alone in the house when fire broke out. Automobile suffocation resulted when the children were left in a car that eventually grew too hot. The bathtub drownings resulted from inadequate supervision while the child was in the tub. Layover suffocation occurred when the mother or other children suffocated the child by rolling over on her during sleep. A child whose nutritional needs were not being met generally died of dehydration or starvation. Finally, inattention to safety needs involved cases where a child died because a mother did not fully consider her safety. For example, one child choked to death on cigarette butts when a mother did not remove them from the ashtray.

In neglect-commission cases, an irresponsible action of the mother caused the death, such as shaking the baby too hard or placing something over the child's head to stop the child from crying. As with the omission cases, the mother did not purposely kill the child.

Meyer and Oberman studied a total of 76 cases of neglect. The average age of mothers at the time when the filicide occurred was 25.46. On average, they became mothers when they were 22.05 years; however, the majority became mothers between the ages of 17 and 20. The fact that these mothers were relatively young may underscore other concerns. For example, a young mother may not have had the opportunity to complete her education. This has many implications for her ability to earn money and her ability to secure other resources. In addition, the overwhelming majority (85 percent) of mothers in this category were single parents, which likely further compounded their economic situation and available resources. There was no second income in the home or second pair of hands to help with the multitude of tasks. Moreover, among the cases reviewed, 41 percent of the families had three or more children. Not surprisingly, 90 percent of the cases in this category involved mothers living in poverty. Mothers could only afford the basic needs. There were no extra funds to pay for safer housing or for a babysitter to provide a respite. Since these mothers generally had weak social support systems, they rarely had any breaks from their children. Finally, in at least 41 percent of the cases the mothers had mental health issues, including mood disorders, such as depression, or chemical dependency.

In short, mothers who commit fatal child neglect are often in need of extensive assistance in numerous areas encompassing both global and specific domains. It is imperative that professionals provide a continuum of care for neglectful mothers. One way to accomplish this is by establishing comprehensive health centers, specifically targeting the zero to three population, as most neglected children fall into this age range. Neglectful mothers must typically travel from agency to agency and town to town as they seek services such as public assistance benefits, prenatal care, medical and dental care, mental health intervention, and parenting skills training. The creation of full service community health care centers would allow for a facility where the needs of both parents and children can be fulfilled. Support for this type of model has already been seen in one innovative program that is dedicated to healthcare delivery to children in the first three years of life. Toward this end, close partnerships are created between mothers and healthcare professionals not only to address the physical needs of the child, but also to address emotional and intellectual growth as well as healthy child development. In addition to physicians and nurses, the model utilizes specialists who have specific training in child development and focus their services on behavioral and developmental issues for children. The specialists have many roles within the program including conducting home visits to support and enhance interactions between the parent and infant, conducting ongoing checkups that assess both child development and family factors, helping mothers manage common behavioral concerns such as fussiness, sleep or discipline problems, facilitating parent education groups, and staffing a telephone information line to answer questions about child development. Essentially, this holistic approach views the promotion of children's development and assistance to parents as primary goals when treating a child's physical illnesses. Certainly, a key feature to each center should be the incorporation of parent education into every single visit.

Although such a program may assist with the stresses neglectful mothers face, an underlying problem is poverty. It is beyond the scope of this chapter to address poverty in the United States. However, we can better understand mothers who kill their children through neglect if we begin to recognize the impact of the lack of power and privilege on disenfranchised groups within American society, such as those living in poverty.

Assisted/Coerced Filicide

Renee had her first child at the age of 13 and by the age of 20 she had four children (two boys and two girls). Renee was convicted of killing her youngest boy in conjunction with her boyfriend. Renee's boyfriend was known for his impatience with Renee's children (none were his biological child) and he had a history of acting out his impatience with them and Renee with an explosive and often violent temper. Renee's youngest child died when he did not obey the boyfriend precisely and the boyfriend struck the child, sending him flying across the room. After the child died, Renee helped dispose of the body because her boyfriend told her if she did not help he would kill all her remaining children. The autopsy revealed the little boy died from an acute trauma to the head. Renee and her boyfriend were each charged and convicted of murder and abuse of a corpse. Renee is currently serving a sentence of 15 years to life.

Renee was molested as a very young child. She describes her childhood as "absolute chaos"
with "constant fighting and brawling" among family members. She has a history of drug and
alcohol abuse and has attempted suicide several times. She describes her circumstances as follows:

"I turned into a revengeful drinker; I was real passive and I couldn't say no when family came
over with friends and they wanted to drink and party. At the time I was caring for the kids and then
I got frustrated and said to hell with it and I started using alcohol.

My kids were very rowdy but I made them that way because I didn't want them pushed around.
Child protective services was called on me and my boyfriend all the time. They would come and
investigate and would see that my kids were fed and clean—no bruises. I just said to hell with the
rest of the world . . . we made it together as a family."

Meyer and Oberman (2001) researched 12 cases in the assisted/coerced category. In
assisted/coerced filicide, mothers purposely kill their child while acting in conjunction
with a partner, generally a romantic partner, who contributes in some manner to the death.
This is a unique category in that most women who kill their children act alone and the
majority of filicide research focuses on women who act alone. Meyer and Oberman subdivided their cases in this category into two subcategories: active and passive. In the active
subcategory, the women were directly involved in their children's death. In the passive category, the women were charged with their children's deaths due to their inability to protect their children.

The characteristics of women in this category are unlike many of the women in other
categories. Most notably, during the time period in which they kill their children, these
women are involved with a partner. The partner also has the tendency to be abusive and
violent. The nature of the violence within these relationships is crucial to understanding
the circumstances of the children's death. The violence perpetrated by the women's partners is generally not comprised of isolated, aggressive events but includes multiple types
of abuse (i.e., physical, psychological, sexual, destruction of property) occurring in a cycle
that often increases in frequency and intensity. The abuse is intended to control and to
invoke fear in the victims.

Women in the partner-involved filicide category, like Renee, are generally involved
with partners who are not the biological parent of the child killed. In addition, the majority
of women in this sample were experiencing a number of social stressors, including poverty
and the presence of multiple children in the home. In the active subcategory, the deaths typically resulted from discipline-related abuse that escalated into death. All of the children in
this sub-sample had been physically abused. The abuse often occurred during times that are
typically stressful for parents, such as toilet training. There are similarities between passive
and active partner-assisted filicide; however, women in the passive category did not kill
their children. Rather, as in Renee's case, they were unable to prevent their partner from
harming the child and/or may not have accurately reported the death to authorities.

One has only to look at the conviction and sentencing data for women from the
partner-involved category to see the criminal justice system's disparate treatment of
women and lack of understanding about the nature of domestic violence. This is most
striking in cases from the passive partner-assisted category, because these involve women
who did not abuse their children. Rather, these women were held responsible for their
child's death because they were expected to be able to prevent their partner from killing
their child. Two of the four women in Meyer and Oberman's sample were not even present
when their child was killed, yet were still blamed for not preventing the death.

Clearly, this category illustrates that merely blaming and punishing women cannot solve the complex problem of partner-involved filicide. Rather, professionals and community members must work together to build resources to address the larger problem of domestic violence, in addition to working to reduce the isolation of mothers and children who are vulnerable to such violence.

Purposeful Filicide and the Mother Acted Alone

Catherine, a Caucasian woman, was approximately 25 years old at the time she committed her crime. Catherine laid out the facts of the case, taking responsibility for her every action. Catherine killed all 4 of her children, one after another over the period of one day. She received 4 charges of murder and 4 consecutive life terms.

Like several of the other women described in this chapter, Catherine had a chaotic and unpredictable young life. She characterizes her early adolescence as "quiet and rebellious." She became sexually active around age 13. At the age of about 14, she ran away with her boyfriend; she later married this man when she became pregnant by him. This man was extremely physically, sexually, and psychologically abusive of Catherine. At one point he attempted to have her involuntarily committed to a psychiatric hospital. They had several separations, the final of which occurred when she was pregnant with their last child. Although their relationship had ended, custody had not yet been decided and a bitter custody battle began. At a time when Catherine was trying to get back on her feet, attending school, living with her parents, and holding down a job, she was raped by an unknown assailant. This assault seems to have triggered a sense of hopelessness and Catherine resolved to kill her children and herself. She attempted suicide but was not successful and she is currently serving out her sentence.

She described her relationship with her children as follows:

"They always came first. They were more of an appendage. I loved them very much. Killing them was not out of hate. It was a suicide. I could never envision them without me. I could not accept that my ex-husband could raise them better than me. I wanted to die and I wanted the kids with me in death. Everything I valued was my kids and if I had them with me in death then there was nothing holding me back and the thought that I could kill them—I was totally worthless and once I started thinking that and felt that way about myself I couldn't stop myself."

Overall, the purposeful filicide cases, as with Catherine's case, are perhaps the most difficult to comprehend. *Although we may not condone it*, it seems somehow easier to understand how a neonaticide could occur or a mother could kill through neglect or abuse. However, it is seemingly incomprehensible how a mother could, acting alone, kill her child on purpose. Although arguably the neonaticides are committed on purpose, there are a host of other factors that set them apart from the purposeful category. For example, in the present category the mothers are older, often kill more than one child, and the children are generally not neonates. To explain these mothers, generally two lay theories are proposed; the mother must be "mad or bad."

Women portrayed as "mad" have been characterized as "good mothers" who have conformed to traditional gender roles and whose crimes seem to be the result of mental illness. In contrast, women characterized as "bad" do not seem to suffer from mental illness nor do they conform to gender stereotypes and are labeled as cold, callous, evil mothers who have often been neglectful of their children or their domestic responsibilities. This dichotomy is easily seen in one woman, Andrea Yates. In 2001, Yates drowned her five children. Yates had a history of mental illness and was discharged from a psychiatric hospital just prior to the murders (see Chapter 4 for an extensive discussion of the Yates case). The prosecutor sought the death penalty suggesting that Yates was "bad" or purposely killed her children and it was not the result of a mental illness. Of course, the defense claimed the opposite that she was "mad" and the deaths were the result of mental illness. Unfortunately, this dichotomy is woefully inadequate and begs the question, just what is a mental illness?

In the legal arena, when the mental status of a defendant comes into question, it generally relates to either the issue of competence to stand trial, or to the defendant's mental state at the time of the offense. In general, the standard for competence to stand trial is whether the defendant understands the charges against her, and the proceedings, so as to be able to aid her attorney in her defense. Andrea Yates was found competent to stand trial. Although competency issues arise in the purposeful filicide cases, more often, mental status issues are at stake.

Mental status at the time of the offense relates to the plea that a defendant makes regarding her mental capacities when she committed the offense. The most commonly used plea relating to mental status at the time of the offense is, of course, the insanity defense. Each state fashions its own definition or test for insanity. However, a common test for insanity is some variant of the M'Naghten test. The M'Naghten test states, in part,

> To establish a defense on the ground of insanity, it must be clearly proved that, at the time of the committing of the act, the party accused was laboring under such a defect of reason, from disease of the mind, as not to know the nature and quality of the act he was doing; or, if he did know it, that he did not know what he was doing was wrong. (10 Cl. & F. 200, 8 Eng. Rep 718 [H.L. 1843])

Arguably, even the most psychotic of individuals knows what she is doing is wrong. Andrea Yates called her husband and 911 to report her crimes. The pivotal terms then involve interpreting what it means to know the "nature and quality" of one's actions. Wisconsin used a variant of the M'Naghten test and found Jeffrey Dahmer, a man who killed numerous victims and then consumed some of their body parts, to be sane.

In order to aid jurors in better understanding the mental capacities of the defendant, and the insanity test used by the state, both prosecution and defense attorneys usually hire mental health experts. This brings definitions of mental illness used by mental health professionals into the legal arena. Unlike the dichotomous legal system where an individual is sane or insane, the mental health system uses the *Diagnostic and Statistical Manual of Mental Disorders - Fourth Edition, Text Revision (DSM-IV-TR;* 2000), which outlines an array of illnesses with specific diagnostic criteria for each one, many of which could apply to mothers who purposely kill their children.

Would Andrea Yates have had a mental illness according to the *DSM-IV-TR?* We did not interview Andrea Yates but read numerous accounts of her behavior. Clearly, she was and had been depressed and suicidal. She was likely grappling with depression the day she killed her children and has continued to grapple with it in prison following the murders. Although Andrea Yates may meet the psychological criteria for mental illness, and in fact was hospitalized for her mental illness, that obviously may not satisfy legal standards for insanity.

Meyer and Oberman struggled with these definitional issues as well. They originally divided this category into purposeful filicide with mental illness and purposeful without mental illness. However, as the above discussion illustrates, there was no way to create exact definitions of purposeful filicide with mental illness and purposeful filicide without mental illness. In fact, they came to view it as a continuum, not a dichotomy, with many exceptions and no rules. For example, if the mother demonstrated signs of mental illness in the past but not at the time of the murder would she represent purposeful filicide with or without mental illness? Or if the mother had no history of mental illness but attempted or successfully committed murder-suicide would it be considered purposeful filicide with or without mental illness? What if the suicide was because of cultural issues or for altruistic reasons such as to spare the child what she believed would be a life of abuse? What if the woman was suffering from a disorder, such as postpartum psychosis, which is not a recognized mental disorder in the *DSM-IV-TR*? They finally decided not to try and separate out cases into subcategories of with or without mental illness but to include them all under a category known as purposeful filicide.

Despite the level of diversity between the cases and the paucity of available information in some instances, striking and clear patterns emerged among the 79 cases Meyer and Oberman reviewed. For example, unlike mothers in other categories, nearly 39 percent of mothers within this category killed more than one child. Additionally, 16 percent of the cases involved serial deaths, where the mother killed multiple children over an extended period. Over one-half (57 percent) of the multiple deaths involved attempted or successful murder-suicides. This large percentage suggests that mothers who are suicidal and commit filicide pose a risk to kill all or the majority of their offspring. Although one cannot definitively state why these mothers killed multiple children, Catherine identified one reason, that she did not want someone else to raise her children. Other reasons include sparing children the pain of growing up without a mother.

These numbers are alarming and highlight the need among the general public for education and awareness regarding mental illness. With education and awareness, the stigma of mental illness may be reduced and seeking treatment for mental illness may increase. Often, the last person to seek help when mental illness strikes is the person with the mental illness. That places the responsibility on her loved ones to be aware of signs of mental illness and act to help her.

In 37 percent of the cases involving multiple killings, mothers chose fire as the primary mode of death. In these instances, mothers set fire to their homes or cars, and in a few cases, killed their children by some other means, such as a gunshot wound or drowning, and then in a final act, set fire to their homes. This phenomenon is unique to the mothers within the purposeful filicide category. Again, it is difficult to determine why these mothers chose fire. Many of these mothers may have felt their lives were spiraling out of control and, in their minds, the fire may have been a final attempt to exert a sense of control over what had been an otherwise powerless existence.

Close to 42 percent of women in this category experienced a recent failed relationship, separation, or divorce prior to the murders. This number increases if expanded to include the death of a loved one. For example, Andrea Yates lost her father shortly before killing her five children. The loss of a relationship should be taken seriously and monitored closely by family members and friends. Clearly with these mothers, it is a warning sign.

Although mothers within this category seem like premeditated murderers who violently killed their children, upon deeper examination, one of the most distinctive features of these women's stories was their devotion toward their children. Catherine describes herself as a loving mother and says she was devoted to her children. While it may seem like an oxymoron to describe women who kill their children as loving mothers, by all accounts that is exactly what most of them were. The overwhelming majority of them had no history of abuse or neglect toward their children and most people who knew them spoke of their undying love for their children.

A very small percentage of mothers within this category suffered from postpartum disorders (8 percent). Since Andrea Yates's case, this issue has received more media attention. The National Organization for Women passed a resolution to increase attention to postpartum disorders and congress has considered increasing funding for research. Still, this continues to be an area in need of research, education, and outreach. Simple interventions could save numerous lives. For example, it could be quite effective and cost efficient to have pediatricians ask and provide education about postpartum syndromes and screen them at well baby checks.

Like most women in this category, Andrea Yates gave many warning signs but they were either ignored entirely or minimized. Friends, family, and the health care system need to understand these signs and learn to take appropriate action to help prevent these tragedies.

CONCLUSIONS

In this chapter we have provided an overview of five different types of mothers who kill their children. Within each type, we have provided some suggestions for changes in policy or prevention and intervention strategies based on the specific circumstances of those mothers. However, there are other important issues and observations we have not addressed which emerged throughout all the categories. The most salient of these relates to the social construction of motherhood and is revealed in the following anecdote.

Once while being interviewed by the media, the first author for this chapter was asked, "Don't you think a mother has a duty to protect her children?" Her response was, "I think every parent has a duty to protect their children." This exchange really embodies the social construction of motherhood. Simply put, on the whole, societal expectations for mothers are different than expectations for fathers. It is beyond the scope of this chapter to argue the value or origins of such expectations but in our research, they often played a part in the tragic circumstances and outcomes. For example, sometimes this related to fears and self-doubt a mother harbored related to her parenting ability but she was reluctant to discuss these concerns so as not to appear to be a "bad" mother or a failure at what everyone termed the "mothering instinct." While we expect new mothers to be facile at these tasks, we may laugh at the inexperience of new fathers, holding mothers to separate unrealistic expectations. The social construction of motherhood is also evidenced in the fact that although many of these mothers were single parenting, the absence of the father or the father's contribution to the crime is rarely addressed in these cases. For example, in many of these cases, the father clearly failed to protect the child but was never charged. Rusty Yates knew his wife was struggling with mental health issues but was never charged with failure to protect his children. This is not to say that he should be charged but women in similar circumstances are charged. For example, if a woman is involved with an abusive partner who kills her child, she is often charged with failure to protect.

Not surprisingly, a mother's feelings of fear and self-doubt are often aggravated by the social expectation that she should be feeling unadulterated joy about being a mother. Frequently, the result of such an expectation is depression, which becomes compounded as the woman withdraws from friends and family. In fact, our research revealed that isolation was a warning sign across all categories from the teen who commits neonaticide to the mothers who experience postpartum syndromes. Although isolation is self-imposed in some women's circumstances, such as in the case of neonaticide, or imposed by others in different circumstances, such as in the case of domestic violence, the end result was the same—devastating isolation. To really consider the impact of such isolation, imagine the number of times each day we ask for social validation from our peers or family. How often do we ask for opinions such as "How did I do?" or "Did you ever feel like that/experience that?" Now imagine it was impossible to obtain that feedback, especially while you were engaging in a new, unfamiliar and exhausting endeavor (like child rearing) that you had never done before (yet everyone expected you to know how to do it).

One of the most frequent comments we heard in our interviews of mothers was that the one thing they had learned in prison was to reach out for help when they needed it, despite their prior socialization experiences that kept them from doing so before. While saying this, they also recognized the danger in reaching out; the social construction of motherhood is institutionalized. Admitting you need help to social services agencies, or that you feel unsure about your ability to raise your child, creates the very real danger you may lose your children through these same agencies. This creates a catch-22 situation: reach out and put oneself at risk or remain isolated and at risk. Fathers who reach out for help may not suffer the same scrutiny. Consider the response when a father is widowed versus when a mother is widowed. When a father is left to raise children through widowhood there is an outpouring of parenting support that we do not usually see for mothers in the same circumstances.

Although it would be grandiose to believe that societal expectations will change with any rapidity, we could increase other support for mothers quite easily. We have identified several ways to do this throughout the chapter. However, the obstacle does not seem to be the venue in which to increase support, but the desire. Our personal commitment to such endeavors seems lacking. When our attention is focused on the issue of mothers who kill their children, there is little exploration into understanding why such an act occurred and much more discussion about what the consequences of her actions should be. For example, the emphasis on Andrea Yates was really not on what led her to kill her children but rather whether she should receive the death penalty. Little progress will be made toward prevention if we do not try to understand causes. And we need to focus on prevention. We found over a thousand reported cases of mothers who killed their children in the 1990s alone. That averages to one case every three days and these were just *reported* cases. Many children were never found or the child was found and the mother could not be identified or the mother was a juvenile and the case was never reported. We can no longer continue to ignore these tragedies.

What was perhaps the most disturbing observation for all of the researchers involved in both the construction of the typology and the interviews was that *on the whole*, these mothers were not atypical prior to the deaths of their children. In the last paragraph of their book, Meyer and Oberman stated, "If there is one central point to this book, it is this: to the extent that we conceive of the crime of infanticide as a rare and exceptional act committed by a deranged or evil woman, we are dangerously wrong" (p. 177). This sentiment was reiterated in numerous interviews. One mother stated,

> People have to stop thinking we are cruel and hard, we just went through an emotional battle. I've had girls tell me that they went through what I went through but they had their husbands and mothers to help them through it. The family has to get involved. People are so closed they don't want to see anything. They see everything in black and white but they really need to see color.

Another mother said,

> I love all my children just like everyone else . . . it devastated me . . . it could have happened to
> any woman. . . . I was wanting to be a mother—something all women want . . . and to be doing
> something that you never thought about doing or being . . . it's not like taking drugs or becom-
> ing an alcoholic and getting behind the wheel of a car and knowing the consequences . . . but
> having a baby which everyone does . . . what kind of mother do people think I am? I have this
> black stain on me.

Few people want to consider themselves capable of unacceptable acts. This is why
Milgram's (1964) findings in the early 1960s, that "good" people would obey an authority
even though it meant harming an innocent person, shocked both his research participants
and himself. It is why the acts of Hitler's army shocked us. Still all of these examples
highlight the fact that given the right set of circumstances, average people can do heinous
things. Most of the mothers in our research were ordinary women who had dealt with
extraordinary circumstances during the course of their lives and just prior to their crimes.

Nothing in this chapter is meant to create an excuse for these mothers or their acts.
The intent of this chapter is to increase understanding of these mothers and the circumstances that are involved in their crimes. In doing so there is an inherent challenge to all of
us to become more attentive to and involved in the lives of other human beings.

REFERENCES

AMERICAN PSYCHIATRIC ASSOCIATION. (2000). *Diagnostic and Statistical Manual of Mental Disorders-IV-TR*. Washington: Author.

CICCHETTI, D. (1989). How research on child maltreatment has informed the study of child development: Perspectives from developmental psychopathology. In D. Cicchetti & V. Carlson (Eds.),
*Child maltreatment: Theory and research on the causes and consequences of child abuse and
neglect* (pp. 377–431). New York: Cambridge University Press.

MCKEE, G. (2006). *When mothers kill: A forensic psychologists casebook*. Oxford: Oxford University Press.

MEYER, C. L., OBERMAN, M. (with WHITE, K., RONE, M., BATRA, P., & PROANO, T., 2001). *Mothers
who kill their children: Understanding the acts of moms from Susan Smith to the "Prom Mom"*.
New York: New York University Press.

MILGRAM, S. (1965). Some conditions of obedience and disobedience to authority. *Human Relations, 18,* 57–76.

MILNER, J. S., ROBERTSON, K. R., & ROGERS, D. L. (1990). Childhood history of abuse and adult
child abuse potential. *Journal of Family Violence, 5,* 15–34.

OBERMAN, M. (1996). Mothers who kill: Coming to terms with modern American Infanticide.
American Criminal Law Review, 1–110.

OBERMAN, M., & MEYER, C. (2008). *When mothers kill: Interviews from prison*. New York: New
York University Press.

RESNICK, P. J. (1970). Murder of the newborn: A psychiatric review of neonaticide. *American
Journal of Psychiatry, 126,* 1414–1420.

WEISBART, C. E. (2002). Listening to women's voices: Women convicted of killing their children.
Unpublished Doctoral Dissertation, Wright State University.

8

Lives in Transition

A Needs Assessment of Women Exiting from Prostitution

Stacy L. Mallicoat

The entry into prostitution is predicated on a combination of individual, contextual, and environmental factors. While the research suggests common pathways to prostitution, such findings do not indicate a single causal factor for prostitution (Bullough & Bullough, 1996). While significant bodies of research document these pathways to prostitution, there are few programs that exist to address the unique and often multiple needs of women involved in prostitution. These limited examples tend to focus on exit strategies for women leaving the streets and are more likely to involve drop-in and referral-based services. While these and other related programs provide valuable resources such as case management, health care, life skills training, therapeutic resources, and drug-/alcohol-related programming, few, if any, provide direct services following an intensive residential program. Despite a growing understanding that women exiting prostitution have multiple needs, few programs specifically design their programs to address the overlap in issues, particularly from a long-term perspective. This results in a fragmented delivery of services and significant limitations for program efficacy (Zweig, Schlichter, & Burt, 2002).

Trends in the literature have addressed the risk issues for women currently in prostitution, as well as the factors that place women at risk for engaging in prostitution. Women exiting prostitution have experiences of poverty, violence, drug addiction, and physical and mental health issues (MMP, 2001). It is important to maintain an awareness of these issues as they may continue to complicate the efforts of women to make healthy choices regarding their lives. These risk factors also increase the difficulties in escaping and remaining free from the lifestyle of prostitution (Nokomis Foundation, 2002). The risk of relapse for this population is high, and women make several attempts to leave prostitution before they are successful (Raphael, 2004). One study found that 80 percent of its program participants had made attempts to leave at some point prior to their current attempts to exit from prostitution (MMP, 2001). For some women, the choice to leave prostitution is an active one, where women seek out interventions to assist them in this transition. For others, the exit is prompted by interventions by the criminal justice system (Dalla, 2000; MMP, 2001). Additionally, the negative social stigma of prostitution has significant implications for a woman's reentry to the "mainstream" society, and challenges the potential for a successful transition (Weiner, 1996).

This chapter focuses on the unique and multiple needs of women as they struggle to exit from a lifestyle of prostitution. Drawing on data from interviews with program providers and women struggling to leave their former lives behind, this chapter highlights the barriers that women face in their efforts to transition to a life beyond the streets. Following a discussion of the risk factors for women in prostitution, there is presented the programmatic challenges in targeting services for women within this multi-systemic need community and presents recommendations for ways to reform these efforts.

RISK FACTORS

The literature on the risk factors for prostitution cites sexual assault as a common precursor for prostitution and related activities. While there is no direct causal link between incest and prostitution, and certainly the majority of incest survivors do not turn to prostitution, research indicates that there is a strong correlation between the two (Nokomis Foundation, 2002). One example of this can be found in one prostitution-recovery program report where 87 percent of the women report that they have a history of incest and/or rape throughout their lives (MMP, 2001). Women emerging from prostitution experience and witness various forms of violence throughout their developmental years (Dalla, Xia, & Kennedy, 2003). For these women, these experiences set the stage for their future where incest became a way in which they learned about sexuality. Sex was a commodity to be traded and the bargaining of sexuality became a means by which these women could feel power in a marginalized community (Raphael, 2004). A history of childhood sexual abuse is also correlated with running away, which in turn places girls at risk for prostitution (Chesney-Lind & Shelden, 1998; Pagelow, 1984).

The cycle of violence that begins with abuse as a child continues throughout a woman's time on the street. Research demonstrates that a modest relationship exists between child sexual abuse and the presence of violence amongst adult sex workers (Surratt, Inciardi, Kurtz, & Kiley, 2004). The level of violence that women experience is significant, and includes behaviors such as robbery, assault, and rape (Nixon, Tutty, Downe, Gorkoff, & Ursel, 2002). Generally, this violence is perpetrated by their dates (Goswami & Schervish, 2002; Raphael & Shapiro, 2004). The second most likely perpetrator is an intimate partner, closely followed by pimps (Raphael & Shapiro, 2004). Many girls are beaten if they refuse to work. For others, the presence of a pimp acts as a barrier against leaving or to accessing services out of the fear of retaliation (Nixon, Tutty, Downe, Gorkoff, & Ursel 2002). As the pressure to make money is increased, women may place themselves in increasingly risky situations with customers (Norton-Hawk, 2004). While the presence of pimps appears to be decreasing (MMP, 2001), the risk of violence remains high. Many women express disbelief that they survived the violence on the streets while some of their peers did not. In addition, many women admit they begin to disassociate themselves from the levels of violence they experience (Nixon, Tutty, Downe, Gorkoff, & Ursel, 2002). These factors present significant implications for women transitioning from prostitution and successful interventions must focus on these common life experiences (Dalla, 2002; MMP, 2001).

The role of substance abuse is central to the discussion of risk factors and treatment options for prostituting women. Seventy percent of women in prostitution indicate issues with drug addiction, the majority of whom began their drug use at an early age (MMP, 2001). Some women began their substance use prior to their entry in prostitution to cope with the pain associated with past or current sexual violence present in their lives. They then resort to prostitution to fund their drug habits (Raphael, 2004; Schoot & Goswami, 2001). For others, substance abuse comes later, in an effort to self-medicate against the fear, stress, and low self-esteem resulting from the selling of sex (Nixon, Tutty, Downe, Gorkoff, & Ursel, 2002; Nokomis Foundation, 2002). As prostitution activity increases, so does substance addiction (Raphael, 2004; Raphael & Shapiro, 2002). Indeed, the relationship between drug use and prostitution may be a self-perpetuating circle (Young, Boyd, & Hubbard, 2000). A sample of women in jail found that women arrested for prostitution had significantly higher rates of drug use, compared to women arrested for non-prostitution-related offenses (Yacoubian, Urbach, Larsen, Johnson, & Peters, 2000).

While drug addiction presents a significant health concern for women in prostitution as a result of their time on the streets, women suffer additional long-term physical health effects. Women are at risk for issues related to HIV, hepatitis, and other chronic health concerns, including dental, vision, neurological, respiratory and gynecological problems (Farley & Barkin, 1998). Condom use appears inconsistently and many women note of their client's refusal to use protection or that they would pay extra for unprotected sex. For most women, the fear of contracting a sexually transmitted disease was of little concern (Dalla, 2002). The age of entry to the streets is significantly related to health issues as those who began their prostitution experiences at a young age experience increased health problems (Raphael & Shapiro, 2002). Finally, the death rate for women in prostitution is 40 times higher than the death rate of overall population (Nokomis Foundation, 2002).

In addition to physical health concerns, mental health issues are a prominent issue. As the levels of violence increase, so do cases of Post-Traumatic Stress Disorder (PTSD). Not only do two-thirds of prostituted women experience symptoms of PTSD (Schoot & Goswami, 2001), but the levels of PTSD for this population are two to three times greater than the levels of PTSD experienced by Vietnam War veterans (Farley & Barkan, 1998). Prostitutes suffering from PTSD may be unable to accurately assess the levels of threat and violence that surround their lives, which in turn places them in increased risks of danger (Valera, Sawyer, & Schiraldi, 2000). While abuse, addiction, and violence are individual risk factors, poverty represents a significant environmental risk factor for prostitution (Farley & Kelley, 2000). Trading sex is often the means for survival when traditional avenues of sustainable employment are limited (Nokomis Foundation, 2002). Coupled with poverty is the issue of homelessness. A majority of the women involved in prostitution report being homeless at various times while working on the street and regularly prostituted for a place to stay (Goswami & Schervish, 2002; Farley & Barkin, 1998). "Because of their restricted access to financial and material resources, some women may resort to prostitution as a resistance or response to poverty" (Hardman, 1997, p. 20). Poverty is also related to a woman's personal wellbeing, and issues of physical health are magnified by the levels of poverty they experience in their lives (Butters & Erickson, 2003).

CURRENT STUDY

The risk factors for prostitution do not disappear when women leave the streets. Indeed, these dangers are multiplied as women struggle to transition successfully from their former conditions. In many cases, the risk factors for women to enter a life of prostitution are the same challenges that women continue to struggle with throughout their lives, even after they shed their former identity. These needs are intertwined with one another, and present a unique challenge for rehabilitation efforts.

In order to effectively meet the needs of women exiting from prostitution, intervention and long-term programming needs to assess the risks of relapse. Women exiting prostitution are faced with issues such as poverty, abuse, and histories of violence and addiction, as well as other barriers to their success, such as physical and mental health concerns, lack of basic life skills and limited job skills, and fragmented employment histories (MMP, 2001). As a result of these numerous barriers, programs should approach the needs of women from a multi-factor correlated perspective and an understanding of the individual, contextual and environmental factors of sex work is invaluable when designing and implementing programmatic interventions for street-level prostitutes.

The current study involves women in a prostitution-recovery program located in a large metropolitan area in a Western state. This community-based organization coordinates two separate but related components aimed at transitioning women from a life of prostitution. The first component involves a residential treatment program where residents participate in intensive therapy and basic skill development. The typical resident stay lasts approximately two years and is linked to the specific needs of the client. The second component involves a therapeutic residential community for the women following the completion of the primary treatment program or other related prostitution recovery programming. The choice to transition to the community residence is based on the individual and is not required for the women who complete the residential treatment program. This study focuses on the role of the community housing project in providing services to the women as they continue throughout their recovery. Drawing from the literature as well as findings from qualitative interviews with board members, program staff and program residents, this chapter seeks to highlight the issues currently facing prostitution recovery programming.

METHODOLOGY

Several individual and focus group interviews were held in August and September 2005 to address the issues currently facing this program. Interview participants included two focus groups with Board Members (n = 9), one focus group with program staff (n = 2), individual interviews with both the Executive Director and the Program Director and one focus group with the women participating in the community housing project and residential programs (n = 6). The community housing project consists of nine apartments, four of which were filled at the time of these interviews.

The Board Members varied in the length of involvement with the Board as well as their pathways to their participation. The composition of the Board is linked to the community of donors who provide substantial support to the project. Much of the donor base comes from a specific denomination of the Christian faith, and several of the board members were actively involved with church leadership activities. One board member had been a resident of the population over twenty years ago and was now involved in the program as an administrative function. Finally, other board members came to the organization out of an interest in offering social service to the program population. The residents in the focus group varied in their length of time since exiting prostitution, ranging from nine months to eighteen years and varied in their pathways to living at the community. Some of the women had resided at the community living facility since their completion of the primary treatment program. Others had previously completed the residential program and later returned to the community residence to benefit from the subsidized housing option that the residence provided. One woman had never participated in the affiliated residential program, but was in need of community housing and came to the shared living program following an exit from prostitution, having received her primary services elsewhere. As part of their transition process and recovery, many of these women had reunited with their children and resided with them at the community residence. Many of these children had been under the care of other family members or in the custody of social services during their mother's careers in prostitution and during their primary rehabilitative program. Finally, two of the study participants were at the ending stages of the residential treatment program and participated in the focus group process as they were assessing whether they would transition to the community residence following the completion of their residential program.

The focus groups and interviews lasted approximately 60–120 minutes in length and all parties were notified of the confidential nature of the information they shared. Groups were asked open-ended questions from a semi-structured interview schedule (Appendix A). This study explores the following issues for discussion: 1) How does the program administration define success for its participants at the community residence? 2) What are some of the factors that contribute to the success of the participants? 3) What are the issues currently facing the community housing project and limit the efficacy in delivering services?

FINDINGS

Defining and Creating Success

One of the primary challenges for the program was to develop a definition of "success" for its program participants. This is not an uncommon issue for programs in evaluating their efficacy. Staff members articulated the following measures of success for the program participants: 1) Maintain a drug and alcohol-free lifestyle; 2) develop a support network; 3) facilitate family reunification for participants with children; 4) improve money management skills (financial stability); 5) continue participation in programming to address continuing needs; 6) transition to sustainable living opportunities outside of the community residence. Given this definition of success, the data indicate several areas where the program and its participants fall short.

In defining success, a disconnection existed between the staff's definition of success and the feelings of success of the residents for their lives. Many staff felt that the residents required significant assistance while residents resented the intervention efforts. This friction impeded the ability of staff to develop meaningful rehabilitation options for the community residents:

> "Well, if you're constantly telling me I've got to have a meeting then you obviously don't feel that I've come to a point where I can do it on my own. But where does it end?" (Resident)

> "They think their lives work, and they don't need that stuff, and of course, we're watching the child abuse, we're watching the poor money management, we're watching the horrible relationship with men, the codependency, we're watching them relapse or be in relapse mode." (Staff Member)

> "Allow me to be an independent, responsible person that moved in here. Allow me to be that and not be on my back." (Resident)

In creating success for the residents of the community, three central themes emerged from the data. First, both residents and staff members agreed that programs and services should be made available to facilitate the continued growth and support of the community housing population. However, these groups disagree on how such resources should be made available and in what context such programming should be delivered. Second, both staff and residents admit that the human resources of the agency are stretched thin and may impact the ability to meet the high needs of the population. Third, staff and board members agree that a key indicator in achieving success for the residents is to transition them from the community residence to living on their own. While this is an expressed function of the program, there have been challenges in achieving this goal. These challenges include concerns about the delivery of therapeutic and life-skills programming, the limited resources of the organization, and the changing definition of the facility from a transitional housing program to a community residence.

1. *Therapeutic and Life Skills Programmatic Concerns.* Historically, the therapeutic resources mandated for residents have been individualized to the unique needs of the women. Staff members noted the importance of circumstances and situations that created an individualized program for each woman. This process allowed staff members to take into account the unique needs of each woman in their journey toward success. Residents felt strongly that services should be made available, particularly for women in the early stages of their transition. In particular, the need for services should be made on a personalized basis in consultation with their case manager, versus a community-wide broad approach. In advocating for an individualized approach, one resident acknowledged why group programming would be ineffective for the population: *My needs are so different from [x]; my needs are so different from [y]; and my needs are so different from [z]. Everybody has a different need.*

In asking residents and staff members about what types of services were needed for the community, suggestions included counseling, 12-step programming, parenting, living skills, job search skills, family reunification, and money management. The women indicated that some programming was helpful, but that their interest in the information was dependent on the types of programming and how it was structured for the community. Presentation from outside providers on topics such as insurance policies was found to generate the greatest interest by the residents. Here, the women were receptive to presentations of information, but admit they shut down when services are presented in an authoritative manner.

One issue that was debated between the staff and resident population was whether participation in therapeutic programming should be a requirement for residency at the community. Staff members felt strongly that residents continued to need programming and case management, yet the resistance to such efforts by the residents was high. Previous attempts to provide life-skills–based classes such as money management and various 12-step programs failed due to lack of interest by the residents in the community. These failures impact the ability and energies of the staff to offer effective services to the population in the future.

> "They didn't want to come. And the ones that did that were here can't really say they wanted to be there. They were disgruntled because this is, you know they ran across this same attitude year after year after year after year, whereas some people had to go; others were just – let slide, or they'd have bad attitudes, so then everybody else would have a bad attitude about just being there." (Staff Member)

For some residents, they believed they did not need a "program" and moved to the shared living residence only for affordable housing and support, and not to participate in a therapeutic community.

> "The rent for me is the only thing that keeps me here, is the affordable rent, and if it got to the point where it got so bad here that I couldn't deal with the program stuff, and all that, I'd move, and I would suffer, and so would my child. And I bite my tongue, and I don't say anything, and all that – mostly for [my child]. Mostly to be able to afford a decent living, you know? Once [my child's] on [their] own, who care if I live in a little cracker box apartment? At least I have a roof over our heads. I need to stay here, but I'm also getting a little tired of all the bullshit that goes on over here." (Resident)

While some of the residents stated they enjoyed having their own lives and time for themselves, particularly in terms of dealing with their psychological health and wellness, they recognized the power of the community for support, especially in meeting the needs of their children.

> "It helps knowing everybody that's in the building, and you feel more secure." "The support, you know? Like, if for some reason. . . . I can't pick [my child] up from school. You know what I mean? You're having the support of the community. Where you know that if something happens to me, [staff] could pick your kids up from school – whatever." (Resident)

2. *Institutional Resources.* Like many non-profit organizations, this community residence relied heavily on its donor base to provide financial support for the organization. Board members were actively involved with fundraising efforts to generate funds for the operational budget. Staff and board members spoke of the difficulty in raising funds for the project outside of a population that was already familiar with the works of the organization. Many of the board members believed that the existence of the community residence served a positive function from a fundraising perspective as it allowed the program

to provide additional opportunities to expand its reach to serve a greater number of women and their families. Given that the project serves such a small population, as well as the lack of successful transitions for the women, board members raised concerns about their ability to be successful in raising funds for the program.

> "For some of our former previously major donors who look at the program in comparison to other things, other kinds of programs where there's a larger volume of results, dare I use the term result. They are very discerning people or whatever, so they bring that same discerning eye with this and challenge us."

Many board members were faced with confronting the social stigma that exists for women in prostitution. One board member commented that many of her efforts in fundraising were thwarted by the "pretty woman" myth perpetuated by popular culture references to prostitution. Additionally, issues with program stability and efficacy impacted the ability to be successful fundraisers. One board member questioned whether the fiscal issues facing the program had contributed to the structural and programmatic issues, which ultimately impacted the ability for women to be successful in their transition.

In addition to issues of fiscal concern, a key concern for both the staff and the residents was the limits of available human resources. Given the small size of the program, staff members wore a number of different hats as part of their daily activities. In addition to managing the case needs of the residents of the community, staff members were faced with the facility maintenance needs for an aging building in a high-risk neighborhood. Many respondents indicated that maintenance had become a full-time issue due to the state and condition of the facility. While the residents acknowledged that some recent effort had been made to repair the building, they were frustrated by the constant need for maintenance. The decaying state of the residence and the effects for the population created additional areas for concern for the already overwhelmed program staff. Indeed, the limited human resources of the project appeared to be taking a toll on both the staff members and the resident population.

> "In my opinion, [my case manager] is doing too much. There's a lot of things to do. I see it being very hard, and I'm healthy. For one person to have so much responsibility when it shouldn't have to be like that." (Resident)

> "Right now, they're just dumping it on me. I said, look, I can't do that and everything else I'm supposed to do, and yet they keep throwing it at me. I put my boundaries up." (Staff)

> "She'll go out of her way. She'll even drop a doctor's appointment for herself and go and pick you up when she should be seeing that doctor, okay? Her health is just as important of mine, because if she's not healthy, then how in the world can she help me." (Resident)

3. *Transitional Housing versus Community Residence.* When the program acquired the apartment building that housed the community residence ten years ago, they created the unique opportunity to provide low income housing options for women who were transitioning from the intervention program. In an effort to fill the available units, decisions were made by the program administration to offer available units to former clients, some of who had been away from the program for a significant period of time. While the intent was to provide assistance for a temporary transitional basis to help reunify women and their children, the reality became less of a transitional living arrangement and program staff began to identify the residence as a community residence. However, the goals of the

program remained tied to its original intent and future policy decisions reflected the continued link toward creating a transitional experience. Many of the board members continue to identify the residential community as a transitional living program with the goal being that women will leave following a contracted period of time. However, history indicates that successful transitions have been rare.

> "Our transitional program hasn't transitioned anyone. Yesterday, a woman moved out for the first time. . . . I think it's five years since anyone transitioned. . . . where the project really took her step by step to completion." (Staff Member)

While most of the staff and board members agree that the goal is to successfully move residents from their subsidized living environment, some wondered if they were providing the women with the necessary skills to ensure a successful transition.

> "I think that there are a lot of things that we could do from the get-go that would make the transitioning more of a transition, not just a jump and then, done. You can't figure out how to deal, you don't know where to go I mean very funny things that I think we take for granted. You know, their life skills . . . really, really basic things that I think sometimes we take for granted, but we're kind of not instilling and teaching from the get-go," (Staff Member)

> "We may have people who really need to have some sort of, dare I use the term, assisted living." (Board Member)

Beyond the personal struggles, staff, board, and residents acknowledge that financial concerns present the greatest barrier in transitioning from the community residence. Staff members indicated that poor money management skills have contributed to the negative financial wellbeing of the women in the community. The option of affordable housing off-set the stress that existed in a region with high rental costs. In addition, debts to child services and related agencies presented a great burden for the women. The availability of the community residence allowed women to gain financial stability, provide a home for their families and allowed for development of their self-esteem.

> "The affordable rent is basically, I feel for me, that's why I'm definitely here, because it helps me tremendously, especially with children. And I would have to definitely have to file for bankruptcy if I was living somewhere else, and I think the rent being so affordable is the main reason that that helps me in life, you know? It gives me hope that one day I will be able to venture out, and for me that's what it is . . . I view this as a transition, because of in the future, I will be able to move elsewhere and help be another part of society, but by this being so affordable, this helps me with clear my debts, and not have to worry about being in the streets again because of those debts." (Resident)

> "A lot of the women that come here . . . they'd have a lot of child support issues, back child support that they owed the State, so these big bills come in the mail and it's like, oh God, how am I going to survive outside of this subsidized rent thing that I've got going on? So it's tough for them." (Staff Member)

Barriers to Success

One of the key challenges for the residents in their recovery is their continuing struggle with sobriety and drug addictions. Historically, the community had allowed residents to remain at the property while they addressed their issues on an outpatient basis. In cases where a resident would leave the community to attend an inpatient drug treatment program off-site, the facility would keep their apartment vacant for their return to the community upon completion of their treatment. While some residents appreciated that the staff and the program stood by them during these relapses, others admitted that the presence of relapsing clients and the chaos that it brought to the community often exacerbated their own struggles.

> "Our approach to relapse has always been to get treatment, so if you relapse, you get group, you get therapy, you get 12-step programs. You get whatever it is you need. We learned early on that the only way their lives are ever going to be better was to be here, and it made no sense to kick them out." (Staff Member)

> "It's hard for you to maintain – well . . . sobriety of whatever it is that you're trying to do when you don't have someone being consistent with you, either, You know what I'm saying? It's oh, the project's going to do this, or the project's going to do that. Blah, blah, blah. And it's all talk and no action, you know?" (Resident)

The struggles of the residents to maintain sobriety throughout the relapse behaviors of their neighbors illustrate a key issue within the community: a lack of consistency in terms of rule development and enforcement. The rules of the facility were relatively unclear and appeared to be applied in a sporadic fashion. Indeed, only a few staff members, residents or board members could articulate the specific expectations of the residents, beyond the following requirements: No illegal behaviors on the property demonstrate employment and income eligibility and no additional live-in adult residents (boyfriends). While all agreed that there needed to be disciplinary action for people who don't follow the rules, some staff and women indicated that a lack of communication and consistency by staff contributed to the lack of effective enforcement of rules in the past.

> "We're not giving them that there are repercussions to your behaviors and your actions, and how to prevent yourself from being in that predicament to begin with." (Staff Member)

> "You shouldn't have let it go as far as it went. It's going on for a long time, and they knew it was going on, and the rest of us who are living here, we're saying, oh, hello. So and so is blah, blah, blah, and this is what's happening. And then four or five weeks later, all of a sudden all hell breaks loose, and then they do something. And in the meantime, the rest of us are suffering." (Resident)

In response to some of the problems in the community, staff members reacted with increased programming and rule enforcement. In many cases, this led to policies that were administered across the board, rather than in the individualized fashion that the residents had grown accustomed to. In an attempt to increase stability in the community, these changes created conflict between the residents and the staff.

> "Everyone has an individualized program. But to a degree, you can't really do it that way. I mean, you do have to take into consideration people's specifics but a program is a program. So I think back away a bit from the individualized. You have to set forth some boundaries and it has to been set in stone . . . and they know what their consequences are going to be." (Staff Member)

> "All of a sudden, everybody here's being drug tested, because one person can't keep their life straight. You know what I'm saying? It's like that's not fair. Don't be watching over me 24/7 just because somebody else did something." (Resident)

"Obviously it works (rule enforcement), because you set your boundaries. Say no, you can't live here. If you're going to use, you can't be here. Get out. You need to get into treatment, or you leave." (Staff Member)

DISCUSSION AND FUTURE CONSIDERATIONS

The greatest asset of this prostitution recovery program is the availability of housing. Homelessness puts women at risk to engage in prostitution and women who return to the lifestyle often do so out of economic necessity (Benoit & Millar, 2001). In order to leave prostitution, women need not only safe and affordable housing, but also ways in which to address the culture of poverty in which they live (Nokomis Foundation, 2002; Raphael & Shapiro, 2002; Schoot & Goswami, 2001). The need for available and affordable housing also has a significant relationship with additional risk factors. "Without reliable housing, it is challenging to escape the cycle of prostituting in order to obtain drugs, and taking drugs in order to numb the humiliation of sex work" (Yahne, Miller, Irvin-Vitela, & Tonigan, 2002, p. 52).

While the stated goal of this community is to provide transitional housing options, it is unclear how "successful" this current venture is. While some residents may have significant difficulties in transitioning on their own, appropriate definitions of transitional housing must be specified to establish the expectations for residents. While the need for affordable housing for women exiting prostitution is paramount to their success, women must also possess the skills and receive support to effectively transition to an independent living environment. These expectations, skills and support begin with the adherence to rules for the community for both the residents and staff alike.

Given the nature of the economy, fiscal concerns may impact the ability to adequately deliver effective programming. The literature recommends that protections should be put in place to protect staff members from becoming overburdened. Therefore, community partnerships should be developed to provide services for interested residents (Zweig et al., 2002). This allows for residents to pursue treatment and skill building in a confidential manner outside of their living environment, while still receiving case management support from the organization. Not only does this practice protect the residents from becoming codependent on their case manager, it provides a relief for the limited number of staff members who may be overwhelmed by the high needs of the resident population.

While there remains an understanding that the specifics of programming may vary based on the needs of the individual, it is important to minimize reactive responses and sweeping regulations. Rule violators must be addressed on an individualized basis in a swift and consistent manner to insure equitable treatment in the community. In addition, staff and residents should continue to work on improving communication skills to encourage the growth of positive working relationships. In doing so, all members of the community need to be open and responsive to possibilities of programmatic changes that will help facilitate success for the residents. One suggestion in the literature is to incorporate the input of residents into rule making and to keep the number of rules to a minimum (Melbin, Sullivan, & Cain, 2003).

It is clear from the words of the program participants and staff members that women exiting from prostitution have multiple needs that impact their attempts toward a healthy life. Each of these struggles build upon each other, as the effects of sexual assault are also related to drug and alcohol addiction and mental health traumas, such as post-traumatic stress disorder and a negative self-identity (Farley & Barkin, 1998; Nokomis

Foundation, 2002; Raphael, 2004). Any successful prostitution recovery program must address the challenges that women face as a result of their substance addictions not only in terms of strategies for remaining drug-free, but also in the correlating social and psychological factors that lead to addiction and relapse (Dalla, 2002; Plummer, Potterat, Muth, Muth, & Darrow, 1996). The literature mandates that while services must be available to address the unique and multiple needs of women in this population, they should be made optional for program participants and not a requirement of residency (Rabinovitch & Stregan, 2004). When programming is viewed as practical and flexible, participants are more likely to feel positively about the program and its effects on their lives. In contrast, when advocates are seen as patronizing and authoritarian, residents are less positive about the relationship between the program and their lives (Melbin, Sullivan, & Cain, 2003). The focus group with program residents echoed this suggestion. The literature also strongly advocates for programming to be developed and managed by prostitution survivors in order to develop connections and trust with program participants (Raphael, 2004; Nokomis Foundation, 2002). Finally, the findings of the focus groups and the literature agree that some services that are most helpful for some women may be less needed for others, indicating that a multitude of services is needed to address the unique needs of women in prostitution recovery (Rabinovitch & Strega, 2004). Together these factors may help to improve the peer culture of the community, skill building and the relationships between community residents and staff members.

In conclusion, it is important to recognize the value that prostitution recovery programming plays in the community. Indeed, the need for treatment always overwhelms the availability of treatment (Nokomis Foundation, 2002). In emphasizing the strengths of the program, board members and staff should continue to focus on the unique nature of affordable housing and the multiple needs of the population as keys to developing avenues for financial support. While financial costs are always a concern, the legitimacy of a program plays a greater role in its ability to continue to serve the population at hand (McNeece & Arnold, 2002). It is important to continue to clarify and improve the successes within the program, as it strives to meet the needs of a population that is significantly underrepresented in current treatment and programmatic options.

APPENDIX A

Interview Schedule

BACKGROUNDS

1. How did you get involved with this program?
2. How long have you been involved with the program?

PROGRAM DESIGN

3. What do you see as your role in the design and implementation of the program?
4. How do you define success for residents? How do we measure this?
5. What kinds of things make up a good program? What is needed to provide these elements?
6. What are the best components of the current program?

7. What specifically can the program provide that is lacking in other arenas or programs?
8. What kinds of help do you think residents need?
9. What are the issues that are arising for residents?
10. What are the obstacles in providing services for residents? How can we overcome these obstacles?
11. Are residents adequately provided with the tools needed to transition into society?

PROGRAM IMPLEMENTATION

12. What are the rules for residency eligibility?
13. Is the program adequately staffed to effectively manage the program and its residents?
14. How should the program deal with issues outside of program structure, staffing, and client management (i.e. building maintenance)?
15. Are our policies and procedures adequate to address the needs of clients and the program? Is there anything that we could be doing, that we aren't?
16. Should there be a time limit for residency?
17. How should rule infractions be dealt with?

REFERENCES

BENOIT, C. & MILLAR, A. (2001). Dispelling Myths and Understanding Realities: Working Conditions, Health Status and Exiting Experiences of Sex Workers. Retrieved September 3, 2008 from Prostitutes Empowerment, Education and Resource Society Website: http://www.peers.bc.ca/pubs.html.

BULLOUGH, B. and BULLOUGH, V. (1996). Female Prostitution: Current Research and Changing Interpretations. *Annual Review of Sex Research* 7: 158–180.

BUTTERS, J. & ERICKSON, P. G. (2003). Meeting the Health Needs of Female Crack Users: A Canadian Example. *Women and Health* 37(1): 1–18.

CHESNEY-LIND, M. & SHELDEN, R. G. (1998). *Girls, Delinquency and Juvenile Justice.* Belmont, CA.: West/Wadsworth.

DALLA, R. L. (2000). Exposing the "Pretty Woman" Myth: A Qualitative Examination of the Lives of Female Streetwalking Prostitutes. *The Journal of Sex Research* 37(4): 344–353.

DALLA, R. L. (2002). Night Moves: A Qualitative Investigation of Street-Level Sex Work. *Psychology of Women Quarterly* 26(1): 63–73.

DALLA, R. L., XIA, Y. & KENNEDY, H. (2003). "You Just Give Them What They Want and Pray They Don't Kill You": Street-Level Sex Workers' Reports of Victimization, Personal Resources, and Coping Strategies. *Violence Against Women* 9(11): 1367–1394.

FARLEY, M. & BARKIN, H. (1998). Prostitution, Violence and Post-Traumatic Stress Disorder. *Woman and Health* 27(3): 37–49.

FARLEY, M. & KELLEY, V. (2000). Prostitution: A Critical Review of the Medical and Social Sciences Literature. *Women and Criminal Justice* 11(4): 29–64.

GOSWAMI, S. & SCHERVISH, A. (2002). Unlocking Options for Women: A Survey of Women in Cook County Jail. Retrieved September 3, 2008 from Chicago Coalition for the Homeless Website: http://cch.issuelab.org/research.

HARDMAN, K. L. J. (1997). A Social Work Group for Prostituted Women with Children. *Social Work with Groups* 20(1): 19–31.

MAGDALENA PILOT PROJECT: MOTIVATIONAL OUTREACH TO SUBSTANCE ABUSING WOMEN STREET SEX WORKERS. *Journal of Substance Abuse Treatment* 23(1): 49–53.

MARY MAGDALENE PROJECT [MMP] (2001). Beyond 2000 Committee Final Report.

MCNEECE, C. A. & ARNOLD, E. M. (2002). Program Closure: The Impact on Participants in a Program for Female Prostitutes. *Research on Social Work Practice* 12(1): 159–175.

MELBIN, A., SULLIVAN, C. M. & CAIN, D. (2003). Transitional Supportive Housing Programs: Battered Women's Perspectives and Recommendations. *Affilia* 18(4): 445–460.

NIXON, K., TUTTY, L., DOWNE, P., GORKOFF, K. & URSEL, J. (2002). The Everyday Occurrence: Violence in the Lives of Girls Exploited Through Prostitution. *Violence Against Women* 8(9): 1016–1043.

NOKOMIS FOUNDATION. (2002). We Can Do Better: Helping Prostituted Women and Girls in Grand Rapids Make Healthy Choices: A Prostitution Round Table Report to the Community. Retrieved September 3, 2008 from Nokomis Foundation Website: http://www.nokomisfoundation.org/documents/WeCanDoBetter.pdf

NORTON-HAWK, M. (2004). A Comparison of Pimp- and Non-Pimp Controlled Women. *Violence Against Women* 10(2): 189–194.

PAGELOW, M. D. *Family Violence.* New York, NY: Praeger, 1984.

PLUMMER, L., POTTERAT, J. J., MUTH, S. Q., MUTH, J. B. and DARROW, W. W. (1996). Providing Support and Assistance for Low-Income or Homeless Women. *JAMA: The Journal of the American Medical Association* 276(23): 1874–1875.

RABINOVITCH, J. & STREGAN, S. (2004). The PEERS Story: Effective Services Sidestep the Controversies. *Violence Against Women* 10(2): 140–159.

RAPHAEL, J. (2004). Listening to Olivia: Violence, Poverty and Prostitution. Northeastern University Press, Boston, MA.

RAPHAEL, J. & SHAPIRO, D. L. (2004). Violence in Indoor and Outdoor Venues. *Violence Against Women* 10(2): 126–139.

RAPHAEL, J. & SHAPIRO, D. L. (2002). Sisters Speak Out: The Lives and Needs of Prostituted Women in Chicago: A Research Study. Center for Impact Research, Chicago, IL.

SCHOOT, E. & GOSWAMI, S. (2001). Prostitution: A Violent Reality of Homeslessness. Retrieved September 3, 2008 from Chicago Coalition for the Homeless Website: http://cch.issuelab.org/research

SURRATT, H. L., INCIARDI, J. A., KURTZ, S. P. and KILEY, M. C. (2004). Sex Work and Drug Use in a Subculture of Violence. *Crime and Delinquency* 50(1): 43–59.

VALERA, R. J., SAWYER, R. G. & SCHIRALDI, G. R. (2000). Violence and Post Traumatic Stress Disorder in a Sample of Inner City Street Prostitutes. *American Journal of Health Studies* 16(3): 149–155.

WEINER, A. (1996). Understanding the Social Needs of Streetwalking Prostitutes. *Social Work* 41 (1): 97–105.

YACOUBIAN, G. S., URBACH, B. J., LARSEN, K. L., JOHNSON, R. J. & PETERS, R. J. (2000). A Comparison of Drug Use Between Prostitutes and Other Female Arrestees. *Journal of Alcohol and Drug Education* 46(2): 12–26.

YAHNE, C. E., MILLER, W. R., IRVIN-VITELA, L. & TONIGAN, J. S. (2002).

YOUNG, A. M., BOYD, C. & HUBBARD, A. (2000). Prostitution, Drug Use and Psychological Distress. *Journal of Drug Issues* 30(4): 789–800.

ZWEIG, J. M., SCHLICHTER, K. A., and BURT, M. R. (2002). Assisting Women Victims of Violence Who Experience Multiple Barriers to Services. *Violence Against Women.* 8(2): 162–180.

9

Abortion

Is It a Right to Privacy or Compulsory Childbearing?

Roslyn Muraskin

Abortion has been an issue that has dominated the American system of laws for many years. When the first edition of this book was published in 1993, there was controversy over the right of a woman to obtain an abortion. Today, there is even more focus on this issue. As stated by a Tulsa lawyer with the Center for Reproductive Rights, "It is one battle in the war, but the war shall continue" (Hardwick, August 20, 2009, p. 19). A very large conservative movement is afoot in the United States. The Supreme Court continues to face cases that restrict the rights of women over the control of their bodies. There continues to be public debate in state courts and the legislatures as well as among the justices of the Supreme Court regarding a woman's right to privacy. This chapter presents the cases and their holdings. Reproductive rights are the focus of the constitutional right to privacy; stated otherwise, is there a constitutional right to privacy? The cases that are evidenced today are good examples of the court's ability to protect the rights of women. Viewed from another perspective the question becomes, is the unborn fetus a person, a person with rights? As of this writing, the U.S. Supreme Court has not made a determination as to when life begins. The fetus is not considered a person; still there is a strong faction attempting to overthrow the Roe decision and to give the fetus certain rights, such as proper medical care. Today the ruling of *Roe v. Wade* (1973) still pervades, giving women the right to abortion based on a sliding scale. However, the sliding scale offered in *Roe* appears to be slipping.

It is fair to say that abortion "has dominated the landscape of procreational discourse and policy in the United States during the twentieth" century and continues into the twenty-first century (MacKinnon, 2001, p. 1212). From Alice Walker, "[a]bortion, for many women, is more than an experience of suffering beyond anything most men will ever know; it is an act of mercy and an act of self-defense. To make abortion illegal again is to sentence

170

millions of women and children to miserable lives and even more miserable deaths" (1989, pp. 691–692). To view abortion as a crime means that many women will die.

MacKinnon (2001) describes a young black woman who had an illegal abortion during a time prior to *Roe*:

> We were very middle class 1950s. . . . There was no spontaneous sex. . . . But on one occasion, in the fall, one of Joseph's apartment mates was away. . . . We were kidding around and we went to [his] room, and we started fooling around. . . . We fell into his bed and had sex, and my period did not come the next time. . . . I liked the guy, but when he started talking about marriage and babies and stuff I wasn't ready. I wanted to finish my education. . . . I decided to ask my stepmother in Des Moines if she could help me. . . . We must have done it on a Friday night. . . . We went to the poor section of town. I remember not seeing anyone—just looking straight ahead.
>
> It was a kitchen table, coat hanger abortion. It took maybe six minutes. I got on the kitchen table. I think my stepmother gave me a drink of brandy or something, and she said, "Now this may hurt a little bit." She held my hand and this woman stuck a piece of coat hanger into my vagina. She stuck the coat hanger in, a piece that had been sterilized or whatever the hell she had done, and then my stepmother said, "Okay, now you get dressed." And what you were supposed to do was leave that in there until you started to abort. And then I left. I remember walking out with this coat hanger between my legs. . . . That evening I started bleeding. . . . I got up very early in the morning and went to the bathroom and there was just this passage of blood and a clot that was slightly bigger than the clots I usually passed during my menstrual period. . . . I should have been more concerned. If for no other reason than for the physical reality. I could have died. I could have become sterile. . . . When I read about people on the kitchen table I say, "I had one of those." (As cited in Messer & May, 1994, pp. 17, 19–23)

This was then. In the 1970s it was estimated that the number of deaths from illegal abortions was eight times greater than that from legal abortion. Reproductive freedom has been joined with such rights as freedom of speech or assembly. There exist those who have come to the conclusion out of simple personal concern that if women do not control their bodies from within, they can never control their lives from the skin out. There are those who feel that women's role as the most basic means of production will remain the source of their second-class status if outside forces continue to either restrict or compel that production. Remember the words of Justice Miller in *Bradwell v. State of Illinois* (1872), where he stated that "[t]he paramount destiny and mission of woman are to fulfill the noble and benign offices of wife and mother. This is the law of the Creator."

The freedom for women to decide when to become a mother and under what conditions is an issue of great concern. Is abortion an issue that affects women only, and is it an example of sex discrimination? Are we to think primarily of the fetus and thus conclude that abortion is murder, thereby involving the criminal courts? Is abortion to be viewed from a religious perspective, thinking of how the legal codes of Western religions treat the subject? Is abortion a question of privacy? Should states be prevented from intruding into the affairs and personal decisions of their citizens? Does there exist under *Reed v. Reed* (1971) a compelling state interest to interfere with a woman's right to choose? If a woman is a victim of rape or sexual abuse, is she entitled to an abortion without interference from the state? Is it an issue of discrimination against the poor, who may need the state to subsidize abortions, or even racial discrimination because of the high proportion of minorities who choose to abort? The question that comes into focus is not "how can we justify abortion?" but "can we justify compulsory childbearing?" Is there a compelling interest on the part of the state to protect what the courts have refused to define as a person?

A new health bill was passed in March 2010 in the United States. It is left up to individual carriers to decide whether to cover women's abortions. The government will not pay for such procedures. The way it works today is that any state-based exchange that will offer coverage for abortion procedures will in and of itself be segregated "from any premium and cost-sharing credits an amount of each enrollee's private premium dollars that is determined to be sufficient to cover the cost of abortion coverage and any money used for abortions would have to come from premiums, not federal tax dollars" (Farley, September 22, 2009, 1a).

What are the issues the courts have faced when we discuss the issue of abortion? There are two significant constitutional issues at stake in judicial bias against women. The first issue has to do with the right to privacy, implied by the U.S. Constitution in the Fourth Amendment. The other issue concerns the Fourteenth Amendment's right to due process and equal treatment. Is the issue simply one of female autonomy over her body? The conflict continues. It is an issue that comes back repeatedly to haunt the courts, the legislators, and the executive branch of government. When can a woman have a partial abortion? Whose rights are we protecting? The U.S. Supreme Court held that laws prohibiting abortion are unconstitutional. In *Roe v. Wade* (1973), the Court held that "no state shall impose criminal penalties on the obtaining of a safe abortion in the first trimester of pregnancy." Women cannot be charged criminally with obtaining an abortion, but there are administrative regulations and legal penalties that prevent her from doing so.

Abortion is an emotional, legal, religious, and highly volatile issue. In December 1971, the Supreme Court heard the *Roe v. Wade* case, brought to it by an unmarried pregnant woman from Texas who complained that the Texas statute permitting abortions only when necessary to save the life of the mother was unconstitutional. (This person has since indicated that women should not be given the option of abortions, that all life is precious, and therefore, if pregnant, a women should not have the right to choose.)

What was held in *Roe* was that a state may not, during the first trimester of pregnancy, interfere with or regulate the decision of a woman and her doctor to terminate the pregnancy by abortion; that from the end of the first trimester until the fetus becomes viable (usually about 24 to 28 weeks), a state may regulate abortions only to the extent that the regulation relates to the protection of the mother's health; and that only after the point of viability may a state prohibit abortion except when necessary to save the mother's life. The Court further permitted the state to prohibit anyone but a licensed physician from performing an abortion.

The Court did not accept the argument that a woman has a constitutional right to have an abortion whenever she wants one and that the state has no business at all interfering with her decision. Rather, the Court established a sliding scale that balanced the right of the woman against the right of the state to interfere with the decision; the state would have to prove that it had a compelling interest to do so. During the first three months of pregnancy, when continuing the pregnancy is more dangerous than ending it, the Court found no such compelling state interest for overriding the private decision of a woman and her doctor. When abortion becomes a more serious procedure, the Court found that the state's interest in the matter increases enough to justify its imposition of regulations necessary to ensure that the mother's health will be safeguarded. In the last trimester of pregnancy, the Court found that the state's interest in the health and well-being of the mother as well as in the potential life of the fetus is sufficient to outweigh the mother's right of privacy except when her life is at stake.

In the language of the *Roe* Court (1973):

> The right of privacy . . . is broad enough to encompass a woman's decision whether or not to terminate her pregnancy. The detriment that the State would impose upon the pregnant woman is apparent. Specific and direct harm medically diagnosable even in early pregnancy may be involved. Maternity, or additional offspring, may force upon the woman a distressful life and future. There is also the distress, for all concerned, associated with the unwanted child and there is the problem of bringing a child into a family already unable psychologically and otherwise to care for it. In other cases as in this one, the additional difficulties and continuing stigma of unwed motherhood may be involved. All these are factors the woman and her responsible physician will consider in consultation.

The Court continued by indicating in *Roe* that the right to terminate the pregnancy at whatever time was not acceptable to the Court. It indicated further that the right to privacy was not absolute.

With regard to the argument presented that the fetus is a person, the Court went on to comment:

> [I]n nearly all . . . instances [in which the word "person" is used in the Constitution] the use of the word is such that it has application only postnatally. None indicates, with any assurance, that it has any possible prenatal application. All this together with our observation . . . that through the major portion of the nineteenth century prevailing legal practices were far freer than they are today, persuades us that the word person as used in the fourteenth amendment, does not include the unborn.

In answering the question of when life begins, the Court further stated:

> It should be sufficient to note . . . the wide divergence of thinking on this most sensitive and difficult question.
>
> In areas other than criminal abortions, the law has been reluctant to endorse any theory that life as we recognize it, begins before live birth or to accord legal rights to the unborn except in narrowly defined situations and except when the rights are contingent upon live birth. In short, the unborn have never been recognized in the law as persons in the whole sense.
>
> We repeat . . . that the State does have an important and legitimate interest in preserving and protecting the health of the pregnant woman . . . [a]nd that it has still another important and legitimate interest in protecting the potentiality of human life.

The Court had decided to allow the mother to abort at the end of the first trimester and then to allow her physician to decide medically if the patient's pregnancy was to be terminated after this period. The judgment was to be effected by a decision free from the interference of the state.

At the same time that the Supreme Court decided the *Roe* case, it decided a second case, that of *Doe v. Bolton* (1973), which involved a Georgia abortion statute that set forth several conditions that were to be fulfilled prior to a woman obtaining an abortion. These included a statement by the attending physician that an abortion was justified, with the concurrence of at least two other Georgia-licensed physicians; the abortion was to be performed in a hospital licensed by the state board of health as well as accredited by the Joint Commission on Accreditation of Hospitals; there was to be advance approval by an abortion committee of not less than three members of the hospital staff; and the woman had to reside in the state of Georgia.

The Court then held that these provisions were overly restrictive, thereby treating abortion differently from comparable medical procedures and thus violating laws that require the husband of a pregnant woman or the parents of a single mother to give their consent prior to having an abortion. Both of these requirements were struck down by the Supreme Court (*Planned Parenthood of Central Missouri v. Danforth,* 1976).

What, then, is to happen when husband and wife cannot agree? Who is to prevail? The courts have argued that the woman should. Since it is the woman who bears the child physically and who is affected more directly and immediately by the pregnancy, the balance would seem to weigh in her favor.

Until this point the state did not appear to have the constitutional authority to give a third party an absolute and possibly arbitrary veto over the decision of the physician and a parent. There has developed the question of the authority that a parent has over a child. It has been well understood that constitutional rights do not mature and come into being magically when one attains the state-defined age of majority. Minors as well as adults are protected by the Constitution and possess constitutional rights.

There exists a suggested interest in the safeguarding of the family unit and of parental authority. The idea of providing a parent with absolute power over a child suggests that a parent has complete autonomy not allowing for any conflict. The Court continues to review cases whereby the parent of the female will make the decision for her regardless of her wishes.

Two other important issues bearing on the ability of women to obtain abortions have been the right of hospitals to refuse to perform abortions and the right of Medicaid to refuse to pay for nontherapeutic abortions. In the case of *Nyberg v. City of Virginia* (1983), a federal court of appeals concluded that a public hospital may not refuse to perform abortions: "It would be a nonsequitur to say that the abortion decision is an election to be made by the physician and his patient without interference by the State and then allow the State, through its public hospitals, to effectively bar the physician from using State facilities to perform the operation." Theoretically, private hospitals may refuse to perform abortions, but it is not always easy to determine when a hospital is private. One needs to review whether the hospital leases its facilities from the local government, whether it is regulated extensively by the state, whether it has received tax advantage, whether it has received public monies for hospital construction, and whether it is part of a general state plan for providing hospital services. Litigation and debate continue.

Under the decision in *Roe v. Norton* (1973), the Court concluded that federal Medicaid provisions prohibit federal reimbursement for abortion expenses unless a determination has been made that the abortion was medically necessary. The Court held that the government is not required by the Constitution to pay for any medical service, but once it does decide to do so, it must not unduly disadvantage those who exercise a constitutional right. Of late, laws have been passed that no birth control clinic that receives funding from the federal government may give information dealing with abortion, although that has not stopped those who are against abortion from using whatever tactics they deem necessary to prevent such information from being disseminated, including bombing abortion clinics.

Those who are against abortion state that when a woman chooses to have sex, she must be willing to accept all consequences. This is much like the criminal law—you are responsible for the natural consequences of your actions. Those who are against abortion will defend the rights of the fetus to develop, to be given life, and to grow, regardless of the wishes of the mother. Those who are against abortion state that whatever the costs, even to those who are victims of rape and incest, there is a life growing, and it is murder to do anything but carry it to full term. Better that any number of women should ruin their health or even die than one woman should get away with not having a child merely because she does not want one.

There have been cases—in the state of Idaho, for example—that have attempted to make physicians criminally liable for performing abortions rather than laying the responsibility on the mother. Under the Idaho proposal, a man who had committed *date rape*, a term describing sexual assault by an acquaintance (although rape is still defined as rape), could conceivably force the woman to carry the child.

Further decisions have been made affecting the woman's right to choose. For example, in the case of *Bellotti v. Baird* (1979), the Court had voted by a majority vote of 8 to 1 that a state may require a pregnant unmarried minor to obtain parental consent for an abortion if it also offers an alternative procedure. In the case of *Harris v. McRae* (1980), the Court upheld by a margin of 5 to 4 the Hyde amendment, which denies reimbursement for Medicaid abortions. And in the case of *City of Akron v. Akron Center for Reproductive Health, Inc.* (1983), the Court voted 6 to 3 that states cannot mandate what doctors will tell abortion patients or require that abortions for women more than three months pregnant be performed in a hospital. In *Thornburgh v. American College of Obstetricians and Gynecologists* (1986), the Court voted 5 to 4 that states may not require doctors to tell women about risks of abortion and possible alternatives or dictate procedures to third-trimester abortions.

In the case of Ohio upholding a law that required a minor to notify one parent before obtaining an abortion, Justice Kennedy wrote that "it is both rational and fair for the State to conclude that, in most instances, the family will strive to give a lonely or even terrified minor advice that is both compassionate and mature." However, Justice Blackmun, who was the senior author of *Roe v. Wade* (1973), wrote in what has been described as a stinging dissent that Kennedy and his adherents were guilty of "selective blindness" to the reality that "not all children in our country are fortunate enough to be members of loving families. For too many young pregnant women parental involvement in this intimate decision threatens harm, rather than promises of comfort." He ended by stating that "a minor needs no statute to seek the support of loving parents. . . . If that compassionate support is lacking, an unwanted pregnancy is a poor way to generate it." And in *Webster v. Reproductive Health Services* (1989), the Court upheld 5 to 4 a Missouri law barring the use of public facilities or public employees in performing abortions and requiring physicians to test for the viability of any fetus believed to be more than 20 weeks old.

Debate over these and other issues has spawned extensive litigation and put the Court in the position of reviewing medical and operational practices beyond its competence. We therefore believe that the time has come for the court to abandon its efforts to impose a comprehensive solution to the abortion question. Under the Constitution, legislative bodies cannot impose irrational constraints on a woman's procreative choice. But, within those broad confines, the appropriate scope of abortion regulation should be left with the people and to the political processes the people have devised to govern their affairs.

The Court stated that Missouri had placed no obstacles in the path of women seeking abortions. Rather, the state simply chose not to encourage or assist abortions in any respect.

Abortion remains a newsworthy and important subject today. Perceptions of the abortion law differ. For the courts, it is a constitutional issue. Others consider it an act of murder and believe that it should be turned over to the criminal courts. And indeed, some states have at one time or other defined abortion as homicide. The focus is on the process. The issue is difficult because most people do not see it as a clear issue of law. Is the issue one that concerns a woman's right to privacy? Is it a case of sexual discrimination? Or are we to look at the issue from the view of the fetus and view it as an issue of murder? Should abortion be viewed from a religious perspective, thinking of how the legal codes of Western religions treat the subject? Is it simply an issue of privacy and telling the states that they cannot intrude into the private affairs of their citizens? Or do we view abortion as a matter of health, of preventing injuries and death to women who undergo abortions? The answer lies in the fact that there are no easy answers and no easy solutions. Abortion is an issue that explodes in the courts, in legislatures, and in the minds of citizens.

In the case of *Rust v. Sullivan* (1991), the Court upheld 5 to 4 the federal government's ban on abortion counseling in federally funded family-planning clinics. In the case of *Planned Parenthood of Southeastern Pennsylvania v. Casey* (1992), the Court decided against the constitutionality of a law passed in Pennsylvania:

Informed Consent

At least 24 hours before the abortion, except in emergencies, the physician must tell the woman:

- The nature of the proposed procedure or treatment and the risks and alternatives
- The probable gestational age of the unborn child
- The medical risks associated with carrying her child to term
- That government materials are available that list agencies offering alternatives to abortions
- That medical assistance benefits may be available for prenatal care, childbirth, and neonatal care

Parental Consent

If the woman is under 18 and not supporting herself, her parents must be informed of the impending procedure. If both parents or guardians refuse to consent, judicial authorities where the applicant resides or where the abortion is sought shall . . . authorize . . . the abortion if the court determines that the pregnant woman is mature and capable of giving informed consent.

Spousal Notice

No physician shall perform an abortion of a married woman . . . without a signed statement . . . that the woman has notified her spouse.

Exceptions

- Her spouse is not the father of the child.
- Her spouse, after diligent effort, could not be located.
- The pregnancy is the result of spousal sexual assault . . . that has been reported to a law enforcement agency.
- The woman has reason to believe that notifying her spouse is likely to result in bodily injury.

Reporting

Each abortion must be reported to the state on forms that do not identify the woman but do include, among other items:

- The number of the woman's prior pregnancies and prior abortions
- Whether the abortion was performed upon a married woman and if her spouse was notified

The government has interpreted the Constitution in many cases to protect the woman from arbitrary gender-based discrimination, yet the struggle continues. The courts continue to hear cases. However, in no instance is reference made to women's rights. Rather, the cases are based on the constitutional theory of the right to privacy, which is subject to interpretation, there being no exclusive right of privacy mentioned in the Constitution. Of the Supreme Court justices, Justice John Paul Stevens has supported abortion rights; Justice Antonin Scalia looks to overturn the decision in *Roe v. Wade* (1973) but has yet to do so; Former Justice Sandra Day O'Connor had taken the middle ground, as articulated in her dissenting opinion in *Akron v. Akron* as well as in the case of *Hodgson v. Minnesota* (1990), where she stated that the right to an abortion is a "limited fundamental right" that may not be "unduly burdened" absent a compelling government interest, but may be burdened less severely upon a rational basis (947 F.2d, at 689–91). To date there have been no new cases involving abortion.

What becomes noteworthy about cases dealing with the issue of abortion is that the motivation of a woman becomes entirely "irrelevant" to a determination of whether such a right is "fundamental." The Supreme Court has refused to overrule the *Roe v. Wade* decision, although erosion has taken place. The Court in their "wisdom" has upheld state restraints on a woman's right to choose an abortion freely, as supported in their decision in *Planned Parenthood of Southeastern Pennsylvania v. Casey* (1992) by a 5 to 4 decision, but the courts have yet to turn the clocks back to 1973, a time when states could make abortion a crime and punish both a woman and her physician. The Court in the case of *Planned Parenthood* did allow states to impose conditions on women seeking an abortion—an "informed consent" provision that includes a lecture to women in an effort to "educate" them about alternative choices to abortion as well as a 24-hour waiting period to "think it over."

The decisions of the Court have given the states considerable leeway that can make abortions costlier and more difficult to obtain. Such requirements by the state certainly continue to prove difficult for the poor woman who lives and works far from abortion clinics. Even a waiting period as short as 24 hours will force some women who cannot afford to stay overnight to make two trips to the clinic. The issue of whether such a procedure will pose an undue constitutional burden to choose remains open. Has abortion become a question of sex equality? As indicated by Reva Siegel, "[a]bortion-restrictive regulation is state action compelling pregnancy and motherhood, and this simple fact cannot be evaded by invoking nature or a woman's choices. . . . A pregnant woman seeking an abortion has the practical capacity to terminate a pregnancy, which she would exercise but for the community's decision to prevent or deter her. If the community successfully effectuates its will, it is the state, and not nature, which is responsible for causing her to continue the pregnancy" (MacKinnon, 2001, p. 1248).

Partial birth abortions entail a still further controversial procedure. Partial birth abortion is the extraction of all the body of the fetus except the head from the uterus and into the vagina. Thereafter, the contents of the skull are taken from the fetus. The dead intact fetus is removed from its mother-to-be. Many states have enacted legislation that bans partial birth abortions except in cases where it can be confirmed that the mother's life was in danger. Such statutes have been found to be unconstitutional because they are void for either being too vague or putting too great a strain on the woman's right to terminate a pregnancy. In *Carhart v. Stenberg*, 192 F.3d 1142, 76 A.L.R.5th 785 (8th Cir. 199), *cert. granted* in part 2000 WL 21145 (U.S. 2000), the Eighth Circuit held a Nebraska statute banning partial birth abortions unconstitutional on the ground that the statute placed an undue burden on a woman's right to terminate a pregnancy because it would prohibit the use of the dilation and evacuation procedure, which is the most common procedure for second-trimester abortions, as well as the dilation and extraction procedure, which is perhaps more commonly thought of as a partial birth abortion (Bower, 2005, p. 1). By the year 1999, about 30 states had in fact enacted statutes restricting partial birth abortions, but the majority have been found to be unconstitutional either because they are vague or because they miss the exception of protecting a woman's health. Yet, where we speak about constitutional protections, such procedures can be banned.

The following cases show the dilemma in granting women the right to a partial birth abortion:

- A statute regulating a method of abortion must include an exception where it is necessary in appropriate medical judgment for the preservation of the life or health of the mother (*Women's Medical Professional Corp. v. Taft* [2000]).
- Illinois and Wisconsin partial-birth abortion[1] statutes were unconstitutional; the laws lacked any exception for the preservation of the health of the mother and imposed an undue burden on a woman's ability to choose a dilation and evacuation (D&E) abortion, thereby unduly burdening the right to choose abortion itself (*Hope Clinic v. Ryan* [2001]).
- Missouri Infant's Protection Act, which banned the intact dilation and extraction abortion procedure, was unconstitutional because it made no exception to protect the health of the pregnant woman (*Reproductive Health Services of Planned Parenthood of St. Louis Region, Inc. v. Nixon* [2004]).
- Failure of the Partial-Birth Abortion Ban Act of 2003 to contain requisite exception for the preservation of the health of the woman warranted issuance of

a temporary restraining order (TRO) against enforcement of the Act (*Carhart v. Ashcroft* [2003]).

- Partial-Birth Abortion Ban Act of 2003 unconstitutionally restricted a particular abortion method without providing an exception permitting use of that method when necessary to protect a woman's health; substantial evidence in record did not support congressional fact findings that the banned procedure was never necessary in appropriate medical judgment for the preservation of the health of the woman (*Carhart v. Ashcroft* [2004]).

- Any abortion regulation must contain adequate provision for a woman to terminate her pregnancy if it poses a threat to her life or health; an adequate health exception is a per se constitutional requirement (*Planned Parenthood of Idaho, Inc. v. Wasden* [2004]).

In *Planned Parenthood of Southern Arizona v. Lawall* C.A.9 (Ariz.) 2002, the case was brought by a family-planning organization and a physician who challenged the facial validity of Arizona's parental consent abortion statute. The Court held that the statute had been constitutional, and there was an appeal. The Court of Appeals held that "judicial by-pass provision of the statute adequately protected minors' right to choose and privacy interest and thus was not facially invalid."

In the case of *Hill v. Colorado* (530 U.S. 703) in 2000, abortion opponents had sought to enjoin enforcement of a statute prohibiting any person from knowingly approaching within eight feet of another person near a health care facility claiming it was a violation of first amendment rights. The U.S. Supreme Court heard the case and held that (1) the statute narrowly tailored content-neutral time, place, and manner regulation; (2) it was not overbroad or unconstitutionally vague; and (3) it did not impose unconstitutional prior restraint on speech.

And so the fight continues.

In the case of *New Mexico Right to Choose v. Johnson* (1999), the court held that a "prohibition by the New Mexico Human Services Department on using state funds to pay for abortion for Medicaid-eligible women who were not covered because of the Hyde Amendment violated the state ERA." Under the right to privacy, accessibility to the use of contraceptive devices cannot be made a crime, but then insurance companies typically do not cover such devices. Is this a form of discrimination against women?

Some argue that abortion is counter to the interests of feminists—that abortion is sexist in nature (Bailey, 1995). The argument goes that a new movement of prolife feminists asserts that abortion is an act of desperation. The argument continues that when women murder their own children, society has done a great disservice to women. There arises the question of whether the act of abortion is "an offensive and sexist notion that women must deny their unique ability to conceive and bear children in order to be treated equally" (Smolin, 1990).

What characterizes the United States is the extreme division on issues such as abortion and sexuality. ". . . laws pertaining to abortion and sexuality are the grist of much political activity and can reflect extreme viewpoints on the degree to which people are legally able to make decisions about reproduction. . . . the claim is that a minority of politically active conservatives has had a strong influence on laws that limit access to abortion and constrain sexuality. [Resulting from this] laws may not reflect majority public opinion, but instead may reflect the preferences of a minority of the population" (Morash, 2006, p. 45).

There have been setbacks on all sides. In April 2004, there was a march of hundreds of thousands in Washington, D.C., showing their support for the right of a woman to choose. These activists were protecting the policies of President George W. Bush at the time. "Contradicting prior Supreme Court decisions, in 2003 the U.S. Congress passed and the president [George W. Bush] signed the Partial Ban Abortion Act of 2003, which restricted abortion in cases when the fetus could be considered viable outside the uterus. (Note this went beyond all prior Supreme Court decisions.) In 2004, the Unborn Victims of Violence Act was signed. The purpose of that act is to allow a separate murder against a person, who, by killing a woman, also kills the fetus she is carrying. The law therefore defines a fetus as a viable person, contrary [to the language in *Roe v. Wade*]" (Morash, p. 46).

As can be rightly concluded there is a trend to give more and more rights to the unborn, taking away a woman's right to control her own body. President Barack Obama supports the rights of women to choose. But yet we have had decisions that women who are indigent and wishing an abortion do not come within the limited category of disadvantaged classes.

It is noteworthy that in states such as New York, the prochoice dialogue appears to have redefined abortion from a criminal issue to a medical issue. Whereas states such as Pennsylvania have the most restrictive legislation regarding abortion. Abortion as a medical issue sees women having more choices. "When abortion is viewed as a legal issue, legislators etch into the law specific circumstances that will limit women's choices" (Morash, 2006).

At the time of this writing another *interesting* issue that has arisen is the issue of health care for all those 35 million Americans who have no health insurance. Current law, reinforced in bills passed by both the House and the Senate, requires a woman to purchase what amounts to a rider policy to cover abortion services. The health bill has been passed and is now law. The debate continues as to whether insurance companies will pay for abortions. As per the American Association of University, women believe that the job of politicians is not to make decisions for women regarding reproductive health care. It is a decision that belongs only to the woman, and to no one else. If this were to occur we would go back to the days of the coat hanger abortions.

Still another issue that attaches itself to the question of abortion is that of federal funding for stem cell research, related to abortion. "Stem cell science offers a wholly new approach to intractable diseases. . . . the issue is deeply controversial. Some opponents simply argue against fiddling with Mother Nature. Others view the use of embryonic stem cells—isolated from embryos—as murder, sure that the life of an individual begins at conception. Thus, it is closely tied to the abortion debate, not soon to be resolved" (Cooke, 2001, p. 1). Some believe that this issue of stem cell research is tied to abortion, because these embryos are defined as humans with rights and privileges attached. Former President George W. Bush indicated that he would allow federally funded research on existing human embryonic stem cells to go forward, but only on cells that already exist. The debate has once again become political. Rather than allowing research to go forward that may find the cures to various diseases, the mere fact that the president has put limits on the research means that research will slow down. According to an editorial by Clymer in *The New York Times* (August 10, 2001, p. A18), "[m]ost people might have trouble seeing a tiny clump of cells in a petri dish as a human being. But some abortion opponents do, and they have argued that the thousands of excess embryos created by fertility clinics every year should be protected and 'adopted' by childless couples. They deserve respect for their beliefs. But they should not be allowed to dictate public policy, especially in an area where the health of so many people might be in the balance. As supporters of the stem cell research keep pointing out, there is more than one way to be pro-life."

From the words of Justice Stewart speaking in the *Roe v. Wade* (1973) decision, "[I]n a Constitution for a free people, there can be no doubt that the meaning of 'liberty' must be broad indeed. The Constitution nowhere mentions a specific right of personal choice in matters of marriage and family life, but the 'liberty' protected by the Due Process Clause of the Fourteenth Amendment covers more than those freedoms explicitly named in the Bill of Rights" (p. 168). And as written by Justice Harlan, "[T]he full scope of the liberty guaranteed by the Due Process Clause cannot be found in or limited by the precise terms of the specific guarantees elsewhere provided in the Constitution. This 'liberty' is not a series of isolated points priced out in terms of the taking of property; the freedom of speech, press and religion; the right to keep and bear arms, the freedom from unreasonable searches and seizures and so on. It is a rational continuum which, broadly speaking, includes a freedom from all substantial arbitrary impositions and purposeless restraints . . . and which must also recognize what a reasonable and sensitive judgement must, that certain interests require particularly careful scrutiny of the state needs asserted to justify their abridgment" (p. 169).

According to the wording in the case of *Borowski v. Attorney General of Canada* (1989), "[t]he Court must be careful not to create a time in a woman's life when, because of her unchosen biological capacities, she is outside the constitutional protection of the expansive equality rights." If we were to recognize the fetus as a person legally, and then grant it legal rights over the woman's body, the woman would no longer have any legal and decision-making rights over her own body (Borowski).

"The relation between a pregnant woman and the fetus within her is not an ancient archetype or a category long fundamental to law. Legal personhood has conventionally begun at birth and ended at death. . . . both birth and death as lines have their ambiguities. Fetal life challenges these demarcations, raising questions of the definition of life and the power over death. . . . The common law traditionally has regarded the mother and fetus or unborn child as a single unit. [Thus] the contemporary discussion over the maternal-fetal relation can be seen as pulled between two poles. One seeks to humanize the fetus, as medicine has advanced its ability to care for unborn life outside the women to ever earlier stages in development" (MacKinnon, p. 1278). Does the woman have a right to privacy?

The Constitution does not explicitly mention any right of privacy. Whether the right of privacy is based on the Fourteenth Amendment's notion of personal liberty or on the Ninth Amendment's reservation of rights to all people, the fact is that if enforced by the state to not allow abortions, women would be the ones to carry a fetus that may be unwanted, or as a result of being a victim of a rape, the question is whether personal privacy includes the right to have an abortion.

As stated by Ellen Chesler (1992), "[I]t has been seventy years since Margaret Sanger claimed that science would make women 'the owner, the mistress of herself.'" The spirit of her words lives on. The struggles of women and their right to choose and not to be punished in criminal courts continue. The final decision is not yet in. But for those who enjoy a safe bet, it is that women during the twenty-first century will be limited in years to come to choose for themselves whether to have an abortion. That battles were fought and won in prior years does not mean that these decisions will remain. Battles won will still be fought. When will women be allowed to decide for themselves who has control over their body, or has that already been decided by the courts?

REFERENCES

BAILEY, J. T. (1995). Feminism 101: A primer for prolife persons. In R. McNair (Ed.), *Profile feminism: Yesterday and today* (pp. 160, 163).

BOWER, C. (2005). American Law Reports. ALR 5th. (Copyright 2000–2004 West Group). Thomson/West.

CHESLER, E. (1992, August 2). RU-486: We need prudence, not politics. *The New York Times, Op-Ed. page*.

CLYMER, A. (1992, July 31). Lawmakers fear amendments on abortion rights. *The New York Times*, p. A11.

CLYMER, A. (2001, August 10). The stem cell battle moves to congress. *New York Times*, p. A18.

COOKE, R. (2001, August 10). Fundamentals of stem cell research. *Newsday*, p. A2.

FARLEY, R. (2009, September 22). Under health reform, public wouldn't pay for abortions. *St. Petersburg Times*, Florida, p. 1A.

HARDWICK (CENTER FOR REPRODUCTIVE RIGHTS). (2009, August 20).

MACKINNON, C. (2001). *Sex equality*. New York: Foundation Press.

MESSER, E., & MAY, K. E. (Eds.). (1994). *Lilia, in back rooms: Voices from the illegal abortion era.* Amherst, NY: Prometheus Books.

MORASH, M. (2006). *Understanding, gender, crime and justice*. Thousand Oaks, CA.: Sage.

SMOLIN, D. (1990). The jurisprudence of privacy in a splintered Supreme Court. *Marquette Law Review*, 75, 975, 995–1001.

WALKER, A. (1989). What can the white man say to the black man? *The Nation*, 75, 691–692.

ENDNOTE

1. D & X is deliberate dilation of the cervix usually over a sequence of days; instrumental conversion of the fetus to a footling breech; breech extraction of the body excepting the head; and partial evacuation of the intracranial contents of a living fetus to effect vaginal delivery of a dead but otherwise intact fetus (*American College of Obstetricians and Gynecologists, January 1997*).

CASES

Akron v. Akron (1983), 462 U.S. 416.

Borowski v. Attorney General of Canada, S.C.R. 342 (1989), 1279.

Bradwell v. State of Illinois, 83 U.S. 130 (1872).

Carhart v. Ashcroft, 287 F. Supp. 2d 1015 (D. Neb. 2003).

Carhart v. Ashcroft, 311 F. Supp. 2d 805 (D. Neb. 2004).

Carhart v. Stenberg, 192 F.3d 1142, 76 A.L.R.5th 785 (8th Cir. 199).

City of Akron v. Akron Center for Reproductive Health, Inc., 462 U.S. 416, 103 S. Ct. 2481, 76 L. Ed. 2d 687 (1983).

Doe v. Bolton, 410 U.S. 179, 93 S. Ct. 739, 35 L. Ed. 2d 201 (1973).

Harris v. McRae, 448 U.S. 297, 100 S. Ct. 2671, 65 L. Ed. 2d 784 (1980).

Hill v. Colorado, 530 U.S. 703(2000).

Hodgson v. Minnesota, 110 S. Ct. 2926 (1990).

Hope Clinic v. Ryan, 249 F. 3d 603 (7th Cir. 2001)

New Mexico Right to Choose v. Johnson, 975 P.2d 841 (1988), *cert. denied*, 562 U.S. 1020 (1999).

Nyberg v. City of Virginia, 667 F.2d 754 (CA 8 1982), *cert. denied*, 462 U.S. 1125 (1983).

Planned Parenthood of Central Missouri v. Danforth, 428 U.S. 52 (1976).

Planned Parenthood of Idaho, Inc. v. Wasden, 376 F.3d 908 (9th Cir. 2004).

Planned Parenthood of Southeastern Pennsylvania v. Casey, 505 U.S. 833 (1992).

Reed v. Reed, 404 U.S. 71 (1971).

Reproductive Health Services of Planned Parenthood of St. Louis Region, Inc. v. Nixon, 325 F. Supp. 2d 991 (W.D. Mo. 2004).

Roe v. Norton, 408 F. Supp. 660 (1973).

Roe v. Wade, 410 U.S. 113, 95 S. Ct. 705, 35 L. Ed. 2d 147 (1973).

Rust v. Sullivan, 114 L. Ed. 2d 233 (1991).

Thornburgh v. American College of Obstetricians and Gynecologists, 476 U.S. 747, 106 S. Ct. 2169, 90 L. Ed. 2d 779 (1986).

Webster v. Reproductive Health Services, 492 U.S. 490, 109 S. Ct. 3040, 106 L. Ed. 2d 410 (1989).

Women's Medical Professional Corp. v. Taft, 114 F. Supp. 2d 644 (S.D. Ohio 2000).

10

Murdering for Motherhood

A New Breed of Female Murderers

Etta F. Morgan

This chapter represents research in progress as we begin to examine the cases of female murderers who killed their victims in order to steal their fetuses. We begin with a brief discussion on female criminality followed by a discussion of the literature on female perpetrated homicides. In the next section, we offer some possible psychological explanations for the behavior of these female murderers along with a discussion of perpetrators of violence. We conclude that the peculiarities of these cases will continue to unfold as we obtain and analyze information.

INTRODUCTION

Society's interest in the study of female criminality has proliferated during the last three decades; however, very few empirical studies have been conducted on violent women. While the occurrences of female perpetrated murders are relatively rare, the lack of systematic attention to violent female offenders may be partially explained by gender stereotyping. A woman who commits a violent act such as a murder is perceived differently than a man who commits a similar act unless the act is perpetrated in a gruesome manner. A woman who commits murder is perceived by society as one who has stepped outside of her socially sanctioned role to commit an unspeakable act of violence that goes against the nature of womanhood. While fewer than 15% of the arrestees for murders committed in the United States are females, history reveals numerous examples of female murderers.

Elizabeth Duncan, Velma Barfield, and Bernadette Powell are a few examples of female murderers who have experienced considerable public attention because of their crimes. Elizabeth Duncan, who was executed in 1962, hired two men to murder her son's pregnant wife; Velma Margie Bullard Barfield (a 50-year-old grandmother) was executed in 1984 for poisoning her fiancé to death by lacing his beer with arsenic; and Bernadett Powell was convicted of killing her husband after unsuccessfully using the battered woman defense. These historical examples of disturbing cases of female murderers continue with Susan Smith's murder of her two young sons in 1994 in South Carolina.

In spite of these violent acts perpetrated by women, very few Americans link violent acts to women, and fewer Americans perceive the violent offender to be a female. Acts of violence are embedded in American culture and homicides perpetrated by women are a part of this broader culture of violence. In an effort to provide a broader understanding of female murderers, this study discusses the development of a typology of females who commit domestic homicides and those who commit nondomestic homicides. The paucity of systematic research on women who commit murder facilitates the need to develop patterns and trends of female homicides. The motive(s) for the commission of murders perpetuated by females, characteristics of those females who are most likely to commit murder and how they actually commit the murder are pertinent in evaluating women who kill in domestic and nondomestic situations.

REVIEW OF LITERATURE

Women commit murder for a number of reasons including anger, exposure to domestic violence, self-defense, the influence of a male, mental illness, a feeling of isolation, and substance abuse. However, research on homicide committed by women suggests that the most common female murderer is one who kills her intimate partner after years of physical, sexual, and psychological abuse (Block, 1985; Goetting, 1988; Jones, 1980; Mann, 1996; Rasche, 1990; Scott & Davies, 2002; Wolfgang, 1958). Women who commit murder are likely to do so in the context of intimate relationships or family stress, suggesting that women, in some situations, kill in self-defense (Browne, 1987; Walker, 1989). Women living in abusive relationships often feel hopeless, despair, have low self-esteem, and a distorted view of reality (Browne, 1987; Walker, 1989) and, in some cases, speak their rage or express their dissatisfaction with their personal situation and the patriarchal society through their murderous act.

While we may think that aggression and violence in females is abnormal, research (Gilbert, 2002; Jack, 2001; Kramer, 2005) suggests that we live in a society that shapes our being through cultural ideology. According to Alvarez and Bachman (2003):

> From its very inception, violence and killing have been instrumental in the formation of American society and its value system. . . . How we define ourselves, the ways in which we respond to conflict, and the values we hold as truths are all guided and shaped by our cultural frames of reference. . . . our violent past affects the nature and distribution of modern American homicide. (p. 24)

Evidence shows that women commit a substantially larger proportion of spousal violence in the United States than in other nations (Wilson & Daly, 1992, p. 190). A look at spousal homicide statistics from 1976 to 1985 reveals that a total of 18,471 individuals were estimated to have murdered their spouses in the United States (Maxfield, 1989; Mercy & Saltzman, 1989) with 10,529 spousal homicides involving wives as victims and 7,888 involving husbands as victims. Thus, while females only comprise 10% of all persons who murder, the number of women who kill their husbands relative to the number of men who kill their wives narrows considerably in the area of domestic homicide. In fact, for every 100 men who killed their wives, roughly 75 women killed their husbands. Wilson and Daly (1992) refer to this quantity as the *Sex Ratio of Killing (SROK)*. While the likelihood of wives killing their husbands is symmetrical to husbands killing their wives, the motives for the murders are entirely different between the sexes. Researchers have found that female and male murderers were more similar than dissimilar although the quality and quantity of stress experienced by both sexes differ (Wilson & Daly, 1992).

The most likely victims of women who kill are people with whom they have had a close relationship: intimate partners, their children, and to some degree other relatives. However, domestic homicides committed by women do not explain all murders committed by females. To a lesser degree, women commit nondomestic homicides involving a stranger or an acquaintance (Scott & Davies, 2002). In the mid-1970s, Alder (1975) and Simon (1975) proposed a liberationist view of women who kill. This perspective suggests that as women are liberated from traditional social roles, their economic and social opportunities in the workforce will increase and, thus, patterns of female offending will become more like those of their male counterparts. Of course, the liberation perspective advanced by Alder (1975) and Simon (1975) has been criticized by others (Daly & Chesney-Lind, 1988; Smart, 1976) who suggest that further research is needed before conclusive statements about the similarities between female offending patterns and male offending patterns can be made and that females patterns will differ from males (D'Cruze, Walklate, & Pegg, 2006). Even in those instances where employment and economic opportunities for women and men are quite similar, gender-based differences are still relevant.

Some research suggests that with changes in the historical and traditional role of women and the need to elevate their economic position, some women kill in circumstances related to a drug market economy rather than in a domestic setting (Brownstein, Spunt, Crimmins, & Langley, 1997; Scott & Davies, 2002). Brownstein et al. conducted a study on females incarcerated for committing murder in the context of economic interests as related to the drug market and they concluded that some women do commit murder to protect or expand their economic interests; however, the commission of the homicide is not solely due to protecting their economic interests. Some women commit homicides for reasons other than the drug economy (e.g., killing in self-defense, killing in anger, and killing to stop abuse). Interestingly, while these women used violence to protect or broaden their economic base in the drug market, they often act violently in terms of their relationship to a man, either killing on behalf of the male or killing out of fear of the male (Scott & Davies, 2002).

WEAPONS OF CHOICE

The woman's choice of weapon in a murder case now resembles those selected by their male counterparts. While knives and other objects are used frequently by women who commit murder, most studies reveal that the handgun is used in over 50% of homicide cases involving women as perpetrators (Mann, 1996; Wolfgang, 1958; McClain, 1982; Formby, 1986; Scott & Davies, 2002). The use of handguns in the current cases follows the same patterns as noted in previous research. It has been substantiated elsewhere that women murderers in southern and western cities were more likely to use guns than their female counterparts in midwestern or eastern cities (Mann, 1996). Generally, women are likely to perpetrate the homicide by using a single weapon to inflict multiple wounds. Surprisingly, strangulation has been used by some female murderers.

A NEW BREED OF FEMALE MURDERERS

Alcohol use and drug use have been cited as factors in homicides (Mann, 1996; Wolfgang, 1958; Ward, Jackson, & Ward, 1979). While the association between alcohol use and female-perpetrated homicide is generally supported by research, it does not appear that the new breed of female murderers are under the influence of any type of mind-altering substances before, during, or after the homicide. This new breed of female homicide perpetrators meticulously plans to surgically remove and steal a fetus from a pregnant female.

In planning to commit these crimes, the perpetrators told spouses, boyfriends, family members, and friends that they were pregnant even though in at least one case (Scott 1996), the perpetrator had a hysterectomy. Plans also included obtaining ultrasounds, feigning morning sickness, having baby showers, and going to doctor's offices to mingle with expectant mothers. To date approximately twelve women have been charged with this crime. The earliest documented case occurred in Albuquerque, New Mexico, in 1987 where Dari Pierce strangled her victim and cut the baby from her abdomen with a car key. This case is perhaps the most gruesome of the twelve. In at least two of the cases Jacqueline Williams (1995) and Tiffany Hall (2006) also murdered or attempted to murder the victims' other children who were present in the home. Erin Kuhn-Brown (2000) and Tiffany Hall (2006) were related to their victims, aunt and cousin, respectively. The latest case occurred during the summer of 2009. The majority of the victims were shot before the child was removed. After removing the fetuses, the perpetrators state that they went into labor during periods that they were alone and therefore had to deliver the baby themselves.

The next step in the plan involved taking the fetuses to the hospital to help validate to others that the perpetrators had in fact had a baby; however, in some cases, it was this step that started the investigation when medical personnel realized that the individual purporting to have given birth did not, yet they had a newborn. As medical personnel questioned and stalled perpetrators, they tended to just leave the hospitals perhaps suspecting that they could not continue the charade without involving the authorities. The final step in the plan was to convince the spouse, boyfriends, family, friends, and anyone willing to listen, that motherhood was the ultimate joy in a woman's life by "showing off" the new baby.

VICTIM PRECIPITATION

According to Wolfgang's (1958) research on homicides in Philadelphia, victims, especially men, were likely to precipitate their own deaths by using threats of physical force or by actually using physical force. In the twelve current murder cases under review, evidence does not suggest that any of the victims used or threatened to use physical force toward the perpetrator. The perpetrators found various ways to become acquainted with their victims. Besides being relatives, some befriended their victims and/or pretended to want to purchase items such as, vehicles or animals from the victims. Perpetrators appeared to pose no threat to their victims and as a result victims were unaware of the danger they were in. Victims were clueless regarding the motive of the perpetrators.

PSYCHOLOGICAL EXPLANATIONS OF THE CRIMES

The uniqueness of these cases make them difficult to understand and explain. The main motive that has been given for these gruesome murders is that the perpetrators desired to be mothers. Whatever the motive, it does not justify the murders. During the preliminary investigation of these cases, we have identified several factors which we believe are important to understanding the perpetrators' state of mind as well as their behavior. These factors include emotions, aggression, violence, and responsibility. According to McInerney (1979), "an emotion is a unitary mental entity" (p. 43) with some common features, namely, subject matter and the evaluation of subject matter viewed as abstractions, not elements. An emotion is aroused through some type of classification process of the subject matter. For example, in these cases, perhaps the perpetrators believed that they would make the best mothers and, therefore, characterized their victims as unfit and unworthy to be mothers. As a result, some emotion, perhaps the need to nurture the baby, caused them to react. McInerney (1979) explains it as thus, "a person's reasons for his emotion are included in the emotion itself via the subject matter" (p. 44).

The subject matter is very important in relation to an emotion and therefore must be evaluated. However, it is possible for numerous evaluations to occur on the same subject matter (McInerney, 1979). "The notion of evaluation abstracts from the descriptive and referential features of what is experienced. What we actually experience in an emotion is a complex evaluated subject matter. . . . The evaluation provides a general orientation for our action" (McInerney, 1979, p. 45–46). The action one takes may or may not be negative and in some instances, persons take no action. However, one should not assume that because a person is experiencing a certain emotion, he/she will be motivated to respond in a particular manner. Although we have no way of knowing the specific emotion that influenced these perpetrators, we do know that the response was vengeful, ruthless, and dehumanizing. Another factor that may help to explain these cases is aggression. In order to fully understand aggression, we must first examine the influence of culture on motivations. One's culture sustains shared values, goals, explanations, world images, and a symbolic environment. It also influences motives and their responses (Alvarez & Bachman, 2003; Staub, 1989). Staub (1989) notes that "many aspects of culture are *processes* that occur *among* individuals" (p. 51, emphasis in original). [Yet], "cultural characteristics modify each other" (Staub, 1989, p. 51). Various studies (Milgram, 1974; Maslow, 1971) have discovered cultural differences which influence numerous social institutions that may cause the mistreatment of others or prosocial actions. A cultural characteristic of great significance in these cases seems to be aggression.

Aggressive behavior develops as a result of cultural influences and life experiences. For some people aggressive behavior becomes a value whereby they tend to find challenges and provocation in the very being of their daily existence. Staub (1989) suggests that *"there are genetic predispositions toward altruism and aggression . . . [which] are shaped by socialization and culture into actual dispositions*" (p. 53, emphasis in original). In societies where aggression has been culturally idealized or used as means to resolve conflict, such as the United States, due in part to wars, television, and film, it merely becomes an acceptable and available way of life (Alvarez & Bachman, 2003; Staub, 1989).

PERPETRATORS OF VIOLENCE

Perpetrators of violence tend to possess either one or both of the following characteristics (a) "potentially antisocial and (b) authority oriented. Upon closer examination of these characteristics, we find that the potentially antisocial person (a) has a poor self-image, (b) views others and social institutions as hostile, (c) he/she may be defensive towards others, and (d) are sensitive to problems in life. This person may have morals and values that differ from the established norms in society, particularly since: harming others can become a value in itself . . . these characteristics can give rise to the motivation to harm or reduce inhibitions against aggression whatever motive it serves, and provide the competencies required for aggression. Aggression becomes a possible avenue to satisfy varied motivations, even a desire for stimulation and excitement" (Staub, 1989, p. 71).

A characteristic shared by both the potentially antisocial person and the authority oriented person is the inability to accept others while denying his/her own faults or failures. We should note that these persons may function as responsible members of society until such time when circumstances become overwhelming and then, they blame others for their problems and may even harm them (Staub, 1989). Family socialization practices, whether it is physical punitiveness or the withdrawal of love, also influence antisocial personality. Perpetrators may also exhibit a characteristic known as authority-oriented personality. Persons who possess this characteristic respect authority, but act "punitively towards people not in authority" (Staub, 1989, p. 73). These persons like exercising power over those persons lower than themselves in hierarchical relationships. There seems to be a need to have order and structure in their world based on power and position in relation to the hierarchy. Again, these characteristics alone do not cause persons to become perpetrators. However, these characteristics coupled with circumstances, associates, and the culture are all influential factors which govern the behaviors of perpetrators. Anyone can become a perpetrator, especially persons who have worked in occupations which have devalued others. In some instances, persons may become perpetrators through a process of "self-selection and selection by authorities of those who possess at least part of a predisposing pattern, especially when the need for violence is evident from the start" (Staub, 1989, p. 69).

Since aggressive behavior extends from childhood into adulthood, persons should be attentive to different acts of harm committed by children toward others. Perhaps, this will allow for some type of early intervention which may assist in decreasing the likelihood of continued harming of others in the life of that particular individual. Without early intervention, the likelihood of the harm-doing behavior becomes more probable (Staub, 1989). According to Staub (1989), "one psychological consequence of harm-doing is further devaluation of victims . . . the just-world hypothesis [states] people tend to assume that victims have earned their suffering by their actions or character" (p. 79). Persons who learn to be aggressive proceed along a continuum which permits the exchange of conventional morals and values for those which tend to be destructive.

Staub (1989) states:

> As the destruction process evolves, harming victims can become "normal" behavior. Inhibitions against harming or killing diminish, and extraneous motives can enter: greed, the enjoyment of power, the desire for sex or excitement. This is helped along by the belief that the victims do not matter and deserve to suffer, and even that any form of their suffering furthers the cause the perpetrators serve. (p. 84)

The closer a person gets to the extreme end of the destruction continuum, the more difficult it becomes to stop the progress because at that point the person is determined to complete the goal. Any interference will add additional tension to the tension that already exists as one nears the completion of a goal (Staub, 1989). Arriving at the extreme end of the destruction continuum will result in some type of harm to another person and, in some instances, will result in violence and death.

Violence is an element that touches the lives of all people whether directly or indirectly. We, as a society, are constantly reminded of acts of violence or the threat of violence. The media, politicians, and public outcry focuses on our fear of violence to (a) increase the marketability of various products, (b) win elections and pass legislation, and (c) control our daily existence. Harris (1980) states:

> violence . . . creates harmony among otherwise warring elements . . . the *status quo* (emphasis in original) breeds violence and merely differ in the cause they attach to it. The rest of us are joined through psychological benefits derived from violence. We thrill to the threat of violent acts, and we tingle with self-assigned blame for them. (p. 10)

Society tends to selectively condemn violence. By this we mean that some acts of violence are not viewed as violence, therefore, they are not condemned. For example, a person's death caused by a crowd is not labeled as a death due to a violent act, but instead it is called an accident. Yet, other acts of violence are more widely publicized and condemned. In the case under study, we find acts of violence that seem to defy reality.

Yet, research has shown that women can be ruthless murderers. Kirsta (1994) notes "that women who kill, whether in the heat of passion or in cold blood, may do so with as much sadistic savagery and overkill as any man" (p. 132). It is believed that the cruel and sadistic nature of the murders reflect inadequacies in the perpetrator's life such as, a lack of power and control within his/her own life (Kirsta, 1994). Previous studies (Haritos-Fatouros, 1988; Haritos-Fatouros, 2003; Staub, 1989) have found that persons who are capable of torturing others must be normal and mentally stable in order to become dehumanized to the point that torture and murder become acceptable and without meaning.

CONCLUSION

These are not typical female murderers and the use of both a gun and a knife attest to the savage nature of the crimes. It is difficult at best to truly understand these cases. How does one go from being a friend to the victim's murderer? Although there are many similarities in these cases, each one also has its own peculiarities. As this research continues, we want to know exactly what caused a productive citizen in the community to turn into a cold, heartless, kidnapper and murderer.

REFERENCES

ALDER, F. (1975). *Sisters in crime: The rise of the new female offender*. NY: McGraw-Hill.

ALVAREZ, A., & BACHMAN, R. (2003). *Murder American style*. Belmont, CA: Thomson/Wadsworth.

BLOCK, C. (1985). Lethal violence in Chicago over seventeen years: Homicides known to police 1965–1981. Chicago, IL: Criminal Justice Information Authority.

BROWNE, A. (1987). *When battered women kill*. NY: Free Press.

BROWNSTEIN, H., SPUNT, B., CRIMMINS, S., & LANGLEY, S. (1997). Convicted women who have killed children: A self-psychology perspective. *Journal of Interpersonal Violence, 12*, 49–69.

DALY, K., & CHESNEY-LIND, M. (1988). Feminism and criminology. *Justice Quarterly, 5*, 497–538.

D'CRUZE, S., WALKLATE, S., & PEGG, S. (2006). *Murder: Social and historical approaches to understanding murder and murderers*. Portland, OR: Willan Publishing.

FORMBY, W. (1986). *Homicides in a semi-rural southern environment*. Unpublished manuscript.

GILBERT, P. (2002). Discourse of female violence and societal gender stereotypes. *Violence Against Women, 8*(11), 1271–1300.

GOETTING, A. (1988). Patterns of homicide among women. *Journal of Interpersonal Violence, 3*, 3–20.

HARITOS-FATOUROS, M. (1988). The official torturer: A learning model for obedience to authority of violence. *Journal of Applied Social Psychology, 18*(13), 1107–1120.

HARITOS-FATOUROS, M. (2003). *The psychological origins of institutionalized torture*. London: Routledge.

HARRIS, J. (1980). *Violence and responsibility*. London: Routledge.

JACK, D. (2001). *Behind the mask: Destruction and creativity in women's aggression*. Cambridge, MA: Harvard University Press.

JONES, A. (1980). *Women who kill*. NY: Fawcett.

KIRSTA, A. (1994). *Deadlier than the male: Violence and aggression in women*. NY: Harper Collins.

KRAMER, L. (2005). *The sociology of gender* (2nd Ed.). Los Angeles, CA: Roxbury.

MANN, C. (1996). *When women kill*. NY: SUNY-Albany Press.

MASLOW, A. (1971). *The farther reaches of human nature*. City: The Viking Press.

MAXFIELD, M. (1989). Circumstances in supplementary homicide reports: Variety and validity. *Criminology, 27*(4), 671–696.

McCLAIN, P. (1982). Black female homicide offenders and victims: Are they from the same population? *Death Education, 6*, 265–278.

MERCY, J., & SALTZMAN, L. (1989). Fatal violence among spouses in the United States, 1976-85. *American Journal of Public Health, 79*(5), 595–599.

MILGRAM, S. (1974). *Obedience to authority*. NY: Harper Row.

RASCHE, C. (1990). Early models for contemporary thought on domestic violence and women who kill their mates: A review of the literature from 1895 to 1970. *Women & Criminal Justice, 1*(2), 31–53.

SCOTT, L., & DAVIES, K. (2002). Beyond the statistics: An examination of killings by women in three Georgia counties. *Homicide Studies, 6*(4), 297–324.

SIMON, R. (2005). *Crimes women commit and the punishments they receive*. Lanham, MD: Rowman & Littlefield.

SMART, C. (1976). *Women, crime and criminology: A feminist critique*. Boston: Routledge & Kegan Paul.

State of Alabama v. Felicia Scott (1996).

STAUB, E. (1989). *The roots of evil: The origins of genocide and group violence.* New York: Cambridge University Press.

WALKER, L. (1989). *Terrifying love: Why battered women kill and how society responds.* NY: Harper & Row.

WARD, D., JACKSON, J., & WARD, R. (1979). Crimes of violence by women. In F. Adler & R. Simon (Eds.), *Criminology of deviant women.* Boston: Houghton-Mifflin.

WILSON, M., & DALY, M. (1992). Who kills whom in spouse killings? On the exceptional sex ratio of spousal homicides in the United States. *Criminology, 30*(2), 189–215.

WOLFGANG, M. (1958). *Patterns in homicide.* Montclair, NJ: Patterson Smith.

11

Trafficking in Women

Ann Janette Alejano-Steele and Liying Li

--- ❖ ---

In recent years, greater attention has been given to human trafficking as a global human rights violation that exploits women as commodities. The violent nature of human trafficking has peaked public curiosity and called for action and protections. What is the scope of this complex crime? How have gendered vulnerabilities resulting from social, political, and economic inequalities led women to circumstances where they are forced, fraudulently led, and coerced into labor and commercial sex? Most important, what comprehensive initiatives and resources exist to address this crime? This chapter will review the crime of human trafficking impacting women in the United States.

The year 2000 was a pivotal legislative year both internationally and nationally, with the creation of the United Nations' Protocol to Prevent, Suppress, and Punish Trafficking in Persons, especially Women and Children. 148 states plus over 140 non-governmental organizations (NGOs) took part in the negotiations leading to the adoption of the "Palermo Protocol" in Italy. The Palermo Protocol was the first to define and criminalize human trafficking in international law.

> "Trafficking in persons" shall mean the recruitment, transportation, transfer, harboring or receipt of persons, by means of the threat or use of force or other forms of coercion, of abduction, of fraud, of deception, of the abuse of power or of a position of vulnerability or of the giving or receiving of payments or benefits to achieve the consent of a person having control over another person, for the purpose of exploitation. (United Nations, 2000, article 3a)

In the same year, the United States' Trafficking Victims Protection Act of 2000 (TVPA) defined human trafficking as "a crime that deprives people of their human rights and freedoms." The most severe form of human trafficking was defined as:

- "Sex trafficking in which a commercial sex act is induced by force, fraud, or coercion, or in which the person induced to perform such an act has not attained 18 years of age; or
- The recruitment, harboring, transportation provision, or obtaining of a person for labor or services, through the use of force, fraud, or coercion for the purpose of subjection to involuntary servitude, peonage, debt bondage, or slavery." (TVPA 2000 106 P.L. 386: 114 Stat. 1470, Sec. 103 (8), United States Congress, 2000)

The TVPA 2000 effectively made the crime of human trafficking a federal offense; created sentencing guidelines for prosecuting human traffickers, and provided trafficking victims access to federal benefits and immigration relief. The most recent reauthorization, TVPRA 2008 (United States Congress, 2008), categorizes human trafficking as an index crime in the Uniformed Crime Reports by FBI.

A multifaceted approach is crucial to understanding the complexities of human trafficking, beginning with distinguishing between elements of the crime, as defined by the Palermo Protocol. The act of trafficking in persons constitutes the *actus reus* (the criminal act) (i.e., "recruitment, transportation, transfer, harboring or receipt of persons") and the *mens rea* (the criminal intent) (i.e., "threat or use of force, coercion, abduction, fraud, deception, abuse of power or vulnerability, or giving payments or benefits to a person in control of the victim"). The motivating purpose of trafficking is "exploitation, which includes exploiting the prostitution of others, sexual exploitation, forced labour, slavery or similar practices and the removal of organs." In addition, the crime encompasses attempts to commit trafficking offence; participation as an accomplice in such an offence; and organizing or directing others to commit trafficking (Organization for Security and Cooperation in Europe [OSCE], 2007; United Nations Office on Drugs and Crime [UNODC], 2009a).

Human trafficking has been termed a form of "modern-day slavery" that leads to and results from a widespread violation of victims' human rights (Department for Global Development, 2003). Trafficked persons have no basic human rights such as the right to life, freedom from slavery or involuntary servitude, and freedom from cruel and inhumane treatment (UN, 1948). Human trafficking affects women and girls disproportionately, comprising approximately 80 percent of all trafficking cases domestically (U.S. Department of State, 2007) and globally (UNODC, 2009a, p6).

Cultural norms exacerbate the vulnerability of women to being trafficked, where gender-based violence is accepted in many countries. Culturally determined gender roles often leave women emotionally and financially dependent upon those who abuse them, forcing women to remain in violent situations (Enriquez, 2006). Many culturally accepted forms of gender violence including bride-burning, wife-beating, and honor killings remain rampant. Widespread poverty, unemployment, lack of opportunities, lack of education, and social, political unrests create vulnerable populations of women upon whom traffickers prey (La Strada International, 2008).

NUMBERS AND SCOPE

Definitions of the crime of human trafficking subsequently beg the question of statistics. How many victims exist globally or in the United States? How are these statistics tracked? Over recent years, the U.S. Trafficking in Persons Report (TIPR) has provided estimates of people trafficked varying from 4 to 27 million. Issued annually by the U.S. State Department, the TIPR provides a global snapshot of efforts to eliminate severe forms of trafficking in persons. The 2009 report features statistics from the International Labor Organization (ILO)—the United Nations agency charged with addressing labor standards, employment, and social protection issues—estimating "at least 12.3 million adults and children in forced labor, bonded labor, and commercial sexual servitude at any given time. Of these victims, the ILO estimates that at least 1.39 million are victims of commercial sexual servitude, both transnational and within countries" (U.S. Department of State, 2009, p8).

In the United States an estimated 14,500 to 17,500 foreign nationals are trafficked into the country. The number of U.S. citizens trafficked within the country each year is even higher, with an estimated 200,000 American children at risk for trafficking into the sex industry (Polaris Project, 2010a). As human trafficking continues to be the fastest growing criminal industry today, it is also one of the most lucrative. An estimated 32 billion is generated in annual revenue from all trafficking activities, taking the sale of individuals and the value of their exploited labor or services are taken into account, with at least a conservatively estimated $7 billion attributed to sex trafficking (U.S. Department of State, 2008, p34).

As with other crimes, statistics attempt to provide an accurate picture of the victimization, the traffickers, recruitment, and survivorship that, in turn, are critical to policy formation, diplomacy, identifying gaps in services, and public awareness initiatives. The most often-cited resources that publish statistics include the US Department of State, the UNODC, the International Organization for Migration [IOM], & ILO. Each of the four organizations shares similarities in their efforts to collect data on a global scale and provide understanding of the scope and nature of the issue of human trafficking[1].

The challenge of quantifying this current human rights issue is that data collection is still in the early stages of development within the anti-trafficking movement. There continues to be lack of consistency between researchers who have historically disagreed on how trafficking should be defined and studied. Because of state, cultural, and political and religious priorities, methodology and ethical standards of proof vary tremendously (U.S. Government Accountability Office, 2006). Additional challenges in measuring human trafficking are its hidden nature and the difficulty of accurately quantifying the number of victims. Victims and survivors come from largely "hidden" populations (e.g., undocumented migrants, women in prostitution, and youth experiencing homelessness, among others), populations "for whom the size and boundaries are unknown, and for whom no sampling frame exists. Furthermore, membership in hidden populations often involves stigmatized or illegal behavior, leading individuals to refuse to cooperate, or give unreliable answers to protect their privacy" (Tyldum & Brunovskis, 2005, p18).

The next best options are to utilize data estimations, averaging "… the various aggregate estimates of reported and unreported trafficking victims published by nongovernmental organizations, governments and international organizations, estimates that themselves are not reliable or comparable due to different definitions, methodologies, data sources, and data validation procedures" (U.S. Government Accountability Office, 2006, p13). In some cases, data sources themselves have gaps, as in the case of U.S. estimates not including internal/domestic trafficking numbers (U.S. Government Accountability Office, 2006).

Currently, tracking systems provided by law enforcement and service providers have yet to be funneled into a single coordinated system. With time, these systems will further develop in order to provide accurate representations of trafficking victims in any given region or country. Until then, inaccurate estimates remain.

TYPES OF HUMAN TRAFFICKING

As noted in the TVPA (2000) and the Palermo Protocol, two categories of human trafficking have evolved—one focusing upon labor for services and the other on commercial sex. Both categories, however, need to be understood within a continuum of exploitation. At one end is workers' voluntary participation where labor rights are honored and upheld and the individual has the freedom to resign from the job. Human trafficking is located on the opposite end of the continuum, where the worker's participation is against their will, labor rights are nonexistent, and the individual is unable to leave on their own volition, due to force, fraud and/or coercion (Polaris Project, 2006). Forms of human trafficking involving women vary between communities, dependent upon location in the global economy.

Major forms of trafficking in persons noted in the TIPR 2009 include categories of forced and bonded labor, debt bondage and involuntary servitude, child soldiers, sex trafficking, and child sex tourism. Each form varies in complexity where minors are considered. Under the category of human trafficking for labor or services, individuals are trafficked into migrant agricultural and farming operations, weaving, sweatshop work, or street peddling. Individuals are subjected to harsh conditions and brutality to keep them in the agricultural fields. Domestic servitude of women includes work as nannies, housekeepers, cooks, and house managers. This form of labor trafficking is complicated by the private "family" setting where abuses are more easily hidden from public view. More recently, sales crews where youth sell items like magazines, candy, perfume, and other foods have been found to have elements of human trafficking present, where youth are beaten physically and sexually and are abandoned in the city when sales quotas are not met (Polaris Project, 2006).

In countries where there is civil unrest, children are commonly recruited as child soldiers who then serve on the front lines of armed conflicts. An estimated 300,000 children are believed to be combatants in some thirty conflicts worldwide, where at least 14 governments have recruited children in auxiliary forces, civilian defense groups or in illegal militias and armed groups acting as proxies for official armed forces (Child Soldiers Global Report, 2008). Thirty percent of the world's armed forces include girl soldiers (Singer, 2006).

One of the less-defined areas of human trafficking includes situations involving "mail-order" brides [MOB]. Although the mail order bride is a lucrative and legal enterprise in many countries (with an estimated 10,000 Internet sites worldwide), the context hides instances of human trafficking. An estimated 2,000–3,500 American men find their wives through MOB agencies each year, and although not every situation may involve trafficking, it provides an opportunity to lure women from abroad, particularly from Southeast Asia and the former Soviet Union (Hughes & Roche, 1999).

Of the two broad categories of human trafficking, sex trafficking receives the greater amount of attention because of its media appeal that combines both violence and sex. Forms of commercial sex include street prostitution, pornography, stripping, erotic/nude massage, escort services, phone sex lines, private parties, gang-based prostitution, interfamilial pimping, and forms of internet-based exploitation. Recent efforts supported by federal funding have focused upon minors in the sex industry. As a replacement for the pejorative term, "child prostitute" that implies willing participation, the term "commercial sexual exploitation of children" or CSEC reframes the issue as a form of child abuse (Girls Education and Mentoring Services [GEMS], 2007). Formally, the definition of CSEC includes: "(the) sexual abuse and remuneration in money, goods, or services, or the promise of money, goods, or services to the child or a third person or persons. The activities are defined by an element of organization and/or intent, and/or the context of the commercial sex industry, whereby the child is treated as a commercial and sexual object" (Girls Education and Mentoring Services [GEMS], 2007). Reframing the language expresses the philosophy that sexually exploited children deserve support services instead of jail sentences, and more accurately represents the scope of the issue and the reality of exploited youth's experiences.

Recent identified risk factors have noted that at least 100,000 to 300,000 youth are at risk for commercial sexual exploitation annually in the U.S., and that the average age of entry into the commercial sex industry in the U.S. is 12 years old (Estes & Weiner, 2001). Given the estimates that 1.6 million children runaways from home each year in the U.S., attention to CSEC is paramount; an estimated one in three teens will be recruited by a pimp within 48 hours of leaving home and becoming homeless (Finkelhor, Hotaling, & Sedlak, 1999, c.f. Girls Education and Mentoring Services [GEMS], 2007).

CAUSES OF HUMAN TRAFFICKING

The dynamics of the human trafficking phenomenon requires multifaceted explanations. Social forces surrounding human trafficking differ from community to community, family to family, and individual to individual. The interplay of the push/pull factors from social, cultural, political, and economic dimensions at community, family, individual level is complex.

Pull Factors

The pull factors mainly fall into two categories: a persistent demand for women's and child's sexual services, and cheap labor. In the U.S., for example, the sex industry is a $10 billion-a-year business, its profits are bigger than those from the NFL, NBA, and major league baseball combined (ABC News/Primetime, 2004). Approximately one in every four video and DVD rentals are pornographic, with annual production of 10,000 hardcore adult videos (Hausbeck & Brents, 1999). Around the U.S. military bases in Korea, more than 5,000 Filipinas and Russian women are estimated to be involved in prostitution (Enriquez, 2006). In the UK, 10 percent of London's male population buys women for sex. In Germany, one million prostitute-users buy women on a daily basis for sex (Herz, 2003). In Australia, women trafficked from Asia are particularly desirable because they are perceived as more tolerant to sexual violence (Project Respect, 2008). One alarming trend is that girls at younger ages are being trafficked into the sex industry, because some men believe that younger girls are HIV negative and many are willing to pay a much higher price to have sex with virgins—the virgin trade (International Organization for Migration [IOM], 2007).

The "voracious" demand for cheap labor, another strong pull fueling human trafficking, is created by profit-driven employers. Poor, young, and less educated population in less developed countries are willing to migrate and fulfill the unmet labor demands in rich countries. Upon arrival in the destination countries, many find themselves imprisoned as slaves (United States Department of State, 2008). The global economic crisis further increases the demand for cheap goods and services. It is expected that more unscrupulous businesses seek to avoid taxes and unionized labor (UNODC, 2009a).

Push Factors

From the supply side, numerous push factors operate in the "origination" countries that provide vulnerable labor for trafficking. First and foremost, we need to understand these push factors within the context that leads people into trafficking situations. At the community level, the consensus in the international community is that human trafficking flourishes in environments characterized by poverty, lack of employment opportunities, population surplus, social and political instabilities, wars and armed conflicts, severe gender inequalities, gender violence, wide-spread government corruption, and a lack of law enforcement anti-trafficking efforts (Bales, 1999a; United States Congress, 2008; William, 2009). Bales (1999b) ranked government corruption, poverty, population surplus, and conflicts and social unrests as most significant push factors contributing to human trafficking.

At the individual level, victims' experiences vary by one's gender, socioeconomic status, education, employment, and personal aspirations—all play a role in the likelihood of being trafficked (IOM, 2008). The intersectional relationships among these factors are crucial. Although social inequalities limit access to resources for both poor men and women, women are further discriminated against in all aspects of life. For example, the double edge of globalization both liberates and marginalizes women in the developing world (Meyer, 2003). For those women who have lost their traditional sources of incomes and found themselves being exploited in low-wage sweatshops, their vulnerability increases.

Family plays a vital role in trafficking victimization. Family dysfunctions, loss of parent or parents or having step parents, and poverty are push factors making family members vulnerable to trafficking situations. Moreover, trafficking may be facilitated by the family (Aid to Children Without Parents, Inc. [ACWP], 2007; Joffres, Mills, Joffres, Khanna, Walia, & Grund, 2008). Some families living in extreme poverty sell their children to traffickers for a fee in exchange for their children's labor. The parents are told that the children will go to work and live in better conditions. In reality, many children become forced child labor working under extreme inhuman conditions (ACWP, 2007). In Somalia, for example, parents paying up US$10,000 to send their children through traffickers or relatives to Western Europe in the hope that their children will be provided for. Many of these "unaccompanied" children end up being trafficked (Humanitarian News and Analysis Service of the UN Office for the Coordination of Humanitarian Affairs, 2003). Further, in some extremely poor and remote areas in the world, prostitution becomes the only source of income for families. As a result, children and women are forced to use their bodies to help with their family survival (ACWP, 2007). In the end however, many women and girls are not accepted by their families because of the social stigma of their work and their label as "bad girls." One disturbing phenomenon is the practice of "the virginity trade" in some Asian countries fueled by high demands. Most girls were either tricked by family members and friends or forced through coercion to sell their virginity between ages 7 and 12. Many foreign businessmen and local men pay as much as $500-600 USD per week for the possession of these girls (ACWP, 2007). According to IOM (2007), the commercial sale of virginity is arguably the largest push factor for young women into commercial sexual exploitation once girls lost their virginity. Clearly in many instances, women and girls are already victims of discrimination and violence long before they enter the process of human trafficking.

Feminist scholars have long argued that human trafficking, specifically trafficking of women and girls, is a gender inequality issue (Dunlop, 2008). As such, the crime of human trafficking needs to be understood within the framework of gender stratification in patriarchal societies, where "gender is fundamentally about power" (Hondagneu-Sotelo, 2003, p6). Gendered power imbalances create patriarchal structures that legitimize the dehumanization and exploitation of women. In turn, this dehumanization shapes labor demand, migration, and human trafficking (Hart, 2007). Within feminist scholarship, women's participation in the sex industry as "voluntary" versus "forced" under patriarchal conditions have been examined and analyzed. However, this debate does not refute the fact that many women in the sex industry work under horrific conditions (Peng, 2005). Further, the issue of consent is only relative and dynamic. The voluntary-forced dichotomy can only disqualify sex workers from human rights considerations if their status is viewed as "voluntary" (Doesema, 1998).

At the community or country level, Shinkle (2007) cites government corruption as one of the most significant push factors. In many countries, local government corruption is endemic or systemic, and institutionalized. Corruption leads to bad governance, a lack of rule of law, and weak law enforcement, all leading to low risks for traffickers being investigated and prosecuted. Corruption also adversely affects government's ability to provide resources to its population. Suffice it to say, corruption causes severe economic hardship and social inequalities in the society, exacerbating the vulnerability of potential victims.

Facilitating Factors

Globally, there are a number of contributing or facilitating factors. Human trafficking is the fastest growing and highly lucrative criminal business. After drug dealing, human trafficking is tied with the illegal arms industry as the second largest criminal industry in the world (U.S. Department of Health & Human Services [HHS], 2006). Trafficking victims can be resold, and each transaction renders profits for traffickers, while drugs or illegal arms only generate profit once. When illegal drugs or arms are seized or confiscated, no further profits can be delivered (UN Emerging Social Issues Division of the ESCAP Secretariat, 2005). There is a lack of effective cross-national anti-trafficking legislation and enforcement resulting in low risks for human trafficking cases to be investigated and prosecuted. For instance, at present, only a handful of countries prosecute most trafficking cases, while the majority of other countries prosecute just a few cases (UNODC, 2009a, 2009b). "In the six years after the TVPA passed, less than 70 cases of sex trafficking were successfully prosecuted," even though thousands of such cases were reported to the DOJ during the same period of time (Neuwirth, 2008).

IMPACT ON VICTIMS

Regardless of the cause of how individuals are forced, fraudulently led or coerced into human trafficking, challenges arise in providing services or building cases that may be dependent upon victim testimony. Each victim has uniquely survived trauma—events that involved actual or threatened death or serious injury, or threats to self or others' physical well-being (American Psychiatric Association [APA], 1994). There is no single profile of victims; each individual will likely have unique combination of physical and mental health problems requiring tailored survival resources. As with many forms of interpersonal violence, sensitivities and cautions are necessary given the possible range of traumatic experiences they have survived, which may impair memory crucial to building cases. Their traumatic experiences may include serious harm, physical restraint, withholding documents (e.g., passport, social security card, driver's license), malnutrition, and threats to family (Polaris Project, 2006). In the case of sex trafficking, the physical abuses may be multidirectional—at the hands of "Johns," (purchasers of sex) who feel entitlement to do what they please (no matter how violent), or at the hands of traffickers (Farley et al. 2003; Zimmerman et al, 2003). For many women in labor trafficking situations, sexual violence may be wielded as a tool of force.

Psychologically, many victims have survived degradation, isolation, induced debility, and exhaustion (Biderman, 1957); consequently, victims feel fear, shame of the unspeakable acts they have been asked to perform, and self-blame for being trafficked. Substance use may be initiated as a control tactic to induce or increase labor productivity. Unfortunately, the resulting addiction can then be used as a form of control maintenance, by continuing to feed the addiction as "reward" (Logan, 2008). In some cases, trauma bonds develop between the victim and their trafficker can be found, where the relationship alternates violence and kindness, isolation, and shame and stigma (Girls Education and Mentoring Services [GEMS], 2007; Zimmerman et al, 2003). Similar to situations of domestic violence, human trafficking survivors may defend her trafficker, whereby the trauma bond is formed as a matter of survival (Farley, 2003).

In order to best serve and support survivors of human trafficking, it is imperative to train service providers on symptoms and red flags that indicate human trafficking. Holistic approaches are required to assess what the victim has survived, and how to provide individualized treatment (Alejano-Steele, 2008). First responders, such as law enforcement or emergency rooms, need to assess the combined presentations of physical trauma, including gang rape, sexually transmitted infections including HIV/AIDS, forced abortions, head trauma, substance abuse and addiction, neglected injuries, and malnutrition. Psychologically, victims may appear passive and silent, particularly if they are accompanied by their trafficker speaking on their behalf, silenced by feelings of humiliation and shame. Socially, survivors may present with varying trust issues and relational skills. Most importantly, victims of trafficking may present symptoms very similarly to rape and domestic violence; sensitively and patiently delivered assessment will be necessary to understand the full story of their victimization. Most of the initial literature on survivorship has focused upon crisis needs after discovery, when safety and security are paramount. It is important, however, to note the long-term impact of human trafficking, where coping mechanisms can vary between survivors.

Anxiety and complex post traumatic stress disorder are common among human trafficking survivors (Herman, 1997), whereby a constellation of symptoms can occur, including reliving the trauma, social withdrawal, hyper vigilance, changes in self-perception and perception of the perpetrator, and difficulties with social relations (Herman, 1997). Self-induced substance use may develop as a coping mechanism, where alcohol or drugs serve as a method of numbing traumatic memories. The challenge therefore lies in providing comprehensive and consistent treatment to support victim survivorship, to prevent them from repeatedly vacillating between social services and the street (McNaughton & Sanders, 2007; Smith & Marshall, 2007).

Human trafficking trauma can destroy a victim/survivor's sense of agency, strength, competence, and autonomy. Clearly, sensitivities are required to provide services and develop legal cases to prosecute traffickers. Given the range of traumas unique to each individual, one singular approach to survivorship will not "fit all," nor is the range of services supported by federal, state, and local resources consistent across communities. Fortunately in the United States, there are provisions for crisis needs and long-term survivorship.

FEDERAL AND LOCAL RESPONSES TO HUMAN TRAFFICKING

Comprehensive and multi-sectoral resources are required to support the needs of human trafficking survivors, particularly through coordination of governmental agencies, non-governmental agencies, and community members. In 2000, the United States Congress enacted a comprehensive federal anti-trafficking law, the TVPA 2000. Reauthorized in 2003 and 2005, and then renamed as the William Wilberforce Trafficking Victims Protection Reauthorization Act of 2008, the TVPRA mandates policy to address human trafficking from a human rights primacy approach (Stolz, 2007). Multiple methodologies focusing on *prosecution, protection, and prevention* (the Three Ps) have since guided anti-trafficking work for government agencies and collaboratives nationwide.

Prosecution efforts support successful investigation and prosecution of traffickers, in large part by strengthening laws and legal responses. According to BJA (n.d.), more than three-fourths of the states have passed criminalization legislation making human trafficking a felony offense since 2002. Several states have since passed legislation to enhance penalties when the crime of human trafficking has involved minors, undocumented migrants, kidnapping, or results in the death of a victim (National Institute on State Policy on Trafficking of Women and Girls, 2005). Joining forces on prosecution efforts, the DOJ and HHS have worked to increase the number of anti-trafficking task forces, coalitions, and outreach efforts across the U.S. By the end of 2009, BJA funded 42 task forces designed to bring together state, local, and federal law enforcement with partners from NGOs. In partnership with local U.S. Attorneys' Offices and community-based organizations, these task forces identify victims; interdict and convict persons engaged in severe forms of human trafficking; and ensure victim safety and access to services.

As awareness of human trafficking has increased throughout the United States, federal resource limitations and capacity have necessitated state-level legislation to secure local resources to handle human trafficking cases. With the assistance of NGOs, model elements of comprehensive state legislation to combat trafficking in persons have helped to shape state-level policy (Polaris Project, 2010b).

Investigative and Prosecutorial Challenges

Despite the number of successful collaborative efforts, many challenges remain that prevent the identification, investigation, and prosecution of human trafficking at the state level, including lack of enforcement of state statutes that criminalize human trafficking. For example, complexities may arise internally from police departments. With limited knowledge of the crime, several departments have not prioritized resources to address human trafficking; most departments have limited capacity, with detectives handling cases on overtime amidst a very heavy case load of a variety of crimes (Ryan, 2007; Boteler, 2009). As found in many government agencies, politics can influence how human trafficking is framed and prioritized.

Comprehensive protocols to investigate and prosecute human trafficking cases are needed across the United States. Local research needs to go beyond tracking of *what* to do to better control trafficking in local jurisdictions, and move to explaining *how* to build strong local or best local practice that complements federal practices. Several states are ideally primed for context-specific research because of unique local factors (i.e., transit/secondary status, immigration issues) and current state and federal resources. Sharing best practices between states will help to guide and streamline coordination of federal and state/local resources. Ideally, state-specific streamlined systems will increase the number of successful prosecutions (Alejano-Steele et al, 2009).

The American criminal justice system entrusts great power and responsibilities in the hands of prosecutors who coordinate the government's response to crime. They make discretionary decisions about whether or not to charge a case, which charges to bring, and what sentence to recommend (Cole & Smith 2004, p303). In prosecuting human trafficking cases, however, prosecutors first and foremost need to be well-informed of all the anti-trafficking legislation and the protection and assistance available to the trafficking victims. Immigration violations or other offenses on the part of trafficking victims should be exempt from prosecution.

Protection efforts provide safety and support for domestic and foreign national victims and survivors from a range of service providers. Initiatives by the United States Department of Justice, Office for Victims of Crime (OVC) are intended to assist victims between the period of time they are encountered by law enforcement or first responders. Benefits and services include shelter, case management, interpretation services, medical care, dental care, crisis counseling, legal/immigration assistance, criminal justice system advocacy, job training, and transportation (United States Department of Justice, Office for Victims of Crime, 2010). Similar resources are also available through the United States Department of Health & Human Services' [HHS] Rescue & Restore campaign, most notably the National Human Trafficking Resource Center [NHTRC], with its 24-hour national hotline: 1-888-3737-888 (NHTRC, 2010).

Resources tailored to the unique needs of foreign national victims are supplemented by HHS' Office of Refugee Resettlement, the agency that issues all certifications and eligibility letters for nonimmigrant T-visas (United States Department of Health & Human Services, Administration for Children and Families, Office of Refugee Resettlement, 2010). Dependent upon cooperation with law enforcement, the T-visa allows individuals to work and live in U.S. for four years, with the possibility of lawful permanent residency ("green card") after three years. General U-visas designated generally for victims of crime are also available. Additionally, the Department of Homeland Security (DHS) provides protections in the form of immigration relief through four of its subdivisions. Once survivors are certified, victims are eligible to apply for benefits and services under any federal or state funded programs, to the same extent as refugees including refugee cash, medical assistance, and social services.

Prevention efforts aim to decrease the number of people trafficked through training and prevention education. Training efforts by BJA and OVC have focused upon law enforcement and nongovernmental/service provider agencies on the identification of victims and trafficking crime scenes, as they are often the first points of contact for trafficked persons. Law enforcement are specifically trained to stop trafficking crimes in progress, manage victims as witnesses, and utilize NGO and community resources for successful investigations. Because of the clandestine nature of trafficking, local law enforcement officers must be trained to identify the crime of human trafficking as unique from smuggling and drug trafficking, due to the dimension of human rights violations.

Most importantly, training content for service providers includes sensitivities to working with vulnerable populations, particularly women and children. Victims are fearful of coming forward and abused to fear police and service providers (Free the Slaves & Human Rights Center, 2006). Special cautions to prevent mislabeling of victims as illegal immigrants or prostitutes who "violate social order" (Limanowska, 2004, p3) are included in trainings, as well as guidelines for specific indicators that help to identify victims (see Table 1).

In tandem to service provider trainings, prevention education and outreach programs are designed to reach vulnerable populations at high risk for human trafficking (e.g., young women, people experiencing homelessness, migrant farm workers, immigration detention centers, residential treatment centers). Funding by HHS' Office of Refugee Resettlement (ORR) supports outreach to provide resources and hotline numbers to caution these groups about the dynamics of human trafficking that begin with false promises and exploitation (United States Department of Health & Human Services, Office of Refugee Resettlement, 2010).

In partnership with these governmental agencies, NGOs provided services and resources, including victim assessment, crisis services, and long-term case management for comprehensive needs. NGOs actively participate on task forces, provide prevention education and training, and advocate by raising public awareness (United States Department of Justice, Bureau of Justice Assistance, 2006). NGOs are especially helpful to cases by restoring dignity to victims, ensuring victim safety, and supporting witness preparation for cases. Community coalition-building is also an important arm of NGO work in the anti-trafficking movement, working to organize community-based responses by building alliances with victim services coalitions, immigrant advocacy groups, human rights groups, crime victim advocacy groups, health care providers, and faith-based community organizations (Venkatraman, 2003). Training of the general public also helps to provide additional eyes and ears to report suspicious activity to local and national hotlines.

TABLE 1   Red Flags and Potential Indicators of Human Trafficking (NHTRC, 2010)

http://nhtrc.polarisproject.org/call-the-hotline/identifying-human-trafficking-.html

This list represents a selection of possible indicators, and is not exhaustive. The red flags in this list may not be present in all trafficking cases and are not cumulative.

Common Work and Living Conditions: The Individual(s) in Question

- Is not free to leave or come and go as he/she wishes
- Is under 18 years of age and is providing commercial sex acts
- Is in the commercial sex industry and has a pimp/manager
- Is unpaid, paid very little, or paid only through tips
- Works excessively long and/or unusual hours
- Is not allowed breaks or suffers under unusual restrictions at work
- Owes a large debt and is unable to pay it off
- Was recruited through false promises concerning the nature and conditions of his/her work
- Is living or working in a location with high security measures (e.g. opaque or boarded-up windows, bars on windows, barbed wire, security cameras, etc.)

Poor Mental Health or Abnormal Behavior

- Exhibits unusually fearful, anxious, depressed, submissive, tense, or nervous/paranoid behavior
- Reacts with unusually fearful or anxious behavior at any reference to "law enforcement"
- Avoids eye contact
- Flat affect

Poor Physical Health

- Presents with unexplained injuries or signs of prolonged/untreated illness or disease
- Appears malnourished
- Shows signs of physical and/or sexual abuse, physical restraint, confinement, or torture

Lack of Control

- Has few or no personal possessions
- Is not in control of her/his own money, no financial records, or bank account
- Is not in control of her/his own identification documents (ID or passport)
- Is not allowed or able to speak for herself/himself (e.g., a third party may insist on being present and/or interpreting)

Other

- Claims of "just visiting" and inability to clarify where she/he is staying or to provide an address
- Lack of knowledge of whereabouts and/or does not know what city she/he is in
- Loss of sense of time
- Has numerous inconsistencies in her/his story

CONCLUSION

Clearly, the complexities of the crime of human trafficking run the gamut when it comes to definitions, causes, measurement, and responses to best serve women victims. The anti-human trafficking field is emerging from its formative years, where protocols and procedures continue to develop. Effective anti-trafficking efforts must continue to focus upon gender justice, society's demand for sex and cheap labor, and the role of the U.S. in globalization—key issues beyond the scope of the chapter. With hope, comprehensive legislation, streamlined statistics, community awareness, and coordinated multi-sectoral responses will collectively begin to stem the growth of this burgeoning human rights atrocity.

REFERENCES

AID TO CHILDREN WITHOUT PARENTS, INC. [ACWP]. (2007). Saving Children in Crisis Program. Retrieved on January 10, 2010, from the ACWP official website http://www.acwp.org/index.php?option=com_content&task=view&id=26&Itemid=59

ALEJANO-STEELE, A. (2008). *Human trafficking: Victim identification and survivor needs*. Human Trafficking and Modern Day Slavery. Metropolitan State College of Denver. Denver, CO.

ALEJANO-STEELE, A., SNAWDER, J., & BICKFORD, D. (2009). *Collaboratives between women's studies and women's centers as long term empowerment resource for survivors of human trafficking*. Paper presented at National Women's Studies Association Conference, Atlanta, GA.

AMERICAN PSYCHIATRIC ASSOCIATION. (1994). *Diagnostic and statistical manual of mental disorders*. 4th Ed. Washington, DC: American Psychiatric Association Press.

BALES, K. (1999a). *Disposable people: New slavery in the global economy*. University of California Press. CA: Berkeley.

BALES, K. (1999b). *What predicts human trafficking?* Proceedings of the United Nations Conference on Human Trafficking, Verona, October.

BIDERMAN, A.D. (1957). Communist attempts to elicit false confessions from Air Force prisoners of war. *Bulletin of the New York Academy of Medicine*, 33(9), 616–625.

BOTELER, J. (2009). *Federal human trafficking investigations*. Human Trafficking Course Metropolitan State College of Denver. Denver, CO.

CHILD SOLDIERS GLOBAL REPORT (2008). *Facts and figures on child soldiers*. Retrieved on September 16, 2009. From Web Site: www.childsolidersglobalreport.org/content/facts-and-figures-child-soliders

COLE, G. F. and SMITH, C. E. (2004). *The American System of Criminal Justice*. 4th Ed. Belmont, CA: Thomson Wadsworth.

DEPARTMENT FOR GLOBAL DEVELOPMENT. (2003). *Poverty and trafficking in human beings: A strategy for combating trafficking in human beings through Swedish international development cooperation*. Retrieved on December 14, 2009, from http://www.sweden.gov.se/content/1/c6/02/02/62/3819f9a2.pdf

DOESEMA, J. (1998). Forced to choose: beyond the voluntary v. forced prostitution dichotomy. In K. Kempadoo and J. Doezema (Eds.), *Global sex workers: Rights, resistance, and redefinition*, pp. 34–50. New York and London: Routledge.

DUNLOP, K. (2008). Human Security, Sex Trafficking and Deep Structural Explanations. *Human Security Journal*. 6, 56–67.

ENRIQUEZ, J. (2006). *Globalization, militarism and sex trafficking*. The International meeting of Women World March, in Lima, Peru, July 4–9, 2006.

ESTES, R.J. & WEINER, N.A. (2001). *The commercial sexual exploitation of children in the U. S., Canada and Mexico*. Executive Summary, University of Pennsylvania.

FARLEY, M. (2003). *Prostitution, trafficking and traumatic stress*. New York, NY: Haworth Press.

FARLEY, M., COTTON, A., LYNNE, J., ZUMBECK, S., SPIWAK, F., REYES, M.E., ALVAREZ, D. & SEZGIN, U. (2003). In M. Farley (Ed.). *Prostitution, trafficking and traumatic stress*. New York, NY: Haworth Press.

FINKELHOR, D., HOTALING, G., & SEDLAK, A. (1999). Missing, Abducted, Runaway, and Thrown-away Children in America (NISMART)—Numbers and Characteristics, National Incidence Studies (Washington: U.S. Department of Justice, Office of Juvenile Justice and Delinquency Prevention).

FREE THE SLAVES & THE HUMAN RIGHTS CENTER. (2006). The challenge of hidden slavery: Legal responses to forced labor in the United States. In K. Beeks & D. Amir (Eds). *Trafficking and the global sex industry*. Blue Ridge Summit, PA: Rowman & Littlefield Publishers, Inc.

GIRLS EDUCATIONAL AND MENTORING SERVICES. (2007). *Training manual on the commercial sexual exploitation of children (CSEC)*. Office of Juvenile Justice and Delinquency Program, U.S. Department of Justice Training. December, 2007 Training: Denver, CO.

HART, A. (2007). *Power, gender, and human trafficking*. Paper presented at the annual meeting of the American Sociological Association, TBA, New York, New York City, Aug 11.

HAUSBECK, K. & BRENTS, B. (1999). The McDonaldization of Sex. In Primis. New York City, New York: McGraw Hill.

HERMAN, J. (1997). *Trauma and recovery: The aftermath of violence—from domestic violence to political terror*. New York, NY: Basic Books.

HERZ, A. 2003. *Investigating and prosecuting trafficking in human beings—with special emphasis on the new German prostitution law*. Freiburg, Germany: Max Planck Institute for Foreign and International Criminal Law. Retrieved on September 26, 2003, from www.iuscrim.de/forsch/krim/herz.html

HONDAGNEU-SOTELO, P. (2003). *Gender and U.S. Immigration: Contemporary Trends*. Berkeley, CA: University of California Press.

HUGHES, D. & ROCHE, C.M. (1999). Making the harm visible. *Global Sexual Exploitation of Women and Girls—Speaking Out and Providing Services*. The Coalition against Trafficking in Women, 1999.

HUMANITARIAN NEWS AND ANALYSIS SERVICE OF THE UN OFFICE FOR THE COORDINATION OF HUMANI-TARIAN AFFAIRS. (2003). *In-depth: Separated Somali children*. Retrieved on January 2, 2010, from http://www.irinnews.org/IndepthMain.aspx?IndepthId=44&ReportId=71069

INTERNATIONAL ORGANIZATION FOR MIGRATION. (2007). *Demand for virgins fueling sex trade in Cambodia*. Retrieved on January 11, 2010, from www.humantrafficking.org

INTERNATIONAL ORGANIZATION FOR MIGRATION. (2008). *Human Trafficking in Eastern Africa*. Geneva, Switzerland: International Organization for Migration.

JOFFRES, C., MILLS, E., JOFFRES, M., KHANNA, T., WALIA, H., & GRUND, D. (2008). Sexual Slavery without Borders: Trafficking for Commercial Sexual Exploitation in India. *International Journal for Equity in Health* 2008, 7:22 doi:10.1186/1475-9276-7-22.

LA STRADA INTERNATIONAL. (2008). *Violation of women's rights, a cause and consequence of traf-ficking in women*. Amsterdam, the Netherlands: La Strada International.

LIMANOWSKA, B. (2004). *Anti-trafficking action in south-eastern Europe: Lack of effectiveness of law enforcement and migration approaches*. The United Nations, Division for the Advancement of Women.

LOGAN, T.K. (2008). *The multiple roles of substance abuse in human trafficking*. National Sympo-sium on the Health Needs of Human Trafficking Victims. September 22–23, 2008. United States Department of Health and Human Services, Office of the Assistant Secretary for Planning and Evaluation. Washington, DC.

MCNAUGHTON, C. & SANDERS, T. (2007). Housing and transitional phases out of "disordered" lives: The case of leaving homelessness and street sex work [online version]. *Housing Studies*, 2 (6), 885–900.

MEYER, L. B. (2003). Economic globalization and women's status in the labor market: A cross-national investigation of occupational sex segregation and inequality. *The Sociological Quar-terly*, 44 (3): 351–383.

NATIONAL HUMAN TRAFFICKING RESOURCE CENTER. (2010). The national human trafficking resource center hotline. Retrieved from http://nhtrc.polarisproject.org/call-the-hotline/who-can-call.html

NATIONAL INSTITUTE ON STATE POLICY ON TRAFFICKING OF WOMEN AND GIRLS OF THE CENTER FOR WOMEN POLICY STUDIES. (2005). Resource Guide for State Legislators Model Provisions for State Anti-Trafficking Laws. Center for Women Policy Studies. Retrieved on January 11, 2010, from www.centerwomenpolicy.org

NEUWIRTH, J. (2008). Another Overview of William Wilberforce Trafficking Victims Protection Reauthorization Act (the TVPRA). Retrieved on December 19, 2009 from http://feministlawprofs.law.sc.edu/?p=4285

ORGANIZATION FOR SECURITY AND CO-OPERATION IN EUROPE. (2007). A Legal Analysis of Trafficking in Persons Cases in Kosovo. OSCE.

PENG, Y. (2005). "Of course they claim they were coerced": On voluntary prostitution, contingent consent, and the modified whore stigma. *Journal of International Women's Studies*, 7(2), 17–35.

POLARIS PROJECT (2010a). *What is human trafficking?* Retrieved on January 2, 2010 from http://www.polarisproject.org/content/view/26/47/

POLARIS PROJECT. (2010b). *Model legislation, summaries and guidelines*. State legislative advocacy and resources. Retrieved on January 2, 2010 from http://www.polarisproject.org/content/view/199/116/

POLARIS PROJECT (2006). *Human trafficking training for victim advocates*. Conference sponsored by The Salvation Army, Office of Victims of Crime grantee. April 2006, Auraria Campus. Denver, CO.

PROJECT RESPECT. (2008). *Why Australia?* Retrieved on December 8, 2009, from http://projectrespect.org.au/our_work/trafficking/why_australia

RYAN, M. (2007). *Sex trafficking investigations*. Human Trafficking Course Metropolitan State College of Denver. Denver, CO.

SHINKLE, W. (2007). Preventing Human Trafficking: An Evaluation of Current Efforts. Policy Brief #3. The Institute for the Study of International Migration (ISIM).

SINGER, P. W. (2006). *Children at war*. Berkeley, CA: Pantheon/University of California.

SMITH, M. & MARSHALL, L. (2007). Barriers to effective drug addiction treatment for women involved in street-level prostitution: A qualitative investigation. *Criminal Behavior and Mental Health*, 17, 163–170.

STOLZ, B. A. (2007). *Implementing the U.S. Trafficking Victims Protection Act: New challenges for law enforcement and prosecutors*. Paper presented at the annual meeting of the American Society of Criminology, Atlanta, Georgia. Retrieved on May 24, 2009 fromhttp://www.allacademic.com/meta/p200415_index.html

TYLDUM, G. & BRUNOVSKIS, A. (2005). Describing the unobserved: Methodological challenges in empirical studies on human trafficking. In E.M. Gozdiziak & E.A. Collett (Eds). *Data and research on human trafficking: A global survey*. International Organization for Migration: IOM.

UNITED NATIONS. (1948). *Universal Declaration of Human Rights*, G.A. res. 217A (III), U.N. Doc A/810 at 71.

UNITED NATIONS. (2000). *Protocol to Prevent, Suppress, and Punish Trafficking in Persons, Especially Women and Children, Supplementing the United Nations Convention against Transnational Organized Crime*. UN GAOR 55th Session, UN Doc.A/55/383 (entered into force on December 25, 2003). http://www.unodc.org/pdf/crime/a_res_55/res5525e.pdf

UNITED NATIONS EMERGING SOCIAL ISSUES DIVISION OF THE ESCAP SECRETARIAT. (2005). Violence against and Trafficking in Women as Symptoms of Discrimination: The Potential of CEDAW as an Antidote. *Gender and Development Discussion Paper Series*, No. 17.

UNITED NATIONS OFFICE ON DRUGS AND CRIME. (2009a). The Global Report on Trafficking in Persons. Vienna, United Nations Office on Drugs and Crime (UNODC).

UNITED NATIONS OFFICE ON DRUGS AND CRIME. (2009b). Anti-human trafficking manual for criminal justice practitioners. Vienna, United Nations Office on Drugs and Crime (UNODC).

UNITED STATES GOVERNMENT ACCOUNTABILITY OFFICE. (2006). *Human trafficking: Better data, strategy, and reporting needed to enhance U.S. antitrafficking efforts abroad.* Report GAO-06-825. Washington DC: Government Accountability Office.

UNITED STATES CONGRESS. (2000). *Trafficking Victims Protection Act of 2000* (TVPA), Public Law 106-386 22 United States Code, § 7102(8).

UNITED STATES CONGRESS. (2008). *William Wilberforce Trafficking Victims Protection Reauthorization Act of 2008* (TVPRA), Public Law 110-457.

UNITED STATES DEPARTMENT OF HEALTH & HUMAN SERVICES. (2006). HHS Fights to Stem Human Trafficking. Retrieved on January 12, 2010, from HHS website http://www.hhs.gov/news/factsheet/humantrafficking.html

UNITED STATES DEPARTMENT OF HEALTH & HUMAN SERVICES, Administration of Children & Families. (2010). *Campaign to rescue and restore human trafficking: Human trafficking.* Retrieved on January 5, 2010 from http://www.acf.hhs.gov/trafficking/about/fact_human.html

UNITED STATES DEPARTMENT OF HEALTH & HUMAN SERVICES, Administration of Children & Families, Office of Refugee Resettlement. (2010). *State Letter #04-12.* Http://www.acf.hhs.gov/programs/orr/policy/sl04-12.htm

UNITED STATES DEPARTMENT OF JUSTICE, BUREAU OF JUSTICE ASSISTANCE. (2006). *Human trafficking in the United States: Promoting law enforcement awareness.* Curriculum for BJA-sponsored trainings. Washington, DC: USDOJ.

UNITED STATES DEPARTMENT OF JUSTICE, OFFICE OF VICTIMS OF CRIME. (2010). *Trafficking in persons: Background of OVC-funded programs.* Retrieved on January 5, 2010 from http://www.ojp.usdoj.gov/ovc/help/tip.htm

UNITED STATES DEPARTMENT OF STATE. (2009). *Trafficking in persons report.* U.S. Dept of State Publication 11407. Office of the Undersecretary for Democracy and Global Affairs and Bureau of Public Affairs. Washington, DC: GTIP.

UNITED STATES DEPARTMENT OF STATE. (2008). *Trafficking in persons report.* U.S. Dept of State Publication 11407. Office of the Undersecretary for Democracy and Global Affairs and Bureau of Public Affairs. Washington, DC: GTIP.

UNITED STATES DEPARTMENT OF STATE. (2007). *Trafficking in persons report.* U.S. Dept of State Publication 11407. Office of the Undersecretary for Democracy and Global Affairs and Bureau of Public Affairs. Washington, DC: GTIP.

VENKATRAMAN, B.A. (2003). A guide to detecting investigating, and punishing modern-day slavery. *The Police Chief*, December, 2003.

WILLIAM, J. L. (2009). *Human trafficking: Preventing, prosecuting, and protecting.* Southern Legislative Conference of the Council of State Governments. Retrieved on January 11, 2010, from http://www.slcatlanta.org/Publications/publications.htm

ZIMMERMAN, C., YUN, K., SHVAB, I., WATTS, C., TRAPPOLIN, L., TREPPETE, M., BIMBI, F., ADAMS, B., JIRAPORN, S., BECI, L., ALBRECHT, M., BINDEL, J., & REGAN, L. (2003). *The health risks and consequences of trafficking in women and adolescents. Findings from a European study.* London: London School of Hygiene & Tropical Medicine (LSHTM).

ENDNOTE

1. For detailed critique of estimations of a "problem of unknown size," see Albanese (2007). A criminal network approach to understanding and measuring trafficking in human beings. In U. Savona & S. Stefanizzi (Eds). *Measuring human trafficking: Complexities and pitfalls.* New York, NY: Springer.

12

Human Trafficking of Young Women and Girls for Sexual Exploitation

Thozama Lutya

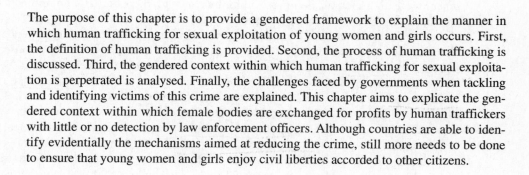

The purpose of this chapter is to provide a gendered framework to explain the manner in which human trafficking for sexual exploitation of young women and girls occurs. First, the definition of human trafficking is provided. Second, the process of human trafficking is discussed. Third, the gendered context within which human trafficking for sexual exploitation is perpetrated is analysed. Finally, the challenges faced by governments when tackling and identifying victims of this crime are explained. This chapter aims to explicate the gendered context within which female bodies are exchanged for profits by human traffickers with little or no detection by law enforcement officers. Although countries are able to identify evidentially the mechanisms aimed at reducing the crime, still more needs to be done to ensure that young women and girls enjoy civil liberties accorded to other citizens.

INTRODUCTION

Human trafficking writers and authors have identified sexual exploitation as the most researched and reported form of human trafficking (Musto, 2009; Segrave, 2009; Department of State, 2009). The majority of trafficked persons are young women and girls (Bhabha, 2005; Raymond, 2002). The United Nations Office on Drugs and Crime estimates that 70% of these young women and girls are trafficked for sexual exploitation (Sakulpitakphon, Crispin, Naebklang, Capaldi, & Madrinan, 2009). Trafficking of young women and girls for prostitution is made more urgent by the perception of this crime as a disruption to social and moral order (Segrave, 2009). Despite the wide recognition placed on human trafficking for sexual exploitation, data on this subject remain limited and are often based on estimates. It is approximated by the International Labour Organisation

(ILO) that at least 56% of the 12.3 million trafficked adults and children attached to some form of forced labor such as commercial servitude and bonded labor are women and girls (Department of State, 2009). The report reveals that 1.39 million of trafficked persons are bonded in commercial exploitation. The income generated through bonded labor is estimated at $12 billion a year (Tommasso, Shima, Strøm, & Bettio, 2009). The secretive nature with which the traffickers commit the crime and the lack of universal connotation to the definition of human trafficking make it difficult for criminal justice authorities to apprehend and prosecute the perpetrators (Hughes, 2003). Human traffickers may have informed networks, informants, and good resources than law enforcement officers that steer them away from prosecution. (Langberg, 2005). However, since the introduction of the Trafficking Victims Protection Act (TVPA) of 2000 the United States of America has conducted 183 investigations, charged 82 individuals for the crime and convicted 77 offenders in 40 human trafficking cases of which 27 were related to sexual exploitation (Department of State, 2009). Despite the lack of legislation to prosecute human trafficking as such, the South African Police Services (SAPS) has recorded 19 cases of trafficking for sexual exploitation for the period of 2008/2009 (SAPS, 2009). In the meanwhile, Farrell and Fahy (2009) are of the opinion that the limited and estimated data as well as low conviction of human traffickers can be attributed to the exaggerated nature in which the crime is reported and recorded. At any rate, the success of preventing and addressing human trafficking for sexual exploitation depends on the accuracy of data and an understanding of the concept. As much as governments are globally making strides preventing its occurrence, protecting victims, and prosecuting human traffickers partially and holistically, human trafficking is an intricate crime with which to tackle.

The factors contributing to the trafficking of young women and girls are gendered. Vulnerability prior trafficking, experiences during trafficking, as well as responses by legal and social institutions to the plight of victims occur within a gendered context. Young women and girls may accept dubious offers from human traffickers as an escape from calamities prevailing within their domestic settings and social context (D'Cunha, 2002; Piper, 2005; Segrave, 2009). Victims of sexual exploitation, of which 90% are young women and girls, encounter a variety of victimizations that intersect gender, race, and class (Farrell & Fay, 2009). Legal and social responses to the sexual exploitation of young women and girls occur within a context of gender discrimination expressed by prosecutors and lawyers toward victims of sexual violence (Segrave, 2009). Accordingly, this chapter aims to provide a gendered framework of sexual exploitation of trafficked women and girls. Firstly, the concept of human trafficking is defined. Secondly, the process of human trafficking for sexual exploitation followed by its gendered occurrence is analyzed. Lastly, intricacies and hindrances encountered by practitioners when identifying and offering protection services to victims of human trafficking are briefly examined.

CONCEPTUALIZATION

The United Nations Palermo Protocol of 2000 defines trafficking in persons as the recruitment, transportation, transfer, harbouring, or receipt of persons, by means of threat, force, coercion, abduction, fraud, and deception; abuse of power; a position of vulnerability; or of giving or receiving payments to achieve consent of a person having control over another for the purpose of exploitation. In this regard, exploitation implies the use of a human being for sexual exploitation, forced labor or services, slavery or services similar to slavery, servitude, or removal of organs. This definition considers a trafficked person taken by surprise at the turn of events at place of destination and it does not cover victims who had known about the form of employment they will perform.

There are two groups of victims of human trafficking for sexual exploitation: voluntary and involuntary sex workers. Voluntary sex workers may have been working as such prior the acceptance of offers from human traffickers (Clark, 2002). It is pointed out by Gülçür and İlkkaracan (2002), Roby and Tanner (2009), Skeldon (2000), as well as Simkhada (2008) that most Asian women in the sex industry had voluntarily accepted offers from human traffickers and were aware of the type of work they shall perform at the place of destination. There usually is no deception, manipulation, or force expressed by human traffickers to this group of women. Meanwhile, involuntary sex workers are forced against their will to perform the work. Nevertheless, the UN Protocol does recognise that human trafficking can occur within the context of consent of the victim whereby the victim was aware of the work to be executed at destination but unaware of the confining conditions within which the work will be performed (Raymond, 2002). In order to ascertain the occurrence of human trafficking for sexual exploitation, victims ought to be controlled, noncompensated, owned by traffickers, as well as bought and sold (Lusk & Lucas, 2009).

The women's organizations in the United States have taken different stances to the definition of human trafficking for sexual exploitation. On the one hand, abolitionists, advocating the end of the sex work, are of the opinion that prostitution is never voluntary because consent to sex work is meaningless (Limoncelli, 2009). Whilst the liberationists, striving for the legalization of prostitution, postulate that the conflation of human trafficking with prostitution jeopardizes the chances of identifying victims for protection (Godziak & Collet, 2005). They are often misguided, paternalistic, and imperialistic; thus denying the agency of young women and girls who enter the profession voluntarily (Limoncelli, 2009). Overall, the U.S. women's organizations agree that recruitment and transportation regardless of force should occur in order to ascertain the occurrence of human trafficking (Godziak & Collet, 2005). Nevertheless, the moralistic and individualistic undertones to the concept bring conflicting connotations to the definition of human trafficking for sexual exploitation (Janic & Finckenauer, 2005).

HUMAN TRAFFICKING PROCESS

There are three ways in which human traffickers lure young women and girls into the sex industry. Human traffickers abduct and kidnap, recruit through false promises of economic prosperity and wealth, as well as coerce young women and girls to work in the sex industry. This process occurs because the demand—male and female users or clients of sex workers—requests brothel owners and managers of sex work outlets to bring new or "fresh girls" or female sex workers into their countries or places. Managers of these outlets either recruit individually or seek services of human traffickers who in turn manipulatively target specific girls for recruitment. A human trafficker can be anyone such as an organized crime gang, parent, loose networks, and brothel owners. There are, to name just a few, Italian Camorra operating in Spain, Russian mafia, Japanese Yakuza gang, and Chinese triads (Raymond, 2002).

Human traffickers are frequently involved in other organized criminal activities such as drug trafficking and weapon smuggling (Raymond & Hughes 2001). Loose clan networks recruit young women and girls from Mozambique into South Africa (Martens, Pieczkowski, & van Vuuren-Smyth, 2003). Albanian organised crime gangs abduct and kidnap young girls for United Kingdom and Russia (Burkley, 2003). Young girls in the sex industry in Asia solicit help from human traffickers to travel for work in Europe, Japan, or America (Simkhada, 2008; Skeldon, 2000). A South African brothel owner recruited young women and girls from the Eastern Cape under false pretences and transported them to Gauteng, Pretoria, to work as prostitutes (Qaba, 2007). Targeted victims could be young women and girls seeking employment and adventure or visiting family members abroad, or dislocated and displaced young girls such as street children, child prostitutes, runaways, drug users, and club revellers (Delport, Koen, & MacKay, 2007).

Victims are usually between the ages of 12 and 24 years. They could be inexperienced and at times ill-informed about human trafficking but driven by the possibility of earning a better income in order to send money back home, buy clothes, entertain themselves, and enjoy a superior lifestyle (Janic & Finckenauer, 2005). Human traffickers may also request, coerce, or force victims already in the industry to recruit other girls into the mould. The youthfulness of victims determines the amount of time they could stay in sexual exploitation. Once they have reached a certain age, they might be dejected and replaced by younger ones (Lusk & Lucas, 2009). They are considered as unappealing and old, and perceived to have exhausted their usefulness (Lusk & Lucas, 2009). Victims are trafficked from Asia, Central America, Africa, Mexico, and Europe into the United States of America (Bertone, 1999; U.S. Department of State, 2009). In some regions such as Asia, women are trafficked from Bangladesh to Pakistan, Philippines to Japan, Nepal to India, and Thailand, Burma, and Cambodia to America (Raymond, 2002). In the meanwhile, whilst a growing number of female traffickers has been identified (Simkhada, 2008; UNODC, 2009) human traffickers remain overwhelmingly male (Hughes, 2000; Roby & Tanner, 2009).

The recruitment tactics include newspaper advertisements, mail order brides, and verbal promises of better economic and employment opportunities at place of destination (Hughes, 2001a; Hughes, 2001b). During the recruitment process, the human traffickers arrange travel documents if the destination is another country. They make use of corrupt state officials who construct and sell legitimate documents in return for cash. Once recruited, with travelling documents, the victims are transported by human traffickers from places of origin to transit or directly to destination. Travelling documents are confiscated on arrival at transit or destination. The transit and destination can be within the borders (noncross border) of the country or outside (cross-border). South African young women and girls are recruited and trafficked from economically deprived areas, namely, rural areas, townships, and informal settlements to economically developed areas such as Cape Town and Johannesburg. Before they reach Cape Town they could transit Port Elizabeth and work in indoor and outdoor sex work establishments as prostitutes for three days then are moved to Cape Town. Furthermore, West African girls earmarked for Italy could be taken to South Africa first before they are taken to Italy (Martens, Pieczkowski, & van Vuuren-Smyth, 2003). It is before they arrive at transit or destination that victims learn the reality of their jobs. Trafficked victims may be told by human traffickers that the victims own a substantial amount of money for travelling, accommodation, and food. The victims will be required to pay back the money by working as prostitutes giving all earnings to the human traffickers. Human traffickers may gang-rape trafficked victims as a form of break-ing their inhibitions especially if trafficked victims refuse to follow instructions or are new in the sex industry. This practice is termed *test-drive* by South African human traffickers (Lutya, 2009). Trafficked victims may be forced to work as prostitutes indoor or outdoor, such as in escort agencies, massage parlors, brothels, hotels, rental rooms, apartments, clubs, and restaurants. (Raymond & Hughes, 2001).

Transported, confined, and tied into debt bondage, victims of human trafficking could be kept in isolation, and fed drugs and alcohol to force them to submit into servi-tude (Moran, 2003). Furthermore, human traffickers may mutilate, murder, throw out of the balcony, and behead a reluctant victim in the presence of other victims as a form of punishment for resisting instructions from human traffickers (Hughes, 2001; Van der Watt, 2009). They are constantly moved from one location to the other in order to evade crimi-nal justice authorities (Lutya, 2009; Van der Watt, 2009). Human traffickers sell victims to brothels, private individual customers, and escort agencies.

Human trafficking violates the human rights of trafficked women. Trafficked vic-tims are not only tied into debt bondage but should also work in appalling conditions, with no freedom of movement and medical care, serving clients who may refuse to wear condoms: thus putting them at risk of contracting sexually transmitted diseases (Bettio & Nandi, 2009; Lusk & Lucas, 2009; Piper, 2005). Most victims may not be aware of their rights (Clark, 2002; Piper, 2005) in this context due to the manner in which they came to these places. Similar to victims of intimate partner violence they often blame themselves for the violence. Trafficked victims are not only deprived of civil liberties but are also physically, emotionally, sexually, financially, and spiritually ruined during the human trafficking process (Musto, 2009; Segrave, 2009). Consequently, some victims exit the process, physically, emotionally, and sexually depleted with no money but shame and embarrassment (Lusk & Lucas, 2009). Common among victims of human trafficking are sexually transmitted diseases such as HIV/AIDS, gonorrhoea, and syphilis, mental health challenges such as anxiety, suicidal thoughts, depression, insomnia, and paranoia as well as economic challenges such as, limited skills to resume a new life once repatriated (Dixon, 2008; Hughes, 2000; Moran, 2003; Muller & Holley, 2009; Tsutsumi, Izutsu, Poudyal, Kato, & Marui, 2008).

The essence of the human trafficking process is the recruitment, transportation, deception and manipulation, harbouring and transfer, as well as debt bondage of a female body by the human trafficker. A female body is an instrument for sexual subjugation, con-trol, and domination in male-dominated societies (Bettio & Nandi, 2009; Butler, 1998; Kelly, 2005). Once caught it is confined and constrained to perform a heterosexual gen-dered role of providing sexual services to males (Hughes, 2001; Hughes, 2003). The sex-ual services are considered as a predestined imperative by males with financial power to acquire the commodified female body (Hughes, 2003). This selling and sexual subjectiv-ity of women is captured by Bertone (1999, p. 7) when she says:

> The patriarchal world system hungers for and sustains the international subculture of docile women from underdeveloped nations. The women themselves, who are forced or lured into the trade, believe that providing international sexual services and sex tourism outfits is the acceptable order of things. The men accept the world order as well, regardless of their background.

Although not all trafficked victims emanate from developing nations, they might likely to be economically deprived persons seeking better alternatives in economically developed places. It should also be considered that human trafficking victims could be sourced internally (noncross border). Regardless, once the female body has reached its usefulness it may be discarded, sold, and replaced by another (Ben-Israel & Levenkron, 2005; Hughes, 2003).

Various countries globally have made strides to respond legally and socially to the crime. Since the September 11 terrorist attacks, the United States has increased its efforts to combat crimes committed by foreign immigrants including human trafficking (Bump & Duncan, 2003; Piper, 2005). The U.S. policies aimed at tackling terrorism have integrated human trafficking and human smuggling. That means human trafficking and smuggling as well as terrorism might be accorded the same status by the legal policy makers. The Intelligence Reform and Terrorism Prevention Act of 2004 has established a Human Smuggling and Trafficking Centre to address illicit travelling such as terrorism, smuggling, and trafficking in persons (Farrell & Fahy, 2009). Considering the threat imposed by the terrorist attacks human trafficking is perceived not only as a threat to human rights (D'Cuhna, 2002; Piper, 2005) but also a threat to national security (Farrell & Fahy, 2009). Human traffickers may transport victims in the same illicit manner as terrorists. It is possible that when victims are discovered in the absence or presence of human traffickers, they could be perceived as criminals.

The Intelligence Reform and Terrorism Prevention Act of 2004 may pose negative connotations to the safety and security of trafficked young women and girls. It could be possible that with threats to national security correlated with human trafficking, restrictions might be imposed to immigration of young women and girls. The main reason trafficked victims agree to travel with human traffickers foremost is to access economic opportunities. The question that needs to be asked is: What are the implications of having policies and legislations that could conflate undocumented, displaced, and dislocated young women and girls to terrorists? How does the Intelligence Reform and Terrorism Prevention Act of 2004 respond to victims of human trafficking? Restrictions could mean any young woman, trafficked or not, entering the United States may have to adhere to strict regulations that seek to safeguard the citizens against terrorism but could see her sent back to the country of origin if she does not meet the requirements of the Intelligence Reform and Terrorism Prevention Act of 2004. Some trafficked women travel unaccompanied and meet traffickers at destination countries. Moreover, the legal policy makers are not able to distinguish between trafficked and nontrafficked victims. Other mechanisms of reducing human trafficking for sexual exploitation such as prevention may not yield negative repercussions to the safety and security of trafficked victims.

Prevention measures in the United States include public awareness programmes facilitated by American Anti-Slavery group, Human Rights Watch, and the Anti-Human Trafficking Task Forces operating across the U.S. states and cities (Lusk & Lucas, 2009). These organizations advocate for policy reform and educate the public about the crime through distribution of pamphlets and brochures detailing the human trafficking process (Lusk & Lucas, 2009). The Department of Homeland Security in 2008 had made use of a Billboard Campaign written in Chinese, French, Russian, Korean, and Arabic languages to inform the public about human trafficking (U.S. Department of State, 2009). As required by the TVPA of 2000, the United States of America supplies a T-Visa to rescued victims of human trafficking if they are willing to assist criminal justice authorities to investigate the crime and prosecute the perpetrators (Lusk & Lucas, 2009; U.S. Department of State, 2009). The T-Visa allows the trafficked victims to stay in the United States for three years after which they will be eligible for permanent citizen status (Bump & Duncan, 2003; McCabe, 2008; U.S. Department of State, 2009). It appears that these visas are issued for direct and indirect victims (McCabe, 2008). According to the U.S. Department of State report (2009) up to date, the United States has issued 247 T-Visas to direct victims and 171 to family members. Furthermore, the Office for Victims of Crime coordinates the Services for Trafficking Victims Discretionary Grant Program which provides medical, and legal assistance, crisis counselling, and advocacy (Aron, Zweig, & Newmark, 2006).

The United Nations introduced the Palermo Protocol to prevent, suppress, and punish trafficking in persons especially in women and children in 2000. The protocol requires of its signatories to devise plans to prevent the crime, identify and rescue victims and support them, formulate partnerships regionally and within countries, as well as introduce legislations to prosecute the crime. Although there are some disparities pertaining to the definition of human trafficking that may hinder international cooperation, the majority of the 116 countries which have ratified the protocol have introduced legislations to prosecute the crime (UNODC, 2008). Human trafficking is a multifaceted crime that necessitates efforts from diverse organizations to address human trafficking for sexual exploitation of young women and girls. Organizations pursuing an end to gender violence integrated human trafficking into their agendas by focussing on poverty, employment, underdevelopment, and comodification of women (Bertone, 2004). Most of these organizations became instrumental during early 1990s with the high contingent of Russian women trafficked to Western Europe subsequent to the collapse of the Soviet Union (Bertone, 2004; Leppänen, 2007; Mameli, 2002). Providing guidance and leadership to address trafficking in persons, the Office of the United Nations High Commissioner for Human Rights (UHCR) educates and conscientizes organizations inside and outside the United States to apply a human rights and gender perspective in the fight against human trafficking (UN Commission on Human Rights, 2002). United Nations Children's Fund (UNICEF), United Nations Development Programme (UNDP), International Labour Organization (ILO), International Organization for Migration (IOM) are some of the international organizations taking up the issue of human trafficking for sexual exploitation. According to the UN Commission on Human Rights (2002), UNICEF partners civil organizations, organizes conferences as well as commissions, and conducts research on human trafficking. Through its Gender and Development Programme the UNDP addresses human trafficking as part of activism against violence toward women and children. ILO, considering child prostitution and commercial sexual exploitation, works to ensure an end to the use of children by adults in child labor and other exploitative activities. IOM with its research, victim protection and repatriation, economic mobilization and awareness programmes has been playing an instrumental role in addressing human trafficking for sexual exploitation. These organizations work successfully with other governmental and nongovernmental partners to respond to the crime. In South Africa, IOM has partnered with civil society, government, and criminal justice departments to form Southern African Counter Trafficking Programme (SACTAP) and Tsireledzani which conduct capacity building workshops, awareness programmes, conferences, and research on human trafficking (Le Roux, 2009a; Le Roux, 2009b).

Prosecution
Evidence

As required by the UN Palermo Protocol of 2000, signatories should produce evidence of prosecuting human trafficking. This principle may only be achieved if countries have legislations instructing the criminal prosecution of human traffickers. The United States of America introduced the TVPA in 2000 (Department of State, 2009). South Africa does not have a human trafficking legislation to prosecute the crime as such but is making use of partial sections from existing legislations to fight the crime. The Criminal Law (Sexual Offences and Related Matters) Act 32 of 2007 as amended and Children's Act 38 of 2005 have sections reserved to respond to human trafficking for sexual exploitation. These sections are temporary and will be removed once the human trafficking legislation has been introduced into law. Other legislations namely, Prevention of Organised Crime Act 118 of 1998, Immigration Act 13 of 2002, as well as Sexual Offences Act 23 of 1957 can also be used to prosecute the crime.

In summary, human trafficking is a clandestine and hidden crime. Trafficked victims are often reluctant to report the crime to criminal justice authorities. In this manner, the crime could occur unabated. Although figures illustrate the rise in the crime are based on estimates, case studies from rescued victims imply a surge in the crime. Human rights, civil society, and governmental departments are making inroads to ensure a decrease in the crime. However, as the number of organizations fighting the crime increases, little is known about the impact such organizations are making to prevent potential victims from becoming victims of the crime. The sexual exploitation of young women and girls by human traffickers occurs within a context of gender violence that receives minimal recognition from criminal justice authorities (Sigsworth, 2008). It may appear that for some victims the acceptance of offers does not necessitate report of victimization by human traffickers to the law enforcement officers. Some victims may interpret victimization as their own responsibility not warrant the attention of the criminal justice authorities. As admirable as the work performed by state departments in the fight against trafficking, some victims still experience gender prejudices and discrimination when reporting the crime.

Ultimately, unequal gendered relationships exist between role players in the human trafficking process—traffickers, clients or users of trafficked victims, husbands of mail order brides, as well as criminal justice authorities—and the trafficked victims. Firstly, once the documents have been confiscated on arrival at transit or destination, the trafficked victim becomes a dependent of the male trafficker (Bertone, 1999). This practice follows the traditional gender stereotypes of women as domesticated, caged beings that depend on men for economic and political resources (D'Cunha, 2002). Caged, isolated, with no documentation to prove their legality in the host country, usually with limited knowledge of the social processes and structure, their movements become constrained (Bertone, 1999; Bokhari, 2009). Furthermore, the relationship between human traffickers and trafficked victims remains inequitable regardless of the manner in which they were trafficked: be it voluntary or involuntary (Bettio & Nandi, 2009). The agency of voluntary prostitutes disappears, with debt bondage, confiscation of travelling documents, and restricted movements.

Diff...
Prostitution

Secondly, the socio-cultural and psychological meaning attached to the female body as well as the lifestyles of clients or users of prostitutes renders the industry an acceptable form of accessing sexual services. According to Ben-Israel and Levenkron (2005) as well as Butler (1998), a female body, a socially constructed instrument to serve certain purposes, carries with it cultural meanings through which men prove their masculine status.

It is amongst prostitutes that traumatized men, usually rejected during childhood and within current relationships, seek services of prostitutes: to sexually dominate weak and vulnerable subjects as well as to validate their masculine status (Ben-Israel & Levenkron, 2005). In this regard, the body of a prostitute does not only carry a significant meaning—sex can be obtained—but its caged and vulnerable context also renders it easily accessible to the client.

Thirdly, young women and girls could be trafficked for the purpose of marriage. They may respond to an advertisement seeking models, waitresses, or au pairs. Hidden behind the advertisement is a man from a developed world seeking a wife. It is on arrival at the place of destination that they learn the facts behind the advertisement. Nevertheless, once the victim assumes the role of the wife, a power imbalance between the couple will prevail, worsened by the fact that the bride has been forced into the marriage through trafficking channels. It is pointed out by Langevin and Belleau (2000) and Simkhada (2008) that the husband is likely to be financially secure, educated, and older than the bride. Meanwhile the bride has been trafficked from a developing world, with little education and financial resources to sustain herself (Simkhada, 2008). Therefore, the bride becomes a dependent of the husband to such an extent that if the marriage fails, she will have to return to the country of origin with no resources but shame and embarrassment. Furthermore, according to Langevin and Belleau (2000), the family of the bride may depend upon her to stay in a developed country in order to fulfil financial obligations of the family. Moreover, she could be the only source of income. Although the mail order bride marriage could be equitable and fulfilling to both partners if the bride is not trafficked, the bride relies upon the husband's citizenship to remain in the developed world.

Lastly, at times, criminal justice authorities may treat human trafficking victims as criminals instead of victims. During brothel raids victims can be seen getting arrested, loaded in police vans, and deposited at detention centres for not producing identity documents. For example, during Operation Gielded Cage in San Francisco, July 2005, the police raided ten brothels and rescued 120 women but placed them in immigration detention despite the provisions of the TVPA of 2000 (Kim & Chang, 2007). Of course their documents may have been confiscated by human traffickers. Human trafficking victims are likely to lose cases whereby the law enforcement officials and prosecutors resumed with arrest of trafficked victims rather than rescue and provide social services (Clark, 2002; Kim & Chang, 2007; Segrave, 2009). The cases are likely to be haphazardly investigated, with victims distrustful of the investigators as well as afraid that human traffickers may know they are testifying against them.

GENDERED CONTEXT OF SEXUAL EXPLOITATION

Young women and girls are trafficked for multiplicity of sexually exploitative purposes such as sex work, sexual slavery, as well as child brides. Trafficking of young women and girls for sexual exploitation is driven by a gendered set of male perceptions about sex, socio-economic, and individual hindrances experienced by young women and girls as well as the ease with which human traffickers are able to capture, confine, transfer, sell, and abuse the labor of young women and girls through debt bondage. A perception that runs across the heterosexual male users of prostitutes is that men need sex (Hughes, 2003; Phinney, 2001). In order to fulfil this need, they should obtain it from women and girls either as partners or sex workers (Ben-Israel & Levenkron, 2005).When women and girls accept misleading offers from human traffickers, they are often forced by a variety of gendered social relations prevailing at countries and places of destination (Croontz & Griebel, 2004).Feminization of poverty and unemployment, dysfunctional family circumstances, gender violence, civil conflict, lack of opportunities for educational and economic advancements, and teenage parenting are some of the gendered factors driving human trafficking for involuntary prostitution (D'Cuhna, 2002; Manohar, 2002; Piper, 2005).

Often the users and the demand for young women and girls are men whose interests are purely to serve a gendered need. The male demand for sex work prefers young girls (Ben-Israel & Levenkron, 2005; UNICEF, 2003). Due to their immaturity and lack of sexual experience, the users or purchasers of sexual services assume them free of sexually transmitted diseases such as HIV/AIDS (Ben-Israel & Levenkron, 2005). Besides, the widespread belief that sexual encounters with virgins cures HIV infected older men of the diseases has seen an increase in abduction of young girls by older men for early marriage and sexual slavery (Dixon, 2008; Kelly, 2005). Recently, the surge in the number of older men in rural areas afflicted by HIV/AIDS has exacerbated a rise in the number of cases of abduction and kidnapping of young women and girls in South African rural areas especially the Eastern Cape. This increase has propelled the South African Law Reform Commission to hold workshops in order to debate the right and wrongfulness of the traditional customs informing the decisions to abduct and kidnap young women and girls for early marriage.

Sexual exploitation of young women and girls occurs within a context of socio-economic and individual experiences of gender inequality. The human traffickers' choice of victims and their circumstances as well as the victims' decision to accept job offers from human traffickers are gender determined. Research has revealed that victims of human trafficking for sexual exploitation could be illiterate, poor, lack access to educational opportunities, ill-informed about human trafficking and human rights, and some are displaced and dislocated prior victimization by human traffickers (Manohar, 2002). The victims accept offers from human traffickers in the hope that they will improve their current socio-economic and individual shortfalls (Piper, 2005). Some victims were exposed to child abuse, incest, marital discord, emotional and physical violence, prior the experience of trafficking (D'Cuhna, 2002). Some victims had been residing in or run away from orphanages, shelters for dislocated and displaced children, street children, and gangs (Manohar, 2002). Often human traffickers target specific women for recruitment based on gender stereotypical perceptions, expected roles to perform, and social expectations of women (D'Cuhna, 2002). For instance, a gendered and ethnically prejudiced perception amongst some male clients is that African women are wild, Asian women are obedient and erotic, and Latin American women are hot (Ben-Israel & Levenkron, 2005). Regardless, the decision to accept or reject an offer from a human trafficker is also dependent upon the type of job offered. For instance, when selecting jobs, low-skilled women—often human trafficker targets for recruitment—are likely to slide toward traditionally feminine jobs such as sex work, waitressing, and domestic labor (D'Cuhna, 2002).

The individual and socio-economic factors experienced by victim's prior sexual exploitation as well as difficulties experienced by criminal justice authorities in successfully arresting and prosecuting human traffickers facilitate an easy recruitment to the trafficking process. Human trafficking victims are willing and able to allow their female bodies to be moved across and within borders to access better economic opportunities whilst human traffickers do so with the intention to take advantage of the biologically determined and natural capabilities of a female body (Segrave, 2009). Having exited their countries to seek advancements, once captured, confined, and defrauded of this goal, victims might least likely to escape human traffickers: If they escape some may continue working as sex workers individually (Lutya, 2009).

CHALLENGES WITH VICTIM IDENTIFICATION AND PROTECTION

Trafficked victims should be identified in order to be eligible for protection services. Law enforcement officers, medical practitioners, as well as border officials are in the position to identify and rescue trafficked victims (Bump & Duncan, 2003). Victims may seek medical and mental health services as well as report cases to law enforcement officers subsequent to the process of human trafficking. For example, a high contingent of Zimbabwean children enters South Africa unaccompanied and at risk of being captured and confined to serve human trafficking purposes (EYE, 2009). Nevertheless, it is pointed out by Bump and Duncan (2003) that some girl children enter the United States as wives of human traffickers: It may not be possible for border officials to ascertain their inevitable circumstances once they have reached their destinations. Moreover, some of the girls are made to inflate their age to make their stories believable to the border officers (Bump & Duncan, 2003).

Identification and protection of human trafficking victims is a difficult task to accomplish. Firstly, the Palermo Protocol neither does make any provisions regarding procedures to identify human trafficking victims nor does it stipulate precisely the characteristics of a victim of trafficking (Clark, 2008). Secondly, trafficked victims do not have legal status in countries of exploitation: therefore may not possess a right to claim medical, mental, educational as well as legal services (Dixon, 2008). It is not possible for human trafficking practitioners to separate victims from local citizens for the reason that physical appearance of victims is similar to the local citizens. Once they exit the human trafficking process, trafficked victims take different alternatives. Foreign victims may seek help from helping organizations or disappear into the country and mingle with the citizens. Thirdly, victim identification is made difficult by the fact that prostitution is a hidden crime and prostitutes are often alienated from the mainstream society (Kim & Chang, 2007; Musto, 2009; Simkhada, 2008). The hidden nature of human trafficking is illustrated by the fact that some victims could be imprisoned in brothels where they cannot be rescued and identified by the criminal justice authorities and other service organizations (Kim & Chang, 2007). On the other hand, victims of internal trafficking are often registered missing to the Department of Social Development and the SAPS. Regardless, victims could be turned into criminals during police raids. It is whilst in detention that some victims learn about the protection services accorded to victims of human trafficking (Aron et al., 2006).

The lack of resources to provide needed services to the victims as well as the victim's inability to succinctly articulate their circumstances in the application forms may thwart their chances of attaining protection from state departments. According to Aron et al. (2006) whilst under the care of victim protection, some victims require services closely related to their culture namely, food, medical, and mental health services that cannot be provided by the country of destination. Furthermore, Bump and Duncan (2003), Clark (2008), and UNODC (2008) state that the harmful experiences endured by the victim during the trafficking process may render them incapable of verbalizing their experiences on paper; thus decreasing the chances of accessing the needed services. According to UNODC (2008), the prolonged traumatic experiences endured by the victims may make them less cooperative, aggressive, and irritable to professionals wanting to learn the details of their experiences. It may not be the victim's fault that services cannot be provided. It remains the responsibility of each country to investigate the types of victims that could need their services and organize their helping capacities accordingly.

CONCLUSION

This chapter aimed to provide a gendered context within which human trafficking of young women and girls occur. Human trafficking is defined, the process of human trafficking is described, the gendered factors contributing to the crime are analyzed. Essentially, the chapter briefly discussed the challenges encountered by practitioners when identifying and providing services to human trafficking victims. It appears that despite the information produced by human trafficking authors, writers, and researchers, differences, contradictions, and gaps still exist. Clark (2008), Hughes (2001), and Piotrowicz (2008) point out that disparities regarding the definition of human trafficking among signatories of the Palermo Protocol can be identified: The definitional differences hinder the international collaborations aimed at responding to human trafficking. As a result of the differences in the definition of human trafficking, practitioners may find it difficult to identify human trafficking victims. This task of victim identification is made worse by the fact that the Palermo Protocol does not provide indicators, guidelines, or procedures to distinguish between human trafficking victims and ordinary citizens (Clark, 2008). Up to date, there is no clear distinction between voluntary and involuntary prostitution (Clark, 2008; Gülçür, & Ìlkkaracan, 2002; Musto, 2009; Segrave, 2009). Human trafficking victims continue to face socio-cultural, political, economic, and individual hindrances when they exit the process of human trafficking. Even before they exit the process users, who could help them exit immediately, hold negative attitudes toward trafficked prostitutes. The majority of respondents in Nami and Keiko (2009) were aware that the prostitutes were trafficked; but still continue to use their services. According to Nami and Keiko (2009), clients perceived trafficked sex workers as poor women from developing countries in need of the money. One aspect that could help the victims to exit the process is the dissemination of human trafficking information to potential users of trafficked prostitutes. Due to the clandestine context within which the human trafficking crime occurs, victims could be reluctant to tell the client about the manner in which they came into contact with the sex work industry (Hughes, 2000). What's more is that it is even difficult for researchers to obtain direct/primary respondents. Certain researchers make use of secondary respondents. According to Godziak (2005), the use of secondary respondents, reliance on overviews and estimates of the number of victim as well as commentary and anecdotal evidence on human trafficking draws an inaccurate picture of human trafficking. Furthermore, there is no obligation in the Palermo Protocol regarding state and nonstate collaborations pertaining to the provision of housing and temporary residence (Bhabha, 2005).

REFERENCES

ARON, L. Y., ZWEIG, J. M., & NEWMARK, L. C. (2006). *Comprehensive services for survivors of human trafficking: Findings from clients in three communities.* Washington: Urban Institute Justice Policy Centre.

BEN-ISRAEL, H., & LEVENKRON, N. (2005). *The missing factor: Clients of trafficked women in Israel's sex industry.* The Hebrew University in Jerusalem: Hotline for Migrant Workers.

BERTONE, A. M. (2004). Transnational activism to combat trafficking in persons. *Brown Journal of World Affairs, X*(2): 9–22.

BERTONE, A. M. (1999). Sexual trafficking in women: International political economy and the politics of sex. *Gender Issues, 18*(1): 4–22.

BETTIO, F., & NANDI, T. K. (2009). Evidence on women trafficked for sexual exploitation: A rights based analysis. *European Journal of Law and Economics.* [O] Available: http://www.springerlink.com/link.asp?id=100264. Assessed 2009/10/05.

BHABHA, J. (2005). *Trafficking, smuggling and human rights.* [O] Available: http://www.migrationinformation.org/Feature/print.cfm?ID=294 Assessed 2009/11/24.

BOKHARI, F. (2008). Failing through the gaps: safeguarding children trafficked into the UK. *Children and Society and Society*, 22: 201–211.

BUMP, N. M., & DUNCAN, J. (2003). Notes and commentary: Conference on identifying and serving child victims of trafficking. *International Migration, 41*(5): 201–218.

BURKLEY, M. (2003). *Baltic girls forced into sex slavery.* [O] Available: http://www.bbc.co.uk. Assessed 209/03/21.

BUTLER, J. (1998). Subjects of sex/gender/desire. In Phillips, A. (ed), *Feminism and Politics.* Oxford: Oxford University Press.

CLARK, A. M. (2002). Trafficking in persons: An issue of human security. *Journal of Human Development, 4*(2): 247–263.

CLARK, A. M. (2008). Vulnerability, prevention and human trafficking: The need for a new paradigm. In UNODC. *An introduction to human trafficking: Vulnerability, impact and action.* Vienna: UNODC.

CROONTZ, P., & GRIEBEL, C. (2004). International approaches to human trafficking: The call for a gender-sensitive perspective in international law. *Women's Health Journal.* [O] Available: http://www.atc.org.yu. Accessed 2009/11/11.

D'CUNHA, J. (2002). Trafficking in persons: a gender and rights perspective. *Promoting Gender Equality to Combat Trafficking in Women and Children*, 7–9 October, Bangkok.

DEPARTMENT OF STATE. (2009). *Trafficking in persons report.* [O] Available: http://www.state.gov/g/tip. Assessed 22/10/2009.

DELPORT, E., KOEN, K., & MACKAY, A. (2007). *Human trafficking in South Africa: Root causes and recommendations.* Paris: United Nations Educational Scientific and Cultural Organization (UNESCO).

DIXON, J. (2008). Vulnerability, prevention and human trafficking: the need for a new paradigm. In UNODC. *An introduction to human trafficking: Vulnerability, impact and action.* Vienna: UNODC.

EYE ON HUMAN TRAFFICKING. (2009). Issue 21. Pretoria: International Organisation for Migration.

FARRELL, A., & FAHY, S. (2009). The problem of human trafficking in the US: Public frames and policy responses. *Journal of Criminal Justice* (2009): 1–10.

GODZIAK, E. M., & COLLETT, E. A. (2005). Research on human trafficking in North America: A review of literature. In IOM. *Data and research on human trafficking: A global survey.* Geneva: IOM.

GÜLÇÜR, L., & ÌLKKARACAN, P. (2002). The "Natasha" experience: migrant sex workers from the former Soviet Union and Eastern Europe in Turkey. *Women's Studies International, 25*(4): 411–421.

HUGHES, M. D. (2000). Men create the demand: Women are the supply. *Lecture on sexual exploita-tion*, November, Valencia, Spain.

HUGHES, M. D. (2001a). The Natasha trade: Transnational sex trafficking. *National Institute of Jus-tice Journal*, (1): 9–15.

HUGHES, M. D. (2001b). The impact of the use of new communications and information technolo-gies on trafficking in human beings for sexual exploitation: A study of the users. *Committee for Equality Between Men and Women*. [O] Available: http://www.uri.edu/artsci/wms/hughes/study_of_users. Accessed 2009/10/20.

HUGHES, M. D. (2003). The demand: the driving force of sex trafficking. *Vital Speeches of the day, 69*(6): 182–183.

JANIC, G., & FINCKENAUER, J. O. (2005). Representations and misrepresentations of human traffick-ing. *Trends in Organized Crime, 8*(3): 24–40.

KELLY, L. (2005). "You can find anything you want": A critical reflection on research in trafficking in persons within and into Europe. *International Migration, 43*(1/2): 235–265.

KIM, K., & CHANG, G. (2007). *Reconceptualising approaches to human trafficking: New directions to perspectives from the field*. Los Angeles: Loyola Law School.

LANGBERG, L. (2005). A review of recent OAS research on human trafficking in the Latin American and Caribbean Region. In IOM. *Data and research on human trafficking: A global survey*. Geneva: IOM.

LANGEVIN, L., & BELLEAU, M. C. (2000). *Trafficking in women in Canada: A critical analysis of the legal framework governing immigrant live in caregivers and mail order brides*. Ontario: Status of Women Canada.

LEPPÄNEN, K. (2007). Movement of women: Trafficking in interwar era. *Women's International Studies Forum*, 30: 523–533.

LE ROUX, S. (2009a). Human Trafficking: A practical perspective. Research Seminar: *A Multi-Discipli-nary approach to Human Trafficking*, Pretoria, 16 September.

LE ROUX, S. (2009b). Trafficking: incidence, trauma and caretaking of the trafficked child in South-ern Africa. *Towards multi-disciplinary expertise in handling child abuse—A focus on Trafficking—* Pretoria: 4–6 May.

LIMONCELLI, S. (2009). Human trafficking: Globalisation, exploitation and transnational sociology. *Sociology Compass, 3*(1): 72–91.

LUSK, M., & LUCAS, F. (2009). The challenge of human trafficking and contemporary slavery. *Jour-nal of Comparative Social Welfare, 25*(1): 49–57.

LUTYA, T. M. (2009). Epi-criminological responses to human trafficking of young women and girls for involuntary prostitution in South Africa. *Journal of Scandinavian Studies in Criminology and Crime Prevention*, 10(Supplement): 60–79.

MAMELI, P. A. (2002). Stopping the illegal trafficking of human beings. *Crime, Law & Social Change*, 38: 67–80.

MANOHAR, J. S. (2002). Trafficking in women and girls. *Promoting Gender Equality to Combat Trafficking in Women and Children*, 7–9 October, Bangkok.

MARTENS, J., PIECZKOWSKI, M., & van VUUREN-SMYTH, B. (2003). *Seduction, sale and slavery: Traf-ficking in women and children in Southern Africa*. Pretoria: International Office for Migration (IOM).

MCCABE, K. A. (2008). *The trafficking of persons: national and international responses*. New York: Peter Lang Publishing.

MORAN, T. (2003). *Health and human trafficking*. Geneva: IOM.

MULLER, K & HOLLEY, K. (2009). "I want to be a different person". The impact of trafficking on children: The story of Elsie. *Towards multi-disciplinary expertise in handling child abuse—A focus on Trafficking*—Pretoria: 4–6 May.

Musto, J. A. (2009). What's in a name? Conflations and contradictions in contemporary U.S discourses of human trafficking. *Women's Studies International Forum, 32*(2009): 281–287.

Nami, O., & Keiko, H. (2009). Japanese perceptions of trafficking in persons: An analysis of the demand for sexual services and policies dealing with trafficking survivors. *Social Sciences Japan Journal, 12*(1): 45–70.

Phinney, A. (2001). *Trafficking of women and children for sexual exploitation in the Americas.* USA: Inter-American Commission of Women.

Piper, N. (2005). *Gender and Migration.* [O] Available: http://www.gcim.org. Accessed 2009/11/11

Piotrowicz, R. (2008). *The UNHCR Guidelines on Human Trafficking.* Oxford: Oxford University Press.

Qaba, N. (2007). Prosecuting trafficking without trafficking laws. *Trafficking in human beings: National and International perspectives*, 17 August, Bloemfontein.

Raymond, J. C. (2002). The New UN Trafficking Protocol. *Women's Studies International Forum, 25*(5): 491–502.

Raymond, J. G., & Hughes, D. M. (2001). *Sex trafficking of women in the United States: International and domestic trends.* Rockville: National Criminal Justice Reference Service.

Roby, J. L., & Tanner, J. (2009). Supply and demand: Prostitution and sexual trafficking in Northern Thailand. *Geography Compass, 3*(1): 89–107.

Sakulpitakphon, P., Crispin, V., Naebklang, M., Capaldi, M. & Madrinan, C. (2009). *Their protection is in our hands: The state of global child trafficking for sexual purposes.* Bangkok: ECPAT International.

Segrave, M. (2009). Order at the border: The repatriation of victims of trafficking. *Women's Studies International Forum, 32*(2009): 251–260.

Sigsworth, R. (2008). *The promulgation of the Criminal Law (Sexual Offences and Related Matters) Amendment Act: Bureaucracy versus Democratisation.* Braamfontein: CSVR.

Simkhada, P. (2008). Life histories and survival strategies amongst sexually trafficked girls in Nepal. *Children & Society*, 22:235–248.

Skeldon, R. (2000). Trafficking: A perspective from Asia. *International Migration*, 2000 (1): 7–30.

South African Police Service. (2009). *Crime situation*: Crime Statistics. Pretoria: South African Police Services.

Tommasso, M. L. D., Shima, I., Strøm, S., & Bettio, F. (2009). As bad as it gets: Well-being deprivation of sexually exploited trafficked women. *European Journal of Political Economy, 25*(2009): 143–163.

Tsutsumi, A., Izutsu, T., Poudyal, A. K., Kato, S., & Marui, E. (2008). Mental health of female survivors of human trafficking in Nepal. *Social Science and Medicine*, 66: 1841–1847.

United Nations (Palermo) Protocol to prevent, suppress and punish trafficking in persons, especially women and children. Supplementing the United Nations Convention against transnational Organised crime. 2000. New York: United Nations.

United Nations Children's Fund (UNICEF). (2003). *Trafficking in human beings especially women and children in Africa.* Italy: UNICEF Innocenti Research Centre.

United Nations Commission on Human Rights (UNCHR). (2002). *Integration of the Human Rights of Women and the gender perspective.* United Nations: Economic and Social Council.

United Nations Organisation for Drugs and Crime (UNODC). (2009). *Global report on trafficking in persons.* Vienna: UNODC.

UNODC. (2008). *An introduction to human trafficking: vulnerability, impact and action.* Vienna: UNODC.

Van der Watt, M. (2009). Trafficking: Best practices, a case illustration. *Towards multi-disciplinary expertise in handling child abuse—A focus on Trafficking*—Pretoria: 4–6 May.

SECTION III
Women: Victims of Violence

13

Women: Second-Class Citizens?[1]

Roslyn Muraskin

The past several hundred years have seen women struggling for equality—struggling to help make changes occur. Today, we still advocate change. Change in the criminal justice system is part of the change needed. What is equality? No society exists that can actually boast about the principles of equality being present. According to Catherine MacKinnon, "the second-class status of women as a group is widely documented to be socially and legally institutionalized, cumulatively and systematically shaping access to life chances on the basis of sex" (2001, p. 2). Using the words of Richard Rorty, a philosopher, a woman "is not yet the name of the way of being human" (MacKinnon, 2001, p. 3).

Women are being arrested at higher rates than ever before, although men are still predominant in correctional facilities. Women are also more often the victims of crimes than ever before. Witness the incidence of domestic violence, rape, and women who find themselves being sexually harassed. The contention is that the continuum of violence against women includes sexual harassment as well as domestic violence. As women gain more equality, they become harassed by their employers in a manner that is akin to criminal violence. During this new century, a strategy must be developed to combat all violence against women. The argument is made that while the public has slowly recognized the dynamics of rape and domestic violence, cases of sexual harassment need to be taken seriously and dealt with seriously.

INTRODUCTION

Historically, laws have discriminated against women. Women have, in fact, sometimes been victimized by policies designed to protect them. During the last decades, women have been especially strong in arguing for equality. The history of women's struggles has taught us that litigation is simply a catalyst for change. A change in attitude is still needed, discrimination still exists, and women continue to struggle. When Abigail Adams wrote to her husband, John, who helped to write the Constitution of the United States, she told him to "remember the ladies." The ladies still wish to be remembered. Controversy still abounds.

Women's issues still infuse every aspect of social and political thought. As early as 1913, Rebecca West stated that she had never been able to find out precisely what feminism is, but added that people called her a feminist whenever she expressed sentiments to differentiate her from a doormat. Women's basic human rights are inextricably linked to women's treatment by and with their participation in today's political world. Due to the fact that the lives of women are reflections of what they do, what they say, and how they treat one another, women as participating members of the human race are ultimately responsible for human affairs.

What, then, is the agenda for change in the criminal law in the twenty-first century? There is no way to guarantee both men and women equal protection under the laws unless we are committed to the elimination of all gender discrimination. The criminal justice system over the years has slowly come to grips with an understanding of women and justice. In the twenty-first century, more and more cases are being heard and will be heard in the courts, where legal procedures and precedents have been established to ensure that complainants will receive a fairer hearing than that envisioned previously. Courts need to allow time for the discovery of evidence as well as the opportunity to hear expert testimony in cases of sexual violence.

The data continue to show that women are involved in the criminal justice system in numbers greater than before. Crimes such as rape, domestic violence, and sexual harassment are all part of the continuum of violence against women. Rape is not a crime of sex; it is a crime of power. It is "an act of violence, an assault like any other, not an expression of socially organized sexuality" (MacKinnon, 1979, p. 218). The fact that rape is acted out in sex does not mean that it is an act of male sexuality. Rape is simply an act of violence. Think of the social construction of battering. "Take a moment and think about the image that comes to mind when you hear words such as *domestic violence, spouse abuse, wife battering,* and *women battering.* Close your eyes and think about an assault between two adults who are in an intimate relationship. Visualize the events leading up to the assault and the event itself. Who is the perpetrator? Who is the victim? What is the context surrounding the assault?" (Eigenberg, 2001, p. 15). Sexual abuse has never been seen as "an act of sex inequality but as a crime or a tort. Neither criminal law nor tort law has taken the social context of sex inequality systematically into account in defining and adjudicating as sexual assaults" (MacKinnon, 2001, p. 766).

Sexual abuse has happened because historically it was neither defined nor treated as a crime. The rules that pertain to cases of sexual abuse such as rape were defined prior to women even winning the right to vote or being allowed to serve on juries. "A sex equality analysis of sexual subordination would seek to understand the place of sexual assault in the status of the sexes, and the role of gender status in sexual assault and its treatment by law" (MacKinnon, 2001, p. 767). The acts of rape and domestic violence have drawn parallels with that of sexual harassment. If sex or sexual advances are unwanted, if they are imposed on a woman who is in no position to refuse, why is this act any different from rape or domestic violence? Some consider sexual harassment a lesser crime, and that in and of itself is questionable, but it is, nevertheless, an act of violence against women. Both women and men spend the better part of their day at work. Sexual harassment is sexual discrimination, and attention must be paid to these acts. In recent years there has been a current of public discussion about the cases of women accused and sometimes convicted of assaulting and killing partners who abuse them. The actual number of these cases is relatively small, but the attention given to these cases illuminates the larger problem for which they have come to stand: the common disparity of power between men and women in familial relationships. What about working relationships? What we need to understand is whether sexual assault is truly based on sex alone.

Looking at the crime of rape, in the words of Susan Brownmiller (1975):

> The rapist performs a myrmidon function for all men
> by keeping all women in a thrall of anxiety and fear.
> Rape is to women as lynching was to blacks: the ultimate
> physical threat by which all men keep all women in a state
> of psychological intimidation.

Can any woman imagine what it must be like to be a victim of rape? In the words of Sue Lees, *Carnal Knowledge: Rape on Trial* (1996, p. xx), in Great Britain:

> Imagine for one moment what it is like, from a woman's perspective, to give evidence
> against a man who has raped you. The case does not come up for a year. You are then obliged
> to relive the whole life-threatening experience, face to face
> with the man who assaulted you, the mere sight of whom brings
> back the horror of the attack. You avoid looking at him. You
> face ranks of barristers in wigs, the judge up high, police
> everywhere, all in the awe-inspiring surroundings of the
> crown court. You have no legal representative of your own,
> and you are not allowed to meet the prosecuting counsel.
> You must describe in intimate detail every part of your body that was assaulted in words
> which would be embarrassing
> To use with friends, let alone in a public setting. The paradox
> Is that the very use of such language is sufficient to render
> A woman "unrespectable." Except in pornography, the kinds
> of detail described in rape cases would never be voiced. It
> is hardly surprising that so many women find court a nightmare.

This could very well explain why crimes of rape are rarely reported in the United States, let alone prosecuted.

If a sexual crime is a crime of power, all these acts constitute the subordination of women to men. This reflects the powerlessness in the criminal law of women as a gender. "If sexuality is set apart from gender, it will be a law unto itself" (MacKinnon, 1979, p. 221). The reasoning still exists that men rape to establish their power and that women are raped because they are still considered the property of men.

According to Katharine K. Baker, "Once a Rapist? Motivational Evidence and Relevance in Rape Law" (1997, pp. 606–608),

the U.S. soldiers left the 11th Brigade patch [in My Lai]
in order to impugn the honor of North Vietnamese men.
The U.S. soldiers could have gotten their sex without leaving
manifest evidence that they had done so. They could have
just killed the women in the same way they destroyed the
villages' animals, property, and elderly men. By making
the fact of their rapes public, the soldiers added further
insult to the enemy. This view explains why rapes during
war time often take place in public or are committed in
front of civilian witnesses, and it explains why rape and
war have gone hand in hand since there has been war.

HISTORY

The United States was founded on two principles that (1) "all men are created equal" and
(2) "governments derive their powers from the consent of the governed." Women were not
included in either concept. The Constitution of the United States did not include women
as citizens or as persons with legal rights. Women were not considered persons under the
Fourteenth Amendment to the Constitution, which guaranteed that no state shall deny to
"any person within its jurisdiction the equal protection of the laws." Remember the words
of Justice Miller in the case of *Bradwell v. Illinois:* "The paramount destiny of women is
to fulfill the noble and benign offices of wife and mother. This is the law of the Creator.
And the rules of civil society must be adopted to the general constitution of things, and
cannot be based upon exceptional cases" (Muraskin, 2007, p. 6). Therefore, in the face of
the law, women had no rights—women did not exist on a legal footing with men.

The women's movement was the most integrated and populist force in the United
States. More than 80 years later, *after* women won the right to vote, a right granted to
women *after* the slaves were freed, women still wait for the promise of the Declaration of
Independence of equality before and under the law.

The "rule of thumb" that existed under the English common law allowed a husband
to beat his wife with a whip or stick no wider than his thumb. The husband's prerogative
was incorporated into the law of the United States. The sad fact is that several states had
laws on the books that essentially allowed a man to beat his wife with no interference from
the courts. Blackstone referred to this action as the "power of correction." For too many
decades women have been victims of sexual assault. Each act of "sexual assault is recognized as one of the most traumatic and debilitating crimes for adults" (Roberts, 1993,
p. 362). The victimization of women has been most prevalent and problematic for the
criminal justice system. As Susan Faludi (1991) points out, women's advances and retreats
are generally described in military terms: battles won, battles lost, and points and territory
gained and surrendered. In times when feminism is at a low ebb, women assume the reactive role—privately and most often covertly struggling to assert themselves against the
dominant cultural tide. But when feminism becomes the tide, the opposition does not
simply go along with the reversal—it digs in its heels, brandishes its fists, and builds wall
and dams.

"Under the federal constitution and most state constitutions, women have not yet
been raised to the status of constitutional protections enjoyed by males" (Thomas, 1991,

p. 95). Gender-neutral language does not solve the problem either. All such language does is to allow employers to hide the discrimination that is prevalent.

Women represent half of the national population, and they deserve the same rights as men. When a rape victim speaks out, she demonstrates that the victim no longer has the facility to control her own personal being. The victim of rape experiences a diminishment in her ego defense. The act of rape, even more so than any other criminal act, deprives the victims and their acquaintances of the protective mantle of privacy, converting their private agony in finding themselves discussing what happened to them in private into what is termed a public forum. There was a time when rape cases required corroboration that denigrated the testimony of women whose claim to have been sexually violated was in and of itself indefensible (Muraskin, 2007, p. 181). The aura of dishonesty was raised because which woman would allow herself to be a victim of a rape? Historically, rape laws, as many other laws that direct their attention to women as victims, have been based on the premise that women are basically liars. After all remember the words of Justice Matthew Hale:

> A charge such as that made against the defendant in this case
> is one which is easily made and once made, difficult to defend
> against, even if the person accused is innocent. Therefore, the
> law requires that you examine the testimony of the female person named
> in the information with caution. (Muraskin, 2007, p. 182)

The quandary that thousands of women who are the victims of rape face is whether to report the rape in the first place. Oftentimes, the answer is not to report, because the reasoning is that "she asked for it." There has evolved a pattern—both the lack of support from the community and the low priority the police and prosecutors give to rape cases— that appears to alienate the victims. Unfortunately, those victims who do persevere to the trial stage have historically found themselves put on trial as the defense attorney has grilled them about their prior sexual history, provided it is relevant to the case. Under the rape shield laws, a victim of rape cannot be questioned about her prior sexual history unless it has relevance to the defense's case.

"Rape is an unbelievably vicious and personal form of attack. Many a female victim fears her assailant will return (and some do). Many a victim is reluctant to return home or to return to her normal home life upon being raped. Rape legislation has had a long-standing and sordid history as sexist legislation designed not to protect women, but rather to protect men's social and property interests in female chastity" (Muraskin, pp. 183–184).

Unfortunately, rape has become an instrument of forced exile for many victims.

Historically, the criminal justice system has been inadequate in responding to the problems of domestic violence as well. Mandatory arrest policies by law enforcement have been established throughout the United States. Like crimes of rape, crimes of domestic violence have been cloaked in secrecy. "Both legal and social institutions reinforced the 'hands-off approach' that characterized early responses to woman battering . . . since the 1970s, efforts initiated by the battered women's movement have successfully propelled the issue of intimate violence into the national spotlight" (see Block & Christakos, 1995; Dobash & Dobash, 1977; Schechter, 1982, in Muraskin, 2007, p. 239).

Similar to cases of rape and all cases of violence against women, responding to disputes of domestic violence has brought on deep feelings of frustration both from those involved in law enforcement and from the women who seek protection. Year after year, "battered women faced police officers who routinely supported offenders' positions and challenged the credibility of victims—often trivializing their fears and even blaming them for their own victimization" (Miller & Peterson, 2007, p. 239). As the momentum has grown toward mandatory arrest policies, we find that the psychological benefits to these victims are great: "Arrest demonstrates an official willingness to assert that battering will not be tolerated" and the factor of mandatory arrests also provide the police with the necessary training and guidance needed in dealing with cases of violence against women (p. 240).

"One potential problem with mandatory arrest policies is that they almost certainly produce unanticipated and negative consequences for women. But due to limited opportunities, resources, and alternatives, men who abuse women from minority or lower socioeconomic groups may be disproportionately arrested in jurisdictions favoring pro-arrest policies, creating additional problems for these battered women" (Miller & Peterson, p. 246).

In establishing policies for women and violence, we understand that the policies of law enforcement cannot subsist in a vacuum. There are examples of alternative programs in dealing with such problems. "It has been suggested that a collaboration of legal sanctions and social services, such as court-mandated counseling, generally tend to complement one another, and correct power imbalances between victims and offenders with a minimum of coercion. Prosecutor's offices have introduced pretrial mediation programs as an alternative to formal criminal processing. The idea behind mediation is to informally educate both the victim and the offender about more effective methods for resolving conflict and to inform both parties about their legal rights" (Miller & Peterson, p. 249).

THE NEED FOR A NATIONAL COMMITMENT TO END VIOLENCE AGAINST WOMEN

Addressing violence against women requires a national commitment and a national remedy. Toward this end, in the early 1990s, Congress began assembling a mountain of data about gender violence. A summary of this data was included in the dissenting opinion of Supreme Court Justice David Souter in *United States v. Morrison* (2000, pp. 1761–1763):

- Three out of four American women will be victims of violent crimes sometime during their lives.
- Violence is the leading cause of injuries to women ages 15 to 44.
- As many as 50 percent of homeless women and children are fleeing from domestic violence.
- Since 1974, the assault rate against women has outstripped the rate for men by at least twice for some age groups and far more for others.
- Battering is the largest cause of injury to women in the United States.
- An estimated 4 million women in the United States seek medical assistance each year for injuries sustained from their husbands or other partners.
- Between 2,000 and 4,000 women die every year from domestic abuse.
- Arrest rates may be as low as 1 for every 100 domestic assaults.
- Partial estimates show that violent crime against women costs the United States at least $3 billion a year.

- Estimates suggest that the United States spends $5 to $10 billion per year on health care, criminal justice, and other social costs of domestic violence.
- The incidence of rape rose four times as fast as the total national crime rate over the past 10 years.
- According to one study, close to one-half million females now in high school will be raped before they graduate.
- One hundred twenty-five thousand college women can expect to be raped during this or any year.
- Three-fourths of women never go to the movies alone after dark because of the fear of rape, and nearly 50 percent do not use public transit alone after dark for the same reason.
- Forty-one percent of judges surveyed in a Colorado study believed that juries give sexual assault victims less credibility than other victims of crime.
- Less than 1 percent of rape victims have collected damages.
- An individual who commits rape has only 4 chances in 100 of being arrested, prosecuted, and found guilty of any offense.
- Almost one-fourth of convicted rapists never go to prison, and another one-fourth received sentences in local jails, where the average sentence is 11 months.
- Almost 50 percent of rape victims lose their jobs or are forced to quit because of the crime's severity.
- The attorneys general from 38 states urged Congress to enact a civil rights remedy, permitting rape victims to sue their attackers because "the current system of dealing with violence is inadequate."

Based on these extensive data, which were collected over four years, Congress has found that "crimes of violence motivated by gender have a substantial adverse effect on interstate commerce, by deterring potential victims from traveling interstate, from engaging in employment in interstate business . . . [and being] . . . involved in . . . [other] . . . interstate commerce" (H.R. Conf. Rep., No. 103–711, 1994, p. 385).

Because of its findings, Congress deemed it necessary to supplement the inadequate state remedies in combating gender violence by creating and passing the Violence Against Women Act (VAWA) in 1994. This Act attacked violence against women in several ways. First, it provided substantial sums of money to states for education, rape crisis hotlines, training criminal justice personnel, victim services, and special units in police and prosecutors' offices to deal with crimes against women. The Act specifically provided incentives for the enforcement of statutory rape laws, the payment of the cost of testing for sexually transmitted diseases for victims of crime, and studies of campus sexual assaults, and the battered women's syndrome. As a condition of receiving federal monies, states would have to demonstrate greater efforts toward arresting and prosecuting domestic violence offenders. Several states changed and strengthened their domestic violence laws and moved from policies of arrest avoidance in domestic cases to mandatory arrest policies.

Second, criminal provisions of the VAWA provide that it is a federal offense to cross state lines with the intent of contacting a domestic partner when the contact leads to an act of violence. In addition, the Act also makes orders of protection enforceable from one state to another.

Third, the civil rights component of the Act permitted a victim of gender violence to sue his or her attacker and seek compensatory and punitive damages for a crime of violence motivated in part by gender animus. Victims of gender violence were thus empowered to bring lawsuits against their attackers even if the prosecutors were unwilling or unable to pursue a criminal action.

Finally, the Act was an important vehicle to raise the consciousness level of the nation to the problem of violence against women. The VAWA was not the millennium, but an important first step by our national government in its commitment to combat gender violence.

Shortly after the VAWA became law, it encountered a significant constitutional challenge. In the Fall of 1994, a young woman named Christy Brzonkala enrolled in college at Virginia Polytechnic Institute. Early in her freshman year, Christy alleged that she was gang raped by two other students named Crawford and Morrison who were varsity football players. Subsequently, Christy reported the attack and became severely emotionally disturbed and depressed. She sought assistance from a University psychiatrist, was prescribed antidepressant medication, stopped attending classes and eventually withdrew from the University. Neither man was ever charged with a crime.

The victim filed a complaint against Morrison and Crawford pursuant to University procedures. Virginia Tech held a hearing and Crawford produced an alibi witness who said that he left the room before any sexual activity occurred. Morrison admitted having sexual contact with Christy even though she had told him twice, "no." After a hearing, Morrison was suspended for two semesters. There was insufficient evidence to punish Crawford.

Subsequently, a University official set aside Morrison's punishment as being "excessive when compared to other cases. . . ." The victim then became the first to file a lawsuit against her attacker and Virginia Tech under the newly created VAWA. Although the case began as a victim suing her alleged rapists, by the time the case reached the United States Supreme Court, some called the case a clash between feminism and federalism. (*United States v. Morrison*, 2000, 350 U.S. 598, pp. 60–61)

Unfortunately, under the concept of federalism (sharing of power between the state and federal government), the U.S. Supreme Court, by a narrow margin (five to four), ruled that Congress did not have the constitutional authority to create this federal civil remedy. Chief Justice Rehnquist writing for the majority said: "[I]f the allegations—[of rape by the football players] . . . are true, no civilized system of justice could fail to provide her a remedy for the conduct of respondent Morrison. But under our federal system that remedy must be provided by the Commonwealth of Virginia, and not by the United States." Four justices disagreed. They contended that "Congress has the power to legislate with regard to activity that in the aggregate has a substantial effect on interstate commerce." The impact of the *Morrison* decision is that civil remedies designed to assist women who have been victims of violence will be balkanized. Women will have to seek legislative approval in communities throughout the United States so that they are authorized to bring lawsuits against their attackers for gender violence. In response to the *Morrison* decision, the city of New York became one of the first U.S. communities to create such a remedy for victims of gender violence.

The VAWA has been an important national vehicle in addressing the issue of violence against women. It is unfortunate that this important federal civil remedy relied on by the victim in *Morrison* has been ruled unconstitutional. Nevertheless, the other provisions of the Act are still intact and billions of federal dollars will still flow to states over the next few years to support various provisions of the Act. Violence against women still requires an urgent national response.

SUMMARY

It may be that sexual equality has been affirmed, but the fact is that it is rarely practiced and is more hypothetical than real. The law has seen and treated women the way that men have viewed and treated women. Like the crime of rape, cases of domestic violence, and as you will see in Chapter 14, sexual harassment are not issues of lust, but remain issues of power. In voluntary sexual relationships everyone should exercise freedom of choice in deciding whether to establish a close, intimate relationship. Such freedom of choice is absent in cases where women are victims of violence. Rape, incest, battering, as well as sexual harassment may be understood as an extreme acting out of qualities that are regarded as supermasculine: aggression, power, dominance, and force. Men who harass are not pathological, but rather they are people who exhibit behaviors that have been characteristic of the masculine gender role. Most cases in which women are the victims of violence start at the subtle end of the continuum and escalate over time. Each year, women experience the unfortunate consequences of being violated, yet cultural mythologies consistently blame the victim for sexual abuse and act to keep women in their place.

Women who speak about victims of violence use terms such as *humiliating, intimidating, frightening, financially damaging, embarrassing, nerve-wracking, awful,* and *frustrating.* These are not words that are used to describe a situation that one enjoys.

Historically, the rape of a woman was considered to be an infringement of the property rights of a man. Cases of violence have been viewed in the same light. The message for this, in the twenty-first century, is the recognition that changes are needed. We can no longer blame the messenger. We need to understand the message. There are no questions that what is referred to as "women's hidden occupational hazard," being victimized as a woman, is nothing less than sexual victimization. The fact that cases of rape and domestic violence exist demonstrates that they must be understood as part of the continuum of violence against women. In a typical case of violence, the female accuser becomes the accused and the victim is twice victimized. This holds true in all cases where women are victims because of their gender and because of the use of power over them. Underlying the dynamics of the situation is the profound distrust of a woman's word and a serious power differential between the accused and the accuser.

What actions are being taken? As noted in this chapter, more and more cases are coming to light. Conduct that many men consider unobjectionable may very well offend women.

AGENDA FOR CHANGE

Litigation is occurring. Although we do not have a federal equal rights amendment, there are states that recognize its potential worth. As an example, the use of male terms to indicate both genders is slowly being examined. Some choose to use gender-neutral terms. Note the use of *reasonable person.* Words are meant to have definitive meaning. "Words are workhorses of law" (Thomas, 1991, p. 116). Sexual harassment, as noted in Chapter 14, is a major barrier to women's professional and personal development and a traumatic force that disrupts and damages their personal lives. For ethnic-minority women who have been victimized, economic vulnerability is paramount. Women feel powerless, not in control, afraid, and not flattered by any act of violence. As stated previously, women's basic human rights are inextricably linked to their treatment by and with their participation in today's political world.

The courts need to continue to look at the totality of circumstances. One action where no evidence of extreme emotional distress exists cannot be construed to be an act of violence regardless of the political atmosphere. Calling an act an act of violence simply because a person makes an accusation will not create the change that is needed.

What, then, is the agenda for change in this century? More needs to be done by elected officials, public policymakers, religious institutions, educational institutions, the criminal justice system, the media, and business and labor organizations. For justice to be gained, everyone must be concerned with the long arduous fight for freedom and equality for everyone. It was Gloria Steinem who noted that cultural myths die hard, especially if they are used to empower one part of the population. We must do whatever is necessary to fight oppression and alleviate repressive conditions wherever they exist. The struggle of women continues under the law. There is no way to allow both genders automatically to enjoy equal protection of the laws unless we are committed to the elimination of all gender discrimination. The criminal justice system over the years has slowly come to grips with the needed understanding of both women and justice. Recent Supreme Court cases regarding violence against women have become "a mathematically precise test," calling for an examination of all the circumstances of a case. In this new century, more cases will be heard, and legal procedures and precedents will be established to ensure that complainants will receive a fairer hearing than ever before. Everyone must be concerned with the long arduous fight for freedom and equality for everyone. Women's agenda is that by representing half of the population, they must be willing to meet the challenge.

If we go back to 1979 and review the tenets of the *Convention on the Elimination of All Forms of Discrimination Against Women* (UN Document/A/REs/34/180), we find the following:

> Recalling that discrimination against women violates the principles of equality of rights and respect for human dignity is an obstacle to the participation of women, on equal terms with men, in the political, social, economic and cultural life of their countries, hampers the growth of the prosperity of society and the family and makes more difficult the full development of the potentialities of women in the service of their countries and of humanity.

It was agreed that the term *discrimination against women* shall mean any distinction, exclusion, or restriction made on the basis of gender that has the effect or purpose of impairing or nullifying the recognition, enjoyment, or exercise of men and women, of human rights and fundamental freedoms in the political, economic, social, cultural, civil, or any other field (MacKinnon, 2003, p. 49).

> Women deserve the same rights and opportunities afforded men. There has existed/does exist/will exist the rhetoric of gender equality (yesterday, today, and tomorrow), but it has yet to match the reality of women's experiences. The question remains: Are men ready? The twenty-first century is here; are we all ready to meet the challenges necessary for much needed change? In the words of Abigail Adams, "Remember the ladies."

REFERENCES

110 Congressional Record, February 8, 1964, 2577. www.jofreeman.com/lawandpolicy/titlevii.htm

BROWNMILLER, S. (1975). *Against our will: Men, women, and rape.* New York: Simon & Schuster.

EIGENBERG, H. M. (2001). *Woman battering in the United States: Till death do us part.* Prospect Heights, IL: Waveland Press.

FALUDI, S. (1991). *Backlash: The undeclared war against women.* New York: Crown Publishers.

MACKINNON, C. A. (1979). *Sexual harassment of working women.* New Haven, CT: Yale University Press.

MACKINNON, C. A. (2001). *Sex equality: Rape law.* New York: Foundation Press.

MACKINNON, C. A. (2003). *Sex equality: Sexual harassment.* New York: Foundation Press.

MILLER, S., & PETERSON, E. S. L. (2007). The impact of law enforcement policies on victims of intimate partner violence. In R. Muraskin (Ed.), *It's a crime: Women and justice* (4th ed.). Upper Saddle River, NJ: Prentice Hall.

MURASKIN, R. (2007). *It's a crime: Women and justice* (4th ed.). Upper Saddle River, NJ: Prentice-Hall.

ROBERTS, A. (1993). Women: Victims of sexual assault and violence. In R. Muraskin and T. R. Alleman (Eds.), *It's crime: Women and justice.* Upper Saddle River, NJ: Prentice Hall.

RUSSELL-BROWN, S. (2002). Rape as an act of genocide. *Berkeley Journal of International Law, 21,* p. 350.

THOMAS, C. S. (1991). *Sex discrimination.* St. Paul, MN: West.

ENDNOTE

1. This chapter appears in the fifth edition of *Visions for change: Crime and justice in the twenty-first century.* Muraskin & Roberts. Prentice Hall (2009).

CASES

Bradwell v. Illinois U.S. Ct. 1740 (2000).

United States v. Morrison, 529 US 598 (2000), 120 S.Ct. 1740 (2000).

14

It's Not Sex, It Is Rape!

Roslyn Muraskin

❖

Rape is an act of power; it has nothing to do with sex. The problem with acts of sexual abuse against women is that they have not traditionally been defined as crime. "This has occurred in part because women have historically been excluded from the authoritative processes through which community rules are defined, interpreted, and enforced—their input in this instance coming mostly in the disempowered role of victim. The criminal law defined the crime of rape long before women were permitted to vote or to serve on juries" (MacKinnon, 2001, p. 766). It is the men who have defined sexual abuse long before women were recognized as persons having the same rights, privileges, and protection as men. When a woman was raped, the perpetrator was either her father or her husband.

When Adam lost his rib, he gained a mate, but it has been a bone of contention ever since.

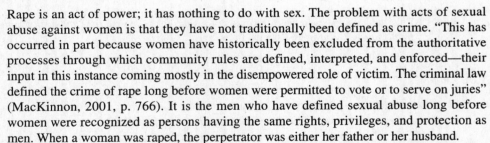

My whole life has been invaded, violated. It didn't happen just to me, but to my husband and children.
Rape, it shatters your sense of self; it leaves you with the feeling of having been defiled, of being stained, of being different.
   I am dirty. There are times when I wish the rapist had killed me, it would have been kinder.
I have changed, the world has changed. I don't see things the way I used to.
I am besieged by fear. I am afraid to stay home alone. I am afraid to go out alone.

When a rape victim speaks about her rape, as noted earlier, she feels that she no longer has the ability to control her own personal self. The victim experiences a diminishment in her ego defense. Rape, more so than any other criminal act, deprives the victims and their relatives of the protective mantle of privacy. They wind up speaking about what they consider a private matter in a public forum, which is embarrassing and uneasy for all women concerned.

As pointed out by Susan Brownmiller (1975), "the rapist performs a myrmidon function for all men by keeping all women in a thrall of anxiety and fear. Rape is to women as lynching was to blacks: the ultimate physical threat by which all men keep all women in a state of psychological intimidation" (pp. 254–255).

The factor that there was a corroboration requirement that denigrated the testimony of women who claim to have been sexually violated is in and of itself indefensible. It evidenced an irrational belief in the dishonesty of women who claimed to have been sexually assaulted. Historically, woman has always been considered the property of man. If she was raped at a young age, the father's property was said to have been defiled, and if the wife was raped, the husband's property was said to have been tarnished. Rape laws have always been premised on the assumption that women are liars, and therefore the law has imposed stricter standards of proof. The woman's words were to be corroborated by other testimony, not so in cases of robbery, assault, arson, and so on. Judges were required to read the following cautionary instructions to the jury:

> A charge such as that made against the defendant in this case is one which is easily made and, once made, difficult to defend against, even if the person accused is innocent. Therefore the law requires that you examine the testimony of the female person named in the information with caution. (Judge Matthew Hale)

Thousands of rape victims face the dilemma of whether to report a rape. For many the answer is *no*. Although regrettable, the response is understandable. The rape victim has long been the victim of the popular but false belief that "she asked for it." Many rape victims have accused police, prosecutors, and medical examiners of insensitive and unsympathetic behavior. Social service agencies are often ill-equipped to deal with rape victims' special needs.

There has always evolved a pattern—both the lack of support from the community and the low priority the police and prosecutors give to rape cases—that appears to alienate the victims. Those victims who do persevere to the trial stage have historically found themselves put on trial as the defense attorneys have grilled them about their own sexual behavior.[1]

What is rape? The definitions of forcible rape have varied from state to state. Two definitions that have been used include "carnal knowledge of a woman forcibly and against her will" and "sexual intercourse with a woman, not the wife of a perpetrator, forcibly and against her will or in circumstances under which she was incapable of giving consent." In nearly every state, the way rape has been treated under the law has been different from the way other crimes have been treated. For reasons beyond understanding, most states have traditionally made it harder for a woman to establish that she has been raped than for any other person to establish that he or she has been the victim of some other crime such as robbery or assault. The reason given is that the woman probably lied.

The rape laws as they have developed reflect fears: fears that vengeful women will charge innocent men against whom they bear grudges, that women who have consented to sexual intercourse and have become pregnant or have otherwise been found out by their husbands or parents will charge a man with rape so that they will escape some punishment, or that some psychotic women who secretly wish to be raped will in fact believe that they have been. The other fear is that some women will simply bring rape charges to gain notoriety. This has resulted in American rape laws seemingly protecting the defendant, while ignoring the rights of the defendant.

"The case attrition rate in rape cases is shockingly high, and very few rapists are convicted of the crime. Victims often do not report the rape largely because they fear overbearing, hostile police and—should a trial ensue—vicious attacks on their character. Although false reports of rape are no more common than of other crimes, justice system officials are highly skeptical of women who have claimed to have been raped by acquaintances. If the rape victim's conduct prior to the crime violated traditional sex-role norms, police commonly disbelieve her report or blame her for the rape. Thus, officials deny justice to woman who have engaged in nonmarital sex, or other 'improper activities such as heavy drinking or hitchhiking" (Bryden & Lengnick, 1997, n.p.).

The words of Judge Hale show that under the common law there existed the belief that chastity was a character trait. This idea fell under the belief that premarital sex was immoral. "Acts of previous illicit sexual relations, like other acts or moral turpitude, could thus be used to impeach the credibility of the complaining witness in a rape case" (n.a., Tanford, 1980, p. 544).

Traditionally, in order for innocent men to be protected, juries were instructed to scrutinize the testimony of a rape complainant closely, where the complaining witness and the defendant were expected to be chaste until time for marriage. The laws then developed not so much to protect the female but rather were developed to protect the property of the male. A woman was considered damaged goods, if she was not a virgin. Men did not desire damaged goods.

It was believed that females were thought to have a definite character flaw; no normal woman would ever consider to rape. No normal woman would exhibit a propensity to have sexual relations with anyone but her husband. Today, rape is still pretty much an unreported crime, but as a reflection of the times, most courts and legislatures appear to have adapted to the times in that they realize that a woman who is unchaste or who indulges in extramarital sexual relationships is no more likely to consent indiscriminately than a woman who is chaste.

In the past the defendant in a rape case commonly introduced testimony about the victim's sexual relations and produced witnesses who would give testimony about the sexual reputation of the victim's chastity. The courts' opinion was if the woman was considered to be promiscuous, then how could she be believed?

Recent years have seen these laws reflecting the outmoded morality and unenlightened male-dominated legal system. Today, a growing awareness of women's equality exists, which have seen the revision of the rape laws. It was always the woman on the witness stand who stood to be "raped" once more, this time by the criminal justice system. The myth is that women do not provoke rape, nor do they ask for it.

In the words of one woman:

I had locked all doors because I was afraid, and I don't know how he got in; it was probably through the screen door. When I woke up, he was shaking my leg. His eyes were red, and I knew he had been drinking or smoking. I thought I would try to talk my way out of it. He started by saying that he wanted to sleep with me, and then he got angrier and angrier, until he started to say "I want pussy." Then, I got scared and tried to push him away. That's when he started to force himself on me. It was awful. It was the most humiliating terrible feeling. He was forcing my legs apart and ripping my clothes off. And it was painful. I did fight him—he was slightly drunk and I was able to keep him away. I had taken judo a few years back, but I was afraid to throw a chop for fear he would kill me. I could see he was getting more and more violent. I was thinking wildly of some way to get out of this alive, and then I said to him, "do you want money, I'll give you money." We had money, but I was also thinking that if I got to the back room, I could telephone the police—as if the police would have even helped. It was a stupid thing to think of because obviously he would follow me. And he did. When he saw me pick up the phone, he tried to tie the cord around my neck. I screamed at him that I did have the money in another room, that I was not going to call the police because I was scared, and that I would never tell anyone what happened. It would be an absolute secret. He said, Okay, and I went to get the money. But when he got it, all of a sudden he got this crazy look in his eye, and he said to me, "now I am going to kill you." (Conference Proceedings, 1981)

Rape becomes an act of aggression in which the victim has been denied her self-determination. Rape is an act of violence, an act of power. It is a form of mass terrorism; the victim of the rape is chosen indiscriminately, but the propagandists for male supremacy broadcast that it is women who cause rape by being unchaste or in the wrong place at the wrong time—in essence *by behaving as if they were free* (Proceedings).

Rape is an unbelievable vicious and personal form of attack. Many female victims fear that their assailant will return (and some do). Many victims are reluctant to return home or to return to their normal home life upon being raped. Rape victims oftentimes find themselves no longer trusting men. Many loving husbands or boyfriends have abandoned their women, even knowing of their innocence after finding that they cannot handle them having been raped.

Rape legislation has had a long-standing and sordid history as sexist legislation designed not to protect women, but rather to protect men's social and property interests in female chastity. Sometime back, two judges in separate cases made judicial decisions that would appear to decriminalize rape. In Wisconsin, the judge sentenced one of three boys involved in a gang rape of a 16-year-old girl to one year of court supervision at home. The judge *in his wisdom* explained that after all the boy was merely reacting normally to an environment of prevalent sexual permissiveness and provocative woman's clothing. The judge continued that "I'm trying to say to women, 'stop teasing.'" In California, a judge voided the conviction of a man charged with raping a hitchhiker: "it may not speak well for the prevailing standard of morality in society, but women hitchhikers should anticipate sexual advances from men who pick them up" ("Decriminalizing Rape," 1977, p. 9).

Rape has become an instrument of forced exile. It has been known to drive a wedge through both community and family (Russell-Brown, 2002, p. 35). It has been known that mediation acts as a tool in acquaintance rape cases.[2] It is used to empower victims while addressing the needs of the offenders. Most rapes (as noted earlier) go unreported and are unsuccessfully managed by the criminal justice system. One out of every six women in the United States has been a victim of rape or attempted rape, and therefore other avenues, such as mediation, are also looked for (Corpus Juris Secundum database, 2004).

Rape trauma syndrome requires only a general fit between the characteristics of the syndrome and the victim's syndrome. Women who suffer from the act of rape and therefore from rape trauma syndrome have recognizable reactions differing from those of other types of trauma. Anxiety and fear are common traits among those who have been raped (Cleary, 2004). Rape trauma syndrome is the "acute phase and long-term reorganization process that occurs as a result of forcible rape or attempted forcible rape. It is an acute stress reaction to a life-threatening situation" (*New York Jurisprudence*, 2nd edition, 2005).

A victim's reputation and sexual activities with men should be irrelevant for the justice system. The concentration that has always existed upon the reputation of the victim as if she were the one whose guilt or innocence was to be determined has been a continuing indication of the bias against the rape victim in the U.S. current system of justice.

Even the extent of the victim's prior sexual relationships with the defendant should have little relevance to the issue of whether a current voluntary relationship existed. Even the career of a prostitute, a woman who engages in an established pattern of indiscriminate sex, should not prevent her from calling "rape," if that is the case. Still some courts as well as commentators continue to express concern that many sexual offense accusations are made by psychologically disturbed individuals, and therefore such evidence should not be deemed reliable by the courts.

The way the rape shield laws work today is as follows:

- Evidence of prior sexual conduct or consensual sexual intercourse between the complainant and the defendant tends to prove that the complainant consented to the conduct in issue.
- Evidence of an established pattern of prior sexual conduct on the part of the complainant tends to prove that the complainant consented to the conduct in issue. Such evidence if known . . . or such evidence, if known to the defendant at the time of the act or acts charged, tends to prove that the defendant reasonably believed that the complaint was consenting.
- Evidence of prior sexual conduct on the part of the complainant so distinctive and so closely resembling the defendant's version of the alleged encounter with the complaint tends to prove that she consented to the conduct in issue.
- Evidence of prior sexual conduct on the part of the complainant tends to prove that a person other than the defendant committed the act or acts charged or caused the complainant's physical condition allegedly arising from these acts. Such evidence shall include proof of the origin of semen, pregnancy, disease, or injury allegedly resulting from these acts.
- Evidence of sexual conduct on the part of the complainant tends to prove that the complainant has a motive for fabricating the charge or charges made.
- Evidence of sexual conduct on the part of the complainant offered as the basis of expert psychological or psychiatric opinion that the complainant fantasized or invented the act or acts charged.
- Evidence of prior sexual conduct on the part of the complainant tends to show that the complaining witness has, on direct examination, made a material

misrepresentation as to the nature of her sexual experience on occasions other than that of the alleged offense. (Tanford, 1980, p. 544)

The rights of the rape victims as viewed by the courts recognize the need to protect a person who takes the stand from attacks designed merely to harass, annoy, or humiliate. "For many [women] the trauma of baring one's intimate past to the eyes of the world—turning one's bedroom into a showcase—overshadows the usual discomfort of testifying or having others testify, to one's biases, lies, or even conflicting criminal acts" (Tanford, 1980).

According to Catherine MacKinnon (2001), "in a case of rape against a city police officer in which the department was found to have implemented a policy of avoiding, ignoring, and covering up complaints of physical and sexual abuse by officers, the judge said that first degree abuse is a violent crime and intrinsically related to other violent crimes: 'if a man whips his child with an extension cord, then dons his police uniform and beats up a prisoner then locks a female prisoner in his squad car and forces her to perform oral sex on him, the acts . . . constitute act of violence' " (see *Parrish v. Luckie*, 963 F.2d. 201, 205, 8th Cir. 1992, p. 782).

The victim of the rape is placed in a false light within the eye of the public. The result is that she is making a public disclosure of private facts that may have no relevance to the present case.

> Suppose that a victim has been "incautious" not in her actions preceding the rape (drinking, hitchhiking, walking alone at night), but her sexual habits and choices. Perhaps she has had extramarital affairs or borne children out of wedlock. Perhaps she has only had one or two premarital encounters but lives in a place where conventional morals are strongly enforced. Should the woman decide to go to court, she faces the prospect of having this personal data disclosed, sometimes directly, sometimes obliquely as reputation, unless of course she was "lucky" enough to have gotten attacked in a state with a stringent rape statute. Although it belies human experience to argue that women will tailor their lives to the image of the model rape complainant, just in case and thus be chilled in their primary conduct, it is not absurd to suggest that exposure of intimate facts in a public courtroom regardless of their degree of relevance imposes a truly harsh penalty on certain types of sexual choices. To say that the woman can always refrain from filing charges and thus avoid unwanted scrutiny is to her the option. (Tanford, 1980, p. 545)

But why should she be put to shame because she was the victim? "Bare the most personal parts of your life or abandon all hopes of legal redress. What the act of rape wholly denies, traditional rules of evidence punish: the right of women as well as men to sexual self-determination" (Berger, 1977, p. 42).

> To the extent that the prosecutrix in rape and related sexual crimes is uniquely subject to painful prejudicial attack on her private life and intimate conduct, one might argue that she has literally been denied the equal protection of the laws. Other complainants can go to court to seek redress for their victimization without incurring this heavy penalty. Rape targets, on the other hand, are disproportionately discouraged from prosecuting their violators. As a result, they fail to receive the law's protection after the fact and probably (though it would be extremely hard to show) before as well, since knowledge of its inefficacy can be expected to lessen whatever deterrent effect the criminal sanction has in this area. Those victims who do invoke the legal process, paying the price in personal exposure, often find that their sacrifice

has netted them absolutely nothing: the jury acquits the man of rape but convicts the woman of loose behavior. (Berger)

With the U.S. system of justice, an act of violence offends against the society at large, not simply the injured individual. As the state rather than the victim formally charges the defendant, there are some who would favor using an independent attorney particularly in rape cases to represent the victim. The fact that all sittings of the court are public gives the opportunity to be heard in public. To ban the public as has been done in some jurisdiction is to seemingly protect the complainant, that is, the victim of the rape. Whatever way the case of rape is handled, it must be held in a manner where the victim's dignity is preserved, only pertinent information is presented, and the decision whether to prosecute or not must be in the hands of the victim.

The *moth-laden* rules of rape have changed. The law converts as well as mirrors cultural norms and expectations. A rape is a rape regardless of whether it is done by someone you know (acquaintance), by someone you do not know (stranger), or by your spouse (marital). It is the use of force against your will for purposes of soliciting sex. However, the authorities will tend more to believe the story if it is a stranger who has raped the female. Andrea Dworkin described rape as an act of terror. "It means that part of the population lives in a state of terror" (1993, pp. 169–171). There are also statutory rape laws that prohibit "sex by men above a certain age with girls below a certain age" (MacKinnon, 2001, p. 856). Regardless of whether consent was given, it is still statutory rape. The exception is when the two (though one is underage) are married.

In 1994 the Violence Against Women Act (VAWA)[3] was passed allowing "rape victims to sue perpetrators civilly for sex discrimination for acts of gender-motivated violence" (MacKinnon, p. 888).

The story is told in Susan Brownmiller's work, *Against Our Will*, published in 1975 but still quoted. The story is about former Israeli Prime Minister Gold Meir who told the following:

> Once in a cabinet we had to deal with the fact that there had been an outbreak of assaults on women at night. One minister suggested a curfew: women should stay home after dark. I said, "[B]ut it's the men who are attacking the women. If there is to be a curfew, let the men stay home, not the women."

And as stated by Brownmiller, "all rape is an exercise in power" (p. 256). The female victim is not to be raped by the criminal justice system.

REFERENCES

BERGER, V. (1977). Notes on rape cases. *Columbia Law Review, 77,* 42.

BROWNMILLER, S. (1975). *Against our will, men, women and rape.* New York: Simon & Schuster.

BRYDEN, D. P., & LENGNICK, S. (1997). Rape in the criminal justice system. *Journal of Criminal Law and Criminology,* 1194.

CLEARY, P. (March 26, 2004). It's time to recognize and deal with footy's silent subculture of misogyny. On Line Opinion Australia's ejournal of social and political debate.

CRIMINAL 225 CORPUS JURIS SECUNDUM. (June 2004). Indictments and Informations XII.

DWORKIN, A. (1993). Letters from a war zone (pp. 169–173). In C. MacKinnon (Ed.), *Sex equality rape law*. New York: Foundation Press.

MACKINNON, C. (2001). *Sex equality rape law*. New York: Foundation Press. New York Woman Against Rape Conference, May 1981.

New York Jurisprudence 2nd edition (2005).

RUSSELL-BROWN, S. (2002). Rape as an act of genocide. *Berkeley Journal of International Law, 21*, 350.

TANFORD, A. J. (January 1980). Rape victims shield laws and the Sixth Amendment. *University of Pennsylvania Law Review, 128*, 544.

ENDNOTES

1. Rape shield laws, a recent phenomenon, prevent the questioning of the female victim about her prior sexual history, unless it has and/or is shown to have relevance to the case.
2. Where both victim and attacker know each other, but he attacks, and she says no, it is still a crime of rape. There is no such crime as date or acquaintance rape. Most states recognize rape as being rape.
3. As a sex discrimination law, it conceived the injury of sexual violation not as a moral wrong, breach of community rules, or gender-neutral personal injury but as a violation of human rights on the basis of sex.

CASE

Parrish v. Luckie 963 F.2d. 201 (1997).

15

Explaining Fear of Crime as Fear of Rape among College Females

An Examination of Multiple Campuses in the United States

Rhonda R. Dobbs, Courtney A. Waid, and Tara O'Connor Shelley

ABSTRACT

Given the fact that women are less likely to experience crime victimization than males, researchers have been puzzled for decades as to why women experience higher levels of fear of victimization. Scholars such as Warr (1984) and Ferraro (1995, 1996) argue that the fear of rape that females experience shadows fear of other crime, as rape is viewed by females as a cotemporaneous offense that may lead to other offenses. The present study examines the impact of fear of rape on the overall fear of crime for men and women on college campuses. While women are significantly more fearful of crime prior to controlling for fear of rape, the findings indicate that once fear of rape is considered, women's higher fear of other crimes seems to diminish such that there are either no sex differences in fear or men are more fearful than women. Relevant policy implications are discussed.

INTRODUCTION

Since the 1960s, the fear of crime has emerged as a significant social issue (Skogan & Maxfield, 1981; Stanko, 1995; Stinchcombe et al., 1980). Scholars such as Clemente and Kleiman (1977), Ferraro (1995, 1996), and Warr (1984, 2000) have articulated theoretical arguments postulating that the fear of crime can be as debilitating as victimization itself, because fear may cause avoidance behaviors similar to those incorporated into one's lifestyle after criminal victimization. Therefore, it can be expected that demographic groups experiencing higher levels of criminal victimization, such as young males, will experience elevated levels of fear. However, research has consistently shown that some groups, especially women and the elderly, are more fearful of crime, despite lower levels of victimization than young males (Clemente & Kleiman, 1977; Ferraro, 1995, 1996; Fetchenhauer & Buunk, 2005;

Fisher & Sloan, 2003; Garofalo, 1979; Parker & Ray, 1990; Parker, McMorris, Smith, & Murty, 1993; Stafford & Galle, 1984; Stanko, 1995; Warr, 1984, 2000). Other scholars have argued that men are affected by social desirability in self-report surveys examining fear; in other words, men may act in accord with the prescriptions of hegemonic masculinity and report lower levels of fear when in fact they may be quite fearful of crime (Smith & Torstensson, 1997; Sutton & Farrall, 2005). Furthermore, in considering social desirability in responding, feminist researchers have proposed that self-report surveys are inadequate in the assessment of abuse by intimate male partners, a form of abuse that may increase fear of criminal victimization among females (Hammer & Saunders, 1984; Kelly & DeKeseredy, 1994; Reid & Konrad, 2004; Riger, Gordon, & LeBailly, 1978; Smith, 1988; Stanko, 1987, 1990a, 1990b).

Nevertheless, the critical question remains: Why are females more fearful of crime? This perplexing trend has caused scholars to question what factors lead to higher levels of fear in women. Two key issues have been examined in the literature: (1) perceived vulnerability to crime and (2) fear of rape. Perceived vulnerability refers to individuals' perceived ability to successfully defend themselves against an attack as well as their perceptions of their own strength and running speed compared to the average male and female (Gordon, Riger, LeBailly, & Heath, 1980; Riger et al., 1978). Some scholars argue that the physical weakness of females (as compared to males) limits self-defense ability (Bennett & Flavin, 1994; Katz, Webb, & Armstrong, 2003; Smith & Hill, 1991). If females feel more vulnerable, they will experience a higher fear of criminal victimization. Whereas perceived vulnerability to crime is a cognitive judgment, the fear of crime taps into an affective/emotional response (Ferraro, 1995). It has been argued that males experience elevated vulnerability to robbery, whereas females exhibit higher level of perceived vulnerability to burglary and sexual assault (Reid & Konrad, 2004). An early study by Gordon and colleagues (1980) indicates that women's fear of crime decreases more than the fear of crime of men after controlling for perceived vulnerability; hence, vulnerability to victimization has more impact on female fear than male fear and may account for differences in levels of fear by sex. However, recent research indicates that the fear of crime for both sexes may serve to increase perceived vulnerability of victimization (Rader, 2004; Rader, May, & Goodrum, 2007).

Specific to fear of rape, research by Culberston, Vik, and Kooiman (2001) and Smith (1988) indicate that females who have experienced sexual assault are more fearful of crime than women who have never been assaulted. Aside from direct experience with sexual assault, rape is viewed by those examining women's fear of crime as a perceptually contemporaneous offense. This means that the offense is "viewed as accompanying or ensuing from" other offense(s) (Warr, 1984, p. 695). Thus, the assumption is that women fear personally threatening offenses other than rape because they view these offenses as events that can lead to rape (Ferraro, 1995, 1996; Gordon & Riger, 1989; Lane & Meeker, 2003; Warr, 1985). Examples of these offenses include begging and burglary (Warr, 1984). Because of this, Warr (1984) contends that for women, "fear of crime *is* fear of rape" (p. 700). Utilizing this perspective, rape is seen as the master offense in explaining women's disproportionate fear of crime (Ferraro, 1995, 1996; Riger et al., 1978; Warr, 1984). Feminist scholars have noted that "gender inequality is associated with a culture of violence against women" (Yodanis, 2004, p. 670); given this, women are constantly aware of the threat of rape and that men control women through the power that ensues from it (Brantingham & Brantingham, 1994; Brownmiller, 1975; Softas-Nall, Bardos, & Fakinos, 1995). Others working in this area contend that because the fear of rape is so powerful for women, it influences their daily routines and social behaviors (Gordon & Riger, 1989; Madriz, 1997; Stanko, 1990a, 1990b, 1992, 1995). This fear can be heightened by societal and media messages, some of which blame the victim in cases of sexual assault, and others that continually stress how females should avoid risky behavior (Gilchrist, Bannister, Ditton, & Farrall, 1998).

The elevated fear of crime that females experience as a result of perceived vulnerability and/or the fear of rape can lead them to engage in either avoidance or protective behaviors. When engaging in avoidance behaviors, a female may choose not to walk alone after dark, avoid dense urban areas and the establishments located in them (Cobbina, Miller, & Brunson, 2008; Garofalo, 1979), or remain inside her home with the doors locked, essentially becoming a prisoner in her own home. In considering females who are victims of sexual assault by a known perpetrator, elevated levels of fear are reported in the home, most likely because the home serves as the setting of the offense (Culbertson et al., 2001; Kelly & DeKeseredy, 1994). Protective behaviors include the purchase of defense aids such as guns and home alarms, and completing self-defense courses (Ferraro, 1995, 1996; Gordon & Riger, 1989; Skogan & Maxfield, 1981). Recent theoretical discussions propose and subsequent research indicates that perceived risk to victimization, defensive/protective behaviors, and avoidance behavior all have reciprocal effects on the fear of crime. In other words, while the three may increase the fear of crime as indicated in previous research (Ferraro, 1995, 1996), the fear of crime may also serve to increase perceived vulnerability, avoidance behavior, and defensive/protective behavior (Rader, 2004; Rader et al., 2007).

Avoidance and protective behaviors may have specific implications for college-age females given the social context of dating relationships and the environmental context in which they interact with male students. Research suggests that women enrolled in colleges and universities "are at a greater risk for rape and other forms of sexual assault than women in the general population or in a comparable age group" (Fisher, Cullen, & Turner, 2000, p. 1). Female social interaction with male students is commonplace, and as Sloan, Lanier, and Beer (2000) note, substance use and abuse common among many social groups on college campuses can precipitate many violent and sex offenses. In a joint National Institute of Justice (NIJ) and Bureau of Justice Statistics (BJS) report published in 2000, many female students are the target of verbal harassment, obscene phone calls, stalking, and forced sexual advances. This study found that in a given academic year, on average, close to 3 percent of females attending the colleges and universities from which the sample was drawn will experience an attempted or completed rape. This would amount to a rape rate of 27.7 per 1,000 female college students. Further, Fisher et al. (2000) found incidence of rape was higher than the victimization rate as 23 percent of the rape victims had been victimized multiple times. While the occurrence of rape among college women may seem rather low when these figures are first examined, Fisher et al. (2000) note that this measure accounts for just over 6 months of the year and does not contextualize the occurrence of rape over a college career. Extrapolating to a calendar year, almost 5 percent of college women are victims of attempted or completed rape (calendar year rate of 35.3 per 1,000). For a campus with 10,000 female students, this would amount to 353 rapes in a year. Applying these estimates to an entire college career, one-fifth to one-quarter of college women will experience an attempted or completed rape (Fisher et al., 2000). It should also be noted that these figures only include occurrence of attempted and completed rape and not other forms of sexual victimization.

Factors increasing the likelihood of these occurrences include living in campus residence halls, being of single status, engaging in drinking with social groups, and prior sexual victimization (Fisher et al., 2000). Because of heightened fear related to these experiences, students, faculty, and staff on campuses across the country engage in avoidance and protective behaviors to prevent sexual victimization. Similar to the extant literature on the general female population, Fisher and Sloan (2003) indicate that female college students view rape as perceptually contemporaneous offense that shadows fear of other face-to-face victimization. Furthermore, their results indicate that perceived risk of rape among this population influences fear of rape and subsequent protective and avoidance behavior, a finding similar to that of Rader and colleagues concerning the general population (2004, 2007). McCreedy and Dennis (1996) note that approximately 30 percent of students avoid night classes when possible, and those with prior sexual assault experience do so at a greater rate. However, another study by Griffith, Hueston, Wilson, Moyers, and Hart (2004) notes that only 8 percent of females employ avoidance and protective behavior while on campus.

Only in recent years have campus sexual assault incidents been considered pubic record. Before the passage of the Crime Awareness and Campus Security Act of 1990, crime incidents on campuses were considered educational records, and thus considered protected information. After the passage of 1990 Act, post-secondary schools were required to report crime statistics, and the schools complying were eligible to receive funding to aid in the endeavor. The Clery Act, passed in 2000, requires colleges and universities across the United States to report campus crime as well as incidents that occur in residential and commercial areas contiguous to campus. Furthermore, the Act calls for schools to receive to receive punishment for nonparticipation in the reporting of these offenses. However, as Wilcox, Jordan, and Pritchard (2007) note, campus crime continues to be underreported, mostly due to "jurisdictional confusion, organizational inefficiency, and concern with student (offender) confidentiality" (p. 222). In addition, some forms of victimization such as interpersonal and dating violence are more likely to go unreported to the police and are consistently unaccounted for in campus crime reports. Related to interpersonal and dating violence is the finding by Turner and Torres (2006) that women often do not feel safe in residence halls. Because of this, students may not become involved in campus activities to the level that they desire (Currie, 1994), which limits the development of positive social networks. It has been established that the majority of offenses against college women occur between acquaintances (Fisher, Sloan, Cullen, & Lu, 1998). Yet, women may be more fearful of crimes they are less vulnerable to, such as stranger-perpetrated offenses for which Clery requires schools to report (Day, 1994; Fisher et al., 2000; Jennings, Gover, & Pudrzynska, 2007; Softas-Nall et al., 1995; Wilcox et al., 2007).

METHODOLOGY

The present study seeks to examine the impact of the fear of rape on the overall fear of crime for both men and women on college campuses. Self-administered surveys were distributed on three college campuses in three different regions of the United States, one in the southeast, one in the southwest, and one in the west. It is expected that different campuses would exhibit different levels of fear of crime and fear of rape, specifically, for a variety of reasons, including but not limited to geographic location, size of the campus as well as the surrounding area, the incidence of crime on campus and in the surrounding area, racial composition of campus, and the proportion of students living on campus. While levels of fear are expected to differ across the campuses, it is less clear whether the impact of fear of rape on the overall fear of crime will be uniform across the campuses. It is possible that the impact of fear of rape will differ across the campuses, which has yet to be examined in previous research. If it does differ, this would have implications for developing an appropriate response that is campus specific.

Surveys were administered on the southwestern campus during a three-week period in April 2007. The total student population at this university is just over 25,000. Data were collected during August 2007 at a university in the southeast with a total student population over 41,000. Surveys were administered during March 2008 at a university in the west with a student population just over 26,000. All three campuses are public four-year universities. Participants were informed that their involvement in the study was voluntary and the results would be anonymous. Surveys were administered in classes that were purposively chosen based on the instructor's willingness to forego class time to administer the survey. Both lower and upper division classes were chosen for survey administration as were classes in several different disciplines. Students in the sample constitute a convenience sample of those who were present on the day of survey administration and who volunteered to complete the questionnaire. A total of 961 students completed the survey, 454 on the southwestern campus, 242 on the southeastern campus, and 265 on the western campus.

FINDINGS AND DISCUSSION

Fear of crime was measured by asking respondents how fearful they were of being the victim of nine specific crimes (murder, attack with a weapon, robbed/mugged, beaten up/assaulted by strangers, approached on street by beggars, home broken into, car stolen, property vandalized/damaged, cheated/conned out of money). Respondents were also asked to rank their perceived likelihood of being the victim of a violent crime and a property crime within the next year. Each of these was measured on a scale of 0–10, with 0 representing no fear and not at all likely, respectively.

Independent variables included in the analysis of fear are presented in Table 1. As shown, respondent's concern about crime, perception that crime has increased, and perceived likelihood of victimization in the next year are included in the analysis. The respondent's victimization experience as well as the victimization experience of close family members is considered. The demographic variables are sex, age, and race/ethnicity. Lastly, respondent's major as being CRCJ (criminology/criminal justice) or not is also included as CRCJ majors have been shown to be less fearful in other fear of crime research on campuses.

T-tests measuring mean differences between men and women in the overall sample as well as each subsample are presented in Table 2. Consistent with previous research on both general populations and college populations, women's fear of crime is generally higher than men's, especially for those offenses that would involve face-to-face interaction (Clemente & Kleiman, 1977; Ferraro, 1995, 1996; Fisher & Sloan, 2003; Garofalo, 1979; Warr, 1984, 2000). There were statistically significant differences by sex for fear of all violent crimes

TABLE 1   Independent Variables Used in Analysis

Variable Description	Coding	Mean (St. Dev.)
Fear rape	0 = not at all fearful; 10 = very fearful	4.68 (3.83)
Concern about crime	0 = not at all concerned; 10 = very concerned	6.93 (2.10)
Victimization experience	0 = no; 1 = yes	.47 (.50)
Family victimization experience	0 = no; 1 = yes	.63 (.48)
Crime has increased	0 = crime decreased/stayed same in last year; 1 = crime increased in last year	.15 (.36)
Likelihood of violent victimization in next year	0 = not at all likely; 10 = very likely	2.33 (2.48)
Likelihood of property victimization in next year	0 = not at all likely; 10 = very likely	3.57 (2.82)
Major	0 = non-CRCJ; 1 = CRCJ major	.35 (.48)
Sex	0 = male; 1 = female	.58 (.49)
White	0 = non-white; 1 = white (reference category)	.60 (.49)
Black	0 = non-black; 1 = black	.14 (.34)
Hispanic	0 = non-Hispanic; 1 = Hispanic	.18 (.38)
Other race	0 = non-other; 1 = other race	.09 (.28)
Age	respondent's age in years	21.12 (3.59)

measured in the total sample as well as in each campus subsample when examined separately. The only item that would involve face-to-face contact that did not result in a statistically significant difference by sex was fear of being approached by a beggar or panhandler for the sample from the southeast campus. For the total sample and each of the subsamples, the largest difference in means was for the fear of rape/sexual assault item. Further, for women, the highest mean for the fear items was for fear of rape for the total sample and two of the three subsamples (southeast and west). For the southwest sample, fear of someone breaking into your home had a slightly higher mean (7.12) than fear of rape (7.08).

Similar to previous research (Reid & Konrad, 2004), fear of each of the property crimes was significantly higher for women in the total and southwest sample. Fear of having your home broken into was the only property crime for which there was a statistically significant difference by sex among the southeast sample. Since the measure did not specify whether the respondent was home when the break-in would occur, it is possible that respondents interpreted

TABLE 2   Mean Differences for Fear and Perceived Risk by Sex

	Total		Southwest		Southeast		West	
	Male	Female	Male	Female	Male	Female	Male	Female
Fear:								
Rape	1.91	6.72***	2.15	7.08***	1.94	6.44***	1.47	6.39***
	(3.05)	(2.97)	(3.21)	(2.93)	(3.22)	(2.99)	(2.52)	(2.77)
Murder	3.21	5.50***	3.67	6.16***	3.35	4.95***	2.25	4.90***
	(3.34)	(3.51)	(3.55)	(3.44)	(3.39)	(3.46)	(2.97)	(3.48)
Attack w/weapon	3.75	6.39***	4.01	7.05***	4.07	5.86***	2.98	5.77***
	(3.13)	(3.01)	(3.26)	(2.93)	(3.16)	(2.93)	(2.72)	(2.99)
Break into home	4.53	6.55***	4.58	7.12***	4.95	6.11**	4.02	6.01***
	(2.99)	(2.99)	(3.09)	(2.85)	(3.05)	(2.93)	(2.71)	(3.11)
Car stolen	4.21	5.54***	4.68	6.46***	3.70	5.00**	3.88	4.50
	(3.23)	(3.27)	(3.20)	(3.07)	(3.10)	(3.22)	(3.31)	(3.22)
Robbed/mugged	3.66	5.67***	3.90	6.50***	3.92	5.29**	2.95	4.66***
	(3.09)	(3.17)	(3.16)	(3.08)	(3.23)	(2.99)	(2.72)	(3.11)
Property vandalized	4.46	5.40***	4.58	6.23***	4.41	4.77	4.30	4.58
	(3.02)	(3.12)	(3.08)	(2.99)	(3.00)	(3.11)	(2.95)	(2.98)
Cheated/conned	3.83	5.07***	4.12	5.91***	3.69	4.31	3.44	4.39*
	(3.22)	(3.23)	(3.40)	(3.24)	(3.21)	(3.11)	(2.84)	(3.00)
Approached by	2.72	4.31***	2.85	5.09***	3.55	4.14	1.63	3.21***
beggar	(2.99)	(3.27)	(3.02)	(3.53)	(3.26)	(3.11)	(2.27)	(2.92)
Beaten up by	2.97	5.01***	3.29	5.89***	3.05	4.32**	2.30	4.18***
strangers	(3.01)	(3.48)	(3.15)	(3.49)	(3.16)	(3.28)	(2.47)	(3.29)
Perceived risk:								
Violent crime	2.19	2.44	2.28	2.73	2.29	1.91	1.94	2.44
	(2.47)	(2.51)	(2.43)	(2.75)	(2.59)	(2.18)	(2.44)	(2.29)
Property crime	3.69	3.49	3.60	3.87	3.81	3.11*	3.74	3.20
	(2.84)	(2.82)	(2.83)	(3.03)	(2.87)	(2.58)	(2.84)	(2.57)

Note: ***p < .001; **p < .01; *p < .05

this as a potential face-to-face victimization. This was also the highest mean fear for each of the samples. For the west sample, there were no significant mean differences for having your car stolen or having property vandalized. While women were significantly more fearful of being conned, this was only at the p < .05 level.

When examining perceived risk of crime, few differences were observed, with the exception of risk of property crime at the southeast campus. Interestingly, it is men in this sample that perceive more risk of property victimization in the next year. While this difference is significant, it should be noted that it is only at the p < .05 level. Perceived risk is generally quite low for both violent and property crimes. This finding is in accord with previous research (Ferraro, 1995, 1996) that suggests perceived risk of crime is generally lower than fear of crime.

   In order to more vigorously test the impact of fear of rape on fear of crime by sex, multivariate OLS models were estimated for each of the fear of crime variables for the total sample and each of the subsamples. Previous research indicates that fear of rape should shadow fear of crimes that involve face-to-face interactions, including murder, robbery, being beaten up, being attacked with a weapon, being approached by a beggar, and possibly home burglary. Theoretically, fear of rape should have less impact on the property crimes (car stolen, property vandalized, and being conned), although Fisher and Sloan (2003) did find fear of rape to shadow larceny/theft. Given the t-test results, fear of rape is expected to shadow fear of violent crimes in each of the samples, but might shadow property crimes less so for the southeast and west samples. Partial results for the OLS models are presented below. Full regression models were estimated for each sample, however, for the sake of conciseness only the theoretically relevant variables of sex and fear of rape are presented in the tables. The other independent variables included in the various analyses are displayed in Table 1.

   The OLS results for fear of each of the specific crimes in the total sample are presented in Table 3. Model 1 represents the best fit model explaining fear of that crime. As shown, women (coded as 1) in the total sample were significantly more fearful of each of the types of crime examined. Model 2 represents the best fit model with fear of rape included. Once fear of rape is included in the model, women are significantly less fearful of eight of the nine types of crime. There were no sex differences for fear of being approached by a beggar once fear of rape was controlled. Fear of rape was significant in each of the models. For all nine offenses, then, women's higher fear was accounted for by their fear of rape.

   The results for the southwest campus are displayed in Table 4. Similar to the total sample, women were significantly more fearful of each of the nine specific crimes in each of the best fit models (Model 1). Again, once included, fear of rape was significant in each model and accounted for this higher fear of crime, with women being significantly less fearful in three of the nine models and no significant sex differences appearing in the other six. Results for the southeastern campus (Table 5) are similar in terms of the impact of fear of rape. Although there were fewer significant sex differences in the initial models than in the total sample and the southwest sample, fear of rape is significant in each of the models when included. Further, women are significantly less fearful for eight of the nine crimes in this sample. As indicated in Table 6, the findings were similar for the western campus, with women generally being more fearful in the initial models and fear of rape being a significant predictor once added to the model. Further, women are significantly less fearful in the second models for seven of the nine crimes and there are no statistically significant results for the other two crimes.

   In each of the samples examined here, fear of rape was generally found to shadow fear of other forms of crime, whether they were violent crimes that would involve face-to-face interaction or property crimes. Once fear of rape is considered, women's higher fear of other crimes seems to diminish such that there are either no sex differences in fear or men are more fearful than women. In order to determine whether fear of rape operates differently on general fear of crime than other crime-specific fears, similar

TABLE 3   Partial OLS Results for Fear of Specific Crimes—Total Sample

	Murder		Attacked w/weapon		Robbery		Beaten up		Approached by beggar	
	Model 1	Model 2	Model 1	Model 2	Model 1	Model 2	Model 1	Model 2	Model 1	Model 2
Sex	1.55***	−1.64***	2.01***	−.84***	1.41***	−1.01***	1.26***	−1.20***	1.26***	.15
	(.21)	(.20)	(.19)	(.17)	(.19)	(.21)	(.21)	(.22)	(.21)	(.26)
Fear of rape		.77***		.66***		.56***		.58***		.25***
		(.03)		(.03)		(.03)		(.03)		(.04)
Adjusted R^2	.36	.66	.41	.68	.35	.55	.35	.54	.21	.25

	Break into home		Car stolen		Property vandalized		Cheated/conned	
	Model 1	Model 2	Model 1	Model 2	Model 1	Model 2	Model 1	Model 2
Sex	1.61***	−.70**	.95***	−1.06***	.61**	−1.17***	.79***	−.94***
	(.19)	(.20)	(.21)	(.24)	(.19)	(.22)	(.21)	(.25)
Fear of rape		.53***		.46***		.40***		.39***
		(.03)		(.03)		(.03)		(.04)
Adjusted R^2	.27	.48	.25	.40	.26	.38	.22	.33

b and (standard error) reported
***$p < .001$; **$p < .02$; *$p < .05$

TABLE 4   Partial OLS Results for Fear of Specific Crimes—Southwestern Campus

	Murder		Attacked w/ weapon		Robbery		Beaten up		Approached by beggar	
	Model 1	Model 2	Model 1	Model 2	Model 1	Model 2	Model 1	Model 2	Model 1	Model 2
Sex	1.91***	−1.65***	2.40***	−.63*	1.91***	−.53	1.96***	−.55	1.89***	.66
	(.32)	(.28)	(.28)	(.26)	(.28)	(.29)	(.30)	(.33)	(.31)	(.39)
Fear of rape		.79***		.67***		.54***		.55***		.27***
		(.04)		(.04)		(.04)		(.05)		(.05)
Adjusted R^2	.36	.69	.41	.70	.42	.61	.40	.57	.28	.33

	Break into home		Car stolen		Property vandalized		Cheated/conned	
	Model 1	Model 2	Model 1	Model 2	Model 1	Model 2	Model 1	Model 2
Sex	1.93***	−.55	1.35***	−.54	1.09***	−.74*	1.27***	−.57
	(.28)		(.30)	(.33)	(.28)	(.33)	(.33)	(.39)
Fear of rape		.55***		.42***		.40***		.41***
		(.04)		(.05)		(.04)		(.05)
Adjusted R^2	.33	.55	.27	.38	.31	.43	.23	.33

b and (standard error) reported
***$p < .001$; **$p < .02$; *$p < .05$

TABLE 5   Partial OLS Results for Fear of Specific Crimes—Southeastern Campus

	Murder		Attacked w/ weapon		Robbery		Beaten up		Approached by beggar	
	Model 1	Model 2	Model 1	Model 2	Model 1	Model 2	Model 1	Model 2	Model 1	Model 2
Sex	2.05**	−1.47***	1.63***	−1.01**	.90*	−1.15**	.76*	−1.63***	.62	−.78
	(.37)	(.35)	(.34)	(.33)	(.37)	(.40)	(.37)	(.38)	(.42)	(.49)
Fear of rape		.80***		.61***		.52***		.59***		.31***
		(.05)		(.05)		(.06)		(.06)		(.06)
Adjusted R²	.34	.66	.33	.61	.26	.45	.32	.54	.01	.09

	Break into home		Car stolen		Property vandalized		Cheated/conned	
	Model 1	Model 2	Model 1	Model 2	Model 1	Model 2	Model 1	Model 2
Sex	1.16**	−.88*	1.06*	−.89*	.25	−1.35**	.18	−1.27**
	(.36)	(.41)	(.40)	(.44)	(.36)	(.42)	(.38)	(.44)
Fear of rape		.47***		.47***		.37***		.35***
		(.06)		(.06)		(.06)		(.07)
Adjusted R²	.22	.39	.14	.30	.23	.34	.23	.31

b and (standard error) reported

***p < .001; **p < .02; *p < .05

TABLE 6 Partial OLS Results for Fear of Specific Crimes—Western Campus

	Murder		Attacked w/ weapon		Robbery		Beaten up		Approached by beggar	
	Model 1	Model 2	Model 1	Model 2	Model 1	Model 2	Model 1	Model 2	Model 1	Model 2
Sex	2.05***	−1.47***	2.12***	−1.06**	1.08**	−1.68***	1.33***	−1.34**	1.50***	.31
	(.37)	(.35)	(.33)	(.31)	(.36)	(.38)	(.37)	(.41)	(.34)	(.45)
Fear of rape		.80***		.73***		.64***		.61***		.24***
		(.05)		(.05)		(.06)		(.06)		(.06)
Adjusted R^2	.34	.66	.39	.69	.25	.50	.23	.45	.13	.18

	Break into home		Car stolen		Property vandalized		Cheated/conned	
	Model 1	Model 2	Model 1	Model 2	Model 1	Model 2	Model 1	Model 2
Sex	1.70***	−.77	.56	−2.21***	.36	−1.46**	.63	−.92*
	(.37)	(.42)	(.40)	(.46)	(.34)	(.43)	(.36)	(.45)
Fear of rape		.54***		.57***		.37***		.34***
		(.06)		(.06)		(.06)		(.06)
Adjusted R^2	.22	.41	.16	.37	.21	.32	.21	.29

b and (standard error) reported
***p < .001; **p < .02; *p < .05

analyses were conducted, although not reported here, that indicated that fear of crimes other than rape did not have this same impact on sex differences related to fear of specific crimes. For example, when modeling fear of murder, controlling for fear of being robbed did not change the direction of the coefficient for sex. Women remained significantly more fearful when fear of being robbed was considered as an explanatory variable for fear of murder. Thus, the data indicate that there is something about fear of rape that drives the fear of other crimes for women. These findings are in accord with previous research examining the impact of the relationship of sex and fear of crime (Clemente & Kleiman, 1977; Ferraro, 1995, 1996; Fetchenhauer & Buunk, 2005; Fisher & Sloan, 2003; Garofalo, 1979; Parker & Ray, 1990; Parker et al., 1993; Stafford & Galle, 1984; Stanko, 1995; Warr, 1984, 2000).

The standardized coefficients (betas) for the fear of rape variable were the highest of all standardized coefficients in each model, indicating that fear of rape is the best explanatory variable included. Examining the change in the R-squares from model 1 to model 2 indicates that the explanatory value of the equations for violent crimes generally increased more so with the inclusion of fear of rape than the property crimes. This is perhaps an indication that fear of rape more strongly shadows fear of violent crimes that are more likely to involve face-to-face contact than property crimes. This was true for the total sample and for each individual campus examined.

The findings presented here also indicate that there are differences across campuses in regard to gender and fear of crime. In the southwestern sample, women were more fearful of all nine types of crime in the initial models, whereas women were more fearful in six of the nine initial models on each of the other two campuses. Higher fear among college women, then, is not uniform across different places. There was some similarity across the other two campuses in terms of what crimes did not yield significant sex differences. Specifically, on the southeastern campus, there were no initial differences between men and women for being approached by a beggar, having your property vandalized, and being cheated or conned out of your money. On the western campus, there were no sex differences for having your car stolen, having property vandalized, or being cheated or conned out of your money.

The gender differences were also not uniform across the campuses in the second models (controlling for fear of rape). Again, the southwestern campus stands out as being somewhat different than the other two. Once fear of rape is controlled, men were more fearful for three of the crimes examined (murder, being attacked with a weapon, and having your property vandalized). For the other six types of crime, there were no gender differences. In the other two samples, men were more fearful once rape was controlled for the majority of the crimes, in eight of the nine models on the southeastern campus and seven of the nine models on the western campus. While the impact of fear of rape is uniform in dampening the fear of other crimes for women, it seems to have a differential impact across campuses. It is unclear exactly why the southwest campus stands out from the other two in terms of fear, although reasonable speculation can be made. While it is the smallest of the campuses in terms of enrollment, it is located in the midst of a large metropolitan area, whereas the other two campuses are located in less populous areas. Previous research has shown fear to be highest in urban areas, so this likely accounts for at least some of the differences in fear across campus. It is less clear why the gender differences would be less pronounced among respondents from the southwest campus.

It could be related to the location of the campus, although it is possible that there are other factors involved.

POLICY IMPLICATIONS

As Jennings et al. (2007) note, physical and social changes are necessary when considering the development and implementation of policies, as one without the other will be insufficient in attempts to reduce fear among females attending colleges and universities today. From a structural/physical standpoint, lighting can be improved, and new buildings can be planned to maximize natural light and allow for optimal space between buildings (Day, 1994). Furthermore, blue-light telephones have been implemented with greater frequency on campuses across the United States in recent years. By and large, this policy has been met with favoritism by administrators and students (Day, 1994; Wilcox et al., 2007).

Social programs provided to students can take a variety of forms, such as awareness programs and education for all students, self-defense courses for female students, and neighborhood watch in residential areas contiguous to campus. As Fisher and Sloan (2003) note, programs should be developed to counter actual and real social risks. If females can understand which crimes and in what situations they are most vulnerable through proactive programming, the lives of women on campuses across the United States will be enhanced, and many will not find interruption in their daily lives. This approach to programming is imperative given the nature of victimization among college females, as many who fall victim to crime do so at the hands of someone they know (Day, 1994; Fisher et al., 2000; Jennings, et al., 2007; Softas-Nall et al., 1995; Wilcox et al., 2007). Awareness and education programs can be required of all incoming students, members of fraternities and sororities, and all student-athletes (Day, 1994; Fisher & Sloan, 2003). These programs are imperative for females who have been victims of sexual assault in the past, as those who have been victimized before are more likely than their counterparts to be sexually victimized again (Jennings et al., 2007). Programs may focus on the consequences of alcohol and substance use/abuse and the accuracy of crime reporting on campus. Programs could also encourage and espouse reporting of crime to campus authorities and assurance that support will be made available to reporting victims. Education and awareness programs have been criticized in the past for advocating avoidance. Scholars such as Day (1994) have noted that much of the sexual victimization awareness promoted on college campuses in the past two decades has largely reinforced gender social norms. Unfortunately, programs of this nature may increase avoidance behaviors, thus serving to remove the female student from the complete college experience (Currie, 1994). For this reason, it is important to create awareness and prevention programs aimed at men and their behaviors and responsibility in regard to sexual violence. In addition to education and awareness, scholars have advocated that self-defense courses are effective in reducing the amount of perceived risk that college females experience. The rationale is that even in situations where the actual likelihood of victimization does not decrease, females completing self-defense programs are likely to feel empowered and in control of various social situations (Weitlauf, Smith, & Cervone, 2000). This is tantamount considering the lives of female college students are largely driven by their social interaction with males of a similar age on campus or in residential or commercial areas close to campus.

REFERENCES

Bennett, R. R., & Flavin, J. M. (1994). Determinants of fear of crime: The effect of cultural setting. *Justice Quarterly, 11*(3), 357–381.

Brantingham, P. J., & Brantingham, P. L. (1994). Surveying campus crime: What can be done to reduce crime and fear? *Security Journal, 5*(3), 160–171.

Brownmiller, S. (1975). *Against our will: Men, women, and rape.* New York: Bantam Books.

Clemente, F., & Kleiman, M. (1977). Fear of crime in the United States: A multivariate analysis. *Social Forces, 56*(2), 519–531.

Cobbina, J. E., Miller, J., & Brunson, R. K. (2008). Gender, neighborhood danger, and risk avoidance strategies among urban African American youth. *Criminology, 46*(3), 673–709.

Culbertson, K., Vik, P., & Kooiman, B. (2001). The impact of sexual assault, sexual assault perpetrator type, and location of sexual assault on ratings of perceived safety. *Violence Against Women, 7*(8), 858–875.

Currie, D. (1994). Women's safety on campus: Challenging the university as a gendered space. *Humanity and Society, 18*(3), 24–48.

Day, K. (1994). Conceptualizing women's fear of sexual assault on campus. *Environment & Behavior, 26*(6), 742–765.

Ferraro, K. F. (1995). *Fear of crime: Interpreting victimization risk.* Albany: State University of New York Press.

Ferraro, K. (1996). Women's fear of victimization: Shadow of sexual assault? *Social Forces, 75*(2), 667–690.

Fetchenhauer, D., & Buunk, B. (2005). How to explain gender differences in fear of crime: Towards an evolutionary approach. *Sexualities, Evolution & Gender, 7*(2), 95–113.

Fisher, B. S., Cullen, F. T., & Turner, M. G. (2000). *The sexual victimization of college women.* Washington, DC: Office of Justice Programs.

Fisher, B. S., & Sloan, J. J. III. (2003). Unraveling the fear of victimization among college women: Is the "shadow of sexual assault hypothesis supported?" *Justice Quarterly, 20*(3), 633–659.

Garofalo, J. (1979). Victimization and the fear of crime. *Journal of Research in Crime and Delinquency, 16*(1), 80–97.

Gilchrist, E., Bannister, J., Ditton, J., & Farrall, S. (1998). Women and the fear of crime: Challenging the accepted stereotype. *British Journal of Criminology, 38*(2), 283–298.

Gordon, M. T., & Riger, S. (1989). *The female fear: The social cost of rape.* Urbana, IL: University of Illinois Press.

Gordon, M. T., Riger, S., LeBailly, R. K., & Heath, L. (1980). Crime, women, and the quality of urban life. *Signs: Journal of Women in Culture and Society, 5*(3), 144–160.

Griffith, J. D., Hueston, E., Wilson, C., Moyers, & Hart, C. L. (2004). Satisfaction with campus police services. *College Student Journal, 38*(1), 150–156.

Hammer, J., & Saunders, S. (1984). *Well-founded fear: A community study of violence to women.* London: Hutchinson.

Jennings, W., Gover, A., & Pudrzynskas, D. (2007). Are institutions of higher learning safe? A descriptive study of campus safety issues and self-reported campus victimization among male and female college students. *Journal of Criminal Justice Education, 18*(2), 191–208.

Katz, C. M., Webb, V. J., & Armstrong, T. A. (2003). Fear of gangs: A test of alternative theoretical models. *Justice Quarterly, 20*(1), 95–130.

KELLY, K. D., & DEKESEREDY, W. S. (1994). Women's fear of crime and abuse in college and university dating relationships. *Violence & Victims, 9*(1), 17–30.

LANE, J., & MEEKER, J. W. (2003). Women's and men's fear of gang crimes: Sexual and nonsexual assault as perceptually contemporaneous offenses. *Justice Quarterly, 20*(2), 337–371.

MCCREEDY, K. R., & DENNIS, B. G. (1996). Sex-related offenses and fear of crime on campus. *Journal of Contemporary Criminal Justice, 12*(1), 69–80.

MADRIZ, E. (1997). *Nothing bad happens to good girls: Fear of crime in women's lives.* Berkeley: University of California Press.

PARKER, K. D., MCMORRIS, B. J., SMITH, E., & MURTY, K. S. (1993). Fear of crime and the likelihood of victimization: A bi-ethnic comparison. *Journal of Social Psychology, 133*(5), 723–732.

PARKER, K. D., & RAY, M. C. (1990). Fear of crime: An assessment of related factors. *Sociological Spectrum, 10*, 29–40.

RADER, N. E. (2004). The threat of victimization: A theoretical re-conceptualization of fear of crime. *Sociological Spectrum, 24*(6), 689–704.

RADER, N., MAY, D., & GOODRUM, S. (2007). An empirical assessment of the threat of victimization: Considering fear of crime, perceived risk, avoidance, and defensive behaviors. *Sociological Spectrum, 27*(5), 475–505.

REID, L., & KONRAD, M. (2004). The gender gap in fear: Assessing the interactive effects of gender and perceived risk on fear of crime. *Sociological Spectrum, 24*(4), 399–425.

RIGER, S., GORDON, M. T., & LEBAILLY, R. (1978). Women's fear of crime from blaming to restricting the victim. *Victimology: An International Journal, 3*, 274–284.

SKOGAN, W. G., & MAXFIELD, M. G. (1981). *Coping with crime: Individual and neighborhood reactions.* Beverly Hills, CA: Sage Publications.

SLOAN, J. J., LANIER, M. M., & BEER, D. L. (2000). Policing the contemporary university campus: Challenging traditional organizational models. *Journal of Security Administration, 23*(1), 1–20.

SMITH, L. N. & HILL, G. D. (1991). Perceptions of crime seriousness and fear of crime. *Sociological Focus, 24*(4), 315–327.

SMITH, M. D. (1988). Women's fear of violent crime: An exploratory test of a feminist hypothesis. *Journal of Family Violence, 3*(1), 29–38.

SMITH, W., & TORSTENSSON, M. (1997). Gender differences in risk perception and neutralizing fear of crime: Toward resolving the paradoxes. *British Journal of Criminology, 37*(4), 608–634.

SOFTAS-NALL, B., BARDOS, A., & FAKINOS, M. (1995). Fear of rape: Its perceived seriousness and likelihood among young Greek women. *Violence Against Women, 1*(2), 174–186.

STAFFORD, M. C., & GALLE, O. R. (1984). Victimization rates, exposure to risk, and fear of crime. *Criminology, 22*(2), 173–185.

STANKO, E. (1987). Typical violence, normal precaution: Men, women and interpersonal violence in England, Wales, Scotland and the USA. In J. Hanmer and M. Maynard (Eds.), *Women, violence, and social control.* London: Macmillan

STANKO, E. A. (1990a). *The case of fearful women: Gender, personal safety and the fear of crime.* Paper presented at the annual meeting of the American Society of Criminology, Baltimore.

STANKO, E. (1990b). *Everyday violence: How women and men experience sexual and physical danger.* London: HarperCollins.

STANKO, E. (1992). The case of fearful women: Gender, personal safety, and fear of crime. *Women and Criminal Justice, 4*(1), 117–135.

STANKO, E. (1995). Women, crime, and fear. *Annals of the American Academy of Political and Social Science, 539*(1), 46–58.

STINCHCOMBE, A. L., ADAMS, R., FLEIMER, C. A., SCHEPPELE, K. L., SMITH, T. W., & TAYLOR, D. G. (1980). *Crime and punishment: Changing attitudes in America.* Jossey Bass.

SUTTON, R. M., & FARRALL, S. (2005). Gender, socially desirable responding and the fear of crime: Are women really more anxious about crime? *British Journal of Criminology, 45*(2), 212–224.

TURNER, K. B., & TORRES, A. (2006). Campus safety: Perceptions and experience of women students. *Journal of College Student Development, 47*(1), 20–36.

WARR, M. (1984). Fear of victimization: Why are women and the elderly more afraid? *Social Science Quarterly, 65*(3), 681–702.

WARR, M. (1985). Fear of rape among urban women. *Social Problems, 32*(3), 238–250.

WARR, M. (2000). Fear of crime in the United States: Avenues for research and policy. In D. Duffee (Ed.), *Measurement and analysis of criminal justice*, Vol. 4 of *Crime and Justice 2000*. Washington, DC: National Institute of Justice.

WEITLAUF, J. C., SMITH, R. E., & CERVONE, D. (2000). Generalization effects of coping-skills training: Influence of self-defense training on women's efficacy beliefs, assertiveness, and aggression. *Journal of Applied Psychology, 85*(4), 625–633.

WILCOX, P., JORDAN, C., & PRITCHARD, A. (2007). A multidimensional examination of campus safety: Victimization, perceptions of danger, worry about crime, and precautionary behavior among college women in the post-Clery era. *Crime & Delinquency, 53*(2), 219–254.

YODANIS, C. L. (2004). Gender inequality, violence against women, and fear: A cross-national test of the feminist theory of violence against women. *Journal of Interpersonal Violence, 19*(6), 655–675.

16

The National Crime Victimization Survey and Rape

Does It Really Measure Rape Better Now That It Has Been Re-designed?

Helen Eigenberg

Critics of the National Crime Survey (NCS) have claimed that the instrument drastically failed to capture rape estimates with any accuracy for several reasons. Most significantly, the NCS screening questions did not specifically ask about rape. The instrument also defined and operationalized rape poorly. As such, most critics concluded that the NCS drastically underestimated rape rates. In the early 1990s the NCS underwent a major revision, and the newly redesigned (and renamed) National Crime Victimization Survey (NCVS) included questions that specifically asked respondents if they had been raped or sexually assaulted. There has, however, been relatively little discussion of the NCVS and its ability to capture rape victimization. This chapter examines changes in the NCVS and concludes that while the redesign has led to improvements, sufficient problems remain and these shortcomings continue to underestimate the amount of rape in the United States.

There are two general types of data that help establish the frequency of rape in the United States: (1) rapes that are reported to the police and (2) victimization studies. Since the Uniform Crime Report (UCR) measures only crimes reported to the police, it underestimates crime in general and rape in particular (Biderman & Reiss, 1967; Gottfredson, 1986; Gove, Hughes, & Geerken, 1984; Koss, Gidycz, & Widniewski, 1987; O'Brien, 1986; Russell, 1984; Skogan, 1975, 1977). For example, recent estimates suggest that only 41% of rapes and sexual assaults are reported to the police (Rand, 2009, p. 6).

Problems associated with the UCR facilitate reliance on victimization surveys. These surveys provide valuable information about criminal activities which are not reported to the police—those crimes which have been called the "dark figure of crime" (Biderman & Reiss, 1967, p. 1). Thus, victimization surveys are often assumed to provide more accurate estimates of the "true" nature of crime (Gottfredson, 1986; O'Brien, 1985,

1986). The National Crime Survey (NCS) and the revised version of it, renamed the National Crime Victimization Survey (NCVS), is the only official (i.e., governmental) source of national victimization data gathered annually in the United States.

The NCS was first delivered to a random sample of United States citizens in 1973. In 1992 a major re-design of the survey took place and the new revisions were fully implemented in 1993 when the instrument was renamed the National Crime Victimization Survey (NCVS). Significant changes were made that affect how crime, and especially rape, is measured.

Each year the Bureau of Justice Statistics (BJS) selects a nationally representative sample. In 2008, 42,093 households and 77,852 individuals aged 12 and older were interviewed (Rand, 2009) and answered questions about their experiences with criminal victimization in the United States. Each housing unit selected remains in the sample for three years and respondents complete seven interviews taking place at 6-month intervals. The first interview is done in person, and as of 2006 subsequent interviews are conducted by telephone using Computer-Assisted Personal Telephone Interviewing (CAPI) (Rand & Catalano, 2007). Each person in the home who is 12 years and older is interviewed. The survey uses a two-stage measurement process which relies upon screening questions which are followed by incident reports. The screening questions ascertain whether or not respondents have experienced victimization, and if they have, many additional questions are then asked to further assess the nature of the victimization, gather details about when it occurred, who the perpetrator was, if there were injuries, if the crime was reported to the police and so on. The results of the survey are used to estimate the likelihood that someone experienced a rape/sexual assault, robbery, assault, theft, household burglary, or motor vehicle theft in the prior year. Estimates of this kind are referred to as incident rates which are different from those studies that examine victimization over a period of time (e.g., a lifetime) which are referred to as prevalence rates.

The genesis for the re-design of the NCS began shortly after the implementation of the initial survey. In the mid-1970s, the National Academy of Sciences recommended several changes including modifications to the screening questions (Bachman, 2000; BJS, 1995). A research consortium was established to make recommendations about the re-design. Input was solicited from universities, private research firms, governmental agencies, and private consultants. The consortium issued its final report in 1986. Changes, including those affecting rape, were phased in later through implementation of a three-step design. Beginning in January, 1989, new screening questions were administered to 5% of the sample. These data were used to identify and correct any problems with the redesign. In January 1992, 50% of the sample was introduced to the new design while 50% completed the old design. Data from this year are referred to as the split sample. Full implementation occurred in July 1993 (Kindermann, Lynch, & Cantor, 1997).

SCREENING QUESTIONS

The newly designed NCVS made several major changes in the screening questions. The NCS used 13 initial screening items to determine whether or not respondents were victims of crime (BJS, 1989a, p. 100). The items quickly identified victims so that detailed questions about their victimization experiences could be gathered. Thus, the screening questions were designed to be thorough, but not too lengthy. Screening questions specifically asked respondents questions to ascertain whether someone had tried to take something from them, rob them, beat them up, attack them with a weapon, or steal things from them. *None of these questions asked whether someone had tried to rape them* (see Eigenberg, 1990). The question that was supposed to elicit rape asked: "Did anyone try to attack you in some other way? (other than any incidents already mentioned)" (BJS, 1989a, p. 100). Thus, respondents were expected to make the connection between a vague reference to attacks and report rapes to interviewers.

Two additional questions were used to try to elicit information about victimizations during the screening process. Respondents were asked whether they had called the police during the last six months to report something that happened which they thought might have been a crime. They also were asked whether anything else happened to them which they thought was a crime even if they did not report it to the police.

Apparently, at the time the NCS was developed, it was deemed "inappropriate for a government-sponsored survey to ask respondents directly about rape" (BJS, 1996, p. 150). Explicit use of the word *rape* was presumed to be "offensive to respondents" and was excluded because of "the sensitivity of the issue" (Dodge & Turner, 1981, p. 3). Researchers were reluctant to directly ask about rape, fearing that a direct question phrased in such "indelicate terms would likely promote public charges of the unbridled insensitivity of government snoopers as well as Congressional outrage" (Turner, 1981, p. 22). Supposedly, then, the less obtrusive form of asking whether respondents had been attacked allowed them to respond "with considerably less embarrassment" (Turner, 1981, p. 22). This approach, however, ignored the fact that victims had to self-disclose rapes which may well have been more difficult than simply responding yes or no to a question which described sexual victimization and asked whether they had experienced the same. Simply put, it probably was harder for a victim to say "I was raped" than to say "yes" when specifically asked about sexual assaults. In addition, respondents had no way of knowing how many screening questions existed and whether an additional one was to follow to ask about rape specifically. They would have no way of knowing that this was their "last chance" to reveal a rape. Respondents also may have concluded that they were not supposed to talk about rape or that the researcher was not interested in that type of crime since it was not directly mentioned. Even worse, they may have concluded that rape was not a serious crime if it was not included in a survey that purportedly was designed to measure crime.

Interestingly, it was clear there was a major problem with the rape question before 1973 and the implementation of the first NCS survey. A reverse record study was conducted to test the initial instrument. Samples of known victims were selected from police records in San Jose, California, and victims were surveyed to evaluate the efficacy of the survey (see Turner, 1981). Theoretically, if victims reported their crime to the police, the survey should capture all (or most) of the victimization when researchers were conducting the survey to test its efficacy. The San Jose study found that only about two-thirds (66.7%) of the rape victims who had reported their rapes to the police subsequently revealed their victimization to interviewers (Turner, 1981). This figure was the second lowest recall of the five crimes measured (assault, rape, robbery, burglary, and larceny); only assault did worse (48.1%).[1]

The NCVS continues to acknowledge that sensitive material (like rape) is difficult to talk about and states that the instrument was redesigned to "make reporting of this kind of information easier for victims" (BJS, 1996, p. 150). The NCVS, as redesigned, includes two broad questions designed to capture violent crime including rape. In the first set of questions targeting violent crime, respondents are asked (BJS, 1996, p. 153):

Has anyone attacked or threatened you in any one of these ways?

a.   with any weapon, for instance, a gun or a knife?
b.   with anything like a baseball bat, frying pan, scissors, or stick?
c.   By something thrown, such as a rock or bottle? (BJS, 1996, p. 153)
d.   [Did the attack] include any grabbing, punching, or choking?
e.   *Any rape, attempted rape, or other type of sexual assault?* (emphasis added)
f.   Any face-to-face threats? OR
g.   Any attack or threat or use of force by anyone at all?

Respondents also are specifically asked to mention any incidents even if they were not certain it was a crime.

The second screening question is designed to deal exclusively with rape and sexual assault. Respondents are told (BJS, 1996, p. 153):

Incidents involving *forced or unwanted sexual acts* (emphasis added) are often difficult to talk about. Have you been forced or coerced to engage in unwanted sexual activity by

a.   someone you didn't know before?
b.   a casual acquaintance?
c.   or someone you know well?

Respondents also are provided with a couple of other questions which might result in disclosure of a rape. They are asked whether they were attacked or threatened, or had something stolen from them and provided with a variety of locations where these events might occur (including home, school, and neighbor's home). Another question provides a different context which attempts to cue respondents to think about behavior committed by intimates. They are informed that "people often don't think of incidents committed by someone they know" (BJS, 1996, p. 154). Respondents are then asked whether they had "something stolen" or if they were "attacked or threatened" by "someone at work or school, a neighbor or friend, a relative or family member, or any other person [they've] met or known?" (BJS, 1996, p. 154).

These new screening questions certainly represent an improvement over the NCS. When data from the two half samples conducted with both the old and new instruments in 1992 are compared, it is clear that the NCVS captured significantly more crime than its predecessor (Kindermann, Lynch, & Cantor, 1997). While the redesign resulted in an overall increase of 49% in violent crimes, rape increased 157%. Expressed in another way, for every rape reported by the NCS methodology, 2.57 were reported by the NCVS methodology (Kindermann, Lynch, & Cantor, 1997, p. 2). This ratio was the highest for any crime, indicating that rape was the crime measured least effectively by the NCS.

Unfortunately, significant problems with the screening questions remain (Koss, 1992, 1993; Russell & Bolen, 2000). In all likelihood these shortcomings result in underestimating rape rates.

First, the NCVS screening questions dealing with rape and sexual assault are not behaviorally specific; in other words, the questions ask if someone has been raped or not. In contrast, behaviorally specific questions describe the victimization in graphic detail using language that describes the elements of the crime (Belknap et al., 1999, Fisher, 2009, Koss et al., 2007; Russell & Bolen, 2000). For example, Belknap and her colleagues devised an instrument using the following question: "Has anyone made you have sexual intercourse by using force or threatening to harm you or someone close to you? Just so there is no mistake, by intercourse, I mean putting a penis in your vagina" (1999, p. 204). When studies, like the NCVS, fail to ask respondents about the types of sexual violence they have experienced by specifically describing the acts, several problems result. Simply asking victims if they have been raped, "assumes that victims have a shared meaning of the word rape and/or sexual assault, that this meaning is consistent with a legal definition of rape and/or sexual assault, and that victims apply these terms to their experiences" (Koss, 1993, pp. 207–208).

In fact, research clearly demonstrates that many women fail to label their experiences as rape, even when their victimization meets the legal criteria to be classified as a rape. Russell (1984) found that only half of the attempted and completed rapes identified in her study of adult women in San Francisco were captured by a single question asking whether respondents had been raped compared to her figures that resulted from asking behaviorally specific questions. Likewise, Koss et al. (1988) asked college women whether they had experienced certain types of victimization by using behavioral descriptions of the incidents and then also asked whether they were raped in a separate question. Koss found that 55% of the women victimized by strangers defined it as rape, but only 23% of those assaulted by acquaintances labeled it rape. Perhaps even more astounding, 29% of those women assaulted by strangers and 62% of those assaulted by acquaintances did not view it as any kind of crime. Similar findings were reported by another study of college women (Fisher, Cullen, & Turner, 2000). Only half (49%) of the women in this study who reported that they had experienced completed intercourse involving force also stated that they had been raped in a separate screening question using that language. Thus, many women seem to reserve the word rape for sexual victimizations that fit the stereotypical notion of a "real" rape (Estrich, 1987)—which is one involving a stranger as a perpetrator.

Research by Fisher, Cullen, and Turner (2000) provides the strongest evidence that the NCVS and its lack of behaviorally specific questions contribute to underreporting by rape victims (see also Fisher, 2009). In this study, the authors selected two nationally representative samples of college women, each of which had approximately 4,500 respondents. Both studies used a two-stage measurement process using screening questions followed by questions about any rape incidents reported. In the first sample (referred to by the authors as the National Violence Against College Women Study [NVACW]), the authors used the existing NCVS methodology and screening questions. In the second sample (referred to by the authors as the National College Women Sexual Victimization Study [NCWSV]), twelve behaviorally specific questions were used. Similar behaviorally specific statements also were used to measure attempted rapes, and both attempted and completed acts including forced oral and anal assaults, penetration by foreign objects, and digital penetration (e.g., by fingers). The results were quite conclusive; rape rates using the NCVS screening questions were ten times smaller for completed rape and six times smaller for attempted rape when compared to the sample using behaviorally specific questions (Fisher, 2009). While other studies (Koss, 1993; Russell, 1984; Tjaden & Thoennes, 1998) also have reported that rapes are underestimated when researchers fail to use behaviorally specific questions, Fisher and her colleagues demonstrate this argument convincingly because of their ability to directly compare the NCVS methodology with a method involving behaviorally specific questions while also using a sample that is about as similar for both groups as is humanly possible in a research environment (see Fisher, 2009).

A second problem with the NCVS screening questions is that there are too few of them. Thus, there is insufficient time to establish rapport so that victims feel comfortable disclosing their experiences. The average interview where no victimization is disclosed lasts only five or six minutes (Russell & Bolen, 2000). The NCVS with its lack of behaviorally specific questions coupled with a relatively short screening instrument, which only specifically discusses rape and sexual assault in two places, requires victims to make quick decisions about whether or not to reveal their experiences. Multiple questions and longer surveys appear to give women time to think over their responses and choose how to reveal their experiences (see Koss, 1993; Koss et al., 2007; Russell & Bolen, 2000). Research also suggests that questions using different language and context may help with memory recall. Researchers might be better able to devise more efficient screening questions if they better understood how memories are stored and knew what types of labels (i.e., sexual assault, rape, unwanted sexual activity, etc.) best cue women to reveal their victimizations. In the meantime, evidence suggests that studies which present *several* behaviorally specific screening questions produce higher rape rates (see Belknap et al., 1999; Fisher, 2009; Koss, 1993, Menard, 2005; Russell & Bolen, 2000).

A third issue with the NCVS screening questions relates to the way it attempts to encourage reporting of victimization by intimates. The NCVS asks respondents to consider unwanted sexual acts committed by people known to the victims including casual acquaintances and people who they know well, though the NCVS fails to specifically name other common perpetrators of sexual assaults in this screening question—including relatives, dates, boyfriends, and husbands for example (Bachman, 2000; Russell & Bolen, 2000).[2] While family members and relatives are expressly mentioned on the broad questions asking about "attacks," strangers are probably more likely to be associated with this wording. If victims hesitate to use the word rape in conjunction with sexual assaults by intimates (as demonstrated by previous research), then some victims may fail to conceptualize these experiences as attacks and the wording of the screening questions does little to encourage victims to think about these types of rape.

Thus, the NCVS screening questions are somewhat improved. The new questions specifically ask victims to think about acts like acquaintance rape and unwanted sexual experiences which victims might be reluctant to identify as a crime. For the first time, the survey also specifically asks "respondents directly about attacks that were perpetrated by relatives or other offenders known to them" (Bachman & Taylor, 1994, p. 504), thereby diminishing the previous concentration on stranger rape. Perhaps most importantly, the NCVS finally specifically addresses rape and sexual assault; victims no longer have to guess that they should mention these experiences in response to a vague question on attacks. However, awkward operationalization and lack of clear definitions of rape and sexual assault continue to make it difficult to ascertain just what precisely the NCVS is capturing with regard to sexual victimization.

DEFINITIONS OF RAPE

The NCS defined rape as "carnal knowledge through the use of force or the threat of force including attempts" (BJS, 1989a, p. 127), although this definition was somewhat irrelevant because it was not provided for respondents (Bachman & Taylor, 1994, p. 506). If respondents indicated that they had been raped based on the ambiguous screening question referring to "attacks" then it was coded as a rape or attempted rape, depending upon the description of the act provided by the victim. If victims were reluctant to provide details about the incident, interviewers were instructed to ask if they had been "raped" or if someone had "tried to rape" them or committed a "verbal threat of rape" (Bachman & Taylor, 1994, p. 506). Thus, some victims may have provided sufficient information to allow interviewers to code the act appropriately, while others may only have reported they were raped and offered no information about their definition of the act. It is difficult, then, to determine precisely what types of acts the NCS captured (see Eigenberg, 1990; Gove, Hughes, & Geerken, 1984). As such, a great deal of discretion was given to interviewers in terms of deciding how to code incidents.

The NCVS attempts to rectify some of these problems. If respondents indicate that they have been a victim of rape, attempted rape, or sexual attack in response to the explicit screening questions, respondents are asked to clarify their experiences by responding to the following question: "Do you mean forced or coerced sexual intercourse?" If the answer is yes, the incident is coded as a rape (Bachman & Taylor, 1994, p. 507). The NCVS also provides a definition of rape that "*can* be used for reference [for interviewers] or *can* be read to respondents at any time during the interview" (emphasis added, Bachman & Taylor, 1994, p. 507). Rape is defined as:

> forced sexual intercourse and includes both psychological coercion as well as physical force. Forced sexual intercourse means vaginal, anal, or oral penetration, by the offender(s). This category also includes incidents where the penetration is from a foreign object such as a bottle. Includes attempted rapes, male as well as female victims, and both heterosexual and homosexual rape. Attempted rape includes verbal threats of rape. (BJS, 2009, no page number)

This definition poses several difficulties. First, it is not clear that respondents who have not had the definition read to them define "sexual intercourse" as broadly as does the NCVS. The more common cultural understanding of intercourse is associated with coitus (vaginal penetration by a penis) which may fail to include oral and anal sexual assaults in the minds of some victims. In fact, one study of about 600 students enrolled at a Midwestern university reported 59% of them did not believe that oral sex qualifies as sex and only 19% thought the same about anal intercourse (Sanders & Reinisch, 1999). Therefore, it is possible that some victims who experienced forced oral or anal assaults may fail to disclose their experiences in response to the first follow-up question which concentrates only on asking about experiences with forced sexual intercourse. The use of the terms heterosexual and homosexual rape in the NCVS definition of rape also is puzzling. The NCVS does not define homosexual rape. Apparently, the NCVS assumes that same sex rapes (men raping men) are homosexual acts or committed by homosexual men. Both of these assumptions are highly questionable.

Second, the NCVS definition of rape fails to include several acts of rape which are commonly included in state and federal law. Two examples include: (1) non-forcible rape with an incapacitated victim (a person unable to give consent because of unconsciousness, sleep, intoxication, or mental or physical impairment) and (2) sexual acts with girls below the statutory age of consent (Koss, 1993, 1996; Koss et al., 2007; Russell & Bolen, 2000). Here again, these exclusions serve to underrepresent the amount of rape as measured by the NCVS.

Third, it is not clear why the NCVS has chosen to include acts involving psychological coercion or verbal threats of rape. As stated previously, the NCS instructed interviewers to ask victims who were reluctant to provide details about the assault if they had experienced rape, attempted rape, or a "verbal threat of rape" (Bachman & Taylor, 1994, p. 506). Not only does the NCVS continue this practice but it expands upon it by including verbal threats of sexual assault. The inclusion of these terms is confusing. While the term psychological coercion may be interpreted to mean verbal threats of bodily harm and rape, which are crimes, the term also might encompass other types of behavior which are not criminal. As Koss notes: "the term may suggest to respondents situations involving false promises, threats to end the relationship, continual nagging and pressuring, and other verbal strategies to coerce sexual intercourse, which are undesirable but not crimes" (1996, p. 60).

In fact, too little attention has been paid to researching how coercion is measured, the words used to describe it, and how these decisions impact rape rates (Belknap et al., 1999; Hamby & Koss, 2003; Koss, 2003; Russell & Bolen, 2000). For example, there is a need to better understand how respondents perceive questions that ask about unwanted versus forced sexual intercourse and how these terms affect disclosure and of what types of acts. Some coerced and/or unwanted sexual acts may have harmful effects on victims (e.g., when partners threaten to break up with them if they don't engage in sex); however, that does not mean they are illegal. Limited research indicates coercion is a complicated concept and that questions which assume a strict dichotomy of force versus non-force significantly hinders our understanding of rape as well as our ability to count it (Belknap et al., 1999; Hamby & Koss, 2005; Koss, 2003).

Fourth, the NCVS has made it more difficult to determine rates of sexual violence by adding a new category of victimization called sexual assault. The NCVS defines sexual assaults as:

> a wide range of victimizations, separate from rape or attempted rape. These crimes include attacks or attempted attacks generally involving unwanted sexual contact between victim and offender. Sexual assaults may or may not involve force and include such things as grabbing or fondling. Sexual assault also includes verbal threats. (BJS, 1996, p. 174)

While it is important to measure sexual abuse in childhood (including fondling, verbally coerced sex, and unwanted sexual contact) which are crimes, some of these acts may not represent legal violations when applied to adult women (e.g., verbal coercion without threats of force). This overly broad definition of sexual assault used by the NCVS to calculate victimization rates for both girls and women is confusing. It is not clear how interviewers distinguish between verbal threats of rape and verbal threats of sexual assault, or what acts besides grabbing or fondling might constitute sexual assaults. Furthermore, the use of the term sexual assault is confusing because it is most often used as a legal synonym for rape (Koss, 1993). As such, the average person reading NCVS tables reporting rates for both rape and sexual assault will probably be confused about the meaning of the data. As such, the definitions of rape and operationalization of the same are not as clear as they should be in the NCVS.

ADMINISTRATION OF THE SURVEY

There also are problems associated with the administration of the NCVS. These issues include identifying context of the survey, collecting the data, training of interviewers, and ensuring confidentiality.

The context in which the NCVS is conducted likely serves to underestimate the frequency of rape reported by respondents. As stated previously, the main context provided by the survey is crime—it includes crime in the name and it is introduced to participants as a survey about crime. Studies that use relationships, personal safety, or health issues as their framework appear to produce higher (and more reliable) estimates of rape (Bachman, 2000; Eigenberg, 1990; Hamby & Koss, 2003; Russell & Bolen, 2000). Here again, Fisher and her colleagues' study, which compares methodologies, provides important evidence of the effect of context. In both samples, respondents were sent a cover letter about two weeks prior to being contacted for the interview. The introductory letter for the NVACW study, where the authors used the existing NCVS methodology, described the context as a study on criminal victimization, while the study using behaviorally specific questions described the context of the study as unwanted sexual experiences. Results (Fisher, 2009) suggested that victims who responded to the study using the NCVS methodology were more apt to report criminal victimization and those using the behaviorally specific methodology reported a wider range of victimization.

It also appears that the interviewing methodology impacts data, though deciphering the exact nature of this effect is complicated. In 1987, interviewers began to supplement paper and pencil interviewing with some use of computer-assisted telephone interviewing using two central telephone facilities to administer the survey (Rand & Catalano, 2007, p. 9). In 2006, the use of the telephone facilities was discontinued. NCVS implemented a fully automated computer-assisted personal interviewing system (CAPI) where field representatives use laptops to administer interviews.

The lack of research on mode of delivery makes it difficult to ascertain what effect the various methods of administration have had upon rape estimates. High estimates of rape have been found in studies using in-person interviews and self-administered questionnaires, but interviews have also produced some of the lowest estimates of rape (see Koss, 1993). One thing is clear, the change in mode of administration had a profound impact upon NCVS data. In fact, BJS is not using any data from 2006 in any of their longitudinal analyses because estimates "varied widely from the estimates of previous years. The differences were too extreme to be attributed to year to year changes" (Rand & Catalano, 2007, p. 7). While other changes related to sampling also likely contributed to these "anomalous" (p. 10) findings,[3] clearly BJS believes that the change to CAPI had a significant impact as it was one of the three reasons given for abandoning any attempt to use 2006 data to evaluate crime trends. It is impossible, though, to determine specifically how this change affected rape rates. More information is needed about how the computer software structures follow-up questions and attempts to clarify victimizations when they are disclosed.

It also is important to know more about the training of interviewers given the changes in mode of delivery. As discussed previously, the ambiguity of definitions of rape and sexual assault and the ways that the screening questions are administered make it critical that interviewers are highly trained and that decisions are made in a consistent manner. Furthermore, without more information about the ways the CAPI software structures the decision making process, it is impossible to determine whether interviewers are administrating screening questions and clarifications of definitions in a consistent manner, nor is it possible to determine what effect these issues have upon the rape estimates. There is a lack of information about the nature and quality of training for interviewers who administer the NCVS (Russell & Bolen, 2000). Training is especially important as it relates to new employees who may have less familiarity with administering the instrument and who, therefore, may introduce error if they fail to count victimizations appropriately (or consistently). BJS reports that 28% of the assignments were completed by new interviewers in 2006 (Rand & Catalano, 2007).

Critics of the NCVS also are concerned that the lack of privacy and confidentiality during the interview may affect disclosure by victims (Koss, 1993; Russell & Bolen, 2000). Telephones, by design, are often placed in central locations of the house to facilitate access. Victims may lack the privacy necessary to comfortably respond to the questions. Furthermore, the perpetrator may be in the room since many rapes are committed by male relatives, current or former spouses, boyfriends, and lovers. Officials state that "many" items can be answered with a yes or no making it difficult for anyone overhearing the interview to follow the conversation (BJS, 1996, p. 150). The notion that yes and no answers will suffice, however, is debatable. As discussed previously, respondents are, theoretically, asked several times whether an act was a rape, attempted rape, or sexual assault. They also are asked to describe incidents to the interviewer. In fact, one BJS publication praises the new screening questions for "avoidance of the yes/no question-and-answer format" which characterized the NCS (BJS, 1994, p. 4). While officials also note that respondents are notified that they can break off the interview and re-schedule at any time during the interview (Bachman & Taylor, 1994; BJS, 1996, p. 150), it is difficult to believe that many rape victims, who generally are reluctant to discuss their victimization, will go to great lengths to re-schedule an interview so they can talk about their experiences.

Confidentiality issues are of special concern when proxy interviews are involved. Proxy interviews may be used when a household member objects to a direct interview of 12- or 13-year-old respondents. Proxy interviews also may be done when household members are incapacitated (those physically or mentally incapable of answering questions) or if they are absent altogether for the entire interviewing period. The NCVS does not report data on the number of proxy interviews; however, it seems reasonable to assume that the use of these interviews will assuredly underestimate the amount of rape. Clearly, any household member who is assaulting a younger child will prevent the child from completing the interview. It also seems reasonable that many non-assaultive parents may insist on being present during the interview. Either situation will greatly inhibit respondents from reporting sexual assaults of any kind.

In general, then, problems with the screening questions, definitions of rape (and operationalization of the same), and administration of the survey raise important questions about the validity of the NCVS data. Several concerns also are evident when the data itself is examined.

PROBLEMS WITH NCVS DATA

For the most part, the NCVS is assumed to have few problems associated with sample selection and response rate; however, both have been declining in recent years. A recent publication (2007) states that about 135,300 individuals aged 12 and older in 76,000 households are interviewed and a current web page with 2008 data reports about 134,000 persons aged 12 and older in 77,200 households are interviewed (BJS, n.d.[a]). These figures contradict other BJS reports. In fact it appears that the number of households has been steadily declining since 1973 (presumably because of budget decreases, Maltz & Zawitz, 1998, p. 7). Another BJS (Survey Methodology, n.d.[b]) reports that the number of households has declined from about 45,000 in 1996 to about 38,000 in 2006. Similarly, the number of persons interviewed has declined from 85,330 to 67,650, and the response rate has declined from 91% to 86%. These changes, in all likelihood, have an important impact on rape rates because of the low number of cases of rape reported annually.

NCVS data are reported in two ways: as rates per 1,000 people and as population estimates, both of which are calculated based on the actual number of victimizations reported in a given year. For example, 2008 data indicate that the rate for rape and sexual assault victimizations (completed and attempted) was .8 victims per 1,000 people. This rate is estimated to represent a total of 203,830 rapes in the United States. These figures, however, are based on the number of victimizations revealed in the sample and should not be confused with the number of rapes actually revealed to the interviewers as both are estimates based on the interviews. Rarely is there information in the BJS publications which allow one to ascertain exactly how many rapes were actually reported by respondents in any given year—in other words the exact number of victimizations reported. Russell and Bolen (2000, p. 71) report that population estimates for rape are typically based on between 60 and 100 reported rapes annually. In fact, prior to the redesign, there were so few cases of rape reported that annual reports did not include rape. Instead, they gathered data for a ten-year period before publishing a report with any details about the crime (BJS, 1985). Since the redesign, many tables in various publications also confirm that the actual number of reported rapes is based on a small number of cases, especially for men. Published tables contain footnotes that caution readers when estimates are based on fewer than ten cases. Since the implementation of the redesign (1993), there has never been a year where there were more than ten cases reported for men (in any of the individual categories of rape, attempted rape, or sexual assault). Novice readers and journalists may not catch this caveat in the data; instead they are apt to look at the population estimates based on these figures (ranging from 10,000 to 20,000) and assume that these numbers of cases were reported annually.

Low numbers of cases of reported rapes, especially reports of less than 10 incidents annually, are problematic because they also introduce error into other statistics and increase the likelihood that estimates are unreliable. Standard error is used to determine how close a figure from a sample is to the "true" value (e.g., the "real" rape rate). Information on standard error has been available in annual publications only haphazardly. From 1996 to 2001, some information about standard error is presented in annual publications discussing changes and trends in crime rates (Rand, 1998; Ringel, 1997; Rennison, 1999, 2000, 2001, 2002), although the information is presented in chart format making it difficult to ascertain exact numbers. Nonetheless, the charts for these five years clearly demonstrate that rape consistently has the most error when comparing estimates between the previous and current year. In addition, they demonstrate the level of error is quite high. One publication provides more detailed specifics. Data indicate there was a reported 17.65% decrease in rape from 1995 to 1996; however, the amount of error means that rape may have decreased by 41% or increased 5.8% (using a 95% confidence level; Maltz & Zawitz, 1998, p. 7). The authors note that for a 10% change in the rape rate to be statistically significant, the NCVS would need a sample of over 500,000 which is more than five times the current sample size (p. 5).[4] Similarly, the reported rape rate for 1996 was 1.4 per 1,000 people, but based on standard error, that rate may have been as low as 1.13 or as high as 1.67. While this change seems relatively small, it would result in a change in population estimates of 100,000 or more victims.[5]

The problems associated with standard error are magnified when looking at the 1992 split sample because one half of the sample was administered the old instrument (NCS methodology) and one half the new one (NCVS methodology). Therefore, the already low numbers of rapes reported annually were further reduced in each sample. The sample that was administered the old methodology reported the lowest rape rates on record, and 42% of the respondents who revealed victimization were male which was "atypically high" and represented an "anomaly" (Russell & Bolen, 2000, p. 70). As a result, there is reason to conclude that there was an unusually high amount of error in these data which is critically important because BJS uses the comparisons between the split sample results for other purposes. BJS uses statistical techniques to calculate adjustments to allow for changes in the NCS and the NCVS that reflect increases in the figures based on changes in the methodology (as opposed to increases in crime). Doing so, theoretically, allows them to maintain longitudinal data allowing for comparisons of victimization rates from 1973 to the present (see, for example, BJS, 2008). In other words, any data that compares results from the NCS and NCVS generally uses data which has been transformed in this matter; it is not using actual NCS rates compared to NCVS rates. Mathematical computations transforming the data under these circumstances seems quite precarious and ill advised, given the large amount of known error in the rape data. Nonetheless, these data are used to produce charts showing annual changes in rape rates over time (BJS, n.d. [a]) which purportedly demonstrate a steady decline in rape over the years. The validity of any trend is questionable.

Another practice of reporting the data affects how rape rates are perceived over time. Until 1992, the NCS reported rape rates per 1,000 females not per 1,000 people. The inclusion of male victims in definitions of rape and the increasing tendency to rely upon

gender-neutral reporting of rape statistics serves to dramatically reduce the overall estimates of rape. Since the overwhelming number of rape victims are women (approximately
90%), reporting rape rates per 1000 people effectively cuts the estimates almost in half.
While most states have enacted gender-neutral laws which include both male and female
victims, the new focus on rape as a gender-neutral crime serves to underestimate the extent
of victimization for women since most of the publications, especially the key facts and
quick overviews, tend to focus on rape in general rather than the rape of women.

CONCLUSION

In sum, then, there are many reasons to doubt estimates provided by the NCVS despite
some improvements made in the redesign. The most recent NCVS data report that 1.3
women per 1,000 persons experience rape, attempted rape, or sexual assault (Rand, 2009).
While comparisons between studies using different populations are always precarious due
to problems associated with generalizability, they do allow some insight into the efficacy
of the NCS and the NCVS. An in-depth review is beyond the scope of this paper; however,
all of the recent studies using random samples and behaviorally specific questions find
substantially larger incident and prevalence rates than does either the NCS or the NCVS.
As a whole, they cast doubt on the validity of the NCVS rape rates and continue to suggest that there is reason to be concerned about the accuracy of the NCVS findings.

Estimates of rape in the 1980s became a central focus of hegemonic debate about
the nature and frequency of sexual violence in the United States. This debate emerged, in
no large part, in response to two groundbreaking studies (Koss et al., 1988; Russell, 1984)
that suggested rape rates were substantially higher than previously believed. Russell
(1984) found that 41% of her sample had been the victim of at least one completed or
attempted rape in their lifetime (prevalence). She also found that her incident rate (e.g.,
annual rate) for attempted and completed rape was 40 per 1,000 females, which is seven
times that reported by the NCS (Russell & Bolen, 2000, p. 39 & 64). Similarly, Koss and
her associates (Koss et al., 1987) surveyed 3,187 female college students nationwide in
1985. They found that 27.5% of the women reported that they had been victims of
attempted or completed rape. The most conservative incident rate calculated was 50 per
1,000 women which is 10 to 15 times greater than that of the NCS.

Several important national studies followed up on the influential research by these
scholars. Kilkpatrick and his colleagues (Kilpatrick, Edmunds, & Seymour, 1992) conducted the National Women's Survey in 1991. They surveyed approximately 4,000 women
and reported that 13% of the women in their study had experienced an attempted or completed rape. While the authors failed to report incident rates, calculations by Koss (1992,
p. 70) suggest that they had a victimization rate of 7.2 completed rapes per 1,000 women.
This figure would have been much higher if attempted rapes were included (as is
the norm). This incident rate is five times higher than the NCS (Kilkpatrick Edmunds, &
Seymour, 1992, p. 2). Tjaden and Thoennes (1998, 2000) conducted the National Violence
Against Women Survey in 1995 and 1996. They report that 18% of the women in their
sample had experienced an attempted or completed rape. This translates into an incident
rate of 8.7 per 1,000 women (Tjaden & Thoennes, 2000, p. 13) which is twice that of the
NCVS (Tjaden & Thoennes, 1998). Most recently, Fisher and her colleagues (Fisher et al.,

2000) conducted the National College Women's Sexual Victimization in 1996 and found that about 20 to 25% of college women were raped. Their data also indicated that their victimization rate is 27.7 per 1,000 women. As stated previously, their completed rape rate was 11 times larger than the comparison study using NCVS methodology and their attempted rape rate was 6 times larger than the rate in the comparison study (p. 8).

In addition, these studies have clearly demonstrated that the vast majority of rapes are completed by someone who is known to the victim—in contrast to the stereotype of stranger rape (see Fisher et al., 2005, p. 494). While some earlier studies (Kirkpatrick & Kanin, 1957) raised this issue quite early in terms of rape research, it was not substantially challenged until the groundbreaking studies by Russell (1984) and Koss et al. (1987) brought this issue into the public consciousness.

Several critics proceeded to challenge these findings claiming that most rape was committed by strangers and that rape was relatively rare. They argued that rape estimates produced by newer research were inflated and that overly broad definitions of rape were used (Bonilla, 1993; Hoff-Sommers, 1994; Paglia, 1993; Roiphe, 1993). Gilbert (1991, 1992, 1994, 2005) has been one of the most prolific critics. He claims that overzealous, radical feminists who use "advocacy numbers" have created a "phantom epidemic" to secure funding for rape-related programs such as rape crisis centers. Gilbert's central claim is that feminist researchers have manufactured excessively high rates of rape, largely by using overly broad definitions. He repeatedly uses incident rates from official statistics, especially the NCS and NCVS, and contrasts them to prevalence rates from other studies in order to claim that the latter are highly inflated. He also argues that feminists use overly broad screening questions which fail to contain the words rape or attempted rape. He contends that respondents should not have their victimizations counted as rape unless they are willing to label the experience as a rape, even when behaviorally specific questions make it clear that they have experienced a rape according to definitions provided by legal statutes. This position is akin to saying that a victim of robbery must know they were robbed and not burglarized in order to count it in a survey even if the victim reported that someone took possessions from them by force.

Without any understanding or in-depth analysis of the shortcomings of the NCS and NCVS, the claims made by Gilbert and other critics are presented by an uncritical media which appears to validate their central theses. Issues such as operationalization of variables, behaviorally grounded screening questions, and differences between incident and prevalence rates are not amenable to 60 second sound bites. As a result, the media often leaves one with the impression that "feminist" studies find drastically higher rates because of overly broad and loose definitions of rape. Rarely, if ever, does media coverage examine the issue in sufficient depth to explain how methodological differences, rather than ideological ones, account for discrepancies in the findings. The NCS and the NCVS continue to play an important role in this debate. Even without the backlash movement, "the prestige and authority with which these costly surveys are imbued, their national scope, their replication every year, and the fact that they represent the official government source on reported and unreported rape statistics" (Russell & Bolen, 2000, p. 256) ensures that the NCVS will continue to assert its influence on the social construction of rape in this country. Unlike the NCS, however, there has been relatively little critical analysis of the NCVS.

It is important to note that the NCVS has made improvements and by doing so has increased the number of reported rapes significantly; however, the weaknesses outlined in this chapter also make it clear that it is far from perfect. In fact, in some ways, the improvements make it harder to demonstrate, especially to a lay audience, that rape rates continue to be measured very conservatively. Intuitively, even those without a research methods background could understand that an instrument which failed to even mention the word rape could not possibly count it with any accuracy. Translated, most people can understand that if you don't ask, victims won't tell. In contrast, those who insist upon arguing that feminist researchers exaggerate rape rates are even better served by the new NCVS which does, finally, at least mention the word rape. These critics are better situated to continue their attacks on feminist researchers using the conservative estimates provided by the NCVS. It is likely that the general public lacks the skills and attention span to dissect the detailed and complicated methodological arguments outlined in this paper. As such, the NCVS may have done more harm than good by making minimal changes to the way it measures rape and sexual assault.

The impact of the NCVS design and its inherent weaknesses also reach beyond the United States as other international victimization surveys model themselves after the NCVS (Koss, 1996; Russell & Bolen, 2000). Furthermore, since problems associated with the NCS were rarely noted and not well publicized even within the discipline (see Eigenberg, 1990), one can only anticipate that the methodological weaknesses associated with the NCVS also will have limited visibility.

It is unfortunate that the revisions made to the NCVS were done without significant input by "diverse groups with expertise on violence against women" (Koss, 1996, p. 67). If BJS had done so, they might have benefitted from some of the suggestions which have been published by experts in the field (Bachman, 2000; Belknap et al., 1999; Hamby & Koss, 2003; Koss, 1993; Koss et al., 2007; Russell & Bolen, 2000; Schwartz, 2000). Studies on rape should start with a clear conceptualization of rape which includes elements of force, non-consent, penetration, and statutory age; use a methodology which allows one to calculate legally defined rapes separate from other types of sexual coercion; and rely upon screening questions which facilitate recall and provide sufficient time for respondents to think about them. Interviewers need to be trained to create a safe climate for disclosure and future research should use a variety of methods so that they can evaluate which methods of data collection are most apt to result in disclosure. Behaviorally specific screening questions are mandatory and researchers should try to use a variety of them. Researchers also need to wrestle with the difficult issue of defining child sexual assault and ways to measure that type of victimization more accurately. For example, some acts which might not qualify as coercive, illegal sexual acts when perpetrated against adults, may qualify as illegal acts of child sexual assault (e.g., fondling). Unfortunately, however, it appears that these suggestions have little practical utility for the administration of the NCVS. It seems unlikely that any further changes to the NCVS will occur in the near future, given that it took almost twenty years before BJS was willing to alter the NCS.

Assuming that any massive redesign is unlikely in the near future, several actions remain that should be taken to ensure that the NCVS data are interpreted properly. Scholars in the field must be acutely aware of the serious shortcoming of the NCVS and they need to educate both lay audiences and students about these problems. Like the NCS, it is critical that the NCVS's deficiencies are cited in introductory textbooks and that they are well advertised within the discipline. Research using the NCVS for secondary data analysis should be required to discuss the weaknesses of this data set in some significant depth if these studies are going to be published. For example, there is the risk that scholars using NCVS data make recommendations that women should or should not fight back in order to best evade a rapist when, in fact, they are making conclusions based on a very weak data set. Most importantly, there must be additional governmental funding for other large-scale studies on rape using national samples. Understanding of the magnitude and prevalence of rape has been greatly influenced by these studies (e.g., Fisher et al., 2000; Kilkpatrick et al., 1992; Tjaden & Thoennes, 1998, 2000). These types of projects need to continue to explore better methodologies and refine our ability to count rape victimization. These data sets, however, are now over ten years old. It is imperative that research on rape remains a high priority if we are to maintain current data sets that continue to improve upon existing studies, but the current economic climate and budget constraints may make this difficult.

Unfortunately, the hegemonic battle over how much rape has obscured many other important research questions. There is still too little understanding or information about men who rape, and we have barely begun to scratch the surface in terms of understanding how women cope with and process rape experiences in their daily lives. Nonetheless, the battle over how much rape exists is critically important to the social construction of rape. While the newer studies on rape suggest high incident and prevalence rates, especially for adolescent and young women, critics continue to try to conceptualize rape as a rare and aberrant event committed by deranged strangers and experienced by a few unfortunate women. In sum, then, this debate is a battle over the hegemonic definition of rape. Newer rape studies provide the ammunition to attack these traditional rape stereotypes. Doing so, however, is a threat to traditional, patriarchal, social structures. In sum, data which suggests that rape is a widespread event and that most perpetrators are acquaintances (including lovers, dates, and husbands) has the power to drastically redefine gender relations and the very nature of intimate relationships—including the family. As such, this battle is not a simple debate over how much rape exists, but rather a much more complex struggle over the definitions of gender, sexuality, and power in our society.

REFERENCES

BACHMAN, R. (2000). A comparison of annual incidence rates and contextual characteristics of intimate-partner violence against women from the National Crime Victimization Survey (NCVS) and the National Violence Against Women Survey (NVAWS). *Violence Against Women, 6*, 839–867.

BACHMAN, R. & TAYLOR, B. (1994). Violence and rape by the redesigned National Crime Victimization Survey. *Justice Quarterly, 11*, 499–512.

BELKNAP, J., FISHER, B., & CULLEN, F. (1999). The development of a comprehensive measure of the sexual victimization of college women. *Violence Against Women, 5*, 185–214.

BIDERMAN, A. and REISS, A. (1967). On exploring the 'dark figure' of crime. *The Annals, 374*, 1–15.

BONILLA, M. (1993). Cultural assault: What feminists are doing to rape ought to be a crime. *Policy Review, 66*, 22–29.

BUREAU OF JUSTICE STATISTICS. (1985). *The crime of rape*. Washington, D.C.: U.S. Department of Justice.

BUREAU OF JUSTICE STATISTICS. (1989a). *Criminal victimization in the United States, 1987*. Washington, D.C.: U.S. Department of Justice.

BUREAU OF JUSTICE STATISTICS (1994). *Technical background on the redesigned National Crime Victimization Survey*. Retrieved from http://www.ojp.usdoj.gov/pub/bjs/asii/ncsrtb.txt

BUREAU OF JUSTICE STATISTICS. (1995). *National Crime Victimization Survey redesign*. Retrieved from http://bjs.ojp.usdoj.gov/content/pub/pdf/ncsrqa.pdf

BUREAU OF JUSTICE STATISTICS. (1996). *Criminal victimization in the United States, 1993*. Washington, D.C.: U.S. Department of Justice.

BUREAU OF JUSTICE STATISTICS. (2008). *National Crime Victimization Survey Violent Crime Trends, 1973–2008*. Retrieved from http://bjs.ojp.usdoj.gov/content/glance/tables/viortrdtab.cfm

BUREAU OF JUSTICE STATISTICS. (n.d.[a]) *Key Facts at a Glance*. Retrieved from http://bjs.ojp.usdoj.gov/content/glance/rape.cfm.

BUREAU OF JUSTICE STATISTICS. (n.d.[b]) *Key Facts at a Glance: Violent Crime*. Retrieved from http://bjs.ojp.usdoj.gov/content/glance/rape.cfm.

BUREAU OF JUSTICE STATISTICS. (n.d. [c]). *Survey Methodology for Criminal Victimization in the United States, 2006* (n.d.). Retrieved from http://bjs.ojp.usdoj.gov/content/pub/pdf/cvus/cvus06mt.pdf

DODGE, R. & TURNER, A. (1981). Methodological foundations for establishing a national survey of victimization. In R. Lehnen and W. Skogan (Eds.), *The national crime survey: Working papers, Volume I: Current and historical perspectives* (pp. 2–6). Washington, D.C.: U.S. Department of Justice.

EIGENBERG, H. (1990). The National crime survey and rape: The case of the missing question. *Justice Quarterly, 7*, 655–671.

ESTRICH, S. (1987). Real rape: How the legal system victimizes women who say no. Cambridge, MA: Harvard University Press.

FISHER, B. (2009). The effects of survey question wording on rape estimates: Evidence from a quasi-experimental design. *Violence Against Women, 15*, 133–147.

FISHER, B., CULLEN, F., & DAIGLE, L. (2005). The discovery of acquaintance rape: The salience of methodological innovation and rigor. *Journal of Interpersonal Violence, 20*, 493–500.

FISHER, B., CULLEN, F., & TURNER, M. (2000). *The sexual victimization of college women*. Washington, D.C.: Bureau of Justice Statistics.

GOTTFREDSON, M. (1986). Substantive contributions of victimization surveys. In M. Tonry and N. Morris, *Crime and justice: An annual review of research, Volume 7* (pp. 251–287). Chicago: University of Chicago Press.

GOVE, W., HUGHES, M. & GEERKEN, M. (1984). Are Uniform Crime Reports a valid indicator of the index crime? An affirmative answer with minor qualifications. *Criminology, 23*, 451–501.

GILBERT, N. (1991). The phantom epidemic of sexual assault. *The Public Interest, 103*, 54–65.

GILBERT, N. (1992). Realities and mythologies of rape. *Society, 31*, 4–10.

GILBERT, N. (1994). Miscounting social ills. *Society, 31*, 18–26.

GILBERT, N. (2005). Examining the facts: Advocacy research overstates the incidence of date rape and acquaintance rape. D. Loseke, R. Gelles, and M. Cavanaugh (Eds.), *Current controversies on family violence* (pp. 117–128). Newbury Park: Sage.

HAMBY, S., & KOSS, M. (2003). Shades of gray: A qualitative study of terms used in the measurement of sexual victimization. *Psychology of Women Quarterly, 27*, 243–255.

HOFF-SOMMERS, C. (1994). *Who stole feminism*. New York: Simon & Schuster.

KILKPATRICK, D., EDMUNDS, C., & SEYMOUR, A. (1992). *Rape in America: A report to the nation*. Arlington, VA: National Victim Center.

KINDERMANN, C., LYNCH, J., & CANTOR, D. (1997). *Effects of the redesign on victimization estimates*. Washington, D.C.: Bureau of Justice Statistics.

MALE AGGRESSION ON A UNIVERSITY CAMPUS. *American Sociological Review*, 22, 52–58.

KOSS, M. (1992). The under detection of rape: A critical assessment of incidence data. *Journal of Social Issues, 48*, 61–76.

KOSS, M. (1993). Detecting the scope of rape: A review of prevalence research methods. *Journal of Interpersonal Violence, 8*, 198–222.

KOSS, M. (1996). The measurement of rape victimization in crime surveys. *Criminal Justice and Behavior, 23*, 55–69.

KOSS, M., ABBEY, A., CAMPBELL, R., COOK, S., NORRIS, J., TEST, M., ULLMAN, S., WEST, C., & WHITE, S. (2007). Revising the SES: A collaborative process to improve assessment of sexual aggression and victimization. *Psychology of Women Quarterly, 31*, 357–370.

KOSS, M., DINERO, T., SEIBEL, C. & COX, S. (1988). Stranger and acquaintance rape: Are there differences in the victim's experience. *Psychology of Women Quarterly, 12*, 1–24.

KOSS, M., GIDYCZ, C., & WISNIEWSKI, N. (1987). The scope of rape: Incidence and prevalence of sexual aggression and victimization in a national sample of higher education students. *Journal of Consulting and Clinical Psychology, 50*, 455–457.

MALTZ, M., & ZAWITZ, M. (1998). *Displaying violent crime trends using estimates from the National Crime Victimization Survey*. Washington, D.C.: Bureau of Justice Statistics.

MENARD, S. (2005). *Reporting sexual assault: A social ecology perspective*. New York: LFB Scholarly Publishing.

O'BRIEN, R. (1986). Rare events, sample size, and statistical problems in the analysis of the NCS city surveys. *Journal of Criminal Justice, 14*, 441–448.

PAGLIA, C. (1993). *New essays: Vamps and tramps*. New York: Vintage.

RAND, M. C. (1998). *Criminal victimization 1997: Changes 1996–97 with Trends 1993–97*. Washington, DC: U.S. Department of Justice.

RAND, M. (2009). *Criminal Victimization, 2008*. Washington, D.C.: Bureau of Justice Statistics.

RAND, M. & CATALANO, S. (2007). *Criminal Victimization, 2006*. Washington, D.C.: Bureau of Justice Statistics.

RENNISON, C. (1999). *Criminal victimization 1998: Changes 1997–98 with Trends 1993–98*. Washington, DC: U.S. Department of Justice.

RENNISON, C. M. (2000). *Criminal Victimization 1999: Changes 1998–99 with Trends 1993–99*. Washington, D.C.: Bureau of Justice Statistics.

RENNISON, C. (2001). *Criminal victimization 2000: Changes 1999–2000 with Trends 1993–2000*. Washington, DC: U.S. Department of Justice.

RENNISON, C. M. (2002). *Criminal Victimization 2001: Changes 2000–01 with Trends 1993–2001*. Washington D.C.: Bureau of Justice Statistics.

RINGLE, C. (1997). *Criminal victimization 1996: Changes 1995–96 with Trends 1993–96*. Washington, DC: U.S. Department of Justice.

ROIPHE, K. (1993). *The morning after: Sex, fear, and feminism*. Boston: Little Brown.

RUSSELL, D. (1984). *Sexual exploitation: Rape, child sexual abuse and workplace harassment*. Beverly Hills: Sage.

RUSSELL, D. & BOLEN, R. (2000). *The epidemic of rape and child sexual abuse in the United States*. Thousand Oaks, CA: Sage.

SANDERS, S. & REINISCH, M. (1999). Would you say you "had sex" if . . .? *The Journal of the American Medical Association, 281*, 275–277.

SCHWARTZ, M. (2000). Methodological issues in the use of survey data for measuring and characterizing violence against women. *Violence Against Women, 6*, 815–838.

SKOGAN, W. (1975). Measurement problems in official and survey crime rates. *Journal of Criminal Justice, 3*, 17–32.

SKOGAN, W. (1977). Dimensions of the 'dark figure' of unreported crime. *Crime and Delinquency, 23*, 41–50.

TJADEN, P. & THOENNES, N. (1998). *Prevalence, incidence, and consequences of violence against women: Findings from the National Violence Against Women Survey*. Washington, DC: National Institute of Justice.

TJADEN, P. & THOENNES, N. (2000). *Full report of the prevalence, incidence, and consequences of violence against women: Findings from the National Violence Against Women Survey*. Washington, DC: National Institute of Justice and Centers for Disease Control and Prevention.

TURNER, A. (1981). The San Jose recall study. In R. Lehnen and W. Skogan (Eds.), *The national crime survey: Working papers, Volume I: Current and historical perspectives* (pp. 22–27). Washington, D.C.: U.S. Department of Justice.

ENDNOTES

1. The problems with measuring assault also are related to the NCS failure to measure interpersonal crime effectively (see Eigenberg, 2000).

2. Obviously, these questions also should have included girlfriends and wives to reflect the gender neutral nature of the instrument.

3. According to BJS, these included introducing a new sample based on 2000 Census data which resulted in shifts in population and hence the sampling process. Introduction of these new households also likely affected bounding estimates (see Rand, 2006, for a more detailed discussion).

4. This figure would clearly be even larger given that the sample size has decreased since this publication was issued.

5. The authors don't provide this figure, but using other data it is possible to make a very rough estimate of the magnitude of the change.

17

Domestic Violence or Intimate Partner Violence

Roslyn Muraskin

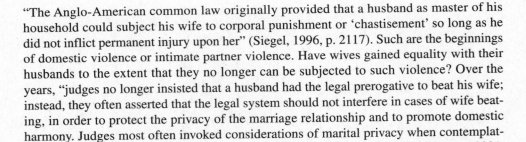

"The Anglo-American common law originally provided that a husband as master of his household could subject his wife to corporal punishment or 'chastisement' so long as he did not inflict permanent injury upon her" (Siegel, 1996, p. 2117). Such are the beginnings of domestic violence or intimate partner violence. Have wives gained equality with their husbands to the extent that they no longer can be subjected to such violence? Over the years, "judges no longer insisted that a husband had the legal prerogative to beat his wife; instead, they often asserted that the legal system should not interfere in cases of wife beating, in order to protect the privacy of the marriage relationship and to promote domestic harmony. Judges most often invoked considerations of marital privacy when contemplating the prosecution of middle- and upper-class men for wife beating" (MacKinnon, 2001, pp. 24–25).

Domestic violence has traditionally been viewed as a private matter rather than as a social matter that requires criminal justice intervention. From a historical perspective, the criminal justice system has failed repeatedly to respond to cases of domestic violence and has been cloaked in secrecy. Mandatory proarrest policies were initiated by many law enforcement agencies. Such cases have evoked feelings of continuous frustration both from law enforcement officers responding to such calls and from battered women seeking protection. The policies followed were mediation or separation, leaving batterers with impunity and victims without sufficient protection. Unfortunately, such policies have led to periods of silence by the victims. These victims have tended to hide their problems and blame themselves. It has been referred to as "women blaming" or "victim blaming." Victim isolation and feeling that they are unique make it harder for abused women to come forward and ask for help.

The Department of Justice continues to reaffirm its commitment to ending any violence against women. In 2009 the 15th anniversary of the Violence Against Women Act (VAWA), which was signed into law on September 13, 1994, was celebrated. According to the Department of Justice, since the passing of the act, countless lives have been saved, whereby the voices of the survivors have been heard, and families continue to be protected somewhat. Yet, domestic violence continues in what some have called epidemic proportions without regard to socioeconomic conditions. In the early 1970s it seemed as if the issue of battered women had come out of the shadow. The VAWA continued to help women feel that they had the right to control their own bodies and lives, and from this women's hotlines and crisis centers were formed. From a historical perspective, crimes against women were professed as anything but crimes. The feeling by judges was "let's kiss and make up and get out of my court."

The passage of VAWA demonstrated that violence against women was to play a major role in the law. On a practical level VAWA offered a remedy that provides for at most times the only legal redress for violence against women. VAWA has avoided the effects of state tort immunities, marital rape exceptions, as well as unduly short statutes of limitations. Constitutional challenges against VAWA were made, but VAWA has withstood most challenges. Taking into account that three out of four women would become victims at one time in their lifetimes, that violence was the leading cause of injury to women ages 15–44, that as many as 50 percent of women and children become homeless as a result of leaving violent situations at home, and that battering was the largest single injury to women in the United States, this act has withstood most challenges to date.

With prevention will come solutions. The recognition that there exists such a problem as domestic violence is a big step. Battered women should have the right to self-determination, including the decision to stay with or leave their partners and pick themselves up and start their lives over without fear of reprisal.

> In both England and the United States, the focus of feminist consciousness raising about domestic violence was on intimate violence in the context of heterosexual relationships. The term first used to describe the problem was "wife abuse," which revealed that it was viewed primarily through the lens of a marital relationship. (Dalton & Schneider, 2001, pp. 20–27)

According to Schneider, the term *domestic violence* was associated with the inferior position of women and her place in the family and as someone who both was discriminated in the workplace and lacked educational opportunities. Whereas the term *intimate violence* has been thought of as coming from a psychological perspective, "this approach which had predated the feminist analysis of the 1960's, had been concerned with how violence is linked to specific pathology in the individual's personality traits and psychological disorders" (2000, pp. 20–27).

Connected to this issue is the enforcement of any laws by the police. "In the early 1970s, class-action lawsuits were filed in New York City and Oakland, California, which challenged police's failure to arrest batterers. This litigation raised the dramatic notion that domestic violence was criminal, sanctionable activity that was harm against the 'public,' the state, not just an individual woman, and should be treated the same as an assault on a stranger" (MacKinnon, p. 51).

There appear to be differences as to the meaning of domestic violence. Richard Gelles and Murray Straus believed that the definition should be limited to physical abuse: "specific, definable acts of omission and commission that are harmful to individuals in families" (MacKinnon, p. 59). We must look at the cycle of violence as representing a pattern of wrongful behavior. Lenore Walker (1989), the author of "Cycle of Violence," broke it into three phases: "the tension-building phase; the acute battering incident; and the tranquil, loving (or at least non-violent) phase. . . ."

> During the tension-building phase, minor battering incidents occur; slaps, pinches, controlled verbal abuse, and psychological warfare may all be part of this phase. The women's attempts to calm the batterer can range from a show of kind, nurturing behavior to simply staying out of the way. What really happens in this phase is that she allows herself to be abused in ways that, to her, are comparatively minor. More than anything, she wants to prevent the batterer's violence from growing.
>
> As the cycle progresses, the battered woman's placatory techniques become less effective. Violence and verbal abuse worsen. Each partner senses the impending loss of control and becomes more desperate, this mutual desperation fueling the tension even more. Many battered women say that the psychological anguish of this phase is its worst aspect. (Some will even provoke an acute incident, just to "get it over with" and, at the cost of grave physical injury, save themselves from real insanity or death.) But, sooner or later, exhausted from the unrelenting stress, the battered woman withdraws emotionally.
>
> During the acute phase—set apart from minor battering incidents by its savagery, destructiveness, and uncontrolled nature—the violence has escalated to a point of rampage, injury, brutality, and sometimes death; the acute battering incident is somehow inevitable.
>
> When the acute battering incident ends, the final phase in the Cycle of Violence begins. In this phase, usually all tension and violence are gone, which both members of the couple experience as a profound relief. This is a tranquil period, during which the batterer may exhibit warm, nurturing, loving behavior toward his spouse. He knows he's been "bad," and tries to atone; he promises never to do it again; he begs her forgiveness. (Walker, pp. 42–45)

Domestic violence or intimate partner violence is much more menacing and multifaceted than any other crime of assault. The problem with these cases is that both the abuser and the attacker are in a close relationship with each other. The victim therefore is rendered helpless and unable not only to use independent judgment but to call for help. What happens is that the victim turns to the assaulter for some kind of connection and/or support.

It was not until the decision in the case of *Tracey Thurman et al. v. City of Torrington et al.* (595 F. Supp. 1521, U.S. District Court for the District of Connecticut, 1984) that action by law enforcement had to take place to protect the victim.

> In October 1982, Charles Thurman attacked plaintiff Tracey Thurman at the home of Judy Bentley and Richard St. Hilaire in the City of Torrington. Mr. St. Hilaire and Ms. Bentley made a formal complaint of the attack to one of the unnamed defendant police officers and requested efforts to keep the plaintiff's husband, Charles Thurman, off their property.
>
> After many altercations between Tracey Thurman and her husband Charles and after Tracey Thurman received an order of protection from the police there still continued to be persistence on the part of Charles Thurman to get to his wife.
>
> On June 10, 1983, Charles Thurman appeared at the Bentley-St. Hilaire residence in the early afternoon and demanded to speak to Tracey. Tracey, remaining indoors, called the defendant police department asking that Charles be picked up for violation of his probation.

After about 15 minutes, Tracey went outside to speak to her husband in an effort to persuade him not to take or hurt Charles Jr. Soon thereafter, Charles began to stab Tracey repeatedly in the chest, neck and throat.

Approximately 25 minutes after Tracey's call to the Torrington Police Department and after her stabbing, a single police officer, the defendant, Petrovits, arrived on the scene. Upon the arrival of Officer Petrovits at the scene of the stabbing, Charles Thurman was holding a bloody knife. Charles then dropped the knife and, in the presence of Petrovits, kicked the plaintiff Tracey Thurman in the head and ran into the Bentley-St. Hilaire residence. Charles returned from within the residence holding the plaintiff Charles Thurman, Jr., and dropped the child on his wounded mother. Charles then kicked Tracey in the head a second time.

Soon thereafter, defendants DeAngelo, Nurkirk, and Columbia arrived on the scene but still permitted Charles Thurman to wander about the crowd and to continue to threaten Tracey. Finally, upon approaching Tracey once again, this time while she was lying on a stretcher, Charles Thurman was arrested and taken into custody. (Dalton & Schneider, pp. 887–888)

At work Charles Thurman had boasted to everyone that he was going to get his wife and kill her. Tracey Thurman sued the Torrington Police Department and received an award of $2.3 million, and her case gave the impetus for mandatory police arrests in cases of violence against intimate partners. This evidence indicated that there was disparate treatment in how police handled such cases of violence. As a result we have seen more police arrests, but we have also seen more women take it upon themselves to kill their abuser and thus become the defendant.

Regardless of our understanding of what battering is or what it does to its victims, usually the women, we have seen the legal system struggle in how to handle these kinds of cases from a legal perspective. According to Schneider, "legal reform for battered women who kill has been one of the most significant areas of feminist lawmaking on domestic violence. In courtrooms around the United States, lawyers have challenged assumptions about battered women in general, and battered women who kill their assailants in particular" (2000, p. 717). Initially women who killed their abusers found themselves being denied equal rights to present the circumstances surrounding the killings, and to this day this is a difficult defense. Sometime ago, it was William Blackstone who noted that "a woman who killed her husband was committing 'treason.' If the baron kills his femme it is the same as if he had killed a stranger, or any other person; but if the femme kills her baron, it is regarded by law as a much more atrocious crime, as she not only breaks through the restraints of humanity and conjugal affection, but throws off all subjection to the authority of her husband" (p. 718).

From all these cases we have seen the development of the battered woman defense. "With respect to battered women who kill, gender bias pervades the entire criminal process. It permeates perceptions of appropriate self-defense and the legal standard of self defense" (p. 718). In situations where the woman has killed, such a defense may very well fall under the rubric of self-defense or excusable action, but such a defense is not yet readily accepted. There is still the feeling that this kind of defense gives women special treatment. This defense is referred to as the battered woman's defense or battered woman syndrome, but such defenses are viewed as being outside the realm of equal treatment.

Although the law of self-defense is purportedly universally applicable it is widely recognized that social concepts of justification have been shaped by male experience. . . . the circumstances in which women kill in self-defense are usually related to physical or sexual abuse by an intimate, not to the conventional barroom brawl or fist fight with a stranger that shapes male experience with self-defense. The acts of men and women are subject to a different set of legal expectations and standards. The man's act, while not always legally condoned, is viewed sympathetically. The law . . . has never protected a wife who killed her husband after finding with him another woman. A woman's husband simply does not belong to her in the same way she belongs to him. (pp. 719–720)

The woman who brings forth a battered woman defense or battered woman syndrome faces tremendous obstacles when trying to demonstrate the reasons for her actions. With the defense of self-defense there is the attribute of retreating in a situation where harm is liable to befall a victim. The root of self-defense is the aspect of sensibleness. This is hard to prove. There has to be the ability to overcome gender-based stereotypes, and stereotypes do not die quickly. A full range of defenses should be available to women who are victims, but the rationale for such a defense is hard to come by.

For example, in the case of *People v. Evelyn Humphrey* (1996), a defendant claimed that she shot her spouse in self-defense. Expert testimony was presented (as is usually the case in such instances), and Dr. Lee Bowker gave testimony with regard to the battered woman syndrome. He indicated that such a syndrome "is not just a psychological construction, but it's a term for a wide variety of controlling mechanisms" (Dalton & Schneider, p. 750). Dr. Bowker had looked at approximately 1,000 battered women and was able to establish that they were incorrectly depicted "as cardboard figures, paper-thin punching bags who merely absorb the violence but didn't do anything about it. He found that battered women often employ strategies to stop the beatings, including hiding, running away, counter-violence, seeking the help of friends or family, going to a shelter, and contacting police" (p. 750).

Most of these women remain in the situation, for they start to blame themselves. They also look for ways to correct the situation so their spouses will stop abusing them. What it comes down to is the physical control the man has over the woman, as well as a question of economics. It is sad that these women who may leave one battering situation repeat their same mistakes in subsequent relationships by always putting the blame on themselves. "Anybody who is abused over a period of time becomes sensitive to the abuser's behavior and when sees a change acceleration begin in that behavior, it tells them something is going to happen" (p. 750).

In this case Hampton was 49 years old, weighed twice as much as the defendant, and was in a relationship that involved the cycle of violence as put forward by Lenore Walker. The defendant was charged with murder. After the judge advised her of what battered woman syndrome consisted of—"whether or not the defendant held the necessary subjective honest [belief,] which is a requirement for both perfect and imperfect self-defense. . . . you may consider the evidence concerning the syndrome and its effects only for limited purpose of showing . . . that the defendant's reactions, as demonstrated by the evidence, are not inconsistent with her having been physically abused or the beliefs, perceptions, or behavior of victims of domestic violence, whether such evidence as presented could exonerate the defendant" (p. 750)—she was convicted of voluntary manslaughter and sent to prison for eight years.

The case of *State v. Kelly* (1984) defines battered woman syndrome as "a series of common characteristics that appear in women who are abused physically and psychologically over an extended period of time by the dominant male figure in their lives" (p. 753).

In the 1980s there was a study conducted in Duluth, Minnesota. This project (Domestic Intervention Project) gained somewhat of a national reputation for being the first to develop what was to be police intervention in cases of intimate partner violence. Not all jurisdictions adopted this plan.

An all-out understanding is needed that this is a very real crime and a crime that involves mostly women who are abused, but men as well. Programs need to be put into place that make it easy to identify such problems and to protect and empower women in such situations. Women should not be afraid to step forward and indicate that they are indeed victims. The law must provide that all people are protected and that women as victims need the same protection as any other person. We have to make it easier for women to come forward and make their claims of violence, be listened to, be counseled, and have the law protect them. We have to have agencies in place that are available to women in need. A coherent policy has to be put in place that protects women from violent acts. A best-practice policy needs to be put in place that is part of an all-exclusive program that responds on the part of both law enforcement and the courts. There must be education and funding so that community members and family members understand this problem and do not turn away. We need to understand not just the physical hurt done to these victims, but also the psychological damage done. And most of all, shelters need to be put in place that do not answer, "sorry, we are filled up today, try us tomorrow."

REFERENCES

DALTON, C., & SCHNEIDER, E. M. (2001). *Battered women and the law*. New York: Foundation Press.

MacKINNON, C. A. (2001). *Sex equality*. New York: Foundation Press.

SIEGEL, R. B. (1996). The rule of love: Wife beating as a prerogative and privacy. *Yale Law Journal*, *105*, 2117–2206.

WALKER, L. E. A. (1989). *Terrifying love: Why battered women kill and how society responds*. Harper Collins Publisher.

CASES

People v. Evelyn Humphrey (1996) 13 Cal. 4th 1073

State v. Kelly (1984) 97 N.J. 178

18

Older Battered Women

Telling the Stories of Four Women Who Lived with IPV for 20 or More Years

Suzanne Faries Lowe and Laura J. Moriarty

3/15/12

❖

ABSTRACT

There has been a great deal of research during the past four decades on the topic of domestic violence. Very little research has been conducted, however, on the effects of long-term intimate partner violence (IPV) on older women. In this chapter, four women participated in an in-depth study where their ages ranged between 63 and 70, and each had been in a violent and abusive relationship for at least 20 years. Two of the women were divorced from their abusers, while two were still married. Each of the women was interviewed twice, for a total of between 4½ and 6 hours. The interview topics included discussions of their childhood, courtship, marriage, and relationships with their now adult children. Social learning, social bond, feminist, and exchange theories were used as a framework for understanding the dynamics involved in these abusive relationships.

INTRODUCTION

Much research has been conducted on the topic of intimate partner violence over the past few decades. Most of it, however, has focused on violence against women generally or that which occurs in homes with children. Very little research has focused on the impact of women living in a violent and abusive intimate partner relationship for twenty years or more. Most of the research on violence against older women does not differentiate between partner violence and caretaker violence. By lumping non-partner and partner violence together, we ignore the special dynamics that have existed in these particular relationships over their entire course of the abuse. In this chapter, we begin with a discussion of what we already know about older abused women. Then we shift the focus to a description of long-term abuse, reporting the results after extensively interviewing four women who were between the ages of 63 and 70, and who had been or are still in a violent abusive relationship for at least 20 years. We conclude with recommendations from the women to those in similar situations to cope with the abuse.

WHAT DO WE KNOW ABOUT OLDER WOMEN WHO ARE ABUSED?

The characteristics of older women victims of intimate partner violence (IPV) include many of the same factors as for younger women. Some factors include low socioeconomic status, minority status, and cognitive impairment (Harrell, Toronjo, McLaughlin, Pavlik, Hyman, and Bitondo-Dyer, 2002). However, for many older women physical frailty due to arthritis, osteoporosis, and the general physical decline associated with aging (Allsworth, Zierler, Lapane, Krieger, Hogan, & Harlow, 2005) exasperates the high toll that living in an abusive relationship for many years has on the mental health of victims (Allsworth, et al., 2000; Astbury, Atkinson, Duke Easteal, Kurrie, Tait, & Turner, 2000; Flannery, 2003).

becomes harder mentally over time

Women who have been in abusive relationships for many years exhibit very low self-esteem and a sense of overwhelming powerlessness (Phillips, 2000). The primary tactic of the successful abuser is to isolate his victim. As a result of having been isolated from family and friends, these women have come to rely on their abuser exclusively for companionship (Brandl & Horan, 2002; Penhale, 1998). Older women tend to be painfully aware of how precarious their financial situation would be if they left (Vinton, 1999; Brogden & Nijhar, 2000) and have often developed an emotional and psychological dependence on their abuser (Wilke & Vinton, 2003; Hattendorf & Tollerud, 1997). Many older women who have tried to escape their abuser in the past found their efforts to be futile and, in some cases, those attempts only served to escalate the violence (Brandl, Hebert, Rozwadowski, & Spangler, 2003). As asserted by Kalmuss and Straus (1990, p. 379), "marital dependency reinforces that women will tolerate physical abuse from their husbands." Rennison and Rand (2003) add that leaving could result in possibly living in poverty and the loss of life and health insurance at a time when that is particularly needed. Plus, "by leaving, these victims risk stigmatization by friends and family and a loss of the social network to which they have belonged for some time" (Rennison & Rand, 2003, p. 1426). For many older women, there is the added fear that if they report the abuse they will end up in a nursing home (Astbury, et al., 2000): A real fear that is not commonly found among younger victims.

Violent relationships evolve over time. People change through their experiences, and even the same event may have a different effect on the people who share it. Women who are abused throughout a relationship sometimes develop what Lenore Walker (1979) refers to as "learned helplessness." Learned helplessness can be defined as a "psychological state induced by previous experiences with situations perceived as uncontrollable. Disturbances in motivation, emotions, and cognitive processing result in symptoms including (a) passivity, (b) depression, and (c) decreased expectations regarding future outcomes" (Hattendorf & Tollerud, 1997, p. 16). Women learn, over time and much abuse, that they have no control over the outcome of their situation. If she fights back, she is beaten more severely. If she passively submits, she will still be hurt, but perhaps not as severely. Passivity becomes synonymous with survival.

It has been noted by researchers that the likelihood of physical violence decreases as the ages of the abuser and victim increase (Wilke & Vinton, 2003; Mezey, Post, & Maxwell, 2002). However, as Mouton, et al. (2004) point out, if verbal abuse is counted in victimization statistics, abuse rates for young and older women are similar (Mouton, Rodabough, Rovi, Hunt, Talamantes, Brzyski, & Burge, 2004). Zink and colleagues (2006) add the caveat that while their study demonstrated that violence often decreases with age, psychological and emotional abuse often escalates (Zink, Jacobson, Regan, Fisher, and Pabst, 2006). Even after physical abuse ceases as a necessary tool of subjugation, the exercise of mastery can usually be maintained with words. The threat of violence is always present as a remembrance to reinforce domination.

Older women are more vulnerable to fractures due to osteoporosis and arthritis (Mouton, Rovi, Furniss, & Lasser, 1999). Allsworth and colleagues (2004), in a longitudinal study of the inception of perimenopause, found that the "experience of abuse was associated with delayed onset" (p. 938) of perimenopause, and that some research has also found it is related to an "increased risk of breast cancer" (p. 942). According to Campbell and colleagues (Campbell, Jones, Dienemann, Kub, Schollenberger, O'Campo, Gielen, & Wynne, 2002), 40–45% of physically abused women are forced into sexual activities by their intimate partners. Victims of abuse are "more likely to have gynecological diseases, vaginal bleeding or infections, fibroids, pelvic pain, and urinary tract infections, all of which are associated with sexual abuse" (p. 1158), as well as STDs, HIV/AIDS, and cervical neoplasia (cancer and pre-cancerous cell changes) (Coker, Davis, Arias, Desai, Sanderson, Brandt, & Smith, 2002; Coker, Sanderson, Fadden, & Pirisi, 2000; Plichta, 2004). The most common locations for physical IPV injuries are the face, neck, upper torso, breast, and abdomen (Banks & Ackerman, 2002).

In an article focusing on the often unrecognized consequences of traumatic brain injuries suffered by victims of IPV battering, Banks and Ackerman (2002) found that brain injuries are cumulative, resulting in greater damage with repeat brain insult. They found that such injuries are often subtle and go unrecognized. These injuries can result in a "disruption in the speed, efficiency, execution, and integration of mental processes" (p. 134). These deficits are often misdiagnosed as dementia, especially in older women.

According to Campbell and colleagues (2002, p. 1158), besides the fear and stress associated with IPV, the major long-term symptoms include "pain or discomfort from recurring central nervous system symptoms such as headaches, back pain, fainting, or seizures." They further found that battered women also showed more "signs of symptoms, and illnesses such as colds and flu, and cardiac problems, such as hypertension and chest pains" (p. 1158), as well as depression, chronic pain, stress, osteoarthritis, gastrointestinal disorders, and gynecological symptoms. Depression and its associated symptoms constitute a major concern for those treating abused women (Miller, 2006; Ozment & Lester, 2001). It is strongly argued by most researchers that the reason for the increase in physical ailments among abuse victims is that high levels of stress are known to have a depressive effect on the immune system (Coker et al., 2002; Carlson, McNutt, & Choi, 2003; Nurius, Macy, Bhuyan, Holt, Kernic, and Rivara, 2003). The overall conclusion then, based on the literature, is that there is similarity between older and younger victims of IPV but the duration of the abuse (20 or more plus years) heightens or exasperates these conditions.

STUDY METHODS

This exploratory research employed in-depth interviewing of four women between the ages of 63 and 70 years. Each woman was interviewed twice for approximately 2–2½ hours each time. Long interviews were used to allow greater depth. The interviews used open-ended questions to encourage unfettered responses and were divided into three parts: the focused life history, the details of the experience, and the subjects' reflections on the meaning of their experience. The research sought to capture the "lived experience" of these women by seeing their lives from their perspective (Padgett, 1998).

Older women victims of IPV are usually reluctant to report such abuse; thus, they seldom seek help at shelters and are often unknown to shelter service providers. This makes finding a sample of women over the age of 55 who have spent at least 20 years with an abuser problematic. Nevertheless, we tried to secure a sample using shelters in the Richmond metropolitan area of Virginia but it proved fruitless. It was decided that using a shelter in a more elderly populous area of Florida would be a better approach. Contacts were made with the Betty Griffin House in St. Augustine, Florida. The shelter staff agreed to post fliers about the study seeking volunteer study participants. Three participants were acquired through the use of this method. Participants contacted the primary researcher using a toll-free number and appointments for interviews were scheduled. Shelter staff arranged rooms in the administrative and counseling services building where the interviews were conducted. Another participant was identified by personal contact, and lived in Richmond, VA. She agreed to participate and was interviewed over two days on the campus of Virginia Commonwealth University.

The criteria for participants required that each subject be at least 55 years of age and have spent at least 20 years in an abusive relationship. All interviews were tape recorded and then transcribed. After transcription, the tapes were destroyed. The names of the participants were changed to conceal their identities.

SUMMARY INFORMATION ABOUT THE PARTICIPANTS

The participants ranged in age from 63 to 70 years of age, with the average age being 66 years. Most of the women were married with half being married to the abuser. The number of years in the abusive relationship ranged from 21 to 47 years, with the average number being 34 (33.75) years. The pseudonyms for the women are Alice, Beth, Cathy, and Dot.

DESCRIPTIONS OF THE ABUSE

The first time Beth was aware that her husband might hurt her was on their honeymoon, when he pushed her against a wall. She said that within three or four months his pattern of physical abuse was established. Dot reported that she did not feel fear of her husband until they had been married for twelve years. He had been verbally abusive the whole time, but had never done anything physically threatening. Since that time, however, he has threatened her with firearms and by drawing his fist back in a motion indicating that he intended to strike her. While he has never actually hit her, she is convinced that he may possibly the next time he gets angry with her. She said that she does not consider pushing or squeezing her arm as physical abuse (clearly, not everyone agrees on the definition of physical abuse). He has told her many times during the 47 years of their marriage that he will kill her.

The first time that Cathy realized that her husband would hurt her was when he returned from Vietnam and their twins were 10 months old. She came home from work and he *was fussing, just mean*. She said she had no experience with people who drank, so she hadn't realized that he was drunk. After she got the kids fed, bathed, and put to bed, she showered and went to get into bed.

> He wouldn't let me get in the bed. I said what is wrong with you, so I attempted to get in the bed anyway. I said I've been sleeping here all along . . . and he strangled me to the point that I began to lose consciousness. What made him stop was the twins. . . . were screaming and crying. They were screaming and crying. They saw him and it scared me so bad, I thought, what was wrong with him?

She slept on the sofa that night, and the next morning he asked her why she was sleeping on the sofa. He claimed to have no memory of the incident. She said *it was like two different personalities*. The next morning she was vacuuming the living room and when she pulled out the sofa she found *a whole line of beer cans and vodka bottles. My mouth fell open. I said this is what was wrong, he'd been drinking. I didn't know he drank, and it was all downhill from there.*

As soon as they married, Alice and her second husband moved to Germany and into Army quarters. They had a disagreement soon after and she tried to leave the home. He refused to allow her to leave and caught her leg in the door to keep her inside. Alice had been born with both hips dislocated. She had both of her hips replaced in 1971, and this incident occurred in 1974. She required surgery to repair her injured hip from this incident. But she said she was embarrassed and didn't want to get her new husband in trouble with the Army, so she told the doctors that she had slipped.

The following incident of what is clearly sexual abuse (coerced sexual activity) occurred during her hospital stay following surgery:

> I laid in the hospital and I laid in the room, and I really shouldn't say this, but we had a private room, the professor said "you just got married, and I let you have a private room over Christmas". Because I had to get surgery just before Christmas, see we got married on the 5th and I had to have surgery on the 16th or such. So, he let him be in the room and My husband would come from behind me from the side and he would say "look, just make love a little bit" and I had just had the hip put in. But you know you don't want to make a scene, and he would be loud and he would be nasty with me, and he wanted to make love, can you believe this?

For all of the women, their abuser was verbally abusive from the very beginning of their marriages. In addition, Alice's husband sold all of the property, including her car, which she had brought into the marriage. He has kept total control of her assets and earned income over the years. He was also physically and sexually violent and coercive. Cathy said that her husband would drink on weekends, and when he drank *he would hit me, he would bite me, strangle me. . . .*

While he employed tactics of shoving, pushing, and some hitting, Beth claimed not to have been too concerned, because her husband never told her that he would kill her. She said that mainly,

> he took it out on other things, for instance he smashed furniture, for instance one time he flipped the dining room table over . . . he punched holes in the walls, so, you know, he just directed it somewhere else.

 All of the men were in the military at the time, where disrespect for women was considered normal and acceptable. Consistent with feminist theory, the pattern of abuse was set immediately. Physical abuse or threats to harm occurred either simultaneously or soon after.

FIRST ASSAULT, WORST AND LAST ASSAULT

The first assaults on Alice and Cathy have already been discussed. Dot asserted that she has never been battered, but she has been pushed, shoved, and threatened with guns and he has told her many times that he is going to kill her. When asked if she believes now that the threat to kill her is real, she answered that she does. She says that obviously he hasn't killed her yet, but she never feels completely safe with him. She seems to accept the risk. This is perplexing to us but it demonstrates how differently women themselves may define abuse compared to most researchers and advocates. Dot appeared to be very isolated emotionally, and she indicated that she has few social connections apart from her family.

> We were only married a couple of months. I don't recall that he was drunk. I think he was just angry and I didn't argue with him. He screamed and yelled and hollered at me, and you know, I didn't do that and I didn't argue with him. If he hurt my feelings, I would cry. I cried a lot. In the beginning, I cried a lot. And then he'd get mad. That's why he slammed me against the wall. Because I was crying and he pushed me, pushed me up against the wall. He couldn't stand it when I cried. (Beth)

Every victim of IPV will have her own idea of the worst abuse she ever suffered at the hands of her abuser. They may not match what others may think of as traditional violent assaults, with broken bones and serious injury. Abuse is very personal, individually felt and interpreted. For instance, when asked about the worst abuse she ever suffered at the hands of her husband, Dot didn't mention the time he held a gun to her head and threatened to kill her. She simply said that he had never beaten her, that what had hurt her the most were the constant put downs and criticisms and his belittling of her to her children.

Beth's assertion in the following passage that *he never beat me up* is particularly poignant. He never injured her so badly that she needed medical attention, but most people would consider being struck, pushed into walls, strangled, and dragged down a hallway by her hair as qualifying. In her response, she said that he struck her across her chest with the side of his open hand, like with a tomahawk.

> He left a big bruise across me that time. And he left bruises on my arms and when he pushed me down. When he shoved me against the wall it would bruise my shoulder or my back, or wherever I hit. But he never beat me up.

The time that Cathy was pregnant with her youngest child she considered the worst because of her concerns for the consequences of the assaults on her unborn son. These two beatings were not the most serious for her well-being, but her fear for her child made them the ones that stood out in her mind.

> The worst to me was the two beatings while I was pregnant. None of them were good, but the worst was, the two that I got when I was pregnant with R. Because I couldn't, I was just real vulnerable and it was near the end of the pregnancy, so I was off balance and you can't even get out of the way, you know.

Abuse is an intimate and usually private event. These responses have shown the variability of interpretations by the participants about how to define abuse, or getting "beaten up." It is by her definition of "abuse" that a woman interprets her situation in a relationship. If she does not consider pushing, shoving, or slapping as abusive, then she places herself in the position of not being able to demand an end to those behaviors. And if she does not consider that conduct to be abusive, then surely her partner will not either.

Strangulation   According to a study published by Plattner and colleagues (2005) of a forensic study of 134 survivors of strangulation in Switzerland, 85% of the victims were female, and all but 2 of their abusers were male (Plattner, Bolliger, & Zollinger, 2005). Strangulation is a particularly intimate form of violence, as the perpetrator must be holding his hands around his victim for the entire time.

Strangulation is one of the most serious forms of physical abuse that a woman can suffer. Not only is there the possibility of death, but there is always the danger of brain damage when a person's oxygen supply is interrupted (Banks & Ackerman, 2002). These risks are particularly severe when the victim is strangled to unconsciousness.

Fortunately, two of the women in this study say they have never been strangled. Beth reported that her husband only did it once, and she never lost consciousness. His ability to exercise the self-control necessary to avoid seriously injuring or causing her to lose consciousness strongly suggest that his violence was purposeful and not the result of uncontrollable anger.

> Well, he realized at the time that he better not go too far. You know, we had all these little people and always he knew that he was going to have make explanations. If I was unconscious or if something really dreadful happened or if I had to go to the hospital, he was going to have to make explanations. . . . He left bruises on me that time. He just grabbed me by the neck. (Beth)

Only one of the participants used strangulation as a regular tactic of violence. Cathy stated that her husband strangled her during the first assault and throughout the marriage. By good luck, she lost consciousness only twice. And while there is no way to know for certain, there is no obvious indication of permanent damage.

Frequency and severity of assaults over time and triggers   While it is common that the level of violence remains the same or intensifies over the years of a relationship, it is also very often the case that the level and frequency of violence decrease with time (Wilke & Vinton, 2003; Mezey et al., 2002). It is thought that after it is established that violence will be used as a means of exerting dominance and control (the purpose of abusiveness, according to feminist theory), the victim becomes so cowed that she submits readily, and the abuser does not feel the need to use force or physical coercion (Feld & Straus, 1990; Rennison & Rand, 2003). The threat remains very real, however. Additionally, with age, there is evidence of a decrease in aggressive behavior in many males as they tend to employ less confrontational tactics as they age (Bookwala, et al, 2005). These factors, accompanied by the infirmities of old age, act to decrease violence in many relationships. However, even when the violence decreased, it has been found that verbal abuse is not reduced (Mezey, et al, 2002; Mouton, et al, 2004) and may actually escalate (Zink, et al, 2006).

Alice's husband has restricted his physical abuse to mainly pushing, shoving, or squeezing her arms. While the physical abuse has diminished over the years, she still expresses the fear that he might hurt her. Beth's husband mainly hit her on her chest, arms, and back and she stated that the violence *stayed pretty much at the same level* during the course of her 34-year marriage. When asked if she ever needed medical attention for her injuries, Beth responded: *No. If I did, I never went because I didn't want to have to explain to anybody.*

On the other hand, Cathy reported that the frequency and severity of the violence got worse throughout the course of her marriage. Usually, Cathy said:

> When I would go to work a lot of times, my side would be sore because I would always try to protect my face so that I didn't go to work with bruises on my face. So I would protect my face and I would go to work with my side hurting or my back hurting from him just hitting me, you know. Fighting me like a man. And even now I think about it and I don't understand it. You know, I don't understand . . . he would sober up and then he would be apologetic and I'm not going to do it again and on and on and on. But it just never stopped.

While Cathy's husband avoided breaking bones, there were times she needed medical attention. *I would go in to the doctor and say I bumped myself or I twisted wrong to get something and I normally would be given muscle relaxants. Because the doctors only go by what you tell them.*

During one assault when the twins were thirteen years old, the children tried to protect her. Cathy's daughter went to her room and got a heavy black baseball bat and

> brought it up and was bringing it down and I threw my arm up and protected his head and she hit my wrist. I had to wear an ace bandage for a long time. She said she was trying to kill him. And I said it's time for me to leave because my children are going to kill him protecting me and somebody's going to jail and somebody's going to go to a cemetery. So I decided then. . . .

To cover up for this incident, Cathy told the ER doctor that she had fallen. He did not question her response.

Animal Abuse   Often, when an abusive man injures his partner's pet, his actions represent displaced anger. He is in effect telling her that he is so angry that he has to hurt something, and the next time it might be the partner or a friend or relative of the partner. While it may be preferable that he hurt a pet to hurting his partner, it is a terrifying display of aggression. It can also be very effective as a means of controlling another person (Walton-Moss, Manganello, Frye, & Campbell, 2005).

Neither Cathy nor Dot ever had any pets threatened or harmed by their husbands. Beth had a small dog that she had since she was a child when she married. Her husband kicked it in anger one day, and the dog died shortly afterward from kidney damage suffered from the blow. Alice had a more frightening tale. Her fear and frustration is evident in her final comment.

> We had a tank with fish, and the fish was running after the other fish so he reaches in and grabs the fish and squashes his head off. He did the same with my bird. I had a big bird for my 60th birthday, and that bird made him angry and he twisted his head off. Now, see, I don't have no marks on me, so how do I get any help with that?

Triggers   A trigger is anything specific that causes abuse. The women all said that anything, anytime could be a trigger. As Dot put it: *I don't think there's special triggers, I think it's whatever is bothering him at the time. I mean yes, there's triggers. He can always find a trigger, I think. An excuse.* In addition, both Alice and Cathy's husbands are/were very jealous and possessive. This possessiveness acts as a trigger for both men.

Perceived effect on self-worth/self-confidence   Women who are in long-term abusive relationships usually have low self-esteem and a sense of powerlessness (Walker, 1979; Astbury, et al, 2000; Hage, 2006). One of the tactics used by most abusers is to isolate their partner from friends and family, thus removing them from the support system that might cause them to report the abuse or leave (Brandl, et al, 2003; Constantino, Kim, & Crane, 2005). There is considerable evidence that victims of abuse display symptoms of depression and stress-related health issues (Campbell, et al, 2002; Nurius, et al, 2003; Coker, et al, 2000).

The constant verbal abuse may explain why these women all remained (or remain) with their husbands for so many years. They grew to believe that their husbands were correct in much of what they said. Without the constant verbal assaults, perhaps they would have been unwilling to tolerate the physical abuse.

All of the women agree that the constant verbal abuse is, or was, devastating to their self-confidence. It was even worse than the physical abuse. As Alice put it:

> It's more painful. I'd rather get a black eye and get it over with. You really don't want the other people to know what's going on, you feel almost embarrassed. You feel guilty, like you do something wrong. After you are so long in a relationship like this, you feel like wait a minute, do I do this wrong, why he treats me like this. Then you lose your self-esteem, totally.

Current lives   Beth has remarried and she says her current husband is not an abuser, either physically or verbally. Cathy expressed a reluctance to become involved in another relationship for fear that she would become trapped with another abusive man. As she put it:

> I dated some after I divorced him. And I met a couple of really nice people who actually wanted to get married. But I never wanted to remarry. Never, ever, ever. Because R did such an about face and it was so shocking over the years and so dreadful that I said I could not trust anybody to do that again. And my doctor and even the therapist said that's really sad, that you will not allow yourself to trust again and that you have so little confidence, lack of confidence in your own judgment. Because I said well, maybe I'm not afraid of other people. Maybe I don't trust my own judgment. I don't know what to look for, how to pick a decent person.

Both Dot and Alice remain with their abusive spouses. Dot said:

> I do get out. I do leave the house and go to the store, do those kinds of things. I guess it was last week one day, I was just going to go to the store, it looked like it was going to rain, and I told him I was going to go to the store, and he said "Nope, you're not going, you just stay

right here." And so then I made sure I got out of the house. I just told him yes that I was going to the store and did he need anything and so on. I left. I think it does him good. I think it, sort of being assertive with him, I'm not, not doing whatever it is he wants me to.

Alice tried to explain what her life is now like:

How do I explain to you, if you don't live this life? Constantly, it's just like if he walks up to you, "get your goddam ass out of the way" or "you bitch this" or "what the hell you in the refrigerator for, close the goddam refrigerator door". It goes from morning to night. It's seven o'clock in the morning, if I get up and open the window or something, he's already chewing me out. He wakes up and he's having a pain or something, it's my fault. F'ing so and so, from morning to night.

The two women who are no longer living with an abuser said that they do feel safe. For the two women who are still with their abusers, however, that is not the case. Far from feeling safe, Alice stated that she is certain that if she were to try to leave her husband, he would find her and hurt her. It is this fear, coupled with her poor health and financial entrapment, which keeps her in the relationship. Her fears are justified. The most dangerous time for a victim of IPV is when she tries or threatens to leave a relationship (Jewkes, 2002). For older women, health issues and financial dependency have been found to be key concerns that often cause them to remain in these abusive partnerships (Spangler & Brandl, 2007; Riggs, Caulfield, & Street, 2000).

For the women who are no longer married to their abusers, the financial picture looks secure. The other two women, however, are still tethered to their abusers by financial concerns. Dot finds that she is unable to live without help apart from her husband. Alice says her husband has total control of all money coming into the home, including her Social Security check.

The issues of safety, health, and financial dependency do not occur singly for older victims of IPV. They occur together and are nearly impossible for the women to separate and consider one at a time. It is the interwoven nature of the concerns and fears that cause individually solvable problems to combine to form a steel web in the minds of victims, trapping them inexorably until death or a nursing home allows escape.

Physical and psychological consequences of long-term abuse   Beth and Cathy suffered far more physical violence than did Alice and Dot, but all four discussed both the physical and emotional toll of their long-term abusive relationships. The women's perceptions of their loss of self-confidence and self-esteem are consistent with the literature on the subject (Astbury, et al, 2000; Hage, 2006). Their experience with depression and stress-related health repercussions is also consistent with long-term abuse (Campbell, et al, 2002; Nurius, et al, 2003; Coker, et al, 2000). Alice expressed the feeling that she was under siege, with no good alternatives. She receives regular counseling from the Betty Griffin House that she said is helpful.

The other women appear to have escaped damage from actual physical assaults, although Cathy feels that the migraine-like headaches that she sometimes suffers from may be related to a head injury she sustained during one particularly brutal assault (www .healthline.com/channel/migraines_headaches_causes; Coker, et al, 2000). She had never had migraines prior to that beating. All of the women do, however, appear to be suffering from stress-related medical problems. Beth has some lingering health issues, primarily digestive problems (Coker, et al, 2000). Dot was diagnosed with fibromyalgia in 1996.

Cathy has been receiving counseling and medication for depression since she was 50 years old. She was also diagnosed as having fibromyalgia several years ago. Her doctor believes that the root of her ailment is the years of stress that she endured during her marriage (www.healthline.com/adamcontent/fibromyalgia; www.nlm.nih.gov/medlineplus) and then later, raising and supporting her three children alone. She has also been diagnosed with chronic fatigue syndrome. She stated that she was told by her doctor and psychiatrist that for some reason, these two maladies tend to occur together. Both are immune system disorders with some overlapping symptoms. She further stated that her symptoms improve with certain of the anti-depression drugs she has been prescribed. This suggests there may be a close relationship between these three problems.

Each of the women has health issues related to stress and age. Beth has had eight major surgeries. She seems to be enjoying good health now, but apparently some of her health problems over the years have been stress related, primarily digestive system ills (Coker, et al, 2000). Cathy and Dot both seem to have stable health situations (mainly fibromyalgia, chronic fatigue syndrome) that do not require the assistance of others.

The only one who has attempted to obtain or seems to need help is Alice. Her doctors have told her that she needs some help in her home because of the dreadful condition of her hips. But her husband's response was: *No way in hell anybody's coming in my house*!

The finding that two of the four women have been diagnosed with fibromyalgia raises the obvious question of how common this malady is in the group of women who have spent many years in abusive relationships. One of the women is still with her abuser, but the other has been divorced from hers for over two decades. Further research is needed to determine how common this problem is for this group of women compared to similar women who report no abuse. Additionally, both of the women suffering from fibromyalgia are also being counseled and treated for depression. If these are problems afflicting many current or former victims of abuse, it could improve their quality of life if health care providers were on the lookout for symptoms and had a course of treatment designed to meet their particular needs.

PARTICIPANTS' ADVICE TO OTHER ABUSED WOMEN

All of the women wanted to share their advice to other women who are living in abusive relationships. Beth's was short and to the point: *Get out while you can*. The advice of the other women was essentially the same, but their words demonstrate their passion based on their hard-won experience. Dot said:

I have this friend from Alanon, and we talk a lot together. She lives in another state. And I just tell her how it is with me, and I tell her how it's always been. You know, we've talked for years, and it doesn't change. She's about 20 years younger than I am. She's got two teenage daughters that are, one's almost finished with high school and the other is going to college. But, I tell her things don't change and people don't change. My husband hasn't changed.

Alice contributed:

I've been thinking about this. I tell you what I thought the other day. If my husband would right now leave me and have another woman, more than likely she would be so in love and not pay attention to matters. I would feel like seeing if she would want to talk to me, and I would just tell her part of his character and to be very careful or run the other way. And she would probably say "oh, she's just jealous or something." You know what I mean? It's so hard, what would I tell a woman if she has family, you have somebody you can run to.

I would just say, if they have relatives or anything, or money, if they can put money away, nowadays all the women work so much more. Put some money away and then get you a lawyer.

Cathy's advice was:

Today, because they have shelters, I would say get out right away and with the first assault you should leave because it's only going to get worse. He'll tell you that, he'll, he'll cry and apologize and tell you what you want to hear, and this is based on experience. But then the beatings get worse, and it's always your fault. So I would say get out. Particularly if you have children, you know, if you have children. Whether you have children or not, you need to just leave. And with men like R, you have to go somewhere where they don't know where you are, because they will come and find you.

When you're married to a person who will beat you and curse you and knock you around they will really harm you. So if you're in a situation [like that], get out of it, don't keep going back.

SUMMARY

Although this study had only four participants, it did provide some interesting insights and questions for future research. The violence and verbal abuse they were subjected to by their abusers significantly impacted all of the women in this study. Some of the common threads in each of their stories are alcoholism, patriarchy and stereotyped gender roles, domination and submission, depression, and fear.

As their stories reveal, intimate partner violence and abuse among older couples is not merely "violence grown old." The forms and frequency of abuse changed over time for these women. As their physical conditions changed, so did their needs and their perceptions of their ability to live apart from their husbands in spite of the abusiveness.

One of the findings of this research was the possible association of long-term abuse to the diagnosis of fibromyalgia in two of the four women interviewed. It is strongly argued by most researchers that the reason for the increase in physical ailments among abuse victim is that high levels of stress are known to have a depressive effect on the immune system. Both chronic fatigue syndrome and fibromyalgia are immune system problems believed to be caused by prolonged exposure to stress.

Two of the women in this study remain tethered in abusive marriages. Their needs help highlight the unique situation that older women face as they become frail and dependent physically and financially on their abuser. A solution to this dilemma needs to be found. We do not know how many women are currently trapped in abusive relationships as a consequence of their age and infirmity.

REFERENCES

ALLSWORTH, J. E., ZIERLER, S., LAPANE, K. L., KRIEGER, N., HOGAN, J. W., & HARLOW, B. L. (2004). Longitudinal study of the inception of perimenopause in relation to lifetime history of sexual or physical violence. *Journal of Epidemial Community Health*. v58 p. 938–943

ASTBURY, J., ATKINSON, J., DUKE, J. E., EASTEAL, P. L., KURRIE, S. E., TAIT, P. R., & TURNER, J. (2000). The impact of domestic violence on individuals. *MJA* (E-journal) v173 p. 427–431. http://www.mja.com.au/public/issues/173_08_161000/astbury/astbury.html

BANKS, M. E., & ACKERMAN, R. J. (2002). Head and brain injuries experienced by African American women victims of intimate partner violence. From *Violence in the Lives of Black Women: battered, black, and blue*, edited by West, Carolyn M. Hawthorne Press Inc.: New York.

BOOKWALA, J., SOBIN, J., & ZDANIUK, B. (2005). Gender and aggression in marital relationships: a life-span perspective. *Sex roles.* v52 n11/12 p. 797–806

BRANDL, B., & HORAN, D. L. (2002). Domestic violence in later life: an overview for health care providers. *Women & Health.* v35 n2-3 p. 41–54

BRANDL, B., HEBERT, M., ROZWADOWSKI, J., & SPANGLER, D. (2003). Feeling safe, feeling strong: support groups for older abused women. *Violence Against Wome*n. v9 n12 p. 1490–1503

BROGDEN, M., & NIJHAR, P. (2000). *Crime, Abuse and the Elderly.* Cornwall, Eng.: Willan Publishing.

CAMPBELL, J., JONES, A.S., DIENEMANN, J., KUB, J., SCHOLLENBERGER, J., O'CAMPO, P., GIELEN, A.C., & WYNNE, C. (2002). Intimate partner violence and physical health consequences. *Archives of Internal Medicine.* v162 p. 1157–1163

CARLSON, B. E., MCNUTT, L. A., & CHOI, D. Y. (2003). Childhood and adult abuse among women in primary health care. *Journal of Interpersonal Violence.* v18 n8 p. 924–941

COKER, A. L., DAVIS, K. E., ARIAS, I., DESAI, S., SANDERSON, M., BRANDT, H. M., & SMITH, P. H. (2002). Physical and mental health effects of intimate partner violence for men and women. *American Journal of Preventive Medicine.* v23 n4 p. 260–268

COKER, A. L., SANDERSON, M., FADDEN, M. K., & PIRISI, L. (2000). Intimate partner violence and cervical neoplasia. *Journal of Women's Health & Gender-Based Medicine.* v9 n9 p. 1015–1023

CONSTANTINO, R., KIM, Y., & CRANE, P. A. (2005). Effects of a social support intervention on health outcomes in residents of a domestic violence shelter: a pilot study. *Issues in Mental Health Nursing.* v26 p. 575–590

FELD, S. L., & STRAUS, M. A. (1990). Escalation and desistance from wife assault in marriage. In *Physical Violence in American Families: Risk Factors and Adaptations to Violence in 8,145 Families.* Edited by Straus, Murray A. & Gelles, Richard J. New Brunswick: Transaction Publishers.

FLANNERY, R. B. (2003). Domestic violence and elderly dementia sufferers. *American Journal of Alzheimer's Disease and Other Dementias.* v18 n1 p. 21–23

HAGE, S. M. (2006). Profiles of women survivors: the development of agency in abusive relationships. *Journal of Counseling and Development.* v84 n1 p. 83–94

HARRELL, R., TORONJO, C.H., MCLAUGHLIN, J., PAVLIK, V., HYMAN, D. J., & BITONDO-DYER, C. (2002). How geriatricians identify elder abuse and neglect. *The American Journal of the Medical Sciences.* v323 n1 p. 34–38

HATTENDORF, J., & TOLLERUD, T. R. (1997). Domestic violence: counseling strategies that minimize the impact of secondary victimization. *Perspectives in Psychiatric Care.* v33 n1 p. 14–23

JEWKES, R. (2002). Intimate partner violence: causes and prevention. *The Lancet* v359 p. 1423

KALMUSS, D. S., & STRAUS, M. A. (1990). Wife's marital dependency and wife abuse. In *Physical Violence in American Families: Risk Factors and Adaptations to Violence in 8,145 Families.* Edited by Straus, Murray A. & Gelles, Richard J. New Brunswick: Transaction Publishers.

MEZEY, N. J., POST, L. A., & MAXWELL, C. D. (2002). Redefining intimate partner violence: women's experiences with physical violence and non-physical abuse by age. *International Journal of Sociology and Social Policy.* v22 n7-8 p. 122–154

MILLER, D. K. (2006). The effects of childhood physical abuse or childhood sexual abuse in battered women's coping mechanisms: obsessive-compulsive tendencies and severe depression. *Journal of Family Violence.* v21 n3 p. 185–195

MOUTON, C. P., ROVI, S., FURNISS, K., & LASSER, N. L. (1999). The associations between health and domestic violence in older women: results of a pilot study. *Journal of Women's Health and Gender-Based Medicine.* v8 n9 p. 1173–1179

MOUTON, C. P., RODABOUGH, R., ROVI, S. L., HUNT, J. L., TALAMANTES, M. A., BRZYSKI, R., & BURGE, S. K. (2004). Prevalence and 3-year incidence of abuse among postmenopausal women. *American Journal of Public Health.* v94 n4 p. 605–617

NURIUS, P. S., MACY, R. J., BHUYAN, R., HOLT, V. L., KERNIC, M. A., & RIVARA, F. P. (2003). Contextualizing depression and physical functioning in battered women. *Journal of interpersonal Violence*. v18 n12 p. 1411–1431

OZMENT, J. M,. & LESTER, D. (2001). Helplessness, locus of control, and psychological health. *The Journal of Social Psychology*. v141 n1 p. 137

PADGETT, D. K. (1998). *Qualitative Methods in Social Work Research: Challenges and Rewards*. Sage Publications, Inc., Thousand Oaks, Ca.

PENHALE, B. (1998). Bruises on the soul: older women domestic violence and elder abuse. *Bold*. v8 n2 p. 16–30

PHILLIPS, L. R. (2000). Domestic violence and aging women. *Geriatric Nursing*. v21 n4 p. 188–193

PLATTNER, T., BOLLIGER, S., & ZOLLINGER, U. (2005). Forensic assessment of survived strangulation. *Forensic Science International*. v153 n2-3 p. 202–207

PLICHTA, S. B. (2004). Intimate partner violence and physical health consequences: policy and practice implications. *Journal of Interpersonal Violence*. v19 n11 p. 1296–1323

RENNISON, C., & RAND, M. R. (2003). Nonlethal intimate partner violence against women: a comparison of three age cohorts. *Violence Against Women*. v9 n12 p. 1417–1428

RIGGS, D. S., CAULFIELD, M. B., & STREET, A. E. (2000). Risk for domestic violence: factors associated with perception and victimization. *Journal of Clinical Psychology*. v56 n10 p. 1289–1316

SPANGLER, D., & BRANDL, B. (2007). Abuse in later life: power and control dynamics and a victim-centered response. *Journal of American Psychiatric Nurses Association*. v12 n6 p. 322–331

VINTON, L. (1999). Working with abused older women from a feminist perspective. *Journal of Women & Aging*. v11 n2-3 p. 85–100

WALKER, L. E. (1979). *The Battered Woman*. Harper & Row, Publishers, Inc.: New York, NY.

WALTON-MOSS, B. J., MANGANELLO, J., FRYE, V., & CAMPBELL, J. C. (2005). Risk factors for intimate partner violence and associated injury among urban women. *Journal of Community Health*. v30 n5 p. 377–389

WILKE, D. J., & VINTON, L. (2003). Domestic violence and aging: teaching about their intersection. *Journal of Social Work Education*. v39 n2 p. 225–235 *www.healthline.com/channel/migraines_ headaches_causes* Retrieved 5/12/08 www.nlm.nih.gov/medlineplus Retrieved 5/12/08

ZINK, T., JACOBSON, C. J., REGAN, S., FISHER, B., & PABST, S. (2006). Older women's descriptions and understandings of their abusers. *Violence Against Women*. v12 n9 p. 851–865.

AUTHOR BIOS

Dr. **Suzanne Faries Lowe** was born in 1944 in Pensacola, Florida. She is divorced with two sons and two granddaughters. She has taught in the public schools in Virginia and as an adjunct at Virginia Commonwealth University. For the past 27 years, she has been a magistrate for the Commonwealth of Virginia. She graduated from James Madison University in 1966 with a BS in history and social studies in secondary education. She received a masters in public administration in 2002 and a PhD in public policy and administration in 2008 from Virginia Commonwealth University.

Dr. **Laura J. Moriarty** is a professor of criminal justice and vice provost for Academic and Faculty Affairs at Virginia Commonwealth University. Her earned degrees include the PhD, Sam Houston State University (1988), the masters of criminal justice (1985), and the bachelors of criminal justice (1984) from Louisiana State University. Her research areas include victims of crime, victimology, fear of crime, and violent crime. She is the author, coauthor, or coeditor of eight books and over 70 scholarly articles, book chapters, and nonrefereed articles.

19

Sexual Harassment and the Law

Violence against Women

Roslyn Muraskin

Sexual harassment remains one of the most pervasive problems of the U.S. legal system. "Sexual harassment law addresses sexual subordination as sex discrimination" (MacKinnon, 2001, p. 908). Sexual harassment is "a problem with a long past but a short history" (p. 908). There are arguments that females have more equality now than ever before. In some cases this may be true; however, unfortunately, females are being victimized in more areas than ever before. As women gain more equality, they become harassed by their employers in a manner that is akin to rape and cases of domestic violence. A strategy needs to be developed that provides law enforcement personnel with a better understanding of the types of crimes committed against women.

Historically, women have been discriminated against by the law, often by policies designed to protect them. During recent decades, women have found themselves in courts of law arguing for equality. The history of women's struggles has taught us that litigation acts merely as a catalyst for change. Litigation does not guarantee results.

The problem of sexual harassment "is probably as old as sex equality. Its known past encompasses feudalism, which entitled lords to the first night of sex with vassals' new wives; [and] American slavery, under which enslaved women of African origin or descent were routinely sexually used by white masters" (MacKinnon, 2001, p. 208).

In 1913, Rebecca West stated: "I myself have never been able to find out precisely what feminism is. I only know that people call me a feminist whenever I express sentiments that differentiate me from a doormat." Women's basic rights are inextricably linked to women's treatment by and with their participation in today's political world. Due to the fact that women's lives are reflections of what they do, what they say, and how they treat one another, women as participating members of the human race are ultimately responsible for human affairs.

Throughout this work, we note that there is no way to allow both genders to automatically enjoy equal protection of the law unless we are committed to the elimination of all gender discrimination. The criminal justice system has slowly come to grips with the needed understanding of women and justice. Today, courts need time for discovery of evidence and the opportunity to hear expert testimony in all cases of sexual violence.

According to the Equal Employment Opportunity Commission:

> Harassment on the basis of sex is a violation of [Title VI]. Unwelcome sexual advances, request for sexual behaviors, and other verbal or physical conduct of a sexual nature constitute sexual harassment when (1) submission to such conduct is made either explicitly or implicitly a term or a condition of an individual's employment, (2) submission to or rejection of such conduct by an individual is used as the basis for employment decisions affecting such individual, or (3) such conduct has the purpose or effect of unreasonably interfering with an individual's work performance or creating an intimidating, hostile, or offensive working environment. [29 C.F.R. § 1604.11(a) (1998)]

Crimes such as rape, domestic violence, and sexual harassment are all part of the continuum of violence against women. Rape is not a crime of sex; it is a crime of power. It is "an act of violence, an assault like any other, not an expression of socially organized sexuality" (MacKinnon, 1979, p. 218). The fact that rape is acted out in sex does not mean that it is an act of male sexuality. Rape is an act of violence. The act of sexual harassment has drawn parallels to the crime of rape. If sex or a sexual advance is imposed on a woman who is in no position to refuse, why is that act any different from the act of rape? Sexual harassment may be a lesser crime in the minds of many, including the courts, but, nevertheless, it is an act of violence against women. Sexual harassment is also gender discrimination, and laws are needed to remedy such disparities. There is a current of public discussion about the cases of women who are accused and sometimes convicted of assaulting and killing their partners who have battered them. The actual number of these cases is small, but the attention given to these cases illuminates the larger problem for which they have come to stand: the common disparity of power between men and women in familial relationships.

The laws of sexual harassment in the United States are deemed an exception. "Unlike the criminal law of rape, sexual harassment grew directly out of women's experiences of sexual violation, rather than from ruling men's notions of that experience. It sees sexual abuse as sex-based abuse: victims are understood to be violated as members of their gender group" (MacKinnon, 1979, p. 913). Further, if a crime of sex is one of power, then taken together, rape, domestic violence, and sexual harassment eroticize women's subordination. This continues the powerlessness in the criminal law of women as a gender (MacKinnon, 1979, p. 221).

From a historical point of view, under the English common law the rule of thumb existed that allowed a husband to beat his wife with a stick no wider than his thumb. The husband's prerogative was incorporated into the laws of the United States as well. The sad fact is that several states had laws on the books that essentially allowed a man to beat his wife with no interference from the courts. Blackstone referred to this action as the power of correction. For too many decades women have been victims of sexual assaults. Each act of "sexual assault is recognized as one of the most traumatic and debilitating crimes for adults" (Roberts, 1993, p. 362). The victimization of women has been more prevalent and problematic for the criminal justice system.

As pointed out by Susan Faludi (1991): "Women's advances and retreats are generally described in military terms: battles won, battles lost, points and territory gained and surrendered. In times when feminism is at a low ebb, women assume the reactive role—privately and most often covertly struggling to assert themselves against the dominant cultural tide. But when feminism becomes the tide, the opposition doesn't simply go along with the reversal, it digs in its heels, brandishes its fists, builds walls and dams."

In past decades we have seen sexual assault reform legislation, resulting "in several long-overdue improvements in the criminal justice processing of sexual assault cases for example, passage of rape shield laws, confidentiality laws to protect communications between the victims and their counselors, and laws designed to preserve medical evidence" (Roberts, 1993, p. 370). In addition, we have seen the establishment of victim assistance programs.

SEXUAL HARASSMENT

Women represent half of the U.S. population. Women deserve the same rights and opportunities afforded to men. There exists the rhetoric of gender equality, but it has yet to match the reality of women's experiences. Women who find themselves in the position of being sexually harassed indicate the forms that it takes:

> Wolf whistles, leering, sexual innuendo, comments about women's bodies, tales of sexual exploits, graphic descriptions of pornography, pressure for dates, hooting, sucking, lip-smacking, and animal noises, sexually explicit gestures, unwelcome touching and hugging, excluding women from meetings, sabotaging women's work, sexist and insulting graffiti, demanding "Hey, baby, give me a smile," sexist jokes and cartoons, hostile put-downs of women, exaggerated, mocking "courtesy," public humiliation, obscene phone calls, displaying pornography in the workplace, insisting that workers wear revealing clothing, inappropriate gifts (for example lingerie), inappropriate invitations (for example to go to a hot tub or nude beach), discussion of one's partner's sexual inadequacies, lewd and threatening letters, "accidentally" brushing sexual parts of the body, pressing or rubbing up against the victim, leaning over or otherwise invading a victim's space, sexual sneak attacks (such as grabbing breasts or buttocks on the run), indecent exposure, soliciting sexual services, demanding sexual services, stalking a victim, [and] sexual assault. (MacKinnon, 1979, p. 915)

Why are females forced to tolerate such unwanted actions to survive economically? The case of Anita Faye Hill, in the hearings to confirm Judge Clarence Thomas to serve as an associate justice of the U.S. Supreme Court in 1991, brought to light the terms of sexual harassment—words that gained new meaning for women. Her testimony regarding Justice Thomas's sexual mistreatment of her while she was employed as his assistant helped to bring forth charges of sexual harassment from thousands of women who then understood the meaning of such actions.

Although we do not have a federal equal rights amendment, certain states recognize its potential value. As an example, the use of male terms to indicate both genders has been under examination for some time. There are those who choose to use gender-neutral terms. However, gender discrimination is masked when gender-neutral terms are used. Words are meant to have definitive meaning. "Words are workhorses of law" (Thomas, 1991, p. 1160). Sexual harassment has become a major barrier to women's professional lives and personal development and a traumatic force that disrupts and damages their personal lives. For ethnic-minority women who have been sexually harassed, economic vulnerability is paramount. Women feel powerless, not in control, afraid, and not flattered by sexual harassment. We need to understand that so much of the harassment that occurs is not sexual. The first case before the Supreme Court was *Meritor Savings Bank, FSB v. Vinson*, a 1986 case, in which it was decided that gender harassment is sexual discrimination and illegal under Title VII of the Civil Rights Act of 1964. *Meritor* (1986) recognized two types of sexual harassment: quid pro quo and hostile environment. *"When sex is exchanged, or sought to be exchanged, for a workplace or educational benefit, called quid pro quo [emphasis mine]* . . . and when conditions of work are damagingly sexualized or otherwise harmful, called hostile environment" (*Barnes v. Costle*, 1977, p. 909).

   Throughout the United States, committees have been established to combat charges of sexual harassment. It was almost as if the Thomas–Hill hearings brought people "out of the closet." Cases that followed include *Wagenseller v. Scottsdale Memorial Hospital* (1985) in Arizona, in which the Arizona Supreme Court overruled earlier law and recognized a public policy exception to discharge at will in the case of an emergency room nurse who was allegedly terminated because she refused to "moon" on a rafting trip.

   A worker who continually harasses female coworkers and is discharged does not have a right to reinstatement for failure of the employer to follow the notice provisions of the contract (see *Newsday, Inc. v. Long Island Typographical Union*, 1991). In the case of *Ellison v. Brady* (1991), the trial court had dismissed as trivial "love" letters that the plaintiff had received from a coworker along with persistent requests for dates. The Ninth Circuit disagreed, however, stating that the perspectives of men and women differ. Women, as indicated by the courts, have a strong reason to be concerned about sexual behavior, as they are potential victims of rape and sexual assault.

   A court in Florida ruled in the case of *Robinson v. Jacksonville Shipyards, Inc.* (1991) that a display of nude women can create a hostile environment and is therefore deemed an act of discrimination. In the case of *Continental Can Co., Inc., v. Minnesota* (1980), the Minnesota Supreme Court upheld an action to stop harassment by fellow employees. In yet another case, *E.E.O.C. v. Sage Realty Corp.* (1981), the court held that an employer may impose reasonable dress codes for its employees, but the employer cannot require its employees to wear "revealing and sexually provocative uniforms" that would subject the employee to a form of sexual harassment. This constitutes gender discrimination.

   The case of *Nichols v. Frank* (1994) involved Teri Nichols, who was deaf and mute. The night-shift supervisor (Francisco) with whom she worked had authority to grant employees leave as well as overtime pay. He was the only supervisor available able to communicate in sign language. At one point after asking Nichols to do some copying for him, "Francisco started kissing Nichols and indicated that he wanted her to perform oral sex on him. She refused his advances, but ultimately complied because she was afraid she would lose her job if she refused. According to Nichols, 'I remember that when this first happened I was just in shock. I was nervous. I was upset. I wasn't happy doing it, and I was hoping it would never happen again. And I just kept that all to myself. But then there was repeats and repeats and repeats, and I was more upset and . . . I didn't want to do it again and again for him, and I didn't know how to say, 'Stop, just stop.'" The court concluded that "a supervisor's intertwining of a request for the performance of sexual favors with a discussion of actual or potential job benefits or detriments in a single conversation constitutes quid pro quo sexual harassment."

In the cases of *Burlington Industries v. Ellerth* (1998) and *Faragher v. Boca Raton* (1998), the court decided a chaotic body of law in the area of sexual harassment, making it easier for women to sue their bosses who harass them under Title VII of the 1964 Civil Rights Act. Patricia Ireland, former president of the National Organization for Women (NOW), stated that "the boss who paws, propositions and warns of retaliation takes away a women's dignity . . . even if he doesn't take away her job" (1998).

In the *Burlington* case the claim was that the female endured a steady stream of sexual harassment from her supervisor's boss, "including pats on the buttocks, offensive sexual remarks and the threat that he could make her work life 'very hard or very easy.'" Despite the employer's argument that she suffered no tangible job loss, the U.S. Supreme Court decided that her case could go forward because it was the employer's burden to prove that the company had taken reasonable steps and that the complainant had failed to follow proper reporting procedures.

In *Faragher*, the complainant, Beth Faragher, claimed that while working at a remote lifeguard station she was harassed by male supervisors, "who repeatedly touched her, called her and other women 'bitches and sluts,' made comments about her breasts and threatened 'date me or clean toilets for a year.'" The city's claim was that she was not entitled to damages, as she failed to go over her supervisors' heads and report the harassment. The U.S. Supreme Court reinstated her damages award, deciding that the city had not taken reasonable steps to prevent and correct the harassment. In the words of Patricia Ireland, "women's rights need to be written into the Constitution. . . . [w]ithout it . . . women do not have a constitutional right to bodily integrity."

Addressing violence against women requires a national commitment. A summary of the data amassed about gender violence was included in the dissenting opinion of the Supreme Court Justice David Souter in *United States v. Morrison* (2000, pp. 1761–1763):

> Three out of four American women will be victims of violent crimes sometime during their lives.
>
> Violence is the leading cause of injuries to women ages 15–44.
>
> As many as 50% of homeless women and children are fleeing domestic violence.
>
> Since 1974, the assault rate against women has outstripped the rate for men by at least twice for some age groups, and far more for others.
>
> Battering is the largest cause of injury to women in the United States.
>
> An estimated 4 million women in the United States seek medical assistance each year for injuries sustained from their husbands or other partners.
>
> Between 2000 and 4000 women die every year from domestic abuse.
>
> Arrest rates may be as low as 1 for every 100 domestic assaults.
>
> Partial estimates show that violent crime against women costs this country at least $3 billion a year.
>
> Estimates suggest that we spend $5 to $10 billion per year on health care, criminal justice, and other social costs of domestic violence.
>
> The incidence of rape rose four times as fast as the total national crime rate over the past 10 years.

According to one study, close to one-half million females now in high school will be raped before they graduate.

One hundred twenty-five thousand college women can expect to be raped before they graduate.

Three-fourths of women never go to the movies alone after dark because of the fear of rape, and nearly 50% do not use public transit alone after dark for the same reasons.

Forty-one percent of judges, surveyed by a Colorado study, believed that juries give sexual assault victims less credibility than other victims of crime.

Less than 1% of rape victims have collected damages.

An individual who commits rape has only 4 chances in a 100 of being arrested, prosecuted and found guilty of any offense.

Almost one-fourth of convicted rapists never go to prison and another one-fourth received sentences in local jails, where the average sentence is 11 months.

Almost 50% of rape victims lose their jobs or are forced to quit because of the crime's severity.

The attorneys general from 38 states urged Congress to enact a civil rights remedy, permitting rape victims to sue their attackers because "the current system of dealing with violence is inadequate." (Muraskin & O'Connor, 2002, p. 432)

Due to these findings, Congress found it necessary to pass the Violence Against Women Act (VAWA) in 1994. This act provided for "substantial sums of money to States for education, rape crisis hotlines, training criminal justice personnel, victim services and special units in police and prosecutors' offices to deal with crimes against women. The act specifically provided incentives for the enforcement of statutory rape laws, the payment of the cost of testing for sexually transmitted diseases for victims of crime, and studies of campus sexual assaults, and the battered women's syndrome" (Muraskin & O'Connor, 2002, p. 434).

In a Supreme Court case, *Pennsylvania State Police v. Nancy Drew Suders*, argued on March 31, 2004, and decided on June 14, 2004, a female who was a former employee of the state police sued Pennsylvania State Police, alleging that she was sexually harassed by her supervisors resulting in constructive discharge, in violation of Title VII. The facts of the case are as follows:

"In March 1998, the Pennsylvania State Police (PSP) hired plaintiff-respondent Suders to work as a police communications operator for the McConnellsburg barracks, where her male supervisors subjected her to a continuous barrage of sexual harassment" (*Pennsylvania*, 2004, p. 2343). "During June 1998 Suders informed the Equal Employment Opportunity officer of her need for help, but nothing was done. After a few months of constant harassment and nothing happening, she complained again to the officer, was told to file a complaint, but not told how to file. Two days later, Suders' supervisors arrested her for theft of her own computer-skills exam papers. Suders had removed the papers after concluding that the supervisors had falsely reported that she had repeatedly failed, when in fact, the exams were never forwarded for grading" (p. 2343). She resigned her post at this point. "The constructive discharge here at issue stems from, and can be regarded as an aggravated case of, sexual harassment or hostile work environment." For such an atmosphere to exist there must be offending behavior that is "sufficiently severe or pervasive to alter the conditions of the victim's employment and create an abusive work environment"

(p. 2399); see also the case of *Meritor* previously discussed. Justice Ginsburg delivered the majority opinion for the court. He agreed with the Third Circuit that "the case, in its current posture, presents genuine issues of material fact concerning Suders' hostile work environment and constructive discharge claims. We hold, however, that the Court of Appeals erred in declaring the affirmative defense described in *Ellerth* and *Faragher* never available in the constructive discharge form. [W]e vacate the Third Circuit's judgment and remand the case for further proceedings consistent with this opinion" (p. 2342).

Justice Thomas, in writing his dissent,[1] stated that "the Court has now adopted a definition of constructive discharge, however, that does not in the least resemble actual discharge. The Court holds that to establish constructive discharge a plaintiff must show that the abusive working environment became so intolerable that [the employee's] resignation qualified as a fitting rule" (p. 2342). He continued by stating that "[b]ecause respondent has not produced sufficient evidence of an adverse employment action taken because of her sex, nor has she proffered any evidence that petitioner knew or should have known of the alleged harassment, I would reverse the judgment of the Court of Appeals" (p. 2359).

In the case of *Jackson v. Birmingham Board of Education*, argued on November 30, 2004, and decided on March 29, 2005, a "former coach of [a] girls' high school basketball team sued the board of education, alleging that it retaliated against him in violation of Title IX" (p. 1497).

The Supreme Court with Justice O'Connor held that:

1. retaliation against a person because that person has complained of sex discrimination is a form of intentional sex discrimination encompassed by Title IX's private cause of action;

2. coach stated claim of discrimination on the basis of sex that was actionable under Title IX;

3. coach could assert retaliation claim even though he was not victim of discrimination that was subject of his original complaints; and

4. Board of Education had sufficient notice that it could be subjected to private suits for intentional sex discrimination in the form of retaliation.

The case was reversed.

Justice Thomas filed a dissenting opinion along with Chief Justice Rehnquist and Justices Scalia and Kennedy. "The Court holds that the private right of action under Title IX of the Education Amendments of 1972. . . . Extends to claims of retaliation. Its holding is contrary to the plain terms of Title IX, because retaliatory conduct is not discrimination on the basis of sex" (*Jackson*, p. 1497).

In the case of *Fitzgerald v. Barnstable School Committee*, argued before the Supreme Court on December 2, 2008, and decided on January 21, 2009, an elementary school student and her parents filed a sexual harassment suit in violation of Title IX and the equal protection clause claiming student to student harassment. The Court held that Title IX was not meant to be an exclusive mechanism for addressing gender discrimination in schools or as a substitute for section 1983. Activists such as Susan Brownmiller are credited with initiating a view of sexual harassment that has changed radically the way sexual harassment complaints are treated under the legal system. To shift the focus of sexual harassment from the belief that males' sexual pursuit of a woman in the workplace or the classroom is essentially biological and that sexual harassment is therefore a normal consequence of attraction between the genders, MacKinnon, Brownmiller, and others advocate a *dominance* approach. Sexual harassment is gender discrimination. It occurs in the workplace wherever women are situated in an attempt to keep them in their place (Corgin & Bennett-Haigne, 1998).

Other cases have recently held that "the protection of the opposition clause of the anti-retaliation provision of Title IX extended to a municipal employee who spoke out about discrimination in the form of sexual harassment allegedly perpetrated against her, not on her own initiative, but in answering questions during an employer's internal investigation of employee's co-workers complaints of sexual harassment." You cannot fire someone who indirectly yells sexual harassment (*Crawford v. Metropolitan Government of Nashville and Davidson County*, Tennessee, 2009).

MacKinnon has questioned whether "sexual harassment cases conceive gender horizontally in terms of sameness and difference, or vertically as hierarchy" (2001, p. 914). "One way women have been stigmatized as inferior is through the identification of a sometimes erroneous, usually exaggerated, always exclusive set of feminine needs. Women's sexuality has been a prime example. It has been hard to avoid branding women as inferior, long enough to balance a grasp of her dignity with an analysis of her enforced inferiority, in order to address the specificity of her situation" (MacKinnon, 1979, p. 144).

LITIGATION

Men who harass are not pathological but rather are people who exhibit behaviors characteristic of the masculine gender role. The first litigation of sexual harassment claims did not occur until the mid-1970s. Title VII of the Civil Rights Act prohibiting sex discrimination in the workplace was followed eight years later by Title IX of the 1972 Higher Education Amendment, prohibiting gender discrimination in educational institutions receiving federal assistance. However, in much of the early adjudication of gender discrimination, the phenomenon of sexual harassment was typically seen "as isolated and idiosyncratic, or as natural and universal and in either case, as inappropriate for legal intervention." It was in 1980 that the Equal Employment Opportunity Commission, in its guidelines on discrimination, explicitly defined sexual harassment under Title VII as a form of unlawful, gender-based discrimination.

As the law has been interpreted, prohibition against sexual harassment in the workplace technically covers any sufficiently severe and pervasive remark or behavior that would affect not only the victim's but also a "reasonable person's" psychological well-being. A 1991 landmark ruling by the Court of Appeals for the Ninth Circuit in California held that the "appropriate perspective for judging a hostile environment claim [was] that of the 'reasonable woman' and recognized that a woman's perspective may differ substantially from a man's." While the 1991 Ninth Circuit Court ruling acknowledged that men and women may interpret the same behavior differently, in application this legal understanding was overshadowed by a grave misunderstanding of the nature of sexual harassment as experienced by its victims. The people doing the judging were in no position to understand the position of those being judged. The powerful were making judgments against the powerless.

But in the case of *Harris v. Forklift Systems, Inc.* (1993), the U.S. Supreme Court specified and refined its standards for hostile environment cases. "The U.S. Supreme Court decided in Harris that an environment of sexual harassment, to be actionable, had to be objectively hostile—one a 'reasonable person,' under all the circumstances, would find hostile or abusive—as well as hostile to the plaintiff herself. It also held that a hostile environment did not need to seriously affect a worker's psychological well-being to be discriminatory" (MacKinnon, 2001, p. 955).

Rape, Sexual Harassment, and the Criminal Justice System

Like the crime of rape, sexual harassment is not an issue of lust; it is an issue of power. Sexual harassment does not fall within the range of personal or private relationships. It happens when a person with power abuses that power to intimidate, coerce, or humiliate someone because of gender. It is a breach of trust. In voluntary sexual relationships, freedom of choice is exercised in deciding whether to establish a close, intimate relationship. This freedom of choice is absent in sexual harassment (Paludi, 1992). Sexual harassment may be understood as an extreme acting out of qualities that are regarded as supermasculine: aggression, power dominance, and force. Men who harass are not pathological but rather are people who exhibit behaviors characteristic of the masculine gender role in U.S. culture. Most sexual harassment starts at the subtle end of the continuum and escalates over time. Each year, 1 percent of women in the U.S. labor force are sexually assaulted on the job. Yet cultural mythologies consistently blame the victim for sexual abuse and act to keep women in their place. Scholars have identified several similarities in attitudes toward rape and sexual harassment, especially revealing cultural myths that blame the victim:

1. Women ask for it.
   Rape: Victims seduce their rapists.
   Sexual harassment: Women precipitate harassment by the way they dress and talk.
2. Women say "no" but mean "yes."
   Rape: Women secretly need and want to be forced into sex. They do not know what they want.
   Sexual harassment: Women like the attention.
3. Women lie.
   Rape: In most charges of rape, the woman is lying.
   Sexual harassment: Women lie about sexual harassment to get men they dislike into trouble.

Women who speak about being victims of sexual harassment use terms such as *humiliating, intimidating, frightening, financially damaging, embarrassing, nervewracking, awful,* and *frustrating.* These are not terms that are used to describe a situation that one enjoys.

Historically, the rape of women was considered to be an infringement of the property rights of men. Sexual harassment needs to be viewed in the same light. The message is that further changes are needed. We can no longer blame the messenger. We need to understand the message. There is no question that what is referred to as "women's hidden occupational hazard," sexual harassment, is gender victimization. The fact that sexual harassment exists demonstrates that it must be understood as part of the continuum of violence against women. In a typical sexual harassment case, the female accuser becomes the accused and the victim is twice victimized. This holds true in cases of rape and domestic violence as well as in those of harassment. Underlying the dynamics of the situation is the profound distrust of a woman's word and a serious power differential between the accused and the accuser. As indicated, sexual harassment is the most recent form of victimization of the woman to be redefined as a social rather than a personal problem, following rape and wife abuse.

SUMMARY

Sexual harassment continues to be a major barrier to women's professional and personal development and a traumatic force that disrupts and damages their personal lives. For ethnic-minority women who have been sexually harassed, economic vulnerability is paramount. Women feel powerless, not in control, and afraid. There is nothing flattering about sexual harassment. Their emotional and physical well-being resembles that of victims of other sexual abuses (i.e., rape, incest, and battering). It must be stopped.

Women's issues infuse every aspect of social and political thought. It was Gloria Steinem who noted that cultural myths die hard, especially if they are used to empower one part of the population. The struggle of women continues under the law. There is no way to allow both genders automatically to enjoy the equal protection of the laws unless we are committed to the elimination of all gender discrimination. Sexual harassment is gender discrimination. The criminal justice system over these many years has slowly come to grips with the need to understand women in the context of justice and fairness.

Women continue to represent half the population. They are owed the same rights and opportunities as are afforded to men. For justice to be gained, the fight for freedom and equality must continue. Prevention is the best tool the criminal justice system has to offer as long as it takes the action mandated by legislators. Dominance takes several forms. As stated so succinctly by Catherine MacKinnon in 1979: "Sexual harassment (and rape) has everything to do with sexuality. Gender is a power division and sexuality is one sphere of its expression" (pp. 220–221). There is no logic to inequality.

REFERENCES

CORGIN, B., & BENNETT-HAIGNE, G. (1998, August 12). Sexual harassment: Open season on working women. Retrieved from: http://www.now.org/nnt/03-97/sexual.html.

FALUDI, S. (1991). *Backlash: The undeclared war against American women.* New York: Crown.

IRELAND, P. (1998). Sexual harassment: Open season on working women. *NOW Times.*

MACKINNON, C. (1979). *Sexual harassment of working women.* New Haven, CT: Yale University Press.

MACKINNON, C. (2001). *Sex equality.* New York: Foundation Press.

MURASKIN, R., & O'CONNOR, M. (2002). Women and the law: An agenda for change in the twenty-first century. In R. Muraskin & A. Roberts (Eds.), *Visions for change: Crime and justice in the twenty-first century* (3rd ed.). Upper Saddle River, NJ: Prentice Hall.

PALUDI, M. A. (1992). Working nine to five: Women, men, sex and power. In R. Muraskin (Ed.), *Women's agenda: Meeting the challenge to change.* New York: Long Island Women's Institute, College of Management, C. W. Post Campus of Long Island University.

ROBERTS, A. (1993). Women: Victims of sexual assault and violence. In R. Muraskin & T. R. Alleman (Eds.), *It's a crime: Women and justice.* Upper Saddle River, NJ: Prentice Hall.

THOMAS, C. S. (1991). *Sex discrimination.* St. Paul, MN: West.

ENDNOTE

1. The appeals court ruled that a constructive discharge, if proved, constitutes a tangible employment action that renders an employer strictly liable and precludes recourse to the *Ellerth/Faragher* affirmative defense.

   Note: Both *Ellerth and Faragher* decided on the same day that an employer is strictly liable for supervisor harassment that culminates in a tangible employment action, such as discharge, demotion, or undesirable reassignment.

CASES

Barnes v. Costle, 561 F.2d 983 (D.C. Cir. 1977).

Burlington Industries v. Ellerth, 123 F.3d 490 (1998).

Continental Can Co., Inc., v. Minnesota, 297 N.W.2d 241 (Minn. 1980), 242.

Crawford v. Metropolitan Government of Nashville and Davidson County, Tennessee, No. 06-1595. Argued October 8, 2008, decided January 26, 2009.

E.E.O.C. v. Sage Realty Corp., 507 F. Supp. 599 (D.C. N.Y. 1981), 243.

Ellison v. Brady, 924 F.2d 872 (9th Cir. 1991), 119.

Faragher v. Boca Raton, 111 F.3d 1530 (1998).

Harris v. Forklift Systems, Inc., 510 U.S. 17 (1993).

Jackson v. Birmingham Board of Education, 125 S. Ct. 1497 (2005).

Meritor Savings Bank, FSB v. Vinson, 477 U.S. 57, 106 S. Ct. 2399, 91 L. Ed. 2d 49 (1986), 239.

Newsday, Inc. v. Long Island Typographical Union No. 915, U.S. 111, S. Ct. 1314, 113 L. Ed. 2d 247 (1991), 195, 241.

Nichols v. Frank, 42 F.3d 503 (9th Cir. 1994).

Pennsylvania State Police v. Nancy Drew Suders, 124 St. Ct. 2342 (2004).

Robinson v. Jacksonville Shipyards, Inc., 760 F. Supp. 1486 (M.D. Fla. 1991), 241.

United States v. Morrison, 120 S. Ct. 1740 (2000).

Wagenseller v. Scottsdale Memorial Hospital, 147 Ariz. 370, 710 P.2d 1025 (Ariz. 1985).

20

Female Victims
and Cyberstalking Legislation

Janice Joseph

❖

The rapid growth of the Internet and other telecommunications technologies is promoting advances in virtually every aspect of society and every corner of the globe. Most of these advances represent positive changes in society. Unfortunately, the Internet has become an attractive medium for criminals. With the increasing availability of computers and online services, more individuals are logging on to the Internet, thereby providing opportunities to be victimized by the cyberstalker.

The purpose of the chapter is to examine the nature and extent of cyberstalking and the extent to which the legal and criminal responses to cyberstalking affect female victims. Specifically, the chapter examines the extent, nature, and effects of cyberstalking on female victims and on the legal responses to cyberstalking. It also discusses the difficulties law enforcement officers encounter when they investigate cyberstalking and includes recommendations.

DEFINITION OF CYBERSTALKING

There is no universal definition of cyberstalking but instead there is a variety of definitions. The 1999 Department of Justice ("DOJ") *Report on Cyberstalking, for example*, refers to cyberstalking as the use of the Internet, e-mail, or other electronic communications device to stalk another person. The DOJ further states that stalking involves harassing or threatening behavior that an individual engages in repeatedly. D'Ovidio and Doyle (2003) view cyberstalking as repeated use of the digital electronic communication device to threaten, frighten, annoy specific individuals. The term generally refers to the use of computer communications to threaten or harass another person directed at another person (National Center for the Victims of Crimes, 2010).

Paul Bocij defines cyberstalking as:

> A group of behaviors in which an individual, group of individuals, or organization uses information and communications technology to harass another individual, group of individuals, or organization. Such behaviors may include, but are not limited to, the transmission of threats and false accusations, identity theft, data theft, damage to data or equipment, computer monitoring, solicitation of minors for sexual purposes, and any form of aggression. Harassment is defined as a course of action that a reasonable person, in possession of the same information, would think causes another reasonable person to suffer emotional distress. (Bocij, 2004:14)

While there is no universally accepted definition of cyberstalking, it can, however, be defined as unwanted, threatening or offensive e-mail, or other personal communication over the computer that is repetitive. It can also include behavior that is aimed at a particular person, but not sent directly to that person. It is "analogous to traditional forms of stalking, in that it incorporates persistent behaviors that instill apprehension and fear" (Ogilvie 2000; p.1). It is also viewed as an extension of, or alternative to, 'traditional' stalking that utilizes a high-tech modus operandi {method of operation} (Petherick, 1999).

Several categories of cyber bullying proposed by Li (2007) could also be included under a definition of cyberstalking. These behaviors include flaming, denigration, masquerade (impersonating someone else online) and outing (publicly exposing private information about an individual online).

METHODS USED IN CYBERSTALKING

Cyberstalkers employ various methods of Internet communication to harass their victims. They are electronic mail (email), chatrooms, bulletin boards, computers, and social networks.

Electronic mail, commonly referred to as e-mail, is a method of exchanging digital messages. It allows an individual to receive and send text, picture, video, and audio files to another person's electronic mailbox. The cyberstalker can stalk an individual by repeatedly sending him/her a text-based, graphic-based, or audio-based message of a threatening, alarming, or otherwise harassing nature.

Chat rooms are virtual rooms where online users send and receive messages on screen. During "chat" conferences, participants type live messages directly to the computer screens of other participants. When a person posts a message to a public newsgroup or forum this is available for anyone to view, copy, and store. In addition, a person's name, electronic mail (e-mail) address, and information about service provider are usually available for inspection as part of the message itself. Thus, on the Internet, public messages can be accessed by anyone at anytime—even years after the message was originally written. A stalker can send harassing messages directly to the victim while conversing in a chat room. However, the message is also delivered to all those users who currently are logged into the chat room (D'Ovidio & Doyle, 2003).

A Bulletin Board System, or BBS, is a computer system running software that allows users to connect and log in to the system using a terminal program. Once logged in, a user can upload and downloading software and data, read news and bulletins, and exchanging messages with other users, either through electronic mail or in public message boards. While communications made in these forums may initially be read only by the members with access, there is nothing preventing those members from recording the communications and later transmitting them elsewhere (D'Ovidio & Doyle, 2003).

With the computer, cyberstalkers can exploit the operating system of another person in order to assume control over the computer of the targeted victim. This computer-to-computer connection allows the online stalker to monitor the computer of the victim. A cyberstalker can communicate directly with his or her victim as soon as the target computer connects to the Internet (Ogilivie, 2000).

Social Networking Sites

Social networking sites such as MySpace, Facebook, LinkedIn, Flickr, Blogspot, and Xanga are virtual communities where people with common interests meet online to share information and build relationships. Visitors to these sites can chat, debate, network, and socialize. On many sites, members may post details about themselves, such as their photos, social background, and relationship status. Others sites promote business, activism, networking, counseling, socializing, or many types of recreational interests (National Center for Victims of Crime, 2008). The use of these sites has increased the users' vulnerability to stalkers and other predators.

CYBERSTALKING VICTIMIZATION

Extent of Cyberstalking

Currently, information on the victims of cyberstalking is limited. Although, anyone can become a victim of cyberstalking, limited studies and anecdotal evidence on cyberstalking suggest that the majority of cyber stalkers are men and the victims are women. Working to Halt Online Abuse (WHOA), a volunteer online organization founded in 1997 to fight online harassment, collects statistics on cyberstalking. According to WHOA, in 2008 there were 220 victims, 78 percent were females, the majority (35%) were between 18–30 years, 74 percent were white, and 31% were single. The majority of victims (34%) were victimized by emails and 72 percent reported the cyberstalking (Working to Halt Online Abuse, 2010).

Sheridan and Grant (2007), in an online international survey of 1051 victims of cyberstalking, found that 86 percent of the victims were females, the mean victim age when the stalking commenced was 32.6 years, the majority (90.7%) were white, and almost all (93.8%) knew their stalker's identity. D'Ovidio and Doyle (2003), who examined cyberstalking cases in New York City between 1996 and 2000 reported that females were victimized in 52 percent of the cases. They also found that approximately 85 percent of victims were white and the average age of the victims was 32 years.

National figures show victims of cyberstalking are females in college between the ages 18–29. A survey of 765 students at Rutgers University and the University of Pennsylvania found 45 percent of stalkers to be female and 56 percent to be male. Men represented over 40 percent of stalking victims in the Penn-Rutgers study (Boyer, 2006).

It is clear from the limited information on cyberstalking that most of the victims are females. There are several reasons for this pattern. The gender inequality that exists in real life exists as well in cyberspace which is a male-dominated environment. Consequently, women are discriminated against in cyberspace. One of such form of discrimination is cyberstalking.

Mustaine and Tewksbury (1999) suggest that women may be suitable targets because cyberstalking victimization is not yet taken seriously by society nor has it received the attention it deserves from the criminal justice system.

TYPES AND NATURE OF THE VICTIMIZATION

Types of cyberstalkers

The victim is subjected to several types of stalkers. Bocij and McFarlane (2003) classify offenders within four categories. These typologies focus on the relationship between the victim and the offender. They are the vindictive stalker, the composed stalker, the intimate stalker and collective stalkers. Vindictive stalkers threaten their victims more than any other group and are likely to transfer their behavior offline. Composed stalkers constantly annoy and irritate their victims and are likely to make threats. The intimate stalker's goal is to win the affections of their victims. These include ex-intimates and those infatuated with the victim. Collective stalkers are characterized by two or more offenders acting together and displaying an advanced knowledge of technology and utilizing techniques such as identify theft, spamming and intimidating media.

Cyberstalkers can also be categorized using Mullen and associates' (1999) five overlapping categories of stalkers: the rejected stalker, intimacy seekers, incompetent suitors, resentful stalker and predatory stalkers. The rejected stalker is the most common and victimizes a former romantic partner or friend who has ended the relationship with the stalker, or indicates that he or she intends to end the relationship. The intimacy seeker attempts to establish an intimate and loving relationship with his victim. He often interprets any kind of response from the victim as love, even negative responses. The incompetent suitor desires a romantic or intimate relationship with the victim but is impaired in their social and courting skills. This stalker may be very narcissistic. The resentful stalker takes revenge against someone who has upset him. It could be someone known to the stalker or a complete stranger. The behaviors are meant to frighten and distress the victim. The predatory stalker is motivated purely by the desire for sexual gratification and power over their victim. The use of offline typologies for classifying online stalker indicates the similarity between online and offline behavior.

Nature of the Cyberstalking

Direct Cyberstalking   In direct cyberstalking, the stalker makes direct contact with the victim. Using email, the cyberstalker can send unsolicited hate, obscene, threatening mail, victim computer viruses, or high volumes of electronic junk mail (Ogilivie, 2000). This is the most common form of cyberstalking (Petrocelli 2005). In chat stalking, a harasser may choose to electronically interrupt a person's chat or otherwise target a chat system, making it impossible for someone to carry on a conversation with anyone else. In other instances, a cyberstalker can send a person's message to multiple recipients. The cyberstalker can engage in live chat harassment of the victim or what is commonly referred to as *flaming*, in which the victim is belittled or demeaned in a live public forum (The National Center for Victims of Crime, 2004).

Recent information indicates that social networks have been used for direct cyberstalking. For example, in the months before the Virginia Tech massacre, the shooter, Seung-Hui Cho, allegedly used Facebook to locate and stalk female classmates (Geller, 2007). In 2006, a University of Kansas student received death threats from someone who found her class schedule online. He posted photos from the victim's MySpace account on his own site, along with insults about her appearance and her major (KUJH-TV News, 2007).

Cybersmearing   The term *cybersmearing* refers to the posting of embarrassing or humiliating rumors about the victim in a chat room, newsgroup, or bulletin board (Bocij & McFarlane, 2003). Discussion forums are typically a place for Internet users to post opinions and comments on one or more subjects. However, discussion boards can also be a place for cyberstalkers to post harmful, negative personal information about the victim, including the victim's name, address, phone number, email address, and other private information (Petrocelli, 2005). The cyberstalker can also post statements about the victim or start rumors which spread throughout the bulletin board system. The most common form of cybersmearing is the posting of false sexual innuendos about the victim (Petrocelli, 2005).

Cyberstalking by Proxy   Even though most stalkers act alone, the Internet has made it much easier for cyberstalkers to conspire and encourage third parties to harass victims in chat rooms, discussion boards, and within Internet public forums (Reno, 1999). This is referred to as stalking by proxy and describes the process in which cyber stalkers encourage others, such as family members and friends to assist in harassing the victim. Some cyber stalkers may even hire private investigators to follow and report on the victim's daily activities and whereabouts (Bocij & McFarlane, 2003).

Enticing Innocent Third Parties to Harass

One of the most apparent differences between cyberstalking and stalking is that cyberstalkers can entice innocent third parties to victim. Cyberstalkers can easily impersonate the victim by taking on the identity of the victim. In addition, a cyberstalker can fool other Internet users into harassing or threatening a victim by posting inflammatory and controversial messages on multiple bulletin boards using the victim's name, phone number, or e-mail address, resulting in subsequent responses being sent to the victim (Gregorie, 2001).

This was what happened to Jayne Hitchcock, who was cyberstalked when she complained about an advertisement from a literary agency. The cyberstalkers, who were connected to the literary agency, impersonated Hitchcock by posting inflammatory comments on Web pages and sending e-mails in her name with the intent to provoke others to harass her. For three years, she was harassed on the internet by strange men wanting to share their sex fantasies (Davidson, 2000).

Also in 1999, fifty-year-old Californian man duped "innocent" third parties to cyberstalk a woman. He used the Internet to solicit the rape of a twenty-eight-year-old woman who had rejected his romantic advances. He then terrorized her by impersonating her in various Internet chat rooms and posting her telephone number, address, and messages that she fantasized of being raped. Because of these messages, on separate occasions, at least six men knocked on the woman's door saying that they wanted to rape her (Ashcroft, 2001).

In a recent case, a Pennsylvania State Trooper posted five nude photographs of his former wife on a bondage and sadomasochistic website in order to seek revenge for a failed marriage. In addition to creating a profile in his wife's name and posting the nude photographs, he also posted his wife's occupation as a school teacher and her date of birth on the bondage website. Posing as his ex-wife, he posted explicit messages on the website soliciting viewers to contact her to engage in violent sexual acts. This offense was revealed after one of the website's visitors decided to contact Heller's ex-wife at her place of employment. The state trooper subsequently pleaded guilty to harassment for placing the images on the bondage site and agreed to quit the Pennsylvania State Police in light of the criminal charges lodged against him (Pittaro, 2007).

Effects of Victimization

The effects of cyberstalking on the victim are numerous. In response to being stalked, some cyberstalking victims may experience changes in sleep and eating patterns, nightmares, hypervigilance, anxiety, helplessness, and fear for their safety (The National Center for Victims of Crime, 2004). Victims may exhibit Posttraumatic Stress Disorder (PTSD) and aggressive and violent behavior (Bocij, 2005). The victim may be anxious, suicidal or homicidal, or suffer mental anguish. Victimization may also interfere with the victim's daily activities, or she may experience large financial burdens (Lamberg, 2001; Finn, 2004).

According to Finch (2002) victims respond in a variety of ways to their victimization. This ranges from amusement or indifference on the one hand to more extreme reactions causing significant psychological damages at the other end of the continuum. Spitzberg and Hoobler's (2002) study of obsessive relational intrusion and cyberstalking revealed that victims have three distinct set of coping mechanisms. These include unilateral protection, which involves various techniques such as changing one's actions, aggressive protection, which includes seeking legal support, and interaction, which includes communicating with the stalker to cease his or her behaviour (Spitzberg & Hoobler, 2002).

In addition to the psychological/emotional affects on victims, cyberstalking can have secondary effects. Pathé and Mullen (1997) found 37% of victims change jobs, schools or careers. Victims of cyberstalking can also incur financial costs, such as seeking professional help, paying legal fees, and missing work (Ashcroft, 2001). Cyberstalking can extend beyond the victim to include friends and family members of the victim (Bocij, 2004). Finch (2002:425) highlights that each case is unique and "there are cases in which no vestige of the victim's life remains unaffected".

LEGAL RESPONSE TO CYBERSTALKING

Federal Laws

There are three major federal laws that apply to cyberstalking: the Interstate Communications Act; the Telephone Harassment Act, as amended by the 2000 Violence Against Women Act (VAWA); and the Interstate Stalking and Prevention Act.

The Interstate Communications Act

Under the Interstate Communications Act, it is a crime to transmit in interstate commerce any communication (for example, by telephone, email, or beeper) that contains a threat to injure anyone (18 USC § 875(c). The punishment for the violation of this law is five years in prison and a fine of up to $250,000.

Although 18 U.S.C. 875 is an important tool, it is not an all-purpose anti-cyberstalking statute. First, it applies only to communications of actual threats, and many cyberstalkers do not threaten the victim. Thus, it would not apply in a situation where a female victim was harassed by a cyberstalker but was never threatened. Also, it is not clear that it would apply to situations where a person harasses or terrorizes another by posting messages on a bulletin board or in a chat room encouraging others to harass or annoy another person. In other words, a female victim who is harassed by a third person because of messages posted on a bulletin board may not be protected by this law.

limited app.

Violence Against Women Act (VAWA)

Certain forms of cyberstalking may be prosecuted under the 1934 Telephone Harassment Act, as amended by the 2006 VAWA. Under this law, it is a crime to anonymously and knowingly use a telephone or internet to transmit in interstate or foreign commerce any message that annoys, abuses, harasses, or threatens a person (47 USC §§ 223 & 223(a)(1)(C)). Violation of this law results in two years or less in prison.

In comparison with 18 U.S.C. 875, it covers both threats and harassment. However, Section 223 applies only to direct communications between the perpetrator and the victim. Therefore, it cannot address third-party cyberstalking where a person encourages others to harass or annoy another person. The statute also requires that the perpetrator not reveal his or her name.

The Interstate Stalking and Prevention Act

According to the 1996 Interstate Stalking and Prevention Act, it is a crime for any person to cross a state line with the intent to injure or harass another person or to travel in interstate or foreign commerce to use the mail, any interactive computer service to engage in a course of conduct that causes substantial emotional distress to another person.

Although a number of serious stalking cases have been prosecuted under Section 2261A, the requirement that the stalker physically travel across state lines makes it largely inapplicable to victims of cyberstalking incidents. This law, therefore, does little to help victims of cyberstalking because it does not involve the physical crossing of state lines.

State Laws

All 50 states and the District of Columbia have enacted stalking and harassment laws. Of these, 46 states explicitly include electronic forms of communication within stalking or harassment laws. The laws vary in terms of the conduct criminalized, standards that may trigger prosecution, penalties for violations, and protections afforded to victims, among other things.

As of January 2007, there were only six states (Illinois, Louisiana, Mississippi, North Carolina, Rhode Island, and Washington) that had laws specifically targeting cyberstalking. These states passed anti-cyberstalking laws even though they already had anti-stalking (offline stalking) laws.

Some states have amended their statutes to cover cyberstalking. About half of the states currently have language in their laws that specifically address harassing by means of electronic, computer, or e-mail communications. However, the type of electronic communications covered by these statutes varies. Some of these states use the term "electronic communications" while others specify the type of communications, such as email, computer communications, or communications on the network.

The anti-stalking laws of some states contain broad language that can be interpreted to encompass cyberstalking behavior. Several states' anti-stalking statutes require physical pursuit and fail to include electronic communications. Finally, there is a group of states that have no laws specifically dealing with cyberstalking.

Issues Regarding State Laws

Although the attempts to address cyberstalking by some states is commendable, these changes are still inadequate to protect female victims from cyberstalking.

First Amendment Right

One of the issues regarding legislation to combat cyberstalking is the issue of free speech protection in the United States. This involves speech over the Internet which has been recognized as an important tool for protected speech activities (Reno, 1999). Although the courts have upheld antistalking legislation that deals with threats because the First Amendment does not protect true threats, it has identified some acts of cyberstalking as being protected by the First Amendment. Consequently, judges may decide not to convict alleged cyberstalkers. This occurred in the case *United States v. Alkhabaz*. Using the pseudonym "Jake Baker", Abraham Jacob Alkhabaz, a student at the University of Michigan posted stories describing the rape, torture, and murder of a woman. In one of his stories, he named the victim as one of his fellow female students. He said he used her name because it rhymed with other words in his stories. Baker was charged with interstate transmission of threats over the Internet and arrested in 1995. While these stories were initially about violence, the courts took into consideration his First Amendment right and the judge dismissed the case against Baker. Free speech advocates state that the Government violated Jake Baker's First Amendment right to free speech by charging him with a crime for writing stories. Others criticized the government on the grounds that the law did not take any action to protect the female listed in his stories. They argued that the courts did not address the slander against her, nor did it address her privacy rights (*United States v. Alkhabaz*, 1997) 104 F.3d 1492 (6th Cir. 1997).

Credible Threat

In a number of states the language of the statute requires a "credible threat" of serious physical injury or death. These laws on cyberstalking apply to behavior that constitutes a direct or credible threat and causes the victim to be fearful for his or her safety. Because "credible threat" is generally considered verbal or written threat of physical harm and the apparent ability to carry out the threat, some forms of cyberstalking, such as email harassment are unlikely to meet this standard. In addition, some cyberstalkers do not overtly threaten their victims, but instead harass their victims without any threats. It is, therefore, difficult for the victim to establish "credible threat" if no actual threat of violence from the cyberstalker was evident. Second, many cyberstalkers often do not threaten their victims directly or overtly or in person; rather, they may engage in techniques that would hide their identity. It is even more difficult proving "credible threat," when the cyberstalker and victim live in two jurisdictions or countries. Since the very nature of cyberstalking allows the cyberstalker to be hundreds or thousands of miles away from his victim, statutes that require a credible threat cannot address the crime.

Limited Protection for Victims

While some of the statutes can cover emails, they are not applicable to chatrooms, bulletin boards or websites and, therefore, cannot protect the female victims of such forms of cyberstalking. The case of Amy Boyer, in 1999, is a good example. Without her knowledge, Boyer's stalker, a fellow student, purchased her social security number over the Internet. With that information, he was able to locate her license plate number and place of employment. He detailed his plans to kill her on a website posted under her name. Within minutes of his last website entry, he drove to her workplace, murdered her, and then committed suicide (CBS, 2000). A case such as this one would be difficult to prosecute in states that include only email stalking in their legislation.

In many states, there is little protection for victims who were stalked by proxy or by innocent third party. Unfortunately, most of the state laws do not address this aspect of cyberstalking since they focus on a genuine victim and not someone impersonating another person as a victim. Consequently, such cases of cyberstalking are difficult to prosecute, leaving the female victim with very little legal protection from the stalker. Perhaps most frightening is that cyberstalkers can incite other "innocent" third parties to do their cyberstalking for them. Only three states, Ohio, Rhode Island, and Washington, have statutes that explicitly address cases where third parties innocently harass the victim at the cyberstalker's bidding (Goodno, 2006).

ENFORCEMENT OF ANTI-CYBERSTALKING LEGISLATION

In addition to gaps in the state and federal laws, there are also barriers in combating the cyberstalking problem. Law enforcement officers face serious limitations when they investigate cyberstalking.

Anonymity

One major obstacle to the enforcement of laws against cyberstalking is the identity of the cyberstalker. Due to the technology, users of the Internet can hide their identities. Cyberstalkers can "mask" their identity on the internet by using Internet Protocol (IP) address and anonymous remailers mail servers that purposefully strip identifying information. The ability to hide one's identity makes it relatively easy for cyberstalkers to send anonymous communications, while making it difficult for victims, internet providers, and law enforcement to identify the person or persons responsible for transmitting harassing or threatening communications over the Internet. By using pseudonyms, the perpetrator could be in another state, in another country, or in the next cubicle at work without the victim even knowing where the perpetrator is located. The perpetrator could be a former friend or lover, a total stranger met in a chat room, or simply a teenager playing a practical joke. The inability to identify the source of the harassment or threats hinders police in their investigation of cyberstalking.

Given the enforcement problems, some people have called for the prohibition of anonymous communications while other have called for restrictions to be placed on anonymity. Opponents of anonymity argue that it facilitates illegal conduct, such as cyberstalking, and allows the perpetrators to evade the consequences of their actions (Ellison & Akdeniz, 1998). However, legislation that restricts anonymity on the internet can be subjected to constitutional challenges. In the United States, attempts to control anonymity on the Internet have been ruled unconstitutional. In *American Civil Liberties Union (ACLU) v. Miller*, for example, the Federal District Court agreed with the ACLU that a Georgia statute was constitutional because it prevents online users from using pseudonyms or communicating anonymously over the Internet (*American Civil Liberties Union v. Miller*, 1997). In the United States, anonymity has historically been recognized as valuable for free speech. The problem, however, is that it can be abused as in the case of the cyberstalker.

Issue of Privacy

Even if the cyberstalker is identified, there is still the issue of the cyberstalker's privacy. In United States, the Federal Cable Communications Policy Act prohibits disclosure of cable subscriber records to law enforcement agencies unless the agency has a court order and has notified the subscriber. Under the CCPA, a law enforcement agency investigating a cyberstalker who uses a cable company for Internet access would have to provide the individual notice that the agency has requested his/her subscriber records. The purpose of the law was to prevent police from abusing their power by checking on the viewing habits of cable subscribers without the knowledge of the persons being investigated. The law was designed to protect individual's privacy, but now it can hinder police investigation of cyberstalkers cyberstalking (Reno, 1999). Although it may be appropriate to prohibit the indiscriminate disclosure of cable records to law enforcement agencies, the government should still allow law enforcement officers to have access to a person's file without his or her knowledge if that person is suspected of cyberstalking.

Jurisdiction and Statutory Authority

The use of the internet is a global phenomenon and internet users have access to the internet anywhere in the world. Because cyberjurisdiction is global, law enforcement officers face the issue of jurisdictional limitations when investigating cyberstalking that involves multiple jurisdictions. Determining the jurisdiction of an electronic stalking case presents difficulties for law enforcement officers when the stalker and the victim live in different states or different countries. For example, if a cyberstalker sends a threatening message from a computer in Michigan, United States to a computer in Seoul, South Korea, the dilemma for the law enforcement officer is to determine which country should investigate: the place where the e-mail originated or the place where the victim lives? While a victim of one country or state where the cyberstalker resides may have some legal recourse, the same victims of a cyberstalker living elsewhere may not have any recourse. So that although the internet may be borderless for the cyberstalker, law enforcement officers are bounded by geographical boundaries. This makes investigating and arresting a cyberstaker outside the jurisdiction extremely difficult. It is clear from the above example that there are difficulties investigating cyberstalking cases that involved multiple jurisdictions.

RECOMMENDATIONS

Cyberstalking is expected to increase as computers and the Internet become more popular. Governments, IPS, law enforcement officers, and internet users need to recognize that cyberstalking is a serious crime. Therefore, more effort should be made to address cyberstalking.

Addressing the Gaps in the Laws

At the present time, many of the federal and state laws against cyberstalking are impractical and ineffective in prosecuting cyberstalkers and protecting female victims. The federal and state governments should enact laws that can effectively address cyberstalking. The fact that cyberstalking behavior may implicate important issues of free speech does not mean that cyberstalking should not be outlawed. Governments have to balance individual free speech and the protection of society. They will have to enact anti-stalking statutes that would not infringe upon free speech.

In addition, governments should develop legislation that would make the prosecution of cyberstalkers easier when it involves multiple jurisdictions. A law dealing with cyberjurisdiction must address whether a act of cyberstalking that crosses different jurisdiction will be controlled by the laws of the state or country where the Website is located, by the laws of the state or country where the Internet service provider is located, by the laws of the state or country where the user is located, or perhaps by all of these laws.

Criminal Justice Response

As cyberstalking becomes more prevalent, specialized investigative skills would be needed. It is, therefore, imperative that law enforcement officers be properly trained to effectively detect and investigate cybercrimes, including cyberstalking. They should have a thorough knowledge of the nature of cyberstalking and the relationship between online stalking and offline stalking.

There are only a few police departments in the United States that have cyberstalking units. Law enforcement agencies should make an effort to establish more cyberstalking units. They should also network with other agencies so that they can share resources and information about cyberstalking.

Victim Services

There are only a few victim advocacy groups available to assist, support, and advise female victims of cyber stalking. More services are, therefore, needed. In addition, these services should use a female-centered approach if they are to effectively assist female victims of cyberstalking. They should also establish multidisciplinary teams consisting of members from law enforcement, women's groups, the medical community, and victim organization. Victim advocates should also be trained on Internet technology and should be familiar with the tactics used by cyberstalkers.

Internet Providers

Internet providers should take a more active role in combating cyberstalking. They should impose stricter regulation for their users. For example, they can create a code of behavior so that when users attempt to connect to the Internet, they would be subject to an agreement that could prohibit certain types of behaviors, including cyberstalking. Failure to comply with the agreement would result in loss of service. Internet service providers also should be responsible for reporting users who abuse their privileges. In other words, internet providers should be made to police their services more effectively.

Research

The lack of comprehensive data on the nature and extent of cyberstalking makes it difficult to adequately understand the phenomenon. Any attempt to address the crime of cyberstalking necessitates a general understanding of the problem. Effective preventive measures or strategies for female victims of stalking cannot be developed unless there is adequate information on cyberstalking. There is, therefore, a need for more research in this area.

More comprehensive research should be conducted on cyberstalking to determine the extent, nature, and effects of this phenomenon. Future studies should examine the effectiveness of the laws, the impact of punishment on perpetrators, the effects of preventive measures on the rate and extent of stalking, and effects of cyberstalking on victims.

Since cyberstalking is a global problem, it is necessary to conduct comparative studies focusing on the international community. Such studies could compare the laws governing the Internet in various countries and their impact on cyberstalking, and law enforcement practices in various countries dealing with cyberstalking. Comparative studies would provide a more comprehensive and holistic overview of the problem of stalking.

SUMMARY

Cyberstalking is a growing problem that transcends international boundaries. As the dependency on computers and electronic forms of communication grows, so will cyberstalking. While governments have attempted to use laws to combat cyberstalking, the global nature of the internet has made many of these laws ineffective. New laws, which can address the unique nature of cyberstalking, need to be created. Internet providers also have to take the initiative to monitor and report the abuses of their users. In general, effective laws and law enforcement strategies and other legal responses to cyberstalking are the best ways to control and protect females against cyberstalking.

REFERENCES

ASHCROFT, J. (2001). *Stalking and domestic violence*. Washington, DC: U.S. Department of Justice.

BOCIJ, P (2004). *Cyberstalking: Harassment in the internet age and how to protect your family*. Westport: Praeger Publishers.

BOCIJ, P. & MCFARLANE, L. (2003). Cyberstalking: The technology of hate. *Police Journal, 76*(3), 204–221.

BOCIJ, P. (2005). Reactive stalking: A new perspective on victimization. *The British Journal of Forensic Practice, 7*(1), 23–45.

BOYER, M. (2006, August 22). Colleges work to combat cyberstalking. Retrieved February 10, 2010 from http://www.foxnews.com/printer_friendly_story/0,3566,209395,00.html

CBS (2000, March 23). An online tragedy. Retrieved May 7, 2007, from Retrieved March 10, 2010 from http://www.cbsnews.com/stories/2000/03/23/48hours/printable175556.shtml

D'OVIDIO, R. & DOYLE, J. (2003). A study on cyberstalking: Understanding investigative hurdles. *FBI Law Enforcement Bulletin, 72*(3), 10–17.

DAVIDSON, A. (2000). Stalking in cyberspace. *Proctor—Journal of the Queensland Law Society*. Retrieved March 2, 2010 from www.uq.edu.au/~laadavid/cyberlaw/april2000.html.

ELLISON, L., & AKDENIZ, Y. (1998). Cyber-stalking: The regulation of harassment on the internet. *Criminal Law Review, Crime, Criminal Justice and the Internet*, pp. 29–48.

FINCH, E. (2002). Stalking: A violent crime or a crime of violence? *Howard Journal of Criminal Justice, 41*(5), 468–483.

FINN, J. (2004). A survey of online harassment at a university campus. *Journal of Interpersonal Violence, 19*(4), 468–483.

GELLER, A. (2007, April 18). VA gunman had 2 past stalking cases. Associated Press. Retrieved July 10, 2007 from www.newsday.com.

GOODNO, N. H. (2006). Cyberstalking, a new crime: Evaluating the effectiveness of current State and Federal Laws. Retrieved March 13, 2010 from http://law.bepress.com/cgi/viewcontent.cgi?article=7936&context=expresso

GREGORIE, M. T. (2001). Cyberstalking: The dark side of the information superhighway. Retrieved December 10, 2009 from http://www.ncvc.org/newsltr/networks_cyberstalking.htm

KUJH-TV News (2006). Facebook used to aid stalkers. Retrieved May 10, 2007 from www.tv.ku.edu/newsd.

LAMBERG, L. (2001). Stalking disrupts lives, leaves emotional scars. *Journal of American Medical Association, 286*(5), 519–523.

LI, Q. (2007). Bullying in the new playground: Research into cyberbullying and cyber victimisation. *Australasian Journal of Educational Technology, 23*(4), 435–454.

MULLEN, P. E., PATHE M., PURCELL R., & STUART, G. W. (1999). Study of stalkers. *The American Journal of Psychiatry, 156*(8), 1244–1250.

MUSTAINE, E. E., & TEWKSBURY, R. (1999). Routine activity theory explanation for women's stalking victimizations. *Violence Against Women, 5*(1), 43–62.

OGILVIE, E. (2000). Cyber stalking. Retrieved January 10, 2002 from http://www.aic.gov.au/publications/tandi/tandi66.html.

PATHÉ, M., & MULLEN, P. (1997). The impact of stalkers on their victims. *British Journal of Psychiatry, 170*, 12–17.

PETHERICK, W. 1999. Cyber-stalking: Obsessional pursuit and the digital criminal. Retrieved December 15, 2009 from http://www.trutv.com/library/crime/criminal_mind/psychology/cyberstalking/2.html

PETROCELLI, J. (2005). Cyber stalking. *Law & Order, 53*(12), 56–58.

PITTARO, M. L. (2007). Cyber stalking: An analysis of online harassment and intimidation. *International Journal of Cyber Criminology, 1*(2), 180–197.

Reno, J. (1999). *1999 report on cyberstalking: A new challenge for law enforcement and industry.* Washington, DC: U.S. Justice Department.

Sheridan, L. P., & Grant, T. (2007). Is cyberstalking different? *Psychology, Crime & Law,* 1477–2744.

Spitzberg, B., & Hoobler, G. (2002). Cyberstalking and the technologies of interpersonal terrorism. *New Media & Society, 4*(1), 71–92.

The National Center for Victims of Crime (2004). Cyber stalking. Retrieved Feb. 18, 2006 from http://www.ncvc.org/ncvc/Print.aspx?PrintableZoneID=Cell_3&PrintableVertionID=WP_P.htm

Working to Halt Online Abuse, 2010; Online Harassment/Cyberstalking Statistics. Retrieved March 5, 2010 from http://www.haltabuse.org/resources/stats/index.shtml.

SECTION IV

Women Incarcerated

21

Disparate Treatment in Correctional Facilities

Women Incarcerated

Roslyn Muraskin

❖

With more than one million women behind bars or under the control of the criminal justice system, women are the fastest growing segment of the incarcerated population increasing at nearly double the rate of men since 1985 (ACLU "Women's Rights" www.aclu.org, December 12, 2007). This is an increase of 57,600 more inmates than state, local, and federal officials held on the same day one year earlier.

Three out of four violent female offenders commit simple assault. An estimated 28 percent of violent female offenders are juveniles. An estimated four in ten women who *juvenile* commit violent crimes are perceived as being under the influence of alcohol and/or drugs at the time the crime was committed. In 1998 alone an estimated 3.2 million women were arrested. And since 1990 the rate of increase in the number of female defendants convicted of felonies in state courts is more than twice that of male defendants (U.S. Department of Justice, 2000).

According to the Bureau of Justice (August 2003), "the lifetime chances of going to prison increased more rapidly for black females (from 1.1% in 1974 to 5.6% in 2001) than for white males. Hispanic females (from 0.4% in 1974 to 2.2% in 2001) and white females (from 0.2% in 1974 to 0.9% in 2001) had smaller increases in their lifetime chances of going to prison."

Providing services and programs is all part of good correctional practice. It ensures that those inmates returned to society can be reintegrated into society. With the number of women incarcerated there exists the need for their proper treatment within the correctional facilities. In this chapter, we review the problems and cases of the past, demonstrating that services legally mandated have not been fully delivered.

OVERVIEW

Based on the self-reports of victims of violence, women account for about 14 percent of violent offenders—an annual average of about 2.1 million violent female offenders. Three out of four violent female offenders are estimated to commit simple assault. An estimated 28 percent of female offenders who are violent are classified as juveniles. It is also likely that an estimated four in ten women who commit acts of violence have been perceived by their victims to have been under the influence of either alcohol or drugs when they commit crime. It is noted that the per capita rate of women who committed murder in the year 1998 (latest date figures are available) was the lowest since 1976. Overall the rate by which women commit murder has been declining since 1980. In 1998 an estimated 3.2 million women were arrested, which accounts for about 22 percent of all arrests during that year. The per capita rate of arrest among juvenile females has been estimated to be nearly twice the adult female rate. It is a fact that since 1990 the rate of increase in the number of female defendants who have been convicted of felonies in various state courts is more than two times that of male defendants. As of 1998 (latest figures available) one million women were estimated to be under the care, custody, or control of correctional agencies—probation or parole agencies supervising 85 percent of these offenders in the community. This total equals out to a rate of about 1 woman involved with the criminal justice system for every 109 adult women in the U.S. population. Disturbing about these statistics is the factor that women who are under the supervision of criminal justice agencies were mothers of approximately 1.3 million minor children (Greenfeld & Snell, 1999, p. 1).

In examining the racial and ethnic composition of the general inmate population, we find that "non-Hispanic black females outnumber non-Hispanic black males by nearly 1.9 million, accounting for more than a quarter of the total difference in the number of males and females in the general population" (Bureau of Justice Statistics, 2000). The average age of females in the general inmate population is about 2 1/2 years higher than that of males. See Table 1 for a comparison of violent crimes committed by females and males. It is interesting to note that among females, Hispanic females have the lowest average age, that of 29.6 years, while white non-Hispanic women have the highest, 39.6 years (Greenfeld & Snell, 1999, p. 1).

TABLE 1   Comparison of Violent Crimes by Gender

Offense	Average Annual Number of Offenders Reported by Victims, 1993–1997		Women as a Percentage of Violent Offenders
	Female	Male	
All	2,135,000	13,098,000	14
Sexual assault	10,000	442,000	2
Robbery	157,000	2,051,000	7
Aggravated assault	435,000	3,419,000	11
Simple assault	1,533,000	7,187,000	18

Based on victims' reports, about one out of seven violent offenders was a female. Women accounted for 1 in 50 offenders committing a violent sex offense, including rape and sexual assault; 1 in 14 committing robbery; 1 in 9 committing aggravated assault; and more than 1 in 6 committing simple assault. Black and white offenders accounted for nearly equal proportions of women committing robbery and aggravated assault; however, simple assault offenders were more likely to be described as white (see Table 2).

With regard to women who murder: "Since 1993 both male and female rates of committing murder have declined. Rates of committing murder in 1998 were the lowest since statistics were first collected in 1976. The estimated rate for murder offending by women in 1998 was 1.3 per 100,000, about 1 murderer for every 77,000 women. The male rate of murder offending in 1998 was 11.5 per 100,000, about 1 murderer for every 8,700 males" (Bureau of Justice Statistics, 2000, p. 10).

"In 1998 there were an estimated 3.2 million arrests of women, accounting for about a fifth of all arrests by law enforcement agencies. Women were about 17% of those arrested for Part I violent crimes (murder, rape, robbery, and aggravated assault) and 29% of those arrested for Part I property crimes (burglary, larceny, and motor-vehicle theft). Women accounted for about 16% of all felons convicted in State Courts in 1996. Women were 8% of convicted violent felons, 23% of property felons, and 17% of drug felons. Women defendants accounted for 41% of all felons convicted of forgery, fraud, and embezzlement" (Bureau of Justice Statistics, 2000, p. 11).

According to Julie Samuels, acting director for the National Institute of Justice, a common observation exists that the criminal behavior of women is not to be deemed an important problem. For many years it has been believed that if women were to commit any crimes, they would commit only minor crimes and therefore have always constituted a small fraction of the correctional population. But these facts have veiled a trend that has attracted everyone's attention. It is well known that although crime rates are down, there is a growing population within correctional facilities as a result of tougher and longer sentences. The number of female inmates, however, is growing at a rate higher than that of men. Among academics there has been a call to redefine justice.

According to Samuels, "Whether justice should promote unalloyed equality, be blind to the circumstances in which crime is committed, and consider only the gravity of offense and prior record, is still a matter of debate. In the current sentencing environment, the view of those who favor equity above all other considerations has won the day. There is another perspective, the belief that sanctions ought to be tailored to the specific characteristics and circumstances of individual offenders" (U.S. Department of Justice, 2000, p. 2).

TABLE 2   Characteristics of Violent Female Offenders

Offense	Percentage by Race of Female Offenders		
	White	Black	Other
Violent offense	55	35	11
Robbery	43	43	14
Aggravated assault	45	46	10
Simple assault	58	31	10

Women in prison are typically young, are poor, come from minority communities, and have "experienced significant problems in their life prior to imprisonment. More simply women in prison have been triply marginalized by race, class, and gender." Over the years women have gone to prison for offenses that appear to differ dramatically from those of male prisoners. "While the increasingly harsh treatment of the drug offender leads to the incarceration of thousands of women and men into the contemporary prison, women have been sent to prison in rates far surpassing those of men. Women are usually incarcerated for nonviolent property and drug offenses and are very often serving their first prison term" (http://law.jrank.org/pages/1803/Prisons-Prisons-Women-Conclusion.html).

The explosion in the number of women entering prison cannot be explained only by the crime rate of women. The low rate of violent crime committed by women as compared to men has to be taken into consideration.

> When women do commit acts of violence, it is most likely against a spouse or a partner. . . . drug offenses have had the most significant impact on female arrest rates. Sharp increases in the numbers of women arrested for minor property crimes, like larceny, fraud, and forgery, have also contributed to the explosion in women's imprisonment. Many women resort to minor property crime in order to support their drug use. In addition to increased prosecution of drug offenses, the lack of viable treatment and alternative community sanctions for women has contributed to this unprecedented increase in women's population. . . . most criminologists see that the war on drugs, . . . accounts for the unprecedented rise in the imprisonment of women. (http://law.jrank.org/pages.1803/Prisons-Prisons-women-Conclusions.html)

LOOKING BACK INTO HISTORY

In the United States, no constitutional obligation exists for all persons to be treated alike. The government frequently does, in fact, treat disparate groups differently. However, this principle does not excuse invidious discrimination among potential recipients (Gobert & Cohen, 1981, pp. 294–295). It is required that where unequal treatment exists, the inequalities must be rational and related to a legitimate interest of the state (Pollack & Smith, 1978, p. 206). Laws have created categories in which some people may be treated unequally. These categories have always included women incarcerated in correctional facilities. The question that still arises is "whether the inequalities by the law are justifiable—in legal terms whether the person upon whom the law's burden falls has been denied equal protection of the law" (pp. 206–207).

Since the decision in *Holt v. Sarver* (1970), in which the court declared an entire prison to be in violation of the Eighth Amendment and imposed detailed remedial plans, the judiciary has taken an active role in the administration of correctional facilities. Many of the landmark cases challenged the inequity of treatment between male and female prisoners.

Ostensibly, the needs of male and female prisoners would appear to be the same. They are not. Although some inmate interests are similar, others are separate and distinct. In many institutions, criteria developed for men were applied automatically to women, with no consideration given for gender differences. Research has shown that female offenders have always experienced more medical and health problems than do male inmates. Classification officials have noted that female offenders have needed help in parenting skills, child welfare, pregnancy and prenatal care, home stability, and understanding the circumstances of their crimes.

But typically, assignments to programs and treatment resources within correctional facilities have always been based on what is available rather than on what should be available.

A review of the literature of the cases and issues that have dealt with disparate treatment has revealed that women historically have represented a small minority in both prisons and jails. Yet the effects of incarceration have been in many but not all respects similar for men and women. Each has suffered the trauma of being separated from family and friends. When either a man or a woman becomes imprisoned, he or she experiences a loss of identity as well as a devaluation of his or her status. Regardless of the inmate's gender, prison life has coerced conformity to an environment alien to the individual, where one's every movement is dictated each and every minute (Muraskin, 1989).

Most challenges to prison conditions have neglected the special needs of female prisoners, especially in the jails, where both males and females are housed together. Traditionally, correctional facilities for women have not received funding comparable to that of correctional facilities for men. Educational and vocational programs for women historically have been and seriously underfunded. "Benign neglect [has] . . . created a situation of unequal treatment in many states" (Hunter, 1984, p. 133). Correctional administrators have insisted that "the small number of female offenders [has] made it too expensive to fund such programs." The courts, however, have ruled that "cost is not an acceptable defense for denying equal treatment" (pp. 133–134). Historically, females have been subject to policies designed for the male offender. Just as "women have deferred to males in the economic, social, political spheres of life, [i]n the legal realm, more specifically in the imprisonment of the female, women have been forced into the status of being less than equal" (Sargent, 1984, p. 83).

REVIEW OF CASES: WOMEN AND EQUALITY/PARITY

When inmates similarly situated find themselves being treated differently, there may exist a violation of equal protection. A review of the cases discussed next demonstrates what established the discrimination against women who are incarcerated.

Constitutionally, no obligation exists for the government to provide any benefits beyond basic requirements. However, this principle should not be an excuse for invidious discrimination among potential recipients (Gobert & Cohen, 1981, pp. 294–295). Case law has held that benefits afforded to some cannot be denied solely on race or gender. In any equal protection challenge, the central question that has been raised is the "degree of state interest which can justify disparate treatment among offenders" (*Reed v. Reed*, 1971). As established, the "classification must be reasonable, not arbitrary and must bear a fair and substantial relation to the object of the legislation or practice" (*Reed*). Courts, for example, have found gender classifications to be irrational because they appear to be enacted solely for the convenience of correctional administrators (see *Craig v. Boren*, 1976;[1] *Weinberger v. Wisenfeld*, 1975;[2] *Eslinger v. Thomas*, 1973[3]). Existing differences in conditions, rules, and treatment among inmates have proven fertile ground for equal protection challenges. Neither administrative convenience (*Cooper v. Morin*, 1979, 1980) nor lack of funds (*State ex rel Olson v. Maxwell*, 1977) is an acceptable justification for disparity of treatment.

Legal uprisings against intolerable conditions in correctional facilities and prisoners' rights litigation were initiated by male attorneys and male prisoners. In the early stages of this litigation, female inmates did not turn to the courts, nor did officials at

Cases 1968 – 1980 = Phase I

female institutions fear lawsuits, condemnation by the public, or inmate riots. With so few women incarcerated, there was little the women felt they could do. This situation has changed. Female prisoners sued and demanded parity with male prisoners. The Fourth Amendment has been the source for issues of violation of privacy, and the Eighth Amendment is used for cases involving cruel and unusual punishment.

Differential sentencing of similarly situated men and women convicted of identical offenses has been found to violate the equal protection clause. A review of cases dealing generally with sentencing in correctional institutions includes prior rulings in the case of *United States ex rel Robinson v. York* (1968), which held that it was a violation of the equal protection clause for women who were sentenced to indeterminate terms under a Connecticut statute to serve longer maximum sentences than those of men serving indeterminate terms for the same offenses. In *Liberti v. York* (1968), the U.S. Supreme Court held that the female plaintiffs' indeterminate sentences of up to three years violated the equal protection clause because the maximum term for men convicted of the same crime was one year. In *Commonwealth v. Stauffer* (1969), a Pennsylvania court held that the practice of sentencing women to state prison on charges for which men were held in county jail was a violation of a woman's right to equal protection.

In *Williams v. Levi* (1976), which dealt with disparate treatment in the issue of parole, male prisoners in the District of Columbia were placed under the authority of the D.C. Board of Parole, whereas women prisoners were placed under the authority of the U.S. Board of Parole's stricter parole standards of violence. In *Dawson v. Carberry* (1973), it was held that there must be substantial equivalence in male and female prisoners' opportunities to participate in work-furlough programs.

In *Barefield v. Leach* (1974), women at the Women's Division of the Penitentiary of New Mexico claimed that conditions there violated their rights to an uncensored press, to have their persons free from unreasonable searches, to be free from cruel and unusual punishment, and to be allowed due process and equal protection of the law regarding disciplinary procedures and rehabilitative opportunities, respectively. The court held that "[w]hat the equal protection clause requires in a prison setting is parity of treatment as contrasted with identity of treatment, between male and female inmates with respect to the conditions of their confinement and access to rehabilitative opportunities." *Barefield* is especially important, as it was the first case to enunciate the standard against which disparity of treatment of men and women in prison was to be measured.

Still further, in *McMurray v. Phelps* (1982), there was a challenge to conditions for both men and women at the Quachita County jail, where the jail ordered an end to the disparate treatment of female detainees. And in *Mary Beth G. v. City of Chicago* (1983), a strip-search policy under which female arrestees underwent a full strip search without reason to believe that a weapon or contraband was present was ruled to be a violation of the equal protection clauses as well as the Fourteenth Amendment.

In *Bounds v. Smith* (1977), the Court held that prisoners' access to the courts was a fundamental constitutional right. The Court noted that there existed an affirmative obligation on the part of state officials to ensure court access to prisoners by providing them adequate law libraries or some alternative involving a legal-assistance program. It was noted further in the Court's decision that females had less access to library facilities than did male inmates. It was ordered that this situation be remedied. In *Cody v. Hillard* (1986), the Court held that inmates at the state women's correctional facility, which had neither a law library nor law-trained assistants, were denied their constitutional right of meaningful access to the courts.

In *State ex rel Olson v. Maxwell*, 1977, a case that dealt with the transfer of female inmates out of state because of a lack of facilities, female inmates filed a petition for a supervisory writ challenging the North Dakota practice of routinely transferring them to other states to be incarcerated, alleging a denial of equal protection and due process. It was held that North Dakota must not imprison women prisoners outside the state unless and until a due process waiver hearing was held or waived, and the state admitted that it could not provide women prisoners with facilities equal to those of male prisoners.

"From a policy perspective, discriminatory distribution of prison privileges . . . will appear counter-rehabilitative, fueling inmate administration animosity and generating inmate peer jealousies" (Gobert & Cohen, 1981, p. 295). In *Canterino v. Wilson* (1982, 1983), it was indicated that "restrictions imposed solely because of gender with the objective of controlling lives of women inmates in a way deemed unnecessary for male prisoners" would not be tolerated. The Court concluded that "males and females must be treated equally unless there is a substantial reason which requires a distinction be made" (1982). Case law has established that discriminatory selection for work release based on race, religion, gender, or even mental impairment is not an acceptable practice. The courts have prohibited any arbitrary or capricious selection for participation in work programs.

Due to the presence of small numbers of women in men's correctional facilities, services and treatment programs have appeared to have been reduced. Such reduced services included medical services as well. Generally, there has always been a wider range of medical services provided for male inmates than female inmates. Both *Todaro v. Ward* (1977) and *Estelle v. Gamble* (1976) were about medical issues. In the former case, the medical system in the Bedford Hills Correctional Facility was found to be unconstitutionally defective, while in the latter, there was found to be deliberate indifference to the medical needs of the females. This was a violation of the Eighth Amendment.

In *Bukhari v. Huto* (1980), the court held that no justification existed for disparate treatment based on the fact that women's prisons serviced a smaller population and the cost would be greater to provide programs equivalent to the men's institutions. Cost could not be claimed as an excuse for paucity of services.

The landmark case on women's prison issues was *Glover v. Johnson* (1979). This comprehensive case challenged a disputed system of educational, vocational, work, and minimum security programs in the Michigan prison systems based on due process and equal protection. The Court ruled that female prisoners must be provided program opportunities on a parity with male prisoners. The case resulted in an order requiring the state to provide postsecondary education, counseling, vocational programs, and a legal education program (in companion case *Cornish v. Johnson*, 1979) as well as other relief. "Institutional size is frankly not a justification but an excuse for the kind of treatment afforded women prisoners" (*Glover*, 1979).

In a facility in Nassau County, New York, in the case of *Thompson et al. v. Varelas* (1985), the plaintiffs asked for

> [d]eclaratory and injunctive relief regarding the discriminatory, oppressive, degrading and dangerous conditions of . . . their confinement within the Nassau County Correctional Center. . . . [A]lleged in their action was the existence of inadequate health care, lack of private attorney

visiting facilities, inadequate and unequal access to employment, recreation and training; unequal access to library facilities and newspapers, and excessive confinement; unsanitary food preparation and service; and, inadequate and unequal access to religious services.

They claimed that lack of these facilities and services violated their rights as guaranteed by the First, Fifth, Sixth, Eighth, Ninth, and Fourteenth Amendments to the Constitution of the United States, but it was not until September 1985 that a consent was entered in the *Thompson* case. *Thompson* made a further argument for the needs of a checklist of standards against which to assess what constitutes disparate treatment in the correctional facilities.

Prior to these cases the female prisoner was the "forgotten offender." A teacher's testimony in the *Glover* case indicated that whereas men were allowed to take shop courses, women were taught at a junior high level because the motto of those in charge was "keep it simple, these are only women."

In the twenty-first century, we find that the courts generally held that it was unconstitutional or unlawful to have gender discrimination in the correctional facilities, jails or prisons; educational and vocational programs as well as employment opportunities; and the interstate transfer of inmates and visiting privileges. However, those cases that involve regulations such as grooming have been held not to be unconstitutional. Where we have cases regarding disparate treatment involving inmates criminally committed to a mental hospital as well as disparate treatment regarding recreational programs offered to both men and women, there is legal authority that holds such treatment to be unequal and unlawful. Most of the cases previously discussed are based on the Fourteenth Amendment to the Constitution as well as its counterparts in the states.

As, for example, in the case of *Batton v. State Government of North Carolina* in 1980,

> the court denied the government defendants' motion for summary judgment as to the female inmates' claim that they were offered vocational training opportunities only in low-paying, dead-end, traditionally female jobs while male inmates were afforded training in a wide variety of occupations. Stating that it had to employ an intermediate level of judicial scrutiny to the inmates' equal protection claims, the court added that a parity of treatment standard provided instructive guidance for analyzing these claims. Although the court noted that the government defendants produced the results of preference polls taken of samples of the female inmate population which indicated a continuing preference for traditionally female jobs, the court stated that the polls were suspect because no systematic explanations were offered of the job characteristics of many of the occupations listed, adding that it would not assume that the survey accurately reflected the desires of the female inmates. (501 F. Supp. 1173)

Subsequently in the case of *Davie v. Wingard* (1997), which dealt with the differences in the regulations that govern the length of the hair of male and female inmates, it was held that such differences were justified by much lower incidence of contraband concealment, escape, gang participation, and the violence by women inmates as compared to male inmates (958 F. Supp. 1244).

In *Klinger v. Department of Corrections* (1994), "female state prison inmates could not maintain class action against [a] prison system on the basis of an equal protection challenge to disparities between services and facilities made available to male and female prison populations, where differences between male and female institutions, such as size, average length of stay, and security levels resulted in women inmates not being similarly situated to males" (31 F.3d 727).

Still in cases that dealt with the unlawfulness of unequal treatment, for example in the case of *Clarkson v. Coughlin* (1995), it was held that though a larger number of male deaf and hearing-impaired inmates may be held in state prisons, this was not a justification for the lack of availability of such services to deaf and hearing-impaired female inmates. They were also entitled to interpretive services as well as assistive communicative devices as needed as part of the normal medical and mental health treatment (898 F. Supp. 1019).

In an important decision (*Gerber v. Hickman*), the Ninth Circuit Court of Appeals held in 2001 "as a matter of first impression that a prisoner's right to procreate survives his incarceration but was subject to restriction based on legitimate penological interests. The court found that a prison's refusing to allow a male prisoner from artificially inseminating his wife was not reasonably related to the asserted legitimate penological interest of treating men and women inmates equally to the extent possible, for purposes of determining whether the prison had violated the prisoner's due process rights. Likewise, the court also rejected the prison's asserted legitimate penological interest in avoiding liability from women prisoners asserting their equal protection rights to challenge the denial of an opportunity for artificial insemination" (2001 WL 1008205).

And importantly, in what is somewhat a continuance of the *Glover* case, in 1999, it was held that "apprenticeship opportunities provided to male and female inmates of state prison were sufficiently comparable and, therefore, did not constitute gender discrimination in violation of [the] equal protection clause, despite [the] fact that male inmates were offered twelve different types of apprenticeships and female inmates were offered seven types; all eligible female inmates could participate in apprenticeship, while only [a] small portion of eligible male inmates could participate" (*Glover v. Johnson*, 35 F. Supp. 1010 [E.D. Mich 1999]).

And in another issue of visiting privileges, it was held that whereas over 90 percent of the jail population consists of males, the county was justified in allowing more total visiting time to males than females, especially since no prisoner, male or female, could be visited for more than 15 minutes at a time. To have allowed a greater percentage of time for the public to visit would have constituted differential treatment (*Morrow v. Harwell*, 768 F.2d 619, 1985).

And so it continues.

Although litigation has provided the opportunity for inmates to have a role in altering their conditions of confinement, a judicial opinion does not necessarily bring about change, then or now. Viewed from a nonlegal perspective, litigation is simply a catalyst for change rather than an automatic mechanism for ending wrongs. All the cases held that invidious discrimination cannot exist.

REVIEW OF THE LITERATURE

The first penal institution for women was opened in Indiana in 1873. By the beginning of the twentieth century, women's correctional facilities had been opened in Framingham, Massachusetts; Bedford Hills, New York; and Clinton, New Jersey. The Federal Institution for Women in Alderson, West Virginia, was opened in 1927, and the House of Detention for Women (the first separate jail for women) was opened in New York City in 1931. All these institutions shared one thing in common, "traditional values, theories and practices concerning a woman's role and place in society. . . . The staffs, architectural design and programs reflected the culturally valued norms for women's behavior" (Feinman, 1986, p. 38).

Historically, disparate treatment of male and female inmates started when state penitentiaries were first opened. "Female prisoners . . . were confined together in a single attic room above the institution's kitchen. [They] were supervised by the head of the kitchen below. Food was sent up to them once a day, and once a day the slop was removed. No provision was made for privacy or exercise and although the women were assigned some sewing work, for the most part they were left to their own devices in the 'tainted and sickly atmosphere' " (Rafter, 1983, p. 135). Female convicts were morally degraded to a greater extent than male convicts. The reformatories built for female prisoners "established and legitimated a tradition of deliberately providing for female prisoners treatment very different from that of males" (p. 148).

"From Lombroso to the present, criminological thought has been wrought with the sexism inherent in assuming that there exist only two distinct classes of women—those on pedestals and those in the gutter" (Lown & Snow, 1980, p. 195). "The differential law enforcement handling seems to be built into our basic attitudes toward women. The operation of such attention can be called euphemistically the chivalry factor" (Reckless, 1967).

The chivalry factor meant that women should be treated more leniently than men. The nature of treatment and programs for female inmates appears to indicate the assumption of such a theory. Theories have always abounded concerning the causes of female offenders' criminality. The chivalry factor, once accepted, does not appear to be held in favor today. Once a woman enters the correctional facility, she has not necessarily benefited from the benevolence of the criminal justice system. Theories of female crime have always emphasized the natural differences between men and women but have failed to explain why women commit the crimes they do. It is clear that female prisoners have historically been treated differently and sometimes worse than male prisoners. Often, as an alternative to differential treatment, the model followed has been that of the male prisons, which has frequently ignored the obvious physical differences of female inmates. An almost total lack of enforcement of standards exists for the confinement of women.

In addition to the historically poor quality and minimal services that have been made available to female inmates, they have continued to suffer the same miserable conditions of incarceration as those of male inmates. Women have suffered even more in the jails, because of the failure of the criminal justice system to classify them according to the seriousness of their crime. Women have always lived in crowded facilities, often finding themselves under squalid conditions, lacking privacy, and faced with insensitive visiting rules, callous treatment, and the threat of, or actual, sexual abuse. Stress on the female inmate also continues to stem from being separated from her family and children.

Much of the neglect in assessing disparate treatment has been attributed by writers believing that the experiences in prison for both men and women are the same and are not areas calling for special investigation. As Rafter indicated in 1983, it was not until the 1970s that literature dealing with women's prisons began to take notice of women's specialized problems (p. 130). Feinman (1982) indicated that for the most part, programs in correctional facilities for women continued to be based on the belief that "the only acceptable role for women is that of wife/mother" (p. 12). The female offender continues to be described as being poor, African-American, Hispanic, or other races; being undereducated; and lacking in both skills and self-confidence. Whereas nearly two-thirds of the women under probation supervision are white, nearly two-thirds of those confined in local jails and state and federal prisons are minorities: black, Hispanic, and other races. The majority of the women who are incarcerated have graduated from high school. About seven in ten women who are in the correctional facilities have minor children. These women are reported to have an average of 2.1 children. These estimates convert into more than 1.3 million children who are the offspring of women incarcerated. Female prisoners demonstrate more difficult economic circumstances than do their male counterparts: About four in ten women in state prison reported that they were employed full time prior to being arrested, while nearly six in ten males had been working full time. The up-to-date figures show that about 44 percent of women who are incarcerated had been physically or sexually assaulted. About half of the women have used alcohol or drugs at the time they were caught. "About 6 in 10 women in State prisons described themselves as using drugs in the month before the offense, 5 in 10 described themselves as a daily user of drugs, and 4 in 10 were under the influence of drugs at the time of the offense" (Bureau of Justice Statistics, 2000, p. 19). In the year 1998, the highest per capita rate of women who were confined was in Oklahoma (1,222), and the lowest was in Maine and Vermont (9 in each) (p. 21). About 138,000 women were confined in correctional facilities in 1998, which represents a "tripling of the number of incarcerated women between the years 1985 and 1997" (latest available figures) (p. 8).

Indications are that in the twenty-first century, more women will be involved in committing crimes than ever before. Yet when prisoners are released back into the community, studies continue to show that men still represent a disproportionate majority in community programs. The way that community programs continue to be structured provides evidence of the lack of sensitivity and the differential treatment afforded to women.

Historically, the women's correctional system was not to replicate that of the men's but rather was to differ along a "number of key dimensions, including its historical development, administrative structures, some of its disciplinary techniques and the experience of inmates" (Rafter, 1983, p. 132). Women's facilities today have changed little from those at the beginning of the twentieth century. Today, women's prisons appear to be smaller and fewer in number (Pollock-Byrne, 1990, p. 97). Characteristically women's prisons are located farther from friends and families; the number of women prisoners is relatively small compared to that of men prisoners, with the "relatively small number of women in prison and jail [being] used to 'justify' low levels of specialization in treatment and failure to segregate the more serious and mentally ill offenders from the less serious offenders" (as is done in men's prisons and jails) (p. 97).

The attitude that has persisted throughout the literature over these many years illustrates that women have been regarded as moral offenders, whereas men have continued to assert their masculinity. "[I]nstitutional incarceration needs to become more reflective of the ongoing changing social climate" (Sargent, 1984, p. 42). Most states continue to have one (in some cases, two) facility for women, which of necessity must be of maximum security; local jails house both men and women. Population size has become a justification for ignoring the plight of women prisoners. However, as pointed out in the decision in

Glover, size is but "an excuse for the kind of treatment afforded women prisoners" (p. 1078). The disparate treatment of female and male prisoners "is the result of habitual and stereotypic thinking rather than the following of a different set of goals for incarceration" (Lown & Snow, 1980, p. 210).

If administrators in corrections continue to assign women's corrections low priority in budget allocation, staff development, and program development, continued conflict can be expected between the needs of the correctional facilities and such treatment afforded to women in this century. It may well be that because of overcrowding in both types of facilities, men's and women's equality will become less of an issue, thereby producing equally undesirable conditions for both. Regardless, disparate treatment continues to permeate correctional institutions. Adequate care and continuity in delivering services to all inmates is important. Standards must be applied equally. Such standards as developed over the years are meant to serve efficiency, provide greater cost-effectiveness, and establish better planning than we have at present.

According to Richie, Tsenin, and Widom (2000), "there is a common perception that the criminal behaviors of women and girls are not serious problems. Women are more likely to commit minor offenses and have historically constituted a very small proportion of the offender population. But these facts mask a trend that is beginning to attract attention. The dramatic rise in the number of prison and jail inmates is fairly well known; less so is that the ranks of women inmates are increasing much faster than are those of their male counterparts. The pace at which women are being convicted of serious offenses is picking up faster than the pace at which women are convicted" (p. 2). These researchers have asked for a redefining of justice. "Whether justice should promote unalloyed equity, be blind to the circumstances in which crime is committed, and consider only gravity of offense and prior record, is still a matter of debate. In the current sentencing environment, the view of those who favor equity above all other considerations has won the day. . . . [W]omen and girls who are caught up in the justice system enter it as a result of circumstances distinctly different from those of men, and so find themselves at a distinct disadvantage" (p. 3).

The current profile of women in prison has remained constant: low income, disproportionately African-American and Hispanic, not educated, unskilled, and unemployed. These women are primarily young and are single parents with two children. Two-thirds of them have children under the age of eighteen years. "Substance abuse, compounded by poverty, unemployment, physical and mental illness, physical and sexual abuse, and homelessness also characterize the women's prison population" (http://law.jrank.org/pages/1804/Prisons-Prisons-Womencomposition-women-s-prisons.html).

From the outset prisons were intended to punish men. There was little or no consideration that women would be incarcerated at the numbers we find. Although the number of women in prisons persists, the programs and policies with the correctional system and the criminal justice system have not kept pace. Lacking such policies and research carries on the tradition of neglect and inattention characterizing the history of prisons for women.

If the cases are the catalyst for change, change must occur. Words have little meaning if actions do not follow (Muraskin, 1989, p. 126).

REFERENCES

BUREAU OF JUSTICE STATISTICS. (2004b, May 27). *Nation's prison population increase largest in four years.* www.ojp.usdoj.gov/bjs

FEINMAN, C. (1982). Sex role stereotypes and justice for women. In B. R. Price & N. J. Sokoloff (Eds.), *The criminal justice system and women* (pp. 131–139). New York: Clark Boardman.

FEINMAN, C. (1986). *Women in the criminal justice system.* New York: Praeger.

GOBERT J. J., & COHEN, N. P. (1981). *Rights of prisoners.* New York: McGraw-Hill.

GREENFELD, L. A., & SNELL, T. L. (1999). *Bureau of Justice Statistics special report, women offenders.* Washington, DC: U.S. Department of Justice.

http://law.jrank.org/pages/1803/Prisons-Prisons-Women-Population-increases.html. Retrieved on May 1, 2010.

http://law.jrank.org/pages/1804/Prisons-Prisons-Women-composition-women-s-prisons.html. Retrieved on May 1, 2010.

HUNTER, S. (1984, Spring–Summer). Issues and challenges facing women's prisons in the 1980's. *Prison Journal, 64*(1).

LOWN, R. D., & SNOW, C. (1980). Women, the forgotten prisoners: *Glover v. Johnson.* In S. L. Fabian (Ed.), *Legal rights of prisoners.* Beverly Hills, CA: Sage.

MURASKIN, R. (1989). Disparity of correctional treatment: Development of a measurement instrument. Doctoral dissertation, City University of New York. *Dissertation Abstracts International.*

POLLACK, H., & SMITH, A. B. (1978). *Civil liberties and civil rights in the United States.* St. Paul, MN: West.

POLLACK-BYRNE, J. (1990). *Women, prison and crime.* Belmont, CA: Brooks/Cole.

RAFTER, N. (1983). Prisons for women, 1790–1980. In M. Tonry & N. Morries (Eds.), *Crime and justice: An annual review of research* (Vol. 5). Chicago: University of Chicago Press.

RECKLESS, W. (1967). *The crime problem.* New York: Appleton-Century-Crofts.

RICHIE, B. E., TSENIN, K., & WIDOM, C. S. (2000, September). *Research on women and girls in the justice system.* Washington, DC: National Institute of Justice.

SARGENT, J. P. (1984, Spring–Summer). The evolution of a stereotype: Paternalism and the female inmate. *Prison Journal, 1.*

U.S. DEPARTMENT OF JUSTICE. (2000). http://www.ojp.usdoj.gov/bjs.pub/ascii/wo.txt

ENDNOTES

1. In *Craig v. Boren* (1976) it was held to "withstand [a] constitutional challenge under the equal protection clause of the Fourteenth Amendment, classification by gender must serve important governmental objectives and must be substantially related to achievement of those objectives."

2. *Weinberger v. Wisenfeld* (1975) was a case in which a widower was denied benefits for himself on the ground that survivors' benefits were allowable only to women under 42 USCS sec. 4029g: "a provision, heard, 'Mother's insurance benefits,' authorizing the payment of benefits based on the earnings of a deceased husband and father covered by the Social Security Act, to a widow who has a minor child in her care." The Court held that "(1) the sex-based distinction of 42 USCS sec. 402(g), resulting in the efforts of women workers required to make social security contributions producing less protection for their families than was produced by the efforts of men, violated the rights to equal protection under the due process clause of the Fifth, and (2) the distinction could not be justified on the basis of the 'non-contractual' character of social security benefits, or on the ground that the sex-based classification was one really designed to

compensate women beneficiaries as a group for the economic difficulties confronting women who sought to support themselves and their families."

3. *Eslinger v. Thomas* (1973) was an action brought by a female law student who alleged that she was denied employment as a page because of her gender. Citing *Reed*, the Court indicated that the "Equal Protection Clause (denies) to States the power to legislate that different treatment be accorded to persons placed by a statute into different classes on the basis of criteria wholly unrelated to the objective of that statute." The Court quoted from an article by Johnson and Knapp (1971) that "on the one hand, the female is viewed as a pure, delicate and vulnerable citizen who must be protected from exposure to criminal influences; and on the other, as a brazen temptress, from whose seductive blandishments the innocent must be protected. Every woman is either Eve or Little Eva—and either way she loses." The decision of the lower court was reversed, there being no "fair and substantial 'relation between the object of the resolution,' which was to combat the appearance of impropriety, and the ground of difference, which was sex."

CASES

Barefield v. Leach, Civ. Action No. 10282 (1974).
Batton v. State Government of North Carolina, Executive Branch 501 F. Supp. 1773 (1980 ED NC).
Bounds v. Smith, 430 U.S. 817 (1977).
Bukhari v. Huto, 487 F. Supp. 1162 (E.D. Va. 1980).
Canterino v. Wilson, 546 F. Supp. 174 (W.D. Ky. 1982) and 562 F. Supp. 106 (W.D. Ky. 1983).
Clarkson v. Coughlin, 898 F. Supp. 1019 (S.D.N.Y. 1995).
Cody v. Hillard, 799 F.2d 447 (1986).
Commonwealth v. Stauffer, 214 Pa. Supp. 113 (1969).
Cooper v. Morin, 49 N.Y. 2d 69 (1979), *cert. denied*, 446 U.S. 984 (1980).
Cornish v. Johnson, No. 77-72557 (E.D. Mich. 1979).
Craig v. Boren, 429 U.S. 190 (1976).
Davie v. Wingard, 958 F. Supp. 1244 (S.D. Ohio 1997)
Dawson v. Carberry, No. C-71-1916 (N.D. Cal. 1973).
Eslinger v. Thomas, 476 F.2d (4th Cir. 1973).
Estelle v. Gamble, 429 U.S. 97 (1976).
Gerber v. Hickman, 2001 WL 1008205 (9th Cir. 2001).
Glover v. Johnson, 35 F. Supp. 2d 1010 (E.D. Mich. 1999).
Glover v. Johnson, 478 F. Supp. 1075, 1078 (1979).
Holt v. Sarver, 309 U.S. F. Supp. 362 (E.D. Ark. 1970).
Klinger v. Department of Corrections, 31 F.3d 727 (1994, CA8 Neb.).
Liberti v. York, 28 Conn. Supp. 9, 246 A.2d 106 (S. Ct. 1968).
Mary Beth G. v. City of Chicago, 723 F.2d 1263 (7th Cir. 1983).
McMurray v. Phelps, 535 F. Supp. 742 (W.D.L.A. 1982).
Molar v. Gates, 159 Cal. Rptr. 239 (4th Dist. 1979).
Morrow v. Harwell, 768 F.2d 619 (1985).
Reed v. Reed, 404 U.S. 71 (1971).
State ex rel Olson v. Maxwell, 259 N.W.2d 621 (Sup. Ct. N.D. 1977).
Thompson et al. v. Varelas, Sheriff, Nassau County et al., 81 Civ. 0184 (JM) (September 11, 1985).
Todaro v. Ward, 431 F. Supp. 1129 (S.D.N.Y. 1977).
United States ex rel Robinson v. York, 281 F. Supp. 8 (D. Conn. 1968).
Weinberger v. Wisenfeld, 420 U.S. 636, 43 L. Ed. 2d 514 (1975).
William v. Levi, Civ. Action No. Sp. 792–796 (Sup. Ct. D.C. 1976).

RELATED CASES

Casey v. Lewis, 834 F. Supp. 1477 (1993, DC Ariz.) Issue of Mental Hospital Commitment.

Forts v. Malcolm, 426 F. Supp. 464 (1977, SD NY) Issue of Grooming.

Pargo v. Elliott, 894 F. Supp. (1995, S.D. Iowa) Issues of Employment, Recreation, Visiting.

Women Prisoners of District of Columbia Dept. of Corrections v. District of Columbia, 93 F.3d 910 (D.C. Cir. 1996) Issue of Employment.

BIBLIOGRAPHY

ALLEN, H. E., & SIMONSEN, C. E. (1978). *Corrections in America: An introduction* (Criminal Justice Series). Encino, CA: Glencoe.

AMERICAN CORRECTIONAL ASSOCIATION. (1985, April). *Standards for adult local detention facilities* (2nd ed.). In cooperation with the Commission on Accreditation for Corrections. Lanham, MD: Author.

ARDITI, R. R., GOLDBERG, F., JR., PETERS, J., & PHELPS, W. R. (1973). The sexual segregation of American prisons. *Yale Law Journal, 6*(82), 1229–1273.

ARON, N. (1981). Legal issues pertaining to female offenders. In N. Aron (Ed.), *Representing prisoners*. New York: Practicing Law Institute.

BELKNAP, J. (1996). *The invisible woman*. Belmont, CA: Wadsworth.

BUREAU OF JUSTICE STATISTICS. (2004a, June 30). *Prison statistics*. Retrieved from http://www.ojp.usdoj.gov/bjs

FABIAN, S. L. (1980). Women prisoners' challenge of the future. In N. Aron (Ed.), *Legal rights of prisoners*. Beverly Hills, CA: Sage.

GIBSON, H. (1973). Women's prisons: Laboratories for penal reform. *Wisconsin Law Review*.

INCIARDI, J. A. (1984). *Criminal justice*. Orlando, FL: Academic Press.

LEWIS, D. K. (1982). Female ex-offenders and community programs. *Crime and Delinquency: Rights of Prisoners, 28*.

MURASKIN, R. (2000). *It's a crime: Women and justice*. Upper Saddle River, NJ: Prentice Hall.

SARRI, R. (1979). Crime and the female offender. In E. S. Gomberg & V. Frank (Eds.), *Gender and disordered behavior: Sex differences in psychopathology*. New York: Brunner/Mazel.

SINGER, L. (1979). Women and the correctional process. In F. Adler & R. Simon (Eds.), *The criminality of deviant women*. Boston: Houghton Mifflin.

WILLIAMS, V. L., FORMBY, W. A., & WATKINS, J. C. (1982). *Introduction to criminal justice*. Albany, NY: Delmar.

WOOD, D. (1982). *Women in jail*. Milwaukee, WI: Benedict Center for Criminals.

22

Gender and Corrections

Comparing Facilities and Programs

Alana Van Gundy

This chapter will utilize data from the American Correctional Association's Directory to examine the current state of corrections in the American system. It will focus on comparing two main aspects of the system by gender: correctional facilities and the programs offered to address offenders' needs. The chapter will discuss background information on the status of females within the criminal justice system, present information on the data source and sample, and present a discussion that compares facilities and programs by gender. The chapter will conclude with implications of the findings, limitations of this comparison, and suggestions for future research.

BACKGROUND INFORMATION

Females are a minority population within the American criminal justice system. They are arrested, tried, and incarcerated at lower numbers than male offenders and have traditionally committed 'gender-specific' crimes such as shoplifting, prostitution, and offenses that are less violent than traditional male offenses. As a result of their low numbers and minority status, female offenders have sparked little interest of those who fund, research, and work within the three core components of the American criminal justice system: the police, courts, and corrections.

Over the last few decades, feminist criminologists have attempted to bring attention to the changes in female criminality to the forefront of the discipline as a means to stimulate advances in the response to the treatment of women in the criminal justice system. They have raised questions as to the adequacy of criminological theory's ability to explain female offending, distinct social status of females within the system, non- and over-classification of female offenders, gender biases in arrest, trial, and incarceration, the intersection between race, gender and crime (in particular, African-American and Hispanic-American women), the lack of appropriate facilities, funding, and access to programming for females, and females' existence and their treatment within the employment sectors of the system.

Between 2004 and 2005, the criminal justice system evidenced a dramatic change, in particular, within the field of corrections. The female prison population doubled from 3% of those incarcerated to 6%. By 2009, it had further increased to close to 8% of our total incarceration rate. Even though they continue to commit violent crimes at lower rates than males, females are now being arrested at higher rates for their involvement with gangs, violent crimes such as aggravated assault and burglaries, embezzlement, vandalism, driving under the influence of alcohol, and drug-abuse violations.

One of the critical components for appropriately responding to female offenders is understanding the gender-specific components to their crimes and their history. Females are more likely to commit a crime in conjunction with a male counterpart such as a boyfriend, a husband, and/or a significant other than are male offenders. They are also significantly more likely to be victims of sexual abuse, engage in drug/alcohol abuse at higher rates, be a single parent, and evidence co-occurring disorders such as bi-polar, depression, and anxiety and panic disorders. Female offenders also evidence different medical needs such as pregnancy, higher rates of breast cancer, ovarian and cervical cancer, increased risks and rates of heart disease, and treatments related to their sexual victimization.

These gender-specific components have led criminologists to study the differences between male and female correctional facilities. With over crowding, increased violence, and distinct subcultures (in particular, gangs) within male facilities, male correctional facilities are structured in a manner that is focused on a custodial model. They are fortress-like buildings with different areas to segregate incarcerated individuals in order to prevent violence. The sheer number of males incarcerated in America's facilities has led them to operate in the form of mass warehousing.

However, studies have shown that this type of facility is not conducive for the incarceration purposes of female offenders. Females are more relational in general, and to place them in a facility in which they are unable to form friendships, pseudo-families, and in facilities which over-classify them as dangerous offenders when they are less violent by nature may accelerate their criminality. Female facilities function in a more appropriate manner when they are structured in a way that increases companionship, the ability to socialize, and are less rigorously secured by correctional guards (community corrections is suggested to work best for female offenders). Despite these findings, women are misclassified to higher security level facilities because they are classified by male classification instruments, they are often times moved into old male facilities because a new male facility has been built (moving them into a structure that is not conducive to controlling the population or treating their needs), and they are imprisoned in facilities that are not able to physically or programmatically address their needs.

It has been suggested these same applications of male models to female offenders exist when examining programming within facilities. Male programming focuses on education and job trades that provide a marketable skill whereas female programming will provide job skills such as seamstress courses or cosmetology courses (both of which perpetuate the low status of females in society and provide skills for a job that as a convicted felon, they are unable to attain because they are unable to earn a license). Conversely, male programming has more funding available and is tailored toward the specific needs of males. In contrast, female facilities offer fewer programs and those that are offered may not focus on the gender-specific needs of female offenders.

Feminist criminologists have been arguing for gender-specific classification instruments, appropriately designed and structured facilities, and gender-specific programs to diagnose, address, treat, and respond to female offenders. Differences in crime methodology and typology, gender-specific histories, unique medical needs, and gender-specific needs and responses should result in less secure facilities for females and gender-specific programming that addresses their unique histories of victimization, their propensity for drug and alcohol addiction, and the distinct mental and emotional needs of incarcerated females. While small-scale research does exist that focuses on the differences between state institutions, this chapter will focus on examining the state of America's corrections from a macro or large-scale approach.

DATA SOURCE/DATA SET

The data source for this comparison is the American Correctional Association's (ACA) 2007 Directory. This Directory provides information as provided by adult and juvenile correctional officials to the ACA on the following data: name of facility and current warden and staff, date the facility was opened, if the facility has been renovated and date of renovation, security level, capacity, actual population, gender, age limit, cost of care per day, amount of staff, type of offender, and programs offered. Data is provided on federal and state adult and juvenile corrections and probation and parole authorities. For the purpose of this chapter, the final data set did not include juvenile and community corrections facilities (if they were reported to be community only they were excluded, but facilities that included a community corrections option were included) or probation and parole authorities. Private facilities and boot camps were also not included in the final comparison.

FACILITY INFORMATION

The Directory originally provided data on 1,971 facilities, but the final data comparison was analyzed with a sample size of 1,336 facilities. As reported in Table 1, eighty percent (80%) of the American facilities housed males only, nine percent (9%) females only, and seven percent (7%) were reported as co-gender. To be considered or reported as co-gender, the facility may have as few as one female or male within it. For example, if a state has a female death row inmate and no facility to house her in, when she is placed in the facility with the appropriate security designation or housing block, it may be reported as co-gender.

TABLE 1   Facility by Gender

	Frequency	Percentage
Male	1,066	80
Female	114	9
Co-gender	91	7

TABLE 2   **Facility by Gender and Security Level**

	Females (Percentage)	Males (Percentage)	Co-gender (Percentage)
Not-specified	5	4	1
Low	0	1	1
Minimum	26	24	28
Medium	10	22	11
Maximum	7	4	4
Super-Maximum	4	6	2
Multiple	40	30	36

This information shows that the availability of correctional facilities is not directly proportionate to the amount of those incarcerated. Ninety-two percent of America's prison population are males, yet 80% of our incarceration facilities are dedicated solely to housing them. This leaves room for speculation as to if the co-gender facilities are primarily designed for males and females are simply placed into the structure, if female facilities are actually slightly over-represented within this sample, or if the female facilities are disproportionate in size to males' prisons, that is, they are much smaller than males' facilities. If America's correctional facilities were to show proportionality, then the facilities would mirror the represented population. That is, 92% of American facilities would be for males, and eight percent (8%) would be for females if they were of an equal size and capacity.

Table 2 provides a presentation of the facilities by gender and security level. Direct proportionality again would show that if females were appropriately classified by their crime typology and violence level, most female institutions would be low to medium security and there would be few female maximum and super-maximum facilities. However, according to the ACA directory, there are no low security public institutional facilities reported for females. One co-gender facility is available for low security female offenders, but it is unclear how many female offenders are housed in that facility. Eleven percent (11%) of female facilities are maximum or super-maximum in comparison to ten percent (10%) of male facilities. Another existing and notable difference is the fact that 40% of all female facilities house multiple offenders, while only 30% of the male facilities are multiple security level facilities. Therefore male facilities may be more customizable to the offender they house.

An important factor to consider when examining the relationship between gender and America's correctional facilities is to investigate the designed and actual capacity of the facilities themselves. As shown in Table 3, all of America's correctional facilities are clearly overcrowded, but there are gender differences here. Female facilities included in the sample reported a range of 24 inmates to 2,934 inmates, but the actual capacity was 16–3,887 inmates (at the high range this is 32% over capacity). The male facilities are designed to hold from 20 inmates to 5,108, but actual capacity is 26–7,628 (49% over capacity). What is most interesting about these findings is that co-gender facilities report being up to 63% over capacity.

Crowding

TABLE 3   Designed and Actual Capacity

	Range	Mean
Designed Capacity		
Female	24–2,934	646
Male	20–5,108	1,019
Co-gender	0–3,924	748
Actual Capacity		
Female	16–3,887	712
Male	26–7,628	1,148
Co-gender	24–6,395	1,062

PROGRAMMING

Facilities that reported program information provided the name of the program only, and if further information was necessary, the state corrections webpage sometimes provided additional information. Common threads throughout both facilities included: academic education, vocational training, sex offender treatment, prison industries, farm camps, substance abuse programs, anger management, psychological counseling and services, mental health programs, life skills, dog programs, violence prevention and cognitive therapy. Facilities reported these in a general manner; for example, most would state "vocational training" instead of identifying a welding program, a cosmetology program etc. The generality with which it was reported makes it somewhat difficult to identify distinct differences from a macro viewpoint; however, a few key differences did emerge.

Of the programs that reported housing all females, the following programs were distinct: Planned Parenthood programs, women helping women, pregnancy wings, character-based programs, moral recognition therapy (also available in one male facility), victim based programs, string orchestra, female chronic disciplinary unit, female security risk group, emotional repair programs, poetry, and challenge incarceration programs. The programs clearly addressed some of the pregnancy and childhood issues that are prevalent in the female offender population, but there are some important programming aspects that are worth mentioning.

Although no male facilities reported focusing on emotional issues, multiple female facilities offer emotion-based programs that operate with the goal of repairing, controlling, and learning to identify emotion. While one male facility reported having a "moral recognition" program and no male facilities reported having a "character-based" program, numerous female facilities appear to focus on the female lack of, recognition of, and development of pro-social morals and character. Also of note, is that female facilities often offer programs that focus on the victim of the offender and they focus on having the female offenders learn to have empathy for the victim and view crime from more of a restorative justice approach. It is critical to note that no facilities reported having programs that focussed on the females as being victims of the abuses that are prevalent within the population, such as sexual abuse and physical and/or emotional abuse.

only

Facilities that house only males reported the following programs that were distinct to all male facilities: horse training, fatherhood initiatives, welding program, mandatory literacy, special management barracks, garage, geriatrics, hospice, gravel harvesting, reduction of sexual victimization program (RSVP), inner change freedom initiative, Braille program, striving for success initiative, conflict anger management, camp for fire suppression, prison outreach, arts in corrections, IMPACT (inmates making a positive attempt to change teens), employment readiness, Inmate Garden, and Project Christmas.

Co-gender facilities reported more detailed information regarding programming offerings, and as some reported focusing on substance use and abuse, academic and vocational training etc, they also were more likely to specify what type of vocational training they offered than the single gender facilities. Within these facilities, there was more detailed information on gender specific offerings such as cosmetology training, seamstress training, and cooking programs, whereas the all-female-only facilities did not specify these forms of program offerings.

In comparison to the female facilities, male facilities focus on more customized, society-based, and outreach programs. This may be a result of the large numbers of male inmates or the availability of funds, but there are clear differences when examining opportunities for male programs versus female programs. One noticeable difference is the availability of geriatric and Hospice programs. While no female facilities reported having these programs available, a large number of male facilities do. Another difference is that programs in male facilities seem to be more focused on outreach. For example, male facilities report programs that focus on going into the community to focus on crime prevention, prison outreach programs, and programs that make an impact on outside society, such as Braille programs, art projects for children's schools etc. Female facilities do not report having programs whose primary focus is to go out into the community to be able to talk to others to try to prevent crimes; the outreach programs that they report are conducted behind bars, and any programs that deal with outside society are also available within male facilities and are therefore not unique to female offenders or facilities.

IMPLICATIONS

Findings of this broad and descriptive overview offer important implications. First, females appear to be over-represented in correctional facilities and high-security facilities. It was reported that there are no low-security facilities for females and there are more maximum and super-maximum facilities available for females than there are for males. According to the type of crimes they are incarcerated for, most female offenders should be housed in lower security facilities or be placed in community corrections. This raises important questions. How many female offenders are being over-classified? How would including community corrections in this sample affect the rates of over or under-population? Lastly, is incorrect classification or lack of available facilities contributing to the changes in female offenders, especially those that recidivate? Regardless of the responses to these questions, this broad overview suggests that females do not have appropriate classification level facilities to be placed into.

Second, the findings regarding co-gender facilities call to light some important issues. As mentioned previously, to be reported as co-gender, the facility only needs one individual that is of the opposite gender as the majority of the population. The co-gender facilities in this sample report being 63% over capacity. Normally this would lead to the conjecture that these are large male facilities that may house a small range of female offenders because there is not maximum or super-maximum facilities available. However, the reported data shows that female facilities offer a higher percentage of maximum and super-maximum facilities than male facilities. Location may be of issue here (in other words, in the female offenders area there are less facilities available and therefore they are placed in the closest male facility), but the data still lends itself to the question of why co-gender facilities report such high levels of over-crowding.

Also at issue was the fact that stereotypical gender programs were not identified in single gender facilities but are specified in the co-gender facilities. Why would co-gender facilities report offering cosmetology and seamstress programs yet female-only facilities do not? One reason could be that the generality of the data offered to the ACA Directory doesn't ask them to specify the vocational program. Other reasons could be that in America's correctional facilities we offer female-specific programming at higher rates in co-gender facilities or that these facilities are primarily housing females but are determined as co-gender because there might be a minority male population. Regardless, these results implicate the need for more specific data provision, a closer examination of the programming actually offered, and a pressing need to investigate America's co-gender facilities.

Third, there is a large concern and implication regarding programming differences. If research shows that females have gender-specific needs, why are the facilities either a) not offering them, or b) not reporting them? When the state websites are visited, some gender-specific programming is detailed, but it is not available as reported to the ACA. When the gender-specific program information is offered online via the state websites, they often times do not focus on the three most important components of female offenders: sexual abuse, molestation, and victimization, alcohol and drug dependency, and the necessity to treat co-occurring disorders such as bi-polar and depression, schizophrenia and panic disorders etc. This neglect seems to evidence that America's correctional facilities as a whole are highly inadequate at treating, responding to, and understanding female criminality.

Lastly, there is also an implication as to the correctional system's approach to criminality in its totality. With 40% of all reported correctional facilities that contain only females housing multiple security offenders (in comparison to 30% of male facilities), it is clear that these facilities are not addressing the needs according to classification levels. Without facilities offering educational components teaching women the risks for particular cancers (breast, cervical, and ovarian cancer for example), heart disease, diabetes, co-occurring disorders, or even offering geriatric and senior programming for long-term offenders, how is the population being educated in a gender-specific manner? How will these females successfully re-enter, re-integrate, and become healthy, productive, and civically engaged citizens?

LIMITATIONS

There are numerous limitations to the discussion presented in this chapter. The most pressing limitation is the availability of reporting. Correctional facilities voluntarily report this information to the ACA, and there may be issues of under or over-reporting. Of the facilities that report data, many don't report complete or specific data. The generality of the

Too general Data

data makes it difficult to differentiate specific aspects of the facility and the programs. As mentioned previously, most facilities reported general information such as "vocational training" or "academic programs" but did not specify if this was GED, high-school, or college programs. If this information was reported, it would allow for a more thorough discussion and analysis of program offerings by gender.

A second limitation is the lack of specificity of other data. An example of this is the access to information on the cost of an inmate per day and the availability of funds. Of the facilities included in the sample, close to 30% of them did not provide the cost per day information, and the available funds are not reported (i.e., federal and state funding amounts), leaving it difficult to compare other variables by gender. To have a complete picture of America's correctional facilities by gender, it would be important to examine the other data that could have been provided.

Other limitations include the age of the data and inclusion of private facilities and community corrections facilities. The ACA directory utilized was the 2007 annual directory, and the data set was narrowed down to public incarceration facilities only. Private facilities included in the original sample provided the names of facilities and specified them as a private institutions, but did not detail any other information, and therefore could not be included in the sample in any form. This is an appropriate way to provide a broad comparison of the facilities, but different findings may result when community corrections or private facilities are included (females are more likely to be in community corrections, so this might lead to even more of an over-representation of females in facilities).

SUGGESTIONS FOR FUTURE COMPARISONS

These limitations could be addressed by future data comparison. A more detailed and thorough descriptive analysis could be provided by collecting data for each institution from a public webpage or from the institutions themselves. Facilities could be contacted and inquiries could be made as to more specific programming details in order to work with a more comprehensive data set (for example, getting all institutions to report cost per day and staff numbers to view the staff to inmate ratio by gender). This form of outreach would be very time consuming, but it would provide enough information to a researcher to allow for a more thorough analysis of America's correctional facilities and to present a better picture of what the broad trends are. This would also be a difficult form of research because other than what correctional facilities have to report, institutions may be uneasy about providing particular information to the public.

Other suggestions for future data comparison include focusing on a longitudinal data set. The population within the field of corrections has drastically changed over the last few decades. Social context and societal concerns have driven society to incarcerate drug offenders, sexual offenders, and non-violent offenders at increasingly higher rates. Of specific interest would be the correctional facilities' responses to the drastic 2004–2005 change in the female prison population. It would be important to examine if gender-specific programming availability and offerings increased after the population surge, how facility capacity was affected, and how this change affected the population, reporting, and programming within co-gender facilities.

Lastly, information on private facilities and community corrections would be a valuable addition to an examination of correctional trends. The information presented in this chapter is a broad description of incarceration facilities in America. However, the filtering aspect of our criminal justice leads to the understanding that this is not a comprehensive view of American corrections. Private facility expense would be a valuable addition because it would allow for a cross comparison of public versus private institution expenditures and funding. Community corrections would be important to include because the majority of offenders (in particular, female offenders) would speculatively be included in these facilities and programs. Until a data set is collected that provides detailed information on these facilities, a thorough cross-comparison by gender, race, funding, program type and availability is difficult.

SUMMARY

In sum, this chapter examined two aspects of American corrections: institutional facilities themselves and programming offerings within those facilities. The American Correctional Association's 2007 Directory provided information for this broad overview and examination of corrections facilities and programming by gender. Nine percent (9%) of American correctional facilities are reported as female-only facilities. Of those facilities, there are no low-security facilities for females and eleven percent (11%) are maximum and super-maximum facilities. In contrast, 80% of all facilities are reported as male facilities, with ten percent (10%) consisting of maximum and super-maximum facilities.

Within the correctional facilities, gender-specific programming is noted, such as horse training programs for males, and moral recognition and character-based programs for females. Co-gender facilities reported offering gender-specific vocational training programs, but all male and all female programs did not provide extensive detail. Of particular note is the lack of programming that addresses the gender-specific needs of women, such as sexual abuse survivor programs, or educational programs for gender-specific diseases and cancers. These programs are offered within some American correctional facilities; however, they have not been reported to the American Correctional facilities and therefore, this overview is unable to capture a true cross-comparison of gender-specific programming. To analyze American correctional trends in a more thorough manner, more detail must be provided by the facilities, information on private facilities and community corrections should be analyzed, and longitudinal data could be examined.

REFERENCES AND RECOMMENDED READING

AMERICAN CORRECTIONAL ASSOCIATION (2007) *American Correctional Association Directory: Adult and Juvenile Correctional Departments, Institutions, Agencies, and Probation and Parole Authorities* 68th edition, copyrighted by the American Correctional Association.

BELKNAP, J. (2001) Programming and Health Care Responsibility for Incarcerated Women. In J. James (ed.) *States of Confinement: Policing, Detention, and Prisons* (pp. 109–123). New York, St Martin's Press.

BELKNAP, (2002) Responding to the Needs of Women Prisoners. In S. Sharp *The Incarcerated Woman: Rehabilitative Programming in Women's Prisons* (pp. 93–106). Upper Saddle River, N.J. Prentice Hall.

BLOOM, B. (1993) Incarcerated Mothers and their Children: Maintaining Family Ties. In *Female Offenders: Meeting the Needs of a Neglected Population* (pp. 60–68). Laurel, MD. American Correctional Association.

BLOOM, B. (2003) *Gendered Justice: Addressing Female Offenders* Carolina Academic Press.

BLOOM, B. OWEN, B., and COVINGTON, S. (2003) *Gender Responsive Strategies: Research, Practice, and Guiding Principles for Women Offenders.* U.S. Department of Justice. National Institute of Corrections.

Bureau of Justice Statistics (1999). *Special Report: Women Offenders.* Washington D.C. U.S. Department of Justice.

CHESNEY-LIND, M. and L. PASKO (2004) *The Female Offender: Girls, Women, and Crime* 2nd edition, Sage Publications.

FEDERAL BUREAU OF INVESTIGATIONS *Uniform Crime Reports 2001–2008.*

JORDAN, B. K, SCHLENGER W. E., FAIRBANK J. A., and CADELL J. M. (1996). Prevalence of Psychiatric Disorders Among Incarcerated Women. *Archives of General Psychiatry* 53(6) 513–519.

MORASH, M., BYNUM, T. S., and KOONS, B. A. (1998) *Women Offenders: Programming Needs and Promising Approaches* The National Institute of Justice Research in Brief.

POLLOCK, J. M. (2002) *Women, Prison, and Crime* 2nd edition, Wadsworth Publishers.

SCHRAM, P. J. and B. KOONS-WITT (2004) *Gendered (In) Justice,* Waveland Press.

SHEEHAN, R., McIVOR, G., and C. TROTTER (2007) *What Works with Women Offenders* Willan Publishing.

SILVESTRI, M. and CHRIS CROWTHER-DOWEY (2008) *Gender and Crime: Key Approaches to Criminology* Sage Publications.

YOUNG, D. S., and DENNIS, L. C. (2006). The Complex Needs of Mentally Ill Women in County Jails. In R. Immarigeon's *Women and Girls in the Criminal Justice System: Policy Issues and Practice Strategies* (pp. 42.1–42.8) Civic Research Institute, Kingston, N.J.

YOUNG, V. D., and R. REVIERE (2006) *Women Behind Bars: Gender and Race in US Prisons* Lynne Rienner Publications.

ZAPLIN, R. T. (2008) *Female Offenders: Critical Perspectives and Effective Interventions* 2nd edition, Jones and Bartlett Publishers.

23

Three Strikes and It's *Women* Who Are Out

The Hidden Consequences for Women of Criminal Justice Policy Reforms[1]

Mona J. E. Danner

Thirty years of "get tough on crime" policies that increase the likelihood and length of incarceration, such as mandatory minimum sentences and three strikes laws, appear to be either gender blind or beneficial to women. In fact, these reforms contain significant consequences for women. A portion of the costs of prison construction and maintenance are paid for by cutting social services from which women benefit. In addition, since social service agencies are more likely to employ women while criminal justice agencies are more likely to employ men, the growth of the criminal justice system at the expense of the social service system places women's employment opportunities in jeopardy. Finally, the incarceration of parents leaves behind children who may be traumatized and whose emotional and economic care is left to women.

The 1994 Federal Crime Control Act marked the 26th year of the "get tough on crime" movement, initiated with the passage of the 1968 Crime Control and Safe Streets Act (Donziger 1996, p. 14). The 1984 crime bill increased penalties for drug offenses thereby engaging the "War on Drugs" and initiating the centerpiece of law-and-order legislative efforts to control crime—mandatory minimum and increased sentence lengths. "Three Strikes and You're Out" laws in particular captured the imagination of the public, the press, and the politicians. State legislators in 37 jurisdictions proposed Three Strikes laws in 1993 and 1994, often as part of their own state crime bills. By the end of 1995, 24 state jurisdictions and the federal government had enacted these laws, and California voters had made Three Strikes part of their Constitution (Clark, Austin, & Henry 1997; Turner, Sundt, Applegate, & Cullen 1995). The new sentencing laws contained in the federal and state crime bills increased the dramatic expansion of the criminal justice system already underway, especially in corrections.

At the end of 2008, the United States recorded over 7.3 million adults in the correctional population, that is, on probation or parole, in jail or prison. Five million adults were on probation or parole (Glaze & Bonczar 2009). More than 1.5 million people were in federal and state prisons, more than a fourfold increase in just 20 years; another 785,000 were in local jails (Sabol, West & Cooper 2009). Over 115,000 of those imprisoned were women, and nearly 1 million women were on probation or parole (Sabol, West & Cooper 2009; Glaze & Bonczar 2009). In the 1980s, the rate of women's imprisonment increased nearly twice as much as that of men's, and 34 new women's prison units were opened (Immarigeon & Chesney-Lind 1992). African-Americans, who account for 13 percent of the population, are 33 percent of those incarcerated (Sabol, West & Cooper 2009). Black men are six-and-a-half times and black women are three times more likely to be imprisoned than are white men and women, respectively (Sabol, West & Cooper 2009); the expansion of mandatory and increased sentences for drug law violations accounts for much of the increase (Mauer 1990). The number of Black women imprisoned for drugs has increased more than three times that of white women, respectively (Bush-Baskette 1998). Young African American men are particularly hard hit by the rhetoric and ensuing policies associated with the war on drugs and Three Strikes laws (Tonry 1995). Nearly all of those behind bars are poor.

The result of "lock 'em up" policies is that state and federal prisons currently operate at, respectively, up to 108 and 135 percent capacity, with some states hitting nearly 200 percent capacity (Sabol, West & Cooper 2009). Across the country, federal and state governments are engaged in an enormous and costly prison construction program. In fact, prisons represent "the only expanding public housing" in our country ("The prison boom," 1995, p. 223). One truism of prison and jail construction remains: "If you build it, they will come." And so, the costs associated with maintaining these facilities and incarcerating citizens—especially geriatrics as lifers age—will quickly dwarf the costs of construction.

The rationale behind the crime bills and the resulting expansion of the criminal justice system cannot be found in the crime rate. Despite political rhetoric at the national and state levels and the carnage presented daily and repeatedly in all forms of news and entertainment media, the violent crime rate remained relatively stable or decreased over the last 30 years as measured by the National Crime Survey (Catalano 2004).

Throughout it all, however, the consequences for women of the expansion of the criminal justice system remain largely unconsidered and invisible in public policy discussions. This chapter makes women visible in the identification of the hidden costs to women of the expansion of the criminal justice system. In brief, I argue that one way or another it is *women* who will pay the lion's share of criminal justice reform.

LOOKING FOR WOMEN

The feminist revolution in society and the academy is about making women visible, interrogating and deconstructing the manner in which women do appear, and calling for progressive action to benefit women. In criminal justice, feminist analysis has largely focused on women as offenders, victims, and workers (Price & Sokoloff 1995), with the issues and debates centered around building theory, containing men's violence against women, and the equality/difference concern (Daly & Chesney-Lind 1988). This chapter advances feminist perspectives in criminal justice in the analysis of the ways in which supposedly gender-blind crime control writ large affects *all* women.

Women are not readily visible in current criminal justice policy debates. The use of a baseball analogy—"three strikes and you're out"—to refer to the policy of mandatory life sentences for those persons convicted of three felonies illustrates the exclusion of women from the crime debates. Although it's called "the national pastime," women don't identify with baseball much, have no significant presence in the sport, and reap few of its economic benefits (facts true of all professional sports). Yet it is in this sense that baseball represents an excellent analogy to the crime bills since women remain largely invisible from the debates surrounding criminal justice reforms. When women do appear, it is often as diversionary props that only barely resemble the realities of the lives of women and girls. Recent public debates in some states regarding increasing the availability of concealed weapons provide one illustration of this phenomenon.

During the 1995 legislative year, Virginia enacted a "right to carry" law requiring that judges grant permits for concealed weapons to nearly anyone who applies (Snider 1995). Lobbyists for the National Rifle Association (NRA) along with sympathetic legislators repeatedly invoked the image of the lone woman walking to her car at night who might need a gun to protect herself from the lurking stranger ready to pounce on her at any moment. This image of a woman served as a diversionary prop to obscure the protests of police and judges who objected to the law because of safety concerns and the restriction on judicial discretion. The image also diverted attention away from the vested interests of the NRA and state politicians who benefit from NRA contributions. This is simply one example of the way in which women are used in debates surrounding criminal justice policies. Women's lives and the realities of potential dangers are distorted, and in the process, women are left out of the debate and policies are enacted which will not only *not* benefit most women, but will, in fact, harm many women.

Nearly all of the political rhetoric about crime focuses on making our streets and neighborhoods safe again and protecting our homes from vicious, dangerous intruders. The focus on stranger crimes ignores the fact that it is the ones whom they know and love who represent the greatest danger to women's lives. Although women are much less likely than men to become victims of violent crimes in general, when women are assaulted, robbed, or raped, the best guess is to look to their loved ones. Of these violent crimes that women experience, the perpetrator is a husband, boyfriend, ex-husband, or ex-boyfriend 19 percent of the time; the comparable figure for men is 3 percent. Adding in other relatives increases the figure for women to 29 percent; for men, it is 8 percent. Expanding the definition to include other persons known reveals that 67 percent of the times that women are the victims of violent crimes, the assailant is known to the victim as either an acquaintance, a friend, relative, or an intimate partner; for men this figure is 42 percent (Catalano 2004). The offender is a stranger in less than one-quarter of the occasions when women are victims of violent crime by a lone offender (Bachman & Saltzman 1995). In violent crimes occurring between spouses, lovers, ex-spouses, and ex-lovers, nearly 90 percent of the time, the victim is a woman. And a woman is the victim in 70 percent of murders between intimate partners (Greenfeld, Rand, Craven, Klaus, Perkins, Ringel, Warchol, Maston, & Fox 1998).

Women need far less protection from strangers than from supposed protectors, especially intimate partners, relatives, and acquaintances. But the debates surrounding the crime bills and recent research demonstrate that women are also at risk from the lawmakers and even some law enforcers (Kraska & Kappeler 1995), most of whom are men, nearly all of them white, and with respect to politicians, legislators, and judges, members of the elite social classes. Lawmakers do not pay attention to the data but, like the public, fall victim to popular myths about crime, especially the myth that it is strangers who are most responsible for violent victimizations, particularly those committed against women. The result is that this myth and others like it are used to shape public debate and craft public policies that ignore women's lives and force women to bear the brunt of the financial and emotional costs for such policies.

The *New York Times* called women the "quiet winners" in the U.S. Crime Bill because of the inclusion of the Violence Against Women Act (Manegold 1994). This portion of the national crime bill budgeted $1.6 billion dollars for a national hot line for domestic violence victims and education programs aimed at police, prosecutors, and judges. It includes provisions that encourage mandatory arrests in domestic violence complaints, sex offender registration programs, and the release to victims of the results of rapists' HIV tests. It had also allowed women to file civil suits in cases of sex bias crimes, although this provision was overturned by the U.S. Supreme Court in *U.S. v. Morrison* (2000).

The Violence Against Women Act makes women's victimization visible and crafts public policies to assist women. The act represents an important step in public recognition of, and response to, male violence against women. But examination of the crime bills and their accompanying public debate reveals no sign of women other than as victims of domestic violence.

Feminist interrogation about how criminal justice policies affect women's lives calls us to make visible more of the ways in which the criminal justice policies affect women. Considering the unintended consequences and hidden costs of the crime bills and current public policies suggests that women are less likely to be quiet winners in criminal justice reforms as a whole, than to be quiet and big-time losers.

And so we return to the baseball analogy. "Three Strikes and You're Out" doesn't just refer to the policy of mandatory life sentences following a third felony conviction. "Three Strikes and You're Out" also refers to three ways in which women will be hurt by, and forced to pay for, criminal justice reform.

STRIKE 1—OFF THE ROLLS

The first strike against women comes in the decisions regarding which government services will be sacrificed to pay for the expansion of the criminal justice system. The emphasis on budget balancing and deficit reduction at the national and state levels means that money targeted for tough-on-crime proposals comes at the expense of other government programs. RAND researchers concluded that implementation of California's Three Strikes law would require cuts in other government services totaling more than 40 percent over eight years—a move that would leave the State of California "spending more money keeping people in prison than putting people through college" (Greenwood, Fydell, Abrahamse, Caulkins, Chiesa, Model, & Klein 1994, p. 34). The hardest hit programs, however, are those in social services, especially those targeted to the poor, most of whom are women and children.[2]

Discussion about entitlements to the poor is to some limited extent a separate debate about the causes of poverty and the state's responsibility, or lack thereof, to help alleviate misfortune and suffering. But, it is also a debate that remains close to the debates about crime and criminal justice. Like criminal offenders and prisoners, women on welfare and their families are demonized as lazy, unwilling to work for their keep, immoral, and criminal. Both groups—composed disproportionately of poor and minority persons—are scapegoated as the source of numerous social ills while public attention draws away from inequitable economic and political conditions (Sidel 1996). Blaming the victims of structural conditions justifies cutting welfare for the poor and funneling savings elsewhere.

Social services that benefit women are sacrificed to accommodate the expenditures associated with the expansion of the criminal justice system. Chesney-Lind (1995) notes that New York continued to build beds in women's prisons at the same time that it had an insufficient number of beds for women and children in shelters. Adequate social services can reduce those life stressors associated with criminality; legal changes and battered women's shelters helped reduce the rates of women's homicide of male partners (Browne 1990, as cited in Chesney-Lind 1995).

The rhetoric surrounding cuts in social programs reveals class, as well as race/ethnic and gender, bias. The Welfare Reform Bill of 1996 imposed a limitation on the length of time that poor women may receive welfare assistance. After two years most women will be kicked off the rolls under the assumption that they will find work. Overall, few provisions are made for ensuring that either jobs or day care are available. We see social class operating here. Politicians, pundits, and religious leaders commonly argue that children should be cared for at home by the mother. Apparently, this is true, however, only for middle-class mothers and their children; poor mothers are admonished and will be legally required to leave their children so that they may return to work in order to save the tax coffers.

In 1994, at the same time that Virginia first instituted welfare reform, the state also passed its crime bill and accompanying criminal justice reforms. Plans called for the building of 27 new prisons at a cost of $1 billion over 10 years (later estimates placed these costs at $2–4 billion) as well as Three Strikes and other provisions for increasing the length of sentences for violent offenses and repeat offenses. The bill also called for the abolition of parole as of January 1st, 1995, but the governor's new parole board had already, in effect, abolished parole as it drastically reduced the number of paroles granted—at a cost of $77 million in just 6 months (LaFay 1994). Virginia prisons were so overcrowded that they could not accept new inmates housed in local jails awaiting transfer to the state system. This, in turn, led to such pressures in the jails that sheriffs sued the state to force it to assume its responsibility and take custody of its charges (Jackson 1995). One way in which Virginia, like all states, deals with the problem of overcrowding is to ship inmates to other States and pay them the costs associated with incarceration (LaFay 1995).

The expenditures associated with the expansion of the criminal justice system are being paid for in part by the savings to come from reforms that cut the social safety net of welfare. Further, an "iron triangle" of interests—politicians, job-starved communities, and businesses which build and service prisons—benefits from tough-on-crime rhetoric and policies (Thomas 1994). Neither military, corporate, nor middle class subsidy programs are targeted for payment in support of the prison industrial complex; rather, social service programs—with their disproportionately poor, minority, and female recipients—remain those responsible for picking up the check.

Women are the majority of direct beneficiaries of various social service programs, but we know that they steer nearly all of those benefits to their dependents, especially their children but also the elderly and disabled adults in their lives. Simply put, women and those who depend upon them will lose their economic and social safety net, in part so that politicians can appear to be tough on crime and imprison more men and women. It is poor women—who are also disproportionately minority, especially African American women—and their families who in this way will pay a disproportionate share of the hidden costs associated with the war on crime and drugs. Strike one.

STRIKE 2—JOBS FOR WHOM?

Women are not only more likely than men to be the recipients of social services, women are also more likely to be employed in social service agencies as social workers, case workers, counselors, and support staff. The implications of this fact represent the second strike against women. Seventy-one percent of social workers are women, and women comprise an even larger portion of front-line case workers and clerical personnel (U.S. Bureau of the Census 2000, p. 416). Thus, as social services are cut back, women workers will be disproportionately affected.

Critics will respond that the expansion of the criminal justice system means increased employment opportunities for women. After all, 26 percent of law enforcement employees in the United States are women (Pastore & Maguire 2000, table 1.56). Even greater opportunities appear to exist in corrections, where 29 percent of employees in adult corrections are women (Maguire & Pastore 1999, p. 81). However, most women employed in law enforcement and corrections agencies work in traditional pink collar ghettos as low wage clerical or support staff. Practically speaking, the *only* way to advance to upper-levels of administration in either policing or corrections is through line employment as a police or correctional officer. And although 71 percent of law enforcement employees are police officers, only 11 percent of police officers are women (Pastore & Maguire 2000, table 1.56), and women make up just 19 percent of correctional guards (Maguire & Pastore 1999, p. 81).

There remains a long-standing bias against women in policing and corrections. Even after more than 20 years of proven effectiveness as officers on the streets and in the prisons, male coworkers and supervisors persist in their bias against women. They use harassment and masculine work cultures that marginalize women to resist efforts to increase the representation of women on these forces (Martin & Jurik 1996; Morash & Haarr 1995).

The attacks on affirmative action in the current political climate further endanger women's employment possibilities in the criminal justice system (Martin 1995). In addition, the definition and nature of work in criminal justice is being restructured to emphasize punitiveness and dangerousness. In Virginia, probation and parole counselors were renamed officers and may now carry weapons (53.1-145 of the Code of Virginia). Virginia's Director of Corrections since 1994 insists that probation and parole clients as well as inmates be called "convicts" or "felons." These moves emphasize punishment and the untrustworthiness of offenders; they stand in sharp contrast to the need to develop positive relationships in order to encourage social adjustment. Such practices also emphasize masculinity as a requirement for the job, thereby creating a climate that further discourages women in the work.

Three Strikes and no-parole policies have at least three implications for police and correctional officers. For the police, Three Strikes may influence people likely to be caught in the web of these laws to take more desperate measures than ever to evade arrest. For correctional guards, abolishing parole first means overcrowding in the prisons; it also means the loss of incentives and rewards for good behavior and the loss of faith in the future. In turn, these conditions produce an increase in the likelihood of prison violence and uprisings.

Thus, real increases in fear and the loss of hope among offenders become coupled with politically inspired attitudes about the dangerousness of offenders and the punitive goals of the work. Combined with attacks on affirmative action, bias against women in traditionally male occupations and the resulting stress on women employees, these factors may be surprisingly effective in bringing about actual *decreases* in women's employment in precisely those positions in policing and corrections that lead to advancement and higher pay.

The crime bills represent a government jobs program—criminal justice is, in fact, "the only growing public-sector employment" ("The prison boom," 1994, p. 223)—but the new jobs created come at the cost of other public sector jobs, such as those in social services, which are more likely to be held by women. And the new jobs created by the expansion of the criminal justice system are overwhelmingly jobs for men. Strike two.

STRIKE 3—FAMILY VALUES?

Men and women who commit crimes for which they are convicted and sentenced to prison have not lived their lives solely in criminal gangs; they do not structure their entire days around illegal activity; they are not *only* criminals. They are also sons and daughters, fathers and mothers. In short, they are responsible for caring for others who depend on them, and most of them do their best to meet these responsibilities because they do, in fact, love their families.

Sixty-five percent of women and 55 percent of men in state prisons in 1997 had children under the age of 18; most of these women (64 percent) and many men (44 percent) lived with their children before entering prison (Mumola 2000). Imprisoned adults cannot contribute to their families' financial or psychological well-being. In a few cases children are committed to foster homes or institutions. But most of the time another family member takes over care of those children and any elderly or disabled adults left behind—and that family member is usually a woman. This fact represents the third strike against women.

Because most of those imprisoned are men, it is the women in their lives—wives, girlfriends, and mothers—who are left with the responsibility for providing for the economic and emotional needs of the children and any dependent adults, a task these women must accomplish on their own. And when women are imprisoned, it is generally their mothers who take over the care of the children.

As we imprison increasing numbers of men and women, we saddle more women with sole responsibility for care of the next generation. The problem is exacerbated when the state, due to overcrowding, moves prisoners out of its system and to other states, thereby leaving the women and children bereft of even emotional support from incarcerated parents.

Today in the United States, "there are at least 1.5 million children of prisoners and at least 3.5 million children of offenders on probation or parole" (Johnston 1995a, p. 311). The women who care for these children, as well as the children themselves, must be recognized as paying some of the hidden costs of punitive criminal justice policies. Parental arrest and incarceration endures as a traumatic event for all involved. It can lead to inadequate child care due to persistent and deepening poverty. In addition, children may suffer from problems with which the women who care for them must cope: developmental delay, behavioral and emotional difficulties, feelings of shame and experiences of stigmatization, distrust and hatred of police and the criminal justice system, and subsequent juvenile delinquency (Johnston 1995b; Carlson & Cervera 1992; Fishman 1990). In effect, children suffer from post-traumatic stress disorder when their parents are imprisoned (Kampfner 1995). Effective programs to address the needs of children of incarcerated parents and their caregivers remain few in number and endangered.

As politicians get tough on crime, it is women and children who do the time, alone. Remembering the first two strikes against women discussed earlier, it emerges as strikingly clear that women will not be able to look to the federal or state government for either public assistance or public employment. Strike three. It's *women* who are out.

FINAL THOUGHTS: AN EVERY WOMAN'S ISSUE

It remains far too easy to be lulled into complacency when it comes to women and criminal justice. After all, women represent a very small number of offenders. And in spite of male violence against women, most victims of crime are men. Yet, the social construction of crime and criminals and the political nature of their control are neither gender blind, nor gender neutral. We are finally and fully confronted by the harsh reality that criminal justice *is* about women, *all* women. Although it occasionally operates as an important resource for women, the criminal justice system most frequently represents a form of oppression in women's lives. It attacks most harshly those women with the least power to resist it. As Jean Landis and I wrote a decade ago:

> it is time to recognize that in real life . . . offenders do not exist as exclusive objects. They are connected in relationships with other people, a major portion of whom are women—mothers, wives, lovers, sisters and daughters. Any woman who fights to keep her wits, and her roof, about her as she helplessly experiences a loved one being swept away by the currents of criminal justice "knows" the true brutality of the system and the extensiveness of its destruction. If she is a racial/ethnic minority person, which she is likely to be, and/or if she is poor, which she surely is, she intuitively knows the nature of the interaction between criminal justice practices and the racist and/or classist [as well as sexist] structure of her society, as well as its impact on her life, her family, and her community. (Danner & Landis 1990, pp. 111–112)

She also knows that precious little assistance exists for her, and those who depend on her, in the form of either welfare or employment from the larger community as represented by the state. In addition, it is every woman, no matter who she is, who will pay for the dramatic expansion of the criminal justice system. Growing the criminal justice system in an era of tax cuts and budget reduction requires shrinking other government services, such as education, health care, and roads, that benefit all members of the public. Clearly, criminal justice *is* a women's issue.

The "get tough, lock 'em up" and Three Strikes policies will not reduce crime nor reduce women's pain associated with crime. They will only impoverish communities as they enrich politicians and those corporations associated with this new prison industrial complex. Although women have been largely left out of the debate, it is women who are the quiet losers—the big time losers—in the crime bills. Criminal justice reforms such as these are politically motivated, unnecessary, ineffective, and far, far too costly. And, finally and most importantly, it is women who receive the least from the wars on crime and drugs, and it is women who bear most of their hidden burdens.

ACKNOWLEDGMENTS

This chapter was originally prepared as the 1995 Women's Studies Junior Faculty Lecture, Old Dominion University; I thank Anita Clair Fellman, director of Women's Studies, for that invitation. Thanks to Marie L. VanNostrand (formerly of Virginia Department of Criminal Justice Services) and Lucien X. Lombardo (Old Dominion University) who were most gracious in providing me with materials. The members of Our Writing Group and COOL provided much encouragement and entertainment. An earlier version was presented at the 1995 American Society of Criminology meetings, Boston, Massachusetts.

REFERENCES

BACHMAN, R. & SALTZMAN, L. E. (1995). *Violence against women: Estimates from the redesigned survey.* Washington, DC: U.S. Department of Justice.

BROWNE, A. (1990, December 11). Assaults between intimate partners in the United States. Testimony before the United States Senate, Committee on the Judiciary, Washington, DC.

BUSH-BASKETTE, S. R. (1998). The war on drugs as a war against Black women. In S.L. Miller (Ed.), *Crime control and women: Feminist implications of criminal justice policy* (pp. 113–129). Thousand Oaks, CA: Sage.

CARLSON, B. E. & CERVERA, N. (1992). *Inmates and their wives: Incarceration and family life.* Westport, CT: Greenwood Press.

CATALANO, SHANNAN M. (2004). *Criminal victimization, 2003.* Washington, DC: U.S. Department of Justice.

CHESNEY-LIND, M. (1995). "Rethinking women's imprisonment: A critical examination of trends in female incarceration." In B. R. Price & N. J. (Eds.), *The criminal justice system and women: Offenders, victims, and workers* (2nd Ed., pp. 105–117). New York: McGraw-Hill.

CLARK, J. AUSTIN, J. & HENRY, D. A. (1997). *"Three strikes and you're out": A review of state legislation.* Washington, DC: U.S. Department of Justice.

DALY, K. & CHESNEY-LIND, M. (1988). Feminism and criminology. *Justice Quarterly, 5,* 497–538.

DANNER, M. & LANDIS, J. (1990). "Carpe diem (Seize the day!): An opportunity for feminist connections." In B. D. MadLean & D. Milovanvovic (Eds.), *Racism, empiricism and criminal justice* (pp. 109–112). Vancouver, Canada: The Collective Press.

DONZIGER, S. A. (Ed.) (1996). *The real war on crime: The report of the national criminal justice commission.* New York: HarperPerennial.

FISHMAN, L. T. (1990). *Women at the wall: A study of prisoners' wives doing time on the outside.* New York: State University of New York Press.

GLAZE, LAUREN E. and THOMAS P. BONCZAR. (2009) *Probation and parole in the United States, 2008.* Washington, DC: U.S. Department of Justice.

GREENFELD, L. A., RAND, M. R., CRAVEN, D., KLAUS, P. A., PERKINS, C. A., RINGEL, C., WARCHOL, G., MASTON, C., & FOX, J. A. (1998). *Violence by intimates: Analysis of data on crimes by current or former spouses, boyfriends, and girlfriends.* Washington, DC: U.S. Department of Justice.

GREENWOOD, P. W., FYDELL, C. P., ABRAHAMSE, A. F., CAULKINS, J. P., CHIESA, J., MODEL, K. E., & KLEIN, S. P. (1994). *Three strikes and you're out: Estimated benefits and costs of California's new mandatory-sentencing law.* Santa Monica, CA: RAND.

IMMARIGEON, R. & CHESNEY-LIND, M. (1992). *Women's prisons: Overcrowded and overused.* San Francisco, CA: National Council on Crime and Delinquency.

JACKSON, J. (1995, January 11). Sheriffs suing state to relieve overcrowding in city jails. *The Virginian-Pilot,* pp. A1, A6.

JOHNSTON, D. (1995a). Conclusion. In K. Gabel & D. Johnston (Eds.), *Children of incarcerated parents* (pp. 311–314). New York: Lexington Books.

JOHNSTON, D. (1995b). Effects of parental incarceration. In K. Gabel & D. Johnston (Eds.), *Children of incarcerated parents* (pp. 59–88). New York: Lexington Books.

KAMPFNER, C. J. (1995). Post-traumatic stress reactions in children of imprisoned mothers. In K. Gabel & D. Johnston (Eds.), *Children of incarcerated parents* (pp. 89–100). New York: Lexington Books.

KRASKA, P. B. & KAPPELER, V. E. (1995). To serve and pursue: Exploring police sexual violence against women. *Justice Quarterly, 12,* 85–111.

LAFAY, L. (1994, December 9). New, low parole rate has cost Va. $77 million. *The Virginian-Pilot,* pp. A1, A24.

LAFAY, L. (1995, February 17). State sends 150 inmates to Texas. *The Virginian-Pilot,* pp. A1, A9.

MAGUIRE, K., & PASTORE, A. L. (Eds.). (1999). *Sourcebook of criminal justice statistics 1998.* Washington, DC: U.S. Department of Justice.

MANEGOLD, C. S. S. (1994, August 25). Quiet winners in house fight on crime: Women. *New York Times,* p. A19.

MARTIN, S. E. (1995). The effectiveness of affirmative action: The case of women in policing. *Justice Quarterly, 8,* 489–504.

MARTIN, S. E. & JURIK, N. D. (1996). *Doing justice, doing gender: Women in law and criminal justice occupations.* Thousand Oaks, CA: Sage.

MAUER, M. (1990). *Young black men and the criminal justice system: A growing national problem.* Washington, DC: The Sentencing Project.

MORASH, M. & HAARR, R. N. (1995). Gender, workplace problems, and stress in policing. *Justice Quarterly, 12,* 113–140.

MUMOLA, C. J. (2000). *Incarcerated parents and their children.* Washington, DC: U.S. Department of Justice.

PASTORE, A. L., & MAGUIRE, K. (Eds.). (2000). *Sourcebook of criminal justice statistics [Online].* Available: [Retrieved May 4, 2001].

PRICE, B. R., & SOKOLOFF, N. J. (1995). *The criminal justice system and women: Offenders, victims, and workers* (2nd ed.). New York: McGraw-Hill.

SABOL, WILLIAM J., WEST, HEATHER C. & COOPER, MATTHEW. (2009). *Prisoners in 2008.* Washington, DC: U.S. Department of Justice.

SIDEL, R. (1996). *Keeping women and children last: America's war on the poor.* New York: Penguin Books.

SNIDER, J. R. (1995, December 13). Have gun, will travel. *The Virginian-Pilot.*

THE PRISON BOOM (1995, February 20). *The Nation,* pp. 223–224.

THOMAS, P. (1994, May 12). Making crime pay. *Wall Street Journal,* pp. A1, A6.

TONRY, M. H. (1995). *Malign neglect: Race, crime, and punishment in America.* New York: Oxford University Press.

TURNER, M.G., SUNDT, J.L., APPLEGATE, B.K., & CULLEN, F. T. (1995). "Three strikes and you're out" legislation: A national assessment. *Federal Probation*, 59, 16–35.

U.S. BUREAU OF THE CENSUS. (2000). *Statistical abstract of the United States 2000*. Washington, DC: U.S. Government Printing Office.

U.S. DEPARTMENT OF JUSTICE. (2004, July 25). Almost 6.9 million on probation or parole or incarcerated in U.S. prisons or jails. Press Release. [retrieved February 1, 2005].

U.S. V. MORRISON. (2000). 529 U.S. 598.

ENDNOTES

1. This chapter is an updated adaptation from the author's chapter in *Crime Control and Women: Feminist Implications of Criminal Justice Policy* edited by Susan L. Miller (Newbury Park, CA: Sage Publications, 1998).
2. Entitlements to the poor include Temporary Assistance to Needy Families (TANF) formerly known as Aid to Families with Dependent Children (AFDC); the Women, Infants and Children (WIC) nutritional program; food stamps; school breakfast and lunch programs; Medicaid; public housing and emergency grants; and social security for disabled and dependent persons, as well as other programs. Each of these programs is under attack and will almost certainly be cut back, just as has welfare.

24

Behind the Walls of Injustice

Assessing the Impact of Maternal Incarceration on Women and Children

Zina T. McGee, Whytnee Foriest, Kadari Taylor-Watson,
Amanda Redd, Tiffany Hampton, and Brittany Kirkland

In the United States, rates of female arrests and subsequent incarceration are increasing. Recent figures suggest that although there are fewer female offenders than male offenders, the rate at which women are being arrested, convicted, and sentenced has steadily increased, with an estimated 1 in every 109 women in the United States under some form of correctional supervision and confinement (Masters, 2004; Grella and Greenwell, 2008; Loper, 2006). Over the past few years, more attention has been given to women's encounters with the criminal justice system, primarily because of the backlash of wars waged against drugs and crime, determinate sentencing, mandatory sentencing, and judicial practices, all of which continue to adversely affect women who often find themselves in dire circumstances because of their participation in low-level drug offenses (Simon and Ahn-Redding, 2005; Allard, 2002; Conklin et al., 2000; Blitz et al., 2005; Cunningham and Baker, 2003; Ekstrand, 1999; Henderson, 1998; Freudenberg, 2008). It has been estimated that half of incarcerated females were engaged in either drug or alcohol abuse at the time their offense was committed, and although they are more likely to display significant substance abuse problems, they are often less likely to receive substance abuse treatment. In other instances, substance abuse treatment may be all that is offered to women suffering from a range of other problems that often speak to the need for increased group therapy, family counseling, reunification programs, and mental health treatment. Further, issues of multicultural counseling awareness, sensitivity, and training are rarely focused on in discussions of what happens to many women who will ultimately be released from jails and prisons, only to recidivate because of lack of proper aftercare (Morton, 2004; Johnson, 2004). This poses a particular problem for women offenders since many of them are more likely to have been sexually abused as children, with mental health issues that were not properly diagnosed and treated prior to incarceration (Alexander, 2000; Kane and DiBartolo,

2002). Yet, research continues to show that when handling female offenders within a correctional setting, less emphasis is placed on dealing with issues of incest, childhood sexual abuse, and neglect despite the fact that many of these women are also mothers with children under the age of 18 (Sharp and Ericksen, 2003; Alemagno, 2001; Kubiak et al., 2004; Voorhis et al., 2004; Kristine and Myers, 2003; Lalonde and George, 2002; Cerncovich and Lanctot, 2008). Instead, the correctional approach continues to focus less on issues of empowerment and reunification and more on the notion that "she should have thought of her children before she committed the crime," prompting many scholars to argue that since parenting is seen as more of a privilege that must be earned, fewer programs will be developed to help women to properly reunite with their children and to assume responsibility for their lives (Morris and Wilkinson, 1995; Young, 1998; McGee, 2000; McGee and Baker, 2003; Zeitzow, 2006; Zlotnick, 1997; Logen et al., 2002; McGee et al., 2007). Female offenders are rarely liberated, and have been forced into subservient positions where they feel powerless and dependent. Many of them have been physically and psychologically battered by husbands and boyfriends and are devoid of the necessary skills to rebuild relationships and provide effective parenting after their release from jails and prisons. While many researchers have suggested that the female criminal is no longer a "forgotten offender" since more attention has been given to her involvement in the criminal justice system, they have also noted that the system continues to ignore the dimensions of prior experiences and trauma that often serve as precursors to her crimes (Chesney-Lind, 2002; Richie, 2002; Enos, 2001; Pollack, 1998; Johnston, 1997; Arditti, 2008).

Regarding motherhood and confinement, almost 60 percent to 80 percent of all incarcerated female offenders have minor children. Most of these women have at least 2 children, and it is estimated that 1 out of 12 women are pregnant during their incarceration (Masters, 2004). Prior to their confinement, many women were either single, divorced, or separated, andwere were the sole providers for their children. Separation from children is deemed as one of the worst situations a female offender can endure as she is faced with the disintegration of her family on the outside while attempting to adjust to a new environment inadequately prepared to give her proper medical care, counseling, and mental health treatment (Enos, 2001; Dunbar et al., 2003; Ho, 2005; Keaveny and Zauszmewski, 1999; McGee and Gilbert, 2009). Moreover, she is often denied the ability to acquire parenting skills to support her children, survival training to face her reintegration into society, and the needed services to assist her with personal responsibility and independence. Many children, like their mothers, will experience a host of emotions such as fear, anxiety, loneliness, anger, and guilt, while researchers have also noted that the incarceration of mothers may produce similar crime patterns among their daughters in that an estimated 44 percent to 64 percent of all girls detained in the juvenile justice system have mothers who have been either arrested or incarcerated (Morton, 2004).

Regarding the treatment of female offenders, characteristics that are important to note when developing programs further illustrate the need for gender-specific programs. When considering mental health issues, for example, studies indicate that 33 percent of female offenders are diagnosed with post-traumatic stress disorder, 12.2 percent are diagnosed with a serious mental illness, and 72 percent present a dual diagnosis. However, despite these statistics, many inmates report inadequate mental health treatment. Research also suggests that 45.8 percent of female offenders have had at least some high school education, 53.5 percent were unemployed prior to arrest, and 50.4 percent were between the ages of 25 and 34 at the time of their arrest (Snell and Morton, 1990; American Correctional Association, 1994; Madem et al., 1994; Lucente, 2001; Mahan, 2003; Messina et al., 2006; Teplin, 1997; White et al., 2006). Unlike the traditional male inmate, women bring a variety of unique health and relationship issues to the prison experience, but without understanding the many characteristics of female offenders, treatment programs cannot be appropriately tailored to address their needs.

While children experience the incarceration of a father more frequently than the incarceration of a mother, the children of incarcerated mothers are more likely to be displaced from their homes and to experience problems associated with the separation from their parent (Bloom and Steinhart, 1993; Brown and Bloom, 2009). Children of female inmates suffer even more trauma since the mother is usually their primary caregiver (Fishman, 1983). Most children, especially young children, are in the primary care of their mother when she is arrested. The degree of disruption in these children's lives upon the arrest of their mothers depends largely on where they go and who takes care of them while she is incarcerated. When fathers go to jail or prison, their children's mothers typically continue to care for them (US Department of Justice, 1993). This is less often the case when mothers are incarcerated. Some mothers in state prisons report that their children are in the care of the father, while the rest report that the child is with a grandmother, another close relative, a family friend, or in a foster home or agency (US Department of Justice, 1993). Children of incarcerated mothers are more likely to engage in lawbreaking behavior and are at significantly increased risk for second generation incarceration (Johnston, 1991; Johnston, 1992; Johnston, 1995; Johnston, 1995a; Johansson and Leonard, 2009). A frequently cited figure notes that children of incarcerated parents are six times more likely than their peers to be incarcerated (US Department of Justice, 1993). In a sample of 100 women in a California jail, it was reported by mothers that 11.4 percent of their children had been arrested and 10 percent had been incarcerated (Johnston, 1991). Incarcerated mothers in Trice's (1997) study of 229 adolescent children reported that 29 percent of their children had been arrested. Despite the degree of trauma these children experience and the amount of research that clearly establishes a linkage between the criminality of children and their parents, the well-being of children of incarcerated mothers is often ignored in policy discussions relating to female offending. Further, maternal health care in the prison system remains limited. Gynecological exams are not routinely performed, and in nearly all correctional facilities, there are no programs for prenatal or postpartum treatment, prenatal nutrition, allocation for methadone treatment, educational support for childbirth and rearing, or preparation for mother-child separation. Maternal incarceration has detrimental effects on children, families, and society (American Bar Association and National Bar Association, 2001; McCabe et al., 2002; Molidor et al., 2002; Moses, 1995). Women and children affected by maternal incarceration are among the most oppressed and vulnerable populations in the United States (Loper, 2006; Luke, 2002; Department of Health and Human Services, 2001; Wells and Bright, 2005), and maternal incarceration damages children during the developmental stages as well as the parent's overall well-being. Children are more likely to enter into the criminal justice system than their peers who do not have incarcerated parents, and a mother who is separated from her children is more likely to recidivate within a short period of time (Crawford, 2003; Mullis et al., 2004; Myers et al., 1999; Poehlmann, 2005; Harpaz-Rotem et al., 2006; Sherman, 2005; Teplin et al., 2002; Thompson and Harm, 2000; Grinberg et al., 2005).

As mentioned earlier, female offenders face a host of health experiences both during and after their periods of incarceration, many of which are often accompanied by unmet medical needs that have severe implications for their overall health and well-being. One problem in particular involves the persistent risk of HIV/AIDS/STD infection since many of these women have consistent patterns of drug abuse and addiction. Braithwaite et al. (2005) have noted that historically, imprisoned women have had health concerns that have been ignored, posing a particular problem for many women since they are at a greater than average risk for high-risk pregnancies and life-threatening illnesses such as HIV/AIDS, hepatitis C, and human papillomavirus, which may increase risk for cervical cancer. The increase in women's imprisonment is largely due to minor property- and drug-related crimes, although drug rehabilitation and health awareness components are rarely addressed in strategies to assist imprisoned women with aftercare upon their release from prison (DeGroot, 2001). Cotton-Oldenberg et al. (1999) found that among women inmates, differential associations between sexual risk factors and types of drug use existed, prompting them to suggest that future prison-based sexual-risk reduction strategies should be tailored to specific types of drug users. Others have noted that discharge planning prior to prison release often excludes effective strategies to assist women with leading healthier drug-free lives to reduce their chances of increased risk for HIV/AIDS/STD infection (Farley et al., 2000; Guyon et al., 1999; Rich et al., 1999). Black and Latina women, in particular, are at the greatest risk for sexually transmitted infections, further suggesting that greater risk-reduction strategies are needed for these prison releasees (Ravello et al. 2006; 2005; Mahon, 1996). Still others have suggested that greater attention be placed on the social-psychological process of movement from neglecting health to self-care among women prisoners prior to their release from prison through a series of health awareness programs and exercises, many of which should be culturally specific to address the needs of all women (for example, see Leenerts, 2003; West, 2001; and Freudenberg, 2008). The life circumstances of incarcerated women are a critical reminder that an HIV/AIDS/STD infected incarcerated woman has many concerns that affect her ability and willingness to engage in the complex course of intervention that is characteristic of effective treatment. Hence, the incarcerated woman's experiences and concerns are the essential framework for providers to construct appropriate management plans for women offenders both during and after their confinement.

Women in prison present a distinct range of health problems, including alcohol or drug abuse, acquired immune deficiency syndrome (AIDS), sexually transmitted diseases, mental health problems, gynecological problems, and chronic health problems including hypertension, diabetes, and heart disease (Young, 1999). As the number of incarcerated women continues to climb at a faster rate than for men, prison health care facilities for women face increasing demands to provide treatment for health conditions that existed prior to incarceration. Problems experienced by women in prison are often prevalent in a greater proportion of the incarcerated population than in the general U.S. population, and while there has been less research on women than on men, even less research is devoted to the study of incarcerated women's health than of men's (Braithwaite et al., 2005). The negative impact of imprisonment on the health of women is evidenced by a prison system primarily designed for men whereby the health needs of women are often not addressed by policies and procedures. Medical issues that relate to reproductive health and psychological issues that address imprisonment of single female heads of households remain overlooked. Women in prison often complain of lack of regular gynecological and breast examinations, while many imprisoned women who are survivors of physical and sexual abuse have lacked previous health care in their communities, placing them at a greater risk for high-risk pregnancies and life-threatening illnesses such as HIV/AIDS, hepatitis C, and HPV/cervical cancer. Other frequent complaints concern access to care during and after incarceration for asthma, high blood pressure, heart disease, and diabetes. Upon release from prison, many women continue to face these conditions that can be seriously dehabilitating, chronic, and, in some cases, life threatening, if not treated properly (Stoller, 2000).

At the community level, further evidence suggests that overpopulating low-income urban communities with ex-offenders without providing adequate services can lead to community disruption and higher crime rates, damaging social cohesion and its health-enhancing effects (Freedenberg, 2002). Despite increased interest in health research on women and minorities, less research has been conducted on the incidence of coronary heart disease from prospective, longitudinal studies on population based cohorts of black women (Gillum, 1998; Grella and Greenwell, 2008). Life events, coping resources, and psychological well-being among female inmates often relate to the health circumstances of poor, black women comprising a disproportionate amount of detainees. Studies of heart disease, in particular, show that compared to white women, black women have higher rates of coronary heart disease (CHD) mortality although they experience similar rates of heart disease morbidity (Leclere et al., 1998; Sekikawa, 2000). Studies have shown that there are several factors that may produce these variations by race, including individual health factors, socioeconomic risk factors, and social structural factors. Leclere et al. (1998), for example, found that women living in communities with high concentrations of female headed families are more likely to die of heart disease, highlighting the importance of neighborhood effects and their social content on mortality. Findlow (2006), in a discussion of the weathering conceptual framework, argues that the early onset of chronic illness in African American women often results from the negative effects of neighborhood and physical environment. Persistent psychosocial stressors including socioeconomic crises, excessive family and kin obligations, and disruption of family unit can each place women at risk for early onset of heart disease and its resulting complications. This problem is particularly pronounced among newly released mothers who are expected to reunite with their families after incarceration despite their histories of physical, mental, sexual, and drug abuse prior to incarceration. The weathering concept suggests that as black women, including released offenders, continually strive to overcome inequality and barriers, their circumstances can worsen their health as they respond to adverse situations that increase their health risks (Findlow, 2006). The hardships and experiences faced by black women are governed by a society marked by racial and gender oppression, making them more susceptible to disease and illness because of their constant exertion to head their households, earn wages, fulfill their responsibilities, and overcome obstacles as they adjust to the social and physical environment upon their release from prison. Hence, chronic stress and negative coping responses further exacerbate the health conditions of women as they are released from prison into society.

In this research, we focus on several factors that are of concern when studying female offenders, particularly African American women. Issues central to the current study are the experiences of women in jail and prison particularly with regard to coping with separation from children. Our intent is to explore the linkage between familial history of incarceration, drug addiction, sexual abuse, mental illness, and treatment among a sample of female inmates studied over a five-year period. Special attention is paid to the degree of contact with children, prior history of substance abuse, mental illness, treatment for drug and alcohol problems, and coping with separation from children. The study uses three primary sources of information: survey data collected from 200 female inmates, in-depth interviews conducted on 20 women who were either incarcerated at the time of the interview or had been released from the correctional setting, and 200 additional surveys as part of a follow-up project on recently released female inmates. The following are findings from a series of studies conducted using the aforementioned data (McGee et al., 2006; McGee and Gilbert, 2009).

Surveys were conducted with 200 women incarcerated in jails in Virginia, Maryland, District of Columbia, and New York. Twenty interviews were also conducted with some of the women currently housed in the jails and a few who had been released from the correctional institution. We recruited women to the study by requesting volunteers within the female housing unit and obtaining information on other women who would be willing to address their experiences after incarceration. We specifically recruited women with children, and the study reports on a convenience sample since random sampling was not available due to considerable transition and court dates. We are unable to report on the participation rate because of the transition within the units and the anonymity of respondents. We obtained informed consent, and research assistants conducted the interviews and distributed the surveys to the women in a private setting within the jails. They also interviewed females released from prison in community centers that provided services to ex-offenders. There was no compensation provided for data collection within the jails; however, women in the community centers who were former jail inmates received $20 for each interview.

Questionnaire items examined familial background characteristics (i.e., living situation while growing up, family history of incarceration, and parental abuse of drugs and alcohol), the inmate's own situations including abuse prior to incarceration, history of drug and/or alcohol abuse, physical illness, patterns of treatment including drug/alcohol treatment, mental health counseling, medical attention, group counseling, parenting classes, and reunification counseling. Items also addressed the mechanisms that female inmates used to cope with their incarceration, particularly in instances where extended separation from children was involved. To further understand the experiences of women in jail and the manner in which they coped with being away from their children, we used a series of open-ended questions for interviews addressing how the female inmates felt about being away from home, the impact that incarceration had on their lives, the degree to which they received support in jail to assist with rehabilitation, the factors that contributed to their ability to cope while in jail, their goals in life prior to incarceration, and the dynamics of dealing with criminal justice personnel. The questions were later modified as a follow-up interview on released offenders to explore how they adjusted to life after incarceration. For this study, women receiving drug abuse and mental health treatment were compared with women who did not.

Results show that at the time of their arrest, most women were between the ages of 35–44 (42%), were divorced (36%), had completed high school (38%), and were employed full time (34%). Most of the women were black (55%), and a vast majority of the women had children under the age of 18 (71%). They were more likely to have been charged with drug possession (46%), followed by larceny theft (34%), fraud (22%), other offenses relating to drugs (20%), and other property offenses (10%). None of the women reported involvement in violent offenses such as murder, negligent manslaughter, and assault. The findings are consistent with previous studies that suggest that many of the women processed through the criminal justice system are nonviolent, first-time offenders (Crawford, 2003; Kubiak et al., 2004; Morris and Wilkinson, 1995).

The study also presents a description of the specific experiences of the women in jail, including information on their family background, history of abuse, relationships with their children, drug addiction, mental health status, physical health, the extent of treatment for drugs and mental illness, participation in specific programs, and patterns of coping with incarceration. Results show that most of the female offenders lived with both parents while growing up (56%), although a substantial number also lived with their mothers in single-family households (34%). Fewer respondents lived in a foster home (10%), and consistent with research that has indicated generational patterns of abuse and incarceration, most reported that they had incarcerated family members (77%), while 44 percent reported having parents who abused drugs (Morton, 2004). Ten percent of the respondents reported having parents who were treated for mental conditions, and a large number of them reported having been physically or sexually abused before their incarceration (70%), with half of them being abused before the age of 18. Consistent with previous research that has examined the extent to which women are faced with a variety of parenting issues from concerns about their children's well-being to their level of contact with their children, the findings show that most of the respondents lived with their children before incarceration (70%), and a majority of them reported that their children were living with a grandparent during their incarceration (35%). While the mothers did report frequent contact with their children (71%), they were less likely to receive visits from their children (41%) compared to phone calls (76%) and mail (76%). This finding is supported by current studies suggesting that one of the major barriers that women face while in prison is maintaining contact with their children, particularly in terms of visitation, which has been linked to the likelihood of recidivism (Beck and Karberg, 2001; Sharp, 2003).

Regarding substance abuse and treatment, results also reveal that most women had a history of prior drug or alcohol abuse (75%), were under the influence of drugs or alcohol at the time of their arrest (52%), and had committed an offense to get money for drugs (60%). Fewer women reported a history of mental illness or psychiatric condition (28%), although it should be noted that the question did not ask if they had been previously diagnosed with any type of mental disorder or mental illness. Eighteen percent of the women reported being under the influence of psychiatric medication at the time of their arrest. Regarding specific types of drugs, a majority of women reported having used marijuana (80%) and/or cocaine (65%) compared to other drugs such as heroin, stimulants, depressants, hallucinogens, antidepressants, and other drugs such as crack. These figures are supported by research suggesting that women offenders with histories of substance abuse present complex clinical profiles with a range of medical, psychological, and social problems (Alemagno, 2001). However, fewer programs have assessed the specific needs of these women and have focused more on the observations of clinicians. In that regard, results from the current study show that while a majority of women have received drug or alcohol treatment at some point in their lives (62%), fewer have received mental health counseling (41%). Additionally, these women were less likely to report that they had received drug or alcohol treatment while in jail (35%) and mental health counseling while in jail (10%). Less than one-fourth of the women received a gynecological examination in jail (23%), while a small percentage reported that they were pregnant at the time that they entered the correctional facility (5%). Few of them reported having received prenatal care while incarcerated (5%).

With reference to family counseling and treatment for mental health conditions, the findings suggest that only one-third of the women have participated in some form of individual/group counseling, with 5 percent reporting that they had received this type of counseling while incarcerated. Twenty-eight percent of the female inmates reported receiving prescription medications while in jail, while 33 percent indicated that they had been admitted overnight to a mental health facility. Fewer of the women offenders in the sample had been treated for a diagnosed mental condition (36%), had been treated for a diagnosed mental condition in jail (23%), had received family counseling or treatment (28%), and had received parenting classes (48%). It must also be noted that none of the women reported that she had participated in a family reunification program. While all of the respondents reported that they were able to use some mechanism to cope with their imprisonment, a majority of them indicated that they relied on their family to help them cope (90%), followed by their friends (79%), their pastor (44%), and their children (32%). Fewer of the women reported that they relied on a counselor (11%) or a physician (11%) to help them cope with their circumstances.

As expected, these findings have treatment policy implications. While there has been an expansion of drug treatment opportunities, fewer women are given access to other services such as mental health counseling, family reunification, parenting classes, and group counseling. Many of these women will ultimately be released without stable housing or legal sources of income. Discussions of the treatment of released jail detainees continue to utilize a pathological framework while denying the multidimensional needs of women who have been victimized by physical abuse and drug addictions. Johnston (1997), for example, argues that the greatest risk for female inmates is their loss of parental rights, which results primarily from maternal substance abuse and the lack of reunification services for women offenders. The likelihood of mother/child reunification declines with prior maternal incarceration, and as women are arrested, convicted, and incarcerated multiple times, the rates at which they will be permanently separated from their children are quickly rising, further suggesting the need to explore additional treatment options for these women beyond the traditional substance abuse programs. The needs of these women are multidimensional, and research findings continue to show that effective treatment programs should be designed to address all aspects of their incarceration and subsequent release.

The research also presents a description of the specific racial differences among the women in jail, including information on their family background, history of abuse, relationships with their children, drug addiction, mental health status, physical health, the extent of treatment for drugs and mental illness, participation in specific programs, and patterns of coping with incarceration. Chi-Square Tests of Independence (χ^2) were conducted for this portion of the analysis, and the study reports all relationships that were significant at the .05 level. Results show that white women were more likely than their black counterparts to report a prior history of drug or alcohol abuse (100%), report a prior history of mental illness or psychiatric condition (40%), indicate that they were under the influence of drugs or alcohol at the time of their arrest (82%), indicate that they were under the influence of psychiatric medication at the time of their arrest (40%), and report that they committed an offense to get money to buy drugs (89%). Compared to black women, they were also more likely to indicate that at some point in their lives they had used marijuana (100%), cocaine (100%), heroin (42%), stimulants (51%), depressants (69%), hallucinogens (51%), and antidepressants (58%). However, with regard to the use of crack, which was categorized as a separate drug from cocaine, black women were more likely to report usage (18%). This finding is consistent with Alexander's (2000) argument that crack cocaine has had a major impact on African American women, particularly those who maintain their own households and are currently receiving AFDC. In this regard, he suggests that the unique experiences of African American women are often dismissed and proposes a feminist model to examine the full context of their lives since successful intervention requires a holistic approach. Further, Alexander (2000) notes that the oppressive intersection of race, class, and gender must be examined within the context of domestic violence and addiction among females, women of color in particular. This is an issue that must be addressed by counselors in an effort to provide effective treatment.

As stated earlier, fewer of the female inmates reported participation in a variety of programs other than those addressing substance abuse. The findings suggest specific racial differences with regard to women's participation in these programs. For example, white women were more likely than their black counterparts to report participation in mental health counseling (58%), to report being diagnosed with a physical illness (40%) and treated by a doctor (40%), to report receiving a gynecological examination in jail (40%), to report participation in individual/group counseling prior to jail (40%) and while in jail (11%), to have received prescription medications in jail (40%), to have been treated for a diagnosed mental condition prior to jail (58%) and while in jail (40%), and to have received family counseling (51%). However, results also show that a large number of black women were more likely to report participation in drug/alcohol treatment in jail (55%). Fewer reported participation in mental health counseling in jail (18%), although the percentage of participation remained higher than that of white women. Additionally, white women reported greater reliance on the following to cope with detainment: family (100%), friends (100%), and a pastor (60%). Black women were more likely to report reliance on their children (50%) in their efforts to cope with their situation. Concepts of familial bonds and kinship care among women of color are supported here, although it must also be noted that the cumulative effects of poverty, racism, and sexism experienced by many black mothers will ultimately become the experiences of their children, thus creating a new generation of youth at risk. Findings of racial differences regarding the types of treatment and services offered to female inmates are further supported by Richie's (2002) assertion that minority women continue to face collateral damage within the penal system as they are forced to bear the burden of punitive policies and extreme sentencing, only to find themselves facing another plight as they are denied effective treatment for the problems that they may experience beyond drug addictions. Their consistent lack of participation in programs such as family/individual counseling and mental health treatment is further supported by the discriminatory practices that will prevent them from achieving outcomes relating to economic independence, family reunification, and reduced criminal involvement.

In an effort to examine the extent to which familial background characteristics (i.e., living situation while growing up, family history of incarceration, and parental abuse of drugs and alcohol) relate to the female inmate's own circumstances such as history of victimization prior to incarceration, history of drug and/or alcohol abuse, and physical illness, bivariate correlations were conducted and suggest that: (1) a moderate association exists between prior victimization of the female inmate and having parents who abused drugs and/or alcohol ($r = .415$, $p < .01$), (2) a weak association exists between prior victimization of the female inmate and having grown up in a foster care setting ($r = .347$, $p < .01$), and (3) a negligible association exists between prior victimization of the female inmate and having parents who were incarcerated (r = .166, p < .05). In other words, female inmates who reported being the victim of abuse prior to their incarceration were also more likely to have grown up in a foster home, and were also more likely to have parents who had been incarcerated and had abused drugs and/or alcohol. Findings also indicate that a negligible relationship exists between the female inmate's abuse of drugs and/or alcohol and having grown up in a foster home (r = .192, p < .01). Those reporting abuse of drugs and/or alcohol were also more likely to report that they grew up in a foster care setting. Finally, results show that a negligible association exists between the female inmate's health status and having grown up in a foster care setting (r = .163, p < .01), and that a weak association exists between the female inmate's health status and having parents who abused drugs and/or alcohol (r = .328, p < .01). Hence, women reporting physical illness were more likely to have grown up in a foster home and were also more likely to have parents who abused drugs and/or alcohol. In order to examine race differences, a separate analysis was conducted to control for the effects of race, and with the exception of the correlation between the female inmate's illness and parental abuse of drugs and/or alcohol, all other correlations increased in value when the race variable was held constant. These findings suggest that race may be a determining factor in the association between physical illness and parental abuse of drugs and/or alcohol among female inmates in the sample. This is further supported by the contention that many minority women are almost unilaterally denied medical services and assessments that address the linkage between their family histories and their present conditions, and that programs addressing childhood events, family history, and traumatic experiences would be more cost effective than incarcerating women in adulthood.

Chi-Square Tests of Independence (χ^2) were conducted to illustrate the need for services and treatment, and the extent to which limited programs can be linked to a variety of problems experienced by female inmates. Results from these analyses reveal the following: (1) female inmates who did not participate in drug/alcohol treatment programs reported having incarcerated family members (87%), (2) female inmates who did not participate in individual/group counseling in jail reported having incarcerated family members (86%), (3) female inmates who did not participate in mental health counseling reported having parents who abused drugs and/or alcohol (58%), (4) female inmates who did not participate in individual/group counseling in jail reported having parents who abused drugs and/or alcohol (49%), (5) female inmates who did not receive family counseling or treatment reported having parents who abused drugs and/or alcohol (54%), (6) female inmates who did not receive parenting classes reported having parents who abused drugs and/or alcohol (65%), (7) female inmates who did not participate in drug treatment programs in jail reported being physically or sexually abused prior to incarceration (77%), (8) female inmates who did not participate in mental health counseling in jail reported being physically or sexually abused prior to incarceration (72%), (9) female inmates who did not participate in individual/group counseling reported being physically or sexually abused prior to incarceration (78%), (10) female inmates who did not participate in mental health counseling in jail reported a history of prior drug or alcohol abuse (78%), (11) female inmates who did not receive parenting classes reported a history of prior drug or alcohol abuse (90%), (12) female inmates who did not participate in drug/alcohol treatment reported a history of mental illness or psychiatric condition (47%), and (13) female inmates who did not participate in individual/group counseling in jail reported a history of mental illness or psychiatric condition (31%). Thus, the findings of these analyses clearly suggest that successful intervention must encompass the full context of women's lives, and programs that inadequately determine the needs of women offenders will prevent them from receiving the comprehensive services necessary to develop the whole person, one who will eventually return to her children to assume responsibility for their lives and her own.

Finally independent-samples t-test compared the aod (alcohol and drug) scores for women who have been physically or sexually abused prior to incarceration and those who have not been. There was a significant difference in the scores: [M = 4.033, 3.78] and [M = 1.75, 2.13] respectively (p < .001). The magnitude of the difference in the means was moderate (eta squared = .08). An independent-samples t-test was conducted to compare the aod scores for women who have been emotionally abused or treated for a mental condition and those who have not been. There was a significant difference in the scores: [M = 4.13, 5.00] and [M = 2.26, 2.911] respectively (p < .001). The magnitude of the differences in the means was large (eta squared = .14).

Partial correlational analyses also revealed that the relationships between foster care status, familial history of drug abuse, drug abuse history, and physical illness are more pronounced for minority females. Further hierarchical regression analyses also show that the effect of minority status increases the negative effect of unemployment on drug use, crack cocaine use specifically, controlling for other sociodemographic factors such as education, age, and marital status. The interactive effect model increases the r squared from .56 to .73 when compared to main effects.

An additional study analyzed the frequency with which women had contact with their children either through mail or through telephone calls in an effort to address research focusing on parenting and communication skills. This was analyzed through the utilization of a created scale that measures frequency of contact with children. The contact with child (cwchild) scale consisted of two items: calls to and from children and mail to and from children. Each item on this scale had to be reversed and recoded to exclude the response indicating that the participant had no children, since all participants were in fact mothers. The cwchild scale had a Cronbach's alpha coefficient of .95.

The second scale created for the analysis of this data is the total treatment (tottreat) scale, which measures the amount of treatment received by participants. The tottreat scale consisted of three items: received prescription medication in jail, received treatment for a physical illness, and received treatment for mental condition in jail. Treatment for physical illness and treatment for mental illness both had to be recoded to combine the initial responses of "not diagnosed" and "no" received into the same negative response. The scale had a Cronbach's alpha coefficient of .93.

When analyzing data set for this project, several tests were run in order to examine predicted correlations. In attempts to answer the research question regarding sociodemographic characteristics and availability to treatment, tests were run to determine if treatment status (tottreat) was correlated to age, number of children, and/or race. An analysis of the relationship between treatment received and communication with children score (cwchild) was also completed to address another research question. Non-parametric (Kruskal-Wallis) tests were run due to the failure of the data to adhere to the assumptions of parametric tests.

When analyzing the relationship of various sociodemographic characteristics and total contact scale, several statistically significant correlations were discovered at the p = .01 level. A negative strong relationship (r = −.804) was observed between age and contact with children scale score. There was a negative moderate relationship found between race and contact with child score ($r = -.695$). Highest level of education was negatively correlated to contact with child scores on a moderate level ($r = -.718$). Living with children under 18 prior to incarceration was moderately correlated to contact with child scores ($r = .596$). The relationships between sociodemographic characteristics and treatment scale scores were also examined. Employment status prior to arrest had a positive moderate correlation to treatment scale score ($r = .506$). There were also several other weak and negligible relationships.

An independent-samples t-test was conducted to compare the treatment scale scores (tottreat) for black women and white women. There was a significant difference in scores for black women ($\underline{M} = 2.27$, $\underline{SD} = .62$) and white women [$\underline{M} = 3.2$, $\underline{SD} = 1.48$; $\underline{t}(114.49) = -5.57$, $\underline{p} = .0001$]. The magnitude of the differences in the means was large. The effect size, computed using eta squared, was .14.

A Kruskal-Wallis test was run to determine if there was a difference in treatment scale scores across the different education levels. There was a statistically significant difference at the $p = .0001$ level. The Chi-Square value was 34.26 and the degrees of freedom were 2. High school graduates were ranked highest ($\underline{M} = 124.61$), women with some high school ($\underline{M} = 85.78$) were next, and women who had some college ($\underline{M} = 85.68$) were last. A second Kruskal-Wallis test was run to compare the treatment scale scores across the different age groups. There was a statistical difference at the $\underline{p} = .0001$ level. The $\underline{df} = 3$ and Chi-Square value is 37.47. The youngest two groups of women ($\underline{M} = 72.50$) had the lowest mean rank and the third group of women, aged 35–44 ($\underline{M} = 119.64$), had the highest score. Women aged 45–54 had a mean score of 101.79.

A Kruskal-Wallis test was aimed at determining if there was a relationship between the participant's age and her contact with her children score (cwchild). Subjects were divided into groups based on their age (Group 1: 18–24; Group 2: 25–34; Group 3: 35–44; Group 4: 45–54). This test showed that there was statistically significant relationship at the $p = .0001$ level in cwchild scores for the four age groups. The Chi-Square value was reported as 91.26 and $\underline{df} = 3$. Group 1 had the highest mean rank (171.00), followed by Group 2 (127.00), Group 4 (79.18), and finally Group 3, which had a mean rank of 74.83. Another Kruskal-Wallis test was performed to explore the impact of number of children on the communication score (cwchild). Subjects were divided into five groups according to the number of children they had (Group 1: one child; Group 2: two children; Group 3: three children; Group 4: four children; Group 5: five or more children). There was a statistically significant difference at the $p = .0001$ level in cwchild scores for the five groups. Chi-Square value was reported as 45.69 with four degrees of freedom. Group 1 was ranked highest (130.33), Group 2 was ranked second (112.15), Group 4 was third with a mean rank of 85.25, Group 5 was fourth (83.50), and the lowest ranked group was Group 3, with a mean rank of 41.50.

There were significant findings when analyzing the relationship between incarcerated woman's mental illness treatment status and communication with children score (cwchild), using a Kruskal-Wallis test, at the $p = .0001$ level. The women were divided into groups based on their mental illness treatment status (Group 1: not treated; and Group 2: treated). The Chi-Square value was 19.01 and $\underline{df} = 1$. The women who were treated for a mental illness (132.50) were ranked higher than the women who were not (90.94). In order to determine the best predictor of contact with children scale scores, a linear regression was conducted with the following variables: age, race, highest level of education, employment status prior to incarceration, and number of children. This model explains

85 percent of the variance in contact with children scores. The best statistically significant predictor was highest level of education ($\beta = -.446$; $p < .001$). Race, age, highest level of education, and employment status were all statistically significant contributors to contact with children scale scores when taken separately. The number of children was statistically nonsignificant and may as well be dropped from the model.

Another Kruskal-Wallis test analyzes the relationship among treatment status for a physical illness and communication with children. Women were compared according to whether they had or had not been treated by a doctor for a physical illness. Again this test compares the women on the basis of frequency of communication with children. The analysis shows that there is a significant relationship between treatment for physical illness at the $p = .0001$ level in cwchild scores for the two groups where the Chi-Square value was 13.97 with one degree of freedom. Women who had been treated for a physical illness had a higher mean rank (132.50) than those women who were not treated (93.48).

The research findings, as supported by previous literature, show that there is in fact a deficit in available treatment programs for women in prison and an even greater lack of programs designed with mothers in mind. In this sample, no one had participated in reunification programs. In regard to sociodemographic characteristics, white women in this sample were more likely to receive treatment in prison than black women. Although the tests did show a significant difference in treatment across the two races, this may be due to the backgrounds of these women and not completely race. This finding does implicate the need for further research in regard to treatment receipt of incarcerated women as it related to race. There were also statistically significant differences across the different age groups when treatment scale scores were analyzed. Because the differences did not exhibit a distinct pattern, further research may address this concern more readily.

Levels of contact with children were compared across several different characteristics. Women in different age groups varied significantly in the average cwchild scale scores; the youngest women had higher mean ranks on the scale. Women with fewer children had higher averages on the contact with children scale, with the exception of women with three children having the lowest average score. The inconsistent patterns of the differences indicate a need for further research to determine if any underlying factors, such as the ability to read, child's placement, and age of child, should be taken into consideration. Women who had not been treated for a physical or mental illness had a lower mean rank than women who did. This may be because women who are willing to receive treatment are more likely to be motivated to keep contact with their children; however, this would need to be verified by further research. Regression analysis showed that the best predictor of contact with children is highest level of education, which can be seen as a measure of socioeconomic status. It was also evident that several sociodemographic characteristics influence the amount of contact an incarcerated woman will have with her children.

Regarding newly released detainees, surveys were conducted with 200 women incarcerated in jails in Virginia, Maryland, District of Columbia, and New York, and the following year, follow-up questionnaires were distributed to the women as they were released. Twenty interviews were also conducted with some of the women currently housed in jails and a few who had been released from the correctional institution. We recruited women to the study by requesting volunteers within the female housing unit and obtaining information on other women who would be willing to address their experiences after incarceration. We specifically recruited women with children, and the study reports on convenience sample since random sampling was not available due to considerable transition and court dates. We are unable to report on the participation rate because of the transition within the units and the anonymity of respondents. We obtained informed consent, and research assistants conducted the interviews and distributed the surveys to the women in a private setting within jails. They also interviewed and surveyed females released from prison in community centers that provided services to ex-offenders. There was no compensation provided for data collection within the jails; however, women in the community centers who were former jail inmates received $20 for each interview.

A series of scales were used to find correlations among variables. A strong positive correlation ($r = .830**$) was found between the problems scale and the length of separation from child. The more problems the mother had, the longer she was separated from her children. A strong negative correlation ($r = -.995**$) was found between problems scale and the amount of time to arrange where her children would live. The more problems a mother had, the less time she had to arrange where her children would live. There was a strong negative correlation ($r = -.973**$) between parenting problems and common reactions from children. The more parenting problems a mother had, the more likely she was to report problems with angry children as opposed to children with behavior problems in school. Another correlation was found with parenting problems and employment status ($r = -.635**$). A mother was less likely to have a job if she struggled with more parenting problems.

A multiple linear regression was also used to find a relationship between variables. The ANOVA was significant at .000. The dependent variable was the problem scale and the coefficients used were the amount of time to arrange for children to live ($\beta = -.823$) and system's involvement in this arrangement ($\beta = .197$). The best predictor for problems the mother had is the amount of time she had to arrange for her children to live. The more time she had to arrange where her children would stay, the less problems she had. The system involved was a predictor for the amount of time she had to arrange for the children to live. In some cases, if the child was a ward of the state then there was little time to arrange where the child would stay. In relation to the common reactions the children felt due to separation of mother and the amount of time to arrange for children to live, a Chi-Square test was used. Mothers who reported that their children were angry (67.6%) had one day or no time at all to find and discuss living arrangements. Mothers who reported that their children had problems in school (32.4%) had a few months to find and discuss living arrangements. A test of significant mean difference showed that having children who were angry at their mothers for leaving ($m = 13.5$) increased the score on the parenting problem scale compared to children who were having problems in school ($m = 7.0$).

In an effort to address the generational effects of maternal incarceration on female delinquency, additional analyses reported are based on responses to self-administered questionnaires completed by 208 adjudicated female youth between the ages of 14 and 16 in the state of Virginia. Census tract data were utilized to obtain a stratified sample selected from various church and community organizations that service youth in the Hampton Roads area of Virginia. Each participating organization serviced inner-city youth in after-school programs. In each instance, students who participated in the youth organizations attended inner-city schools that had encountered gun-related violence (as victims, perpetrators, bystanders) out of school and had a record of delinquent behavior having been adjudicated delinquent within the past year. Parental income, educational status, and occupational status served as measures of the adolescents' socioeconomic background. Surveys were distributed by research assistants to 20–30 youth at a time during group sessions, many of which involved focus group and debriefing sessions after survey completion. The survey was introduced to students as a study of youth violence in the state of Virginia. Written permission to participate was obtained from parents and students.

Recent studies have also pointed toward predictors of ODD among female adolescents (Johansson and Leonard). Hence, results from a multiple linear regression show that 7.3 percent of the variation in oppositional defiant disorder is explained by having a mother in jail or arrested and living status. The overall model is significant ($F = 8.099$, sig. $= .000$). Family background factors do have a significant input on the development of oppositional defiant disorder. Findings show that not having mother in jail or arrested, decreases the female adolescent's chances of developing ODD ($\beta = -.182$), controlling for living status. Living in a household that is not single parent also decreases the likelihood of developing ODD ($\beta = -.164$), controlling for having a mother in jail or arrested. Finally, an additional regression shows that 7.2 percent of the variation in female adolescents being suspended is explained by having family problems with police and their friends being arrested. The overall model is significant ($F = 230.143$, sig.000). Friends being arrested ($\beta = .483$) is the best predictor of the female adolescent being suspended ($\beta = .483$), controlling for family problems with police ($\beta = -.657$).

As expected, our findings have treatment policy implications. While there has been an expansion of drug treatment opportunities, fewer women are given access to other services such as mental health counseling, family reunification, parenting classes, and group counseling. Many of these women will ultimately be released without stable housing or legal sources of income. Discussions of the treatment of released jail detainees continue to utilize a pathological framework while denying the multidimensional needs of women who have been victimized by physical abuse and drug addictions. Even less emphasis has been placed on the overall impact that the mother's incarceration has on the child, particularly females, since studies highlight a marked increase in the number of female juvenile detainees when the mother goes to prison or is placed under arrest. Johnston (1997), for example, argues that the greatest risk for female inmates is their loss of parental rights, which results primarily from maternal substance abuse and the lack of reunification services for women offenders. The likelihood of mother/child reunification declines with prior maternal incarceration, and as women are arrested, convicted, and incarcerated multiple times, the rates at which they will be permanently separated from their children are quickly rising, further suggesting the need to explore additional treatment options for these women beyond the traditional substance abuse programs. The needs of these women are multidimensional, and research findings continue to show that effective treatment programs should be designed to address all aspects of their incarceration and subsequent release.

Regarding findings from the in-depth interviews with female offenders in the jails, a variety of themes surfaced from the participants' interview responses. Among them were concerns about their children and visitation, having limited support and treatment for mental health and substance abuse, being undereducated with few resources, and facing lengthy sentences for nonviolent crimes. The voices of these women made it apparent that regardless of their race, educational status, criminal involvement, income level, and addictions, these women were still mothers. The themes that emerged from the interviews with these women were consistent with the literature and supported the notion that a woman's experience in jail may be affected by the multiple dimensions of her life such as past abuse, domestic violence, separation from children, and other concerns unique to women in our society. Despite the limited research on the linkage between diminished contact with children while incarcerated and repeat offending, scholars continue to note that the issue of mother-child contact is critical to the understanding of women's criminality after incarceration. Many of the respondents reported feelings of depression, shame, and guilt, yet reported receiving no counseling to assist them with their mental health status. Many of the women also indicated that the only treatment that they had received in jail was for substance abuse, and very few services had been provided to them that addressed group counseling, family reunification, mental health treatment, and post-release counseling. Pollock (1998) contends that where there is a lack of appropriate counseling and treatment, women will never be able to experience the normal aspects of parenting because of the haze of addiction or because they have transferred their responsibilities to other family members. The findings of this research demonstrate the need for effective intervention programs that must be made accessible to women in jails and prisons if they are to reunite with their families and become successful in their efforts to become resocialized within society.

REFERENCES

ALEMAGNO, S. (2001). Women in jail: is substance abuse treatment enough? *American Journal of Public Health*, 91, 798–801.

ALEXANDER, R. (2000). *Counseling, treatment, and intervention methods with juvenile and adult offenders*. Belmont, CA: Brooks/Cole Thomson Learning.

ALLARD, P. (2002). *Life sentences: denying welfare benefits to women convicted of drug offenses*. Washington, D.C.: The Sentencing Project.

AMERICAN BAR ASSOCIATION AND THE NATIONAL BAR ASSOCIATION. (2001). *Justice by gender: the lack of appropriate prevention, diversion and treatment alternatives for girls in the justice system*. Washington, DC: American Bar Association and the National Bar Association.

AMERICAN CORRECTIONAL ASSOCIATION. (1994). *The female offender: what does the future hold?* Lanham, MD: St. Mary's Press.

ANDERSON, T. L. (2006). Issues in the availability of health care for women prisoners. [Electronic reference]. Retrieved September 10, 2006, from www.dc.state.11.us/pub/females/opplan/health.html).

ARACHWAMETY, T. & KATSIYANNIS, A. (1998). Factors relating to recidivism among delinquent females at a state correctional facility. *Journal of Family Studies*, 7, 59–67.

ARDITTI, J. & FEW, A. (2008) Maternal distress and women's reentry into family and community life. *Family Process*, 47, 303–321.

BALDWIN, K. & JONES, J. (2000). *Health issues specific to incarcerated women: information for state maternal and child health programs*. Washington, D.C.: Department of Health and Human Services.

BECK, A. J. & KERNBERG, J. C. (2001). *Prisoners at midyear 2000*. Washington, D.C.: US Department of Justice.

BLITZ, C., WOLFF, N., PAN, K. & POGORZELSKI, W. (2005). Gender-specific behavioral health And community release patterns among New Jersey prison inmates: implications for treatment and community reentry. *American Journal of Public Health*, 95, 1741–1746.

BLOOM, B. & STEINHART, D. (1993). *Why punish the children: a reappraisal of the children of incarcerated mothers in America*. San Francisco, CA: National Council on Crime and Delinquency.

BRAITHWAITE, R., TREADWELL, H. & ARRIOLA, K. (2005). Health disparities and incarcerated women: a population ignored. *American Journal of Public Health*, 95, 1679–1681.

BREMS, C., KUKA-HINDIN, C. & NAMYNIUK, L. (2001). Ethnic difference in substance use patterns in a sample of pregnant substance-using women in treatment. *Journal of Addictions & Offender Counseling*, 21, 50–67.

BROWN, M. and BLOOM, B. (2009). Reentry and Renegotiating Motherhood. *Crime and Delinquency*, 55, 313–336.

CAUFFMAN, E., FELDMAN, S., WATERMAN, J. & STEINER, H. (1998). Posttraumatic stress disorder among female juvenile offenders. *Journal of the American Academy Child & Adolescent Psychiatry*, 37, 1209–1216.

CENTERS FOR DISEASE CONTROL. 2006. HIV/AIDS Among Women. [Electronic Reference]. Retrieved June 1, 2006, from www.cdc.gov/hiv/topics/women/resources/factsheets/women.htm

CERNCOVICH, S. & LANCTOT, N. (2008). Predicting adolescent and adult antisocial behavior among adjudicated delinquent females. *Crime and Delinquency*, 54, 3–33.

CHESNEY-LIND, M. (2002). Imprisoning women: the unintended victims of mass imprisonment. In M. Chesney-Lind & M. Mauer (Eds). *Invisible punishment: the collateral consequences of mass imprisonment*. New York, NY: New Press.

CONKLIN, T., LINCOLN, T. & TUTILL, R. (2000). Self-reported health and prior health behaviors of newly admitted correctional inmates. *American Journal of Public Health*, 90, 1939–1941.

COTTON-OLDENBERG, N., JORDAN, B., MNRTIA, S. & KUPPER, L. (1999). Women inmates' risk sex and drug behaviors: are they related? *American Journal of Drug & Alcohol Abuse*, 25, 129–150.

CRAWFORD, J. (2003). Alternative sentencing for female inmates with children. *Corrections Today*, 65, 708–812.

CUNNINGHAM, A. & BAKER, L. (2003). *Waiting for mommy: giving a voice to the hidden victims of imprisonment*. London on N6A 5P6 Canada: Centre for Children and Families in the Justice System.

DEAL, S. & GALAVER, J. (1994). Are women more susceptible than men to alcohol-induced cirrhosis? *Alcohol, Health, and Research World*, 18, 189–191.

DEGROOT, A. 2001. HIV among incarcerated women: an epidemic behind walls. *Corrections Today*, 63, 77–91.

DEPARTMENT OF HEALTH AND HUMAN SERVICES. (2001). *Women, injection drug use, and the criminal justice system*. Atlanta, GA: Centers for Disease Control.

DUNBAR, A., BROWN, R. & BUTLER, T. (2003). The effects of continuous and repeated Incarceration: depression and hopelessness in long-term prisoners. *Australian Journal of Psychology*, 55, 101–102.

EKSTRAND, L. (1999). *Women in prison: issues and challenges confronting U.S. correctional systems*. Washington, D.C.: United States General Accounting Office.

ENOS, S. (2001). *Mothering from the inside: parenting in a women's prison*. Albany, NY: State University of New York Press.

FARLEY, J., ADELSON, M., LALLY, M., BURZYNSKI, J., TASHIMA, K., RICH, J., CU-UVIN, S., SPAULDING, A., NORMANDIE, L., SNEAD, M. & FLANIGAN, T. 2000. Comprehensive medical care among HIV positive incarcerated women: the Rhode Island experience. *Journal of Women's Health & Gender Based Medicine,* 9, 51–56.

FINDLOW, J. (2006). Weathering: stress and heart disease in African American women Living in Chicago. *Qualitative Health Research*, 16, 221–237.

FISHMAN, S. H. (1983). Impact of incarceration on children of offenders. *Journal of Children in Contemporary Society*, 15, 89–99.

FREUDENBERG, N. (2008). Coming home from jail: the social and health consequences of community reentry for women, male adolescents, and their families and communities. *American Journal of Public Health*, 98, 5191–5202.

FREUDENBERG, N. (2002). Adverse effects of US Jail and prison policies on the health and well being of women of color. *American Journal of Public Health*, 92, 1895–1899.

FRITSCH, T. & BURKHEAD, J. (1981). Behavioral reactions of children to parental absence due to imprisonment. *Family Relations*, 30, 83–88.

GABEL, S. (1992). Behavioral problems in sons of incarcerated or otherwise absent fathers: the issue of separation. *Family Process*, 31, 303–314.

GAUDIN, J. & SUTPHEN, R. (1993). Foster care vs. extended family care for children of incarcerated mothers. *Journal of Offender Rehabilitation*, 19, 129–147.

GILFUS, M. (2002). Women's experiences of abuse as a risk factor for incarceration. *Applied Research Forum*, 1, 1–12.

GILLUM, R., MUSSOLINO, M. & MADANS, J. (1998). Coronary heart disease risk factors and attributable risks in African American women and men: NHANES I epidemiologic follow-up study. *American Journal of Public Health*, 88, 913–917.

GRELLA, C. & GREENWELL, L. (2008). Treatment needs and completion of community-based Substance-abusing women offenders. *Women's Health Issues*, 17, 244–255.

GRINBERG, I., DAWKINS, M., & FULLILOVE, C. (2005). Adolescents at risk: an initial validation of the life challenges questionnaire and risk assessment index. *Adolescence*, 40, 573–599.

GUYON, L., BROCHU, S., PARENT, & DESJARDINS, L. (1999). At risk behaviors with regard to HIV and addiction among women in prison. *Women & Health*, 29, 49–69.

HAGEN, K. & MYERS, B. (2003). The effect of secrecy and social support on behavioral problems in children of incarcerated women. *Journal of Child and Family Studies*, 12, 229–242.

HALPERIN, R. & HARRIS, J. (2004). Parental rights of incarcerated mothers with children in foster care: a policy vacuum. *Feminist Studies*, 30, 339–352.

HANLON, T., BLATCHLEY, R., SEARS, T., O'GRADY, K., ROSE, M. & CALLAMAN, J. (2005a). Vulnerability of children of incarcerated addict mothers: implications for preventive intervention. *Children and Youth Services Review*, 27, 67–84.

HANLON, T., O'GRADY, K., BENNETT, T. & CALLAMAN, M. (2005b). Incarcerated drug-abusing mothers: their characteristics and vulnerability. *American Journal of Drug and Alcohol Abuse*, 1, 59–77.

HARPAZ-ROTEM, I., ROSENHECK, R. & DESAI, R. (2006). The mental health of children exposed to maternal mental illness and homelessness. *Community Mental Health Journal*, 8, 1–10.

HENDERSON, D. (1998). Drug abuse and incarcerated women: a research review. *Journal of Substance Abuse Treatment*, 15, 579–587.

HENRIQUES, Z. (1995). African-American women: the oppressive intersection of gender, race, and class. *Women and Criminal Justice*, 7, 56–79.

HENRIQUES, Z. (1996). Imprisoned mothers and their children separation-reunion syndrome dual impact. *Women and Criminal Justice*, 8, 77–95.

HENRIQUES, Z. & MANATU-RUPERT, N. (2001). Living on the outside: African American women before, during, and after imprisonment. *The Prison Journal*, 8, 145–163.

HO, J., PAULTRE, F. & MOSCA, L. (2005). The gender gap in coronary heart disease mortality: is there a difference between blacks and whites? Data from the U.S. Cohorts Pooling Project. *Journal of Women's Health*, 14, 117–127.

HOUCK, K. & LOPER, A. (2002). The relationship of parenting stress to adjustment among mothers in prison. *American Journal of Orthopsychiatry*, 72, 548–559.

JOHANSSON, P. and LEONARD, K. (2009). A gender specific pathway to serious violent and chronic offending? *Crime and Delinquency*, 55, 216–240.

JOHNSON, H. (2004). Key findings from the drug use careers of female offenders study. Trends & Issues in *Crime and Criminal Justice*, 289, 1–6.

JOHNSTON, D. (1991). *Jailed mothers*. Pasadena, CA: Pacific Oaks Center for Children of Incarcerated Parents.

JOHNSTON, D. (1992). *Helping children of offenders through intervention programs*. Lanham, MD: American Correctional Association.

JOHNSTON, D. (1995). *Effects of parental incarceration.* In K. Gabel & D. Johnston (Eds) Children of incarcerated parents. Boston, MA: Lexington Books.

JOHNSTON, D. (1995a). Parent-child visits in jail. *Children's environments,* 12, 25–38.

JOHNSTON, D. (1997). Developing services for incarcerated mothers. In C. Blinn (Ed) *Maternal ties: a selection of programs for female offenders.* Lanham, MD: American Correctional Association.

KANE, M. & DiBARTOLO, M. (2002). Complex physical and mental health needs of rural incarcerated women. *Issues in Mental Health Nursing,* 23, 209–229.

KEAVENY, M. & ZAUSZNIEWSKI, J. (1999). Life events and psychological well-being in Women sentenced to prison. *Issues in Mental Health Nursing,* 20, 73–89.

KRISTINE, H. & MYERS, B. (2003). The effects of secrecy and social support on behavioral problems in children of incarcerated women. *Journal of Child and Family Studies,* 12, 229–242.

KUBIAK, S. P., YOUNG, A., SIEFERT, K. & STEWART, A. (2004). Pregnant, substance abusing, and incarcerated: exploratory study of a comprehensive approach to treatment. *Families in Society: The Journal of Contemporary Human Services,* 85, 177–198.

LALONDE, R. & GEORGE, S. (2002). *Incarcerated mothers: the Chicago project on female prisoners and their children.* Chicago, IL: The University of Chicago.

LECLERE, F., ROGERS, R. & PETERS, K. (1998). Neighborhood social context and racial Differences in women's heart disease mortality. *Journal of Health and Social Behavior,* 39, 91–107.

LEENERTS, HOBBS. (2003). From neglect to care: a theory to guide HIV positive women in self care. *Journal of Association of Nurses in AIDS Care,* 14, 25–38.

LOGAN, T., WALKER, R., COLE, J. and LEUKEFELD, C. (2002). Victimization and substance abuse among women: contributing factors, interventions, and implications. *Review of General Psychology,* 6, 325–397.

LOPER, A. (2006). How do mothers in prison differ from non-mothers? *Child and Family Studies,* 15, 83–95.

LUCENTE, S., FALS-STEWART, W., RICHARDS, H. & GOSCHA, J. (2001). Factor structure and reliability of the revised conflict tactics scales for incarcerated female substance abusers. *Journal of Family Violence,* 16, 437–450.

LUKE, K. (2002). Mitigating the ill effects of maternal incarceration on women in prison and their children. *Child Welfare,* 81, 692–702.

MADEM, A., SWINTON, M. & GUNN, J. (1994). A criminological and psychiatric survey of women serving a prison sentence. *British Journal of Criminology,* 342, 172–191.

MAHAN, S. (2003). Pregnant girls and moms in detention. *Justice Policy Journal,* 1, 41–58.

MAHON, N. (1996). New York inmates' HIV risk behaviors: the implications for prevention policy and programs. *American Journal of Public Health,* 86, 1211.

MANN, C. R. (1995). Women of color and the criminal justice system. In B. R. Price & N. Sokoloff (Eds) *The criminal justice system and women: offenders, victims and workers.* (2nd ed) New York, NY: McGraw-Hill.

MASTERS, R. E. (2004). *Counseling criminal justice offenders.* (2nd ed) Thousand Oaks, CA: Sage Publications.

McCABE, K., LANSING, A., GARLAND, A. & HOUGH, R. (2002). Gender differences in psychopathology, functional impairment, and familial risk factors among a adjudicated delinquents. *Journal of the American Academy of Child & Adolescent Psychiatry,* 41, 860–867.

McGEE, Z. T. (2000). The pains of imprisonment: long-term incarceration effects on women in prison. In R. Muraskin (Ed) *It's a crime: women and justice.* (3rd ed) Upper Saddle River, NJ: Prentice Hall.

McGEE, Z. T. and GILBERT, A. (2009). Treatment programs for incarcerated women and mother child communication levels." Manuscript under review for publication in *Journal of Contemporary Criminal Justice.*

McGEE, Z. T., JOSEPH, E., ALLICOTT, I., GAYLE, T., BARBER, A. & SMITH, A. (2006). From the inside: patterns of coping and adjustment among mothers in prison. In R. Muraskin (Ed) *It's a crime: women and justice.* (4th ed) Upper Saddle River, NJ: Prentice Hall.

McGEE, Z. T. & BAKER, S. R. (2003). Crime control policy and inequality among female offenders. In R. Muraskin (Ed) *It's a crime: women and justice.* (3rd ed) Upper Saddle River, NJ: Prentice Hall.

MESSINA, N., BURDON, W., HAGOPIAN, G. & PRENDERGAST, M. (2006). Predictors of prison-based treatment outcomes: a comparison of men and women participants. *The American Journal of Drug and Alcohol Abuse*, 32, 7–28.

MOLIDER, C., NISSEN, L. & WATKINS, T. (2002). The development of theory and treatment with substance abusing female juvenile offenders. *Child and Adolescent Social Work Journal*, 19, 209–225.

MORRIS, A. & WILKINSON, C. (1995). Responding to female prisoners' needs. *Prison Journal*, 75, 295–306.

MORTON, J. B. (2004). *Working with women offenders in correctional institutions.* Lanham, MD: American Correctional Association.

MOSES, M. (1995). *Keeping incarcerated mothers and their daughters together: girl scouts beyond bars.* Washington, DC: U.S. Department of Justice.

MULLIS, R., CORNILLE, T., MULLIS, A. & HUBER, J. (2004). Female juvenile offending: a review of characteristics and contexts. *Journal of Child and Family Studies*, 13, 205–218.

MUMOLA, C. (2000). *Incarcerated parents and their children.* Washington, DC: US Department of Justice.

MYERS, B., SMARSH, T., AMLUND-HAGEN, K. & KENNON, S. (1999). Children of incarcerated mothers. *Journal of Child and Family Studies*, 8, 11–25.

NELSON-ZLUPKO, L., KAUFFMAN, E., & DORE, M. (1995). Gender differences in drug addiction and treatment: implications for social work intervention with substance-abusing women. *Journal of Social Work*, 43, 34–47.

POEHLMANN, J. (2005). Incarcerated mothers' contact with children, perceived family relationships and depressive symptoms. *Journal of Family Psychology*, 19, 350–357.

POLLOCK, J. (1998). *Counseling women in prison.* Thousand Oaks, CA: Sage Publications.

POLLOCK, J. (1999). *Criminal women.* Cincinnati, OH: Anderson Publishing.

RAVELLO, L., BRANTLEY, M., LAMARRE, M., QAYAD, M., AUBERT, H. & SAGUE, C. (2005). Sexually transmitted infections and other health conditions of women entering Prison in Georgia, 1998–1999. *Sexually Transmitted Diseases*, 32, 247–252.

RAVELLO, L., BRANTLEY, M., LAMARRE, M., QAYAD, M., AUBERT, H. & SAGUE, C. (2006). Sexual behaviors of HIV seropositive men and women following release from prison. *International Journal of STD & AIDS*, 17, 103–109.

RICH, J., DICKINSON, B., MACALINO, G., FLANIGAN, T., TOWE, C., SPAULDING, A. & VIAHOV, D. (1999). Prevalence and incidence of HIV among incarcerated and reincarcerated women in Rhode Island. *Journal of Acquired Immune Deficiency Syndromes*, 22, 161–167.

RICHIE, B. (2004). Feminist ethnographies of women in prison. *Feminist Studies*, 30, 1–7.

RICHIE, B. (2002). The social impact of mass incarceration on women. In M. Chesney-Lind & M. Mauer (Eds) *Invisible punishment: the collateral consequences of mass imprisonment.* New York, NY: New Press.

SEKIKAWA, A., & KULLER, L. (2000). Striking variation in coronary heart disease mortality in the United States among Black and White women aged 45–54 by state. *Journal of Women's Health & Gender-Based Medicine*, 9, 545–558.

SHARP, S. F. (2003). Mothers in prison: issues of parent-child contact. In S. Sharp (Ed) *The incarcerated woman: rehabilitative programming in women's prisons.* Upper Saddle River, NJ: Prentice Hall.

SHARP, S. F. & ERICKSEN, M. E. (2003). Imprisoned mothers and their children. In B. H. Zaitzow & J. Thomas (Eds) *Women in prison: gender and social control*. Boulder, CO: Lynne Rienner Publishers.

SHERMAN, F. (2005). *Detention reform and girls: challenges and solutions*. Baltimore, MD: Anne E. Casey Foundation.

SIMON, R. J. & AHN-REDDING, H. (2005). *The crimes women commit and the punishments they receive*. (3rd ed) Lanham, MD: Lexington Books.

SNELL, T. & MORTON, D. (1994). *Women in prison*. Washington, DC: Bureau of Justice Statistics.

STOLLER, N. (2000). *Improving access to health care for California's women prisoners*. Santa Cruz, CA: California Program on Access to Care.

TEPLIN, L., Abram, K. & McClelland, G. (1997). Mentally disordered women in jail: who receives services. *American Journal of Public Health*, 87, 604–609.

TEPLIN, L., ABRAM, K., MCCLELLAND, G., DULCAN, M. & MERICLE, A. (2002). Psychiatric disorders in youth juvenile detention. *Archives of General Psychiatry*, 59, 1133–1143.

THOMPSON, P. & HARM, N. (2000). Parenting from prison: helping children and mothers. *Issues in Comprehensive Pediatric Nursing*, 23, 61–81.

TRICE, A. D. (1997). Risk and protective factors for school and community problems for children of incarcerated women. Paper presented at the biennial meetings of the Society for Research in Child Development, Indianapolis, IN.

UNITED STATES DEPARTMENT OF JUSTICE. (1993). *Jail inmates*. Washington, DC: Bureau of Justice Statistics.

VIGILANTE, K., FLYNN, M., AFFLECK, P., STUNKLE, J., MERRIMAN, N., FLANIGAN, T., MITTY, J. & RICH, J. (1999). Reduction in recidivism of incarcerated women through primary care, peer counseling, and discharge planning. *Journal of Women's Health & Gender-Based Medicine*, 8, 409–415.

VIRGINIA COMMISSION ON YOUTH. (2002). *Children of incarcerated parents*. Richmond, VA: Commission on Youth.

VOORHIS, P. V., BRASWELL, M. & LESTER, D. (2004). *Correctional counseling and rehabilitation*. Cincinnati, OH: Anderson Publishing.

WELLS, D. & BRIGHT, L. (2005). Drug treatment and reentry for incarcerated women. *Corrections Today*, 67, 98–111.

WEST, A. (2001). HIV/AIDS education for Latina inmates: the delimiting impact of culture on prevention efforts. *Prison Journal*, 81, 20–22.

WHITE, M., GALIETTA, M. & ESCOBAR, G. (2006). Technology-driven literacy programs as a Tool for re-connecting incarcerated mothers and their children: assessing their need and viability in a federal prison. *Justice Policy Journal*, 3, 1–20.

YOUNG, D. (2000). Women's perceptions of health care in prison. *Health Care for Women International*, 21, 219–234.

YOUNG, D. (1998). Health status and service use among incarcerated women. *Family and Community Health*, 21, 3–19.

ZAITZOW, B. (2006). Empowerment not entrapment: providing opportunities for Incarcerated women to move beyond "doing time." *Justice Policy Journal*, 3, 1–24.

ZLOTNICK, C. (1997). Posttraumatic stress disorder (PTSD), PTSD comorbidity, and childhood abuse among incarcerated women. *The Journal of Nervous and Mental Disease*, 185, 761–763.

25

Witnessing through Memoir

A Restorative Justice Tool

Erika Duncan

I f I let you into my life, will you not judge? If I let you into my life, will you not look at me with those forgiving eyes? Please just listen. Do not have sympathy for me, for your sympathy I do not need. Just know the words on this page [is] my life. It's neither good nor bad. It's my life.

The women of "Herstory Inside" Writers Workshop are reading today, not only for their intimate group made up of women who once, on the streets, had been rival gang members. Seated on the honey-colored wooden pews of the Riverhead Correctional Facility alongside the women in their greens are members of the grants committee of Long Island Unitarian Universalist Fund, who have come to listen to the stories that have been crafted with rare diligence week after week, as their authors pursued the study of what would create empathy in a reading stranger.[1] On each lap is a regulation pebble-covered composition folio containing a book in progress, whose lines each participant fills to capacity while time seems to stand still in her cell. At one time, these notebooks were confiscated in shakedowns, but now they are treated by the prison authorities as an important part of the recovery program.

"My story unfolds in a small afterhours called Papa T's. Papa T's was a backwoods watering hole with illegal gambling . . .," a new voice joins the medley to allow the assembled listeners into what is affectionately known in Herstory lingo as "the Page One Moment."

"They keep telling me it's orders to come outside," another voice chimes in. "She says, 'I'm not telling you what you're arrested for until you're handcuffed . . .' " One minute the women are laughing with a freedom that makes one forget that all of this is taking place in jail. The next, they are handing around tissues. A guard passes—one of the sympathetic ones—then another, more surly, but the women are unstoppable. They are writing not only for their own healing, but so that they can be heard in a way that might undo the cycles of violence and pain they have known all their lives.

Linda Coleman and Lonnie Mathis, Herstory's prison workshop facilitators, move slowly, stopping to put their arms around a woman who needs reassurance, as she reads of a difficult moment. Their arms touch for a moment, Lonnie's dark and large enough, it seems, to hold the whole wide world and Linda's so very, very white in this place of overcoming barriers across race, class and culture through writing side by side. The reader they comfort wasn't going to write about what happened with her uncle, but when she began to understand that it would help other people, she decided she would do it, no matter how hard it would be.

"At three months old I was left on a doorstep," another voice picks up, as even the surliest of the guards has stopped pacing, while those prison authorities who have mothered the women have tears in their eyes. "My great-grand-aunt is what I called her. She was my grandmother's aunt, my mother's aunt, which made her my aunt. Get your ass over here. . . ."

As the voices subside, I think of how the Herstory project[2] began—not in a prison but in the cultural center of an affluent Long Island village hall when I asked a group of women from "the other side of Dune Road" (as one would later name her book) to find a moment in the larger stories that they wished to tell that would evoke empathy in such a way that the "Stranger/Reader" would be a stranger no more. What I was asking, although I couldn't have articulated it at the time, was that the "dare to make another person care" be passed along from one woman to another in every aspect of the writing process, with each workshop member playing the role of helper/listener and writer in alternation. It would take another almost fourteen years (at the time of this writing) to develop the multiplicity of tools that would allow us to engage over 2000 women in what would become a life-changing journey, involving community building, skills mastery and the fight for social justice alike. At the time that I posed this dare, I could not have imagined that soon I would be driving 300 miles a week to facilitate workshops in labor halls, counseling centers and senior residences, while the words "Stranger/Reader," and "Imaginary Page One" would echo in Spanish and behind prison bars.

THE DARE TO CARE

Too often when someone is in jail, the first question that comes up is "What did that person do?" It comes up before that person is allowed a face or a voice or a story that is her own creation. In the case of women especially—and beyond this for those coming from backgrounds of poverty, violence, and discrimination—we must train ourselves to reframe our questions, thinking from the onset "What happened to them? Who are they, and what can they teach us?" What would happen if we were to make a commitment to linger until the story of each incarcerated woman found its rightful space—resisting all temptations to rush toward resolutions, wisdom or repentance that might not yet (or ever) be part of her truth—what might we be able to learn from the process? What would happen if we were to welcome with wide open arms, not the stories we might wish for, but those that come out when we give the permission to drop all pretending? Could this make a difference, not only to those who find healing in bringing their past selves back to life on the page, but to a society that doesn't know what to do with its own violence and pain?

Herstory was only a couple of days old when I realized the therapeutic effects of helping victims of severe trauma to stay with each scene until it came alive for a reading stranger. For, while the direction "to love one's inner child" has little meaning for those inexperienced in love, the dare to write about a past self so fully that another can inhabit your skin provides those who haven't developed compassion for themselves a back-door entry into accepting the selves they have been.[3]

Now, take that dare "to help another person to truly care" a step further, to imagine what it must have meant to women who had been incarcerated—discarded not only inside their own hearts, but by family and the larger society? Imagine how foreign this must have sounded at first, but also how it startled the women into a whole new way of thinking and acting. Imagine the dare being enacted around the written word—of all things—in an environment where the majority of women were convinced they had no writing skills. However, I will argue, it was the very oddness of the mandate, as well as the depth of the expectation ("*You can do it! With each line that you write, let me come inside you! Let me walk in your shoes!*"), which, in the end, brought such powerful results.[4]

By the time Linda Coleman and Lonnie Mathis went into the prisons—seven years into the Herstory project—we had a pretty good idea of the power of our empathy-based method with women coming from all walks of life. However, we could not have imagined the sense of family, community and healing that it would create "in a place where," as one member put it, "there was none."

What started out as a single workshop in Riverhead Correctional Facility in New York's Suffolk County quickly turned into two, with long waiting lists on the cell block as word of mouth spread. Not only were rival gang members writing together, but family members—forbidden by prison rules to touch one another as they passed on the tiers—were suddenly coming to know the stories and secrets that had perpetuated cycles of violence and despair. The work soon spread to a second correctional facility at Yaphank, where in a DWI trailer women slept, defecated and ate in the same quarters, and where the program was made a compulsory part of every resident's recovery plan. While there was a lot of very fine work being done with writing in prisons all over the country, what made what we are doing a little bit different was our focusing people on writing a book—a strange thing to suggest to someone who has never written. Here again, I believe, it was the audacity of that added dare that allowed so many of the women to keep writing an actual book in their wish list, so that whether they were released back to neighborhoods where temptations abounded or were sent to serve long-term sentences upstate, the project became a lifeline.

In 2007 Herstory published our first magazine of prison writings that was passed around from cell to cell, as new inmates kept joining the group. It soon became the basis for readings and sales on the outside as well. In 2008 we established our first "Bridge Workshops" as welcoming sites for women who had begun to write with us in jail, who would now have an opportunity to take their stories to the next level with Herstory's full community of writers—politicians, school teachers, graphic artists, teen mothers, foundation heads, nurses, and nannies—a full spectrum of women who might never have come together save for their desire to convert their memories into chapters that would come alive for another. While many of the writers from the prison project had little formal education, what they brought in the way of raw access to their feelings and the willingness to take risks became a guiding beacon for those who were used to performing to please a teacher, an editor, or a supervisor.

In 2009, through an Education and Activism grant from the Long Island Fund for Women and Girls, we were able to publish a second issue of *Voices* in an expanded journal format, designed not only to give the women whom our society incarcerates a face but to raise the most important questions facing families undergoing cycles of imprisonment, rupture of relationships, and closed doors. We created a series of mini-forums, classroom presentations and readings for students of criminology, sociology, and law. Each time the former inmates had a chance to read to the larger community, they came away strengthened by the response, eager for more dialogue. It was as if our promise, that they could really move a "Stranger/Reader," came true, so that they gradually saw their writing as true source of empowerment, as the drive to continue writing grew stronger. We made both issues available at a price that would be affordable for those students whose future careers would one day influence decisions about incarceration, re-entry, and parole, further discounted for classroom and prison use, with all proceeds going back to our prison project.[5]

TRANSFORMATIVE WITNESSING/A RESTORATIVE JUSTICE TOOL

"Why read these stories?" Linda Coleman wrote in her introduction to Volume Two of *Voices*. "They are not easy stories to read. They are each riddled with darkness, but also with light— the light of each woman's resilience, her humanity, her intention to heal and resume her roles as mother, daughter, partner, and citizen in a productive way. We believe that each of us wants to be of use to others! But when life events land you in prison, the chances of resuming these roles, and of healing wrongs of commission or omission, become increasingly difficult. Statistics tell us that 70 percent of those incarcerated once will return to prison. Seventy percent equals a failed experiment in anyone's book, and yet we continue to throw away the key on millions of parents and their children[6] who are also 'doing time' in their absence.

"We are strange beings, we humans—powerfully creative, potentially wise, compassionate and loving, and then alternately capable of the darkest abuses inflicted upon ourselves or on others of our kind, even those we love the most dearly. Those of us who have not experienced physical violence, abuse, and attack often have an avid curiosity about how others survive it, what scars are left—physically, mentally, spiritually—we want to look, can't help but look, unless it's too gruesome, too disturbing, and then we have to turn away. We can't take it. We'd rather not carry the knowledge that such events happen every minute somewhere on the planet, especially when we are powerless to stop them.

"While it's true that we have no control over the many assaults that occur even as we read this—each of us in our own way has the power to effect change in both future occurrences and the healing of those perpetrators and victims after the fact. But no change will occur without awareness first. Not just awareness of statistics—those too easily become lost in the fog of numberless faces—but instead through the intimate communications of another, through the various paths that bring these experiences into our hearts and minds. That is the great offering of art in its many forms—to allow us to experience the 'other' and to see a part of ourselves in each author."

In his groundbreaking book, *The Wounded Storyteller*,[7] Arthur Frank writes: "One of our most difficult duties as human beings is to listen to the voices of those who suffer. . . . Listening is hard, but it is also a fundamental moral act. . . . The moment of witness in the story crystallizes a mutuality of need, when each is for the other."

Could guided memoir writing with the goal of empowering each inmate to create her own narrative truth be used more formally as a restorative justice tool? This was a question that Professor Natalie Byfield of St. John's University began to explore when she engaged 100 students of sociology in three classes in studying the approach.[8]

"In his speech at the Vera Institute for Justice in July 2009, Attorney General Eric Holder implored everyone to 'concede that [incarceration] is not the whole answer,' " Professor Byfield wrote. "Could this memoir-writing process, based on developing empathy in a stranger, hold part of the answer?

We hope that these selections from both issues of *Voices* will give you a bird's eye view, not of easy answers, but of possible ways to begin to search for them as we seek to build family where it has been ruptured, to build bridges, and to dare others to enter worlds they might otherwise have pushed away.

VIOLENCE AGAINST WOMEN: WHAT HAPPENS WHEN WOMEN FIGHT BACK!

When Linda and Lonnie began their work with the women incarcerated in Riverhead Correctional Facility, they were unaware of the extent to which violence of all kinds had shaped their lives—sexual abuse as children, beatings carried forth from childhood into their adult relationships with men (all too often confused with "proof of love"), and as victims of rape. While the statistics they collected are shocking—indicating that virtually all of the women had experienced more than one kind of violence—the stories that they helped the women to shape are vital in our understanding of why cycles of repetition are so common, regardless of whether the women are passive victims or more active perpetrators trying to fight back.

In the following piece, Melody Roker Sims has used the window of her first arrest to bear witness to what happens to women who fight back. Many women say, "But how can I write a book if I have never learned to spell?" I have chosen to reproduce this piece just as Melody gave it to us, to demonstrate that it is possible to work with narrative form regardless of whether the mechanics of spelling and paragraph placement have been mastered.[9] Regardless of whether women have written before, they immediately take to the idea of planning how one story will act as a container and another as a springboard for the larger stories that they wish to tell. The desire for mastery of the finer writing techniques comes after one is able to create a moving story, not the other way about. As you read this story, I invite you to "listen" to the deeper structure that was very carefully crafted in several planning sessions before Melody even started to write.

Roll Up Melody Roker/Roker, Roker-Roll Up

by Melody Roker Sims

Bedford Hills has come for you excited but scared and disoriented as I begin to focus I look to see what it is on the clock outside the bars on the walkway 4:30 am. People I've gottn too know and became close with are waking up as the guards begin to wake up another female on the opposite housing unit that will be my partner going upstate, I guess. Bedford Hills wants her too. As I begin to give away my clothes and a pair of sneakers with the exception of my outfit I put aside for this day I pray silently.

> Dear Lord,
> Thank you for waking me up and Dear Lord please do not let no harm or danger come to me in this unknown place. What I'll soon have to call my home and please Lord protect me don't let me get raped or beat up. Lord thank you for reliving me from myself. In Jesus Name Amen. . . .

Before starting on the ride to Betty's house (Bedford Hills) in a sheriff's car a woman and male deputy are my escorts. While holding my mug shot the female deputy asks me my name, date of birth, home address and social security number. After giving the information she requested of me, her partner handcuffs me and then he puts the front shackle on my ankles which makes it very hard for me to move so he helps me into the backseat of their squad car and while they do the same thing to my partner while listening I learn her name is Patricia. I wonder is she just as scared as me? Is she an addict like me? What's her charge? She looks like a baby. As the officer helps her in the car I notice that the tears are pouring down her face, instantly my heart goes out to her and I don't feel my fear. I can't help but to say too her it's going to be okay, don't cry. She says I'm trying not to while sobbing she asks me have I been upstate before. I tell her no but I hear it's better up there than here the air, the food and although you're locked up you're allowed more freedom. She says promise me that you won't leave me. Well I don't know if I can make that promise but I will promise to be with you for as long as I can but since this is our 1st time upstate maybe we will be sent to the same facility. She asks me what am I in for. I tell her for selling drugs to an undercover cop and for possession. She asks me how long do I got to be locked up for. I tell her 3 to 6 years but my lawyer got the Judge to give me the Shock program. I asked her how old was she. She replied 17. I asked her was those her sisters and brothers in the picture she held in her hand, she said no they are my 3 children. I thought to myself 17 with 3 children. UNBELIEVABLE. I asked her what she was in for. She said Manslaughter. I couldn't believe what she just said. She then explained to me that her children's father was 20 years her senior and used to beat her everyday, started when she was 4 months pregnant with their 1st born and when he started beating her kids which in the end she lost custody of them she made a vow that the next time he raises his hands to beat her she would kill him and she did just that. I wondered would or could I ever commit a crime like that. I asked her how much time did she get and she said 25 years to life. I almost fainted but instead I shedded tears for the innocence lost and stolen from this child and for the childhood she never had. I would learn later that she was 1 of thousands that I would meet on my journey to finding myself again, while at Betty's house. Patricia and I sat there silent, lost in our won worlds as the deputies were talking and driving. To break the silence I said Well Hi, I'm Melody the first smile I see when she says pleased to me you, Hi I'm Patricia. Somehow I knew I made of my 1st friend on this journey but I also knew life would never be the same again for either one of us.

Melody left Riverhead Correctional Facility in time to be a reader at Herstory's 10th Anniversary Celebration in 2007, where she expressed the wish to live as a writer and to train someday to be a facilitator, which led her to join our bridge workshops, where she worked for well over a year. I often wonder if it was the opportunity to write on level ground with powerful community movers and doers that allowed her to shift into the witnessing role. Although Melody disappeared shortly after she was awarded a special scholarship, we know that the writing experience was something that changed her forever. We will not be completely surprised if she shows up in one of our workshops again.

THE SPECTER OF REPETITION/WORKING TO BREAK THE CYCLE

One day, as I was teaching my Wednesday night workshop, a young woman came in and said she had started writing in jail. Now that she was out, she "needed a new Page One Moment" she said. Like Melody, she had written about other things when she was actually in prison, and only now was ready to look at a moment of witnessing, again through the moment of her first arrest.

The Lesson

by Sandy Beltran

"What precinct is this?"

"The 4th precinct." The officer said.

"Oh." I said with my head down in shame. I have been here before and I was twelve years old at the time. My aunt used to work here and she brought me here once. Her name was Beth and she was a police detention attendant. She was 5ft tall, if that, always kept a short hair cut, never wore makeup . . . let alone a smile, and she was big busted and that's how you could tell she was a woman. She brought me here to this precinct when I was younger as a lesson in life to never wind up here. Right now I think it was a jinx.

I remember my visit here like it was yesterday. It was the midnight shift too. I walked in nervously holding Beth's hand and we had to get buzzed in. I was so small I couldn't even see who was over the counter. I got introduced to all of the officers and they were really nice. She gave me the grand tour; the cells, where they take the mug shots and I even got my fingerprints taken. Then we sat in her office. I looked up and saw the cameras that were videotaping the inmates. At that time nobody was there yet but soon enough a woman showed up. This woman was complaining from the minute she came in. She kept saying that she didn't belong there. She had shabby hair, a very sad face and kept coughing a lot. Beth then had to search her and asked the inmate to remove her clothing. I turned my face in embarrassment but couldn't help but listen to it all.

"Strip, Squat, and Cough."

The lady was sobbing the whole time. After the strip search was over Beth locked her in the cell. She didn't let her keep her shoes, jacket or belt for safety reasons. Beth sat down next to me in the office and started lecturing me on why most of the prisoners belong here and what crimes they have done, "Basically almost everything has to do with drugs. Drugs are the path of destruction . . ." a statement that I never forgot.

While we were talking I heard the lady in the background yelling that she was cold and she was begging for some warmth. Beth went to a closet and pulled out a plastic coated yellow foam thing. She kept crying though, to the point that auntie told her a few times to be quiet and she didn't say it so nice. She told the woman, "Shut up or I'll make you shut up" which didn't surprise me because she spoke to me the same way.

I was concerned and scared but auntie reassured me. "They all act this way. They broke the law and this is where they belong. If you stay good you will never have to worry about coming here."

The inmate kept crying though and she began to throw up too. I couldn't take it anymore. I began crying and I begged Beth to get her help and to call the ambulance. Beth looked at me with a concerned look and said "Ok but I know the lady is fine and she will be back soon with nothing wrong." She gave me a kiss on the cheek and told me to stop crying. About an hour later Beth got a call and it just so happens that the lady died on the way to the hospital. I wanted to leave immediately, this place was scary, I felt desperation to run out of there but Beth didn't let me. She had to finish her shift. I was so mad that she made me come here. She told me to fall asleep on a cot she had up against the wall and I did.

That was a long time ago and now I'm 25 walking in here. Wow. Where's auntie when I need her now. I bet she wouldn't help me anyway.

The female officer came out and told me to go in the picture room. It was just the way I remembered it. As she took the picture I saw my reflection, it wasn't the reflection of a 12 year old that's for sure. I looked drained, my hair was unkempt. I couldn't even smile for the picture. I got my fingerprints taken. The next step was to go to the cell area. Before I walked in I glanced at the office hoping I would find auntie there but I knew damn well she was retired.

"Strip, Squat, and Cough," I obeyed, teary eyed, but I did it as fast as possible. Damn it's cold in here and I can't even keep my shoes or jacket. I'm supposed to be at work right now. This is ridiculous. Locked up in this little cell and I'm claustrophobic. All I can do now is pray. "Oh God I'm sorry. . . . Please just let me go home tomorrow and I'll be good and please don't let me die in here. . . ."

Oh my God, it's so cold in here I'm shivering. I hollered to the officer that I was cold but I didn't get a response. I kept hollering so loud that it turned to sobbing and I got a flashback of that lady sobbing and sobbing. It was like déjà-vous. . . . like I could hear her echo . . . like I felt her spirit. The officer finally came and threw me this plastic coated yellow foam thing and told me to shut up.

I shut up and lay down on the hard wooden bench and covered myself up. I was still shivering but I tried not to think about it.

And then a thought came to my head—If she only could see that this criminal was once a child.

"SO IT WON'T HAVE TO HAPPEN TO ANOTHER GIRL . . ."

Adeline Acevedo was one of the first students to participate in Herstory's prison project. The harrowing tale we reproduce here tells of another kind of witnessing, as under duress Addy allows the police to photograph her wounds, to protect other young girls from the predator who has nearly murdered her. Notice how this piece—written shortly after Addy began to work with us—transfers control of how the violence perpetrated against her will be witnessed, as she takes on the role of storyteller instead of the one who must passively stand before the camera. Was it this capacity—first to be witnessed for the good of others, and then to become a witness, still for the good of others—that led Addy to continue writing her story over a six-year period that included time with Herstory, time in two other correctional facilities, and finally, as of this time writing, over a year of writing with Herstory on the outside? Since her release she has become one of the main spokeswomen for Herstory's prison project, whether speaking to religious congregations, funders or students.

I often like to say that, while we all know our stories, it is not until we actively shape them that we begin to know our journeys. I will return to the more recent parts of Addy's journey at the end of this article.

Excerpt from a longer work

by Adeline Acevedo

The detective leads me to a small room with only a desk and one chair for me and one for him. My back is to the door and his is to the back wall. Directly above him is a tinted pane of glass. I guess that's what a two-way mirror looks like. There's a red flashing light in there.

The detective sees me looking up and says, "Okay Adeline, I'm Detective Johnson and this is going to be recorded on video for your safety and mine, okay?"

"Do I have any choice?"

"No, you don't."

"So why ask if it's okay then?"

He didn't respond to that. Detective Johnson had one of those push-to-the-side haircuts that most men his age wear, and glasses hanging on the tip of his nose. When he spoke to me he looked down through his glasses and down his nose. "Well, I know you don't want to talk to me. I'm not here to judge you, okay? I have a daughter your age and I wouldn't want this to happen to her. If you don't talk to me, he'll keep doing this to other girls too. These are all girls you go to school with, girls you know, and he's going to continue to do this if no one talks. A friend of yours was raped by him yesterday. She doesn't want to talk, but she told a friend that you both have in common—the same one and only person you told. And since neither one of you want to tell, she told. She doesn't want this to happen to anyone else."

"I don't want it to either."

"Did he threaten you?"

"Yes . . . he said he'd finish what he started."

"What do you mean?"

"He'll kill me. I can't say anything."

"Oh honey, what did he say to you?" he said gently, caringly. "We'll put him in jail, he can't hurt you there. Please tell me what he did to you so next time he can't hurt one of your friends the way he wanted to hurt you."

"Do you promise he'll go to jail and never hurt me?"

"Yes I do."

I stood up and lifted the back of my shirt, turned and showed him the still angry red scars from the knife jabs to my back.

"Oh honey, God, what did he do to you?" he said, a little choked up.

I turn back toward him, I see his eyes watery and his expression tender, hurt, and his skin a little paler. "And here," I say softly as I lower my turtleneck collar and smudge the make-up from my throat where I still have white and pink lines. "I have more but I can't show those places."

He pulls a Polaroid camera from his desk, gets up, and opens the door. He yells to a woman detective. "Janis! Can you take this young lady to the head? She's a vic. And she has scars she needs photographed. Adeline, please show her." I nodded my head and followed her.

When I walk back into the small room he's sitting there looking at the photos. He puts them down, I guess out of respect. "Is anyone else gonna talk? The other girls?" I say as I resume my seat.

"If you do, they will too—someone has to make the first step. So far he hasn't hurt any of the others as bad as he's hurt you, but sooner or later he will.

"Okay, what do you want to know?"

"You have to tell me everything that happened."

"Okay."

For the next two hours I told him everything I remembered. He wrote it down as I spoke slowly.

I slept with my mom that night.

"Mommy, you won't let the boogie man get me, right?"

"Well, if he comes through the window," she said giggling, "he'll get you first!"

"Mom, he's real!"

"No Christina, I won't let him get you." She drew me closer and held me. She'd never held me to sleep before. I lay as close as to her as possible. I may be fourteen, but yes, I was still scared of the dark and monsters under the bed. I lay there forever, before I slipped away into sleep.

MOTHERS AND CHILDREN

So many of the women with whom Linda and Lonnie were working had become un-mothered mothers when they were barely out of childhood themselves. Though daring to touch longings for their own mothers—as is so poignantly illustrated in Addy's turning to her mother at the end of the piece you just read—they were able to begin to forgive themselves for looking for love and recognition in all of the wrong places, leading to new ways of being mothers and lovers themselves.

In *Voices, Volume 2,* Linda writes of how "a coffee-skinned, green-eyed, Muslim beauty, Renee enters a room with the grace and reserve of a queen. It is hard to imagine that she has lived her early years as a child making her own way on the streets by the age of eleven. When she first began to write with us and witnessed how powerfully her words affected others, she asked us one night after class, 'Do you think I really could write my story?' I've never thought, never believed I could do anything but sell crack for a living because that is all I've ever done.' "

"Renee never smoked crack, but she successfully built a life on that income and a home for her children until she lost it all. One night during Black History Month, while incarcerated in RCF, she watched other women inmates perform in a talent show. She saw how much intelligence and potential was locked up in the jail alongside her and realized that, as a crack dealer, she had helped to put them there. Later she came to us and said, 'When I go home I don't have to sell drugs for a living. . . . I'm going to go to college. I can write!' "

I, Me, Who Is Thee?

by Ricarda Renee Diamond

The weather was beautiful. The sunrays were shining upon my face, leaving school after a good day. The weather only added to the goodness of the day. After saying Hello to the bus driver, I headed to the back of the bus. The last seat was my regular. Looking out the window I began to think of how excited I was to be going to the doctor with my mom. I loved going places with Mommy, wherever it might be. I was just grateful for the time with her.

Heading off the bus saying goodbye to the driver, "Hey, Ma," I greeted her with a hug. Mommy always walked me to and from the bus stop.

Looking at Mommy standing there with her pink pretty summer flower dress on, her sea blue eyes and her pale white skin, she was really pretty.

She placed a soft kiss on my forehead. "Hey Bambino," her voice very low and sweet and motherly. She took my book bag and we headed home, or should I say to the house.

Before we headed to the doctor's, Mommy called for Tia to come from her bedroom. "Tia, come in here for a minute, Baby." Tia is my older and only sister. She had two babies of her own at this point already. Mommy started to speak: "Tia and Mommy's Bambino, I love you two with all my heart. Mommy's health isn't good. So if something were to happen to me, promise to always stick together." With that said, me and Mommy were off to the doctors . . . her not realizing the promise wasn't ever really made.

Mommy checked in at the window. I headed for the magazines. All of the nurses knew me by name. They adored me. Mommy asked Nurse Mary to watch over me for a moment, as she proceeded to the examination room.

As I was reading the magazine my mind began to wander. I found no more interest in the magazine. I placed it back on the table. I entered a daze, my mind taking me back to what Mommy said. *If anything were to happen to me.* Starting to reflect on all the regular trips to the doctors, my stomach got an instant knot.

My daze was broken by Mommy reaching for my hand. In the car Mommy didn't look at me once or utter a single word. Silence along with worry filled the car. By the time we reached the driveway, Mommy's tears were nonstop and her pain very obvious. I began to cry along with Mommy, her pain instantly became mine.

We entered the house. I did as I was told. I went into my bedroom, even though I yearned to just be held by Mommy and fall asleep to the melody of her heartbeat. I turned my TV on as low as possible. I listened to Mommy telling Tia she is very sick . . . "Tia, the doctors have informed me that I have AIDS along with a form of cancer. Tia, I don't believe that I have much longer." At 11 years old I'm unaware of what cancer or AIDS is. But I'm aware that it is killing my Mom. This is the one condition in life I never grew an understanding of . . . for love to equal pain.

Their voices faded and recent good memories escaped my mental index, replaced with bad ones . . . rather heart aching horrible ones, my first flashback hitting me. My mental is taking me back to when I was about seven years old. That was the first time I found a dirty needle—my enemy. Myself along with the other children are jumping on the bed, playing around. I'd rather be eating dinner, along with getting attention from Carole (Mommy), but she and company are in the living room "doing what grown folks do" like always.

On the very last jump is when I saw this needle along with what appeared to be a huge rubber band. Looking back now I ask myself, Is this why Mommy was always napping? Is this the reason I was always in harm's way? Here was the answer to my many questions. My tears flowed and my physical was filled with rage. . . .

This year goes by so fast. It seems as quick as a blink of an eye. Mommy is in and out of the hospital, CPS is a regular. It's routine for me to enter various foster homes as she enters the hospital, me being put in harm's way again and again. Tired of being violated in the wee hours of the night by "foster dad," tired of being beat by "foster mom," I decide that I'm going to make do on my own. I won't hurt myself. Me is all I have. I have to take care of me; after all Child "Protective" Services isn't protecting me.

Now school is a faded memory. Smoking weed is a part of my everyday.

I have been watching Tia's kids' father along with other older cats. I was extremely observant of their actions in the drug game. Tired of being hungry, needing and wanting, I was ready to put thought into action, getting money that is. I recall walking in the kitchen, the smell smacking me in my face, smelling as if nail polish remover is cooking. All the other females in the house are in the living room speaking on hair, nails, men. That girly stuff is of no interest to me. My interest is in here in the kitchen with the older cats. I grabbed a mask and joined Poppy at the stove.

"What's this, coke?"

"Yeah, but it won't be in a minute. It'll be crack. It's money and power in this pot."

"Let me stir it. Show me how to do it." Poppy shows me what I think is magic. Whipping the coke around in the pot made me feel like a natural chef. I learned how to do so in minutes as if I was born to do it. Taking the pot off the stove, placing it under cold running water, zoning into the water. It felt as if it was only me and the crack in the room. Thinking of all the moves I needed to make to be on.

"Poppy, let me borrow a pack."

"Alright, but slow down, let me dry it and show you how to cut it."

"Good looking out, Poppy."

"Alright, be careful out there, Shorty."
With that said I was on my bike headed to the "block."

I'm moving like a grown woman but at the same time thinking like a wounded child. This silent killer called AIDS has attacked my mother. Mommy cannot speak now nor can she walk—she has gone into a stage of a baby mentally as well as physically.

In between shifts on the block I go tend to Mommy. I bathe her, change her diapers and brush what is left of her pretty blond hair. It makes me feel good to help her but helpless because I can't cure her. My wishful thinking tells me that the more crack I sell the better chances are for me to heal her.

Mommy points to the wheelchair. She directs me to the kitchen. Mommy desires so badly to be my mother. She wants to cook a meal for her "bambino." The heart wrenching truth is that she doesn't remember how. She is not mentally or physically capable of doing so. She sits in front of the stove, her head hanging low in shame. Her pretty sea blue eyes crying an ocean. Her heart is shattered along with mine. I'm unable to think of any words of comfort. The pain in my heart seals my mouth. I lay Mommy down, tucking her in, I lie beside her as close as our two bodies can get. As sickly as Mommy is, she still smells the same . . . good and sweet. My body so tired from being up for days, my mind racing beyond the limits won't allow me to sleep.

I am a child turned warrior all before my 12th birthday. There is a child captured and held prisoner inside this woman that wants to be free. This child wants to play with dolls, jump rope and go to school. This woman has to sell this pack out to survive.

I'm tired as hell, but have nowhere to go. I go to Ms. Lucy's house to get a few hours of sleep. It's a hot spot so of course I won't be completely asleep . . . one eye must always be open.

Back outside to the block. The fiends are coming so the bread is flowing. The block is moving smooth today, no arguing over sells and no blue and whites patrolling. It was August 31, 1993. The day was going okay . . . sitting on the step with my glass of Remy with some cats on the block, Uncle Ricky walks up to us. No one from the family ever comes to look for me. Before Uncle Ricky could say it I knew it. The glass left my hand. It shattered everywhere.

"Damn, Renee! What's up with you?"

I can see their mouths moving but I can't hear a word. I asked Uncle Ricky not to say what I already know.

"Uncle Ricky, please, let's just get in the car."

By the time me, Tia and Uncle Ricky reached the hospital to view Mommy's body we were told it was too late. Looking at this woman in her white nurse's uniform, my blood boiled. "What the fuck do you mean it's too late to see my mother? It's my mother!"

"It's too late. It's too late . . ." is all I keep hearing.

My vision is blurry, my chest is so tight, thought pattern cloudy, "Why? Why me . . ." is the question I'm asking this life that I'm in. . . . "Mommy please, I just want to be your 'bambino'" is what I'm crying out. "Mommy please! I have something to tell you!"

The very next time I held my mother was in a white box that contained her beings. These last few days have been filled with unbearable pain, wounds to my soul that cannot be healed. The pain along with being lost causes me to self-destruct, to search for comfort, except it's in all the wrong places . . . on the block selling crack and inside the arms of men old enough to be my father, with end results being still no direction, and my physical being used for all the wrong reasons.

Talking to this dude by the name of God, figuring maybe he do exist, he just forgot that I exist, too. "God, why was I given life? I'm not living. Who are you? Where are you? Where were you when I was being raped, when my innocence was stolen, when I was hungry and cold? Where are you now that I have no one? I only want to simply be loved." I need a hug after crying out and still not receiving comfort from this dude that everyone glorifies. "Yeah I didn't think you were up there. I'm on the way to my Mommy's funeral. You could at least come with me."

While entering the funeral home I don't know if I'm depressed, angry, or both. As I approach the white box which contains Mommy's ashes, there is a picture of Mommy on top. She was in her mid-twenties and her beauty was flawless, breathtaking . . . looking into this picture my physical cried quietly while my inner beings screamed out loud.

The service was very short. Only about six chairs were filled. After all, no one wanted to arrange it.

As I'm leaving the service I receive a tap on my shoulder. It's Ms. Harris, the woman who's supposed to be my grandmother.

"Here she is." She's handing me my mother in a damn box.

I couldn't get "Grandma" to roll off my tongue. "Ms. Harris, I don't have anywhere to bring my mother."

"Well, if I take her now, I take her for good."

"Can you please just hold her until I get a respectable place to bring her?"

"No, I cannot. If you wasn't out there selling drugs, you would have somewhere to bring her."

I'm thinking to myself, the nerve of this bitch. She doesn't feed me. She won't be my grandmother. "You know what, lady? I don't have an argument in me. You're right. Keep her. She was never mine. Goodbye, Grandma."

From that moment on . . . there was no turning back. This is when I was forced to be an adult, forced to put the little scared child in me to rest. This was the very beginning of my addiction to this game . . . selling drugs, with a weight on my shoulders as heavy as a ton of bricks. I was headed from my mother's funeral to the hood. I needed comfort, whether it be from fiends, spending their money, or men twice my age. I was empty. Sitting on the stoop making sells, smoking a blunt and thinking on everything that had taken place in my 11 years on earth, I'm thinking, "Now what . . .?"

October 20, 1993, my 12th birthday. Nothing is happy about it. Another day in hell on earth. I'm a runaway from CPS, no mother, no father, no nobody. . . . Let me roll another blunt . . . wishing I could be home, playing with the neighborhood kids, singing "Happy Birthday," blowing out candles on my birthday cake. Instead it's only about 3 pm. I'm drunk and high as hell, posted on the block, selling crack. . . .

Something within me this morning wants to go see the house that I can't label home anymore. Riding up on the bike, I pause . . . the sight of the house made every hair on my body stand at attention. Once I work up the nerve, I enter the house, looking around at what was once a beautiful three bedroom home which was so beautifully kept by Mommy. Now it's deserted and filled with pain and agony. Entering Mommy's bedroom that was once fit for a queen made me drop to my knees. From the emptiness of the house I can hear my cries bouncing off the walls. Memories started to invade my mind. I hear the laughter and the cries that once shaped this place. I see the lights blinking from the Christmas tree. I hear Mommy singing as the aroma from her home-cooked meals filled the air. My chance has been taken away. I will never be able to tell Mommy those three very important words, "I love you."

"IF I LET YOU INTO MY STORY, WILL YOU NOT JUDGE . . ."

Over and over, we have seen in our Herstory workshops, both inside and outside the prison walls that when material is difficult, early drafts often come out in a detached or disturbingly skeletal form, creating a map to be gradually filled in as the writer dares to endow each moment and scene with her being. It is in filling out these moments that the deep humanity of the person who is undergoing situations that might alienate a reading stranger starts to glow through what would otherwise drive the reader away.

TyNeisha Johnson was only able to work with Linda and Lonnie for several months before she was sent upstate to do time. Although she was able to map out a remarkable confession, touching on areas of degradation with an honesty that is startling and sad, she had only just begun to take the Herstory process to the stage that would have allowed her to explore bit by bit and scene by scene what it really was like for the young girl who repeatedly left her child to follow the call of her addiction, as she bent in self-abdication both before the draw of her pipe and the needs of the men towering over her.

We know from other workshop experiences that had TyNeisha had time to take the process far enough to have lingered over the call of a bird or the memory of a song, or to insert the tale of the grandmother whose image comes to her so fast we can't catch it, to turn single sentences first into five pages and then ten, as others had the opportunity to do, she would have learned love and forgiveness for the girl she had been. This in turn would have allowed us to stay with her more completely, no matter how painful the places into which she would lead us.

For without this deep entry, none of us are protected, either from our own ghosts or the ghosts of another. This was a process TyNeisha had become increasingly willing to enter, as the goals of the workshop became clearer to her. We can see this in her words when she tells us, "I was told to get gully with this story," as her confession shifts from the slavery to her abusers that marked her own childhood into slavery to an addiction whose demands overshadow those cries of her baby, so that often she cannot tell whether it is her child crying or herself.

"I really would love to avoid this part of my life. It won't hurt so much if it's untold. But to move on, I must do this," she continues, as she shows one degradation after another, all coming so quickly that those who can't extrapolate from their own experiences aren't given a chance to "become" her but must watch her from without.

We return to the words with which we started this article, "If I let you into my story, do you promise not to judge?" Do we risk that people will judge TyNeisha, when we publish her story as it came out in her first powerful purge? This is the risk, I believe, of all unformed stories, which is why we started Herstory to help each teller to go deeper and deeper and deeper still, so that we would never have to look from the outside. And yet, TyNeisha here is doing something very particular, as she violates the most taboo subjects and breaks her own silence. She is giving us something in the making that we can only imagine will grow, as the tiny chinks of self reflection expand into paragraphs and pages. We know from TyNeisha that this writing helped her reach out to reconnect with her son and even with her mother.

As we read her last lines, that her punishment will end when she really feels what her son felt, we can see how the quest for these feelings will come into each new scene and each new detail, if only her life grants her the opportunity to continue with this project. Meanwhile, we have decided that her bravery and courage to speak her hard truths will help others to speak theirs, for she speaks of the lives of so many of the incarcerated women! We cannot have Healing—whether personal or societal—without Knowing. So that for all that it leaves out—as it must—this piece seems to constitute a first step.

Excerpts from Untitled Piece

by TyNeisha Johnson

I can remember always wanting a woman to woman connection with my mother. I feel very lonely in the inside. My mother never said she loved me when I was younger but I know she do. I love her back too, but I choose to stay away from her because. . . . She say things like, "You just like him. I can't stand you." "You make me sick." She doesn't know how to say nothing nicely.

When my mother talked, I would never look at her. I was scared of her. And I was always thinking of a slap whenever she said something, because that's all she do is scream and swing. And that's when I would turn on automatic blockage of my mother. After a while when my mother talked, I didn't hear nothing she said. But this morning, she wasn't screaming. She was talking softly, and asked me to sit down. I wasn't used to this. I felt very uncomfortable. In over twelve years my mother finally talked to me. I was so not used to looking her in the face. While she talked I kept my head down the whole time and actually listened to her. She just out of nowhere started telling me about her past. How out of five kids she was the only one my grandmother gave to her father. I'm not sure if she said her father died or not, but she ended up with her aunt, her father's sister. She had a lot of kids. My mother had to raise and cook for all of them. All her aunt did was scream and beat her. After my mother fed all her cousins, there was no more food. My mother had to go to stores and open up groceries to eat, right there in the store.

When she finished her story I felt sad and sorry for her. I kissed her on the cheek, and that time I kissed her because I wanted to, not just because she was my mother.

Well, I was told to get gully with this story. I really would love to avoid this part of my life. It won't hurt so much if it's untold. But to move on, I must do this.

I can remember when Jaquan was just born. He was more my baby doll than my child. I was 16. A kid myself. I had no woman model around to lead me through this so I just did the best I could. All I did was change his bibs, pampers, and clothes a thousand times a day. He was mine. I enjoyed him but didn't love him the way a mother was supposed to love her child. But how would I know how to love him if my mother didn't show me no love? So I just bared with what I knew by raising my brother and sister. Made sure they weren't hungry. Gave them a bath. Did their hair and changed their clothes. And that's all I did with Jaquan. No hugging, no kissing, no nurturing his soul with love. I felt I was doing the right thing because that's all I knew.

Everytime something happen to Jaquan I would just cry. I didn't know that if you didn't give a baby no water when they had a fever and the runs that they'd dehydrate. I'm looking at his box of Pampers getting lower and lower. You know, I'm starting to wonder if he goes through these Pampers, how I'm going to get another bag of weed? I buy Jaquan's stuff weekly. I know exactly how long everything is going to last, but this is becoming a problem now with his Pampers getting low. I'm not even really concerned about what is happening with my baby, I'm more worried about getting my high on.

Well, I've been gone three months now. Not out of town or anything. Just in the woods. I'm seventeen years old and strung out on crack. I'm not even thinking about my one year old baby I left at home. I always hear him crying whenever I take a hit. But I continue degrading myself for a hit.

All the men are happy to see me because they know what time it is and so do I. I feel real anxious. I'm getting my pipe ready first. I'm holding my pipe in my right hand, holding it up high while I'm starting to suck. I won't take my eyes off his hands, watching him break a piece of the crack off to put it in my pipe. Now he takes his hit. His hand is behind my head while he's looking all around, high as hell. I wait to make sure he's really high before I snatch my mouth off to take my hit.

I need another to get Jaquan off my mind. Every time I take a hit I think I hear my baby crying because I'm so guilty in the inside for leaving him by his self and he only one year of age.

I never experienced this before. I'm having such a hard time doing this time. I don't know where my son is. I feel lonely, abandoned, and lost. I never knew what my son felt like when I would relapse. Leaving him with the unknown feeling: is Mommy dead? Am I going to hear from her again? What does she look like now? I miss her. . . . I wish she would just call or write me.

Now I finally know how he feels because I feel like that right now. My spirits are so low. How can I keep scaring my baby like this? He didn't ask to come into this world.

I just keep beating myself up mentally. I feel like shit. But I keep saying everybody makes mistakes.

But not the same mistake over and over like me.

Then I try to make myself feel better. At least, (I think to myself), when I was out there smoking crack, I wasn't even thinking about Jaquan. Now I'm locked up, he's all I can think of, and I want everything to fall into place. . . . Yeah. . . . right.

Well I came to accept these feelings and put everything in God's hands. This process of getting things right is not going to happen when I want it to. It's when God feels I've been punished enough, when I really really feel how my son felt.

I apologize, Jaquan.

BEYOND THE MIRROR/ WHERE ACTIVISM STARTS TO TAKE SHAPE

Memoir is about the past and nowhere is the shadow of the past more present than in the prisons, where one pays for what cannot be rewritten. Normally I shy away from mirror pieces, for they are far too easy to evoke. They exist far too often outside of the context of what we in Herstory lingo call "Book Time," denoting the moment in which reflections are illuminated by what has actually happened on the page.

The following mirror piece by Adeline Acevedo was written six years after she wrote the piece about being photographed. Yet in "Book Time" it returns to that moment of being fourteen years old. Does the reflection come after the violation or before it? Addy doesn't tell us this in the piece. However, when we dare her to place it, she will have connected more dots.

Note the difference in tone and self-awareness as Addy, now free and now working with "Herstory Inside Out," returns to that moment when her life took the turn that left such a shadow. This is the first piece Addy read to me when she visited one of my workshops, although I had heard her read numerous times in prison before.

I stand looking in the mirror. To anyone other than myself, it would be thought that I was admiring my pretty face and beautiful fourteen-year-old body. I don't like to think of that girl in the mirror as myself. To the outside world she is beautiful, but to herself she is ugly. Her ugliness comes from being empty inside. And so, she stands in the mirror, not looking at herself, but through herself. She sees herself transparent like a ghost . . . the ghost of a person that should have been, but never was. She has never felt loved, and so, would not begin to know why or how to express it truthfully to any other. She is a loner, with no good reason to find a life bond with anyone. People, to her, are only good for the time they are needed or are still fun to be around. She is weary of new people because she is unsure if they will accept her with all the darkness she is made of. She knows she contains no light inside of her and that nothing good will ever come to her in life. She despises the light she sees in others, because she knows they are destined to be happy in life and she is not.

And so, everyday is a constant struggle for her to prove that she is alive inside. She lives every day to what she considers the fullest; having fun in her own twisted way, taking chances because of the excitement value. She feels no remorse for what she does. She can't possibly exhibit any care for anyone, as she can't for herself. She laughs but there is no happiness in her laughter. Only knowing that she causes misery toward other is what makes her smile shine the brightest.

But now let us move away from the 14-year-old self Addy recreated on the page into where the process took the writer. "I started writing reflections on my own feelings sitting here," Addy wrote in a holiday letter to Linda and Lonnie, as she was completing her sentence upstate.

I want to write about my contemplations and epiphanies on what my past has been, my present, and on what I want to make of my future. I want my words to inspire someone else who has lost a child after loving them, to be able to move on without turning to negative influences. I want to touch young kids like late teens and children, so that they never touch heroine. I want to touch them into knowing that anything can go wrong in an instant in the hustling game, to know that a normal average every-day next door neighbor kid can lose themselves to the point of being far gone. And that they can always come back from the dead and stop dying on a daily basis. That is going to be my mission in life, and, of course, to live my dreams and write.

Everything I write sets me freer with every page. I want to be truly free, because this cross I carry is too heavy. I'm done dying everyday. I feel like I've died a million deaths already and haven't even truly lived. I want to take my disappointments and turn them into a success story. I felt very different growing up and want other young teens to know that they are not crazy for going through it, they're just sick. And that it's okay to feel all those emotions and learn to handle them instead of Dying inside. And to have self-esteem and know that they can grow up to be anything they can imagine in this world.

Well I am going to keep writing now until I run out of supplies. Supplies are low though because they took 5 marble notebooks from me, and all my story ideas. I really need those books—it's crucial to my writing. . . .

Could this all have happened, had Addy and the others in the project not found the tools to take them moment to moment and scene by scene into their pasts, with the goal ever present of daring a stranger to care? As she sat in her cell worrying about whether she would have enough paper on which to continue to write, little could Addy have known that in another couple of months she would be writing on level ground with women who were far from the prison world she knew, nor that she would become one of Herstory's most cherished public speakers.

It was on the way home from a standing room only reading at St. John's College, following by a Q & A period where the former inmates held their own with students and faculty from sociology, psychology, creative writing, criminology and law, that Addy and a few of the others who figure in this article said to Lonnie and Linda, "This is the first time in my life that I felt that something I was doing had meaning.

I close with the words of Jonathan Scherr, who runs the DWI trailer at Yaphank Correctional Facility.

At first I was uncomfortable to listen to these women share their lives, fears and needs. But I have come to understand that we all need to hear the words of these women, they are our mothers, sisters, wives, and friends. The women who raised us, loved us and supported us, even now, deserve no less.

If they could change hearts and minds of their prison guards and the students who could one day be making the decisions that would impact the lives of those our society incarcerates, even as they changed themselves, then they could be quite sure that they wouldn't turn backward.

In the fall of 2010, *Voices*—the journal containing the writings of the women represented in this article—was purchased in quantity by the rehabilitation department of Riverhead Correctional Facility. In a groundbreaking decision, brought about by the officers who had witnessed such changes in their attitudes through hearing the women's stories in formation, it was included in the mandated syllabus for every incoming corrections officer in their training academy.

ENDNOTES

1. An elaboration of the terms and notions that mark the Herstory approach can be found in *Paper Stranger: Shaping Stories in Community* by Erika Duncan, Herstory Writers Workshop, Centereach, 2008.

2. Founded in 1996, Herstory Writers Workshop provides opportunities through guided memoir writing that empower women from all walks of life (regardless of age, race, religion, financial status or sexual orientation, whether incarcerated or free) to turn their intimate stories into works of art crafted so that others can hear. Herstory is committed to providing an environment of intensive instruction which, in addition to creating literary works, upholds our values of empathy, inclusiveness, self-guided healing, safety and the search for social change in the expression of voices that historically have been most profoundly silenced.

3. Duncan, "Lost Voices/Found Words" *International Journal of Applied Psychoanalytic Studies* 3(3): 255–276 (2006). Published online in Wiley InterScience (www.interscience.wiley.com) **DOI**: 10.1002/aps.104

4. "Getting Results" *New York Community Trust Newsletter*, October, 2009.

5. The complete prison journals, *Voices: Memoirs from Suffolk County's Correctional Facilities, Volumes One and Two* are available through Herstory's website at www.herstorywriters.org, with special discounts for classroom and prison use.

6. As of February 2008, 2.3 million adults were incarcerated in the United States, or 1 in 100 Americans. 1.2 million women are either incarcerated or on parole. Of this population, 70 percent are nonwhite. If recent incarceration rates remain unchanged, 1 in 15 persons will be incarcerated sometime in their lifetime. *Sources: New York Times* and Department of Justice statistics.

7. *The Wounded Storyteller: Body, Illness, and Ethics* by Arthur W. Frank, University of Chicago Press, Chicago and London, 1995.

8. Byfield, Natalie "The Relationship between the Discourse of Restorative Justice and the Carceral State in the U.S." A paper to be delivered in the summer of 2010 at the International Sociology Association Conference in Sweden. For more information contact Professor Natalie Byfield at byfieldn@stjohns.edu

9. The remaining memoir excerpts that appear in this article are reproduced exactly as they appear in *Voices Volumes One and Two,* only lightly edited for some mechanics such as spelling and punctuation. Our editors deliberately refrained from making major changes in syntax, vocabulary, and grammar, in order to preserve each writer's voice and rhythm.

26

Female Recidivists Speak about Their Experience in Drug Court While Engaging in Appreciative Inquiry[1]

Michael Fischer, Brenda Geiger, and Mary Ellen Hughes

This qualitative study gives voice to 11 out of 18 female recidivists enrolled in phases two and three in a Northern California Drug-Court Program. Empowered as researchers in an appreciative inquiry, these women looked at current and past experiences to assess their program and envision future program innovations. From their perspective, the strongest component of drug court was being surrounded by staff dedicated to their progress and recovery. When treated with respect, these participants appreciated rather than resented the graduated supervision and accurate drug testing received. Wraparound services, resources and referral, treatment facilities that accepted children, and individualized treatment plans and therapy for offenders, who are ex-addicts and preferably females, allowed for involvement and active participation in recovery. Progressing through three phases, acquiring skills, a job, and visitation rights to see their children, or regaining custody, increased these women's sense of self-efficacy. They gained confidence in their ability to lead a drug-free, meaningful life. Findings show the importance of qualitative criteria in evaluating drug-court participants' progress and the process of recovery.

Keywords: female drug offenders' subjective experience; appreciative inquiry; drug-court qualitative assessment.

Authors' Notes: All three authors have contributed equally to the writing of this article. The authors thank Howard Kinlaw for his technical and editorial support.

BACKGROUND

The criminal justice system has seen a dramatic rise in female drug-related offenses and resultant incarceration of women. From 1999 to 2003, arrests for drug-related offenses increased 34.8 percent for women and only 19.9 percent for men (Belknap, 2007, p. 99).

From 1980 to 1994, while women's rate of incarceration increased by 386 percent, that of men rose by only 214 percent (Belknap, 2001, p. 167). From 1995 to 2005, the total number of female prisoners increased by 57 percent as compared to a 34 percent increase of male prisoners (Harrison, Paige, & Beck, 2006, p. 4). By the end of 2007, the female inmate population comprised 7.2 percent of state and federal prison populations as opposed to 6.1 percent in 1995 (Harrison, Paige, & Beck, 2006, p. 4; West & Sabol, Feb. 12, 2009). Cecil reported that of the approximately 200,745 incarcerated women, 106,174 resided in state and federal facilities and the remaining 94,571 in county jails (2007, p. 304).

Drug and drug-related convictions were the most frequent convictions for females (Chesney-Lind & Pasko, 2004). Between 33 percent and 82 percent of the female arrestees tested positive by urinalysis for at least one drug at the time of their arrest (Roll, Prendergast, Richardson, Burdon, & Ramirez, 2005). Of all the women incarcerated, 41.8 percent had participated in some form of drug treatment a month prior to committing their offense (Chesney-Lind & Pasko, 2004). These figures highlight the growing number of drug-dependent female offenders going through the revolving door of the criminal justice system for drug-related offenses (Alvarado, 2004; Merlo & Pollock, 2006; Vessey, 1998). They also suggest that the current interventions of getting tough on crime, increased social control, and punitive sanctions neither eliminate drug-related crimes nor address the underlying needs of female offenders (Belknap, 2007; Chesney-Lind & Pasko, 2004).

Female offenders' life trajectory has been shown to be paved with victimization. These women often are the survivors of sexual and/or physical abuse (Belknap, 2007; Chesney-Lind & Pasko, 2004; Chesney-Lind & Shelden, 2004). Many of them have lived through teen pregnancy and homelessness. Most female offenders are mothers of minor children and many have lost custody because of abandonment, drug abuse, and prison sentence (Fischer, Geiger, & Hughes, 2007; Geiger & Fischer, 2003, 2005). These women often exhibit symptoms of depression, suicidal ideation, eating disorders, bipolar affective disorder, anxiety disorders and co-morbid psychiatric disorders (Belknap, 2007; Chesney-Lind & Pasko, 2004; Chesney-Lind & Shelden, 2004; Kassebaum, 2004). Aware that some female crime and drug addiction are related to the above problems, several communities have implemented community-based drug-court programs that aim at promoting recovery from substance abuse and criminal activity while avoiding the detrimental effects of incarceration (Berman & Feinblatt, 2005).

DRUG-COURT EVALUATIONS

Drug courts receiving federal funding must be evaluated every six months. Although the levels and criteria of success vary, these evaluations consistently show that drug-court programs have been successful in their efforts to rehabilitate drug offenders (Goldkamp, 2000; Goldkamp, Weiland, & Moore, 2001; Gottfredson & Exum, 2002). Among the variety of process and outcome measures included in program evaluation are retention rates, urinalysis results, healthy babies, employment, and recidivism. Cost-benefit analysis also indicated significant savings over incarceration or standard rehabilitation programs. Equally as important is the report of lower recidivism rates (Bouffard & Richardson, 2007; Garrity, Prewitt, Joosen, Tindall, Webster, & Leukefeld, 2008; Goldkamp, 2000; Goldkamp, Weiland, & Moore, 2001; Gottfredson & Exum, 2002; Gottfredson, Najaka, & Kearley, 2003; Sanford & Arrigo, 2005).

Random assignment and meta-analysis studies also indicated process and outcome evaluations with varying rates of success depending on the type of offenders and offense committed. Some researchers claim that drug offenders' successful rehabilitation could be predicted by their criminal history and criminogenic needs such as drug addiction, anti-social attitudes and values, and the presence and influence of drug-abusing peers (Andrews, Zinger, Hoge, Bonta, Gendreau, & Cullen, 1990; Bouffard & Richardson, 2007). Research also indicates that employment at the time of enrollment was the strongest predictor of drug-court program graduation. In contrast, an extensive history of illicit intravenous drug use predicted program failure (Roll, Prendergast, Richardson, Burdon, & Ramirez, 2005).

Most of the findings on drug court have been based on the compilation of statistics related to various objective criteria of success. Rarely, if ever, has research focused on the subjective experience of female offenders participating in drug-court programs. Gendreau, Little, and Goggin's (1996) research findings indicated that the most effective rehabilitation programs are those that match treatment to the specific needs of homogeneous groups. Patton (2002) furthermore argued that more than just numbers are needed to judge the effectiveness of a program, "In judging the effectiveness of this program and making decisions about its future, it can be as important to understand the stories behind the numbers as to have the statistics themselves" (p. 152). Therefore, based on the advice of Gendreau et al. (1996) and Patton (2002), the authors concentrated their research efforts on those invisible but most important actors in drug-court programs—their female participants. Female drug-court participants were invited to engage in an appreciative inquiry (Bushe, 1995, 1997) to evaluate the Northern California drug-court program in which they were enrolled.

The main tenets of appreciative inquiry are: (a) the focus on positive and effective components of a program, and (b) the amplification of what participants want more of, even if what they want more of exists in only a small quantity (Cooperrider, 1990; Cooperrider & Srivastva, 1987; Whitney & Cooperrider, 2000). Congruent with the tenets of appreciative inquiry, this study adopts a social constructivist perspective that views people as continuously reconstructing social reality (Gergen, 1990, 1994).

The importance of this bottom-up research was to empower female drug-court program participants as co-researchers. As co-researchers, these women could evaluate the characteristics of the people and processes that from their own perspective and subjective experience had been conducive to their recovery. As change agents they were viewed as having the ability to evaluate and create new and better programs simply by talking, dreaming, and envisioning new future programs (Barrett, Thomas, & Hocevar, 1995; Cooperrider & Srivastva, 1987).

NORTHERN CALIFORNIA DRUG-COURT PROGRAM DESCRIPTION

The Northern California drug-court program under study enrolled 119 felony convicted offenders, of whom 30 were women. After individual assessment by the case manager, clients are provided with resources and referrals to various treatment facilities. Clients progress through three phases, each lasting for six months, and aftercare also lasting approximately six months. Participants are urine and breathalyzer-tested twice a week, with the days of the test randomly selected. Continuous graduated intensive supervision and monitoring for compliance with treatment are made possible by the joint collaboration of a judge, three probation officers, 12 treatment providers, two case managers, and two counselors. A mental-health specialist-court liaison plays the dual role of case manager and liaison to evaluate and report to the judge the client's progress. The client appears in court three times a week in phase one, twice a week in phase two, and once a week in phase three. Satisfactory progress is symbolized by advancement through the three phases. Compliance with the program requirements leads to a decrease in the intensity of supervision and to an increase in autonomy and individual choice. Graduated sanctions for noncompliance range from explanation and planning, being dropped to a previous stage or remaining longer in a phase, or being sent to jail.

METHODOLOGY

Subject Selection

The sample selection criteria for our research and evaluation were (a) being female, (b) having repeat drug or drug-related offenses, (c) being enrolled in the drug-court program for at least seven months, and (d) being in phases two or three of the program. Based on the opinion of the probation officers and case managers, the above criteria were to guarantee that only clients with sufficient experience and knowledge of the Northern California drug court would participate in our study. Eighteen of the 30 female participants in the drug court under study satisfied these criteria, with eleven of them consenting to participate in the present appreciative inquiry.

The age range of the 11 female participants was between 23 and 47 years, with a mean age of 34.1 and a median age of 32. All the participants had been convicted for drug-related offenses such as drug dealing and use, possession of drug paraphernalia, child endangerment, driving under the influence, possession of firearms, hit and run, embezzlement, forgery, or possession of stolen credit cards or other property.

The reported average number of years of drug addiction was 13.4 years, with 64 percent of the women starting their drug history between ages 12 and 16. The drug of choice for 10 of these women was methamphetamine (meth). Five of them had survived incest, rape, and/or had a family history of drug and alcohol abuse. The remaining six women did not report any family history of drug abuse or incest. In the words of Kim, "A lot of us are from the middle class, without a drug history."

All research participants were mothers of one to five children, with a mean of 2.5 children. All had experienced separation from their children, of whom they had either temporarily or permanently lost custody.

Aside from using drugs to numb the pain, suffering, and anger related to incest, rape, or loss of a parent, boyfriend, or children, these women often continued to use drugs, especially meth and cocaine, because of the tremendous feeling of power and energy the drugs had allowed them to experience. In the words of Paula,

> I liked the high. It was a rush. It was a major rush. I am not kidding. The first time I tried it, it literally put me on my butt. It was a rush I had never felt before. I liked it so much I spent 196,000 dollars on it in eight months.

Instrument

A semi structured in-depth interview that included an interview guide was the main research tool of our appreciative collaborative inquiry. Aside from background information and a history of drug and sexual abuse, questions inquired about participants' experience in the criminal justice system, their experience in the present drug-court program, and the components which were conducive to their progress and recovery. Additional questions allowed these women to envision innovative aspects of future drug-court programs. In order not to interfere with the flow of the narrative, the order of questions in the interview guide was not always adhered to (Brunner, 2004; Denzin, 1989; Patton, 2002; Plummer, 1995).

PROCEDURE

Before obtaining participants' consent, the two researchers conducting the interviews introduced themselves as designated drug-court evaluator and coordinator from another state. The researchers indicated the importance of listening to the participants tell in their own words about the components, activities, and people in the program that had assisted them to succeed and change. It was also specified that participation was voluntary. The interviewers' absence of therapeutic role and the informal nondirective style of the interview eased and facilitated rapport (Baron & Hartnagel, 1997; Hagan & McCarthy, 1992). Anonymity and confidentiality were also guaranteed. All identifying places and names were replaced by pseudonyms. Interviews lasting approximately two hours were conducted with each participant separately. Permission to record the interview was granted.

CONTENT ANALYSIS

Content analysis of the interviews followed the constant comparative method (Brunner, 2004; Glaser & Strauss, 1967; Patton, 2002; Strauss, 1987). Major themes concerning the clients and staff's attitude and behavior and the structural components of the program that lead to participants' successful recovery were inductively drawn from the participants' interview narratives (Denzin, 1989; Holsti, 1969; Kvale, 1996).

Contrary to quantitative studies, the question of establishing the validity of the participants' report did not arise. The researchers were interested in the subjective truth—the truth as these women perceived it from their own perspective and the meaning and interpretation these women gave to their experience in drug court (Denzin, 1989; Gergen, 1994; Holsti, 1969; Patton, 2002). To increase reliability of the findings, the three authors discussed the themes that had been inductively drawn by one of the authors until they reached an agreement concerning the importance of each topic and its inclusion in the final version of their report. Information-rich quotes were used throughout the text without any modification or edition to echo these women's perspectives as truthfully as possible and to support the inductively drawn themes (Lincoln & Guba, 1985; Patton, 2002).

RESULTS

Research participants were in awe of what drug court had offered them in their community. In the words of Paula, "Our drug court here is absolutely incredible. I never want them to retire. We are losing one gal due to budget cutbacks, and that will hurt us all."

In trying to comprehend what makes drug court so unique, these women often compared negative past experiences with positive present experiences. To them it was the drug-court staff that made their program so special and so different from previous experiences in the criminal justice system, and in a few cases, from other drug courts. Whether in drug court, the treatment program, or aftercare, these women felt the support of people who really cared about them. The judge emerged in the foreground as one of the most, if not the most, important figure. He was described as fair, helpful, encouraging, and concerned about the client's progress. In Arlene's words, "He is really nice, encouraging, doing something positive! He makes it much known to everybody. Actually, it makes you feel good."

Despite a rich past in the cogwheels of the criminal justice system, it was the first time that these women felt they were treated with dignity. The judge was talking to them, not past them, or about them to someone else. He genuinely listened to what they had to say about their progress. In the words of Candy, "I think the judge is very fair and honest. He always treats me with respect. He does not talk to me as if I am some worthless addict. I think it is helpful to go in front of the judge." Similarly, Theresa explained while comparing past and present drug-court judges,

> There is a big difference. This time he actually wants you to talk to him. You get up in front of him and report how you are doing weekly, or how your program is going, and if you have a relapse, and if there is any trouble. You can tell him what the problem was and how you solved it. Before they called your name and you stood up and they have this piece of paper and the probation officer and drug court counselor would read it to the judge and say you are doing OK. Bye! It was the drug court staff talking.

The judge was described by participants as exhibiting a unique personality that combined empathy, professionalism, and a wide knowledge about recovery. Sharon states, "He is very compassionate, understanding, and knowledgeable about recovery. He has our best interests and our welfare at heart." The drug-court probation officer and counselor were also appreciated for their concern and respect. In their presence these women no longer felt as a number, but they were actually people who deserved to be listened to. In their own words,

> You see them [probation officer and case manager] once a week. And they ask how are you doing, they want to know what's going on—and a regular probation officer isn't necessarily like that. They want to know everything, which is kind of nice because you know that they really care. You are not just a number. (Arlene)
> I go in and test on Tuesdays and Fridays. But it's just like, whenever I need to talk, I will go in and talk, and they will sit down and talk to me. They are always helpful. (Candy)

Comparing past and present probation officers, Sharon remembered the indifference of her previous probation officer. She comments, "The probation officer before, she did not have any compassion. These guys even though they had to send me to jail, they are still smiling."

Treatment providers and counselors of the drug-court program in which they were currently enrolled were also mentioned in a positive light by the research participants. By being attentive to their needs, treatment providers and counselors gave these women the feeling that they were there for them 24 hours a day. Paula contributes,

> I couldn't say enough good things about this treatment staff. They are very conscientious about recovery. When I lost my last sister two months ago, they told me to go home, but I needed to be with people. They just gave me my space, whatever I needed, all I had to was ask.

Similarly, the availability of sponsors in aftercare and Narcotics Anonymous was another significant component mentioned. Kim explains,

> A counselor may not be available all the time, but somebody is always available from 12 Steps. The people in the meetings have been very supportive. I did not realize how much support there is around here.

Paula agrees,

> On weekends you have sponsors you may call. Mine lives right up the street. I have had a sponsor for the last 10 months.

REWARDS FOR PROGRESS

One of the most rewarding experiences for the program participants was the recognition and praise for progress given by the judge in court in front of peers. Sharon claims,

> I've been in drug court for 17 months now, and I guess the most positive experience for me is going to court every month and hearing the judge say, "You are doing a good job. Keep up the good work." That's positive, then you know, and you know that they know, that you are doing well. That it's going to be OK.
>
> It is before friends in a group, and everybody knows that you are doing well.

The public announcement of their progress made these women feel good. Candy sums up, "In drug court I feel great. I have accomplished more than I did in all of my life."

CLEAR RULES AND CONSEQUENCES FOR RULE TRANSGRESSION

For these women, intensive supervision, structure, and consequences for rule transgressions and delinquent behavior in the drug court and treatment program were accepted to set limits and helpful as long as they preserved the dignity of these women.
Kim states,

> And the structure, having to be tested twice a week, forces you to be off of drugs. There are consequences. That helped me clean up long enough to get my bearings.

Teresa confirms,

> New Beginnings is one of the most structured programs. But it's a neat program. They treat me very well.

Testing positive—relapsing—could require remaining longer at a stage or being moved back to a prior stage, and, in serious cases, being sent to jail. In drug court, participants realized that it was pointless to cheat; they had to play by the rules. Paula explains,

> They don't take any crap off of you. If you are going to be defiant and are not going to follow the rules, you'll have a bracelet slapped on you in a heartbeat.

Kathy continues,

> When you try to take advantage of the court you will get caught. They do not like it. You can only play games for so long. They will put you right in jail. Once you stop using, and stop playing games with them, you realize how good it is.

ACCURATE DRUG TESTING

Participants' confidence in the drug-court system increased because of the knowledge that new drug-testing procedures were accurate and that reliable laboratory results protected them from false positives. Theresa remarks, "They sent it to the lab to break it down, to determine if it was drugs, and they figured out that it was a false positive." Similarly, comparing past and present testing procedures, Theresa explains,

> Back in 1997 tests were not accurate. They accused me of using pot, and told me I was really in denial. "You had a dirty test, and you are going to jail." Today tests are very accurate. If you get a false positive, they send it to the criminal lab and they test it; they break it down. It costs the client 45 dollars to send it to them, whereas it costs six dollars to do the regular test.

For these women punishment and accurate testing were, nevertheless, insufficient to prevent rule transgression and promote active participation in recovery. Piaget (1948) often mentioned in the context of moral education that it is not authority, firmness or punishment that makes people follow the rules. It is rather the love and respect for those who communicate the rules that will make people recognize the fairness and moral validity of those rules (Hirschi, 1969; Piaget, 1948). The women in this research expressed the same sentiment. Kim states,

> You know not to mess up. You can feel the support. People in the front row, you can tell if they have screwed up or not.

Paula concurs,

> The judge will pull a lot of people's collars and put them in jail. They are not serious about recovery. But for those of us who are, he has a lot of respect for us.

Sharon expresses a similar opinion about the probation officer, "Maxine is also tough; don't get me wrong, she makes no bones about it. But if you work with her, she will do anything she can for you."

The realization that drug court had their best interest at heart motivated these women to be honest. Being honest often meant communicating their failure. It meant reporting drug use and alcohol consumption even when they were sure that such use would not be detected by the test. Candy recounts,

> Around Mother's Day, I used marijuana, I got sick to my stomach, I got dizzy, and I had to sit down. What do I do? Do I tell, or not? I drank a 32-ounce bottle of cranberry juice to clean my system out. I had to tell XX it's not truthful and honest. I walked in there and told them. I just talked to them about it, and they made me write a little piece of paper about who I was with, and where I was. They tested me, and my test came back clean. It just set me back two months.

Kathy reveals,

> Alcohol gets out of your system really fast. I could drink on weekends and get away with it. Alcohol is the one thing you can get away with in drug court. All the other drugs will show in your system even after three days.

In drug court these women had learned to assume responsibility for their failings and progress. In case of relapse, the judge would ask for the client's input and plans to prevent future drug and alcohol use. Thelma says,

> The judge asks you, "So what are you going to do next time? How can you stop it from happening again?" I answer, "I am going to do this and going to do that. I am not going to hang around with those people.

Assuming responsibility also meant accepting the consequences of relapse, which at times resulted in returning to jail. Thelma admits,

> I did use; I did get a dirty test a couple of times. I told them I slipped up and used meth. I was sent to jail a couple of times. Now I am doing real good.

Sabina adds,

> I spent 68 days in jail, and I have done 90 days in jail, a week in jail, a couple of months. I know when I will have a dirty test, I have messed up. I will tell them about it, and they will arrest me right then and there.

These women emphasized the crucial difference between drug and house-rule violations. In comparison to the complaint about rigid house-rule violations, consequences for drug violation were accepted as rational and fair. These women requested flexibility in rule transgressions that were not directly related to drug treatment program and supervision. Sending a program participant to jail for technical violations such as smoking or drinking coffee was for these women irrational, harsh, and unfair. Arlene claims,

> Well, when I was in jail pregnant with my son, I was not arrested for using. I was arrested for being kicked out of a program for smoking cigarettes and drinking coffee, and it was a non-smoking program. So I had a really hard time with it, that was a violation, I hadn't used, but I had violated. . . . Actually I did go to jail for four months. And they were going to send me to prison for three years. But the judge decided to give me another chance.

Candy states,

> I call it [treatment facility] boot camp: no coffee, no soda, or cigarettes, or chocolate. You get one cup of sugar. Nobody can know where you live, your phone number.

PERSONAL ATTITUDE AND MOTIVATION TO CHANGE

As they progressed in the interview, the interviewees emphasized the importance of the drug-court participant's personal attitude and motivation as sine qua non conditions for successful recovery. Participants must be ready to change and mature out of drugs. Kathy explained,

> And if you are not ready to change it, then you are not going to last long. And the turnover is like crazy. There have been over 100 people in this treatment facility in the six months I have been coming, and I have seen maybe six people graduate since I have been there.

Thelma agrees, "Drug court and New Beginnings. Everyone can say I have to quit all they want, but you have to do it." These women understood that no matter how much support they received from relatives, friends, or professionals, the desire to change had to come from within. If one is not ready to change, no change will occur. Kristine, who had been surrounded by many caring relatives, knew this well and says,

> If you want drugs, you will take drugs. I had everybody around me telling me to change; I had people trying to help me, my mother, my ex-husband, and everybody else. I did not want to hear it. I still went out to drink.

According to Paula, being ready means "wanting off those chemicals" whatever the reason one had for starting or continuing. The women in this study stated that to change one had to hit bottom. Paula clarifies,

> When I entered New Beginnings we had 11 people in the outpatient program. Now we have 4. That's how many have left to use drugs. They were not serious. I think you have to hit rock bottom. . . . Each person's bottom is different.

For these women the phrase "hitting bottom" meant being tired of the vicious circle of drugs, prostitution, crime, and jail. Candy elaborates,

> The same vicious circle, the lies, the stealing, not knowing where I am going to sleep. I have slept on people's cars, bushes, porches. I have prostituted to get my drugs. I am not ashamed of what I did, just some of what I have gone through, you know, is crap. I am 24 years old and I have not accomplished anything but being a drug addict.

"Hitting rock bottom" also meant coming close to losing it all, children, family friends, and oneself. Paula states,

> It devastated my life. I went from having everything in the world to having nothing. . . . Looking backward, my relationship with my family, my sobriety is more important than any drug in the world.

Only at rock bottom could they grasp the immensity of losing it all, including their life. Such an understanding was not related to knowledge about the devastating effects of drugs. Rather, it came from the depth of their being and experiencing the darkness of chaos. Candy reveals,

> Drug court is a big motivator and a big help, but you have to be ready, from in here [showing her chest]. Not just from your head, but from your heart too. You must really want to change from the inside. You must be ready to grow up.

To come out from chaos requires pulling our own self out and taking responsibility for our fate. Candy continues concerning her parents,

> Mom was also a heroin user. My father would dabble in alcohol, marijuana, heroine, methamphetamines. And I used meth and marijuana with my dad. I feel that they had something to do with how I started off my life, but the problems that I created for myself with the law were my own doing.

Research participants also searched for the components of community-based residential and aftercare treatment programs conducive to these participants' progress and recovery.

INDIVIDUALIZED TREATMENT PLAN

All these women reported that only an individualized treatment plan could provide the services and supervision they needed. In their eyes, the intake interview with a case manager was an essential step in this process. Thelma explained,

> He assesses, determines which program you should enter, whether you need to live in a residential facility. If there is a problem, he will ask you what's going on, etc. If you are doing well, you only have to test once a week, otherwise three times a week. Then both drug court and probation will test you if you need that much supervision.

Remembering past negative experiences, Kim resented her previous counselor, who was too rigid and deaf to her wishes and excluded her from the decision-making process. She states,

> My counselors in Prop 36 wanted me to go into a battered women's shelter with my 17-year-old son, but he could not move in because he was too old. When I would have gotten out of there, I would have been homeless. It made absolutely no sense to me, so I did not sign their paper, and so I got a probation violation. I got kicked out of the program because I was being insubordinate. It frustrated me so much that I screwed up and used again.

Learning from past experiences in drug-court programs in which they had failed, these women stressed that decisions about treatment plans had to involve the client and take into consideration the client's needs, concerns, and preferences. Furthermore, they required periodic assessments of the clients' needs. Clients' needs change and so do their needs for services and supervision. Kim elaborates,

> When you are originally assessed you may need more intensive treatment. However, going through the process of recovery, whether you are waiting to go to jail or waiting to get into that treatment facility, you have changed. You may no longer need an intensive treatment facility. Without being reassessed you may be sent to a place that does not fit you any longer.

TREATMENT FACILITIES THAT ACCEPT CHILDREN

Separation from their children and concern for their welfare was one of the major preoccupations of the interviewees. To these women, especially for those who did not have close relatives to assume custody, there was an eminent need for facilities that accepted children. Kathy was one of the lucky few enjoying a dedicated mother ready to help and a treatment facility that accepted children. She recounts,

> My mom moved into my apartment to take care of the kids when I was in jail. Then they came with me to the residential center. I was extremely lucky, as this is one of the few programs that accept children over the age of four. So my son and daughter came to live with me.

In contrast, Theresa had no close relatives to take care of her children and was not in a residential facility that accepted them. For lack of an alternative, her children were put up for adoption. Embittered by the loss, Theresa claims,

> They put me in a program where I could not have my kids, knowing that I was running out of time and that if they put me in a program where I could not have my kids, I would lose my kids. I have a real problem with that. If they would have put me in a treatment facility with my children back then, maybe it would have made a big difference. But I wasn't in drug court yet, and it took me a few years to get to drug court. Even then they put me in a place where I could not have my children. That kind of screwed me and my children up.

RESIDENTIAL FACILITY'S IDEOLOGICAL ORIENTATION

The research participants spoke about the residential facility's ideological orientation. Christian facilities were appropriate for some, but not for others. Several of the women wanted more therapy and less preaching of Christianity. Candy says,

> It is Christian based, lots of praying, nothing to do with drug abuse.

Arleen adds,

> It was a Christian drug treatment facility. It was more based on the Bible than substance abuse. I wanted more about substance abuse. At the Christian treatment, they are Bible thumpers [bangs on table]. Sin and stuff like that. Really negative.

CHOICE OF THERAPY

The research participants often mentioned intensive therapy and counseling as instrumental to their recovery. It was helping them understand the source of their problems. Kim explains,

> It does make a difference to find the root. They may say it's because your parents drank or you used drugs, but a lot of it isn't. A lot of us are from the middle class, without a drug history. Now I understand myself more, and feel more confident with myself, not to let people push me around.

These women also mentioned the need to match therapy (group and/or individual) with the client's needs and inclination. A mismatch often led to regression. Candy who wanted individual therapy complained about her past treatment facility. She recounts, "It's always in a group. No one-on-one. They really don't work with you on an individual basis. They work with you in a group, and then they judge you individually."

ISSUES ADDRESSED IN THERAPY

Group therapy was often judged helpful to confront past sexual abuse and unresolved anger. Thelma states,

> We worked through a lot of underlying issues, a lot of anger that we had. That I did not know I had. If you learn to hide it at a younger age, drugs just mask it at an older age. With me it was incest.

Arlene also remembers,

> I had a lot of abuse in my past, and I get very anxious and angry, and so I have been in there and talked to people. I didn't really know where the anger was coming from, but they kind of helped me get down to the bottom of it, after I steamed off, like where is this anger coming from, which is really from abuse years ago. And that was really helpful. Because I had no idea as to why I was so angry, I was just mad at everything. And they helped me figure it out.

These women also felt that therapy was needed to deal with the separation and loss of the children and the consequent feeling of guilt and self blame that emerged from this loss. Having lost custody of her children, Thelma explains,

> Separation from the children creates more issues of guilt and shame, issues that a woman cannot face, and it's going to hurt, and she just wants to use more. To heal the family would be to heal the person.

Candy found herself wondering whether any therapy could help her deal with the feeling of loss over her children. She recounts,

> I regret the loss of my children. I lost them for drugs. [Silence for 10 seconds]. I feel very messed up in the head over it. That I have lost them all, I lost them for drugs. It makes me sad, makes me think. Drug court does not really help with the feeling part.

TREATMENT STAFF: PREFERENCE FOR COUNSELORS WHO ARE EX-ADDICTS

The interviewees viewed as superior the treatment facilities that offered a comprehensive set of services. Project Innovation was often cited as the prototype for such a facility. Unfortunately, it had to close for lack of funding. In the words of these women,

> Project Innovation was from 8 until 4, with an hour for lunch, Monday through Friday. We had an hour of Alcohol and Other Drugs (AOD) program in group, and then a break, and then relapse recovery for an hour. . . . A speaker came in. It was a job thing and we learned how to do resumes. It was a really good program. (Arlene)

> It offered family recovery, women's issues, individual, or group therapy, parenting, anger management, art therapy, and relapse prevention. If you needed legal assistance, there was a counselor who would give it. If you needed medical assistance, they would provide it. If you needed a ride, they had a car. They would get you there and make sure you could get back. (Thelma)

RESOURCES AND REFERRALS

The program participants also appreciated the resources and referrals that enabled them to become more independent. Kathy says, "They give you the resources and the referrals, and you take the steps." Theresa adds,

> They are hooked up with the EDD [Employment Development Department] place, and they should also be hooked up with Voc Rehab, which is different from the job place. It actually gets you started in something you want to do, hooks you up in school or finds you a job, or pays for tools if you do not have them, if you cannot get on your feet.

Sensitivity to the participants' financial problems was also mentioned as an asset. In case of need, drug court provided financial assistance to pay for drug rehabilitation, testing, counseling, and transportation. Kathy remarks,

> When you are in a residential program drug court helps you with your finances, when you can't pay for bus tickets, they will pay.

Arlene concurs,

> They pay for my drug rehabilitation, my books [for drug rehabilitation] and stuff; they pay for my aftercare, 10 dollars every time I go. They pay for the one-on-one counseling, if that's what you need; people here in the office will help you get it.

SKILL ACQUISITION AND VOCATIONAL TRAINING

For these women skill acquisition and vocational training were also crucial. The only way to leave welfare as a way of life was to acquire a job. Paula states,

> There are women here who need help and training to get skills and stuff like that. To get them off of welfare, to feel better, stronger. But me, I am happy with what they have done for me.

Thelma adds,

> People should be made to do something, where they get a skill, such as a welder. Then they could go to work when they get out rather than going back on the streets and drugs. Most of the people who end up incarcerated it's because they don't have a job, or a good job, a good paying job.

Receiving wages during vocational training was an additional incentive to enroll. Kathy, who had enrolled in a vocational training project, explains, "They will pay your wages for up to three months; they will pay you for school if you need it."

CONTINUING EDUCATION

Several of the women interviewed expressed the wish to continue their education. Unfortunately, convicted drug felons are not usually eligible for federal financial aid. They have to finish the program to get their conviction expunged or dropped in order to be able to obtain financial aid. Thelma explained, "Being a drug felon, I am not entitled to get financial aid. I will try to work to pay for it. And also I will try to get it dropped, but it's hard to do that, and even if it is dropped, it's hard to get financial aid."

Thanks to the caring and concerned professionals, paraprofessionals, and mentors encircling them, intensive treatment, and therapy, drug court had empowered these women to move from despair to hope. They were now able to take charge of their own lives as free and responsible beings. In the words of these women,

> I think that if it hadn't been for drug court, I would be back doing the same kind of things I was doing. Drug court taught me that my life is in my hands. That's what I want. And New Beginnings as well, they teach you life's lessons. They teach you to be out on your own. (Sharon)

> It was for me time to put the past behind: I regret a lot of the choices I have made. But the past is the past and you must move on. (Thelma)

> I feel embarrassed. I feel that I was stupid. I almost lost everything. I almost lost my family. You can't live in the past, you can't live in regret. I do not regret using because it made me the person I am today. (Sharon)

They were now able to enjoy the present without drugs, and plan for the future. Kathy concludes,

> I wasted a lot of years, but I am glad it's behind me. I am glad I have two beautiful children, and if it was not for drug court, I don't think I would be here right now. Drug court saved me from messing up and losing the kids. I came so close to losing my kids.

The prospect of being with or seeing their children while remaining clean and sober renewed their hope and faith in life. When asked what would help them remain clean, Jasmine answered: "My daughter!" Similarly, Kathy explained, "For 17 years I was either doing meth, alcohol, or just getting high. And now I am sober, for me, and for them." Candy who was about to receive 4-hour-visitation rights, was very excited by the prospect. She remarks, "I really only have contact with one of my children. I am excited. I am so happy. It starts on his birthday."

One of the indicators of recovery was the wish to become productive and gain employment. Kim explains that she enjoyed her work,

> I am a waitress. I am getting ready to go back to work. I like work. It keeps me busy. I was stagnant then, it was a lot of wasted time, and I was not using my potential. I have been like this for too long.

Candy was very excited to have, for the first time, a paying job. Even if it was only partial employment on weekends and such an employment could result in her losing all governmental aid, she was ready to take the chance. She comments, "I really want to work; it's my first job ever. I have never had a job. And I just started two weeks ago and I really like it."

Another indicator of recovery was to give in return by helping other drug addicts. For Paula this was a way to express gratitude to all those who had helped her recover. She explains,

> I had wonderful people support me in my recovery, and it's important to give it back, to close the circle. I take them out shopping, or help them with reading, or take them to a movie. It's

really important to get that support. These young people don't have the opportunity to get out. I have my freedom, my own space.

DISCUSSION

This qualitative study engaged, as co-researchers in an appreciative inquiry, female repeat offenders enrolled in a Northern California drug-court program. Eleven out of 18 females enrolled in phases two and three of the program were given a voice to talk about the strengths of the program and of the key persons who had helped them change. Empowered as change agents, these women looked at their past and present experiences in drug court and the criminal justice system. They could look forward to the future and envision new drug-court innovations. From these women's perspectives, the strongest component of the drug court they were enrolled in was being surrounded by many caring people who listened to them and who were genuinely concerned about their progress. These women did not mind the intensive supervision and graduated and immediate sanctions as long as they were imposed fairly by people who did not want to punish or humiliate them. Wraparound services, resources and referral, treatment facilities that accepted children, and individualized treatment plans were some of the essential components of a successful program. Group and individual therapy and counselors, who were ex-addicts and preferably women, helped these women fully understand their drug addiction and address issues of incest, anger, and guilt over separation from children. In drug court they were empowered to look at the past without fear of relapse and to envision a new life without drugs. They avoided drugs and stayed clean and sober as they moved through the three phases of treatment and aftercare. Acquiring skills, finding a job, and obtaining visitation rights or regaining custody of their children increased confidence in their ability to lead a drug-free, meaningful life.

One of the drug court's basic tenets is that clients' involvement can be achieved through coerced court and community intervention without the requirement of a high level of motivation (Prochaska, DiClemente, & Norcross, 1992). Another tenet is that motivation can be cultivated by suspended sentences and by having participants remain for longer periods of time than is customary in drug-rehabilitation programs (Satel, 1998, 2000). The findings of this study did indicate that clients' participation in drug court increased their motivation when they were supported and rewarded for progress through the phases. The public announcement of such progress was also found to enhance self-efficacy perception (Bandura, 1977) and motivation to complete recovery. Nevertheless, and contrary to past findings (Voorhis, Braswell, & Lester, 2006), our research reveals from the participants' perspective that initial motivation is a sine qua condition for program completion. Participants must want to mature out of drugs, stop being deceitful, and be honest with themselves.

It is possible that the drug-court program presently being examined was successful with the 11 women because they were already in the process of maturing out on their own. Greater insight concerning the level of motivation and readiness of female drug-court participants to mature out of drugs could be obtained by conducting future research. Comparison of subjective experience of female drug-court participants not having gone beyond phase one because of failing or dropping out of the program with those of female drug-court participants who had progressed beyond it could expand our research findings on the topic of motivation.

The women interviewed in this research repeatedly mentioned the human element of care, concern, and fairness of drug-court and treatment staff. What these people gave them could not be compared with any other experience in the criminal justice system, and in a few cases, in other prior drug-court programs. Given the unique personal characteristics of drug court's personnel in the present study, it is recommended to replicate this appreciative inquiry with women participating in other drug-court programs throughout Northern California. Such a replication would allow us to find out whether the uniqueness of the drug-court team was related to the adoption of a therapeutic jurisprudence philosophy or to a single phenomenon related to the special mix of personal characteristics of drug-court staff and clients.

In conclusion, despite the small and selected sample of women who engaged in this appreciative inquiry in one drug court in Northern California, this research expands our knowledge in the field by showing the benefits of a drug-court program from the female participants' perspective. The components of quality care of drug court and of the process of recovery go beyond traditional criteria of success, which are lack of recidivism and sobriety statistics thus far compiled on drug courts. Good affect such as from caring drug-court staff concerned with the client's recovery, respect, and honesty, bottoming out, wanting off of chemicals, relapsing and trying again, putting the past behind and having hope for the future, wanting therapy to deal with the roots of the drug problems and with the feeling of guilt consequent to separation with children, developing a sense of efficacy that increases motivation to take care of the children, work, and giving in return to other drug addicts are some of the many criteria of successful recovery that can only be understood through qualitative research. This study, therefore, shows the invaluable data obtained by conducting qualitative evaluations of drug-court programs.

REFERENCES

ALVARADO, R. (2004). *Strengthening America's families: Programs that work for justice-involved women with co-occurring disorders.* National Gains Center for People with Co-occurring Disorders. Delmar, New York.

ANDREWS, D., ZINGER, I., HOGE, R., BONTA, J., GENDREAU, P., & CULLEN, F. (1990). Does correctional treatment work? A clinically relevant and psychologically informed meta-analysis. *Criminology, 28,* 369–404.

BANDURA, A. (1977). *Social learning theory.* Englewood Cliffs, NJ: Prentice Hall.

BARON, S. & HARTNAGEL, T. (1997). Attributions, affect, and crime: Street youths' reactions to unemployment. *Criminology, 35,* 409–434.

BARRETT, F. J., THOMAS, C. F., & HOCEVAR, S. P. (1995). The central role of discourse in large-scale change: A social construction perspective. *The Journal of Applied Behavioral Science, 31,* 352–372.

BELKNAP, J. (2001). *The invisible woman: Gender, crime and justice* (2nd ed.). Belmont, CA: Wadsworth.

BELKNAP, J. (2007). *The invisible woman: Gender, crime and justice* (3rd ed.). Belmont, CA: Wadsworth.

BERMAN, G. & FEINBLATT, J. (2005). *Good courts.* New York: The New Press.

BOUFFARD, J. & RICHARDSON, K. (2007). The effectiveness of drug court programming for specific kinds of offenders: Methamphetamine and DWI offenders versus other drug-involved offenders. *Criminal Justice Policy Review, 18*(3), 274–293.

BRUNNER, J. (2004). Life as narrative. *Social Research, 71*(3), 691–711.

Bushe, G. R. (1995). Advances in appreciative inquiry as an organization development intervention. *Organization Development Journal, 13*(3), 14–22.

Bushe, G. R. (1997). *Attending to others: Interviewing appreciatively.* Vancouver, BC: Discovery and Design Inc.

Cecil, D. (2007). Looking beyond caged heat. *Feminist Criminology, 2*(4), 304–326.

Chesney-Lind, M. & Pasko, L. (2004). *The female offender: Girls, women, and crime* (2nd ed.). Thousand Oaks: Sage.

Chesney-Lind, M. & Sheldon, M. (2004). *Girls, delinquency, and juvenile justice* (3rd ed.). Belmont: Wadsworth.

Cooperrider, D. L. (1990). Positive image, positive action: The affirmative basis of reorganizing. In S. Srivastva & D. Cooperrider Z. (Eds), *Appreciative management and leadership* (pp. 91–125). San Francisco: Jossey-Bass.

Cooperrider, D. L. & Srivastva, S. (1987). Appreciative inquiry in organizational life. In R. Woodman & W. Pasmore (Eds), *Research in organization change and development* (vol. 1. pp. 129–169). Greenwich, CT: JAI.

Denzin, N. K. (1989). *Interpretive Interactionism.* Newbury Park, CA: Sage Institute.

Fischer, M., Geiger, B., & Hughes, M. E. (2007). Female recidivists speak about their experience in drug court while engaging in appreciative inquiry. *International Journal of Offender Therapy and Comparative Criminology, 51*(6), 703–722.

Garrity, T., Prewitt, S., Joosen, M., Tindall, M., Webster, J., & Leukefeld, C. (2008). Baseline subjective stress predicts 1-year outcomes among drug court clients. *International Journal of Offender Therapy and Comparative Criminology, 52*(3), 346–357.

Geiger, B. & Fischer, M. (2005). Naming oneself criminal: Gender differences in offenders' identity negotiation. *International Journal of Offender Therapy and Comparative Criminology, 49*(2), 194–220.

Geiger, B. & Fischer, M. (2003). Female Repeat Offenders Negotiating Identity. *International Journal of Offender Therapy and Comparative Criminology, 47*(5), 496–515.

Gergen, K. (1990). Affect and organization in postmodern society. In S. Srivastva & D. Cooperrider Z. (Eds), *Appreciative management and leadership* (pp. 153–174). San Francisco: Jossey-Bass.

Gergen, K. (1994). *Toward transformation in social knowledge* (2nd ed.). Thousand Oaks, CA: Sage.

Gendreau, P, Little, T., & Goggin, C. (1996). A meta analysis of the predictors of adult offender recidivism. What works. *Criminology, 23*, 575–607.

Glaser, B. G. & Strauss, A. L. (1967). *The discovery of grounded theory: Strategies for qualitative research.* New York: Aldine.

Goldkamp, J. S. (2000, October). *What we know about the impact of drug courts: Moving research from "do they work?" to "when and how they work"* Testimony before the Senate Judiciary Subcommittee on Youth Violence. US Department of Justice, Bureau of Justice Assistance.

Goldkamp, J. S., Weiland, D., & Moore, J. (2001). *The Philadelphia treatment court, its development and impact: The second phase (1998–2000).* Philadelphia, PA: Crime and Justice Research Institute.

Gottfredson, D., Najaka, S., & Kearley, B. (2003). Effectiveness of drug treatment courts: Evidence from a randomized study. *Criminology and Public Policy, 2,* 401–426. College Park, MD: The University of Maryland.

Gottfredson, D. & Exum, M. L. (2002). The Baltimore city drug treatment court: One year results from a randomized study. *Journal of Research in Crime & Delinquency 39*(3), 227–356.

Hagan, J. & McCarthy, B. (1992). Streetlife and delinquency. *British Journal of Sociology, 43*, 433–561.

Harrison, P., Paige, M., & Beck, A. (2006) *Prisoners in 2005.* Washington, DC: Dept of Justice, Office of Justice Programs, Bureau of Justice Statistics.

Hirschi, T. (1969). *Causes of delinquency.* Berkeley: University of California Press.

HOLSTI, O. (1969). *Content analysis for social science and humanistics.* Reading, MA: Addison Wesley.

KASSEBAUM, P. A. (2004). *Substance use treatment for women offenders: Guide to promising practices.* DHHS Publication (SMA) 04-3929. Rockville, MD. Substance Abuse Mental Health Administration.

KVALE, S. (1996). *InterViews.* Thousand Oaks: Sage.

LINCOLN, Y. S. & GUBA, E. G. (1985). *Naturalist Inquiry.* Newbury Park, CA: Sage.

MERLO, A. & POLLOCK, J. (2006). *Women, law, and social control* (2nd ed.). Boston: Allyn & Bacon.

PATTON, M. Q. (2002). *Qualitative research and evaluation methods* (3rd ed.). Thousand Oaks, CA: Sage.

PIAGET, J. (1946). *The moral judgement of the child.* Glencoe, IL: Free Press (originally published 1933).

PLUMMER, K. (1995). Life story research. In J. N. Smith, R. Harre, and L. V. Langenhove (Eds), *Rethinking methods in psychology* (pp. 50–63). London: Sage.

PROCHASKA, J. O., DiCLEMENTE, C. C., & NORCROSS J. (1992). In search of how people change: Applications to addictive behavior. *American Psychologist, 47,* 1102–1114.

ROLL, J. M., PRENDERGAST, M., RICHARDSON, K., BURDON, W., & RAMIREZ, A. (Nov 2005). Identifying predictors of treatment outcome in a drug court program. *American Journal of Drug and Alcohol Abuse, 31*(4), 641–657.

SANFORD, J. & ARRIGO, B. (2005). Lifting the cover on drug courts: Evaluation studies and policy concerns. *International Journal of Offender Therapy and Comparative Criminology, 49*(3), 239–359.

SATEL, S. L. (2000, Winter). Drug treatment: The case for coercion. *National Drug Court Institute Review, III*(1), 1–57. Alexandria, VA: National Drug Court Institute.

SATEL, S. L. (1998, Summer). Observational study of courtroom dynamics in selected drug courts. *National Drug Court Institute Review, 1*(1), 56–87.

STRAUSS, A. (1987). *Qualitative analysis for social scientists.* Cambridge: Cambridge University Press.

VESSEY, B. M. (1998). Specific needs of women diagnosed with mental illnesses in US jails. In B. L. Levin, A. K. Blanch, & A. Jennings (Eds). *Women's mental health services: A public health perspective.* Thousand Oaks, CA: Sage.

VOORHIS, P. V., BRASWELL, M., & LESTER, D. (2006). *Correctional counseling and rehabilitation* (6th ed.). Cincinnati: Anderson.

WEST, C. & SABOL, W. (2009, February 12). *Prisoners in 2007.* United States Department of Justice (NCJ-224280). Washington, DC: US Dept. of Justice.

WHITNEY, D. & COOPERRIDER, D. L. (2000). The appreciative inquiry summit: An emerging methodology for whole system positive change. *Journal of the Organizational Development Network, 32,* 13–26.

ENDNOTE

1. Updated version of article published in *International Journal of Offender Therapy and Comparative Criminology 51*(6), Dec. 2007, 703–722. Editor provided permission to reproduce as a chapter in a book.

27

Mentally Ill Women in Jails

Asylums for the Invisible

Rosemary Gido and Lanette Dalley

Dorothea Dix is well known as the 19th century *reform advocate* for the mentally ill. From her first experience in 1841 in the East Cambridge, Massachusetts jail, where she encountered the mentally ill living in deplorable conditions, to her *research tour* of jails and almshouses across Massachusetts the following year, Dix would build the foundation for the treatment of the disadvantaged mentally ill that lasted through the mid-20th century (Frontline, 2005).

Prior to Dorothea's tireless involvement, a Massachusetts Congregationalist minister, Reverend Louis Dwight, had lobbied 25 years earlier for the removal of the mentally ill from jails. A report issued by a Committee of the Massachusetts legislature resulting from Dwight's work recommended that "confinement of mentally ill persons in the state's jails should be made illegal" (Frontline, 2005). That, 185 years later, jails once again house the mentally ill, the greater percentage of whom are women, is the focus of this chapter. Two failed national social policy initiatives of the last 50 years, *deinstitutionalization* and the *War on Drugs*, are in large measure responsible for jails once again being termed "the new asylums" (Frontline) and jailed mentally ill women labeled as "the most invisible of females in the justice system" (Gido and Dalley, 2009, p. xix). This chapter reviews the last 30 years of research and policy initiatives that have attempted to address the needs of today's female offenders in local jails.

THE ROAD TO DEINSTITUTIONALIZATION

Morrissey and Goldman (1986) have identified three major historical cycles in U.S. mental health care reform. The first cycle introduced the 19th century asylum and a focus on "moral treatment" (Luchins, 1992). Next came the *mental health movement* and the establishment of the psychopathic hospital in the early 20th century. Deinstitutionalization and the replacement of state psychiatric hospitals with community mental health centers were set in motion from the mid-1950s (Schull, 1976). It is this third cycle that has resulted in *trans-institutionalization*—placing the mentally ill back in jails.

Most accounts of the five previous decades during which deinstitutionalization has been unfolding emphasize changes in ideology and medicine as well as civil rights movements which called attention to the plight of the institutionalized mentally ill and rallied for their more humane treatment (Lamb & Bachrach, 2001). With the post-World War II introduction of neuroleptic drugs in large mental hospitals, the door was opened to a "community care model" for the mentally ill. Congress, responding to lobbying by community mental health care advocates, passed the Mental Health Study Act of 1955, which led to the passage of the Community Mental Health Care Centers Act of 1963 (Mechanic and Rochefort, 1992, p. 130).

The initial era of "emptying" state hospitals, 1955 to 1965, resulted in a 15 percent patient population decrease. The real *impact* was to come between 1965 and 1975 when 60 percent of mental health hospital residents were released (Mechanic and Rochefort, 1992, pp. 130–131). Civil commitment law changes and the passage of Medicare, Medicaid, and Supplemental Social Security Income laws allowed the states to transfer the deinstitutionalized mentally ill to community nursing homes (Morrissey and Goldman, 1986, p. 22).

In assessing the "disaster" of deinstitutionalization, Talbot (2004, p. 6) notes the lack of planning, little consensus on the meaning of deinstitutionalization for the chronically mentally ill, the failure of community facilities to keep pace with the outflow of patients, and a slow-to-develop network or system of ancillary services to serve the mentally ill and their families upon release. The result has been a failed social experiment, and one that has, for the most part, overlooked its critical effects on mentally ill women (Bachrach, 1984). While the effects of deinstitutionalization varied state by state, the period 1970 through the present brought other social problems related to deinstitutionalization—homelessness, housing shortages, substance abuse, victimization, violence, and, ultimately, *criminalization of mental illness,* as the mentally ill re-populated jails and prisons (Lamb and Bachrach, 2001, pp. 5–24; Palermo et al., 1991; Slate and Johnson, 2008; Teplin et al., 2005).

THE WAR ON DRUGS

Since President Richard Nixon's 1972 "declaration of war on drugs," the United States War on Drugs policy has come to represent a body of legislation promulgated at the national and state level in the name of "zero tolerance" of particular types of drugs (Gido, 2002: 3; Merolla, 2008). In the last decade, criminologists and policy analysts have primarily examined the War on Drugs' effects on prison and jail overcrowding. Related to both federal and state mandatory minimum drug sentencing laws, the chances of receiving a federal or state prison term for a drug offense and a longer drug-offense-related sentence have risen dramatically (The Sentencing Project, 2007: 7). Similarly, drug offenders in local jails increased from 17,200 in 1980 to 493,800 in 2003 (TSP, 2007: 10).

Despite the national mobilization of resources to launch and continue the War on Drugs in targeted interdiction and enforcement, the majority of incarcerated drug offenders have been *low-level offenders*. One consequence of this policy is incarcerated women are "more likely than men to have been convicted of a drug offense" (*A 25-year quagmire*, 2007: 13), and Black and Hispanic women are more likely to be incarcerated in prison or jail than white women (p. 1).

TRANS-INSTITUTIONALIZATION: THE MENTALLY ILL IN JAILS

Research and Policy Initiatives—1970 to 2000

With the flow of the formerly hospitalized mentally ill into communities, research began to emerge that documented the growing presence of mentally ill and seriously mentally ill individuals in jails across the United States.

A 1973 study in California's Santa Clara County found a 300 percent increase in the county jail, four years after the closing of Agnews State Psychiatric Hospital in that county. Across California, the number of jailed mentally ill increased 300 percent for the period, 1965–1975 (Frontline, p. 16). Such increases in jailed and imprisoned mentally ill occurred throughout the United States (Pfeiffer, 2007, pp. 38–44; 146–149; 187–203).

One of the first comprehensive national surveys of jail inmates in 1978 found a correlation between the nation's jail inmate profile and the profile of groups underserved by the new community mental health system (Goldkamp, 1978). Policy makers, too, were beginning to take notice of the phenomena at the local, state, and national level with workshops, grants, and studies emerging during the period 1976–1980 (Morgan, 1981: pp. 268–269).

On April 2, 1990, the National Coalition for the Mentally Ill in the Criminal Justice System, in conjunction with the National Association of Counties and Community Action for the Mentally Ill Offender, sponsored a "national work session." The gathering brought together 50 mental health, correctional, and law enforcement professionals, as well as families and consumers, to address specific issues of mentally ill persons in local jails. Reviewing major research findings and program reviews, the participants published a monograph of *policy recommendations* to "mark a more productive course for the 1990s that hold the promise of improvements in the world of mentally ill persons in the criminal justice system . . ." (The National Coalition for the Mentally Ill in the Criminal Justice System, 1990; preface).

Interestingly, the work group that focused on in-jail issues recommended a number of policy initiatives that have become the "standard set"* of action agenda items for advocates over the years (p. 125):

Development, endorsement and local adoption of national standards

Dissemination of screening tools, techniques and model programs by national organizations and agencies

Advocacy for local funding of mental health services in both the community and jail

Development of centralized information systems within mental health jurisdictions**

---

*It has been argued that the global economic downturn and the internationalization of the U.S. War on Drugs have resulted in a greater likelihood of arrest, detainment, prosecution, and imprisonment of poor women of color around the world. See Reynolds (2008)—Ed.

**What is referred to today as "best practices"? Among the leading contributors of the gathering were Drs. Henry Steadman and Linda Teplin who continue today to lead research efforts on mentally ill offenders in the criminal justice system. Dr. Steadman heads Policy Research, Inc. of Delmar, NY, which operates the GAINS Center, funded by the Center for Mental Health Services (CMHS) of the Substance Abuse and Mental Health Services Administration (SAMHSA)—Ed.

By the year 2000, the national policy discussion began to turn to the critical issue of the impact of incarceration and *reentry* on children, families, and communities (Travis and Waul, 2003). Notably, Joan Petersilia (2003) recalled the 1995 study that found 75 percent of parole administrators reporting no special programs for released mentally ill clients (p. 38). Of particular concern were returning "dual diagnosed" individuals, with co-occurring disorders, and their higher rates of recidivism (p. 38). The need to invest in community mental health/criminal justice partnerships for returning mentally ill prisoners, particularly the seriously mentally ill, as well as the need to create *jail diversion systems for the mentally ill* was becoming apparent (Lurigio, 2000).

The combined effects of deinstitutionalization and the war on drugs on jails were becoming evident. The prevalence of mentally ill offenders in jails was found to be higher in jails (60 percent) than in prisons (49 percent). The rate of female offenders to jails increased at a faster rate than for males—42 percent compared to 24 percent (James & Glaze, 2006).

With the establishment of the Substance Abuse and Mental Health Services Administration (SAMHSA) and the National GAINS Center for People with Co-Occurring Disorders in the Justice System, nine jail diversion sites were studied between 1998 and 2003 for program effectiveness under three separate models—pre-booking, court-based pre-booking and jail-based pre-booking. The evaluation found jail diversion programs did link those diverted to community-based services without, unfortunately, finding whether "the type, amount, and mix of services, including evidence-based practices" were those needed to improve mental health symptoms (*What can we say*, 2004, p. 7).

As the War on Drugs came to be tagged "the war against women," the policy arena began to finally recognize "that a substantial proportion of women offenders have experienced trauma and that this plays a vital and often unrecognized role in the evolution of a woman's physical and mental health problems" (Bloom and Covington, 2009, p. 161). The National Institute of Corrections funded research that introduced the concept of "gender-responsive" into the policy discussion of diversion, treatment, and programming for jailed and imprisoned women, underscoring the criticality of an array of mental health services to address trauma and PTSD (Bloom and Covington, 2003; McCampbell, 2005, p. 6). Yet, most studies have found that despite the multiple problems of female offenders, and the added issues of child rearing and parenting problems, "there has been little movement to redesign programming and services to meet the needs of women" and "they are typically underserved in all types of jail programming" (*Addressing the Needs*, 1999: p. 1).

What follows is an in-depth review of research specific to jailed women's mental health care needs, featuring emerging models and initiatives that are addressing the issues.

RESEARCH ON JAILED WOMEN'S MENTAL HEALTH NEEDS

Types, Etiology, and Lack of Treatment

A study conducted by Teplin et al. (1996) was one of the first endeavors to provide an in-depth analysis of women's pervasive mental health problems in jails. As Ross and Lawrence (2009) note, this "landmark" study uncovered a hidden population that had not been well researched until this time (p. 121).

Teplin et al. (1996) administered the Diagnostic Interview Schedule Version III-R to 1,272 pretrial women jail inmates in Chicago's Cook County Jail. The findings were significant in that more than 80 percent of the women met the criteria for one or more lifetime psychiatric illnesses. Additionally, 70 percent of the women were abused or drug dependent. Perhaps even more telling is Teplin's (1997) follow-up of the study data that found only 25 percent of the severely mentally disordered jailed women obtained mental health services.

More recent studies document the acceleration of trans-institutionalization to local jails, as confirmed by the findings of the 2006 Special Report of the Bureau of Justice Statistics on "mental health problems of prison and jail inmates" (James and Glaze, 2006). Female inmates in local jails reported a greater incidence of mental health problems than jailed males (75 percent of females and 63 percent of males). This rate for jailed women compared to 12 percent of females in the general population who met the criteria for mental health disorders (Bloom & Covington, 2009; James & Glaze, 2006, pp. 1 and 3). Not surprisingly, in 2006, the National Alliance for Mental Illness (2006) described jails as "psychiatric emergency rooms" (p. 72).

Over time, the research has continued to document that PTSD, mood disorders, anxiety disorders, and borderline personality disorders are the most common mental health problems presented by jailed female offenders (Green, Miranda, Daroowalla, & Siddique, 2005; James & Glaze, 2006; Broner, Kopelovich, Mayrl, & Bernstein, 2009). Ross and Lawrence (2009, p. 122) have warned of added stressors in jail environments that contribute to PTSD. Linked to the availability of "street drugs" and jail sentences related to drug offenses, mentally ill jailed women are also likely to have co-occurring illnesses that worsen their mental illness symptoms (Haywood et al., 2000; James and Glaze, 2006). A 2005 study (Green et al) found that more than one-third of 100 jailed female inmates had a psychiatric diagnosis, and the majority of the women (74 percent) reported having substance abuse problems. Research by Abram, Teplin, and McClelland (2003) underscores the prevalence of comorbid disorders among jailed women, with the incidence rate, 72 percent, significantly higher than that of the psychiatric population, 30–50 percent. Clearly, incarceration exacerbates mental illness symptoms (Battle, Zlotick, Najavitis, & Winsor, 2003; Trestman, Ford, Zhang, & Wiesbrock, 2007). One of the potential outcomes of comorbid and psychiatric disorders is suicide and suicidal ideation (Charles, Abram, McClelland, & Teplin, 2003).

Suicide: Ideations and Attempts

In general, most studies have focused only on inmates who have successfully committed suicide and have neglected to include inmates who have *attempted* suicide or have suicidal ideations (Charles et al., 2003). This may suggest that the prevalence of suicides (or attempted suicides) is underreported. Regardless of whether an inmate commits suicide or attempts suicide, both pose challenges to jail administrators and staff.

The Bureau of Justice Statistics most recent special report on suicides trends in jails (Mumola, 2005) found the 2002 jail suicide rate was over 3 times greater than the rate in state prisons (p. 1). By 2002, the jail suicide rate had fallen sharply to one-third of the 1983 rate (Mumola, 2005).[1] In addition, BJS discovered that the size of the jail was related to the suicide rate, with the nation's smallest jails (less than 50 inmates) reporting a suicide rate of 5 times that of the largest U.S. jails. Men in jail were also 56 percent more likely to commit suicide as compared to jailed women (32 percent). However, this study did not measure *attempted* suicides or suicidal ideations that are commonly associated with female inmates.

As researchers have noted, incarcerated women may be at a higher risk for suicide, particularly *attempted* suicide, than incarcerated males (Blaauw, Arensman, Kraaij, Winkel, & Bout, 2002; Charles, Abram, McClelland, & Teplin, 2003). In fact, the rate of suicide attempts in the general population is higher for women than for men (Harrison & Rogers, 2007; James & Glaze, 2006). Female jail inmates also mirror similar higher rates of attempted suicides or suicidal ideation as compared to their male counterparts.

In a study of 1,418 female offenders detained in Chicago's Cook County jail, Charles et al. (2003) identified three risk factors related to suicide attempts or ideation by jailed women:

1. *History of previous suicidality.* As other studies have validated, a previous suicide attempt is one of the strongest predictors of attempted suicide in the general psychiatric outpatient population (Brown et al., 2000). Strongly associated with suicidal history is mental illness, particularly for females who more frequently have a higher rate of mood disorders compared to men (www.mental-health.samsha.gov/publications/allpubs/fastfact6/default.asp). More than 50 percent of the jailed women in the Charles et al.'s study (2003) said they had suicidal thoughts and previous suicide attempts. On the basis of these findings and the average daily number of women in jails (98,577), 49,000 women in U.S. jails today are at risk for attempted suicide (James & Glaze, 2006).

2. *Unemployment.* Researchers have consistently shown that individuals who are employed are less likely to attempt or commit suicide in both the general population and outpatient psychiatric population (Brown et al., 2000; Kposowa, 2001). The Charles et al.'s (2003) study found those jailed women who were unemployed were also more likely to have suicidal ideations and attempted suicides.

3. *Marital status.* Research suggests that individuals who are married are less likely to have suicidal tendencies. However, offenders are much less likely to be married (Bonner, 2000; James, 2004). "Even if an inmate is married, the isolation from relationships and the breakdown in communication can increase the risk of suicide" (Charles et al., 2003, p. 67). Specifically, Charles et al. (2003) learned that women who had been previously married (i.e. divorced, separated, widowed) were more likely (44 percent), compared to those currently married (21 percent), to have suicidal ideation or attempts of suicide. Women who were never married also had a higher likelihood of suicidal ideation or attempts.

Other risk factors associated with female inmates' attempted suicides and suicidal ideations are the *traumatic events* they experienced as children, as adults, or as both. In the general population, childhood physical abuse and sexual abuse substantially increase the risk for suicide by as much as 5 times (Dube, Anda, Felitti, Chapman, Williamson, & Giles, 2001 as cited in Charles et al. 2003, p. 67). In one study, jailed women offenders who had a higher rate of sexual and physical abuse during childhood were more likely to be suicidal than those women who had not experienced these traumatic events as children (Blaauw, Arensman, Kraaij, Winkel, & Bout, 2002). A further examination of these risk factors suggests that there is a causal link between traumatic events, mental illnesses, and comorbidity (Bloom & Covington, 2009).

Linking Trauma to Mental Illness and Comorbidity

Recent research posits a correlation between female offenders' pervasive histories of trauma and mental illness and drug abuse (Bloom and Covington, 2009; Green et al., 2005; Pollock, 1998; Trestman et al., 2007). As Bloom and Covington (2009) point out, while mental illness, substance abuse, and trauma have been "therapeutically linked," they have traditionally been treated separately (Bloom & Covington, 2009, p. 161). Increasingly, researchers have identified a pervasive pattern of trauma in lives of these women, strongly linking trauma to female offender criminal pathways and mental illness and comorbidity (Bloom & Covington, 2009; Broner et al., 2009, p. 164). Essentially, women who experience trauma and are mentally ill will often attempt to self-medicate to extinguish feelings of depression and anxiety by using illicit drugs (Bloom & Covington, 2009; Pollock, 1998).

It has been well established that female offenders have substantially higher rates of sexual and physical abuse and mental illness as compared to females in the general population (James & Glaze, 2006; Messina & Grella, 2006) and as well as to male offenders (Gido & Dalley, 2009; James, 2006; Pollock, 1998). Battle and her associates' (2002) literature review confirmed extensive trauma histories among incarcerated women. Green et al. (2005) found that women in jails have extensive exposure to trauma. Of 100 women interviewed, almost half (49 percent) reported being sexually abused; 25 percent were neglected, and 26 percent were physically abused as children. Many of these women continued to experience trauma later in their adult lives. For example, 71 percent had been involved in a violent domestic relationship, 55 percent had been threatened with a weapon, and almost 60 percent had witnessed someone being injured or killed (Green et al., 2005). Connected to these traumatic events was the fact that over one-half had a mental illness and 74 percent had substance abuse problems. In addition, female offenders are more likely to experience poverty, homelessness, and health problems as compared to the general female population or to their male imprisoned counterparts (Broner et al., 2009; Freudenber, Daniels, Crum, Perkins, & Richie, 2005; Gido & Dalley, 2009; James & Glaze, 2006). Again, these obstacles in combination with issues associated with mental illness and comorbidity dramatically increase the likelihood of recidivism and adherence to criminal lifestyles for jailed female offenders. This is especially so for female inmates who received treatment for their mental health disorders but not for their trauma-related experiences (Jordan et al., 2002).

Finally, the most recent comprehensive study of the prevalence of serious mental illness among jail inmates found the rate for male inmates was 14.5 percent, compared to the rate for jailed females of 31 percent (Steadman, Osher, Robbins, Case, & Samuels, 2009, p. 761).

IMPLICATIONS FOR TREATMENT

Treatment Programs for Jailed Women

The U.S. Supreme Court has determined that prisoners have a constitutional right to adequate mental health treatment as provided under the 5th Amendment (due process) and 8th Amendment (cruel and unusual treatment) (Osher, Steadman, & Barr, 2003; Steadman et al., 2009; Trestman et al., 2007).[2] However, "adequate care" was not clearly defined by the Court, leaving it to the states to determine what is *adequate* (American Psychiatric Association, 2000). Despite the dramatic growth in jail populations and the legal mandate to provide treatment to increasing numbers of mentally ill confined in them, jails continue to be underfunded and understaffed, particularly when addressing the mental health and addiction needs of offenders (Trestman et al., 2007).

It is apparent that women's higher rates of mental illness, comorbidity, and trauma call for a different role for local jails that house them (Osher et al., 2003; Steadman et al., 2009; Trestman, et al., 2007). Jails are primarily funded locally and do not typically have access to a reliable stream of state and federal funding. In times of economic "downturn" when local tax revenues decrease, jail budgets typically reduce costs in the areas of prisoner assessment and programming (Kubiak, Beeble, & Bybee, 2009). As Trestman (2007) and his associates suggest, "the combination of limited mental health resources, rapid turnover of unsentenced offenders, and the substantial stress of dislocation from community care, support, and resources, places adults [especially females] detained in jails at-risk of clinically significant distress and functional impairment" (p. 491).

Intake and continued assessment   Offenders are primarily placed in jails after they have been arrested. They are held for short periods of time pending their arraignment, trial, conviction, or sentencing. Jails also serve as holding facilities for mentally ill persons who are awaiting transportation to appropriate mental health facilities (James & Glaze, 2006). Essentially, individuals in jail may be held only a few hours until bond is posted, or as much as one year upon their conviction. Thus, the nature of jails is dramatically different when compared to prisons. By far, jails have higher *daily* admissions and releases of offenders than prisons (James, 2004). Jail administrators and correctional officers are more often confronted with inmates whose mental "stability" deteriorates quickly upon their incarceration (Harrison & Rogers, 2007). As a result, inmates become more difficult to manage and to discipline and staff become frustrated with little understanding of the causes and methods to apply to such behaviors (Dalley & Michels, 2009; Kubiak, Beeble, & Bybee, 2009). The most recent national Bureau of Justice Statistics study (James & Glaze, 2006) found that 28 percent of U.S. jail inmates identified with a mental illness had disciplinary problems, as compared to only 13 percent of the inmates who were not identified with a mental illness (p. 10).

Compounding the inmate's mental health problems further is the potential for inmate suicidal gestures or completed suicides (Blaauw et al., 2002; Harrison & Rogers, 2007). In fact, the previously cited report on suicides by the Bureau of Justice Statistics (James & Glaze, 2006) concludes that almost half of all jail suicides occurred during the inmate's first week, with suicide rates particularly concentrated on the first and second day of jail admission. Suicides were also concentrated after 60 days of admittance—24 percent (p. 8). Based on these data, *timely* and *continued* assessment is essential to suicide prevention (Kubiak et al., 2009). Yet, research from the last 12 years shows that inmates who are mentally ill or who are at-risk for attempted or completed suicides are largely undetected during intake or throughout their period of incarceration (Charles et al., 2003; Harrison & Rogers, 2007; Teplin et al., 2005).

> One likely cause of the lack of services during incarceration, or a continuum of care that follows them into the community, is the absence of a consistent screening process that occurs immediately during or closely following booking into the jail. Important to note that screening is the first step in identifying mental health needs, preceding more in-depth assessment and costly evaluation by mental health professionals. (Kubiak et al., 2009, p. 2)

Research also suggests that jails particularly fail to identify and treat mental illness, substance abuse and suicidal ideation among jailed women, creating further problems for managing this population. In fact, it is not uncommon for the women's mental health symptoms to escalate after jail incarceration (Dalley & Michels, 2009; Kubiak et al., 2009; Trestman et al., 2007). Unfortunately, there are no national statistics gathered to report the actual number of jails that *consistently* provide assessment of mental health, addiction, and suicidal ideations. An early national study of jails found that 88 percent of the 1,500 jails surveyed provided some type of assessment for mental illness, although the assessment instrument's quality and reliability varied greatly (Veysey et al., 1998). More recent studies have confirmed that this trend continues in today's jails; that is, a variety of assessment instruments are in use. More importantly, some of the more common instruments in use may not be effective in identifying at-risk individuals for symptoms of mental illness, suicidal ideations, or other risk factors (i.e., trauma, comorbidity, unemployment, and marital status) (Kubiak et al., 2009; Trestman, 2007).

For example, the Referral Decision Scale is one of the more common assessment instruments used in jails to identify inmates who have major mental illnesses (Harrison & Rogers, 2007; Veysey et al., 1998). The Referral Decision Scale is a 14-item questionnaire that takes 5 minutes to administer. However, two studies cite a weakness associated with this instrument in that it measures only *chronic* mental health disorders rather than the inmate's current or acute symptoms (Veysey et al., 1998). Harrison and Rogers (2007) also stated that it lacked rigor in identifying high suicide risks.

In contrast, Harrison and Rogers (2007) found that the Mental Disorder Suicide Intake Screening (MDSIS) instrument was effective in identifying high-risk suicidal offenders. This instrument consists of 12 interview items and 7 associated observation items. It can be administered in less than 5 minutes and is inexpensive to purchase. Although the findings are promising regarding the effectiveness of the MDSIS, additional testing is recommended by the researchers to support the validity of the MDSIS.

Another instrument, the Brief Jail Mental Health Screen (BJMHS), has been shown to be a reliable instrument in identifying mental illnesses for both men and women in jail. The Screen is an 8-item instrument that can be administered in less than 5 minutes (Steadman et al., 2009). Two recent studies conducted by Steadman and his colleagues (2007, 2009) have indicated that it was highly accurate in identifying women who had serious mental illnesses. In the first study involving 10,562 male and female jail inmates, the BJMHS correctly identified 80 percent of males and 72 percent of females as mentally ill. Their later assessment in 2009 confirmed these findings as well.

As previously discussed, offender mental health symptoms are often exacerbated in jail, and offenders may exhibit symptoms that are not associated with their chronic mental illness (Veysey, Steadman, Morrissey, Johnson, & Beckstead, 1998). This also has treatment implications for those inmates who are unidentified as at-risk for mental health symptoms and suicidal ideations and are also less likely to receive treatment (and intervention). In fact, the most recent national study on mentally ill jailed inmates found that only 7 percent of them received therapeutic treatment for mental health problems (James & Glaze, 2006). Ironically, this same study also reported that 23 percent of inmates in prison nationally were receiving treatment for mental health problems, even though prisons had a lower rate of mentally ill offenders (56 percent) as compared to jails (64 percent). Developing and administering reliable assessment tools to identify at-risk women as well as providing gender-responsive programming for jailed women has not advanced greatly in the last 20 years (*A call to action,* p. 5).

JAIL DIVERSION AND CONTINUITY OF CARE

Each year, more than 10 million people are incarcerated in jails, of which three quarters will be released in a matter of hours to as long as 12 months (Freudenber, Daniels, Crum, Perkins, & Richie, 2005). Yet, public scrutiny has largely been focused on the 600,000 people returning to society from prison, rather than the 7 million returning from jail. From 2000 to mid-2006, the number of adult females in local jails increased by 40 percent, compared to a 22 percent increase for adult males (James & Glaze, 2006). The average daily female jail population is 98,577 (James, 2004). Essentially, more than three quarters of these women will return home within a year's time without having their pre-jail mental health issues addressed (Freudenber, Daniels, Crum, Perkins, & Richie, 2005; Harrison & Rogers, 2007). For the greater number of these women, unsuccessful or inadequate treatment extends to the community and is associated with re-entry back to jails or prisons.

Although the "ACA's [American Correctional Association's] standards for mental health treatment in jail settings describe essential treatment components, research into treatment efficacy for incarcerated women is scarce" (Haywood et al., 2000, p. 321). Existing data suggest that, with a few exceptions, treatment modalities in jails continue to be male-oriented (Haywood et al., 2000). However, as this chapter illustrates, female inmates required specialized treatment targeting their trauma and related mental health and comorbidity disorders (Battle et al., 2005; Green et al., 2005; James & Glaze, 2006).

One major obstacle confronting jail programming is the very short periods of time individuals spend in the jail (less than 72 hours for those who are awaiting bail or initial appearances in court or who are serving short sentences). Thus, those individuals who are on the "fast track" (jailed for less than 72 hours) or subject to the unpredictable nature of jail discharges are clearly more difficult to target for treatment/intervention (Osher et al., 2003, p. 80). In sum, shorter periods of time in jails require more rapid assessments, treatment/interventions, and transitional planning. However, "this challenge may be offset by the fact that jail inmates are less likely than state prisoners to have lost contact with treatment providers [and significant others/families] in the community" (Osher et al., 2003, p. 80).

Most mental health and correctional experts agree that given the complexity of women offenders' problems, a gender-responsive program must include the following essential components (Bloom & Covington, 2009; Charles et al., 2003; Steadman et al., 2009; Teplin et al., 1997):

- *Case management:* Particularly in large, highly populated jails, case management is essential in addressing the needs of female offenders. Given the added concerns of child care, housing, and continuation of treatment facing women leaving jail, the case manager should be responsible for tracking initial assessments, types of treatment/interventions provided and response to treatment. Based on this information, the case manager should refer women to the appropriate services to ensure continuity of treatment/intervention and support in the community upon her release. As experts in mental health and corrections assert, given the unique needs of these women, treatment must be in-depth and continue well beyond their time spent in jail (Bloom & Covington, 2009; Green et al., 2005; Osher et al., 2003; Pollock, 1998).

Some states, like Maryland, have totally invested in transitional case management services at the jail level, with at least one case manager in each local jurisdiction who screens jailed mentally ill individuals and monitors them through release to community-based service providers (Conly, 1999, p. 9). During the last seven years, there have been major federal and state initiatives launched to divert the seriously mentally ill from jails. A recent review of the effectiveness of intensive case management (ICM intervention) has found it to be an essential component of jail diversions for the seriously mentally ill but not sufficient to prevent their return to the system (Loveland & Boyle, 2007).

- *Trauma:* Reinforcing safety to women (both environmentally and psychologically) is the first stage of treatment for trauma victims (Herman, 1997 as cited in Bloom and Covington, 2009). Trauma may result in skewed perceptions that may impact how these women interact with jail staff and participate in programs/interventions. Support includes educating women on their symptoms of mental illness, offering techniques for coping with their symptoms (relaxation, breathing exercises), and validating their responses as normal reactions to trauma.[3] The most recent report of the National Leadership Forum on Behavioral Health/Criminal Justice Services emphasizes that "Gender-specific services that reflect a trauma-informed culture must be developed in all institutional and community services to respond to the frighteningly high rates of mental illness among women in contact with the criminal justice system (*A call to action,* 2009, p. 5).

- *Addiction:* Gender-specific issues related to addiction (including the social, physiological, and psychological consequences of addiction and factors related to the onset of addiction) should be the focal point of addiction treatment (Bloom & Covington, 2009). Many women entering jails experience withdrawal symptoms and are physically and psychological distressed. Therefore, it is necessary to provide them with coping skills to handle the withdrawal. In extreme cases, they also may need to be seen by a physician to further evaluate their withdrawal symptoms. The National GAINS Center has acknowledged the success of the Wicomico County Maryland Phoenix Project as an on-site jail diversion program model for its integrated mental health and substance abuse treatment for women (*Addressing the Needs*, 1999).

- *Mental illness/suicidal ideation:* Women at risk for mental illness and/suicidal ideation should be under close supervision, since 80 percent of suicides occur within the inmate's cell (Mumola, 2005). In addition, since women may lack an understanding of their mental health symptoms, educating women about their mental illnesses could reduce anxiety-provoking behaviors such as suicide. In addition, systematic treatment throughout their incarceration and *after* their release is essential (Charles et al., 2003).

- *Health:* While this chapter did not focus specifically on the health care needs of women, it is widely known that female offenders often have poor health as a result of drug use and its associated lifestyle (Pollock, 1998). For example, because women have a higher rate of IV drug abuse, they are also at greater risk for contracting HIV/AIDS as compared to male offenders. Therefore, women need to be treated for chronic and often life-threatening health problems.

Most importantly, studies have found that a history of mental illness and addiction and the failure to address these problems is one of the strongest predictors of recidivism for women offenders who are being released into the community (Gido & Dalley, 2009; Holfreter & Morash, 2003).

TRANSITIONAL CARE: CONTINUITY OF SERVICE AND TREATMENT

Between 1998 and 2003, SAMHSA (CMHS) federal funding for persons with co-occurring mental illness and substance abuse disorders resulted in the screening and assessment of almost 2,000 dual diagnosed individuals, diverting 1,000 of these from the jail setting (*What can we say*, 2004, p. 3). Significantly, diverted participants were "more likely to be female, have a primary diagnosis of schizophrenia or a mood disorder with psychotic features . . . and be less functionally impaired (p. 5). The previously cited Wicomico County Maryland jail diversion program resulted in the hiring of eight permanent jail trauma specialists, training for criminal justice staff throughout the state in identifying and educating jailed women on child abuse, as well as other initiatives to serve women and their children (Conly, 1999, p. 3).

The APIC Model

Based on earlier studies, the American Association of Community Psychiatrists continuity of care guidelines (2001) and the American Psychiatric Association Task Force (2000), Osher and his associates (2003) designed the APIC Model, a transitional planning tool now considered a "best practice re-entry approach" for jailed inmates with co-occurring disorders. This model provides realistic and "doable" treatment objectives and goals that most if not all jail facilities and communities could incorporate into their system for offender care. It is a tool most applicable for meeting the needs of jailed mentally ill women as profiled throughout this chapter.

The APIC Model is designed to incorporate the offender's admittance into jail, initial assessment treatment/intervention, coordination of treatment/resources (*prior* to the inmate's release), and to coordinate services for when the inmate is released into the community. Thus, the APIC Model is a continuum of care model and is presented in Table 1:

TABLE 1   The APIC Model

Item	Description
Assess	**A**ssess the inmate's clinical and social needs and public safety risks
Plan	**P**lan for the treatment and services required to address the inmate's needs
Identify	**I**dentify required community and correctional programs responsible for postrelease services
Coordinate	**C**oordinate the transition plan to ensure implementation and avoid gaps in care with community-based services

Adapted from: Osher, Steadman, & Barr, 2003, p. 83.

As with most continuum of care models, there must be a commitment from all social and criminal justice systems in the community that have the potential for providing services to the offender. This calls for mental health and addiction agency systems, the social welfare system and the criminal justice system to work together and divide treatment responsibilities (Osher et al., 2003). The division is particularly important to ensure that offender treatment services are not duplicated. As emphasized above, timely strategies for assessment, treatment/intervention, and transitional planning will vary depending on the length of time spent in jail. However, at the very least, for those "fast track" offenders who spend 72 hours or less in jail, assessment, crisis intervention, and transitional planning must be completed before the inmate is released. Osher et al. (2003) recommend that a "team or person" follow the inmate's case throughout the time of confinement to establish a rapport with the offender so that the offender will be more accepting of the treatment and intervention in jail, but also upon her release. Some states such as New York have developed case manager systems within jails because of the complicated needs that offenders present and to also ensure that offenders are appropriately treated (Osher et al., 2003).

Not surprising, as Osher et al. (2003) and other experts (Bloom & Covington, 2009; Gido & Dalley, 2009; Pollock, 1998) assert, inmates will often need a great deal of coordination of services prior to their release in order to be successfully integrated into the community. These often include many if not all of the following (Osher et al., 2003):

- Housing
- Integrated outpatient and inpatient mental health and addiction treatment
- Health referrals for medication for mental illness and health problems
- Food and clothing
- Transportation
- Child care
- Social services (financial assistance—Medicaid, SSI, TANF, etc.)

Osher et al. (2003) also recommend that prior to the offender's release, the community case manager transitioning the offender have a face to face meeting in the jail to begin building the necessary rapport with the woman. Offenders will be more likely to follow through with treatment recommendations if this is done. The APIC Model is a continuum of care model that provides specific components that if provided "as a whole or in part are likely to improve outcomes for persons with co-occurring disorders who are released from jails."

Trauma-Informed Integrated Models for Jailed Women Offenders   Having documented that the profile of a jailed woman is a female offender most likely to need treatment for mental and substance abuse disorders, *has a state of the art trauma-informed integrated model of treatment been developed for jailed women*?

The most positive response comes from the research by the GAINS Center studies on jail diversion programs for persons with co-occurring disorders (*What can we say*, 2004). Two monographs have been published focusing on the creation of such a treatment model and examples of programs in existence (Gillece, 2002; Hills, 2004).

In addressing model interventions for female offenders, The GAINS Center notes the current trend in increased availability of clinical resources to address trauma/PTSD interaction with other mental and substance use disorders (Hills, 2004, p. 14). Diversion and specialty courts* are advised to review and then adapt gender-responsive policies and procedures, screening and assessment approaches, treatment plans, assessments of woman/child transportation, educational and vocational needs, and the *introduction of co-occurring disorder and trauma-specific treatment services*. Related peer support and counseling programs, sex abuse support and domestic violence support groups, parenting classes and school system assistance are also on the list of what is involved in *a fully-integrated model of treatment* (Hills, 2004, pp. 16–18). *Continuity of care* is the final component to ensure long-term continuous care and a break in the cycle of recidivism (p. 18).

It is clear that most jail jurisdictions in the United States will not have the resources to take on this integrated model of care. SAMHSA funding has established several such "model programs" in Hartford, Bristol, and New Britain, Connecticut, as well as the TAMAR and TAMAR Children's Program in Maryland (Trauma, Addictions, Mental Health, and Recovery) that, with other funding sources from the state and private foundations, have served jail (and state prison) pregnant and post-partum women offenders and their children and women who experienced trauma (Gillece, 2002, pp. 3–4; Hills, 2004).

The second response comes from the leadership of the Center for Gender and Justice, LaJolla, CA. Co-Director Dr. Stephanie Covington notes that "while gains have been made in the understanding and development of gender-responsive services, there is still a lag in implementation."**

Dr. Covington has developed a *Women's Integrated Treatment Model (WIT)*, focused on the linkage between substance abuse and trauma (Covington, 2008). One completed study in a residential program for women with their children reported a significant decrease in both depression and trauma at the completion of a 17-session *Helping Women Recover* program, followed by the *Beyond Trauma* program (Covington et al., 2008).***

The WIT model is undergoing further evaluation studies through funding by the National Institute on Drug Abuse (Covington et. al., 2008, p. 397).

CONCLUSION

In conclusion, this chapter provides a summary of the needs of jailed mentally ill women that are just beginning to be addressed with emerging models of integrated, trauma-informed treatment for co-occurring disorders. As initial research underwrites the success of these services, they represent a glimmer of hope as jails and prisons across the United States continue to incarcerate mentally ill women, the most invisible offenders in today's "new asylums."

REFERENCES

A call to action: Ending and American Tragedy: Addressing the needs of justice-involved people with mental illnesses and co-occurring disorders (September, 2009). National Leadership Forum on Behavioral Health/Criminal Justice Services. Delmar, NY: The CMHS National GAINS Center.

Addressing the needs of women in mental illness/substance use disorder jail diversion Programs: The Wicomico County Maryland Phoenix Project. (1999). Delmar, NY: The National GAINS Center.

*A comprehensive review and discussion of mental health and related special courts is beyond the scope of this chapter—Ed.
**Personal Communication: Dr. Stephanie Covington, February 14, 2010—Ed.
***See Messina et al., 2010 forthcoming, where these training curricula were delivered by Dr. Covington in a state prison setting. The experimental pilot study found the GRT participants to exhibit greater reductions in post-release drug use, longer residential aftercare, and lower recidivism than participants in a standard prison therapeutic community—Ed.

BACHRACH, L. L. (October, 1984). Deinstitutionalization and women: Assessing the consequences of public policy. *American Psychologist*, 39 (10), 1171–1177.

BATTLE, C. L., ZLOTICK C, NAJAVITIS, L. M., & WINSOR C. (2002). Posttraumatic stress disorder and substance use disorder among incarcerated women. In P. C. Ouimette & P. J. Brown (Eds.). *Trauma and substance abuse: Causes, consequences, and treatment of comorbid disorders* (pp. 209–226). Washington, D.C.: American Psychiatric Association.

BLAAUW, E., ARESMAN, E, KRAAIJ, V, WINKEL, F. L., & BOUT, R. (2002). Traumatic life events and suicide risks among jail inmates: The influence of types of events, time period, and significant others. *Journal of Traumatic Stress*, 15 (1), 9–16.

BLOOM, B. & COVINGTON, S. (2009). Addressing the mental health needs of women offenders. In R. L. Gido & L. Dalley (Eds.). *Women's mental health issues across the criminal justice system* (pp. 160–176). Upper Saddle River, NJ: Pearson Prentice Hall.

BLOOM, B. & COVINGTON, S. (2003). *Gender-responsive strategies: Research, practice, and guiding principles for women offenders*. Washington, D.C.: National Institute of Corrections.

BONNER, R. L. (2000). Correctional suicide prevention in the year 2000 and beyond. *Suicide and life-threatening behavior*, 30 (4), 370–377.

BRONER, N., KOPELOVICH, S., MAYRL, D. W., & BERNSTEIN, D. P. (2009). The contribution of childhood trauma to adult psychopathology in dually diagnosed detainees: Implications for gender-based jail and reentry on trauma-informed services. In R. L. Gido & L. Dalley (Eds.). *Women's mental health issues across the criminal justice system* (pp. 129–159). Upper Saddle River, NJ: Pearson Prentice Hall.

BROWN, G. K., BECK, A. T., STEER, R. A., & BRISHAM, J. R. (2000). Risk factors for suicide in psychiatric outpatients: A 20-year prospective study. *Journal of Consulting and Clinical Psychology*, 68 (3), 371–377.

CHARLES, D. R., ABRAM, K. M., MCCLELLAND, G. M., & TEPLIN. L. A. (February, 2003). Suicidal ideation and behavior among women in jail. *Journal of Contemporary Criminal Justice*, 19 (1), 65–81.

CONLY, C. (1999). *Coordinating community services for mentally ill offenders: Maryland's Community Criminal Justice Treatment Program*. NIJ Program Focus. Washington, D.C.: National Institute of Justice, U.S. Department of Justice.

COUNCIL OF STATE GOVERNMENTS (2002). Criminal justice/mental health consensus project. http://consensusproject.org/the_report/. Retrieved January 23, 2010.

COVINGTON, S. (November, 2008). Women and addiction: A trauma-informed approach. *Journal of Psychoactive Drugs*. SARC Supplement 5, 377–382.

COVINGTON, S., BURKE, C., KEATON, S., & NORCOTT, C. (November, 2008). Evaluation of a trauma-informed and gender-responsive intervention for women in drug treatment. *Journal of Psychoactive Drugs*. SARC Supplement 5, 387–397.

COWELL, A. J., BRONER, N., & DUPONT, R. (2004). The cost-effectiveness of criminal justice diversion programs for people with serious mental illness co-occurring with substance abuse. *Journal of Contemporary Criminal Justice*, 30 (3), 292–315.

DALLEY, L. & MICHELS, V. (2009). Women destined to failure: Policy implications of the lack of proper mental health and addiction treatment of female offenders. In R. L. Gido & L. Dalley (Eds.). *Women's mental health issues across the criminal justice system* (pp. 177–195). Upper Saddle River, NJ: Pearson Prentice Hall.

DITTON, P. (1999). *Prior abuse reported by inmates and probationers*. Washington, D.C.: Bureau of Justice Statistics/U.S. Department of Justice.

Diverting the mentally ill from jail (July, 2009). Presentation at National Association of Counties Conference. Washington, D.C.: Pretrial Justice Institute.

DUBE, S. R., ANDA, R. F., FELITTI, V. J., CHAPMAN, D. P.,WILLIAMSON, D. F., & GILES, W. H. (2001). Childhood abuse, household dysfunction, and the risk of attempted suicide throughout the life span. *Journal of the American Medical Association*, 286 (24), 3089–3096.

Emerging strategies for the mentally ill (April, 2000). http://www.ncjrs.org/html/bja/mentalhealth/intro.html. Retrieved November 6, 2005.

Freudenber, N., Daniels, J., Crum, M., Perkins, T., & Richie, B. (2005). Coming home from jail: The social and health consequences of community reentry for women, male adolescents, and their families. *American Journal of Public Health*, 95 (10), 1725–1735.

Frontline: The New Asylums: Deinstitutionalization (2005). Special Reports: A psychiatric Titanic/PBS. Retrieved January 3, 2010.

Gido, R. (2002). Turnstile justice: American corrections in the new millennium. In R. L. Gido & T. Alleman (Eds.). *Turnstile justice: Issues in American corrections* (pp. 1–5). Upper Saddle River, NJ: Prentice Hall.

Gido, R. & Dalley, L. (2009). *Women's mental health issues across the criminal justice system.* Upper Saddle River, NJ: Pearson Prentice Hall.

Gillece, J. (2002). *Leaving jail: Service linkage and community re-entry for mothers with co-occurring disorders.* In Davidson, S. & Hills, H. (Eds.) *Series on women with mental illness and co-occurring disorders.* Delmar, NY: The National GAINS Center.

Goldkamp, J. S. (1978). *Inmates of American jails: A descriptive study.* Working Paper Albany, NY: Criminal Justice Research Center.

Grading the states: A report on America's health care system for serious mental illness (2006). Arlington, VA: National Alliance for Mental Illness.

Green, B. L., Miranda, J., Daroowalla, A., & Siddique, J. (2005). Trauma, exposure, mental health functioning, and program needs of women in jail. *Crime and Delinquency*, 51 (1), 131–151.

Harm, N. J. (April, 1992). Social policy on women prisoners: An historical analysis. *Affilia*, 7, 90–108.

Harrison, K. S. & Rogers, R. (2007). Axis I screens and suicide risk in jails: A comparative analysis. *Assessment*, 14 (2), 171–180.

Haywood, T. W., Kravitz, H. M., Goldman, L. B., & Anderson, F. (2000). Characteristics of women in jail and treatment orientations. *Behavior Modification*, 24 (3), 307–324.

Herman, J. (1997). *Trauma and recovery.* (Revised Edition). New York: Basic Books.

Hills, H. (2004). *The special needs of women with co-occurring disorders diverted from the criminal justice system.* Delmar, NY: The National GAINS Center.

Holfreter, K. & M. Morash (2003). The needs of women offenders: Implications for correctional programming. *Women and Criminal Justice*, 14, 137–160.

Ill equipped: U.S. prisons and offenders with mental illness (2003). Human Rights Watch. www.hrw.org/reports/2003/USA. Retrieved February 6, 2010.

Jail diversion for the mentally ill: Breaking through the barriers (1990). Washington, D.C.: The National Coalition for the Mentally Ill in the Criminal Justice System.

Jails and the mentally ill: Issues and analysis (September 17, 2009). Sacramento, CA: The California Corrections and Standards Authority.

James, D. (2004). *Profile of jail inmates special report.* Washington, D.C.: Bureau of Justice Statistics, U.S. Department of Justice.

James, D. & Glaze, L. (2006). *Mental health problems of prison and jail inmates.* Washington, D.C.: Bureau of Justice Statistics, U.S. Department of Justice.

Jordan, B., Schlenger W., Fairbank, J., & Caddell, J. (2002). Lifetime uses of mental health and substance abuse treatment services by incarcerated women felons. *Psychiatric Services*, 53 (3), 317–325.

Kposowa, A. J. (2001). Unemployment and suicide: A cohort analysis of social factors predicting suicide in the U.S. national mortality study. *Psychological Medicine*, 31, 127–138.

Kubiak, S. P., Beeble, M. L., & Bybee, D. (2009). Testing the validity of the K6 in detecting major depression and PTSD among jailed women. *Criminal Justice and Behavior*, 20 (10), 1–17.

Lamb, H. R. & Bachrach, L. L. (August, 2001). Some perspectives on deinstitutionalization. *Psychiatric Services*, 52, 1039–1045.

Lord, E. (August, 2008). The challenge of mentally ill female offenders in prison. *Criminal Justice and Behavior*, 35 (8), 928–942.

Loveland, D. & Boyle, M. (2007). Intensive case management as a jail diversion program for people with a serious mental illness: A review of the literature. *International Journal of Offender Therapy and Comparative Criminology*, 51 (2), 130–150.

Luchins, A. S. (1992). The cult of curability and the doctrine of perfectibility: Social context in the nineteenth century American asylum movement. *History of Psychiatry*, iii, 203–220.

Lurigio, A. J. (2000). Helping the mentally ill in jails adjust to community life: A description of a post-release ACT Program and its clients. *International Journal of Offender Therapy and Comparative Criminology*, 44 (5), 532–548.

Mauer, M. & King, R. S. (2007). *A 25-year quagmire: The "war on drugs" and its impact on American Society*. Washington, D.C.: The Sentencing Project.

McCampbell, S. W. (April, 2005). *The Gender-responsive strategies project: Jail applications*. Washington, D.C.: National Institute of Corrections, U.S. Department of Justice.

Mechanic, D. & Rochefort, D. A. (Spring 1992). A policy of inclusion for the mentally ill. *Health Affairs*, 11 (1), 128–150.

Merolla, D. (2008). The war on drugs and the gender gap in arrests: A critical perspective. *Critical Sociology* 34 (2), 255–270.

Messina, N. & Grella, C. (2006). Childhood trauma and women's mental health outcomes in a California prison population. *American Journal of Public Health*, 96 (10), 1842–1848.

Messina, N., Grella, C, Cartier, J., & Torres, S. (March, 2010 forthcoming). A randomized experimental study of gender-responsive substance abuse treatment of women in prison. *Journal of Substance Abuse Treatment*. Author Manuscript, 1–17.

Minton, T. D. & Sabol, W. J. (March, 2009). *Jail Inmates at Midyear 2008*. Washington, D.C.: Bureau of Justice Statistics, U.S. Department of Justice.

Molnar, B. E., Berkman, L. F., & Buka, S. L. (2001). Psychopathology, childhood sexual abuse and other childhood adversities: Relative links to subsequent suicidal behavior. *U.S. Psychological Medicine*, 31, 965–977.

Morgan, C. (September, 1981). Developing mental health services for local jails. *Criminal Justice and Behavior*, 8 (3), 259–273.

Morrissey, J. P. & Goldman, H. H. (March, 1986). Care and treatment of the mentally ill in the United States: Historical developments and reforms. *ANNALS of the American Academy of Political and Social Science*, 484 (1), 12–27.

Mumola, C. (2005). *Suicide and homicide in state prisons and local jails special report*. Washington, D.C.: Bureau of Justice Statistics, U.S. Department of Justice.

Osher, F., Steadman, H., & Barr, H. (2003). A best practice approach to community reentry from jail for inmates with co-occurring disorders: The APIC model. *Crime and Delinquency*, 49 (1), 79–96.

Palermo, G. B., Smith, M. B., & Liska, F. J. (1991). *Jails versus mental hospitals: A social dilemma*, 35 (2), 97–106.

Petersilia, J. (2003). *When prisoners come home: Parole and prisoner reentry*. New York: Oxford University Press.

Pfeiffer, M. B. (2007). *Crazy in America: The hidden tragedy of our criminalized mentally ill*. New York: Carroll and Graf publishers.

Pollock, J. (1998). *Counseling women in prison*. Thousand Oaks, CA: Sage Publications.

Psychiatric services in jails and prisons: A task force report (2000). Washington, D.C.: American Psychiatric Association.

Reynolds, M. (2008). The war on drugs, prison building, and globalization: Catalysts for the global incarceration of women. *NWSA Journal*, 20 (2), 72–95.

Ross, P. H. & Lawrence, J. E. (2009). Women in jail: Mental health care needs and service deficiencies. In R. L. Gido & L. Dalley (Eds.). *Women's mental health care issues across the criminal justice system* pp. 117–128. Upper Saddle River, NJ: Pearson Prentice Hall.

Sclull, A. T. (January, 1976). The decarceration of the mentally ill: A critical view. *Politics and Society*, 6, 173–212.

SLATE, R. N. & W. W. JOHNSON (2008). *Criminalization of mental illness: Crisis and opportunity for the justice system*. Durham, N.C.: Academic Press.

STEADMAN, H., OSHER, F. ROBBINS, P., CASE, & SAMUELS, S. (2009). Prevalence of serious mental illness among jail inmates. *Psychiatric Services*, 60 (6), 761–765.

STEADMAN, H., ROBBINS, P., ISLAM, T., & OSHER, F. (2007). Revalidating the brief jail mental health screen to increase accuracy for women. *Psychiatric Services*, 58 (12), 1598–1601.

TALBOT, J. A. (October, 2004). Deinstitutionalization: Avoiding the disasters of the past. *Psychiatric Services*, 55, 1112–1115.

TEPLIN, L., ABRAM, K., & MCCLELLAND, G. (1997). Mentally disordered women in jail: Who receives services? *American Journal of Public Health*, 87, 604–609.

TEPLIN, L., ABRAM, K., & MCCLELLAND, G. (1996). Prevalence of psychiatric disorders among incarcerated women: Pretrail jail detainees. *Archives of General Psychiatry*, 53 (6), 505–512.

TEPLIN, L. MCCLELLAND, G., ABRAM, K., & WEINER, D. (August, 2005). Crime victimization in adults with severe mental illness: Comparison with the national crime victims survey. *Archives of General Psychiatry*, 62 (8), 911–921.

TORREY, E. F. (1997). *Out of the shadows*. New York: Wiley & Sons, Inc.

TRAVIS, J & WAUL, M. (Eds.) (2003). *Prisoners once removed: The impact of incarceration and re-entry on children, families, and communities*. Washington, D.C.: The Urban Institute Press.

TRESTMAN, R. L., FORD, J., ZHANG, W., & WIESBROCK, V. (2007). Current and lifetime psychiatric illness among inmates not identified as acutely mentally ill at intake in Connecticut's jails. *The Journal of the American Academy of Psychiatry and the Law*, 35, 490–500.

VEYSEY, B. M. (1998). Specific needs of women diagnosed with mental illness in U.S. jails. In B. L. Levin, A. K. Blanck, & A. Jennings, (Eds.). *Women's mental health services: A public health perspective* pp. 368–389, Thousand Oaks, CA: Sage Publications.

VEYSEY, B. M., STEADMAN, H. J., MORRISSEY, J. P., JOHNSEN, M., & BECKSTEAD, J. W. (1998). Using the referral decision scale to screen mentally ill jail detainees: Validity and implementation issues. *Law and Human Behavior*, 22, 205–215.

What can we say about the effectiveness of jail diversion programs for persons with co-occurring disorders? (April, 2004). Delmar, NY: TAPA Center of Jail Diversion/GAINS Center.

WHITE, M. D., GOLDCAMP, J. S., & CAMPBELL, S. P. (September, 2006). Co-occurring mental illness and substance abuse in the criminal justice system: Some implications for local jurisdictions. *The Prison Journal*, 86 (3), 301–326.

Women and depression fact sheet (2000). National Mental Health Information Center. www.mental-health.samsha.gov/publications/allpubs/fastfact6/default.asp. Retrieved January 20, 2010.

Women in the criminal justice system: An overview (2006). Washington, D.C.: The Sentencing Project.

ENDNOTES

1. See Bureau of Justice Statistics Special Report, *Suicide and Homicide in State Prisons and Local Jails* (2005), that found the 1983 suicide rate for jail inmates was (129 per 100,000 inmates); by 1993 that rate had been cut by more than half (54 per 100,000 inmates), and illness/natural cause (67 per 100,000) had become the most common cause of jail deaths. By 2002, the jail suicide rate (47 per 100,000) had fallen to nearly a third of the 1983 rate (p. 1).

2. See *Estelle v. Gamble*, 429 U.S. 97 103 (1976); See also *Ruiz v. Estelle*, 503 F. Supp. 12156, 1323 (S.D. Tex. 1980).

3. See Dalley & Michels (2009). "Women Destined to Failure: Policy Implications of the Lack of Proper Mental Health and Addiction Treatment of Female Offenders." In *Women's Mental Health Issues Across the Criminal Justice System*. Pearson Prentice Hall. Upper Saddle River, New Jersey for strategies to offer women coping with trauma. See also Covington, S. (2003) *Beyond trauma: A healing journey for women*. Center City, MN: Hazelden.

28

"Doing HIV/AIDS Time"

Health Care Needs of Women Prisoners

Barbara H. Zaitzow, Ph.D., and Mark M. Lanier, Ph.D.

Women are the fastest-growing population incarcerated in the United States due to more expansive law enforcement efforts, punitive drug sentencing laws, and post-conviction barriers to reentry that uniquely affect women. One of the by-products of the "confinement era" within criminal justice is the influx of ill and generally unhealthy female offenders into this nation's correctional institutions. In addition to tuberculosis (TB) and Hepatitis B (HBV) and C (HBC), one of the pressing public health concerns facing correctional systems today is human immunodeficiency virus (HIV)/Acquired Immune Deficiency Syndrome (AIDS). While no segment of the incarcerated population is immune to this infection, an alarming number of female inmates have been shown to test positive for HIV at higher rates than male inmates (Maruschak, 2009). The high rates of HIV infection and AIDS among women offenders are essentially the result of intravenous drug use, trading sex for drugs and money, sexual abuse, living under conditions of poverty, and other gender-specific conditions of their lives including the physiological finding that the female anatomy makes them more prone to HIV infection. The resulting challenges associated with caring for women with HIV/AIDS impact correctional healthcare providers for disease management and infection control within correctional facilities, but also for the prisoners' home communities where they will need health care, drug and alcohol rehabilitation services, housing, and employment. This chapter presents recommendations for effective HIV/AIDS policy, programming, and establishing partnerships between practitioners and academicians in a variety of domains. Epidemiological Criminology (EpiCrim) provides the explicit merging of health with justice issues and consequently may serve as a bridging framework for each of these domains. This chapter concludes with highlights of effective HIV/AIDS prevention interventions as well as programming options for women prisoners.

INTRODUCTION

Women's issues and prison issues are part of the same struggle. Prison issues are important because individual women are being oppressed by prison and, in a wider context, because the judicial/prison system exists to support the larger power structure that oppresses us all. The popularity of imprisonment as a sanctioning tool has significant implications for corrections, which traditionally has allocated few resources to ensure the enforcement of institutional safeguards (e.g., including policies and procedures) to keep incarcerated women safe from harm while serving prison time. Moreover, the exponential growth in the number of incarcerated women in America's prisons and jails has resulted in thousands of women being trapped in a system that is designed for and dominated by men (Zaitzow, 2004). On any given day, more than 100,000 women are living behind prison or jail walls. Thousands of these women are dependent on correctional authorities for their health care, and correctional authorities are legally obligated to meet those needs. The reality of the situation, however, is that even when the constitution is on their side, HIV-positive women (and men) behind bars face special difficulties in exercising those rights and receiving the regimented treatment necessary to control the disease.

It would not be fair to say that imprisonment is worse for women than it is for men. But, imprisonment is definitely *different* for women because women are different from men. To what extent, if any, a prison's policies address HIV/AIDS-related services is one important indicator of how that facility treats women in its custody. There is a need to address how institutional policies contribute to the continuation of the disadvantaged status of women prisoners. After all, women's prisons increase women's dependency, stress women's domestic rather than employment role, aggravate women's emotional and physical isolation, can destroy family and other relationships, engender a sense of injustice (because they are denied many of the opportunities and legal protections available to male prisoners), and may indirectly intensify the pains of imprisonment. Nowhere is this more evident than in the provision of health care to imprisoned women and, in particular, the provision of health care to women prisoners with HIV/AIDS (Lanier, 2006). This chapter illustrates the increasing convergence of public health care issues with that of correctional systems in particular and criminal justice in general. As more people become incarcerated—as more women are locked up—programmatic challenges associated with variations in prison populations' health concerns will only increase in magnitude. Here, Epidemiological Criminology (EpiCrim) is put forth as a means by which to link public health efforts with criminal justice policy and practice. This chapter also explores the healthcare needs of imprisoned women and highlights the need for legislative and regulatory protection for HIV/AIDS-infected women prisoners in the United States.

DEMOGRAPHIC AND CRIME-RELATED CHARACTERISTICS OF FEMALE OFFENDERS

Since mandatory sentencing began in the mid-1980s, the United States prison system has seen a dramatic upswing in incarceration rates. The staggering reality is that 1 in 100 adults are in prison. Currently, women represent the fastest growing segment of prison and jail populations even though their crime rate is not increasing dramatically. Among women ages 35–39 years old, one in 265 are incarcerated. The racial breakdown in that age group shows that one in 355 are white women, one in 297 are Hispanic women, and one in 100 are black women (Pew, 2008).

Incarcerated women are characteristically women of color, poor, unemployed, and single mothers of young children. Imprisoned women tend to have fragmented families, other family members involved with the criminal justice system, significant substance abuse issues, and multiple physical and mental health problems (Bloom, Owen, & Covington, 2003). Since 1995, the number of women being held in the nation's prisons has increased 50%, and at year-end 2007, 115,779 women were imprisoned in state or federal prisons—6.9% of the total prison population (Bureau of Justice Statistics, 2008).

Nearly half of all women in prison are currently serving a sentence for a non-violent crime. The increased incarceration of women appears to be the outcome of forces that have shaped U.S. crime policy over the past two decades: government policies prescribing simplistic, punitive enforcement responses for complex social problems; federal and state mandatory sentencing laws; and the public's fear of crime (even though crime in this country has been on the decline for nearly a decade). "Get tough" policies intended to target drug dealers and so-called kingpins has resulted not only in more women being imprisoned, but also women are serving longer and harsher prison sentences.

Far from the stereotypes of incarcerated women in B-movies and on television, imprisoned women are the most vulnerable in the country: people who have health issues, have suffered abuse, and typically have been unable to get the help they need. Within these numbers are mothers, sisters, daughters, and friends, all facing the variety of health issues any woman "on the outside" may face. The only difference is that they face them while incarcerated with prison policies being weighed against their health care rights.

WOMEN WITH HIV AND AIDS

According to the Centers for Disease Control and Prevention (CDC), between 2000 and 2004, the estimated number of AIDS cases in the United States increased 10 percent among females and 7 percent among males. In 2004, women accounted for 27 percent of the 44,615 newly reported AIDS cases among adults and adolescents. HIV disproportionately affects African-American and Hispanic women. Together they represent less than 25 percent of all U.S. women, yet they account for more than 79 percent of AIDS cases in women.

Worldwide, more than 90 percent of all adolescent and adult HIV infections have resulted from heterosexual intercourse. Women are particularly vulnerable to heterosexual transmission of HIV due to substantial mucosal exposure to seminal fluids. This biological fact amplifies the risk of HIV transmission when coupled with the high prevalence of non-consensual sex, sex without condom use, and the unknown and/or high-risk behaviors of their partners.

Women suffer from the same complications of AIDS that afflict men but also suffer gender-specific manifestations of HIV disease, such as recurrent vaginal yeast infections, severe pelvic inflammatory disease (PID), and an increased risk of precancerous changes in the cervix including probable increased rates of cervical cancer. Women also exhibit different characteristics from men for many of the same complications of antiretroviral therapy, such as metabolic abnormalities.

In addition to facing unique clinical issues, women living with HIV/AIDS are often challenged by social isolation, poverty, discrimination, and lack of access to quality health care.

Frequently, women with HIV infection have great difficulty accessing health care and carry a heavy burden of caring for children and other family members who may also be HIV-infected. They often lack social support and face other challenges that may interfere with their ability to obtain or adhere to treatment. As daunting as these factors are for those who are not imprisoned, these challenges along with institutional constraints add additional barriers that impact women prisoners in profound ways.

HIV/AIDS IN CORRECTIONAL FACILITIES

Just as the "war on drugs" was gaining momentum in the 1980s, the AIDS crisis broke. By targeting the people who are at high risk for HIV, whether because of drug use or sex work, anti-drug policy has dramatically increased the number of people with HIV behind bars (Maddow, 2002). Each year, as many as one in every four Americans living with HIV passes through a correctional facility. At year-end 2008, a reported 22,144 inmates held in state or federal prisons were HIV positive or had confirmed AIDS, accounting for 1.5% of the total custody population. When these figures are broken down by gender, among states that reported data for both 2007 and 2008, 1.5% (20,231) of male inmates and 1.9% (1,913) of female inmates (Maruschak, 2009) were diagnosed with HIV/AIDS. Moreover, a disproportionate number of those individuals are people of color. African-Americans represent 45 percent of all new HIV infections in the United States, and HIV/AIDS is the number one killer of African-American women ages 25 to 44. The soaring incarceration rates for African-American women and an increase in HIV infection rates, in general, in the black community hint at a connection between the two disturbing trends. But it has been hard to explain the exact relationship between being HIV-positive and being incarcerated. Too many people wrongly believe that skyrocketing HIV rates among black people result from drug-addicted inmates engaging in indiscriminate sexual activity behind bars, acquiring HIV in prison or jail then taking it home and spreading it through an unsuspecting community. On the contrary, a 2006 CDC study noted that about 90 percent of people with HIV in the state of Georgia's male prison population were HIV positive before they were incarcerated. The statistics were similar for women.

While many inmates with HIV contract infections prior to incarceration or through non-sexual activity in prison, such as needle-sharing, tattooing, HIV risk behaviors and occasionally HIV infection during incarceration have been reported (Krebs, 2006). However, sparse information is available on HIV transmission within large state prison systems in general and on inmates' risk modification after HIV diagnosis, HIV transmission networks, or antiretroviral drug resistance in particular. We do know that sexual violence behind bars occurs and is a clear source of transmission (Hensley, Castle, & Tewksbury, 2003; Tewksbury & West, 2000). According to the best available research, as many as 20 percent of male prisoners have been pressured or coerced into sex, and ten percent have been raped (Macher et al., 2006). In one women's facility, more than a quarter of the women studied said they had been pressured into sex (Hammett, 2006). Contracting HIV through sexual assault can transform even a relatively short time in prison into an un-adjudicated death sentence. Even where sex is consensual the absence of condoms and dental dams within prisons and jails makes HIV infection a very real threat.

It should be noted, however, that no precise count of HIV cases in prisoners is available as brief incarceration, particularly in jails, limited access to health care, and lack of universal screening hinder the identification and diagnosis of inmates with HIV infection (Lanier, 2006). Also, arrestees may choose not to declare their HIV/AIDS status. Hence, even with the implementation of new record-keeping systems by various governmental agencies, our knowledge about HIV/AIDS in correctional settings must be understood within the context of reporting constraints.

WOMEN PRISONERS DOING HIV/AIDS TIME

Prison is a dehumanizing experience that erodes people's self-esteem and taxes their resilience. When one group controls another, the unbalanced social structure makes things volatile. Add to that the perception of prisoners as "bad women" who deserve whatever they get, and it is easy to imagine how prisons can become a fertile breeding ground for both physical and mental abuse. Female inmates make adjustments to prison life. For many, faced with years behind walls, life becomes a strategy of survival. The most obvious fact of life in women's prisons is that women are dependent on the officers for virtually every daily necessity including food, showers, medical care, feminine hygiene products, and for receiving "privileges" such as phone calls, mail, visits, and attending programs. To ask another adult for permission to do things or to obtain items of a personal nature is demeaning and humiliating (Zaitzow, 2006).

Although life is rarely easy for any inmate, it is often made even more difficult by being HIV-positive. McTighe (2009) discovered that people with HIV in prison often leave sicker than when they were first locked up. This is because prisons fall short of addressing essential HIV needs. Prisoners lack medications. They lack knowledgeable doctors who can prescribe effective regimens. They lack regular delivery of medications (interruptions can lead to drug resistance). When they do take their medications, prisoners often lack proper food, and that can amplify side effects. They lack drug resistance testing, which can cause them to take an ineffective HIV regimen. And they lack viral load and CD4 tests, which can show the medications are working and, therefore, provide incentives for patients to adhere to medication routines. Part of this is due to the inherent conflicts between custody and treatment. For example, if a facility is in a "lock down" mode then medications cannot be dispersed and treatment may be denied. Even "normal" daily routines make it difficult to take medications according to mandated times since most HIV medications, to be most effective, must be taken in a specified time period. The custodial mandates of security and control of imprisoned populations, at times, conflicts with the health care needs of those who reside in their custody.

Another common dilemma is that co-infection with Hepatitis C—a common killer of HIV-positive people behind bars—may go untreated because prisons do not want or are unable to pay for expensive Hepatitis C medications.

In addition, inmates with HIV/AIDS are often segregated, abused, and stigmatized. A daily diet of indignities, coupled with the added pressures of being HIV-positive, can trigger a slew of emotional and health care issues that can exacerbate their current HIV status and which they often carry with them when they go home to their communities. Moreover, with limited access to learning more about the disease, many HIV-positive prisoners are in the dark about what HIV/AIDS is, how to treat it, and how to avoid getting, or spreading, it both inside—and outside—prison walls (Zaitzow, 2001).

The continued stigmatization of prisoners with HIV/AIDS makes inmates less likely to get tested while inside, or, if they do, to disclose their HIV/AIDS status upon release. Fear of stigma may also prevent people from seeking treatment. When people do not seek treatment, they are more likely to have higher viral loads and are, therefore, more sexually infectious. But, there are success stories of women who have fought for their dignity and life and the lives of others. Meet Waheedah Shabazz-El, an HIV-positive ex-prisoner whose diagnosis and time in prison fuel her work as an HIV educator and advocate.

Waheedah Shabazz-El, a loyal and devoted employee of the U.S. Postal Service for more than 20 years, made decent money and lived an exciting life that included a big house in the West Oak Lane section of Philadelphia. She drove a Nissan Elantra, dressed in only designer clothes, vacationed in the Bahamas and enjoyed plenty of male companionship. She also did drugs, mostly marijuana and crack cocaine—and she was no stranger to the more expensive powdered stuff. "Back in the day, my house was the party place," Shabazz-El says. "There were always a lot of people, music, drugs and alcohol at any time of the day or night." One day in 2003 an army of Philadelphia police officers raided her house, rounded up everyone, and took them to jail. Shabazz-El was sentenced to six months at the Cambria Correctional Center (CCC) in Philadelphia for drug possession with intent to distribute a controlled substance. She was placed on five years probation. Shabazz-El discovered that she was HIV-positive during a routine examination at the correctional facility. "Discovering that I was HIV-positive and being in jail at the same time was almost too much to bear," she says.

"The tester blurted out that I was HIV-positive in an open room with a large window and no curtains," she recalls. "Everyone walking by could see me. I sobbed and wanted to kill myself." Uneducated about HIV/AIDS, Shabazz-El never thought that the disease could directly affect her (Townes, 2008).

Some might have written off Shabazz-El, a 55-year-old, Muslim, HIV-positive mother of three and grandmother of four. But she did more than survive prison and HIV—she fully integrated into society after doing her time. Perhaps that's why her story of survival resonates so deeply. But it's an important story because it illuminates the link between incarceration and the spread of AIDS. As noted by McTighe (2009), although HIV is transmitted by specific behaviors, research indicates that the risk of HIV is more closely related to socioeconomic inequities. Specifically, one's position on the economic social ladder impacts the available choices and ability to protect one's health both inside and outside of prison.

MEDICAL SERVICES FOR WOMEN IN PRISON

Women in custody often require more medical attention than men. This is especially true for women who enter prison pregnant and require prenatal care. Their pregnancies are often considered to be high-risk, and many are complicated by drug and alcohol abuse, smoking, and sexually transmitted infections. These factors, if combined with poor social support and histories of abuse, put these women and their newborns at even greater risk for increased perinatal and postnatal morbidity and mortality.

Adequate provision of medical care remains one of the most pressing problems facing women prisoners. While women suffer many of the same illnesses as do their male counterparts—HIV/AIDS, hepatitis, sexually transmitted diseases, tuberculosis, and other communicable diseases and mental illnesses—they have specific health needs, mainly related to reproductive health. Naturally, these needs vary according to a woman's age and situation. For example, the needs of a young girl, a pregnant woman, a woman who has just given birth, a mother accompanied by young children, or an elderly woman are all different. A review of existing studies on health care services for women inmates reveals that (1) access to treatment for both general and drug-related health problems is limited; (2) the health care provided to women prisoners is mediocre; and (3) prison medical professionals are often under-skilled (Maeve, 1999; Lindquist & Linquist, 1999). Such issues have been the subject of litigation. Many of these cases led to consent decrees mandating better treatment, but a lack of follow-up on the enforcement of the legal rulings has allowed the unlawful treatment of imprisoned women to continue.

Throughout the 1980s—and continuing to present—a number of lawsuits were filed on behalf of women prisoners who had been seen as "complainers" and denied adequate health care and protection by prison staff members. Many of these cases led to consent decrees mandating better treatment. In the past few years, prisons nationwide have been confronted with the challenges associated with treating the growing numbers of HIV positive inmates, and most have been slow to respond to their new, complex, and ever-changing needs. In some prisons, campaigns by AIDS activists and class-action lawsuits alleging gross violations of inmates' civil and constitutional rights have instigated change. Faced with court-ordered consent decrees requiring them to improve their medical care, some prison systems, such as the Connecticut Department of Corrections, have made impressive improvements. Others, such as the Alabama Department of Corrections, remain health-care backwaters, where treatment and care are dangerously inadequate. As a result, the type of health care for those with HIV in state prisons ranges from relatively good to cruelly poor. Since inmates are often moved from one institution to another and denied access to basic information and services, such uneven care poses a significant health hazard, not just to prisoners but to the public at large as well.

EPIDEMIOLOGICAL CRIMINOLOGY

As we have shown in the preceding narrative, correctional health care is a multifaceted, complicated, expensive, and often elusive goal. Luyt (2005) noted that:

> Irrespective of how one approaches the matter, HIV in prisons worldwide remains part of the public health and influences the wider community directly. Reaching critical proportions, this public health crisis requires urgent attention and action from all governments. Governments have a moral and ethical obligation to prevent the spread of HIV/AIDS in society, including the prison society. (cited in Lanier, 2009:63)

Virtually all inmates will, at some point, be released. It is not only ethically mandated, but economically imperative, to therefore reduce the spread of HIV/AIDS among this vulnerable and often defenseless (Hensley, Castle, & Tewksbury, 2003) population. Academicians' first objective should be the creation of theoretical principles that may guide this effort.

Government, correctional administrators, staff, academic researchers, and ultimately incarcerated women may all benefit from a unifying perspective, as opposed to the contemporary inherent conflict between health care and custody. This may assist with focusing attention as Luyt argues. Epidemiological Criminology is one means of providing a linking framework. EpiCrim was developed as a bridging mechanism and synthesizing framework between public health and criminal justice. Lanier (2009) noted that "it is ironic that the core of both criminal justice and public health—the correlates to crime and to health disparities—are identical (e.g., poverty, minority status, lack of education, family history, neighbourhood characteristics, geography, and other psycho-social indicators, etc.) . . . the contemporary practice is that crime causation and health behaviours are only discussed from a particular ideological perspective . . . (p. 64)." The dilemmas faced by female inmates with HIV/AIDS provide an excellent illustration of the utility of EpiCrim and how the two disciplines can mutually benefit from a uniting focus.

EpiCrim has a brief but meaningful history. Emile Durkheim first identified crime as being a "health" issue and used crime as an indicator of the health of an overall society. Donald Cressey first linked the two domains of Epidemiology and Criminology in 1960. Akers and Lanier then outlined the need for and coined the phrase "Epidemiological Criminology" in 2009. The term was operationally defined and applications listed later the same year (Lanier, 2009). According to Lanier, "Epidemiological Criminology is the explicit merging of epidemiological and criminal justice theory, methods and practice. Consequently, it draws from both criminology and public health for its epistemological foundation. As such, EpiCrim involves the study of anything that affects the health of a society, be it: crime, flu epidemics, global warming, human trafficking, substance abuse, terrorism or HIV/AIDS" (2010:72). Recently, two major seminars have been convened on the subject (Pack, 2008), several university courses have been taught, and several publications have appeared. Perhaps it is an idea whose time has come. For years health care workers and correctional staff have been at odds and served competing agendas. The advent of the HIV/AIDS crisis has forced each to reconsider the value of the other. The seriousness of HIV/AIDS at many levels—the fiscal cost to government, the social cost to society and the individual loss of life and health for victims, as well as the impact this has on family members and friends of those with HIV/AIDS—necessitates a reconceptualization of how we address health care issues within the criminal justice system. The unique problems facing incarcerated women only strengthen the argument for this synthesization. There are several reasons why this is important.

First, there is the fact that correctional systems have Machiavellian (2004) means of defining and using health (Lanier, 2010). Polizzi questioned if "the health concerns of incarcerated individuals are fundamentally predicated upon the way in which these individuals find themselves constructed by the meaning-generating process of the criminal justice system. If we construct this group of individuals as dangerous but damaged, our strategies of intervention can become overly focused on the assessment of risk and less on the humanity of the individual" (Lanier, 2010: 78). This observation provides further affirmation of the conflicting demands of treatment and custody. Incarcerated women, compared to men, are even more negatively impacted by the terms and conditions of their incarceration.

Second, as we have stressed throughout this chapter, compared to men, women have greater health care needs and requirements (Zaitzow, 2005). This is due to female physiology and economic inequalities. Both public health and criminal justice staff need greater sensitivity to this fact. Rather than making the reality worse for women, by utilizing EpiCrim, and thereby working in conjunction with each other instead of in opposition, health workers and corrections staff can focus more on the different needs of female inmates. The programs cited below have all made strides toward addressing these inequalities.

EXAMPLES OF RESEARCH/PROGRAMS THAT HELP

Good prison health is good public health. The vast majority of people committed to prison eventually return to the wider society therefore reducing the transmission of HIV in prisons is an important element in reducing the spread of infection in society outside of prisons. Protecting and promoting the health of people in prison benefits not only the prisoners, but also increases workplace health and safety for prison staff. Researchers in the United States continue to do cutting-edge research, including on interventions to improve access to care, reduce transmission risk behavior and recidivism in HIV-infected prisoners following release. Some examples of programs that have been proven to be beneficial to HIV-infected women (and male) prisoners include the following:

- In New York, WORTH (Women on the Rise Telling HerStory) is an advocacy/consultant group comprised of formerly and incarcerated women, who have the expertise and understanding to engage, navigate, and challenge policies and perceptions concerning incarcerated women. As a well-organized and sustainable group, WORTH is a visible and powerful voice for formerly and currently incarcerated women in public conversations and policy debates (King, 2009).

- Also, in New York, Project UNSHACKLE is a groundbreaking cross-movement effort that was launched in May 2008 and links people who are formerly imprisoned, community members, researchers, HIV policy advocates, prison reform and social justice organizers, coalition-building veterans, and other allies working together at the intersection of HIV and mass imprisonment (McTighe, 2009).

- In North Carolina, preliminary results of the BRIGHT (Bridges to Good Health and Treatment) study indicate that a case management intervention for HIV-infected prisoners spanning the periods prior to and after prison release is successful in increasing access and utilization of HIV medical care, reducing emergency room utilization, and reducing early recidivism. This confirms that more intensive release preparation programs spanning the continuum of both pre- and post-release are needed, and that these programs should not only provide HIV-related care and support services, but a broader spectrum of support including substance abuse prevention and treatment and community supports (Wohl, 2008).

- In Rhode Island, Project Bridge engages HIV-positive inmates while they are still in prison. By linking HIV-positive prisoners to community-based medical care prior to release, 95 percent of ex-offenders were retained in health care for a year after being released from incarceration. In addition to encouraging the continuum of medical care, Project Bridge links participants with community resources that help them find housing, employment, transportation, and other social services (Holmes, 2007).

As a community, it is important to address the needs of women leaving prison. Many women leave prison in denial of their HIV status and continue with behaviors that endanger their own health and that of others. Increasing HIV infection rates in women are linked to another reproductive health issue, intimate partner violence, and intimidation. Many women in heterosexual relationships with men do not feel empowered to ask or demand that a condom be used. Coordinators of HIV programs for women report a common story: women feel that their male partners will not allow condom use or open discussion of safe sex measures, without it turning into accusations of her infidelity, or worse. Many women experience physical abuse and partner rape, while trying to assert their right to be in control of their own bodies, health, and reproductive rights.

CONCLUSION

Incarcerated women face a myriad of social, economic, psychological, and medical problems. Infection and the threat of infection with HIV and AIDS create additional stress. Obviously, sane, humane, and realistic care of women infected with HIV is necessary. However, it is also critical that effective preventive programs be implemented and evaluated. Due to the vast diversity found among incarcerated women, no single strategy can be considered effective. Instead, a combination of efforts including but not limited to case management, individual counseling, group sessions, and constant reinforcement of HIV prevention education for incoming inmates and reinforcement of HIV prevention messages for all inmates is essential to reducing HIV risk among prisoners. Moreover, specialized programmatic needs for HIV-infected inmates and a system that ensures their uninterrupted medical care during incarceration and upon release should be public health priorities. Finally, correctional agencies should partner with public health agencies to assess and improve existing HIV prevention and treatment programs for all inmates. This partnership is where EpiCrim may prove most useful. EpiCrim, once further developed, may well facilitate the merging of theoretical and multi-disciplinary strategies and applications, which may prove to be more effective with women under correctional supervision, and with community-based contributions (Pack, 2008). Both Public Health and Criminal Justice researchers have embraced the concept but for it to be most effective it must be applied where most needed—correctional settings. This mixture of strategies and use of a theoretical basis may prove effective with women under correctional supervision.

POLICY RECOMMENDATIONS

Under intense public scrutiny, prisoner health is and will continue to be covered by the news. News coverage has a strong impact on how policymakers perceive social issues and influences legislative decision-making. A strategic media advocacy plan should be put forth to take advantage of current news coverage to place issues important to women prisoners onto the agendas of policymakers. As advocates become more effective at promoting healthier public policies towards female prisoners, policymakers will have to take note. Among the issues that require immediate attention:

1. Developing alternatives to imprisonment

The living conditions and health care services faced by women, especially in overcrowded prisons, are such that efforts to promote HIV prevention and education may not be very effective. Therefore, any comprehensive strategy in response to HIV in prison settings should seek to reduce overcrowding as it can create conditions that can lead to sudden outbreaks of violence, including sexual violence. Prisons can be responsible for major damages and disruption to the lives of vulnerable women and their families. Most of them are in prison for non-violent offenses and pose no risk to the public. Therefore, consideration should be given to the development and implementation of non-custodial strategies for women, particularly during pregnancy, or when they have young children.

2. Preventing violence, in particular sexual violence

Prison authorities are responsible for combating gender-based sexual violence, the exploitation of vulnerable prisoners, and all forms of prisoner victimization. They must, therefore, take all measures necessary to protect women from sexual violence, including training personnel to identify and stamp out such abuses, by ensuring adequate staffing levels, training, effective surveillance, and disciplinary sanctions.

3. Providing safe and appropriate health services

Health services, including gynecological and dental clinics, should be appropriately equipped, supplied, and maintained. Sexual and reproductive health care services should be available for women in prison. Health care service providers should be trained to follow the guidelines of universal precautions to prevent the transmission of HIV through medical practices (injections, procedures, or examinations).

4. Providing equivalent health services to those available in the community

It is important to recognize that people in prison are entitled, without discrimination, to health care, including preventive measures, of a standard equivalent to that available in the outside community. This is important, both for prisoners and for the community outside prisons, as the vast majority of people who enter prisons will eventually return to the community.

5. Encouraging and supporting the participation of women prisoners

The involvement of women prisoners in developing and providing health services increases the capacity of prisons to respond to HIV and AIDS. For example, health authorities in prison should encourage and support the development of peer-based education initiatives and educational materials designed and delivered by prisoners themselves. Prison authorities should also encourage the development and support of self-help and peer-support groups that raise the issues of HIV and AIDS from the perspective of the women themselves.

6. Providing a safe environment for prison staff

All prison staff and health care providers as well as anyone in regular contact with prisoners should be given timely access to relevant information and educational material on HIV, universal precautions, and post-exposure prophylaxis (PEP). In addition, prison staff and their families should be provided with the information on modes of transmission and prevention of HIV, medical and psychological treatment availability for those with sexually transmitted infections, and also on voluntary counseling and testing.

7. Promoting effective national responses to meet the special needs of women in prisons

It is essential that the correctional administrative system in any given jurisdiction work and collaborate very closely with other relevant community groups, government agencies, and national AIDS programs for addressing the health, social, and other special needs of prisoners in general, and in particular, for the women in prisons.

Gender-sensitive legislative frameworks, penal policies, and prison rules are necessary to ensure that the needs of women in prisons are addressed in a systematic and sustainable way. A comprehensive framework should also address their psychological, social, and physical welfare—all crucial in managing and minimizing HIV transmission in prisons. Tailored programs addressing gender-specific issues need to be formulated to respond to the challenges of women in prisons—in particular programs targeted at women who face multiple vulnerabilities and who are living with HIV. Every effort should be made to involve women prisoners and non-governmental organizations in the development of HIV prevention, treatment, care, and support programs in prison, as well as to create links between prison programs and community HIV prevention and treatment services.

8. Increasing professional capacity-building opportunities on HIV in prisons

Regular capacity-building programs of prison staff are essential to build knowledge on HIV prevention, treatment, care, and support for women in prison. This training should not be limited to general prison staff but also to the medical service providers (medical doctors, nurses, lab technicians, and pharmacists, etc.), drug dependence counselors, social workers, and other professionals who may contribute to HIV programs in prisons. These programs should also be included as part of the regular training curricula for prison staff. In addition to HIV, issues such as gender-specific needs, human rights with a particular focus on its link to HIV, and stigma and discrimination should also be part of the curriculum. Women prisoners should be trained as peer educators to provide information, prevention commodities, care, and support to other inmates.

9. Monitoring and evaluation

HIV risks for women in prison and responses provided should be monitored and evaluated on a regular basis. Research on HIV and women in prisons should be encouraged and conducted to fill the evidence gap on these issues.

A CALL TO ACTION

The prevalence of HIV infection and drug dependence among women prisoners, combined with a variety of risk-taking behaviors, makes prisons a high-risk environment for the transmission of HIV. Ultimately, this may contribute to HIV epidemics in the communities to which women prisoners return on their release. Women who did not receive testing, counseling, and treatment in prison are unlikely to have the knowledge, skills, or access to the resources needed upon release to protect themselves and their loved ones. In short, infectious disease among detainees is a serious public health issue.

All inmates need more and better services to help them make successful transitions to the community, resist relapse to substance use, and avoid a return to high-risk behavior and criminal activity. This is especially true for women inmates with HIV disease, who might benefit from a range of services including continuity of health care, stable housing, drug treatment, assistance gaining eligibility for benefits, and job training and placement services.

Correctional systems cannot be expected to take full responsibility for addressing the serious public health problem or exploiting the important public health opportunity represented by the related epidemics of infectious diseases in correctional facilities. Public health departments, community-based organizations such as AIDS service organizations and community-based substance abuse treatment agencies, and other community-based providers have critical roles to play as well. There is increasing collaboration among these entities, but there remain far more opportunities and needs for working together. There are differences in philosophy and priority among these organizations, to be sure, but there are also growing examples of overcoming the barriers and forging successful collaborations to provide needed services to inmates and releasees as well as to benefit the public health and serve the interests of society at large.

REFERENCES

AKERS, T. & LANIER, M. (2009). "Epidemiological criminology: Coming full circle." *American Journal of Public Health* 99(3):397–402.

BLOOM, B., OWEN, B., & COVINGTON, S. (2003). "Gender-responsive strategies: Research, practice, and guiding principles for women offenders." Washington, DC: U.S. Department of Justice, National Institute of Corrections, June. [Online]. Available: http://www.nicic.org/pubs/2003/018017.pdf.

CRESSEY, D. (1960). "Epidemiology and individual conduct: A case from criminology." *Pacific Sociological Review*, 3:47–58.

DURKHEIM, E. (1951). *Suicide*. New York, NY: The Free Press.

HAMMETT, T. M. (2006). "HIV/AIDS and other infectious diseases among correctional inmates: Transmission, burden, and appropriate response." *American Journal of Public Health* 96(6):974.

HENSLEY, C., CASTLE, T., & TEWKSBURY, R. 2003. "Inmate-to-Inmate Sexual Coercion in a Prison for Women." *Journal of Offender Rehabilitation*, 37(2): 77–87.

HOLMES, L. (October & November 2007). "Project Bridge: A transitional case management program for HIV-infected men and women." Infectious Diseases in Corrections Report. Available [online]: http://www.idcronline.org/archives/octnov07/spotlight.html

KING, D. (May 8, 2009). "Bills seek to help women prisoners rebuild lives." Gotham Gazette.

KREBS C.P. (2006). "Inmate factors associated with HIV transmission in prison." *Criminology and Public Policy* 5(1):113–136.

LANIER, M. (2006). *The impact of HIV/AIDS on criminology and criminal justice*. The International Library of Criminal Justice, Criminology and Penology. Ashgate Publishing: Hampshire, England.

LANIER, M. (2009). "Epidemiological criminology: A critical cross-cultural analysis of the advent of HIV/AIDS." *Acta Criminologica* 22(2):60–73.

LANIER, M. (2010). "Epidemiological criminology (EpiCrim): Definition and application." *Journal of Philosophical and Theoretical Criminology*. 2(1):63–103.

LUYT, W. (2005). "A critical View on HIV/AIDS in South African prisons within the framework of the Dublin declaration on HIV/AIDS in prisons." *Acta Criminologica* 18(2):71–89.

LINDQUIST, C. & LINDQUIST, C. (1999). "Health behind bars: Utilization and evaluation of medical care among jail inmates." *Journal of Community Health* 24(4):285–303.

MCTIGHE, L. (2009). "Project UNSHACKLE: Confronting HIV and mass imprisonment." Available online: http://www.champnetwork.org/media/Project_UNSHACKLE_Organizing_Toolkit_PILOT_1-09_Laura-McTighe.pdf

MACHER A., KIBBLE D. & WHEELER D. (2006). "HIV transmission in correctional facility." *Emergency Infectious Disease* 12(4):669–671.

MADDOW, R. (2002). "Pushing for progress: HIV/AIDS in prisons." Washington, DC: National Minority AIDS Council.

MAEVE, M. K. (1999). "Adjudicated health: Incarcerated women and the social construction of health." *Crime, Law, and Social Change* (31):49–71.

PACK, R. (2008). Criminology and Public Health: Toward Common Ground. Invited presentation for EPI 1892XX: Epidemiologic Criminology. American Public Health Association; San Diego, CA.

TEWKSBURY, R. & WEST, A. (2000). Research on Sex in Prison during the Late 1980s and Early 1990s. *The Prison Journal* (80), 4: 368–378.

TOWNES, G. (November 2008). "Free at Last?" *POZ Magazine*. Available [On-Line]: http://www.poz.com/articles/hiv_prisoners_feature_2261_15439_2_of_5.shtml

WOHL D. A. (October–November 2008). "BRIGHT." Piedmont HIV Health Care Consortium.

ZAITZOW, B. H. (December 2001). Whose Problem Is It Anyway?: Women Prisoners and HIV/AIDS. *International Journal of Offender Therapy and Comparative Criminology*. (Vol. 45, No. 6): 673–690. Appears in M.M. Lanier (2006). *The Impact of HIV/AIDS on Criminology and the Criminal Justice System*, *Criminology and Penology*. Hampshire, England: Ashgate Publishing (Chapter 11).

ZAITZOW, B. H. (Fall/Winter 2004). Pastel Fascism: Reflections of Social Control Techniques Used With Women in Prison. *Women's Studies Quarterly*'s special Winter 2004 issue on "Women, Crime, and the Criminal Justice System" (Vol. 32, Num. 3 & 4): 33–48.

ZAITZOW, B. H. Women's Health. (2005). *Encyclopedia of U.S. Prisons and Correctional Facilities* (Vol. 2): 1047–1050. Sage Publications.

ZAITZOW, B. H. (Spring 2006). "Empowerment not entrapment: Providing opportunities for incarcerated women to move beyond 'doing time.' "*Justice Policy Journal*, 3, (1). Available at: http://www.cjcj.org/jpj/index.php.

29

Women's Reentry Experiences

Resources from Network Relationships

Hoan N. Bui

This study examines network relationships, network resources, and their roles in women's successful reentry experiences. Women in the study were not only able to access emotional and material support from their families but they also received assistance from parole officers, the clergy, friends, and treatment peers. Separations caused by incarceration and prison experiences contributed to women's shift to pro-social networks that provided positive resources important for successful outcomes. These findings highlight the significance of resources from both strong-ties and weak-ties relationships, but material assistance was not often available from intimate relationships, and parole services seemed to be ineffective in connecting women to work, substance abuse treatment opportunities, and other sources of material assistance. The study suggests the importance of enhancing women's ability to expand their pro-social relationships and access needed resources as well as ensuring that these resources are available and accessible in the community.

INTRODUCTION

Social networks can play a significant role in women's reentry experiences. Families as a major element of personal networks have been considered important to prisoners and the prevention of recidivism (Hairston, 2003). Serving as anchors to life in the community while inmates are in prison, families offer a source of stability, support, and encouragement during the difficult transition from prison to home (Travis & Waul, 2003). While maintaining positive family contacts during and following incarceration can foster integration into the community and reduce recidivism (Petersilia, 2003; Waul, Travis, & Solomon, 2002), returning prisoners often place a greater value on the role of family in their reintegration process after prison release than they did when they were still incarcerated (Naser & La Vigne, 2006). Indeed, most persons released from prison manage to maintain some ties to adult family members that they can rely on for understanding, advice, material aid, company, and affection (Flavin, 2004). For many former prisoners, emotional support and immediate housing assistance after release are the two most critical aspects of family support (Travis & Waul, 2003), and strained familial relationships always pose a challenge to female offenders (Covington, 1998). The importance of families also lies in their long-term availability of assistance. While government services and interventions are short term, families are around for the long haul and can provide access to potential resources that can be helpful in the integration process (Flavin, 2004).

Prior studies on women's experiences with post-incarceration adjustment and recidivism have focused on the role of families and intimate relationships (Bonta, Pang, & Wallace-Capretta, 1995; Brown, 2006; Danner, Blown, Silverman, & Vega, 1995; Griffin & Armstrong, 2003; Henriques & Manatu-Rupert, 2001; Leverentz, 2006; Miller, 1986; O'Brien, 2001; Simons, Steward, Gordon, Conger, & Elder, 2002), but less attention has been paid to the understanding of resources available from network relationships. In addition, relationships with parole officers, ex-inmate friends, treatment peers, and mentors as part of female returnees' social networks as well as resources from these weak-ties relationships have not been systematically studied. Moreover, little is understood about changes in network relationships and available resources as a result of incarceration. Imprisonment can disrupt prior relationships due to forced separations, but new relationships established in the prison setting can be a source of support and may continue after release. To fill the gap in the literature, the present study examines network relationships and resources during and after incarceration among female parolees. The goal is to improve understandings of the availability of resources from women's network relationships and their roles in women's reentry experiences.

NETWORK RELATIONSHIPS, RESOURCES, AND REENTRY EXPERIENCES

Social network literature shows that women tend to have small and less diverse social networks (Campbell & Rosenfeld, 1985). Gender experiences and social-role expectations often restrict women's opportunities for establishing social connections. Due to women's kin-keeping role, responsibility for ensuring continued family interactions, and lack of occupational opportunity, women's social networks are commonly associated with family ties, intimate relationships, neighbors, or nearby friends (Ajrouch, Blandon, & Antonucci, 2005; Curley, 2009). Involvement in the criminal justice system, however, can influence women's network relationships in different ways. A criminal label and the stigma associated with it can restrict social connections (Carter & Feld, 2004). In addition, incarceration can disrupt family ties and other relationships because of separation. Remote prison locations, a lack of transportation, and correctional policies and practices that govern contacts between prisoners and their families often impede the maintenance of family ties (Bloom, Owen, & Covington, 2003; Hairston, 2003). On the other hand, incarceration may strengthen family ties because the family may have to pull together for the well-being of female offenders' children and to help these women get back on their feet

(Arditti & Few, 2006). Prison experiences and parole programs may also stimulate new relationships and diversify women's social networks to include the clergy, prison volunteers, parole officers, treatment peers, and inmate friends (Bui & Morash, 2010).

One major aspect of social networks is the resources ensuing from network relationships, and the availability of network resources often varies with the strength of network connections (Granovetter, 1973). Strong-tie networks, marked by bonding, include intimate relationships in small and closed social circles, such as those among family members, intimate partners, relatives, and close friends who can provide an intense, multi-stranded form of support (Granovetter, 1973; Halpern, 2008). Weak-tie relationships, which involve acquaintances, serve as crucial bridges between individuals and groups and have a special role in a person's opportunity for social mobility (Granovetter, 1973). Through contacts with acquaintances, individuals make many more social connections from which they can get information and learn about opportunities. For women returning from prisons both strong-ties and weak-ties networks can be a major source of emotional and material support during the transition from prison to the larger society. Research has showed that affection, supervision, and advice from families can prevent reoffending and drug-use relapse (Dowden & Andrew, 1999; O'Brien, 2001; Slaght, 1999). Families can also provide other instrumental assistance, including transportation, child care, connections to job opportunities, food, and financial assistance, to facilitate a smooth re-integration process (Arditti & Few, 2006; O'Brien, 2001; Petersilia, 2003; Travis & Waul, 2003). Good relationships with law-abiding spouses or intimate partners can ease the reentry process when they contribute to women's financial security and reinforce their sense of competency (Leverentz, 2006; O'Brien, 2001). Moreover, law-abiding spouses and intimate partners can serve as emotional role model to prevent crime and substance use (Giordano, Cernkovich, & Schroeder, 2007).

Besides potential resources from families and intimate partners, different types of assistance may be available from relationships with parole officers, the clergy, ex-inmate friends, and treatment peers. Parole supervision is considered a resource for reintegration because community correctional officers can address offenders' needs by using state and community capital, or providing information about assistance available elsewhere (Holfreter, Reisig, & Morash, 2004; Morash, 2010). Supervision styles that promote women's transition to the free world and are responsive to women's needs have been found associated with successful outcomes (O'Brien, 2001). Religion and the clergy can play a role in the reentry process because association with religion can facilitate internal changes necessary for crime desistance (Giordano, Cernkovich, & Rudolph, 2002; Shover, 1996). Research suggests that material and spiritual supports from the clergy in prison and those from faith-based programs in the community can be a key factor in women's successful reentry (Parsons & Warner-Robbins, 2002). Despite concerns about negative influences from associations with former inmates or ex-offenders (Larson & Nelson, 1984), ex-inmate peers can serve as valuable resources for knowing the ropes and potential obstacles after release (Leverentz, 2006); they can also provide emotional support during rehabilitation treatment as well as some material assistance, including housing or shelter (Arditti & Few, 2006; O'Brien, 2001). In addition, the informal social supports women develop with each other while in prison can be helpful in creating and maintaining a non-criminal identity because they reinforce positive attempts to reestablish themselves after release from prison (O'Brien, 2001). In short, a thorough examination of strong-ties and weak-ties relationships among women returning from prison will improve understanding of the availability of resources from different types of social networks and their roles in women's reentry experiences.

METHODS

Sample and Data

The present study used a qualitative research method to capture the complexity of network relationships and resources as well as their roles in women's reentry experiences. Data were obtained from in-depth interviews conducted in 2007 with women selected from a parole program located in a mid-size city in a southern state. Women who had spent at least one year in a state prison and one year on parole were eligible to participate in the interview. The selection criterion of at least one year in prison is consistent with the amount of time necessary for women offenders to be involved in prison programs and establish new relationships, and thus it allows the study to examine the impacts of social networks in prison on women's reentry experiences. As almost half of women on parole are returned to prison within one year after release (Langan & Levin, 2002), the criterion of at least one year on parole allows the observation of a certain degree of post-release success.

At the time of sample selection, a total of 38 women met the selection criteria, and 20 women agreed to participate. During the interview process, 3 women dropped out from the study, and to maintain the target number of 20, 3 other women who had a parole time less than 12 months were included (the times these women had served on parole were 11 months, 10 months, and 3 months). To ensure that women who had been on parole for less than a year prior to the interview were indeed successful, parole records were checked 18 months after the interviews. At that point, all but 1 woman were either successfully discharged or doing fine on parole. Only 1 woman was re-arrested for a new offense, and this happened more than 3 years after her release. Thus, all of the women participants had no official record of crime for at least 21 months after their release from prison (13 women had been released for 3 years or more, and 7 women for 21 months to 3 years). Compared to the average re-arrest rates of 44% within 1 year and 59% within 3 years after prison release (Langan & Levin, 2002), the study participants can be considered successful in their reentry experience.

Data for the study were collected through retrospective interviews, which are useful for reconstructing women's past experiences from responses to questions that ask them to recall their life course. Although there are concerns about people forgetting or filtering past events, the retrospective interview is reliable when it is dealing with crucial events or transitions, such as marriage, divorce, arrest, incarceration, and release from prison (Ruspini, 2002). The interviews were conducted by two trained interviewers. Depending on the choice of the women participants, interviews were conducted in a public place or at a private room in the parole office.[1] Each interview, which lasted two to six hours, began with the women's current situations and took them backwards in time. The underlying idea is that an individual's life course can only be understood when it is placed into the context of the trajectory of his/her social life (Fetterman, 1998). Besides demographic and economic characteristics, the women were asked about their network relationships (e.g., family and intimate relationships, friends, acquaintances, and civic participations); network resources available to them prior, during, and after incarceration; and their criminal behavior prior and after incarceration.[2] Depending on the women's life circumstances, most of the interviews took place in one or two sessions, with each session lasted no more than two hours; a few interviews were extended to three sessions. Each participant was paid $25 for each interview session.

Sample Characteristics

Women in the study had diverse demographic characteristics and criminal justice records. Their ages ranged from 25 to 50 years. Thirteen women were whites; five were Blacks; one was Hispanic, and one reported a mixed racial/ethnic identification. At the time of the interview, two women had not finished high school; nine had completed high school (four of them had completed a GED program in prison); and nine had some college education (two of them took college courses in prison). Two women were married and nine were divorced, separated, or widowed. Of nine women who were never married, two lived with an intimate partner. Of 15 women who had children, six women had children under 18, though one did not have custody due to substance abuse. Most of the women worked except four, who experienced different forms of physical disabilities that prevented them from working. Most of those who worked had full-time manual or service jobs with earnings ranging from $400 to $2,500 per month, and half of these women earned above the minimum wage ($1,250–$2,500 per month).

The women had committed a wide variety of offenses, including driving under the influence of intoxicants, theft, fraud, burglary, drug offenses, robbery, and homicide. A majority of them ($n = 14$) had been charged and convicted for more than one offense, and seven had juvenile records. Prior to prison incarceration, a majority of the women ($n = 12$) had been placed on probation and had violated their probation one to six times. Most of the women ($n = 16$) had one prison incarceration, and four had two to six prison incarcerations. The time these women had spent in prison ranged from 12 months to 12.5 years. Prior to their prison experiences, a majority of the women ($n = 12$) also had one to ten incarcerations in jail, which lasted a few days to several months. Most of the women ($n = 17$) had one parole experience, and three had been on parole more than once. By the time of the interviews, most of the women ($n = 17$) had been in the community 1 to 14 years (1–3 years: 11 women; more than 3 years: 6 women); as noted above, only three women had been released less than 12 months prior to the interview.

Data Analysis and Findings

The analysis focused on resources available from women's strong-ties and weak-ties relationships during and after incarceration. The analysis was also carried out to reveal changes in network relationships and resources. Interviews with the women indicated that family relationships were far more important than intimate relationships as a source of tangible and intangible support during incarceration and after prison release. In addition, the correctional setting significantly influenced women's weak-ties relationships and network resources. Positive and supportive relationships established in prison with fellow intimates, the clergy, and mentors continued after prison and became an important source of emotional and material support. For several women, parole supervision was also an intangible resource.

Resources from Strong-Ties Networks

Intimate Relationships   Data from the study showed that husbands'/partners' character-istics influenced the availability of resources from intimate relationships during incarceration and after prison release. Prior to incarceration, most of the women participants (n = 17) were married or involved in intimate relationships. Abusive, criminal, and exploitative were com-mon characteristics of husbands/partners described by these women. A majority of the women with relationships (n = 11) reported that their husbands/partners engaged in criminal activities and were charged, convicted, and incarcerated prior to or during these women's incarceration. Of 14 women who stayed in the relationships at the time of incarceration, two thirds (n = 10) maintained some contacts with their husbands/partners while in prison. Being abandoned or divorced by husbands/partners resulted in no contact for three women, and one woman refused to contact her abusive husband with the intent to end the abusive relationship.

The women's relationships with husbands/partners during incarceration were mainly maintained through telephone calls, cards, and letters. Husbands'/partners' sporadic incomes or incarceration tended to limit personal visits and material assistance. Seven women had personal visits by husbands/partners, and the visit occurred only once for most of these women. For example, four women and their husbands/partners were incarcerated at the same time, and these women had only one visit from their husbands/partners who were brought to the visitation area by prison officials. Of those women whose husbands/partners were not incarcerated, only three received gift packages and/or money placed in their prison accounts from their husbands/partners. A few women indicated that their husbands/partners did not send money or gift packages because they were not working.

After prison release, most of the women experienced change in intimate relationships. For several women (n = 4), the abusive relationships existing prior to incarceration were dis-continued by divorce, abandonment by their husbands/partners, or husbands'/partners' decease. In addition, the separation caused by incarceration, including husbands'/partners' imprisonment, provided an opportunity for several women (n = 6) to end the abusive rela-tionships. Eleven women were involved in intimate relationships after release, including four women who stayed with their husbands/partners and seven who had new relationships. These women described the relationships as good, loving, and/or supportive, and they placed high values on the emotional and particularly material support from their husbands/partners at the beginning of the integration process. As Respondent 13 explained:

> [Husband's name] was a big support. He got me back on my feet, bought clothes, gave hous-ing and car, etc. This was a good start. He took two weeks off from work and we took care of everything, got SS card, etc. He helped me get the driver license. Without him, it was hard to get everything.[3]

Most of the women with relationships, however, did not usually get material assistance from their husbands/partners during their reentry experience. Only five women mentioned some financial support or housing assistance. In addition, only three women were able to move in with husbands/partners when they needed housing assistance upon prison release.

Family Networks   Prior to incarceration, the women's relationships with their parents and siblings were not always positive. One third of the women (n = 7) lived in households with fathers or mothers who were abusive, alcoholic, drug users, or involved in criminal activities; several women (n = 3) spent years in their early age in group homes or with relatives because of their parents' deviant and criminal behaviors. Many women (n = 6) reported strained relationships with their families because of parent-child conflicts or their own drug use. Despite these negative relationships, the women had more positive contacts and support from their close relatives than from their husbands/partners during incarceration. Most of the women, except one, frequently received cards, letters, and telephone calls from their children, parents, siblings, grandparents, and cousins. A substantial majority of the women (n = 14) reported personal visits from their relatives. Most of the women's minor children were taken care by their parents or other relatives. Child care by relatives also helped maintain family relationships as relatives often tried to take children to prison for visiting. The long distance between home and prison, the loss of custody, as well as relatives' physical health and poor economic situations often prevented personal visits and limited telephone conversations. However, most of the women were able to talk to relatives at least once a month, and several women had visits from relatives who spent several hours to almost a day driving to the prison. For example, Respondent 10 said,

> My mom, dad, two sisters and my niece came at one time. It took them 16 hours to get there (prison) for two four-hour visits, one on Saturday and one on Sunday. This was because they were out of state.

Relationships with relatives brought many tangible and intangible benefits to these women. Telephone calls, letters, cards, and personal visits provided them a great deal of emotional support during incarceration. Contacts and personal visitations also helped improve family relationships that had been strained because of their criminal activities and drug use. Positive relationships with families also entailed material assistance. Two thirds of the women (n = 13) received material support from parents, children, relatives who sent them gift packages through prison catalogs or placed money in their prison accounts.

For most of the women, positive relationships with families were maintained after prison release, and resources from family networks continued to be available. A substantial majority of the women (n = 16) indicated that the relationships with their relatives became much better, especially when they were clean. As family relationships improved, more women reported positive resources from relatives. A majority of the women (n = 13) received short-term housing support from relatives when they needed housing assistance after release; more than half of the women (n = 11) also got long-term housing assistance, financial help, or both from parents, siblings, and grandparents. Half of the women also reported emotional support from their relatives. They emphasized the significance of love and encouragement by family members and the opportunity to share their feelings to get through stressful situations. Although many of these women had received emotional and materials support from their relatives prior to and during incarceration, they considered post-incarceration assistance as particularly important in helping them rebuild their lives and keeping them out of trouble. These women talked about the importance of material assistance as follows:

> Money from aunt, uncle, and mom helped me until I got on my feed. Also housing. . . . It helped a lot just to have someone there for you. Having that support when you first get out helps a lot. It determines if you'll succeed when you get out. I've known people who haven't had the support. They ended up right back in. . . . Community resources are not important. Family support has been most important. (Respondent 11)

Mom didn't help much, but grandparents helped a lot, getting me back on my feet. They gave me car, which helped with finding jobs. These helps were very important because if they weren't there to support me I could have gone right back doing the same things as before. (Respondent 20)

Financial and emotional supports are very important. Sometimes you have good days and bad days, you need someone to talk to and get through that. If I hadn't had that I'd probably violate parole (using drugs) and be back in prison. (Respondent 9)

Resources from Weak-Ties Relationships

Parole Officers   The relationships of the women with their parole officers were, in most part, professional (job-oriented) with more emphasis on supervision but less tangible support. Referral services from parole offices were available, but the women did not consider them helpful. Although most of the women needed work at some point, they did not rely on job placement services recommended by the parole office because, as Respondent 19 said, "It was of little help." In addition, free drug treatment and computer training were available in the parole office, but only three women attended the computer training and two women the drug treatment program (other women used drug treatment programs in private clinics). Despite a lack of material and network assistance, a majority of the women participants (n = 15) indicated "good" and "supportive" relationships with their supervising officers. For these women "good relationships" meant that the officers treated them fairly and reasonably, were not mean to them, and did not cause them trouble by imposing difficult conditions. The women also considered the relationship as supportive when the officers were flexible and addressed their needs to help them succeed parole, for example, by giving them permission for going out of town, or rescheduling their report days if necessary. For several women (n = 3), "supportive" also meant "tough love" when the parole officers closely monitored their activities or even intervened in their personal lives in an effort to help them avoid parole violations. As these women explained:

I think he is supportive. He questions me a lot. I think he just wants to make sure I'm on the right track. I'm sure they get a lot of people just creeping their ways through. (Respondent 8)

[Parole officer's name] is tough on me, but this is a good thing as it helped me stay out [of trouble]. He could have sent me back [to prison] this last time but he didn't. He rides me hard. Sometimes, I can't stand it. All pressure from everywhere. But it's good and he's fair. It's a pain, but it's good. (Respondent 15)

Another example of "supportive relationship" is related to the experience of Respondent 20 who had a new boyfriend after prison release. Her parole officer strongly discouraged the relationship because the man's ex-girlfriend, due to jealousy, had created many troubles, including inciting a physical fight that caused Respondent 20 to violate her parole conditions. At first, Respondent 20 was not happy with the interference, but she finally considered the intervention as good in helping her avoid further parole violations. For Respondent 20, "having a good parole officer makes a difference."

The Clergy, Ex-Inmate Friends, and Treatment Peers   A significant factor in the reentry experiences of women in the study was the existence of new weak-ties relationships.

While only half of the women reported pre-incarceration relationships with friends, who were also involved in substance use and/or criminal activity, a substantial majority of the women (n = 16) indicated post-incarceration relationships with pro-social friends, treatment peers, church members, co-workers, as well as church and civic organization volunteers. Many of these relationships were rooted in their prison experiences.

Relationships with the clergy were an important source of support for many women inside and outside the prison setting. A majority of the women (n = 12) reported church attendance during incarceration, and most of these women (n = 11) had good relationships with their chaplains and prison volunteers. These women indicated that they went to church for help, and the opportunity to express their feelings and the emotional support from a spiritual leader helped them get through with their time in prison. Through relationships with the clergy, these women received emotional support and tangible assistance, including holiday gift packages, and sometimes free phone cards and clothes. This material assistance, though small in financial values, was important in the prison setting. Prison volunteers, who were often associated with the clergy, also assisted these women with release plans by providing information about various reentry programs in the community or by helping them make connections with community reentry programs to prepare for the release. Most of the women who maintained relationships with the clergy and prison volunteers emphasized the importance of spiritual and emotional support and viewed their clergypersons as teachers and volunteers as mentors who gave them good advice that saved their lives.

Because of supportive relationships from the clergy in prison, many women continued their contacts with the church after release. Almost half of the women (n = 8) reported that they went to church frequently, attended Sunday schools, and participated in advocacy programs organized by the church. Through their relationships with the church and church members, they accessed material and emotional support, information on housing assistance, constructive activity, and positive guidance. For several women, their mentors in prison setting became their long-term mentors after release. These women talked about their experiences as follows:

> [In prison] The clergy was very positive. I attended church 5 days a week. They provided Serenity classes—a 12-step self-help program. It made you open up and look at yourself. Look at life on life's terms up front. . . . Very positive and helpful. I had really good relationships with the chaplain. She got me hooked up with different programs, such as helping with my current job and housing. She saved my life. [After prison] I participated in Success Ministry Mentor Program and received training to be a mentor for [prison] inmates. I stayed in the program for two years. The clergy [woman] is my mentor. I talk to her everyday. We had a very positive relationship. She provided emotional support and knew everything about life. (Respondent 6)

> [In prison] I participated in "Hands of Grace" program and attended church. Part of the Serenity [program] was to talk to the clergy. They were nice. [After prison] My friend's mom in Hands of Grace program really looked out for me. She bought me clothes and took me to the half-way house. . . . She and people from the church bought me the first car after release. I'm still with Success Ministry. Great support. They helped me stay out of trouble. (Respondent 8)

The women's friendship networks underwent a great deal of change after incarceration and included fellow inmates. During incarceration, only four women had contacts with outside friends who came to visit, sent letters, or provided some financial assistance, but new friendships developed in prison. Although a majority of the women indicated that they had problems with or did not trust other inmates, many (n = 7) established positive relationships with selected inmates and considered them as their best friends or close relatives (e.g., fictive sisters). Inmate friends often provided emotional support and shared spiritual information, but they also shared the gift packages received from families. Often time, mutual experience and the support from each other in prison facilitated long-term relationships that continued beyond the prison setting as illustrated in the experience of Respondent 11 and Respondent 15.

> One of my best friends, I met her in prison, and she is out. I keep in touch with another girl who is still in. We help each other with emotional support. [After incarceration] I still have the best friend I met in prison. She got out 6 months before I did. My best friend and I went through this together. It helped a lot to have someone who understands. (Respondent 11)

> I developed some long-term relationship but very few. We were all kind and helped each other emotionally and materially. (Respondent 15)

Work and participation in treatment programs in the community also provided opportunity for new relationships. Several women (n = 5) met new friends at treatment programs (Narcotic Anonymous) or the workplace, and they described the relationships as positive and an important source of emotional support. As these women said,

> I participated in Narcotic Anonymous and attended regularly. It's where new friends were coming from. It was very important to have someone who is understanding. (Respondent 15)

> I had new friends at work. They're supportive. I also went to NA [Narcotic Anonymous] and became active in that community. Most people there were recovered. That's your support system. (Respondent 17)

Although resources from friends/ex-inmates were intangible in most part, one woman reported crucial material support from friends after release:

> A friend helped with housing for 90 days. My friend I met in prison helped with transportation for finding job. The assistance was very important. If it wasn't for the housing I wouldn't have got out and if it wasn't for the other I wouldn't have gotten a job. (Respondent 18)

Many women also reported positive relationship with co-workers and job supervisors who had no problem with the women's incarceration. These positive relationships helped reduce the stigma associated with the criminal label and improved these women's self-esteem.

CONCLUSION

The study highlights the importance of resources from strong-ties and weak-ties relationships among women who experience successful reentry experience. These women were not only able to access tangible resources from families, which other studies found to be very important for success after release (Dowden & Andrew, 1999; Leverentz, 2006; O'Brien, 2001; Slaght, 1999), but also emotional support and material assistance from parole officers, the clergy and its volunteer service, friends, and treatment peers. Separations caused by incarceration and prison experiences contributed to women's shift to pro-social networks that provided positive resources important for successful outcomes. However, material assistance was not often available from intimate relationships, and parole services seemed to be ineffective in connecting women to work, substance abuse treatment opportunities, or other sources of material assistance.

It is important to interpret the study findings with awareness that women who failed on parole were not included in the study. Given the high proportion of incarcerated women who recidivate nationally (Langan & Levin, 2002), it is clear that the prison experience does not uniformly facilitate pro-social networks with positive resources. Internal transformation may facilitate women's determination to change, but women's willingness to straighten their lives needs to be supported by outside resources to help them overcome multiple barriers to reintegration (Giordano et al., 2002). Women who were not successful might find that the programs and resources available in prison and the community, which seemed to emphasize church-delivered services, or the parole supervision styles they experienced did not meet their needs. Employment and education were also important. Success might have resulted in part because nearly all of the women in the study had at least high school or equivalent education, with several had some college education, and all women had legitimate incomes, with half of them could earn above the minimum wage. Reasonable well-paying jobs enable women meet their financial needs and can help them avoid resorting to illegal means for generating incomes (Jurik, 1983; Koons, Burrow, Morash, & Bynum, 1997; O'Brien, 2001; Voorish, Salisbury, Wright, & Bauman, 2008). In addition, earnings can serve as a springboard for everything else that women leaving prison have to do because they provide a sense of personal reward, autonomy, competence, and confidence (O'Brien, 2001).

Despite the limitation on generalizability, the study is important in drawing attention to the availability of resources as well as potential benefits from women's various pro-social relationships. Intimate relationships, which are often associated with abuse, violence, and exploitations, do not often entail tangible resources. Families of origin are an important source of intangible and tangible assistance, but family networks may not always be able to address the material needs of women returnees because deficit in network resource tends to be associated low socio-economic status experienced by most women offenders (Lin, 2000). Alternative sources of resources can include pro-social friends, civic organizations, the clergy, treatment program peers, and parole officers who use innovative methods to help their clients succeed. The experiences of women in the study suggest that enhancing women's ability to expand their pro-social network relationships and access needed resources, as well as ensuring that needed resources are available and accessible in the community, is important for increasing their chance for successful reintegration.

REFERENCES

Ajrouch, K. J., Blandon, A. Y. & Antonucci, T. C. (2005). Social networks among men and women: The effects of age and socioeconomic status. *Journal of Gerontology: Social Sciences,* 60b, S311–S317.

Arditti, J. A. & Few, A. (2006). Mothers' reentry into family life following incarceration. *Criminal Justice Policy Review*, 17, 103–123.

BLOOM, B., OWEN, B. & COVINGTON, S. (2003). *Gender-Responsive Strategies: Research Practice, and Guiding Principles for Women Offenders.* Washington, DC: National Institute of Corrections.

BONTA, J., PANG, B. & WALLACE-CAPRETTA, S. (1995). Predictors of recidivism among incarcerated female offenders. *Prison Journal, 75,* 277–294.

BROWN, M. (2006). Gender, ethnicity, and offending over the life course: Women's pathways to prison in the Aloha state. *Critical Criminology, 14,* 137–158.

BUI, H. N. & MORASH, M. (2010). The impact of network relationships, prison experiences, and internal transformation on women's success after prison release. *Journal of Offender Rehabilitation, 49,* 1–22.

CAMPBELL, K. E. & ROSENFELD, R. A. (1985). Job search and job mobility: Sex and race differences. *Research in the Sociology of Work, 3,* 147–174.

COVINGTON, S. S. (1998). The relational theory of women's psychological development: Implications for the criminal justice system. In R. T. Zaplin (Ed.), *Female Offenders: Critical Perspectives and Effective Interventions* (pp. 113–131). Gaithersburg, MD: Aspen.

CURLEY, A. M. (2009). Draining or gaining? The social networks of public housing movers in Boston. *Journal of Social and Personal Relationships, 26,* 227–247.

CARTER, W. C. & FELD, S. L. (2004). Principles relating social regard to size and density of personal networks, with applications to stigma. *Social Networks, 26,* 323–329.

DANNER, T. A., BLOWN, W. R., SILVERMAN, J. & VEGA, M. (1995). The female chronic offenders: Exploring life contingency, and offense history dimensions for incarcerated female offenders. *Women and Criminal Justice, 6,* 45–66.

DOWDEN, C. & ANDREW, D. (1999). What works for female offenders: A meta analysis review. *Crime & Delinquency, 45,* 438–452.

FETTERMAN, D. M. (1998). *Ethnography: Step by Step, Second Edition.* Thousand Oaks, CA: Sage.

FLAVIN, J. (2004). Employment counseling, housing assistance . . . And aunt Yolanda?: How strengthening families' social capital can reduce recidivism. *Criminology and Public Policy, 3,* 209–216.

GIORDANO, P. C., CERNKOVICH, S. & RUDOLPH, S. (2002). Gender, crime, and desistance: Toward a theory of cognitive transformation. *American Journal of Sociology, 107,* 990–1064.

GIORDANO, P. C., S. A. CERNKOVICH, & R. D. SCHROEDER. 2007. Emotions and crime over the life course: A neo-median perspective on criminal continuity and change. *American Journal of Sociology, 112,* 1603–1661.

GRANOVETTER, M. (1973). The strength of weak ties. *American Journal of Sociology, 78,* 1360–1380.

GRIFFIN, M. L. & ARMSTRONG, G. S. (2003). The effects of local life circumstance on female probationers' offending. *Justice Quarterly, 20,* 213–239.

HAIRSTON, C. F. (2003). Prisoners and their families: Parenting issues during incarceration. In J. Travis & M. Waul (eds.), *Prisoners Once Removed* (pp. 259–282). Washington, DC: The Urban Institute.

HALPERN, D. (2008). *Social Capital.* Malden, MA: Polity.

HENRIQUES, Z. W. & MANATU-RUPERT, N. (2001). Living on the outside: African American women before, during, and after imprisonment. *The Prison Journal, 81,* 6–19.

HOLTFRETER, K., REISIG, M. D. & MORASH, M. (2004). Poverty, state capital and recidivism among women offender. *Criminology and Public Policy, 3,* 185–208.

Jurik, N. C. 1983. The economics of female recidivism. *Criminology, 21,* 603–622.

KOONS, B. A., BURROW, J. D., MORASH, M. & BYNUM, T. S. (1997). Expert and offender perceptions of program elements linked to successful outcomes for incarcerated women. *Crime & Delinquency, 43,* 512–532.

LANGAN, P. A. & LEVIN, D. J. (2002). *Recidivism of Prisoners Released in 1994. Bureau of Justice Statistics: Special Report* (NCJ # 193427). Washington, DC: Office of Justice Programs.

Larson, J. H. & Nelson, J. 1984. Women's friendship and adaptation to prison. *Journal of Criminal Justice, 12*, 601–615.

Leverentz, A. (2006). *People, Places, and Things: The Social Process of Reentry for Female Offenders* (NCJ # 215178). Washington, DC: NCJRS—Department of Justice.

Lin, N. (2000). Inequality in social capital. *Contemporary Sociology, 29*, 785–796.

Miller, E. M. (1986). *Street Women*. Philadelphia: Temple University Press.

Morash, M. (2010). *Women on Probation and Parole: A Feminist Critique of Community Programs and Services*. Boston, MA: Northeastern University Press.

Naser, R. L. & La Vigne, N. G. (2006). Family support in the prisoner reentry process: Expectations and realities. *Journal of Offender Rehabilitation, 43*, 93–106.

O'Brien, P. (2001). *Making It in the "Free World": Women in Transition from Prison*. New York: State University of New York Press.

Parsons, M. L. & Warner-Robbins, C. (2002). Factors that support women's successful transition to the community following jail/prison. *Health Care for Women International*, 23, 6–18.

Petersilia, J. 2003. *When Prisoners Come Home: Parole and Prisoner Reentry*. New York, NY: Oxford University Press.

Ruspini, E. (2002). *Introduction to Longitudinal Research*. London: Routledge.

Shover, N. (1996). *Great Pretenders: Pursuit and Careers of Persistent Thieves*. Boulder, CO: West View.

Simons, R. L., Steward, E., Gordon, L. C., Conger, R. D. & Elder, Jr. G. H. (2002). A test of life-course explanations for stability and change in antisocial behavior from adolescence to young adulthood. *Criminology, 40*, 401–434.

Slaght, E. (1999). Family and offender treatment focusing on the family in the treatment of substance abusing criminal offenders. *Journal of Drug Education, 19*, 53–62.

Travis, J. & Waul, M. 2003. The children and families of prisoners. In J. Travis & M. Waul (eds.), *Prisoners Once Removed* (pp. 1–29). Washington, DC: The Urban Institute.

Van Voorhis, P., Salisbury, E., Wright, E. &, Bauman, A. (2008). *Achieving Accurate Pictures and Identification Gender Responsive Needs: Two New Assessments for Women Offenders*. National Institute of Correction Library. URL: http://www.nationalinstituteofcorrections.gov/Library/022844. Access 1/12/09.

Waul, M., Travis, J. & Solomon, A. L. (2002). The effect of incarceration and reentry on children, families, and communities. Urban Institute. URL: http://www.urban.org/url.cfm?ID=410632. Access 05/11/2006.

ENDNOTES

1. Many women participants chose the private room in the parole office because it was convenient for them to do the monthly report with their parole officer and participate in the interview in the same location.
2. Data were collected for a larger project, and data on network relationships and resources were used for the study.
3. To protect the identity of the women in the study, their real names are not reported.

30

Women on Death Row

Etta F. Morgan

Capital punishment is a controversial issue in society, yet it is the most severe punishment that our courts can administer. The purposes of this chapter are to (a) provide an historical overview of capital punishment; (b) explain capital punishment using Girard's theory of culture; (c) examine the influence of the Supreme Court regarding capital punishment; (d) discuss the importance of gender in the criminal justice process; and (e) review the literature on executed females as well as share some of the experiences and problems of female death row inmates.

INTRODUCTION

Ironically, every aspect of our society is influenced by the social and cultural perspectives that dominate our being. These influences are also prevalent in the administration of our prisons. Women, as second-class citizens in society, carry this status into the penal system, which openly ignores their needs in more ways than one. One prime example would be that most states have only one prison for women, and some have none. Female criminality and experiences have often been described based on men's experiences. Previous research (Erez, 1989; Kruttschnitt, 1982; Mann, 1984; Pollock, 2002; Visher, 1983; Zingraff & Thompson, 1984) suggests that, as a group, women have been treated more leniently in the criminal justice system than men. If this is true, then it may explain the disproportionate number of women sentenced to death in relation to the number of men sentenced to death. Female offenders have often been a forgotten population in research as well as in reality.

Limited research has focused on women sentenced to death. Victor Streib publishes a quarterly report, which details demographics about the offender, a brief statement about the offense, and the current status of the inmates (i.e., reversals, commutations). Gillespie (1997), O'Shea (1999), and O'Shea (2000) provide historical data about the lives of women sentenced to death, their crimes and trials, various legislation affecting women sentenced to death, and the period leading up to the executions and the actual executions. Other authors (Fletcher, Shaver, & Moon, 1993; Mann, 1984) tend to devote only a few pages in textbooks to a discussion of women on death row. Perhaps this is due to the fact that women do not commit violent crime at the same rate as men.

There appears to be an increase in female crime based on the current Uniform Crime Reports (UCR), but it is unclear as to whether this increase is due to actual offenses or changes in reporting practices by law enforcement agencies. Cautiously interpreting the UCR data, there seems to be an increase in violent crimes by females, but basically, female crime is still concentrated in the area of property crimes. Upon closer examination of violent crimes, it is found that women homicide offenders tend to kill persons of the same race, usually an intimate male associate. As a group, women murderers are not as common as their male counterparts, which could possibly influence the treatment they receive in the criminal justice system. In examining the imposition of death sentences in this country, it is obvious that women are not sentenced to death or executed at the same rate as men.

The death penalty has and continues to be a controversial issue in the United States. It is the ultimate sentence that can be imposed for a criminal offense. Proponents of the death penalty suggest that it is needed in order to deter would-be criminals, while opponents believe that it is an inhumane act on the part of society in administering justice. In the past, the death penalty was withdrawn because some states were unfairly targeting specific populations of offenders. Although it was reinstated by the Supreme Court in 1976, the controversy has not been settled as to whether or not the death penalty should be used a form of punishment.

HISTORICAL OVERVIEW

Capital punishment is a controversial issue nationally as well as internationally. It is believed to have been in existence before societies became organized. After the organization of society, legal codes were established in an attempt to provide rules and regulations for social control. Capital punishment has been included in legal codes since the period of the Old Testament continuing on to the Code of Hammurabi, Assyrian laws, Athenian Codes, European laws, and the code established in the thirteen colonies (Koosed, 1996).

Capital punishment in the United States has been greatly influenced by English traditions, and research has shown it to be an Anglo-American custom (Paternoster, 1991). The practice of capital punishment in the colonies reflected the ideology of the American people in regards to the types of crime which were considered capital offenses. Because there was no uniform criminal code throughout the colonies, each state had different capital statutes (Kronenwetter, 1993; Paternoster, 1991). In some instances, states declared fewer offenses (5–8) capital offenses if committed by whites while identifying seventy (70) offenses as capital offenses if committed by blacks (Paternoster, 1991). After the

American Revolution, states began to restrict the number of offenses that could be classified as capital offenses. States also narrowed the application of capital punishment by establishing degrees of murder and giving juries more discretion in sentencing, thereby, permitting the jury to sentence people to death in only the most serious murders (Paternoster, 1991).

Along with the passage of discretionary statutes for capital crimes, this period of American capital punishment has two distinct characteristics. First, executions were public events, and second, local authorities were responsible for performing all executions. Executions were performed as public events until the end of the 1800s although some public executions were performed as late as 1936 and 1937 (Paternoster, 1991). At the turn of the century we find a shift from public executions controlled by local authorities to executions controlled and conducted by the state (Paternoster, 1991).

Capital punishment's historical significance is not only related to punishment but also to social control. Capital punishment was often administered upon those identified as members of problem populations. It was believed that these populations did not respect established authority. In many instances, these populations were viewed as threatening or dangerous to established authority. Capital punishment also had an extralegal form that was lynching. According to Paternoster (1991), "[l]ynching, primarily by vigilante groups, was frequently used by majority groups to keep minorities oppressed (p. 8)." The use of this extralegal form of capital punishment claimed more lives than legal executions (Paternoster, 1991). Although we experienced a decline in lynchings with the centralization of the death penalty, there were more executions between 1930 and 1940 than were noted for the following twenty years. During the 1960s and 1970s, there was a decline followed by a moratorium on capital punishment (Paternoster, 1991).

Over time, there have been regional differences in the imposition of the death penalty. Historically, the South has performed more executions than any other region. In examining capital offenses and capital statutes during the Pre-Modern Era, Paternoster (1991) states, "one interesting feature about the imposition of capital punishment for different offenses is that the region of the country and the race of the offender has been, at least in the past, an important correlate (p. 15)." Statistics (Flanagan & Maguire, 1989) suggest that race may have been an overriding factor in the imposition of the death penalty for particular offenses in the South resulting in racially biased applications of the death sentence. It has also been suggested, as in previous years, that capital punishment continued to be used as a form of social control for specific groups.

Capital punishment, as the ultimate sentence, has also created problems for juries. Specifically, juries were at odds with the harshness of the laws and as a result found themselves mitigating that fact instead of the case. In later years, juries were given discretionary powers with the understanding that they were to consider any and all factors related to the case which could support a death sentence as well as factors supportive of a noncapital sentence (Paternoster, 1991). This unbridled reign led to irrational and discriminatory practices in the imposition of death sentences. The uncontrolled sentencing freedom enjoyed by juries and the misapplication of death sentences "led to the temporary suspension of the death penalty in the United States (Paternoster, 1991, p. 17)."

The Modern Era of capital punishment represents the return to the imposition of death sentences. During the moratorium on capital punishment, the Supreme Court ruled that the discretionary powers given to juries were unconstitutional along with the procedures used for the imposition of death sentences. A thorough examination of the Supreme Court's position as it relates to capital punishment will be examined in more detail later using Girard's theory of culture.

THEORETICAL ANALYSIS

The debate over capital punishment remains unresolved in American society. Some believe that capital punishment deters would-be criminals while others contend that persons should be punished based on the doctrine of retribution. Another possible explanation for the existence of capital punishment in our society may be the need for ritualized violence as a method of social control. Although controversial, Rene Girard's theory of culture (1977) based on religious thought, anthropology, psychology, literary criticism, and other social sciences appears to explain the importance of the death penalty in our society. According to Girard (1987):

> In the science of man and culture today there is a unilateral swerve away from anything that could be called mimicry, imitation, or mimesis. And yet, there is nothing, or next to nothing, in human behavior that is not learned, and all learning is based on imitation. If human beings suddenly ceased imitating, all forms of culture would vanish. . . . The belief is that insisting on the role of imitation would unduly emphasize the gregarious aspects of humanity, all that transforms us into herds. There is a fear of minimizing the importance of everything that tends toward division, alienation, and conflict. If we give a leading role to imitation, perhaps we will make ourselves accomplices of the force of subjugation and uniformity. (p. 7)

The theory that human behavior is, to some extent, learned behavior resulting from imitating the behavior of others has also been advanced by theorists, such as Aristotle, Plato, Tarde, and Sutherland. Although Plato's description of imitation, as well as his followers, failed to identify specific behaviors involved in appropriation, Girard (1987) states that, "if imitation does indeed play the fundamental role for man, as everything seems to indicate, there must certainly exist an acquisitive imitation, or, if one prefers, a possessive mimesis whose effects and consequences should be carefully studied and considered" (p. 9) not overlooked. It is indisputable that imitation brings about conflict, but, in many instances, persons have learned to control and dispense imitated behavior in acceptable ways.

Society determines which behaviors are authorized, thereby identifying behaviors that may or may not be imitated. In other words, there are restricted imitations. These prohibitions exist because some behaviors are just plain absurd or they threaten the safety of society (Girard, 1987). It has been suggested that primitive societies understood that there was a relationship between mimesis and violence unlike modern society (Girard, 1987). The theory of culture advanced by Girard (1987) claims that:

> [T]here is a connection between conflict and acquisitive mimesis. Modern society tends to view competition and conflict differently from primitive society mainly because we tend to see difference emerge from the outcome of a conflict. . . . [and] we tend to focus on the individual act. (pp. 11–12)

By focusing on the individual act, instead of the act and its context, we (modern society) are able to view violence as an isolated crime. In doing so, we fail to truly understand the context in which the act was committed and its relationship to the violence experienced. Instead, we depend upon the power of our judicial institutions to mandate adherence to the rules of social order which does little, if anything, to increase our understanding of imitative violence or the importance of external factors to violent behavior(s). The purpose of these judicial institutions seems to imply that all persons in a society will abide by the laws which have been established and agreed upon by the members of society, but this is not true, especially, since laws tend to represent the wishes of those persons who have power and wealth in society (the elite) in an attempt to control the masses.

It has been suggested that without these institutions, "the imitative and repetitious character of violence becomes manifest once more; the imitative character of violence is in fact most manifest in explicit violence, where it acquires a formal perfection it had not previously possessed" (Girard, 1987, p. 12). For example, in previous societies, a murder expanded substantially in the form of blood feuds. Violent acts, such as, the blood feuds and other rivalries, had to be curtailed in order to reunite the community, and the solution had to be dramatic and violent. Basically, the idea was and remains violence begets violence.

In *McGautha v. California*, 1971, a violent solution was also suggested by one justice as the only means by which violence could be ended even though it was noted that violence is self-propagating. Fortunately or unfortunately, our society has established a judicial institution in the form of the death penalty as a means to end violence (sanctioned self-propagating violence). Society has proscribed the method, time, and deliverer of the punishment for the sanctioned ritualized killing of another individual (Girard, 1987). As such, the death penalty is a dramatic and violent solution used to reunite the community, but fails, unless the targeted community is the victim's family, not society as a whole. Beschle (1997) states, ". . . modern legal systems seek to break the cycle of imitative violence by directing the punitive urge of all members of society toward a common enemy" (p. 521). The common enemy becomes the "new victim" in the community sanctioned ritualized violence.

In order to proceed through the various phases of the ritualized killing, there must first be some type of relationship established between the "new victim" and the community. As part of the ritualized killing, it is important that the person to be executed (the new victim) is viewed as the cause of the community's discord and that his or her death will somehow restore peace in the community. Girard (1987) also suggests that "at the moment when violence ceases and peace has been established, the community has the whole of its attention fixed on the victim it has just killed" (p. 81) which leads one to surmise that, in some instances, there is a fascination with some executed individuals such as Gary Gilmore and Ted Bundy.

In addition to the symbol of intense interest in the executed victim, there are many symbols associated with the death process. For example, the tradition of the *last meal* is viewed as a special privilege or a ritualized privilege granted by the community to one who for a brief period is perceived as special and worthy of this treatment. Additionally, the person who has received the death sentence most often is a typical member of the community, but is also significantly different because of his or her criminal act. This being the case, most members of the community lack compassion for and do not identify themselves with the offender. Having used Girard's theory of culture to explain the symbolism in the death process, we will now use his theory to examine the shift in the rulings of the Supreme Court.

Girard's (1987) theory can be used as a plausible explanation for the shift in the courts from being concerned with guilt to focusing more on expediting executions. As

Justices are replaced on the Court, we find that the new member is expected to bring to the Court a particular view that is shared by the controlling political party. The Justice, then, merely advances the opinions shared by those who are not in office that share the same beliefs. In many instances, Justices have been accused of relying on personal feelings or previous policy decisions, which purportedly expressed the public's desires, in order to write opinions for various cases. This being the case, it is safe to assume that some of the opinions rendered by the Court not only have been influenced by public opinion, but also mirrors public opinion thereby extending the theory of imitation to the Court. For this reason, we are able to link Girard's theory of culture to the shift in Supreme Court decisions based on the makeup of the Court and the political climate under which it has operated. Girard (1987) noted that society does not desire to be perceived as in a state of constant revenge, but is more interested in providing an effective judicial system, which allows permissible social constraints. The apparent shift in the Supreme Court suggests that some, if not all, of the justices believe that there must be little or no interference from the Supreme Court in lower court decisions. This "hand off" approach has evolved over time as the Supreme Court has decided various cases. In the following sections, we will briefly discuss this evolutionary process of the Supreme Court.

THE INFLUENCE OF THE SUPREME COURT

One phase that the Supreme Court entered into can be identified as the period of constitutionality. By this, we mean that the Court was concerned with the issue of whether or not the death penalty itself was against the Constitution of the United States. *Powell v. Alabama* (1932) (the right to appointed counsel in capital cases) is said to represent the beginning of the Court's reform efforts concerning the death penalty. It is during this period that the Court used broad interpretations of the Fourteenth Amendment to bring about changes in criminal justice systems throughout the states in relation to capital cases. However, the main issue of whether or not the death penalty was in violation of the Constitution was often *not discussed*. It was not until Justice Goldberg's dissenting opinion in *Rudolph v. Alabama* (1963) that there was even any hint of a constitutional issue.

The Court continued to avoid the issue of constitutionality until there was an active campaign against the death penalty initiated by the NAACP Legal Defense Fund, which resulted in a moratorium against executions. During this period, the Court, in *Witherspoon* (1968), ruled that juror exclusion could not be based solely on an individual's personal objections to the death penalty. It is also in *Witherspoon* that we find the first written opinion (by Justice Stewart) in a case decision that questions the propriety of the death penalty. Without ruling specifically on whether or not the death penalty was against the Constitution of the United States, the Court suggested that morally sound jurors would not impose the death penalty upon another human and, therefore, a decision concerning the matter was not warranted by the Court (Burt, 1987). The Court presumed that American society was harmonious and stable and would work in such a manner as to maintain social order (Burt, 1987). The implication was that the maintenance of social order would deter and/or reduce crime and there would be no need for administering the death penalty. Therefore, the Court would not have to address the constitutionality issue concerning the death penalty.

However, four years later in *Furman* (1972), the majority of the Justices declared that the death penalty as administered was in violation of the Eight Amendment protection against cruel and unusual punishment. The rationale for this conclusion varied among the Justices, but the main concern was the application of the death penalty under the existing standards at that time. The Court failed, however, to declare the death penalty unconstitutional based on a different set of standards. By 1976, the Court in *Gregg*, *Proffitt*, and *Jurek* ruled that the sentence of death was not an unconstitutional punishment and for a brief period began scrutinizing imposed death sentences upon appellate review. According to Burt (1987), "this kind of closely detailed, sustained observation by the Supreme Court was itself 'aberrational' " (p. 1780).

Beginning in 1983, the Court turned resolutely away from this pursuit, instead appearing intent on affirming capital punishment in order to suppress "the seeds of anarchy—of self help, vigilante justice, and lynch law" (Burt, 1987, p. 1780). The Court not only seemed to support capital punishment, but it also began closing avenues previously open to inmates seeking federal constitutional relief. State Appellate courts were encouraged to: (a) spend less time reviewing cases, (b) overlook admitted errors in death penalty proceedings, and (c) disregard the proportionality review process (Burt, 1987). Then, in 1985, the Court made another shift in the capital punishment debate.

In *Wainwright v. Witt* (1985) the Court dismantled the opinion it rendered in *Witherspoon* concerning death-qualified jurors and instead concluded that there was a presumption of correctness on the part of state judges in excluding jurors. This action by the Court blocked federal constitutional review unless the defense attorney could show that the trial judge had erred. Given the resources available to defense attorneys in capital cases, the likelihood of a challenge to the presumption of correctness lies moot. The Court continued to tear down the tenets of the *Witherspoon* decision in its ruling of *Lockhart v. McCree* (1986). It ruled that even if a death-qualified jury is more conviction prone than other juries, that fact alone *does not* raise a constitutional issue for review by the Court. According to Burt (1987), the Court's ruling in *Lockhart* reveals that "the Court is now content on suppressing rather than exploring doubts about capital punishment" (pp. 1788–89).

The twenty-first century has been interesting to say the least in regards to the Supreme Court's rulings on death penalty cases. In *Atkins* (2002), the Court held "executions of mentally retarded criminals are "cruel and unusual punishments" prohibited by the Eight Amendment" (pp. 5–17). The Supreme Court in its ruling suggested that society no longer approves of executing the mentally retarded individuals, noting that consistently states are passing legislation declaring that death is not an acceptable punishment for these individuals. In another landmark decision, the Supreme Court ruled in *Roper* (2005), "the Eighth and Fourteenth Amendments forbid imposition of the death penalty on offenders who were under the age of 18 when their crimes were committed" (pp. 6–25). Again, the Court notes that their decision is based upon the evolving standards of decency that has been expressed by enactments of legislatures and the Court's own judgment noting "that the death penalty is a disproportionate punishment for juveniles" (pp. 10–21). It is apparent that some state legislature and the Supreme Court have begun to listen to the voice of the people in regards to certain legal issues; however, we must also remember that each case that comes before the court must stand on its own merit. The debate over capital punishment is not over; for now, two crucial issues have been resolved until they are once again challenged in the courts.

It is not surprising that the controversy surrounding capital punishment continues when the Justices of the Supreme Court cannot effectively deal with the issue. If there are constitutional safeguards to ensure that inmates are afforded those rights, why should judges be instructed to overlook such safeguards? Does this mean that the Justices of the Supreme Court view persons convicted and sentenced to death as less than human and, therefore, should not be afforded the rights guaranteed by the Constitution? It seems fair to say that the chaos that has plagued the Court concerning capital punishment is representative of the confusion and inconsistencies that prevail in society about capital punishment. Perhaps, the chaos that plagues us (society) could be diffused by simply treating those persons sentenced to death as human beings until death, if an execution is forthcoming. After all, what does society have to lose, if death is what one seeks. Does acknowledging that these people are human stir up emotions that one tries hard to suppress? Is that why we prefer not to read or hear about the conditions of incarceration? Facing the reality that death row inmates are humans, just like any of us, makes it hard to accept the inadequacies of prison life.

THE ADMINISTRATION OF LAW

Laws, in any society, define behaviors, which are deemed unacceptable based on the morals and values of the community at large. They also determine who will be punished (Flavin, Price, & Sokoloff, 2007). In societies which are not very complex, informal rather than formal methods are used as means of social control. Both society and individuals are presumably protected by the laws. These laws may prescribe punishments, direct or restrain certain actions, and access financial penalties (Reid, 2009). Flavin et al. (2007) state "the law protects what those in power value most" (p. 14). Laws are created and passed by legislative bodies composed mainly of rich, white men and persons who share their interests (Flavin et al., 2007). Laws tend to be the mechanism by which the dominate class ensures that its interests will be protected (Quinney, 1975). However, challenges to specific laws are not uncommon (Flavin et al., 2007).

Historically, women have been considered the property of their fathers or husbands without full acknowledgment of them as individuals with rights granted by the Constitution (Flavin et al., 2007). Several cases have come before the Supreme Court concerning the rights of women. In the landmark case of *Reed v. Reed* (1971), the Supreme Court ruled that women were indeed persons and should be treated as such under the United States Constitution. The Court stated that the Fourteenth Amendment clause:

> does not deny to States the power to treat different classes of persons in different ways. . . . [it] does, however, deny to States power to legislate that different treatment be accorded to persons placed by a statute into different classes on the basis of criteria wholly unrelated to the objective of that statute. A classification "must be reasonable, not arbitrary, and must rest upon grounds of difference having a fair and substantial relation to the object of the legislation. . . ." (*Reed v. Reed*, 404 U.S. 75, 76, 1971)

According to the Justices, preference based on sex which is used merely to reduce the number of court hearings that could arise because two or more persons are equally entitled is directly in violation of the Fourteenth Amendment clause forbidding arbitrariness nor can sex be used as a preventive measure against intrafamily controversies (*Reed v. Reed*, 1971). Based on this ruling, the Court recognized women as individuals with the right to individualized treatment, but it did not identify sex in relation to the suspect-classification argument under the Fourteenth Amendment.

It was not until *Frontiero v. Richardson* (1973) that the Court ruled that sex was a suspect-classification which "must be subjected to strict judicial scrutiny" (677).[1] This case involved differential treatment of men and women in the military in regards to their respective spouses being classified as dependents. The ruling by the Court also stated that the current statute was in violation of the Due Process Clause of the Fifth Amendment. Justice Powell suggested that the Court should not rule on sex as a suspect-classification because the Equal Rights Amendment (ERA) had been approved by Congress and it would eliminate the need for such a classification (*Frontiero v. Richardson*, 1973). Unfortunately, the States did not ratify the ERA. It is difficult to imagine the extent to which sex discrimination would have evolved without the protection afforded to women in *Frontiero*.

Women were still seeking equal rights during the Ford and Carter administrations. Although the Court ruled in *Craig* that "classification by gender must serve important governmental objectives and must be substantially related to achievement of those objectives" (*Craig v. Boren*, 429 US 190, 197, 1976). Yet, this case did not a have true impact on Constitutional law; instead, it most notably suggested that there were changes in alliances among the Justices. These cases represent only small legal gains by women.

According to Hoff (1994):

> Some of the most disturbing gender-biased decisions the Supreme Court has reached in the last seventeen years have involved pregnancy cases. . . other recent decisions are either discouraging or disquieting for the cause of complete female equality, especially where redistributive economic issues are at stake. (p. 251)

Knowing that many households are now headed by women has not moved Congress or the Supreme Court to properly address the comparable worth issue. Instead, they avoid the comparable worth issue as though it was a plague. Women must decide "whether they prefer equal treatment as unequal individuals (when judged by male standards) or special treatment as a protected (and thus implicitly) inferior group" (Hoff, 1994, p. 274). The legal system has not always treated women and girls fairly, and this could be due in part to the perceptions men (who are the majority in the legal system) have of females (Flavin et al., 2007). Roberts (1994) states, "the criminal law most directly mandates socially acceptable behavior. Criminal law also helps to shape the way we perceive women's proper role" (p. 1). Women who do not adhere to prescribed gender roles and commit criminal offenses are viewed differently by our criminal justice system. This issue will be discussed more fully in the following section on female criminality.

FEMALE CRIMINALITY

Female crime is not as prevalent as that of males and previously had not been considered a social problem (Belknap, 2007). Women are also more likely to commit fewer and less serious violent crimes than males (Belknap, 2007; Mann, 1984; Pollock, 2002; Simon & Landis, 1991). Yet, we have been led to believe that female crime has reached outlandish proportions and far exceeds male crime. The basis for this information has been the Uniformed Crime Reports (UCR) complied by the FBI from data supplied by law enforcement agencies.

According to Steffensmeier (1995), these data (UCR) are problematic in assessing female crime patterns. Steffensmeier (1995) suggests the following: (a) the changes in arrest rates may be related more to "public attitudes and police practices . . . than actual behaviors," (b) because of the broadness of categories they include "dissimilar events and . . . a range of seriousness," and (c) the definition of serious crime as used by the UCR tends to lead one to believe that serious female crime has risen dramatically, when in fact, women have been arrested more for the crime of larceny, "especially for shoplifting" (p. 92) than any other Type I offense. Previous research (Mann, 1984; Naffine, 1987; Simon & Landis, 1991; Steffensmeier, 1980) has revealed that overall female crime rates have remained fairly stable in most areas. The notable changes are in the areas of "less serious property offenses and possibly drugs" (Belknap, 2007, p. 58).

In order to better assess the rate of female crime, Steffensmeier (1995) completed a 30-year study of arrest statistics. Although the study examined trends in individual offenses, of particular importance here are the trends by type of crime based on male/female arrests. The types of crimes chosen to develop trends for male/female arrests were "violent, masculine, index ("serious"), and minor property" (Steffensmeier, 1995, p. 94). He found that female participation in masculine crimes increased slightly which led to more arrests, but this was not the case for violent crimes. Steffensmeier (1995) again attributes the increase in arrests for index crimes to an increase in the number of women committing larcenies. Women have also had an increase in arrest rates for minor property crimes (Belknap, 2007; Steffensmeier, 1995). Simpson (1991) suggests that violent behavior varies among females and it is difficult to separate the individual influences of race, class, and gender because they are so intermingled. For the purposes of this chapter, we will only examine the influence of gender in the administration of law.

Having examined briefly female criminality, we will now turn our attention to the processing of female criminal cases by the criminal justice system. It has been suggested (Chesney-Lind, 1982; Farnworth & Teske, 1995; Frazier, Bock, & Henretta, 1983; Harvey, Burnham, Kendall, & Pease, 1992; Spohn & Spears, 1997; Steffensmeier, 1980) that women receive differential treatment during the processing of criminal cases. The differential treatment may be negative or positive. For example, Steffensmeier (1980) suggested that the likelihood of future offending and the perceived danger to the community influenced the preferential treatment of women in the criminal justice process and as a result increased their chances of receiving probation instead of prison. Yet, Chesney-Lind (1982) discovered that female juveniles have always received negative differential treatment. She noted that the females were processed into the juvenile justice system as a result of status offenses and received institutionalization more often than male juveniles.

Frazier, Bock, and Henretta (1983) examined the affect of probation officers in determining gender differences in sentencing severity. In their study, they collected data from presentence investigation reports with various information concerning the offender as well as recommendations from the probation officers regarding sentences. According to Frazier et al. (1983), "there is a strong relationship between gender of offender and final criminal court disposition. . . probation officers' recommendations have major effects and . . . being female greatly increases the likelihood of receiving a nonincarceration sentence recommendation " (pp. 315–316). Harvey, Burnham, Kendall, and Pease (1992) in an international comparison of gender differences in criminal justice found that women were processed out of the criminal justice system more often than men. Their study also revealed that men who were processed through the criminal justice system were convicted and imprisoned at a higher rate than women worldwide. Harvey et al. (1992) note "that criminal justice worldwide operates differentially by gender (but not necessarily in a discriminatory way)" (p. 217).

In another study, Farnworth and Teske (1995) found some evidence of gender disparity in relation to charge reductions if there was no prior criminal history. The absence of prior offending was noted to increase the possibility of probation for females. Based on the selective chivalry thesis, Farnworth and Teske (1995) discovered "that white females were twice as likely as minority females to have assault charges changed to nonassault at sentencing" (p. 40). There was also supportive evidence, which suggested that the use of discretionary powers influenced informal rather than formal decisions (Farnworth & Teske, 1995).

More recently, Spohn and Spears' (1997) study of the dispositions of violent felonies for both men and women revealed that more men (71.4%) than women (65.0%) were prosecuted, but their conviction rates were very similar and major differences appeared in sentencing. For example, males were incarcerated 77.4% of the time versus 48.2% for females. Overall females normally served "428 fewer days in prison" (p. 42) than males. This study also found that charge reduction or total dismissal of charges was more likely for females than males. Spohn and Spears (1997) state:

> Females were more likely than males to have injured their victims. . . . Female defendants were much less likely than male defendants to have a prior felony conviction. Females were charged with and convicted of less serious crimes and were less likely . . . to be charged with or convicted of more than one offense . . . less likely than males to have used a gun to commit the crime or to have victimized a stranger. . . females were more likely to have private attorneys and to be released prior to trial. (p. 42)

Based on their findings, Spohn and Spears (1997) suggest that violent female offenders are looked upon differently by judges for various reasons such as, (1) females may be perceived as less dangerous to the community; (2) females may have acted as an accomplice instead of being the primary perpetrator; (3) the risk of recidivism is less for females; and (4) there is better chance of rehabilitating female offenders.

WOMEN AND CAPITAL PUNISHMENT

The imposition of the death penalty is not just racially biased, but it is also gender biased. Streib (1990) states that gender bias is associated with two main sources: (a) "the express provisions of the law and (b) the implicit attitudes, either conscious or subconscious, of key actors involved in the criminal justice process (p. 874)." Although gender is not mentioned specifically in state statutes, there are certain considerations which may be applied differently based on gender (Streib, 1990). For example, most male criminals have prior criminal histories that include violent acts, while women, on the other hand, do not have significant prior criminal histories and they tend to be less violent than their male counterparts. When women are arrested for murder, it is usually their first offense. Because there tends to be an absence of criminal behavior on the part of women, Mann (1984) and

Steffensmeier (1980) suggest that women are not viewed as a threat to society. Another factor considered in capital cases is the defendant's mental state. Allen (1987) suggests that a commonly held belief is that female murderers are emotionally unbalanced at the time of the crime. Additionally, women are usually not the primary perpetrator; therefore, they are able to request consideration for this mitigating factor. According to Streib (1990), "even when all of the specific aggravating and mitigating factors are the same for male and female defendants, females still tend to receive significantly lighter sentences in criminal cases generally (p. 879)."

In examining the treatment of female defendants in the criminal justice system, Gillespie and Lopez (1986) found:

> in one area, however, women have constantly been treated with unquestionable deference because of their sex—that of the death penalty. Women have been traditionally been considered a separate class, deserving of a brand of "justice" all their own. Rather than execute them, they have been lectured, even released to the supervision of their husbands, and often never brought to trial. (p. 2)

It has been suggested that this deference is directly related to the paternalistic attitudes of male power brokers in the criminal justice system. However, this idea only explains why some women receive preferential treatment. It is not useful in explaining the absence of this same treatment towards other women. It is this difference in the treatment received by other female defendants which makes them susceptible to harsh treatment in the criminal justice system. Research (Mann, 1984; Streib, 1990) has shown that women who are uneducated, poor, members of a racial minority group, and of the lower socio-economic group tend not to receive preferential treatment in the criminal justice system. It is the women who have any or all of the aforementioned factors that are more likely to be condemned to death and in some instances, executed in our society.

Historically, we find that there is and has been an acceptance of executing female offenders in this country. Although executions of female defendants are rare, there have been 533 confirmed executions of women since 1632. This represents 2.7% of all executions in this country. Yet, when we examine executions of females from other centuries, we find that fewer executions take place today than in the past. For example, women comprised only 0.5% of the executions during the twentieth century (Streib, 1998). In the following section, we will briefly discuss the characteristics of executed women.

We find that sixty-eight percent of the women who have been executed were white and thirty-two percent were black. Although some defendants were over fifty, the average age was 38.7 years old. In terms of previous criminal history, only one had a prior homicide conviction while the others had only minor criminal histories. The motivation for the crimes was profit and emotion, but they were not always domestic situations (Gillespie & Lopez, 1986). Several patterns emerged related to executed women and the crimes. First, there was usually nothing unique or particularly heinous about the crime. Second, collecting insurance was the primary motive for the murder in many cases, and in most instances, there was a male accomplice. Next, there seemed to be no established relationship between the victim and the defendant. Finally, the South has executed more women than any other region while New York[2] leads the states in the execution of women (Gillespie & Lopez, 1986).

In examining death sentences from 1973 to 1997, we find that women only received 117 death sentences compared to over 6,210 death sentences for men (Streib, 1998). During the seventies, women received only 21 death sentences, but there was a dramatic increase (29) in the number of death sentences imposed on women in the eighties for a overall total of fifty death sentences in the two decades following the resurgence of the death penalty. During 1989, there were eleven death sentences given to women representing the single highest total of death sentences given to women in any one year from 1973 to 1997 (Death Penalty Information Center, 1998). In the nineties, the number of death sentences imposed on women exceeded (56) the combined total (50) of the two preceding decades. It is interesting to note that seventy-two of the death sentences imposed during 1973–1997 were either commuted to life imprisonment or reversed while three of the death sentences were actually fulfilled (Death Penalty Information Center, 1998; Streib, 2009). Since 1998, there have been 47 death sentences imposed on women with 8 sentences in 2000 and 7 sentences in 1998. Five sentences per year were imposed during the years 2002, 2004, 2005, and 2006. During 1999 only four death sentences were imposed followed by three death sentences in 2008. The fewest death sentences, two per year, were recorded in 2001 and 2003 (Streib, 2009). According to Streib (2009), "the wide fluctuations in annual death sentencing rates (from one to eleven in a given year) are unexplained by changes in statutes, court rulings, or public opinion" (p. 5).

Currently (as of July 1, 2009) there are 3,219 males and 60 females on death row. Women constitute 1.8% of the total death row population (Criminal Justice Project, 2009). Some women are no longer legally under a death sentence but may continue to be housed on death row pending additional appeals and therefore should not be counted in the above total. If this population is eliminated, then there are 53 females on death row (Streib, 2009). Since capital punishment was reinstated in 1976, there have been 1168 executions. Of these executions, only 11 women (Velma Barfield, 1984; Karla Faye Tucker, 1998; Judy Buenoano, 1998; Betty Lou Beets & Christina Riggs, 2000; Wanda Jean Allen, Marilyn Kay Plantz, & Lois Nadeen Smith, 2001; Lynda Lyon Block & Aileen Wuornos, 2002; Francis Elaine Newton, 2005) have been executed representing 0.9% of the total number of executions. Oklahoma leads the nation in executing women with three in 2001 followed by Texas and Florida with two each (Streib, 2009).

Upon closer examination, we find that the women on death row range in age from 25 to 76. Thirty-five percent of the women on death row were between the ages of 20 and 29 at the time of the criminal act. Thirty-six percent of the women were between 30 and 39 years old at the time of the crime. The racial breakdown of defendants reveals that sixty-four percent of the inmates are white while twenty-three percent are black. Latinas represent eleven percent and Native Americans two percent of the female death row population (Streib, 2009). Briefly, we should note that the victims were sixty percent white, thirteen percent black, twenty-three percent Latinas, and four percent Asian. Overwhelmingly, the victim was male (56%) and could be placed into one of two age categories (a) 0–10 (32%) and (b) 18–49 (47%) (Streib, 2009).

The women who are currently serving a death sentence are subjected to the same inadequate environmental conditions as other women in prison, namely, poor medical care, inhumane treatment, and isolation from family. In many instances, people who are in correctional facilities become socialized to believe that they are (a) not human, (b) worthless, and (c) cannot be rehabilitated. In other words, they will always be criminals. Some critics also suggest that we should not permit persons on death row access to rehabilitative programs because they are serving a death sentence. We disagree, especially since the reversal rate on appeal for women is 97%.

Although the reversal rate for women is high, until their sentences are reversed, these women must survive within the confines of the institution. A major concern for death row inmates is medical care. First, a death row inmate has to wait until an officer makes a security check in order to secure a form requesting a doctor's visit. Then a nurse decides whether or not the request will be granted. In many instances, this decision is based solely on the nurse's opinion, not on a preliminary evaluation of the inmate's medical condition. Inmates state that they often do not seek medical assistance because the officers accuse them of trying to get attention. One inmate was so worried that the officers were going to accuse her of trying to get attention that she did not seek medical assistance at the onset of a heart attack. Her cellmate finally called an officer against the sick woman's wishes to take her to the infirmary. Unfortunately, the nurse in the infirmary said there was nothing wrong with her and had the inmate returned to her cell. The inmate died later that night of a massive heart attack. This is only one story of the lack of concern shown by some people who are employed to provide medical care to inmates. Yet, the media suggests that inmates have the best medical care available.

Death row inmates, like other inmates, are seldom treated like persons by correctional officers and staff. Instead, they are made to feel like a burden that everyone wishes would go away. Because death row is isolated from general population, the correctional officers are the only people these inmates interact with during the day. If an inmate is housed in the same cell unit as another death row inmate, they may visit and talk to each other. Some correctional officers speak to inmates in a manner that creates problems. By this, we mean that inmates expect to be treated like humans not animals or objects. Although their daily activities are programmed by the institution, some correctional officers add to the humiliation of the inmates by their conduct and handling of the inmate. It is times like these that inmates need to be able to turn to family to cope with the dehumanization characteristics of prison life.

In some instances, families cannot withstand the pressures associated with having a family member incarcerated. In far too many cases, family relationships are strained because there is little to no contact with the incarcerated person. Research (Mann, 1984; Pollock, 2002) shows that women tend to lose contact with their families more often than men because women's facilities are in rural, remote areas of the state. Visitation days are normally during the weekdays, and family members would have to take off. As a result, visitation is more difficult and more restricted for death row inmates. Women also experience a severe emotional separation from family and friends due to their socialization process. Family support adds to the inmate's sense of humanity. Without this support, inmates do not have a buffer from the institutional process of dehumanization.

CONCLUSION

The reversal rate on appeal for women sentenced to death is approximately 97% (Streib, 1998). Because of the high reversal rate associated with female offenders, we have been lulled into believing that women would not be executed; however, for a brief period, we experienced an increase in the number of women executed. We believe that this increase occurred because of the "ever lingering get tough on crime" mentality that dominates our society along with legislation in Congress limiting appeals for defendants.

CHAPTER QUESTIONS

1. What were some of the problems associated with capital punishment because there were no uniform codes?
2. Discuss Girard's Theory of Culture in relation to capital punishment.
3. Explain the Supreme Court's apparent avoidance of the constitutionality issue surrounding the death penalty.
4. What is the significance of *Reed v. Reed*?
5. At what stages of the criminal justice process does gender have an affect?

REFERENCES

ALLEN, P. (1987). Rendering them harmless: The professional portrayal of women. In P. Carlen and A. Worrall (Eds.). *Gender, crime and justice*. UK: Open University Press.

BELKNAP, J. (2007). *The invisible woman: Gender, crime and justice* (3rd ed.). Belmont, CA: Wadsworth.

BESCHLE, D. (1997). What's guilt (or deterrence) got to do with it?: The death penalty, ritual, and mimetic violence. *William and Mary Law Review, 38*(2), 487–538.

BURT, R. (1987). Disorder in the court: The death penalty and the Constitution. *Michigan Law Review, 85,* 1741–1819.

CHESNEY-LIND, M. (1982). Guilty by reason of sex: Young women and the juvenile justice system. In B. Price and N. Sokoloff (Eds.), *The criminal justice system and women* (pp. 77–105). NY: Clark Boardman.

CRIMINAL JUSTICE PROJECT OF THE NAACP LEGAL DEFENSE AND EDUCATIONAL FUND, INC. (Summer, 2009). Death Row, New York, NY, U.S.A.

DEATH PENALTY INFORMATION CENTER (1998). Facts about the Death Penalty. Washington, D.C.

EREZ, E. (1989). Gender, rehabilitation, and probation decisions. *Criminology, 27*(2), 307–327.

FARNWORTH, M. & TESKE, Jr., R. (1995). Gender differences in felony court processing: Three hypotheses of disparity. *Women and Criminal Justice, 6*(2), 23–44.

FLANAGAN, T. & MAGUIRE, K. (1989). *Sourcebook of criminal justice statistics*. Washington, D.C.: U.S. Department of Justice, Bureau of Justice Statistics.

FLAVIN, J., PRICE, B. & SOKOLOFF, N. (2007). The criminal law and women. In B. Price and N. SOKOLOFF (Eds.)., *The criminal justice system and women: Offenders, victims, and workers* (3rd ed) (pp. 11–29). NY: McGraw-Hill.

FLETCHER, B., SHAVER, L., & MOON, D. (1993). *Women prisoners: A forgotten population*. Westport, CT: Praeger.

FRAZIER, C., BOCK, E., & HENRETTA, J. (1983). The role of probation officers in determining gender differences in sentencing severity. *The Sociological Quarterly, 24,* 305–318.

GILLESPIE, L. & LOPEZ, B. (1986). What must women do to be executed: A comparison of executed and non-executed women. Paper Presented at the American Society of Criminology, Atlanta, GA.

GILLESPIE, L. (1997). *Dancehall ladies: The crimes and executions of America's condemned women.* New York: University Press of America.

GIRARD, R. (1977). *Violence and the Sacred* (Patrick Gregory, translator). Baltimore: Johns Hopkins University Press.

GIRARD, R. (1987). *Things hidden since the foundation of the world.* London: The Athlone Press.

HARVEY, L., BURNHAM, R., KENDALL, K., & PEASE, K. (1992). Gender differences in criminal justice: An international comparison. *British Journal of Criminology, 32*(2), 208–217.

HOFF, J. (1994). *Law, gender & injustice: A legal history of U.S. women.* NY: New York University Press.

KOOSED, M. (1996). *Capital punishment: The philosophical, moral, and penological debate over capital punishment.* NY: Garland Publishing.

KRONENWETTER, M. (1993). *Capital punishment: A reference handbook.* Santa Barbara, CA: ABC-CLIO.

KRUTTSCHNITT, C. (1982). Respectable women and the law. *The Sociological Quarterly, 23*(2), 221–234.

MANN, C. (1984). *Female crime and delinquency.* Tuscaloosa, AL: The University of Alabama Press.

NAACP LEGAL AND EDUCATION FUND. (1998). Death Row, U.S.A. NY: NY.

NAFFINE, N. (1987). *Female crime: The construction of women in criminology.* Sydney, Australia: Allen & Unwin.

O'SHEA, K. (1999). *Women and the death penalty in the United States, 1900–1998.* Westport, CT: Praeger.

O'SHEA, K. (2000). *Women on the row: Revelations from both sides of the bars.* Ithaca, NY: Firebrand Books.

PATERNOSTER, R. (1991). *Capital punishment in America.* NY: Lexington Books.

POLLOCK, J. (2002). *Women, prison, and crime* (2nd ed.). Pacific Grove, CA: Brooks/Cole.

QUINNEY, R. (1975). *Class, state and crime: On the theory and practice of criminal justice.* NY: Longman.

REID, S. (2009). *Criminal law (8th Ed.).* USA: Oxford University Press.

ROBERTS, D. (1994). The meaning of gender equality in criminal law. *The Journal of Criminal Law and Criminology, 85*, (1), 1–14.

SIMON, R. & LANDIS, J. (1991). *The crimes women commit, and the punishments they receive.* Lexington, MA: Lexington Books.

SIMPSON, S. (1991). Caste, class, and violent crime: Exploring differences in female offending. *Criminology, 29*(1), 115–135.

SPOHN, C. & SPEARS, J. (1997). Gender and case processing decisions: A comparison of case outcomes for male and female defendants charged with violent felonies. *Women & Criminal Justice, 8*(3), 29–59.

STEFFENSMEIER, D. (1980). Assessing the impact of the women's movement on sex-based differences in the handling of adult criminal defendants. *Crime and Delinquency, 26*, 344–357.

STEFFENSMEIER, D. (1995). Trends in female crime: It's still a man's world. IN B. Price and N. Sokoloff (Eds.)., *The criminal justice system and women: Offenders, victims, and workers* (pp. 89–104).

STREIB, V. (1988). *American executions of female offenders: A preliminary inventory of names, dates, and other information* (3rd ed.). Cleveland: Author.

STREIB, V. (1990). Death penalty for female offenders. *University of Cincinnati Law review, 58*(3), 845–880.

STREIB, V. (1998) *Capital punishment for female offenders, names, dates, and other information* (3rd ed.). Cleveland: Author.

STREIB, V. (2009). Death penalty for female offenders, January 1, 1973 through June 30, 2009. Ada, Ohio: Author.

VISHER, C. (1983). Chivalry in arrest decisions. *Criminology, 21*(1), 5–28.

ZINGRAFF, M & THOMSON, R. (1984). Differential sentencing of men and women in the U.S.A. *International Journal of the Sociology of Law, 12*, 401–413.

ENDNOTES

1. However, the vote in the *Frontiero* case was 4–4 with one justice recusing himself, therefore this was a plurality decision negating the decision as law. A majority is needed to make law.
2. Since this time New York no longer uses the death penalty.

CASES CITED

Atkins v. Virginia, 000 U.S. 00-8452 (2002)
Craig v. Boren, 429 U.S. 190, 197 (1976)
Frontiero v. Richardson, 411 U.S. 677, (1973)
Furman, 408 U.S. 238 (1972)
Jurek, 428 U.S. 262 (1976)
Lockhart v. McCree, 106 S. Ct. 1758 (1986)
McGautha v. California, 402 U.S. 183 (1968)
Powell v. Alabama, 287 U.S. 45 (1932)
Proffitt, 428 U.S. 242 (1976)
Reed v. Reed, 404 U.S. 71, 92 S.Ct. 251, 30 L.Ed.2nd, 255, (1971)
Roper v. Simmons, 000 U.S. 03-633 (2005)
Rudolph v. Alabama, 375 U.S. 889 (1963)
Wainwright v. Witt, 469 U.S. 412 (1985)
Witherspoon v. Illinois, 391 U.S. 510 (1968)

BIOGRAPHICAL INFORMATION

ETTA F. MORGAN, Ph.D., is the Interim Chair and an associate professor in the Department of Criminal Justice and Sociology at Jackson State University, Jackson, Mississippi. Her interests include female criminality, race and gender discrimination, correctional administration and courts.

SECTION V
Women and Criminal Justice Professions

31

Early Policing in the United States

"Help Wanted—Women Need Not Apply!"

Martin L. O'Connor

In the early nineteenth century the United States was a collection of agriculturally based communities. Although these communities employed sheriffs, constables, and a night watch (Bartollas & Hahn, 1999, p. 7), there were no police departments per se. Nevertheless, these communities were strongly influenced by English traditions and practices. Therefore, in 1829, when the English Parliament created the London Metropolitan Police Department and organized a paid police force, the United States took notice. The need and desire for a paid police force in U.S. communities became apparent. In 1833, the city of Philadelphia created its first police department, and in 1844 the New York State Legislature authorized municipalities to create police forces. Soon police departments were created throughout New York (Bartollas & Hahn, 1999). Similar police departments were created in Baltimore, Boston, Cincinnati, Newark, and New Orleans (Richardson, 1974). The personnel policies of the newly created police departments mirrored the discrimination in U.S. society. Simply stated, all police departments were composed exclusively of white males (Bouza, 1992). During the nineteenth and most of the twentieth centuries, the recruitment efforts of American police agencies with respect to women could be summarized as: "Help wanted—women need not apply!"

WOMEN BEGIN TO KNOCK AT THE POLICE DOOR

In the mid-nineteenth century the prison system in the United States was staffed almost exclusively by males. Their male guards sexually exploited a number of female inmates and the attendant publicity created efforts for change. Under pressure from the American Female Moral Reform Society to reform the system, in 1845 the city of New York hired six matrons for its jails (Schultz, 1995). Later, the same effort to place matrons in police stationhouses to assist in processing female arrestees was opposed by the Men's Prison Association (Berg & Budnick, 1986). Although women were not welcome in the male club of policing, the growing need for women to assist police agencies with some of the problems of delinquent children and prostitutes led to the police appointment of a woman "safety worker" in Portland, Oregon, in 1905. Safety Worker Lola Baldwin, although not classified as a police officer, was the first documented appointment of a woman with some police power (Bartollas & Hahn, 1999). In 1910, Alice Stebbins Wells, a social worker, was appointed by the Los Angeles Police Department as a detective to work with women and children. Soon thereafter, police departments throughout the country began employing policewomen in support positions to assist in police work associated with women and children. These women were welcomed into police departments in their support roles (Hale, 1992). In 1922, there were 500 policewomen in the United States, and by 1960 their number had grown to 5,617 (Schultz, 1995). Although women began to see a crack in the police personnel door, the resistance of the male police culture to an expanded role for women in policing was strong and well organized (Martin, 1994). Most of the 17,000 U.S. police agencies did not employ women. Sixty years after the appointment of Alice Stebbins Wells as the first policewoman, the role of women in policing was still confined to support functions or work with juveniles and women. Furthermore, women employed in these positions were frequently required to have greater education than male police officers, and women were not permitted to compete with male officers for promotions (Milton, 1972) and were not given patrol assignments (Price, 1996). Some major U.S. police departments did not employ female officers in any capacity until 1966.[1]

During the 1960s a great wave of social change took place in the United States. The civil rights movement, the antiwar movement, the due process revolution, and the feminist movement were seriously questioning the nation's values. The patriarchal order that had dominated society for thousands of years was under sustained attack.

> The resistance toward women in policing must be ultimately viewed in terms of the patriarchal society. . . . Western society, as well as most other cultures, has been based on social, philosophical, and political systems in which men by force, direct pressure, or through tradition, ritual, custom, language, etiquette, education, and law determine what part women shall or shall not play. . . . In policing, women had the "audacity" to desire entrance to an all male occupation, one that male officers perceived to demand the traditionally masculine attributes of dominance, aggressiveness, superiority and power. (Bartollas & Hahn, 1999, p. 286)

In the United States, women were kept in check by social norms, and legislatures created statutes embodying social values that restricted various opportunities for women. These statutes were generally approved by the courts (*Minor v. Happersett* [1875]: women do not have the right to vote in federal elections; *Hoyt v. Florida* [1961]: women can be exempted from jury service and do not have to fulfill the duties of citizenship; *Bradwell v. Illinois* [1873]: qualified women can be excluded from certain occupations, such as lawyer, simply because of their gender; *Goesaert v. Cleary* [1948]: access of women to certain occupations can be limited; *Radice v. New York* [1924]: women can be prohibited from working nights; *U.S. v. St. Clair* [1968]: women can be exempted from the responsibilities of military service). In the 1960s and 1970s a feminist wave began sweeping the United States. The feminist movement gained the attention of the U.S. Supreme Court when it ruled for the first time that sex-based classifications were "subject to scrutiny under the equal protection clause" (*Reed v. Reed*, 1971). In addition, the feminist movement was given powerful impetus by Betty Friedan, who touched a nerve by what she called "The Problem That Has No Name." In essence, she described the role of American women and their dissatisfaction with a nation that limited their roles in society. She raised the question: "Is this all?" (Friedan, 1963). The same question "Is this all?" could be applied to the second-class role of women in policing where they were principally confined to clerical positions and working with children. The issue was: Are woman going to be able to compete in a police career on an equal footing with their male counterparts? The resounding answer from the police organizational culture in the United States was clear, direct, and powerful. No! In the late 1960s, police officers in the New York City Police Department were asked what they thought about women becoming patrol officers. Some of their responses included the following: "Ptl. Paul DiStephano said, 'The idea of a woman driving a radio car is enough to make you want to quit the job. . . .' Ptl. James Miller said, 'It's a bad arrangement. A woman just isn't built to handle situations that confront policemen. They're not physically equipped to do a job that sometimes demands muscle. . . .' Ptl. George Hall said, 'A woman's place is definitely not in a radio car—it's in an office. I'll even go a little further than that—a woman belongs at home, taking care of the kids.' " (Fyfe, Greene, Walsh, Wilson, & McLaren, 1997). The attitude voiced by these officers in the 1960s fairly reflects the overwhelming sentiment of the U.S. police culture of its day. Women were simply not wanted as full partners in the policing enterprise.

LEGAL FORCES BEGIN TO OPEN POLICE DOORS TO WOMEN

In 1964, Congress passed the most historic and sweeping civil rights legislation ever enacted, 42 U.S.C., § 2000. Title VII of this legislation dealt with discrimination in employment on the basis of race, color, religion, national origin, and sex. It is of interest to note that the legislation was designed primarily to address racial discrimination and the word *sex* was added to the bill at the last minute on the floor of the House of Representatives by opponents of the measure in an attempt to prevent its passage (Freeman, 1991, p. 163). Notwithstanding enormous opposition in Congress, the Civil Rights Bill became law in July 1965. The legislation did not affect discrimination against women in most police departments immediately because the act exempted municipal governments from its coverage. However, the act was a very important legal force with respect to discrimination in U.S. society. Women began to believe that it might be possible for the barriers to equal employment in policing to be removed. In 1968, two women in Indianapolis became the first in the nation to be appointed to regular patrol duties in a marked police car (Lord, 1995). Very few municipalities followed the Indianapolis lead. In fact, in some states legal statutes still prohibited women from becoming patrol officers.[2] Therefore, even if an enlightened police official in these states wanted to appoint a female to patrol duties, state statutes and civil service requirements prevented such action. Finally, in 1972, Title VII was amended to apply to state and municipal governments, thereby providing protection against discrimination in employment for women seeking entry to police departments.

However, the legal battle was not yet over. Women soon found that there were additional barriers preventing them from assuming the role of police officer. These hurdles were the numerous height, weight, and physical fitness standards that were in effect in police departments across the nation. It was not uncommon for these standards to require that applicants be 5 feet 7 inches to 5 feet 10 inches in height. Also, applicants had to pass an obstacle course test, a standing broad jump, pull-ups, a sit-up while holding a weight on one's shoulders, and one-handed dumbbell presses (Fyfe et al., 1997). These standards excluded most women from entering the police profession. The relevancy of these standards was highly questionable and almost all of these standards were eliminated as a result of the U.S. Supreme Court decision in *Griggs v. Duke Power Company* (1971). In *Griggs*, the Court unanimously approved the disparate impact method of analyzing discrimination claims. Therefore, a policy or practice may be discriminatory if it has a disproportionate effect upon a particular group and is not job related or justified by business necessity. Hence, height, weight, and physical fitness standards that were facially neutral in their treatment of different groups but, in fact, fell more harshly on women violated Title VII because these standards could not meet the job-related test of *Griggs*. Since *Griggs*, law enforcement agencies have repeatedly tried to justify some measure of height, weight, and physical fitness requirements but have been unable to do so (see also *Dothard v. Rawlinson*, 1977).[3]

THE POLICE DOOR IS LEGALLY OPEN TO WOMEN

After state laws banning women from policing were overturned by the mandates of Title VII and height, weight, and physical fitness standards were removed because they could not meet the test of *Griggs*, women began entering the police profession in increasing numbers. Some women entered police departments and did not encounter great difficulties.[4] Nevertheless, many women encountered enormous resistance from the police organizational culture. Women experienced this resistance very early in their police careers and frequently upon their entry to police academies. In some police academies the physical fitness routine that was geared to male officers was used to demonstrate that females lack the physical strength to be police officers. The lack of upper body strength prevented many female recruits from doing as well as their male counterparts on some physical fitness regimes. In addition, some police academy trainers reluctantly agreed to provide remedial firearms training to female recruits because of a female's unfamiliarity with weapons and a lack of hand strength.

Occasionally, police academy instructors have stood in front of police academy classes and stated, "I don't care what they say, women don't belong on the job."[5] In police academy role-play exercises, female recruits who did not act in an aggressive manner like their male counterparts were considered to have "no command presence." Civility by female recruits was viewed as a sign of weakness. In some police academies it was required that recruits get into a boxing ring with boxing gloves and actually fight a male officer. One training officer in a major police agency suggested that this was necessary to see if a female officer "could take a punch."[6] Some women claimed that they were boxed right out of the police academy (*Newsday*, December 1986).

When female officers graduated from police academies and assumed their role as patrol officers, it was not uncommon for male officers to continue their hostility. Male officers viewed patrol work as "men's work" (Balkin, 1988; Milton, 1974). The hostility toward women on patrol has been based primarily on stereotypes regarding the ability of women to do what is considered a man's job (Bell, 1982). A number of studies were conducted in several cities throughout the United States to determine whether women can perform patrol work as effectively as men. The results of these studies demonstrated overwhelmingly that women are capable of successful performance as patrol officers (Bartell & Associates, 1978; Bartlett & Rosenblum, 1977; Bloch & Anderson, 1974; Sherman, 1975). The problem with these studies is the question that is raised: Can women perform patrol work as successfully as men? This question presupposes that there is a male way of policing. There is not. Although some males may be more aggressive than some females, both males and females bring their own individuality to the problems of policing. Some males are not suited for police work and some females are not suited for police work. Individual knowledge, skills, and abilities are the most important determinants of whether a person can be an effective patrol officer, not gender.

WOMEN IN POLICING: THE TWENTY-FIRST CENTURY

In 2006 the Bureau of Labor Statistics indicated that women account for almost 59 percent of the workforce in the United States. Approximately 33 percent of the legal profession is now comprised of women. The most recent reports of the U.S. Bureau of Justice Statistics indicate that there are approximately 730,000 full time law enforcement officers in the United States and these officers work for some 17,700 state and local law enforcement agencies. In 1999 women held approximately 14 percent of our nation's law enforcement positions, 8.8 percent of supervisory positions and 7.4 percent of the top command positions (International Association of Chiefs of Police [IACP], 1998). The number of women in policing seems to have peaked in 1999 at 14 percent and today women represent approximately 12 percent of the officers in policing (Lonsway, 2003). Policing continues to be an overwhelmingly masculine enterprise. Some argue that the gains for women in policing have been very slow and that women will not reach a gender balance in policing for another seventy years (Martin, 1990, p. 3). Others contend that women are discouraged from applying to law enforcement agencies because of policing's aggressive authoritarian image, an image based upon an outdated paramilitary model of law enforcement (Lonsway, 2001). There are those who believe that widespread bias in police hiring, selection practices, and recruitment policies keep women out of law enforcement. The National Center for Women & Policing (NCWP)[7] argues that entry exams with an overemphasis on upper body strength still wash out many qualified women. Many women never consider a career in policing due to a misunderstanding of the nature of the job and aggressive authoritarian images portrayed in the media (Felperin, 2004). The NCWP contends that "it is critical that police agencies remedy the disproportionate negative impact of physical agility tests on women versus men in the selection process" (Lonsway, 2003). In a study of numerous police agencies that still use push-ups, sit-ups, wall climb, trigger pull, ladder climb, vehicle push, swimming, ammunition load, agility test, 1.5-mile run, and dummy drag, there was no consensus on the types of tests that should be used. It has been cogently argued that entry-level physical agility testing can be eliminated, as many law enforcement agencies have done without apparent negative consequences and replaced with a health-based screening to assess general physical fitness (Lonsway, 2003). Police agencies need to determine whether or not any stage in their selection process screens out women in larger numbers than men and if so, ascertain the reason (Polisar, 1998). It is well known that very few police departments in America require police officers who are no longer on probation to undergo yearly physical agility tests. Hence, it is doubtful that thousands of seasoned police officers who are successfully performing their duties in America could successfully complete the various agility tests that are currently obstacles for new police recruits. If this is the case, why should an institution create entry-level physical agility barriers that the average police officer may not be able to pass? Patrol officers have successfully functioned in their fifties and sixties. In San Francisco, a 56-year-old grandfather was hired as a new police officer in 2008 (Scoville, 2008). Because of these facts alone, it is unlikely that entry-level physical agility tests that are imposed upon some new police recruits can meet the job-related requirements mandated by the United States Supreme Court in *Griggs*.

When new recruits are appointed to police departments they are usually assigned to a police academy for several months of training. Upon assignment to the academy, a recruit is introduced to the military model of policing that is still widespread in the United States. Some large police agencies employ the psychoauthoritarian stress-training model of recruit training that is closely associated with the training in some military boot camps. This "in-your-face" training model frequently involves screaming, extraordinary profanity, and demeaning actions by police trainers toward police recruits and it turns off a certain number of males and females who may be interested in police careers. This psychoauthoritarian training model has been criticized by some of the most prominent members of the police community.[8] Hopefully, during the twenty-first century, police administrators will finally realize that this Neanderthal model of police training keeps talented men and women from the police profession, is incompatible with the concept of community policing, and is detrimental to effective policing in a free society. There is an urgent need for improved police training, with a focus on human communication to develop officers who are capable of helping citizens identify and solve problems in their communities (Birzer & Tannehill, 2001).

The International Association of Chiefs of Police (IACP) established a committee to examine the role of women in policing. The committee, utilizing the resources of the Gallup Organization, conducted a survey of some of its 14,000 members. The survey confirmed critical information regarding the status of women in policing. While recognizing that the number of women in policing is growing, it also revealed:

- There are few women in policing compared to their male counterparts.
- Women still face bias from male officers.
- Many police departments lack strategies for recruiting women.
- Women officers may face gender discrimination and a "glass ceiling" that inhibits promotion.
- Sexual harassment still occurs in many police departments.
- Although the need is great, there are very few mentoring programs for women officers.

Early in the twentieth century, the IACP endorsed the employment of women only in support roles in policing, not in patrol functions. Therefore, it is an extraordinary change for this major international police organization to now state that "it is essential to strengthen the position of women in policing—their professional development, their progress to positions of leadership and their contribution to the public service . . ." (IACP, 1998).

Some of the specific recommendations of the IACP study are as follows:

1. Police agencies should be educated regarding the value of gender diversity in policing.
2. Police agencies should advertise and recruit qualified women.
3. Police agencies should train members regarding gender discrimination and sexual harassment and adopt a zero-tolerance approach to discrimination and sexual harassment.
4. Police agencies should establish policies to improve the role of women in policing.
5. Police agencies should mentor female officers and strengthen their potential for longevity.
6. Police agencies should improve promotional strategies for women and move women into police leadership positions.

The IACP has concluded that while a number of agencies have welcomed women officers, "many simply have not . . . [and] women have often had to bring litigation against departments to overcome resistance" (IACP, 1998). The IACP survey disclosed that 17 percent of the agencies surveyed had no female officers and 55 percent of the agencies surveyed had between one and four female officers. Ninety-one percent of the police departments surveyed had no female officers in policy-making positions. In addition, 28 percent of the departments surveyed express concern that "women lack sufficient physical strength, capacity for confrontation, size, strength and force" (p. 13). This finding is troubling in light of the overwhelming evidence that policing is more cerebral than physical and it suggests that the myth that one must be big, strong, and physical to be a police officer still has support in the police organizational culture.[9] Perhaps, that is why women continue to be disproportionately assigned to support positions rather than patrol (Martin, 1990). Another factor may be paternalism, which involves male officers protecting or excusing women from undesirable tasks. This practice of assigning women to nonline functions suggests that women can't be "real cops," and it stigmatizes female officers in general and creates resentment among male officers (Padavic & Reskin, 1990).

It has taken almost 150 years for women to represent 12 percent of our nation's police forces (Scoville, 2008). The police road they have traveled in the latter half of the twentieth century has been difficult for many. Nevertheless, despite the pessimistic views of some regarding the future of women in policing, there is much to be optimistic about in the twenty-first century. Today, women work in every phase of police work: patrol, investigations, emergency services, street crime units, undercover units, and on SWAT teams. A number of legal and cultural barriers to women in policing have been jettisoned. Women are showing an interest in police careers. Studies in numerous areas, New York, California, Washington, D.C., and Denver clearly indicate that women are quite capable of successful performance as patrol officers (Martin, 1996). Female officers rely less on physical force and more on communication skills and potentially violent confrontations are less likely to occur or escalate into excessive force situations (Report of the Independent Commission on the Los Angeles Police Department, 1991). Female officers are less likely to use deadly force (Horvath, 1987) or excessive force or incur citizen complaints (Lonsway, 2002).

PIERCING THE BRASS CEILING

In 1985, Penny Harrington of the Portland Oregon Police Department became the first female Chief of Police (Schulz, 2003). Females have also been appointed as chiefs of police in Houston, Atlanta, Washington, D.C., San Francisco, Detroit, Cleveland, Tampa, and Milwaukee. In 2009 there were 212 female chiefs of police in our nation. (*Chicago Tribune*, 2009). Because this is a small number it does not adequately describe the success of many women who have pierced the brass ceiling in police departments. There are countless women throughout the United States who have reached top administrative levels in their police departments. They have become police captains, deputy chiefs, assistant chiefs, chiefs of detectives, chiefs of patrol, chiefs of investigative services, chiefs of support services, deputy police commissioners, and deputy police superintendents. For example, early in this chapter it was noted that in the late 1960s several police officers in the New York City Police Department provided negative views concerning the ability of women to function as police officers. Ten years after those negative comments, Joanne Jaffe joined the New York City Police Department as a patrol officer in the 75th precinct. She quickly rose through the ranks of the department by becoming a sergeant, lieutenant, captain, deputy inspector, inspector, and assistant chief. Joanne worked in eight of the department's police precincts, the narcotics division, the street crime unit, the detective bureau, and the Office of Management Analysis and Planning. In 2010 Chief Joanne Jaffe is in charge of the housing bureau and is one of the highest ranking chiefs in the department. (NYPD, 2010). Similar stories can be told about female officers in the Nassau County, New York Police Department, where the highest ranking uniformed officer is a woman (NYPD, 2010), the Suffolk County, New York Police Department, the Chicago Police Department, and other police departments throughout the country where women have significant positions in the command staff of their agencies. At least one study found that female police executives were more flexible, emotionally independent, self-assertive, self-confident, and creative than their male counterparts (Price, 1974). Being a police chief, like being a CEO in other professions, is not an easy job. It involves a great deal of time, effort, study, and sacrifice. Ascending a career ladder in a police department involves working nights, weekends, holidays, and being away from one's family on special occasions such as birthdays and anniversaries. One study found that family and child care responsibilities, among others, played a more significant role in women's decisions to forego promotional opportunities than they did for men (Whetstone, 2001). A recent headline in the *New York Times* captured the essence of the success of women in policing: Female Police Chiefs, a Novelty No More (*New York Times*, 2009).

A number of studies demonstrate that female officers utilize a less authoritarian style of policing and rely less on physical force (Worden, 1995). The cult of machismo in policing is changing, albeit at a glacial pace. Unlike some of their predecessors, male officers now recognize that women make "good cops." Major police departments and police organizations have expressed the desire to recruit, employ, and promote more women in policing.[10] Studies reported by The National Center for Women in Policing documented advantages to hiring and retaining female officers. These reasons include the following:

- Female officers are less likely to use excessive force, deadly force, or incur citizen complaints resulting in fewer lawsuits for their departments.
- Physical strength has not been shown to predict general police effectiveness or the ability to handle dangerous situations.
- Female officers can help implement community policing.
- Employing female officers assists in improving the police response to violence against women.
- Because of their interpersonal skills, female officers can de-escalate potentially violent situations.
- The presence of women reduces the problems of sexual harassment because sexual harassment is more prevalent in male-dominated environments.

LAWS THAT ASSIST WOMEN IN THE POLICE PROFESSION

The U.S. Supreme Court has established guidelines regarding sexual harassment that significantly increase the chance of employer liability if employers do not rid their workplace of sexual harassment (*Burlington Industries v. Ellerth*, 1998; *Faragher v. City of Boca Raton*, 1998). The Court has said that even a sitting president of the United States is not immune from charges of sexual harassment (*Clinton v. Jones*, 1997). Almost all police departments have established sexual harassment policies (IACP, 1998).

Women in policing may become pregnant and during their pregnancy they may not be able to perform all of the duties of police officers. The law is quite clear that employers may not enact fetal protection policies that exclude women from hazardous jobs (*UAW v. Johnson Controls*, 499 U.S. 187, 1991). Decisions about what is best for the unborn child are the responsibility of the parent. Hence, police administrators cannot exclude a female member of the force who is pregnant from working as a police officer. The Federal Pregnancy Discrimination Act 42 U.S.C. section 2000e(k) requires that employers treat women who are pregnant the same as other employees who are temporarily disabled. Thus, if "light duty" assignments are available for other officers who are temporarily disabled, they must also be extended to women who are pregnant. The Family Medical Leave Act of 1993 29 U.S.C. sections 2601–2654 provide pregnant women with twelve weeks of leave for pregnancy and they cannot be required to forfeit their job.

CONCLUSION

Female police officers have come a long way in the past forty years. There are no longer overt signs that women are not wanted in the policing enterprise. In the past twenty-five years, many women have successfully completed their police careers and are now enjoying retirement. New female recruits enter police academies every year. They probably do not know of the extraordinary efforts of the female officers who preceded them. Female police organizations, which did not exist in the past, have been created to assist women in their police careers. These organizations include, but are not limited to, The International

Association of Women Police (IAWP), Women in Law Enforcement, National Center for Women & Policing (NCWP), Women in Federal Law Enforcement (WIFLE), and various state and local female police organizations. Female police officers are also becoming involved in predominantly male police organizations such as the International Association of Chiefs of Police (IACP) and in 2010 a female chief of police became the first female President of the California Police Chiefs' Association.[11] The increased representation of women in all aspects of law enforcement is almost certain to transform the authoritarian military climate of police agencies and hopefully make American policing kinder, gentler, and more sensitive to individual rights and the envy of the world.

REFERENCES

BALKIN, J. (1988). Why policemen don't like policewomen. *Journal of Police Science and Administration, 16*(1), 29–38.

BARTELL & ASSOCIATES. (1978). *The study of police women competency in the performance of sector police work in the city of Philadelphia.* Author.

BARTLETT, H. W., & ROSENBLUM, A. (1977). *Policewomen effectiveness in Denver.* Denver, CO: Civil Service Commission.

BARTOLLAS, C., & HAHN, L. D. (1999). *Policing in America.* Needham Heights, MA: Allyn & Bacon.

BELL, D. J. (1982). Policewomen: Myths and reality. *Journal of Police Science and Administration, 16*(1), 29–38.

BERG, B. L., & BUDNICK, K. J. (1986). Defeminization of women in law enforcement: A new twist in the traditional police personality. *Journal of Police Science and Administration*, 314.

BIRZER, M. L., & TANNEHILL, R. (2001, June). A more effective training approach for contemporary policing. *Police Quarterly, 4*(2), 233–252.

BLOCH, P. B., & ANDERSON, D. (1974). *Policewomen on patrol: Final report.* Washington, D.C.: Urban Institute, pp. 1–67.

BOUZA, A. V. (1992). *The police mystique: An insider's look at cops, crime and the criminal justice system.* New York: Plenum Press.

FELPERIN, J. (2004, May 18). "Women in Law Enforcement: Two Steps forward, three steps back." Northridge, CA. reported in PoliceOne.Com News, available at http://www.policeone.com/.

FREEMAN, J. (1991). How "sex" got into Title VII: Persistent opportunism as a maker of public policy. *J.L. & Equality, 9*, 163.

FRIEDAN, B. (1963). *The feminine mystique.* New York: Norton.

FYFE, J. J., GREENE, J. R., WALSH, W. F., WILSON, O. W., & McLAREN, R. C. (1997). *Police administration* (5th ed.). New York: McGraw-Hill.

HALE, D. C. (1992). Women in policing. In G. W. Cordner & D. C. Hale (Eds.), *What works in policing? Operations and administration examined.* Cincinnati, OH: Anderson/Academy of Criminal Justice Sciences.

INTERNATIONAL ASSOCIATION OF CHIEFS OF POLICE. (1998). *The future of women in policing: Mandates for action.*

JAFFE, J. (2010, January). NYPD, New York's Finest. Retrieved January 4, 2010, from Police Department City of New York: http://nyc.gov/html/nypd/html/administration/housing_co.shtml.

LONSWAY, K. (2001). *Equality denied: The status of women in policing: 2001.* Arlington, VA: National Center for Women & Policing.

LONSWAY, K. (2002). *Men, women and police excessive force: A tale of two genders—A content analysis of civil liability cases, sustained allegations & citizen complaints.* Arlington, VA: National Center for Women & Policing.

LONSWAY, K. (2003). *Hiring & retaining more women: The advantages to law enforcement agencies.* Arlington, VA: National Center for Women & Policing.

LORD, L. K. (1995). Policewomen. In *The encyclopedia of police science* (2nd ed.). New York: William Bailey.

MARTIN, S. E. (1990). *On the move: The status of women in policing.* Washington, DC: Police Foundation.

MARTIN, S. E. (1994, August). Outsider within the station house: The impact of race and gender on black women police. *Social Problems,* 41.

MARTIN, S. E. & JURIK, N. C. (1996). "Doing Justice, Doing Gender: Women in Law and Criminal Justice Occupations," Sage Publications, Thousand Oaks, California.

MILGRAM, D. (2002, April). "Recruiting Women to Policing: Practical Strategies That Work." *The Police Chief Magazine.*

MILTON, C. (1972). *Women in police.* Washington, DC: Police Foundation.

MILTON, C. (1974). *Women in policing: A manual.* Washington, DC: Police Foundation.

MROZ, J. (April 6, 2008). Female police chiefs, a novelty no more. NY: New York Times.

PADAVIC, I., & RESKIN, B. (1990). Men's behavior and women's interest in blue-collar jobs. *Social Problems, 37,* 613–628.

POLISAR, J., & MILGRAM, D. (1998, October). Recruiting, integrating and retaining women police officers: Strategies that work. *The Police Chief Magazine.*

PRICE, B. R. (1974). *A study of leadership strength of female police executives: Police perspectives, problems, prospects.* New York: Praeger, pp. 96–107.

REPORT OF THE INDEPENDENT COMMISSION ON THE LOS ANGELES POLICE DEPARTMENT (1991).

RICHARDSON, J. F. (1974). *Urban police in the United States.* Port Washington, NY: Kennikat Publishing.

RICHIE, M. (September 18, 2009). *It's not so rare for new top cops to be women:* The U.S. counts 212 female police chiefs, still a vast minority. Chicago, IL.: Chicago Tribune, quoting a spokesperson from the National Center for Women in Policing.

SCHULTZ, D. M. (1995). *From social worker to crime fighter: Women in United States municipal policing.* Westport, CT: Praeger.

SCHULTZ, D. M. (2003). Women Police Chiefs: A Statistical Profile. *Police Quarterly,* Vol 6, No. 3, September 2003, p. 332.

SCOVILLE, D. (2008, February). The State of American Law Enforcement—The Blue Mosaic "Policies meant to diversify law enforcement agencies have changed police demographics and will continue to do so in the future." *Police Magazine.*

SHERMAN, L. J. (1975). An evaluation of policewomen on patrol in a suburban police department. *Journal of Police Science and Administration, 3*(4), 434–438.

TUOMEY, L. M. (2009, June). Step Up to Law Enforcement: A Successful Strategy for Recruiting Women into the Law Enforcement Profession. *The Police Chief: The Professional Voice of Law Enforcement.*

WHETSTONE, T. S. (2001). Copping Out: Why police officers decline to participate in the sergeant's promotional process. *American Journal of Criminal Justice,* 25(2), 147–159.

WORDEN, R. E. (1995). The causes of police brutality: Theory and evidence on police use of force. In *And justice for all: Understanding and controlling police abuse of force.* Washington, D.C.: Police Executive Research Forum.

ENDNOTES

1. The Nassau County Police Department in New York is the seventh largest police department in the United States, with a force of more than 3,000 sworn officers. This department did not hire women in any supporting role until the mid-1960s.

2. See New York Civil Service Law, § 58, which specifically provided that only a "male" could become a patrol officer in New York. The male restriction was not removed by the New York state legislature until 1972, when Title VII of the Civil Rights Act of 1964 was amended so that it applied to state and municipal governments.

3. The Civil Rights Act of 1991 further strengthened Title VII after the decision of the U.S. Supreme Court in *Wards Cove Packing Co. v. Antonio* (1989).

4. The author has interviewed several female officers in different police departments who believe that they were treated quite fairly. However, some women in the same police academy class have had very different experiences and perceptions regarding their acceptance by the male police culture.

5. The author was involved as a police administrator in two major police agencies in the United States. During a career of more than 30 years there were several occasions in which statements like this were reported to have occurred during formal training sessions. In some cases, police instructors readily admitted making the statements. In addition, anecdotal information of similar statements being made in other police academies across the country was not uncommon.

6. By parity of reasoning, one police observer suggested (tongue in cheek) that trainers should shoot police recruits to see if they can take a shot.

7. The National Center for Women & Policing (NCWP), a division of the Feminist Majority Foundation, promotes increasing the numbers of women in all ranks of law enforcement as a strategy to improve police response to violence against women, reduce police brutality and excessive force, and strengthen community policing. Since 1995 the NCWP has attempted to educate criminal justice policy makers and produce and disseminate original research on issues relevant to women in the field of law enforcement. http://www.womenandpolicing.org/aboutus.asp.

8. Herman Goldstein, former chief of police Joseph McNamara, and the late Daniel P. Guido, the former commissioner of police of the Nassau County New York Police Department, and the Suffolk County New York Police, the Westchester County New York Police Department, the Yonkers New York Police Department, and the Stamford Connecticut Police Department. Numerous other police officials have also condemned this extreme paramilitary model of police training.

9. Physical strength has not been shown to predict general police effectiveness (Sherman, 1975), or the ability to handle dangerous situations successfully (Bell, 1982).

10. Police departments in Albuquerque and Tucson have dramatically increased their female recruits (Polisar & Milgram, 1998) and 25 percent of the Madison, Wisconsin, Police Department now is composed of female officers. In addition, the International Association of Chiefs of Police is making a major effort to encourage its members to recruit, employ, and promote women in policing.

11. San Mateo Police Chief Susan Manheimer will be the first female police chief installed as the associations' president, California Police Chiefs Association, http://www.cpcaconference.com/, accessed January 4, 2010.

CASES

Bradwell v. Illinois, 88 U.S. 130 (1873).
Burlington Industries v. Ellerth, 524 U.S. 742 (1998).
Clinton v. Jones, 520 U.S. 681 (1997).
Dothard v. Rawlinson, 433 U.S. 321 (1977).
Faragher v. City of Boca Raton, 524 U.S. 775 (1998).
Goesaert v. Cleary, 335 U.S. 464 (1948).
Griggs v. Duke Power Co., 401 U.S. 424 (1971).

Hoyt v. Florida, 368 U.S. 57 (1961).
Minor v. Happersett, 88 U.S. 162 (1875).
Radice v. New York, 264 U.S. 292 (1924).
Reed v. Reed, 404 U.S. 71 (1971).
UAW v. Johnson Controls, 499 U.S. 187 (1991).
U.S. v. St. Clair, 291 F. Supp. 122 (1968).
Wards Cove Packing Co. v. Antonio, 490 U.S. 642 (1989).

32

The Policies of United States Police Departments

Equal Access, Equal Treatment?

Corina Schulze

❖

INTRODUCTION

The work-related policies of institutions establish standards of employment and subsequent evaluation standards, as well as employee rights. Despite equal access and job-related policies and rights, gendered barriers in employment proved insurmountable for many women who were excluded from leadership positions, were denied equal pay, and were victims of discrimination in the workplace. Efforts of feminist groups in the 1960s allowed women to enter previously barred occupations. Though there was an explicit assumption of equality, implicitly this was not the case. Feminists battled discrimination in and outside the legal and political system. These feminists, though comprised of diverse groups, are generally classified according to whether or not they felt policies should be gender-neutral (thus stressing "equality") or whether they should acknowledge the biological and socially constructed gender differences (thus stressing women's "difference") (Freeman, 1988). Policies today are a reflection of this dichotomous philosophical disagreement because some prescribe equal treatment, such as mandatory written tests for employment, and others do not, such as policies that focus on the recruitment of women.

Some studies have found that when polled regarding predominately "women's" issues, female police officers hold distinct views from their male counterparts (Homant & Kennedy, 1985; Stalans & Finn, 2000; Sun, 2007), demonstrating their potential to affect their organization's culture. In a recent study of perceptions concerning job-related policies, Colvin (2009) found that though homophobia is still inherent to policing, this type of discrimination appears to be lessening over time. The increasing cultural diversity of police departments might signify important changes for women as well. The future of women in policing is in large part dependent on the policies that allow their entry as equals while recognizing their "difference" and unique contribution to the changing workplace.

Two police departmental policies regarding equal access and employment rights are discussed in this chapter: the physical fitness tests recruits are required to pass before graduating and the department's family leave policies (having to do with a birth of a child). Police departments are a microcosm of society at large in that masculine qualities dominate and employment policies serve to reinforce collectively agreed-upon gender roles. Written tests for men and women are the same whereas physical agility tests, which tend to favor masculine attributes, vary by department in content and in their level of gender specificity. That is, some departments mandate separate tests for men and women and some do not. This current state of affairs remains relatively unquestioned by academics and police officers alike. It is simply assumed that women's "difference" warrants this type of unequal treatment. Indeed, separate physical testing requirements are posited to benefit women in entering the profession. The ramifications of such a policy, as well as the possibility that there are better, gender-neutral physical tests, have not received sufficient attention.

Once women gain access to police work, they find, for the most part, that job-related policies are so constructed so as to downplay gender differences. Women's child-bearing capability is touted as uniquely feminine by society and feminists alike, but police departments have overwhelmingly denied it as a condition warranting a policy should a police officer become a parent. The survey of U.S. police departments presented in the following confirms this policy void in law enforcement.

Retention of female employees should be considered as important as recruitment efforts. The solution seems obvious: Family leave policies should be drafted and be sufficiently accommodating to female officers who become parents. Another solution, though more dramatic in the type of organizational change required, would accommodate male officers who become parents as well, thus signifying a radically different relationship between employer and employee.

Increasing women's representation in law enforcement will do little to improve gender relations if police culture is not modified to adapt to the ongoing evolution of gender roles in greater society. As King (2005) articulates best, "while increasing the number of policewomen is an essential precursor to change, changing the culture of the police is also crucial if policewomen are to reach their full potential" (p. 218). Formal policy change, though perhaps at first lackluster in effect, will eventually spur changes. For now, at the very least, we can continue to evaluate current policies and raise awareness of their gendered implications. The following examines family leave and physical testing as two very important policies that serve to draw attention to gender differences and, at the same time, undercut feminine qualities and tout masculine attributes as best suited for the job of policing.

FAMILY LEAVE POLICIES: CAN POLICE DEPARTMENTS ACCOMMODATE PREGNANCIES?

The United States lags in family leave policy comprehensiveness to a significant degree. The Project on Global Working Families (2004), supported by the Ford Foundation, found that:

> 163 countries around the world offer guaranteed paid leave to women in connection with childbirth. The U.S. does not. The only other industrialized country which does not have paid

maternity or parental leave for women, Australia, guarantees a full year of unpaid leave to all women in the country. In contrast, the Family and Medical Leave Act (FMLA) in the U.S. provides only 12 weeks of unpaid leave to approximately half of mothers in the U.S. and nothing for the remainder. 45 countries ensure that fathers either receive paid paternity leave or have a right to paid parental leave. The United States guarantees fathers neither paid paternity nor paid parental leave. (p. 1)

This dearth in policy is especially damaging to women, and men, in "nontraditional" fields like law enforcement. The profession's overt demands for loyalty discourage police officers from taking leave for family-related reasons. Women are particularly affected by this type of culture because, if extrapolation from the general public to police officers is appropriate, they are primarily responsible for child-care-taking activities (U.S. Census Report Bureau, 2004).[1]

In 1993 women were permitted under national protection, without fear of dismissal or demotion, to take time from work so that they could give birth or take care of a sick child or an elderly parent. Federal law, in the form of the Federal Family Leave Act (FMLA), mandates that public employers must provide their employees with a minimum of twelve weeks of unpaid leave for the birth or adoption of a child.[2] Employees are also given the discretion to substitute paid vacation, personal, or family leave for FMLA leave so that the time taken is not a financial hardship (29 CFR 825.207).[3] FMLA's design is gender-neutral, so "family leave" policies of police departments must indicate that both fathers and mothers are able to take time off for the birth of a child. However, family leave policies are not gender-neutral, either in design or outcome, and traditional notions of police work and gender role expectations saturate police departments. The underlying presumption of FMLA, and the resulting family leave policies of local and state governments, is that women and men are equally responsible in parenting, an assumption with no factual support.

Despite FMLA's rather meager provisions, or perhaps *because of*, police departments tend to rely solely on its provisions typically having no local or state policy in place to guide the construction of a policy that would accommodate expecting mothers. In a study of departmental family leave policies, I found that a number of women, who helped draft the policy in their departments, were also the first officers to become pregnant (Schulze, 2008). In relatively uncharted waters, these women adapted to their work-environment, without much compromise on the part of the administration. In the survey, women were asked to describe their accommodations, which ranged from light duty and maternity pay to none at all. Most of the responses fell on the latter part of that continuum.

Some studies suggest that women have a difficult time entering male-dominated professions because of their parental responsibilities (Beggs, 1995; Blau et al., 1998; Brown & Pechman, 1987; Fiske & Glick, 1995; Reskin, 2000; Taylor, 2000; Walsh, 1993). Furthermore, women are generally the primary caretakers in a family (Fitzpatrick & Gomez, 1997; Kanter & Stein, 1979; Lechner, 1994; Waldfogel, 1998; Walsh, 1993) signifying a need for comprehensive leave policy. Research suggests that women resign from law enforcement due to child care issues (Seagram and Stark-Adames, 1992).

Law enforcement has a propensity, as a profession, to downplay the dual role of parent and police officer. Masculine institutions have been shown to discourage overall rates of family leave taking in both men and women, creating a climate that devalues parenthood and celebrates the time-honored bread-winner model (Kim, 1998). Police departments urge their employees to work long hours while their spouses are tasked with the majority of the familial responsibilities. Women's obvious physical incapacitation, brought on by pregnancy and child birth, would seem to necessitate policy that is sensitive to their needs. It would seem that such a policy should incorporate knowledge that a disproportionate share of the familial responsibilities are borne by working mothers (Fitzpatrick & Gomez, 1997; Kanter & Stein, 1979; Lechner, 1994; Waldfogel, 1998; Walsh, 1993).

Women police officers desire more comprehensive family leave policies but some evidence suggests that these women desire leave policies that emphasize the gender-neutrality of care taking (Schulze, 2008). By drawing attention to a woman's pregnancy and her parenthood, police departments inadvertently transform what should be an important employee issue into a "women's issue." This stereotype, that mothers create more a disruption in the workplace by their motherhood than men do, as evidenced by their need for "special" policies, serves to reinforce stereotypes of women's disruption to law enforcement.

Parenthood's secondary status is evident in the lack of codified departmental family leave policies. In studying the family leave policies of 203 major United States police departments, one finds an overwhelming tendency of departments to defer to city policy, not having a codified version of their own (Schulze, 2008). Only 11.0 percent of the sampled police departments were found to have a clear, administrative policy in place explicating the department's handling of an employee who becomes a parent. Some of these policies simply mirrored federal or city law. Limited duty assignments were found in 5.4 percent (11/203) of the police departments. Given the physical and emotional demands of police work, the lack of accommodating family leave policies is surprising. The women police officers, all of whom were parents, expressed a deep dissatisfaction in their administration's insensitivity. The excerpt below from one of the study's respondents perhaps conveys this sentiment best:

> Hell yes it needs [to be] improved. Females should be able to work investigations, records, or property after they can no longer effectively do their job on the street. There is plenty of work that needs to be done in these areas to make us more effective while we're pregnant. Let's face it, does it do the dept any good to have us sit at home for 6 months while we, well, gestate? It's a danger to the female officer that doesn't have the time to take off or can't afford to take the disability pay and stay on the street longer than they should. We're basically punished for wanting a family, but the male officers that want kids can have their cake and eat it too. I worked until the day before I delivered for both of my pregnancies, but there wasn't a day that went by that I didn't question the safety of my baby. I did everything I could to protect myself, but this is an inherently dangerous job. I couldn't give in and take the time off and by my second pregnancy I didn't have any time left (my girls are 16 months apart.) I actually had to take a few weeks off without pay the second time around.

A lack of policy does not necessarily indicate a department's purposeful denigration of motherhood, or parenthood in general. Cultural conceptions of what police work demands and the liberal American work ethic discourage any meaningful questioning of these policies. Any accommodation counter to these conceptions, like altered shifts, gives the impression that women are not as hardworking and are overly demanding. The women respondents in this study displayed significant awareness of these social forces. Many of them mentioned wanting policies that treat men and women equally responsible as parents, thus drawing attention away from a woman's leave taking and concentrating instead on what should be the societal importance of the family unit, and a parent's responsibility in upholding that value. One officer writes:

> I think the leave policy would be better if men could be paid for 30 days leave for the birth of a new child. I also think better training for our management to understand maternity leave would be good. Now that I am back [from] maternity leave, every time I ask for time off or to go to a training class I get the response of "you are never here." [N]o one considers the fact I was gone on maternity leave. They just talk about how I am gone all the time.

In a later study, included are both men and women parents finding a similar consciousness regarding the importance of parenthood and the difficulties in balancing the role of parent and as police officer (Schulze, 2010a). One female officer wrote:

> When I had my children, I felt as if it was a huge inconvenience for the Department. I was in patrol at the time and when I went on light duty during my pregnancy and then took off for family leave, my squad was left short on manpower. This creates resentment among the other officers who then could not take off as much time as they wanted. I have also seen this resentment [directed toward] male officers who elect to take off more than a couple days when their child is born.

Nevertheless, even male parents were cited as uninformed about the difficulties faced by mothers due to their often unequal share of the familial responsibilities. A female officer in the study explains:

> Most males and supervisors do not understand that even though I am a co-worker and police officer, I am still a mother and a wife that does all the same "wife" duties at home as their wives do [who] usually do not work full time jobs.

The women in the study placed more emphasis on comprehensive, paid leave and accommodating work schedules than the male respondents did. In other words, parenthood had more an effect on a woman's cognitive perception of her role in the home and in the workplace and rights as an employee.

Police departments are not front-runners in any effort to dispel myths about parental responsibilities, but evidence of their willingness to accommodate pregnant women exists (Schulze 2008, 2010a). By virtue of the job's rigorous demands, departments are arguably compelled to accommodate women who become mothers (some more than others).

FAMILY LEAVE IN THE COURTS

The most recent court cases involving maternity and family leave have centered on accusations charging a violation of the Pregnancy Discrimination Act.[4] The 1978 Pregnancy Discrimination Act, an amendment to Title VII of the Civil Rights Act of 1964, prohibits employers from treating pregnant employees differently and mandates that maternity leave affords the same rights and treatment as medical leave. Demonstrating "adverse employment action," a requirement for a successful suit, has proven to be difficult. In such a case, *Traci Raciking v. City of New Kensington, Frank Link and Charles F. Korman* (2008), police officer Traci King claimed she was discriminated against because of her pregnancy.

She stated that she did not receive sufficient accommodation, having received only one month of light duty instead of the four she had originally requested. Unable to show an "adverse employment action," she lost the case.

It was the fact that the female police officer was forced (in contrast to a request) to take on light duty that generated legal scrutiny in *Tilson v. City of Lawrence* (2008). Claiming sex and pregnancy discrimination, Sergeant Tonya Tilson was four months pregnant when she was, not by her consent, reassigned to the administration office. From there, the mayor reassigned her to dispatch, a position that Tilson claimed was "more stressful" than an alternative assignment would have been. Again, however, the plaintiff was unable to show "adverse employment action" and lost the case.

New York Suffolk County women police officers sued their department arguing that they have a right to limited duty assignments (*Lochren v. Suffolk County,* 2007). They won the right to six months light duty, and a financial settlement. As McDonough (2006) points out, this decision is contrary to what other courts are ruling. The Sixth Circuit Court ruled in *Reeves v. Swift Transportation Co.* (2006) that women should not be given light duty for pregnancy, arguing that such assignments are reserved for those on disability. While the court admits, "pregnancy-blind policies of course can be tools of discrimination," they write, "but challenging them as tools of discrimination requires evidence and inference beyond such policies' express terms" (p. 4). Clearly, light duty is not considered a universal right and demonstrating gender bias must go beyond procuring medical evidence of her incapacitation and documented requests for accommodation (as did the plaintiff in this case).

The plaintiffs in *Cynthia Orr, Patricia Paiz, Stephen Orr v. The City of Albuquerque; Mary Beth Vigil (2005),* after a protracted court battle in the lower courts, were able to demonstrate adverse employment action. Police officers Cynthia Orr and Patricia Paiz claimed that their family leave time adversely affected their eligibility for early retirement and overtime. Their supervisors had forced them to use all accrued sick leave before using their vacation time (a not uncommon stipulation found in city and police departmental family leave policies; Schulze, 2008). The appellate court found:

(i) they were required to use sick leave for their maternity leave at a time when;

(ii) the regulations in force permitted the use of vacation time for leave under the Family and Medical Leave Act (FMLA), 29 U.S.C.S. § 2601 et seq., and

(iii) other employees seeking FMLA leave for purposes unrelated to a pregnancy were routinely allowed to use vacation or compensatory time.

These recent court cases reflect the ambiguity surrounding the role of women working in law enforcement, their role as mothers, and the role of the employer. Broadly speaking, two types of cases involving compulsory leave taking have been examined by the courts. Either women have claimed a right to decide when or how to take leave, arguing that mandatory leave is inequitable, or women, when denied leave time, have brought suit for insufficient accommodation. Seemingly contradictory, both types of demands reflect the desire for choice in how women want to take time from work for caretaking. Both entail the recognition that motherhood should not be viewed as an employment inconvenience, nor simply a "disability." Rather, *parenthood* is a right, which should be socially valued and legally protected.

The family leave policies of cities and police departments are, for the most part, found to be gender-neutral, but their application is not (Schulze 2008, 2010a). This may be due to a police culture that devalues parenthood and men and women's potential for equitable parenting responsibilities. By not allowing men equal legitimacy in fatherhood, police departments inadvertently perpetuate the conception that women are a potential drain on the department. Berggren's (2008) recent work suggests that if employers institute comprehensive family leave policies, views concerning familial roles will become more egalitarian. Unfortunately, as Berggren points out, a person's educational background, ideology, and occupation seems to influence attitudes regarding gender roles more so than any kind of official policy change could exact.

LOOKING AHEAD

Former president Bush amended FMLA in 2008 (this bill was reauthorized by President Obama for 2010) so that the:

> spouse, son, daughter, parent, or next of kin to take up to 26 workweeks of leave to care for a "member of the Armed Forces, including a member of the National Guard or Reserves, who is undergoing medical treatment, recuperation, or therapy, is otherwise in outpatient status, or is otherwise on the temporary disability retired list, for a serious injury or illness." (The National Defense Authorization Act for FY 2008)

In other words, 14 more weeks of protected leave time is allocated to qualifying cases. Parents, or immediate relatives of the severely ill, are not given the same consideration. Though the utility of *unpaid* leave policy is debatable, suffice it to say, parental rights and obligations have generally just received lip service from public officials.

Interestingly, family leave policies tend to be gender neutral whereas many physical tests are not. Though there are many proponents of gendered physical testing due to women's biological "disadvantage," similar arguments are not made for family leave policies. Obviously men are affected by pregnancy differently than women. Biologically speaking, though, they are not affected at all. Yet, policies insist on neutralizing these differences in favor of "family leave," which tends to accommodate fathers with a partner at home more so than the women most impacted by what required the family leave in the first place: the quality of being pregnant for 8–9 months. The next section discusses a policy that has, prima facie, been receptive to gender differences. What the physical testing policy has done in fact and what its utility has been has, as of yet, largely remained unquestioned.

THE PHYSICAL FITNESS REQUIREMENTS OF LAW ENFORCEMENT TRAINING ACADEMIES

The literature remains sparse in this area. Undeniably, physical fitness is an indispensable component of police work and should thus be tested for. However, not all academies test applicants and no clear uniformity in testing requirements exists and academies are free to set the requirements. In a 2002 census of local and state law enforcement training academies, the Bureau of Justice Statistics (BJS) found that 85 percent of the 626 academies surveyed utilized some type of physical fitness test, but did not specify what, specifically, the test entailed.

Emerging research casts doubt on the real-world applicability of physical tests; some even demonstrating their utility in predicting work performance (White, 2008). There is also some legal precedent that suggests such physical tests may be unlawful (*United States v. City of Erie*, 2005; *United States v. City of Erie*, 2004). Though some requirements, like being able to scale a 6-foot wall, could be considered germane to employment, others, like executing some specified number of push-ups, are dubious indicators of an applicant's viability.

As in many instances involving a group's civil rights, the courts have been asked to arbitrate (e.g, *United States v. City of Philadelphia*, 1978; *Roller v. San Mateo*, 1977). The Civil Rights Act of 1964 prohibits discrimination based on race, color, sex, national origin, or religion whereas Title VII of this act concerns the workplace and any loss of benefit resulting from the discrimination. The Supreme Court refused to review a New York City Police Department case even though men passed the physical test at twice the rate as women. On appeal, the U.S. Court of Appeals Third Circuit ruled that if employees are capable of performing their jobs safely, physical tests these same employees cannot pass are not valid (*Lanning v. SEPTA*, 2002). On remand, the district court affirmed its earlier refusal to declare the mandatory 1.5-mile run in 12 minutes imposed by the Southeastern Pennsylvania Transportation Authority invalid. The effect of these civil rights lawsuits on women's rights has been mixed.

THE CONTENT OF PHYSICAL FITNESS TESTS

The National Center for Women & Policing (NCWP) identifies three categories that physical tests can be grouped under: general fitness (gendered testing), job task based (dummy drag, tiring changing, etc.), and task-based physical tests (sit-ups, etc.). The NCWP recommends that the physical tasks of policing be identified and the tests bear some resemblance to everyday police work plus appraise the overall fitness of an applicant. These fitness tests should be gendered due to the anatomical and physiological differences between men and women.

However, by gendering *task-based* tests, as most police academies currently do, the impression is that women are less capable of managing the physical aspects of the job. Despite the fact that doing 20 push-ups has little to do with policing, a policy that mandates men do 40 while women do 20 clearly illustrates women's expected inferiority in this area. A case could be made that if the number of push-ups is equal for both genders, women may be afforded more respect precisely *because* of their "expected inferiority." That is, a woman who demonstrates the ability to reach a masculine goal will be treated more positively than a woman meeting a goal set for her gender.

Training amplifies preexisting gender disparities to the detriment of women (Brown & Heidensohn, 2000). Despite the reality of police work infrequently demanding violent action, the public views police work as dangerous (Price, 1996; Messerschmidt, 1993). In part due to these cultural biases, women face being stereotyped as unsuitable for law enforcement (Greenberg & Berger, 1983; Moulson-Litchfeld & Freedson, 1986, Stanish, Wood, & Campagna, 1999). Prokos and Pradavic (2002) argue that training is dominated by male values where women learn that their "difference" is a disadvantage. This is illustrated in the lower academy completion rates for women. According to the BJS (2002), 88 percent of men completed academy training compared to 81 percent of women.

Perhaps it is the content of training that explains the fewer number of women applicants in policing. The 2002 BJS report found that 99 percent of academies devoted a median number of 60 hours to firearms training and 44 hours to self-defense skills. Noting that the 2002 report showed significant improvement in the number of community policing courses, BJS nevertheless reported that 64 percent of academies provide a median number of 6 hours to problem-solving methods. Though 83 percent of the academies reportedly offer courses in mediation skills and conflict management, the median number of hours relegated to such courses is only 8 hours.

Unfortunately, the BJS report does not provide statistics on the proportion of male to female staff in law enforcement training academies.[5] Law enforcement trainers tend to be veterans of the field and generally lack formal training in teaching (Birzer, 2003; Thomas, 2003). Where there are women instructors, they are found in areas that focus largely on "feminine" skills (NCWP). Most time is spent on masculine activities like shooting and control tactics. In a study of weapons training Vuković1 et al. (2008) find that some modification of instruction resulted in differing affects for men and women's shooting scores. Recognition that learning itself is gendered (Birzer & Tannehill, 2001) may suffice in producing a more female-friendly environment, regardless of the masculine skills being taught. Regardless of the apparent intractability of law enforcement's veneration for the military, the mode in which information is delivered might influence the gendered differential in entrance and attrition rates.

There is, similar to the BJS report, a large amount of variation in the content of physical fitness tests. The Topeka Police department, for example, requires that an applicant be able to pass the obstacle course whereas all that is needed for the Jefferson County Sheriffs Academy is a physician's note. On the other end of the spectrum are academies, like the Nebraska State Patrol Training Academy, which subject applicants to a barrage of physical tests in addition to more job-related task tests like a dummy drag (165 lb—39 ft—20sec) and an obstacle course. Some academies, like the Arkansas Training Academy, reported no minimum requirements at all. To illustrate the variation, four of the most commonly used tests were chosen: sit-ups, push-ups, 1.5-mile run, and obstacle course.

Out of the 96 academies examined, 31 (~32%) had gendered physical fitness tests in which separate minimum requirements were in place for men and women. Sixty-five (~68%) academies did not make a distinction between men and women. All but two of the academies, which had gendered physical fitness tests, age-normed their tests as well. That is, academies had separate requirements for applicants from different age groups in 29 academies. Nine of the 96 academies required applicants to produce a doctor's note attesting their suitability for law enforcement.

The descriptive statistics for the minimum number of sit-ups, push-ups, and minutes required for the 1.5-mile run are provided in the table below. Only the academies requiring the aforementioned tests are replicated in the table. The range indicates that the minimum requirement for academies listed in the row falls within that interval. The actual numbers required for each academy are available from the author by request. Reproducing each academy's minimum requirements would have resulted in a much larger table.

The minimum number of sit-ups and push-ups were surprising. The lowest number of sit-ups an academy required was 14 whereas the lowest number of push-ups required was 4. The minimum numbers of minutes required to complete the 1.5-mile run are reported in descending order because, in this case, larger numbers indicate less exertion. One academy reported their minimum completion time as 21 minutes whereas another academy set their minimum at 11.13, more than an 8-minute mile pace. The largest number of academies (28%) required applicants to complete the 1.5-mile run in 15–15.55 minutes, about a ten-minute mile pace.

Number of academies requiring a designated number of sit-ups, push-ups, and 1.5-mile run

Minimum number of sit-ups		Minimum number of push-ups		Minimum number of minutes to complete a 1.5-mile run	
# of academies		# of academies		# of academies	
14–20	7 (10%)	4–14	5 (7%)	18–21	7 (10%)
21–26	18 (25%)	15–20	23 (32%)	16.28–17.17	9 (13%)
27–30	15 (21%)	21–22	13 (18%)	15–15.55	19 (28%)
31–36	16 (22%)	24–28	13 (18%)	14.05–14.57	8 (12%)
37–40	12 (17%)	29–33	12 (17%)	13–13.58	13 (19%)
41–50	4 (6%)	40–52	6 (8%)	11.13–12.51	11 (16%)
	n = 72		n = 72		n = 67

Note: Percentages may not total 100% as the figures in parentheses are rounded up.

Academies that mandated separate tests for men and women were studied. Of the 6 gendered academies requiring sit-ups, 4 academies required a minimum of 35, 1 academy required 42, whereas the other 44. Of the 9 gendered academies requiring a 1.5-mile run, 1 required applicants to finish in a minimum of 16:11 minutes, 4 required 17:11 minutes, another required 17:18 minutes, 1 academy 17:53 minutes, 1 academy 18:23 minutes, and 18:39 minutes for the last academy. Of the 6 gendered academies requiring push-ups, 2 required applicants to complete a minimum of 20 and the remaining 4 academies required a minimum of 23, 28, 29, and 31 push-ups. Not one academy, in any of these categories, had a minimum requirement that falls below the lowest score for a non-gendered academy. That is, while one academy allowed their female recruits 18:39 minutes to complete a 1.5-mile run, the longest amount of time given in a non-gendered academy was 21 minutes. Whereas the lowest amount of push-ups for academies is 4, the lowest amount women are required in gendered testing is 20. Clearly, the standards are arbitrary, not driven by any scientifically calculated minimums of what women are capable of.

Different standards indicate different capabilities. In an institution that is dominated by masculine values, such standards may serve to undermine women's qualifications. At the same time, by stressing such values, the profession suffers from an overemphasis on skills that may be unrelated to much of what police work is. The findings contribute to the growing skepticism concerning the occupational application of such physical tests by illustrating the diversity in requirements. Moreover, they reveal that gendered tests are more stringent than some other tests that assess men, bringing to question women's physical limitations. In other words, the point of gendered testing, to consider women's inferior upper-body strength for example, is mute in light of these disparate tests.

Simply rectifying these discrepancies in minimum requirements is inadequate because this would still not address the fundamental assumptions of their scientific and occupational efficacy. Instead of debating how many push-ups a woman should be able to complete (or rather how many less push-ups than a man that would be), policy makers should assess the importance of such a test to police work. In deciding this matter, the gendered ramifications of such policies should also be taken into consideration. All other questions aside, the negative stereotyping that results from such testing arguable outweighs, if any, possible benefit to be had from these physical tests.

CONCLUSIONS AND POLICY IMPLICATIONS

Workplace policies can serve to highlight differences between men and women police officers. Examined were two policies in policing that perpetuate gender stereotypes by devaluing women's work as parents and their rights to pursue such work while employed as police officers and by undermining women's strengths through the overvaluing of men's. Police work is dominated by paramilitary values and masculinity (Belkin & McNichol, 2002; Miller, Forest, & Jurik, 2003) and any policy discordant with these values is therefore suspect.

Women's equal job performance and job-related behavior are found to be similar as men's (Feder, 1997; Robinson, 2000; Robinson & Chandek, 2000; Stalans & Finn, 2000), likely because of the historically resilient masculine culture (Crank, 2004; Guyot, 1991; Rabe-Hemp, 2008). However, their potential in contributing their gendered social attributes may be invaluable to the almost universally embraced policing philosophy known as community policing; as Miller (1998) writes, "The feminine attribute of caring may need to be deskilled and neutered before it can be embraced by a male-dominated police force" (p. 167). Communication and conflict management are standard in many public agencies (i.e., Rape Crisis and Domestic Violence centers and agencies providing alternative dispute resolution). Proficiency in these areas of public service is heralded whereas confrontational behavior is discouraged. The philosophical underpinnings of community policing are congruent with many other organizations that serve the public. Law enforcement training centers should inculcate a number of resources, easily found in the public sector, when designing the core curriculum.

The move to community policing has made it necessary to reevaluate instruction, with emphasis on communication and conflict management skills (McCoy, 2006). Community policing values could be described as "feminine" (Kruger, 2006), but little attempt has been made to isolate relevant skill sets and incorporate them into training. Instead, police academies follow traditional instruction plans, departing very little from design and content. It is easy to understand how the public and the law enforcement institution could believe that adequate protection of the public requires warrior-like skills. Upon closer inspection, however, the reality of police work today renders such imagery and Dragnet-inspired daydreaming naïve and antiquated.

REFERENCES

BELKIN, A., & MCNICHOL, J. (2002). Pink and blue: Outcomes associated with the integration of open gay and lesbian personnel in the San Diego police department. *Police Quarterly, 5*(1), 63–95.

BERGGREN, H. (2008). Parental Leave Policies in Europe and Men's Attitudes toward Work-Family Feminism: Accelerating the Rise in Support. Paper presented at the Midwestern Political Science Association, 2008 Annual Meeting.

BIRZER, M. L. (2003). The theory of andragogy applied to police training. *Policing: An International Journal of Police Strategies & Management, 26*(1), 29–42.

BIRZER, M. L., & TANNEHILL, R. (2001). A more effective training approach for contemporary policing, *Police Quarterly, 4*(2), 233–252.

BROWN, M., & BLOOM, B. (2009). Reentry and Renegotiating Motherhood. *Crime & Delinquency, 55*(2), 313–336.

BROWN, J., & HEIDENSOHN, F. (2000). *Gender and policing.* Hampshire: MacMillan Press Ltd.

BUREAU OF JUSTICE STATISTICS. (2002). 2002 Census of Law Enforcement Training Academies.: Barriers and Opportunities in the Law Enforcement Work Environment. *Police Quarterly, 12*(1), 86–101.

CRANK, J. (2004). *Understanding police culture.* Cincinnati, OH: Anderson.

FEDER, L. (1997). Domestic violence and police response in a pro-arrest jurisdiction. *Women & Criminal Justice, 8*(4), 79–99.

FREEMAN, J. (1988). Social revolution and the equal rights amendment. *Sociological forum, 3*(1):145–152.

GORAN V., DOPSAJ, M., RADOVANOVIĆ, R., & JOVANOVIĆ, A. (2008). Characteristics of shooting efficiency during a basic shooting training program involving police officers of both sexes. *Police Quarterly, 11*(1), 27–49.

GREENBERG, G. J., & BERGER, R. A. (1983). A model to assess one's ability to apprehend and restrain a resisting suspect in police work. *Journal of Occupational Medicine, 25*(11), 809–813.

GUYOT, D. (1991). *Policing as though people matter.* Philadelphia, PA: Temple University Press.

HOMANT, R., & KENNED, D. (1985). Police perceptions of spouse abuse: A comparison of male and female officers. *Journal of Criminal Justice, 13*, 29–47.

MCCOY, M. R. (2006). Teaching style and the application of adult learning principles by police Instructors. *Policing: An International Journal of Police Strategies & Management, 29*(1), 77–91.

MCDONOUGH, M. (2006). Pregnant pause. *American Bar Association Journal, 92*(8).

MESSERSCHMIDT, J. W. (1993). *Masculinities and crime: Critique and reconceptualization of theory.* Lanham, MD: Rowan & Littlefield Publishers, Inc.

MILLER, S., FOREST, K., & JURIK, N. (2003). Diversity in blue: Lesbian and gay police officers in a masculine occupation. *Men and Masculinities, 5*, 355–385.

MOULSON-LITCHFELD, M., & FREEDSON, P. S. (1986). Physical training programs for public safety personnel. *Clinics in Sports Medicine, 5*, 571–587.

PASCARELLA, J. E. (2006). Health performance and age restriction policies in policing. *International Journal of Police Science & Management, 8*(1), 9–32.

PRICE, B. R. (1996). "Female Police Officers in the United States." *College of Police and Security Studies.* Accessed January 1, 2010. http://www.ncjrs.gov/policing/fem635.htm.

PROKOS, A., & PADAVIC, I. (2002). There oughtta be a law against bitches: Masculinity lessons in police academy training. *Gender, Work & Organization,* 9(4), 439–459.

RABE-HEMP, C. E. (2008). Female officers and the ethic of care: Does officer gender impact police behaviors? *Journal of Criminal Justice, 36*(5), 426–434.

ROBINSON, A. L. (2000). The effect of a domestic violence policy change on police officers' schemata. *Criminal Justice and Behavior, 27*(5), 600–624.

ROBINSON, A. L., & CHANDEK, M. S. (2000). The domestic violence arrest decision: Examining demographic, attitudinal, and situational variables. *Crime & Delinquency, 46*(1), 18–37.

SCHULZE, C. (2008). Maternity Leave Policy in U.S. Police Departments and School Districts: The impact of descriptive and social group representation in a context of gendered institutions. Doctoral dissertation. University of New Orleans.

SCHULZE, C. (2010a). Law enforcement and parenting: women's "difference" in U.S. police departments. Unpublished manuscript. University of South Alabama.

SCHULZE, C. (2010b). The masculine yardstick of physical competence: The fitness tests of U.S. police academies. Unpublished manuscript. University of South Alabama.

SEAGRAM, B. C., & STARK-ADAMES, C. (1992). Women in Canadian urban policing: Why are they leaving? *The Police Chief*, October, 120–127.

STALANS, L., & FINN, M. (2000). Gender differences in officers' perceptions and decisions about domestic violence cases. *Women and Criminal Justice, 11*, 1–24.

STANISH, H. I., WOOD, T. M., & CAMPAGNA, P. (1999). Prediction of performance on the RCMP physical ability requirement evaluation. *Journal of Occupational and Environmental Medicine, 41*(8), 669–677.

SUN, I. Y. (2007). Policing domestic violence: Does officer gender matter? *Journal of Criminal Justice, 35*(6), 581–595.

THOMAS, K. T. (2003). Understanding educational process in leadership development, PhD Thesis, Deakin University, Geelong, Vic.

WALDFOGEL, J. (1999). The Impact of the Family and Medical Act. *Journal of Policy Analysis and Management, 18*(2), 281–302.

WHITE, M. D. (2008). Identifying good cops early. *Police Quarterly, 11*(1), 27–49.

ENDNOTES

1. According to the U.S. Census, there were 5.5 million "stay-at-home" parents last year, 5.4 million of which were moms and 98,000 were dads. (http://www.census.gov/PressRelease/www/releases/archives/families_households/003118.html, last accessed December 30, 2009).

2. There are many caveats to this. A private company only falls under the act if it employs at least fifty people and that company can deny an employee leave if she falls within the salary range of the top ten percent of paid workers (Conway et al., 1999: 78). In order to qualify, an employer has to have worked for at least one year.

3. Similarly, workers' compensation can be counted as FMLA leave. If an employer has a plan allowing "paid time off," it denotes that an employee will use their own accumulated paid leave.

4. In 2008, the U.S. Equal Employment Opportunity Commission received more than 6,000 complaints of pregnancy discrimination, recovering 12.2 million dollars in damages (http://www.eeoc.gov/types/pregnancy.html, last accessed December 30, 2009).

5. The BJS (2002) reported 12,200 full-time and 25,700 part-time trainers or instructors in 2002.

CASES

Cynthia Orr; Patricia Paiz, Plaintiffs - Appellants, And Stephen Orr, Plaintiff, v. The City Of Albuquerque; Mary Beth Vigil, Defendants-Appellees, United States Court of Appeals for the Tenth Circuit (2005).

Lanning v. SEPTA, United States Circuit of Appeals for the Third Circuit (2002).

Lochren v. Suffolk County, Eastern District of New York (2007).

Reeves v. Swift Transportation Co., United States Court of Appeals for the Sixth Circuit (2006).

Roller v. San Mateo, United States Court of Appeals for the Ninth Circuit (1977).

Traci King, Plaintiff, v. City of New Kensington, Frank Link, and Charles F. Korman, Defendants, United States District Court For The Western District Of Pennsylvania (2008).

Tonya Tilson, Plaintiff, v. City of Lawrence, United States District Court For The Southern District Of Indiana, Indianapolis Division (2008).

U.S. v. City of Erie, Western district of Pennsylvania (2005).

U.S. v. City of Philadelphia, United States Court of Appeals for the Third Circuit (1978).

33

A Paler Shade of Blue?

Women and the Police Subculture

Kim M. Lersch and Thomas Bazley

INTRODUCTION

The occupation of policing is quite unique. It is the job of police officers to make arrests, detain individuals accused of criminal activity, and, under certain circumstances, deprive individuals of their constitutionally guaranteed freedoms. They also have the right to use deadly force, if need be, in order to gain compliance. Police officers, most of whom still only possess a high school education, have an incredible amount of authority and influence over the daily lives of citizens. In addition to their unique powers, officers charged with street-level law enforcement see a world that many of us can only imagine, one filled with human suffering, violence, exploitation, and constant challenges to their authority.

Because of the unique characteristics of police work, a distinct subculture has evolved, one that permeates every aspect of policing, including recruitment and selection, behavioral aspects of officers in the field, and overall acceptance of officers into the profession. In this subculture, the display of attributes associated with masculinity and toughness is rewarded; physical and emotional weakness, fear, compassion, and other qualities labeled as "feminine" are devalued. Given the nature of the police subculture, it is not surprising that women have had limited representation among law enforcement personnel. The occupation of policing has been described as one of the most resistant to the acceptance of women, who have summarily been denied access to the informal policing peer groups (Bartollas and Hahn 1999; Belknap and Shelley 1992; Lanier 1996). In this chapter we begin with a discussion of the elements of the police subculture. We then explore the impact of this subculture on women entering police work. We close with an examination of the resultant changes in the subculture and occupation of policing as women enter the profession in larger numbers.

THE SUBCULTURE OF POLICING

A very popular sociological explanation that is often provided to better understand police behavior involves the subculture of policing. Proponents of this perspective (Herbert 1998; Skolnick 1966, 2002; Stark 1972; Westley 1970) discuss law enforcement officers as being affected by the norms, values, expectations, and regulatory principles of their occupation. While the term *subculture* is usually applied to lower-class youth gangs, a subculture may be defined as a group that maintains a distinctive set of values, norms, and lifestyles that sometimes differs from the overall culture of society. For a variety of reasons, the distinct occupational characteristics of the law enforcement officer tend to be in conflict with and isolated from the community in which they are employed.

From the very beginning, individuals seeking employment as law enforcement officers are a distinctive group. Prospective officers are carefully screened using a variety of mechanisms, including extensive background checks. Applicants must demonstrate that they possess "good moral character" and have no felony convictions, nor any misdemeanor convictions related to perjury or providing false statements. They must pass a physical examination and demonstrate that they are physically able to perform the required tasks. Some researchers have argued that the screening mechanisms used to select appropriate candidates for law enforcement employment are designed to weed out those who have not demonstrated a clear adherence to middle-class norms and values. Successful candidates form a homogeneous cohort of individuals who, from the very start, have been selected because they share a common worldview. As a result of the selection process, law enforcement personnel tend to be white, conservative, middle-class males (Kappeler, Sluder, and Alpert 1998).

Once employed, young recruits find themselves in a different lifestyle from most of their nondepartmental friends. Because they are low in seniority, many new officers must work the night shift. At a time when most young couples or individuals are developing friendships and socializing, the pool of available people declines due to the odd hours that the officer works. Officers are forced to rely heavily on their coworkers for companionship, which further serves to isolate them from society.

The dangerous nature of law enforcement work fosters an environment based on friendship and trust. While violent police–citizen encounters are rare, the threat of danger is always present and the authority of the officer is always being challenged (Skolnick and Currie 1970). Officers must rely on each other for protection; norms that stress the importance of teamwork, cooperation, and mutual responsibility are extremely high among officers (Stark 1972; Westley 1970). Officers turn to each other for support and understanding. Outsiders from mainstream society are viewed as unsympathetic and hostile toward officers, and the officers must have someone to turn to in order to alleviate the stress of their occupation (Stark 1972).

Officers are thrust into the personal lives of complete strangers and rarely see people under the best of conditions. Officers tend to become cynical and hardened, and their conversations tend to focus on violence and crime (Van Maanen 1980). They tend to develop a distinctive way of looking at the world that sets them off from normal citizens and further contributes to their social isolation. Ultimately, a sort of "bunker mentality" develops in which the officers view the world in an "us versus them" fashion. Officers can only trust other officers for friendship, support, understanding, and loyalty.

MASCULINITY AND THE POLICE SUBCULTURE

One of the consistent themes that has emerged among policing scholars in research on the police subculture is that of masculinity. In order to be accepted into the police ranks, an officer must exhibit "macho" traits, including toughness, confidence, bravery, emotional detachment, and aggressiveness (Crank 1998; Garcia 2003; Martin 1980). Kappeler, Sluder, and Alpert (1988), in an oft-cited essay, stated that bravery was a central component of the police subculture. Bravery has been defined as a special form of masculine behavior (Crank 1998). Throughout the tenure of an officer on the streets, exhibitions of bravery can "make or break" him or her. New officers are not truly accepted until they have successfully maneuvered their way through a dangerous situation. When faced with hazardous challenges and threats to their authority, police officers must never back down. Instead, the officers must "show balls" and deal with the situation head-on. In the worldview of patrol officers, backing down is a sign of weakness that reflects poorly not only on the individual officer but on the entire force as well. Officers who demonstrate cowardice face ostracism from the informal peer groups and are not accepted as "good" police officers.

Herbert (1998) described several normative orders that characterize the social world of the police. Included among these normative orders, which Herbert defined as "a set of rules and practices centered around a primary value," was adventure/machismo. In his ethnographic study of the Los Angeles Police Department, Herbert described two labels that officers applied to other officers: "hardchargers" and "station queens." Hardchargers aggressively seek out dangerous situations such as vehicle pursuits and crime-related calls for service. These officers enjoy the adrenaline high that accompanies such unpredictable, potentially explosive encounters. According to Herbert (1998:356), "Hardchargers are police warriors and exemplify such typically masculine characteristics as courage and strength."

Conversely, officers who tend to avoid danger are labeled as "station queens," a term that is less than flattering given the masculine nature of the occupational culture. As noted by Herbert, the use of the term "queens" feminizes these officers, who prefer the safety of the station house to the dangerous environment of the streets. Femininity, therefore, is associated with weakness, fear, and cowardice. While acts of bravery are revered and rewarded, expression of "feminine" traits violates the rules and expectations for behavior. It was perhaps Crank who summarized it best in his essay appropriately titled "No Place for Sissies." According to Crank (1998:180), "Masculinity is a theme that runs through the occupation, affects social status, reinforces group solidarity, and infuses officers' self-images as men's men."

Beyond the world of academic research, the theme of masculinity in policing has been picked up by the popular media as well. Hollywood depictions of the role of police-women tend to reinforce stereotypes that women are weaker and less effective than male police officers. Whereas male cop action heroes are portrayed as tough, masculine, all-knowing, and independent, females in similar roles tend to rely on "women's intuition" and consistently fail to recognize the truth (Dresner 2007; Gates 2006; Inness 1998; Rafter 2006). In an analysis of police action films that were released from 1973 to 2005, males were projected as the hero in 267 films, while only 24 films included women in this role (King 2008). King also found that women were more likely to be portrayed as rookies and hunters of serial killers. These fictional female characters relied more on mental intellect and communication in their crime-fighting roles than men, who tended to rely on physical prowess and combat. As noted by King, "filmmakers appear to be telling stories that cast women as talented and attractive rookies who work far from the halls in which the most dramatic struggles for power take place" (2008:256).

MAINTAINING MASCULINITY: NO GIRLS ALLOWED

The masculine theme that defines the occupational culture of policing has flourished because of (1) the demographics of police departments and (2) the misconceptions surrounding the true nature of police work. Together, these factors have kept women from enjoying full status in law enforcement circles.

One of the primary reasons that the masculinity theme has prospered relates to the demographics of police agencies, especially in the early years. Prior to the early 1970s, it was quite difficult to find women among the ranks of sworn law enforcement officers. A survey of the largest municipal police agencies in 1967 revealed that there were fewer than 1,800 females with full law enforcement powers (Roberg, Novak and Cordner 2005). The 1972 Equal Employment Opportunity Act (EEOA), which extended the protections provided by the 1964 Civil Rights Act to state and local governments, marked the beginning of a new era in many law enforcement agencies (Martin and Jurik 1996). Discrimination was now prohibited based on race, color, and gender. Some have gone so far as to say that without the benefit of the 1972 EEOA mandate and other protections such as Affirmative Action, women would have been denied entry to police patrol duties (Hale and Lanier 2002).

In theory, the Act would open many doors to persons of color and to women who wished to pursue a career in law enforcement. In practice, it has been difficult to undo the impact of nearly 150 years of an all-white, all-male occupational culture. It was not uncommon for agencies to have formal policies restricting the employment and advancement of women as police officers. Highly respected policing experts, including O.W. Wilson, spoke out on the abilities of women to fully serve as police officers. In his influential textbook on police management (which Walker and Katz, 2002:39 described as the "informal bible" of police administration), Wilson and his coauthor McLaren stated that men were more effective administrators who were better able to perform under stressful conditions (see Wilson and McLaren 1963, cited in Roberg, Novak, and Cordner 2005).

Despite the EEOA protections, women continue to be underrepresented as police officers. While exact statistics vary, it is estimated that women hold between 11.3 and 14.2 percent of all sworn law enforcement positions in this country (Hickman and Reaves 2006; National Center for Women and Policing 1999). This is despite the fact that women comprise 46.5 percent of the labor force (Felperin 2004). The representation of women in U.S. law enforcement lags behind the levels found in England and Wales, where women comprise 20 percent of total officer strength and hold 8 percent of the senior rank positions (Christopherson and Cotton 2004; Silvestri 2007). In a study of the distribution of women in Florida police agencies, Poulos and Doerner (1996) found that 20 percent of the smaller agencies in the state did not employ a single female officer. While it should be mentioned that there have been gains in the representation of women in law enforcement, the growth has been slow, with an average annual increase of 0.5 percent. If the representation of women continues to grow at this same slow rate, it will take about 70 years for women to reach equal standing in the police profession (Bureau of Justice Assistance and National Center for Women and Policing 2000).

Hiring standards are often blamed for maintaining gender imbalances on police agencies. As argued by Kappeler, Sluder, and Alpert (1994), police employment standards are designed to screen out candidates who do not possess certain values, traits, and characteristics. Among other things, these hiring standards may assist in determining an applicant's "physical prowess, sexual orientation and gender identification" (1994:89). Applicants who fail to demonstrate their conformity to traditional, conservative ideals were excluded from employment, as were those who did not fit the "macho" expectations associated with the image of a "good" cop.

Physical agility tests were also an effective means of maintaining a masculine force. Because of the potentially dangerous nature of police work, it was felt that we would need very large, imposing individuals to serve as police officers (Haarr 1997). For many years, police agencies screened for these characteristics. First and foremost, applicants for positions as law enforcement officers had to meet a minimum height requirement in order to be considered for employment. For the majority of agencies, the minimum height was 5'8". This was significantly higher than the average height for females, thereby eliminating the majority of women from employment consideration (President's Commission on Law Enforcement and Administration of Justice 1967; Walker and Katz 2002; Holladay 2002). Even if a woman was tall enough to meet the minimum standards, she would then face a rather imposing physical ability test that for years overemphasized upper-body strength. Applicants were asked to complete a variety of military-style physical challenges in a specified amount of time, such as push-ups, sit-ups, and bench presses of one's own weight. Women failed these exams at significantly higher rates than their male peers and thus were eliminated from the "qualified" applicant pool (Hale and Wyland 1993; Swanson, Territo and Taylor 1998).

MAINTAINING MASCULINITY: THE MYTH OF THE CRIME FIGHTER

The question remains: Why were such big and strong men needed in order to perform the duties of police officers? This need is largely based on erroneous assumptions about the everyday duties of a patrol officer. The public often assumes that police work is dangerous, violent, and unpredictable (Austin and Hummer 1999). Popular movies and television shows regularly portray officers in precarious situations dealing with criminals who are often brutal and dangerous. Similarly, in their quest for ratings, newspapers and television news shows overemphasize the violent aspects of policing. Officer-involved shootings are front-page news stories, fueling the belief that police work is much more dangerous than it actually is. Police officers themselves tend to exaggerate the danger of their work, telling and retelling "war stories" and focusing their conversations on crime and violence (Manning 1977; Skolnick and Currie 1970; Westley 1970).

Additionally, the need for big, strong aggressive men was fueled by the traditional crime control model of law enforcement. Under this model, police work is defined by a constant war on crime and little else. The crime control model has been credited with maintaining a subculture that encourages police to view their jurisdiction as a combat zone where only the aggressively masculine can survive (Appier 1998). Walker and Katz (2002) describe the inaccurate assumptions regarding the police work as "the myth of police officers as crime fighters."

In reality, instead of being focused on fighting crime, most police work is concerned with service-related issues (Hale and Wyland 1993; Garcia 2003). In an analysis of more than 26,000 calls for service to three metropolitan police agencies, only 2 percent of the calls were related to what would be considered serious violent crime: murders, rapes, robberies, etc. Conversely, a third of the calls were related to various information or minor assistance problems, such as citizens needing directions, complaints over barking dogs, or other relatively trivial, often noncriminal events (Walker and Katz 2002; see also Scott 1981). Similarly, Parsons and Jesilow (2001) stated that only about 10 percent of policing work involves the law enforcement component, and dangerous activities involve less than 1 percent of citizen-initiated complaints.

Despite evidence to the contrary, the myth of the "police as crime fighters" has persisted, and police work has been summarily categorized as "man's work." The maintenance of the crime-fighting image has undermined most attempts to reform the police. For example, there is a great deal of research that has examined the resistance of the police subculture to reforms associated with community policing, a form of policing that has not been viewed as "real" police work (see, for example, Moore 1992; Wood, Davis, and Rouse 2004). Furthermore, the crime-fighting image has been particularly detrimental to the integration of women into the occupation.

IMPACT OF THE POLICE SUBCULTURE

When women first entered patrol work, they were met with open hostility and organized resistance from their male peers. It was not unheard of for male supervisors to refuse to train female recruits, or for female officers to be denied back-up in dangerous situations (Hunt 1984; Martin 1980; Martin and Jurik 1996).

Today, many female officers continue to face discrimination and prejudice in the workplace (Barker 1999; Haarr 1997; Hale and Lanier 2002; Hunt 1990; Martin 1994). Barker (1999), in a twenty-year ethnographic study of the Los Angeles Police Department, observed that officers noted clear distinctions between the "Old Police," or those hired prior to 1972, and the "New Police." The "New Police," which included many women and minority officers, were viewed by the "Old Police" as being less competent, not as committed, and less qualified to hold their positions.

Barker's findings are not atypical. The literature is consistent with respect to reports of prejudice and disparate treatment of women in patrol by their male counterparts. Despite the gains made by women, male coworkers and supervisors continue to resist females on patrol (Hale and Wyland 1993; Lanier 1996). The hostility has been so great that a report published by the U.S. Department of Justice concluded that "research consistently demonstrates that the negative attitude of male colleagues is the single most significant problem reported by female officers" (Bureau of Justice Assistance and National Center for Women and Policing 2000:22).

The boys-only clubhouse mentality has contributed to a climate in which sexual harassment is commonplace and acceptable. A majority of women in law enforcement have reported incidents of sexual harassment, which include being the target of inappropriate jokes and sexually charged comments, being exposed to pornography, and experiencing unwanted sexual advances (Haarr 1997; Martin 1980, 1992; National Center for Women & Policing 1999).

This chapter began with an overview of the stressors experienced by all law enforcement personnel, including danger, hostility from the general public, and the requirement to handle calls for service involving human tragedies and suffering. In fact, policing is often described as one of the most stressful occupations (He, Zhao, and Archbold 2002). Female officers experience additional stress due to the fact that they have been marginalized within the field (Haarr 1997; Lanier 1996; Wexler and Quinn 1983). Because they are denied access to the informal social structure that exists among law enforcement officers, women do not benefit from the support male officers enjoy from the company and camaraderie of other officers. While sporting clubs and other recreational activities are common among male police officers, women are often denied access to these informal gatherings. For example, in a qualitative study of a Midwest Police Department, Haarr (1997) observed that officers segregated themselves based on race and gender. During roll call, white male officers sat at tables and interacted with other white male officers. Additionally, Haarr noted that female officers were disproportionately assigned to "A cars," or a one-person patrol car. Not only were these women isolated from social interactions with other officers, but they were also relegated to more menial patrol functions, such as writing tickets and responding to calls regarding stolen vehicles.

The unique stress placed on female law enforcement officers manifests itself in a number of ways. Due to their marginalization, women become less likely to assert themselves and engage in self-directed activities. This lack of initiative may lead to a negative downward cycle as male officers then view the women as lazy and unmotivated, which only adds to the disparate treatment of the female officers (Haarr 1997). Ni He et al. (2002) found that female officers reported higher levels of depression and hopelessness, or the level of discomfort related to physical problems such as aches and pains, as well as complaints related to cardiovascular and gastrointestinal disorders than their male counterparts. Occupational related stress may spill over into officers' private lives. Rates of divorce and separation are higher among female officers than their male counterparts (Kirschman 1997). As a result of the special problems facing female officers, the turnover rate of women exceeds that of men (Peak 2003).

THE FUTURE OF WOMEN POLICE: CHANGING THE SUBCULTURE

More contemporary research studies on the subculture of policing have begun to question the absolute, unwavering existence of a single, unified value system held by all officers (Barker 1999; Cochran and Bromley 2003; Herbert 1998; Morrison 1993; Wood et al. 2004). As law enforcement agencies become more and more diverse, values and attributes of the more traditional police subculture may be on the wane. While the greater influx of underrepresented groups (including women, minorities, and homosexuals) to the ranks of police officers has had an impact, other factors influencing changes in the occupational culture within police agencies include the leadership of the agency, changing political climates, lawsuits concerning hiring practices and the treatment of citizens, and the evolving mission of the police from a crime control philosophy to community policing/problem oriented policing (Herbert 1998; Wood, Davis and Rouse 2004). Instead of a single value system identified among early all-male police departments, researchers have identified multiple subcultures that compete with and, in some cases, may be more influential than the more traditional model.

In a four-year ethnographic study, Wood and his colleagues (2004) identified seven competing police subcultures in the "Sunbelt City Police Department." While some officers still held fast to the traditional norms, the existence of other subcultures, including the "opportunistic," "paramilitary," "administrative," "civilian," "expert COP," and "community-oriented policing" subcultures ensured that frontline officers were no longer indoctrinated into a single world view. Interestingly, women had gained some level of acceptance by the more traditionally minded officers, although their entry into the paramilitary subculture was largely denied. The paramilitary subculture embodies many of the same values as the traditional subculture, only it is much more aggressive. Officers in this group were described as "competitive soldiers" and "one-dimensionally masculine." Subcultures associated with community policing models, while present, did not exert a particularly strong influence on the department personnel as a whole.

Similarly, in an analysis of a Southern Sheriff's Department, Cochran and Bromley (2003) identified three different subcultures: "Subcultural Adherents," "COP Cops," and "Normals." Subcultural adherents comprised a relatively small group within the agency, with only one-sixth of the officers aligning themselves with more traditional beliefs. The COP Cops were more likely to report support of the service-oriented functions of police agencies and accounted for nearly one-third of the respondents. Finally, the Normals, who comprised nearly one-half of the deputies, were not strongly committed to either subculture.

Clearly, the influence of a single, traditional normative order among police officers is being challenged. The successful acceptance of women into policing as full, equal professionals may ultimately rest upon which subculture becomes dominant. Will the more traditional subculture that is based on a crime control model regain its singular dominance, or will the influence of community policing elicit lasting change on the value systems of officers? Certainly, no one can argue that the popularity of community-oriented/problem-solving policing has grown exponentially over the past twenty years. This form of policing is built on communication and mutual respect between officers and local citizens. It is in this type of policing that women may find unique success (Miller, 1999). A number of researchers have concluded that female police officers are less authoritarian, less brutal, more nurturing, better communicators, and that due to differential socialization, possess a greater pacifying quality than do their male counterparts (Bell 1982; Grennan 1987; Rivlin 1981; Van Wormer 1981; Weldy 1976). Furthermore, a recent report by the U.S. Department Justice (2000) concluded that because on their unique traits, female officers may be especially suited to performing the type of policing functions associated with community policing (see also Bazley, Lersch, and Mieczkowski 2004).

If community policing remains popular, it would follow that female police officers would be more accepted and achieve greater success in this type of policing function. Additionally, the traditional police subculture, which is based on an "us versus them" distrust of citizens and fueled by a crime control doctrine, is incompatible with the underlying philosophy of community policing. It would be more and more difficult to follow the doctrine of a traditional police subculture in an agency that has truly seized upon the community policing model. Of course, the question remains: Will community policing last, or is it simply another flash in the pan? The question is open for debate (see Skogan 2004). Only time will tell which police service model—and which subculture—will emerge as the dominant value system among law enforcement personnel.

IS THE GLASS HALF FULL?

Before we leave this chapter, it is important to note that several researchers have found that the situation for female police officers may be improving (Carlan and McMullan 2009). For example, based on structured interviews with 14 policewomen employed in a large Midwestern police agency, Archbold and Schulz (2008) found that more than half of the female officers (9/14) indicated that they had been treated like a "token" female officer one or more times during their employment and that they were treated differently than their male counterparts by other male officers. Half of the respondents indicated that their most common sources of frustration stemmed from dealing with disrespect and a lack of full acceptance by their male counterparts. While this may sound discouraging, these results would indicate that approximately half of the female officers did *not* voice such disparaging comments regarding their experiences. In fact, a number of female officers noted positive experiences and perceptions of their advancement opportunities. More than half of the female officers did not report any difference in the calls for service they received. Eight of the respondents reported that the availability of promotions to female officers was either "good" or "very good" and nine reported that they would recommend policing as an occupation to other women. Perhaps most encouraging was the fact that the majority of the female officers indicated that they did not feel isolated from their male counterparts based solely on gender.

Similarly, in a study of 117 female officers Somvadee and Morash (2008) found that 58.2 percent of the respondents reported that they had been a victim of sexual harassment on the job. About half (46.1 percent) reported exposure to sexist or suggestive materials or jokes, while 68 percent had experienced crude sexual comments from their male colleagues. Just over half (53.8 percent) indicated that they had been put down because of sex. Again, we are faced with the "half empty" issue: While about half of the women do report significant issues related to their treatment by male colleagues, about half do not.

Is the situation for female officers improving or not? On a more discouraging note, it should also be noted that some have argued that the treatment of women officers may not actually be improving, but women officers may simply have become more tolerant to jokes, remarks, and other questionable actions (Seklecki and Paynich 2007; Somvadee and Morash 2008; Westmarland 2001). In order to better fit in with their male colleagues, female officers may simply ignore such treatment and just view it as part of the job. Should we view encouraging survey results with optimism or skepticism? The jury is still out.

CONCLUSION

Progressive agencies are welcoming diversity within their ranks, recognizing the importance of recruiting and retaining a police department that demographically reflects the community it serves. This welcome mat is extended not only to women, but to minorities, gays, and lesbians as well. Gains have been made in the recruitment of minorities to policing, especially among Hispanic populations (Scoville 2008). Openly gay and lesbian individuals are also finding policing to be a more welcoming occupation. For example, Miller, Forest, and Jurik (2003) noted that up until a few years ago an officer could be dismissed for being openly gay or lesbian. Now, a number of large agencies including Boston, New York City, Philadelphia, Atlanta, and San Francisco are directly recruiting gay and lesbian officers.

Officers from underrepresented groups, including women, people of color, and gays and lesbians each face their own unique challenges as they enter the realm of an occupation that was and continues to be dominated by white males (Colvin 2009). As Waddington (1999) notes, sexism is not a trait that is exclusive to police culture. The police simply are a reflection of the patriarchal beliefs of the larger society in which masculine traits are valued over femininity (Garcia 2003). Traditionally, through our laws and cultural standards, men have had the power to dictate which positions women are allowed to hold in society (Bartollas and Hahn 1999; Martin and Jurik 1996). It was not all that long ago that women were not allowed to attend college, own property, manage their own financial affairs, or vote. Clearly, sexism among the police is not unique. It exists not only in male-dominated occupations, but across society as well. While great advancements for women have been made, there is still room for improvement. This is especially true in the field of policing.

BIBLIOGRAPHY

APPIER, J. (1998). *Policing women: The sexual politics of enforcement and the LAPD*. Philadelphia: Temple University Press.

ARCHBOLD, C., & SCHULZ, D. M. (2008). Making rank: The lingering effects of tokenism on female police officers' promotion aspirations. *Police Quarterly, 11*(1): 50–73.

AUSTIN, T., & HUMMER, D. (1999). What do college students think of policewomen? An attitudinal assessment of future law enforcement personnel. *Women and Criminal Justice, 10*(4): 1–24.

BARKER, J. (1999). *Danger, duty, and disillusion: The worldview of the Los Angeles police officers*. Prospect Heights: Waveland Press.

BAZLEY, T., LERSCH, K. M., & MIECZKOWSKI, T. (2004). Female patrol officers and use of force: Community policing considerations. Presented at the annual meetings of the American Society of Criminology, November, Nashville, Tennessee.

BELKNAP, J., & SHELLEY, J. K. (1992). The new Lone Ranger: Policewomen on patrol. *American Journal of Police 12*: 47.

BELL, D. (1982). Policewomen: Myths and realities. *Journal of Police Science and Administration 10* (1): 112–120.

BARTOLLAS, C., & HAHN, L. (1999). *Policing in America*. Boston: Allyn and Bacon.

BUREAU OF JUSTICE ASSISTANCE AND NATIONAL CENTER FOR WOMEN AND POLICING (2000). *Recruiting and Retaining Women: A Self-Assessment Guide for Law Enforcement*. Washington, D.C.: United States Department of Justice.

CARLAN, P. E., & MCMULLAN, E. C. (2009). A contemporary snapshot of policewomen attitudes. *Women & Criminal Justice, 19*(1): 60–79.

CHRISTOPHERSON, O., & COTTON, J. (2004). *Police Service Strength in England and Wales, 31 March 2004*. Home Office Report, Stationary Office, London.

COCHRAN, J. K., & BROMLEY, M. L. (2003). The myth(?) of the police subculture. *Policing: An International Journal of Police Strategies & Management, 26*: 88–118.

COLVIN, R. (2009). Shared perceptions among lesbian and gay police officers: Barriers and opportunities in the law enforcement work environment. *Police Quarterly, 12*(1): 86–101.

CRANK, J. P. (1998). *Understanding police culture*. Cincinnati: Anderson.

DRESNER, L. M. (2007). *The female investigator in literature, film, and popular culture.* Jefferson, NC: McFarland.

FELPERIN, J. (2004, May 18). Women in law enforcement: Two steps forward, three steps back. Available online at http://www.policeone.com/police-recruiting/articles/87017-Women-in-Law-Enforcement-Two-steps-forward-three-steps-back/

GARCIA, V. (2003). "Difference" in the police department: Women, policing and "doing gender." *Journal of Contemporary Criminal Justice, 19:* 330–344.

GATES, P. (2006). *Detecting men: Masculinity and the Hollywood detective film.* Albany: State University of New York Press.

GRENNAN, S. (1987). Findings on the role of officer gender in violent encounters with citizens. *Journal of Police Science and Administration, 15:* 78–85.

HAARR, R. (1997). Patterns of interaction in a police patrol bureau: Race and gender barriers to integration. *Justice Quarterly, 14*(1): 53–85.

HALE D., & LANIER, M. (2002). New millennium: Women in policing in the twenty-first century. In R. Muraskin and A. R. Roberts (eds.). *Visions for change: Crime and justice in the twenty-first century* (3rd ed.), pp. 480–497. Upper Saddle River: Prentice Hall.

HALE, D., & WYLAND, S. (1993). Dragons and dinosaurs: The plight of patrol women. *Police Forum 3*(2): 1–6.

HE, N., ZHAO, J., & ARCHBOLD, C. (2002). Gender and police stress: The convergent and divergent impact of work environment, work-family conflict, and stress coping mechanisms of female and male police officers. *Policing: An International Journal of Police Strategies & Management, 25*: 687–708.

HERBERT, S. (1998). Police subculture reconsidered. *Criminology, 36*: 343–369.

HICKMAN, M. J., & REAVES, B. A. (2006). *Local Police Departments 2003.* Washington, D.C.: Law Enforcement Management and Administrative Statistics.

HOLLADAY, A. (December, 2002). Wonderquest. Available online at http://www.wonderquest.com/size-women-us.htm. Accessed February 1, 2004.

HUNT, J. (1984). The development of rapport through negotiation of gender in field work among police. *Human Organization, 43*: 283–296.

HUNT, J. (1990). The logic of sexism among police. *Women and Criminal Justice, 1*: 3–30.

INNESS, S. A. (1998). *Tough girls: Women warriors and wonder women in popular culture.* Philadelphia: Temple University Press.

KAPPELER, V. E., SLUDER, R. D., & ALPERT, G. P. (1998). *Forces of deviance: Understanding the dark side of policing.* Prospect Heights: Waveland Press, Inc.

KING, N. (2008). Generic womanhood: Gendered depictions in cop action cinema. *Gender & Society, 22*(2): 238–260.

KIRSCHMAN, E. (1997). *I love a cop: What police families need to know.* New York: Guilford.

LANIER, M. (1996). Evolutionary typology of women police officers. *Women and Criminal Justice, 8*(2): 35–57.

MANNING, P. (1977). *Police Work.* Cambridge: MIT Press.

MARTIN, S. (1980). *Breaking and entering: Policewomen on patrol.* Berkeley: University of California Press.

MARTIN, S. (1992). The changing status of women officers: Gender and power in police work. In I.L. Moyer (ed.) *The changing role of women in the criminal justice system* (pp. 281–305). Prospect Heights, IL: Waveland.

MARTIN, S. (1994). "Outsider within" the station house: The impact of race and gender on black women police. *Social Problems, 41:* 383–400.

MARTIN, S., & JURIK, N. (1996). *Doing justice, doing gender: Women in law and criminal justice occupations.* Thousand Oaks: Sage.

MILLER, S. (1999). *Gender and community policing: Walking the talk.* Boston: Northeastern University Press.

MILLER, S., FOREST, K, & JURIK, N. (2003). Diversity in blue: Lesbian and gay police officers in a masculine occupation. *Men and Masculinities, 5*(4): 355–385.

MORRISON, R. D. (1993). The police subculture: Myth or reality? *Law & Order, 41:* 87.

MOORE, M. (1992). Problem solving and community policing. In M. Tonry and N. Morris (eds.) *Crime and Justice: An Annual Review* (pp. 99–158). Chicago: University of Chicago Press.

NATIONAL CENTER FOR WOMEN AND POLICING (1999). Equality denied: The status of women in policing. Available online at http://www.womenandpolicing.org/Final_1999StatusReport.htm. Accessed January 15, 2004.

PARSONS, D., & JESILOW, P. (2001). *In the same voice: Women and men in law enforcement.* Santa Ana: Seven Locks Press.

PEAK, K. J. (2003). *Policing America: Methods, issues, challenges.* (4th ed.). Upper Saddle River: Prentice Hall.

POULOS, T., & DOERNER, W. (1996). Women in law enforcement: The distribution of females in Florida police agencies. *Women in Criminal Justice, 8*(2): 19–33.

PRESIDENT'S COMMISSION ON LAW ENFORCEMENT AND ADMINISTRATION OF JUSTICE (1967). *Task Force Report: The Police.* Washington, D.C.: United States Government Printing Office.

RAFTER, N. H. (2006). *Shots in the mirror: Crime films and society.* 2nd ed. New York: Oxford University Press.

RIVLIN, G. (1981). The last bastion of macho. *Update on law-related education, 5:* 22–24, 65–67.

ROBERG, R., NOVAK, K., & CORDNER, G. (2005). *Police and society.* (3rd ed.). Los Angeles: Roxbury Publishing Company.

SCOTT, E. (1981). *Calls for service: Citizen demand and initial police response.* Washington, D.C.: U.S. Government Printing Office.

SCOVILLE, D. (2008, February 1) *The State of American Law Enforcement: The Blue Mosaic.* Accessed online at http://www.policemag.com/Channel/Patrol/Articles/2008/02/The-Blue-Mosaic.aspx

SEKLECKI, R., & PAYNICH, R. (2007). A national survey of female police officers: An overview of findings. *Police Practice and Research, 8*(1): 17–30.

SILVESTRI, M. (2007). "Doing" police leadership: Enter the "new smart macho." *Policing and Society, 17*(1): 38–58.

SKOGAN, W. G. (2004). *Community policing: Can it work?* Belmont: Wadsworth/Thomson Publishing.

SKOLNICK, J. (1966). *Justice without trial.* New York: John Wiley & Sons Inc.

SKOLNICK, J. (2002). Corruption and the blue code of silence. *Police, Practice and Research, 3*(1): 7–19.

SKOLNICK, J., & CURRIE, E. (1970). *Crisis in American institutions.* Boston: Little Brown.

SOMVADEE, C., & MORASH, M. (2008). Dynamics of sexual harassment for policewomen working alongside men. *Policing: An International Journal of Police Strategies & Management 31*(3): 485–498.

STARK, R. (1972). *Police riots: Collective violence and law enforcement.* Belmont, CA: Wadsworth Publishing Company, Inc.

SWANSON, C., TERRITO, L, & TAYLOR, R. (1998). *Police administration: Structures, processes, and behavior* (4th ed.). Upper Saddle River: Prentice Hall.

VAN MAANEN, J. (1980). Beyond account: The personal impact of police strategies. *Annals of the Academy of Political and Social Science, 452:* 145–156.

WESTMARLAND, L. (2001). *Gender and policing: Sex, power, and police culture.* Portland, OR: Willan Publishing.

VAN WORMER, K. (1981). Are males suited to police patrol work? *Police Studies 3:* 41–44.

WADDINGTON, P. A. J. (1999). Police (canteen) sub-culture: An appreciation. *British Journal of Criminology, 39*: 287–309.

WALKER, S., & KATZ, C. (2002). *The police in America: An introduction*. 4th edition. Boston: McGraw Hill.

WELDY, W. (1976). Women in policing: A positive step toward increased police enthusiasm. *The Police Chief, 43:* 46–47.

WESTLEY, W. (1970). *Violence and the police*. Boston: MIT Press Books.

WEXLER, J. G., & QUINN, V. (1983). Sources of stress among women police officers. *Journal of Police Science and Administration, 13:* 98–105.

WILSON, O. W., & MCLAREN, R.C. (1963). *Police administration* (3rd ed.). New York: McGraw Hill.

WOOD, R. L., DAVIS, M., & ROUSE, A. (2004). Diving into quicksand: Program implementation and police subcultures. In W. Skogan (ed.) *Community policing: Can it work?* (pp. 136–162). Belmont: Wadsworth/Thomson Learning.

34

The Career Trajectories of Female Police Executives

Cara Rabe-Hemp

While women currently comprise about ten percent of the nation's police executives, over 50 percent of municipal agencies report no women in the top command or supervisory ranks (National Center for Women & Policing, 2001). As the first generation of female police executives, who joined the policing occupation amidst the rise of community policing, consent decrees, and affirmative action suits (Martin, 1991) retire, many questions about their successful careers remain. These female police executives who have succeeded in an "all boys club" despite early and continued opposition from colleagues, isolation in the organizational culture, and difficulty climbing the proverbial administration ladder (Hunt, 1990; Martin, 1980; Price, 1985; Rabe-Hemp, 2008) necessitate a discussion of the pathways or trajectories successful female police administrators employ to achieve rank. Specifically, this study explores: the importance of mentors, the mechanisms employed to overcome obstacles including sex discrimination and inter-organizational mobility, and the costs and triumphs of delayed career or family goals.

THE NATURE OF POLICE PROMOTION

Borrowed from the military, the occupation of policing is a hierarchically structured bureaucracy, signified by the uniform, rank structure, and the legal authority to use deadly force. The police organizational structure, a conglomeration of military and bureaucratic models, is characterized by an authoritarian command structure in which the greatest discretion is held by command and administrative ranks. The police organization is characterized by strict subordination, a rigid chain of command, and a formal provision for moving up the ranks (Bordua & Reiss, 1965). The hierarchical command starts at the bottom with patrol officer, followed by the Corporal, Sergeant, Lieutenant, Captain, Deputy Chief, and Chief.[1] One of the major ways that policing differs from other careers is that administrators work up through the ranks to become leaders of their organization. To become a police administrator (Captain, Deputy Chief, Chief, Colonel, Lt. Colonel), an officer must have started as a patrol officer, and almost always held a middle management position previously (Commander, Sergeant, Lieutenant).

Making rank or moving from one rank to another is a process with several stages. Police administration requirements vary from agency to agency, but may consist of a written assessment, an oral interview, and a review of past job evaluations. The first stage is based on self-selection. Individual officers' inducements to apply include greater organizational power and prestige, benefits, and salary. Eligible officers undergo a written assessment created by a civil service committee. Scores on the assessment are ranked and placed on an eligibility list. In the selection stage, the Chief may choose any candidate from the top 10 percent of the list or may chose the top scored, depending on department practice or policy. Regardless of the department particulars, gaining promotion always requires strong testing capabilities, along with administration support (Scarborough, Van Tubergen, Gaines, & Whitlow, 1999).

Promotion opportunities in many police agencies are scarce (Archbold & Schulz, 2008). The very few administrative positions in police agencies and the civil service system that regulate promotion contribute to the lack of mobility in police agencies. A 1981 study by the Police Executive Research Forum suggested that civil service regulations that require officers to serve a certain number of years at each rank (typically between 2 and 5) before becoming eligible for promotion to the next rank is partly responsible for the lack of upward mobility in police agencies. This is exacerbated by the practice of offering promotion exams at irregular intervals based on department needs and fiscal health. To understand how these practices contribute specifically to the promotional experiences of policewomen, an understanding of how history and past institutional practices contribute to the reproduction of the social structure in the modern era is necessary.

FEMALE POLICE EXECUTIVES

In 1963 Felicia Shpritzer and her colleagues from the New York Police Department sued and won the right to test for the Sergeant's promotional exam. Her accomplishment broke the barrier for policewomen across the nation. Since that time women have legally challenged entry requirements, selection criteria, and promotional processes that blocked opportunities for women to progress through the police ranks (Martin, 1991; Sulton & Townsey, 1981). The result was affirmative action programs that were adopted in many police agencies in the 1980s. These policies, along with the expanded police role of the community policing model, led to the increased representation of women in policing from 4.2 percent of municipal officers in 1978 to 8.8 percent in 1986 (Martin, 1990). Women's representation in supervisory positions also increased during this time from 1 percent to 3.3 percent.

Despite early gains, today the average police department has no women in top or command positions (National Center for Women & Policing, 2001). Women comprise only 10 percent of administrative positions in large municipal agencies (National Center for Women & Policing, 2001) and 1 percent of chiefs positions nationwide (Schulz, 2006).

Those percentages are low considering that women consist of 17 percent of large municipal departments (Bureau of Justice Statistics, 2006), especially when bearing in mind that those numbers represent a few large, municipal agencies. Dubbed the "brass ceiling" by Dorothy Schulz (2006), women are not well-represented in the administrative ranks in policing. Many factors have been suggested to explain the lack of proportionate representation of women in the administrative ranks of policing including harassment and discrimination (Burligame & Baro, 2005; Franklin, 2005; Garcia, 2003; Hunt, 1990; Martin, 1980), tokenism (Belknap & Shelley, 1992; Kanter, 1977), lack of role models and mentoring (Martin, 1980; Wexler & Logan, 1983), and conflict with familial responsibilities (Wertsch, 1998; Whetstone & Wilson, 1999).

Harassment and Discrimination

Male police officers' resistance to female officers has been amply documented (Brown & Heidensohn, 2000; Haarr, 1997; Harrington, 2002; Hunt, 1990; Lonsway & Alipio, 2008; Martin, 1980). Martin (1980) found, "most women officers have experienced both sex discrimination and sexual harassment" and frequently these behaviors were "blatant, malicious, widespread, organized, and involved supervisors; occasionally it was life-threatening" (p. 290). Hunt (1990) examined the underlying logic of police sexism among police when she researched the hesitation of male police to accept women into the rank-and-file. Discrimination and harassment influences the promotional opportunities of policewomen by maintaining women as "outsiders" in police work, which limits opportunities necessary for promotion and leads to the isolation and intimidation of potential leaders.

The structure of hegemonic masculinity, which reinforces the power of men both on the cultural and collective levels in policing, celebrates masculine values that engender particular views of women, and defines roles for which men and women officers are believed to be most suitable (Dick & Jankowicz, 2001). Historically women have been deemed most suitable in positions that emphasize feminine and caretaking qualities. Through academy and field training experiences, female officers are acculturated to the hyper-masculine values and attitudes of policing which restrict women's behavior to feminine tasks, mostly involving women and children (Garcia, 2003). By adopting the roles for "women's work," female officers maintain the hegemonic masculinity operating in the police occupation. These positions rarely lead to field experiences, which are important to move up the proverbial ladder. In a study of a medium-sized police department in the Pacific Northwest, policewomen reported being trapped in gender-appropriate roles was a major barrier to upward mobility (Wertsch, 1998).

Tokenism

The token status of women in police organizations may also contribute to the under-representation of women in the administrative and command ranks. When a group makes up less than 15 percent of an organization, they perceive themselves to be highly visible, attracting disproportionate attention to themselves, and being perceived as "in but not of" the organization (Belknap & Shelley, 1992; Kanter, 1977). In organizations with less female representation, the behaviors of female officers are more salient and draw more attention as novelties than those of male officers, which is especially relevant in non-urban agencies where women are especially un-common.[2]

While women consist of approximately 17 percent of police officers in large municipal agencies nationwide (Bureau of Justice Statistics, 2006), no agency to date comes close to Kanter's balanced ratio of 60:40 (Kanter, 1977). Krimmel and Gormley (2003) tested tokenism in a number of police departments in New Jersey and Pennsylvania. They found that although women were generally happy with their profession, women in departments with less than 15 percent female officers had lower levels of job satisfaction, higher levels of depression and lower levels of self-esteem than women in departments where women comprised more the 15 percent sworn personnel. A recent test of Kanter's (1977) theory of tokenism was undertaken by Archbold and Schulz (2008), who found mixed support for tokenism. In keeping with past research (Wertsch, 1998), the majority (79 percent) of female officers reported that they had to work harder than male officers in the agency and 64 percent reported they had been treated like tokens at some point during their law enforcement career (Archbold & Schulz, 2008). Interestingly, many policewomen reported they had been encouraged toward promotion solely because of their gender. This had the unintended consequence of singling them out, drawing negative attention from male patrol officers, and ultimately discouraging them from the promotion process (Archbold & Schulz, 2008).

Role Models and Mentoring

Role models and mentors are integral to the integration and career progression of female officers (Cox & Nkomo, 1992; Kanter, 1977). In policing, Martin (1980) argues that a lack of variety of female role models in higher ranks is a major obstacle to younger female officers. Without the guidance of seasoned female veterans to teach rookies the ropes, female officers are excluded from informal networks that are essential to forming mentoring relationships that lead promotion recommendation (Martin, 1980; Wexler & Logan, 1983).

Conflict with Familial Responsibilities

Due to the increasing numbers of women in the workplace in the past decade, much attention has been centered on how motherhood influences the career paths of young women (Bureau of Labor Statistics, 2006). In 1989, Felice Schwartz coined the term "mommy track" to describe two divergent paths to leadership: a fast one for those who are childless and a slower one where mothers pause or stay in middle-level management. While no research to date has explored how motherhood influences the career trajectories of police executives, several recent studies have suggested that familial obligations influence officers' decisions to take the important first step of promotion exams (Rabe-Hemp, 2008; Werstch, 1998; Whetstone & Wilson, 1999). In their study of officers eligible for promotional exam, Whetstone and Wilson (1999) argue family and child-care issues play a large role in women's decisions to forego promotional opportunities, reflected in a preference to stay in their current assignment and job shift. Cooper and Ingram (2004) reported that the most often cited reason policewomen gave for leaving their current posts was domestic responsibility. Due to civil service systems, union influences, and police tradition, officers bid for shifts based on seniority within rank. In Rabe-Hemp (2008), many female officers reported a hesitancy to take the promotional exam, because a promotion would mean the loss of a traditional 9-to-5 schedule creating difficulties with child care. This research highlights the concerns female officers express in considering promotional opportunities. While past research highlights the obstacles policewomen face progressing up the police ranks, little research identifies what strategies and personal characteristics permit female police executives to overcome these obstacles to rise to the top. That is the primary focus of this research.

METHODS

The sample consists of 14 female officers, each with varying police experience ranging from 17 to 35 years. In an attempt to determine the experiences of female police executives, only officers with the civil service rank of Lieutenant and above (Captain, Colonel, Deputy Chief, and Chief) were interviewed (mean years served were 25.7). All of the respondents were White. The sample included 5 municipal officers, 4 campus police officers, and 5 state police, from all over the United States. The position held included: 4 Chiefs, 1 Colonel, 5 Captains/Commanders, and 4 Lieutenants.

The most difficult aspects of researching female officers are finding them and making initial contact. To encourage honesty and frankness by female officers, department administrators were not contacted seeking lists of possible interviewees. Instead, due to the rarity of the population being examined,[3] potential participants were identified by "snowball sampling."

The interview protocol consisted of open-ended questions designed to examine female officers' perceived acceptance and integration in their departments, difficulties associated with the police roles and organization, and coping mechanisms utilized to overcome resistance. Since the study concerns women's subjective perceptions and assessments of their experiences as female police executives, the questions allowed the respondents to elaborate on their experiences and the events that shaped their tenures.

During each interview, notes were taken, and each interview was taped with the subject's consent and then typed verbatim for qualitative data analysis. Each transcript was analyzed for emerging themes, concerns, and phrases that had been presented by the participants. These were coded using an open-ended approach. After the first reading, tags corresponding to relevant research issues were placed on the transcriptions by hand. The issues covered by the tags were very broad in nature (i.e., promotion, obstacles and accomplishments, and mentoring) and left a great deal of scope for establishing variability in participants' responses that were later organized into categories that represented the participants' distinctions. The themes within each tagged topic were refined and reorganized through multiple re-readings of the transcripts. In the last step, representative quotes were pulled to illustrate the major themes reported by the participants (Padgett, 1998; Tutty, Rothery, & Grinnell, 1996).

These findings should be evaluated in light of the study's methodological limitations. First, in any interaction, the audience has the potential to affect the presentation of the descriptive experiences described. Despite all attempts by the researcher not to lead or interfere with the officers' responses, the context of discursive control alone influences the accounts given (Presser, 2005; Stokoe, 2006). Second, although the study utilized a wide variety of agency and police officer types in comprehensive interviews, a small number of police women are represented. Third, women of color are not represented in this study. Previous research suggests that African-American women report higher levels of discrimination in the promotion process (Whetstone & Wilson, 1999). This could limit the applicability of the overall findings.

RESULTS

To determine the length of time it took women police executives to climb the leadership ladder, four important steps of the career trajectory were analyzed (Sergeant, Lieutenant, Captain, and Chief). Due to the civil service system and the use of military ranks, promotion opportunities are highly structured. Sergeant is the first civil service rank after patrol officer, followed by Lieutenant, and Captain. Positions such as Detective, Deputy Chief, or Chief are appointed at the discretion of the highest agency administrator and/or city council and are not considered civil service promotions. The results suggest the career trajectories of female police executives were quite similar with few exceptions. Most of the women in the study began policing in the 1980s (range 1974 to 1992) and took an average of 7 years to accomplish (range 14–4) the first civil service promotion to the rank of Sergeant. Many officers were promoted to appointed positions (most often Detective) prior to Sergeant. The second civil service promotion to Lieutenant took an average of 16 years (range 24–9). Of the 7 who achieved the rank of Captain, the average length of service before the Captains promotion was 19 years (range 20–16.5). Finally, of the 5 who achieved the rank of Chief, the average length of service before that promotion was 19 years (range 30–4).

Due to the scarcity of available leadership positions, female police executives reported serving multiple positions and/or agencies throughout their careers. Executives ranged from 4 to 15 different positions (appointed and civil service) in their careers and 0 to 8 physical relocations. The average number of positions held by executives at leadership rank was seven. That is change in position every three to four years. Physical moves (i.e., agency or district changes) were less common, but still averaged 2.5 moves per career. Women executives serving in state police agencies were the most likely to transfer to a variety of districts (mean = 5.5). This may be due to the strong paramilitary structure of state police agencies and traditional management theory which holds that employees should work up through the ranks to build loyalty and respect.

Colonel, State Police:	I've been moved around quite a bit in the agency. I've spent time in just about every work unit there is, and that was because of directors before and I think this is a good thing. One director in particular had a military background and so he felt that in order for you to be a well-rounded leader, you needed to experience that agency from all facets.
Captain, State Police:	When you get the upper ranks, a lot of times it requires you to move.
Deputy Chief (Lieutenant), Municipal:	Once you get to the Lieutenant level, the Chief kind of moves the puzzle pieces around so I have been moved to a lot of different jobs as a Lieutenant.
Chief, Municipal:	I worked in or supervised every part of this organization.

Another strategy suggested was to serve in more "women friendly" police agencies. Echoing Peter Horne's (2006) suggestion that campus police departments are more "female friendly," many in the sample suggested the university police agencies had better opportunities for female officers. As one University Chief mentioned:

> Women move within university police departments further and faster. They are more open to women in leadership roles. Definitely more so than municipalities.

Harassment and Discrimination

Police executives in this study overcame a variety of obstacles, including sexual harassment, discrimination, or disrespect, all of which impeded their successes and acceptance in police work. Surprisingly, most participants suggested the serious obstacles they faced, such as physical assault and obstacles to promotion, had occurred early in their careers and had desisted after several years experience; often to re-surface following a new assignment or promotion.

Captain: And I wasn't getting those positions even though I had a really good work record and I had really good relationships with my co-workers and peers. One of the guys that got a position that I didn't get was a complete idiot. So I started to say, you know that the writing is on the wall. They are not going to let me go into what I want to do, there is still some stigma going on here. There was still some issues with where they wanted females to go.

Chief: He said "Rick's a boy." I said, yeah I have been doing this job. He said I can't promote you over a man.

Captain: Always a bridesmaid, never a bride. And I think part of that was my mindset and part of it was the department's mindset. I would settle for the second position instead of the top position. And I am not sure why I did that.

Lieutenant: I interviewed for 13 different positions with my department over the course of the years and was always denied.

Many police executives reported frustration following their promotions that they were required to re-negotiate their acceptance and position in their departments, suggesting that acceptance was not a level of achievement, but a fluid, dynamic status that must be negotiated on a day-by-day basis to be maintained. Female police executives perceived this process as something unique to female administrators.

Captain, State Police: It's a continual process; you are never accepted based on your merits. It's like all you know. And I'll tell you I felt like I could not call in sick. Because it's there she goes, she is probably having her period.

Police Chief, Municipality: After a new assignment, I had to prove myself all over again.

Captain, State Police: When I came back to my home district I had to prove myself all over again. And if I were a male it would have been like, Oh Hallelujah, he is here.

| Captain, Municipal: | Acceptance on a police department when you are a female is something that you never completely obtain but you kind of constantly strive towards to some extent. |

Tokenism

The female police executives represented reported accomplishing many "firsts" including being the first female officer, first officer of rank, and first Police Chief for their respective departments. Being the first is a highly vulnerable, but exciting position in any organization. Officers commonly mentioned the advantages and disadvantages of being highly visible.

Police Chief:	It gets old being the first. Everyone looks at you. It's like being in a fishbowl.
Captain, State police:	Well I am a female in a male-dominated organization. I'm not particularly tall. I'm not particularly short. I'm not particularly fat . . . So what sets me apart? My gender does . . . It's an advantage if it gives you visibility.
Colonel, State Police:	I had a lot of opportunities because being a woman in [names agency], back then I was very unique. So I think I had the opportunity to do a lot of things. Opportunities the others may not have had. In part because the department was showcasing me. You know, I looked good in a uniform, but sometimes you would get frustrated because they would not take you seriously.

Successes

When asked what had contributed to their success, female police executives mentioned several mechanisms employed to overcome obstacles and ascend through the police ranks. Many women described a "survive and thrive" model for success based on overcoming adversity and turning negatives into positives.

| Captain, State Police: | Drive. From day one. |
| Captain, Municipal Police: | Heart. A lot of heart and a high tolerance for adversity. |

Other female officers attempted to better themselves through education to be more competitive for potential and future police positions as a way of overcoming obstacles in police work. Almost of all the women interviewed had attained Bachelor's degrees, 6 had achieved Master's Degrees, and one had a PhD. Educated officers may not be unusual for police recruits today, but was rare for police recruits of the 1980s (Carter, Sapp, & Stevens, 1989; Harrington, 2002). Many women suggested their degrees helped them move up the proverbial slow administrative ladder, which may explain the high degree of administrators in the sample.

Colonel: If you think women have to be twice as good just to be considered aver-age, then don't spend your energy complaining about it, just spend your energy being twice as good . . . I knew education was a door for me, so I knew I had to do that.

The women police officers interviewed acknowledged they are often trapped in gender appropriate roles. In an organizational culture which prizes law enforcement above all other police roles, gaining experience in the more aggressive roles were important for female officers to gain legitimacy in the paramilitary organization.

Deputy Chief: I think in particular for women to get the experience to become supervisors, they need to be placed in positions like drug units, tactical units, less traditional and into in the sexual assault and juvenile unit . . . They gain the knowledge of the position, they gain the respect of superi-ors, and that will assist them later on.

Captain, Municipal: More street experience. It would have made it easier for me to go up the chain. I would have had respect starting out as opposed to having to earn it once I made rank. That's a mistake a lot of females make. They don't get guided in the right direction. You need to stay on the street for about five years before you leave.

Colonel, State Police: Then a boss took a risk and put me into the field as a field commander and said, "You need this field experience in order to give you creditability."

Captain, State Police: On paper you would not know I was a woman. I am a crit-ical incident instructor. I am a tactical officer, you know things that women aren't traditionally involved in.

Role Models and Mentoring

Mentors and role models were important to the success of almost all the women inter-viewed. Because almost all of the officers in this analysis were from what Dorothy Moses Schulz (2003) calls the first generation, almost all their mentors were men. The roles that mentors played in these officers' career trajectories varied from role model, advisor, or supervisor. The commonality in each experience was that the mentor directed the officer's navigation through the steps of career progression.

Captain, State Police: I had a field training officer that took me under his wing like a little sister. He said always always, always take the promotional test because you never know. And they're not going to promote you if you are not ready, but if you don't take the test then you are not in the game.

Police Chief: And he told me, 'don't take that shit from no one.'

Lieutenant, Municipal: [Mentors] were supportive of women in policing. They were supportive of me in particular. They kind of said, 'hey, we want to give you the confidence to move ahead, we want to take you under our wing, we want to open up some opportunities for you, you know . . . I've talked you up to other people, you know, you have the ability, you have the talent.'

Conflict with Familial Responsibilities

The challenge of balancing family responsibilities with career was a common theme reported by police executives in the analysis. The work-life balance in police work has been revived in the past decade, with a variety of studies suggesting that policewomen face unique stressors in police work (Kurtz, 2008; McCarty, Zhao, & Garland, 2007). Female police executives confirmed Kurtz's (2008) findings that the demands of family life are especially difficult for female police.

Police Chief, Municipal: Police work is disruptive to family life.

Colonel, State Police: Your personal life becomes very showcased, and I did not like that, so needless to say my second marriage, he was not a member of the department.

To explore the notion that the trajectories of female police executives were impacted by motherhood, women police were asked if they faced any gender-specific obstacles such as: child-care issues, pregnancy, and uniform difficulties. Of the fourteen officers interviewed, five had children. Early in their career trajectories women with children, compared to their childless counterparts, do not seem to differ significantly early their careers (i.e., the time from hire to Sergeant). The length of time was approximately 7 years for both groups. However, differences emerged at the rank of Lieutenant. Those with children took an average 3 years longer to make Lieutenant than those without children. Interestingly, there was only a year difference in delay at the rank of Captain for those with children. These results are explained by the officers' narratives which suggested they worked hard to overcome the concern that motherhood would be perceived as a lack of organizational commitment, impacting their perceived work ethic competency to lead.

Police Chief: I was the first female in my work unit to have children. After a tussle in my unit, the guys spoke to my supervisor who subsequently put me on light duty. I was disappointed in the guys. The supervisor told the guys, 'See, this is why women should not be in law enforcement.' After I came back I did not miss a beat. I needed to make up for lost time.

Balancing the work and family was reportedly difficult for the women in the sample who did have children (5 of 14 had children), especially given the lack of maternity policies in agencies in the 1970s and 1980s. One childless police executive reported that she would have been fired had she gotten pregnant.

Captain, State Police:	When your chief legal advisor tells you that being pregnant is actually no different that someone breaking their ankle, we figure we might have a problem.
Lieutenant, University:	That's why I was Sergeant for a year and a half on midnights. After I got done with my degree I said, 'I don't want to be on midnights for the next 20 years. I have got a 5-year-old at home. So I gave up my Sergeant stripes and went back to Corporal and now I am on days. And that was a personal choice, what was best for my family.
Chief, University:	We said okay we are considering having families. Could we be assigned to desk duty during our pregnancy and our job. And his answer was no, I would have to fire you if you couldn't go on and do your job.

The Next Generation

Women police executives were reflective about the generations of female leadership coming up through the ranks. Many expressed concern about future generations. There is some empirical support for their concerns. As consent decrees have expired in many of the major cities, police departments are not hiring women at the rate at which the first generation is retiring (Horne, 2006).

Captain, State Police:	When we go, there is nobody behind us.
Captain, State Police:	We have to be careful because a lot of time we are a lot harder on each other, specifically to women. . . . My expectations are huge and it's negative in one aspect and positive in another. The negative side of that is that I try desperately not to do this, but as you raise through the levels of ranks, you have a tendency to compress because it has taken you so long to get there.
Colonel, State Police:	I would say we are about to see another big brain drain. . . . I don't think they have done a lot to prepare that young leadership to move up.
Police Chief, Municipal Police:	Women of higher rank look at female colleagues and instead of being mentors and inclusive, they are mean, nasty, and spiteful. To the point of making you look bad makes me look better. Very catty.

DISCUSSION

The purpose of this study was to explore the pathways or career trajectories successful female police administrators employed to achieve high ranks. To that end, female police executives were interviewed to allow the women to articulate their own experiences. Their "success stories" have many commonalities including the struggles associated with proving their skills and capabilities first as officers and then as administrators, the mechanisms and strategies employed to be successful, and the costs and triumphs of delayed career or family goals associated with achieving high rank in modern police agencies.

The career trajectories of women in the sample included many transfers and moves to different agencies or districts, in the case of State Police agencies, to overcome a lack of inter-agency mobility. This is consistent with past literature suggesting that leadership-driven policewomen either move up or move out (Fry, 1983). In her groundbreaking study of female Chiefs, Schulz (2003) reports that most of the women in her sample relocated in order to achieve the rank of Chief, ranging from one to five relocations. Over one-third of her sample became Chief in the agency in which they began their careers. This is also consistent with management literature which reports that, on average, women move between organizations more often than men (Valcour & Tolbert, 2003). While this practice afforded women promotional opportunities, Valcour and Tolbert (2003) reported that in the long term, this practice negatively impacted women's earnings. In addition, the practice of moving to a variety of agencies or district no doubt exacerbated the difficulties women faced in continually proving themselves to new agencies and colleagues. The process of constantly negotiating acceptance and respect compelled administrators to be in a constant state of self-awareness, which may explain the higher than average rates of stress, burnout, and turnover reported by female officers (Haarr, 1997; Kurtz, 2008; McCarty, Zhao, & Garland, 2007). Future research should assess the cumulative benefits and detriments of moving up or moving on.

Consistent with past research, education provided women in this study with an advantage in promotion exams and led to supervisory and administrative positions. Carter, Sapp, and Stephens (1989) reported that women typically enter law enforcement with higher education levels than men. The higher education level of women officers was also noted by Schulz (2003) in her study of police chiefs and sheriffs, which found that the women were exceptional in their educational levels. Elevated educational levels may influence promotional opportunities in multiple ways. In their study of Texas law enforcement officers in advanced or specialized positions, Polk and Armstrong (2001) found that higher education reduced the time required for movement in rank and was positively correlated to promotion into supervisory and administrative posts, suggesting that extended education provided an advantage during promotion assessment. Some agencies give preference in the civil service promotion system to those with college degrees (Travis, 1995). These findings suggest that women who invest in their education may greatly increase their opportunities for advancement in policing.

Mentors and role models are also integral to the success of women to integrate into organization and progress into leadership roles (Cox & Nkomo, 1992). Past research has suggested that a lack of female role models in higher ranks is a major obstacle to younger female officers (Martin, 1980). As this generation of female police executives leaves policing, the legacy of their leadership for future generations of policewomen is yet to be seen. If the culture of policing becomes more accepting of female police officers, the "thrive and strive" mentality that drove modern policewomen to success may be replaced with new leadership models (Wachs, 2001).

Tokenism may also impact the promotion opportunities of future generations. In their sample of promotion-eligible policewomen, Archbold and Schulz (2008) reported that policewomen were encouraged to highlight their token status in the department, to exaggerate their skills as being polarized to their male officers, and to become highly visible in their respective departments. Rabe-Hemp (2008) reported women in her sample, who had attempted to market themselves as unique from their male counterparts, were most successful in gaining promotion. Unique, however, need not be the more feminized forms of policing. Linda Wirth (2001), author of *Breaking Through the Glass Ceiling: Women in Management,* warns that the inability of women to break through glass walls is due to them being moved into feminized areas of their fields, away from the core activities of their organizations. Women in the present study raised similar concerns suggesting that women with leadership aspirations should seek high-profile positions that are career enhancing (i.e., SWAT, Special Weapons, Investigations, Counter-terrorism).

If the numbers of women in police increase, and gender loses its visibility in police agencies which appeared to assist women in obtaining promotional opportunities, the next generation of female police executives may have very different promotion experiences. It is difficult to predict how those potential changes will impact the future of female police executives. Recent research suggesting that women are opting out of the promotional process will further exacerbate the gap or "brain drain" many female executives mentioned in this study. Due to the civil service regulations that require officers to serve a certain number of years at the each rank combined with the practice of offering promotional exams at irregular intervals, crucial decisions that may affect the ability to move into management must be made early in one's career. Timing is important. Since women are likely to postpone early promotional opportunities for family and child care reasons, they may simply miss those early opportunities. A recent survey of almost 2,500 high-achieving women by Sylvia Ann Hewlett (2007) found that 37 percent of women stop working for a period, or temporarily "opt out" of the workforce. In addition, to the loss of early promotion, behaviors such as having kids and taking time out of the workplace also constitute career risks because they are perceived as a lack of organizational commitment (Williams, 2000). Stereotypes associated with competency and commitment of mothers leads to lessened employer career investments as well as advancement opportunity (Epstein, Seron, Oglensky, & Saute, 1999). Delaying childbirth and limiting family size are associated with greater career success in the form of advancement (Mason & Goulden, 2002; Valcour & Ladge, 2008).

Despite a small sample, this study finds some evidence of a "mommy track" in policing, underscoring the need for additional research which maps the trajectories of successful police executives. Currently, most police agencies do not systematically collect information on the proportion of women in different roles and ranks that allows for a large-scale empirical analysis of positions, tasks performed, and the time taken to attain promotion. The best methodological attempt is to ask officers to retroactively record promotions. Future research should attempt to capture a cohort of women whose career progressions can be tracked. This methodology would allow researchers to follow those women who depart from police work and record their career stages and purposes of their departures (i.e., resigned, retired, removed).

These findings have implications for the future of the police promotional process. Police agencies may have to reconsider the inducements to achieving civil service rank for men and women. Much of the current research suggests that relationship building and familial time is much more important to employees of this generation than material wealth

(Campbell, 2009; Galinsky, Aumann, & Bond, 2009). Unique to policing, both Whetstone (2001) and Scarborough et al. (1999) recently reported that large contingencies of eligible officers declined to participate in the promotional process. The generation of parent employees now in their twenties, dubbed the millennials (Strauss & Howe, 1991), is spending considerably more time with their children than previous generations. For example, today's millennial fathers spend an average of 4.3 hours per workday with their children under 13, significantly more than their age counterparts in 1977 who spent an average of 2.4 hours per workday with their children. Mothers are also spending considerable more time with their children (Galinsky, Aumann, & Bond, 2009). To maintain the best and brightest as administrators, police departments may need to consider family-friendly inducements such as maternity/paternity leave, flex time, and in-house day care options to stay competitive with the private sector.

In conclusion, the voice of this cohort of women and their legacy is heartening. Female officers' integration into policing has forced police officials to rethink traditional practices in selection, training, and performance evaluation, and has improved the quality of police services for the community (Miller, 1999; Sherman, 1975). Further, female police executives have the potential through their administrative policies and statures to exact change in how police "do" justice and gender. The potential for enduring change in the field of policing is great as women continue to make strides in achieving high ranks, breaking down assignments barriers, and ensuring just opportunities for future generations of policewomen.

REFERENCES

ARCHBOLD, C. A. & SCHULZ, D. M. (2008). Making rank: The lingering effects of tokenism on female police officers' promotion aspirations. *Police Quarterly, 11(1),* 50–73.

BELKNAP, J. & SHELLEY, J. K. (1992). The new lone ranger: Policewomen on patrol. *American Journal of Police, 12(2),* 47–75.

BORDUA, D. J., & REISS, A. J. (1965). *Command, control and charisma: Reflections on police bureaucracy.* University of Michigan: Working Papers of Center for Research on Social Organization.

BROWN, J., & HEIDENSOHN, F. (2000). *Gender and policing: Comparative perspectives.* Hampshire, UK: MacMillan Press Ltd.

BURLIGAME, D., & BARO, A. L. (2005). Women's representation and status in law enforcement: Does CALEA involvement make a difference? *Criminal Justice Policy Review, 16(4),* 391–411.

BUREAU OF JUSTICE STATISTICS. (2006). *Local police departments, 2003.* Washington, DC: Law Enforcement Management and Administrative Statistics.

CAMPBELL. (2009). *Advice from the top.* Santa Barbara, CA: Praeger.

CARTER, D. L., SAPP, A. D., & STEPHENS, D. W. (1989). *The state of police education: Policing directions for the 21st century.* Washington, DC: Police Executive Research Forum.

COOPER, C., & INGRAM, S. (2004). *Retention of police officers: A study of resignations and transfers in ten forces.* London, England: Home Office.

COX, T., & NKOMO, S. M. (1992). Candidate age as a factor in promotability ratings. *Public Personnel Management, 21(2),* 197–210.

DICK, P., & JANKOWICZ, D. 2001. A social constructionist account of police culture and its influence on the representation and progression of female officers. *Policing, 24,* 181–199.

EPSTEIN, C. F., SERON, C., OGLENSKY, B., & SAUTE, R. (1999). *The part-time paradox: Time norms, professional lives, family and gender.* Hampshire, UK: Routledge.

FRANKLIN, C. (2005). Male peer support and the police culture: Understanding the resistance and opposition of women in policing. *Women & Criminal Justice, 16(3),* 1–25.

FRY, L. (1983). A preliminary examination of the factors related to turnover of women in law enforcement. *Journal of Police Science and Administration, 11(2),* 149–154.

GALINSKY, E., AUMANN, K. & BOND, J. T. (2009). *Times are changing: Gender and generation at work and at home.* New York: Families and Work Institute. Retrieved from http://familiesandwork .org/site/research/reports/Times_Are_Changing.pdf

GARCIA, V. (2003). Difference in the police department: Women, policing, and doing gender. *Journal of Contemporary Criminal Justice, 19(3),* 330–344.

HAARR, R. (1997). Patterns of interaction in a police bureau: Race and gender barriers to integration. *Justice Quarterly, 14,* 53–85.

HARRINGTON, P. (2002). Advice to women beginning a career in policing. *Women & Criminal Justice, 14(1),* 1–13.

HEWLETT, S. A. (2007). *Off-ramps and on-ramps: Keeping talented women on the road to success.* Cambridge, MA: Harvard Business School Press.

HORNE, P. (2006). Policewomen: Their first century and the new era. *Police Chief, 73(9).* Available at: http://policechiefmagazine.org/magazine/index.cfm?fuseaction=display_arch&article_id= 1000&issue_id=92006

HUNT, J. (1990). The logic underlying police sexism. *Women & Criminal Justice, 1(2),* 3–30.

KANTER, R. (1977). *Men and women of the corporation.* New York, NY: Basic Books.

KRIMMEL, J. T. & GORMLEY, P. E. (2003). Tokenism and job satisfaction for policewomen. *American Journal of Criminal Justice, 28(1),* 73–88.

KURTZ, D. (2008). The gendering of stress and burnout in modern policing. *Feminist Criminology, 3(3),* 216–238.

LONSWAY, K., & ALIPIO, A. M. (2008). Sex discrimination lawsuits in law enforcement: A case study of thirteen female officers who sued their agencies. *Women & Criminal Justice, 18(4),* 63–103.

McCARTY, W., ZHAO, J., & GARLAND, B. (2007). Occupational stress and burnout between male and female police officers: Are there any gender differences? *Policing: An International Journal of Police Strategies and Management, 30,* 672–691.

MARTIN, S. (1980). *Breaking and entering: Police women on patrol.* Berkley, CA: University of California Press.

MARTIN, S. (1990). *One the move: The status of women in policing.* Washington, DC: Police Foundation.

MARTIN, S. (1991). The effectiveness of affirmative action: The case of women in policing. *Justice Quarterly, 8(4),* 489–504.

MASON, M. A. & GOULDEN, M. (2002). Do babies matter: The effect of family formation on the life-long careers of academic men and women. *Academe, 88(6),* 21–27.

MILLER, S. (1999). *Gender and community policing: Walking the talk.* Boston, MA: Northeastern University Press.

NATIONAL CENTER FOR WOMEN & POLICING. (2001). *Equality denied: The status of women in policing.* Los Angeles, CA: Author.

PADGETT, D. K. (1998). *Qualitative methods in social work: Challenges and rewards.* Thousand Oaks, CA: Sage.

POLK, O. E. & ARMSTRONG, D. A. (2001). Higher education and law enforcement career paths: Is the road to success paved by degree? *Journal of Criminal Justice Education, 12(1),* 77–99.

POLICE EXECUTIVE RESEARCH FORUM. (1981). *Survey of police operational and administrative practices.* Washington, DC: Police Executive Research Forum.

PRESSER, L. (2005). Negotiating power in narrative and research: Implications for feminist methodology. *Signs, 30,* 2067–2090.

PRICE, B. R. (1985). *Sexual integration in American law enforcement.* In W. C. Hefferman & T. Stroup (Eds.), Police Ethics (pp. 205–214). New York, NY: John Jay Press.

RABE-HEMP, C. (2008). Survival in an all boys club: Policewomen and their fight for acceptance. *Policing: An International Journal of Police Strategies and Management, 31(2)*, 251–270.

SCARBOROUGH, K., VAN TUBERGEN, N., GAINES, L. & WHITLOW, S. (1999). An examination of police officers' motivation to participate in the promotional process. *Police Quarterly, 2(3)*, 302–320.

SCHULZ, D. M. (2003). Women police chiefs: A statistical profile. *Police Quarterly, 6(3)*, 330–345.

SCHULZ, D. M. (2006). *Breaking the brass ceiling*. Santa Barbara, CA: Praeger.

SCHWARTZ, F. (1989). *Management, women and the new facts of life*. Cambridge, MA: Harvard Business Review.

SHERMAN, L. J. (1975). An evaluation of policewomen on patrol in a suburban police department. *Journal of Police Science and Administration, 3(4)*, 434–438.

STRAUSS, W., & HOWE, N. (1991). *Generations: The history of America's Future. 1584 to 2069*. New York, NY: Morrow.

STOKOE, E. (2006). On ethnomethodology, feminism, and the categorical reference to gender in talk-in-interaction. *Sociological Review, 54*, 467–494.

SULTON, C., & TOWNSEY, R. (1981). *A progress report on women in policing*. Washington, DC: Police Foundation.

TRAVIS, J. (1995). *Education in law enforcement: Beyond the college degree*. Paper presented at the 1995 Forum on the Police and Higher Education, Chicago, Illinois.

TUTTY, L. M., ROTHERY, M. A. & GRINNELL, R. M. (1996). *Qualitative research for social worker.* Boston, MA: Allyn & Bacon.

VALCOUR, M. & LADGE, J. J. (2008). Family and career path characteristics as predictors of women's objective and subjective career success: Integrating traditional and protean career explanations. *Journal of Vocational Behavior, 73(2)*, 300–309.

VALCOUR, P. M., & TOLBERT, P. S. (2003). Gender, family, and career in the era of boundarylessness: Determinants and effects of intra- and interorganizational mobility. *International Journal of Human Resource Management, 14(5)*, 768–787.

WACHS, E. (2001). *Why the best man for the job is a woman*. Harper Collins.

WERTSCH, T. L. (1998). Walking the thin, blue line: Policewomen and tokenism today. *Women and Criminal Justice, 9(3)*, 23–61.

WEXLER, J., & LOGAN, D. (1983). Sources of stress among police women police officers. *Journal of Police Science and Administration, 11*, 46–53.

WHETSTONE, T. S. (2001). Copping out: Why police officers decline to participate in the sergeant's promotional process. *American Journal of Criminal Justice, 25(2)*, 147–159.

WHETSTONE, T. S., & Wilson, D. (1999). Dilemmas confronting female police officers promotional candidates: Glass ceilings, disenfranchisement, or satisfaction? *International Journal of Police Science and Management, 2(2)*, 128–143.

WILLIAMS, J. (2000). *Unbending gender: Why work and family conflict and what to do about it*. New York, NY: Oxford University Press.

WIRTH, L. (2001). *Breaking through the glass ceiling: Women in management*. Geneva: ILO.

ENDNOTES

1. Depending on the level of department presented, rank structure varies. Although the large and varied number of federal, state, and local police departments and sheriff's office have different ranks, a general model, from highest to lowest rank, would be:
   - Chief of police/police commissioner/superintendent/sheriff
   - Deputy Chief of police/Deputy Commissioner/Deputy Superintendent/undersheriff
   - Inspector/commander/colonel
   - Major/deputy inspector

- Captain
- Lieutenant
- Sergeant
- Detective/Inspector/Investigator
- Officer/Deputy Sheriff/corporal

2. While women make up 17 percent of large urban municipal agencies, women make up less than 6 percent of small urban police agencies (Bureau of Justice Statistics, 2006).

3. The National Center of Policing reports municipal agencies typically have between 6–17 percent female officers. However, due to the tenure requirement for this sample, the population of possible officers was significantly smaller. For this reason, snow ball sampling was the only way to access this under-utilized population. In addition, most previous research exploring female officers' experiences come from one agency, so comparisons based on department type and culture is difficult. This research fills that research gap as women from 10 diverse agencies were interviewed.

35

The Dislike of Female Offenders among Correctional Officers

A Need for Specialized Training

Christine E. Rasche, Ph.D.

Work with *women* offenders? Oh, they are the *worst*! I hate to admit it, but I would rather have a caseload of male rapists than a caseload of WOMEN petty offenders!—Female Community Corrections Officer

There is a widespread phenomenon in corrections which has not been well researched scientifically. Anecdotally, this phenomenon shows up in conversations with correctional line staff, both those who work in prisons and in community corrections. While correctional leaders seem to mostly regard it as a curiosity with little real relevance to correctional practice, this phenomenon *does* have an impact on correctional officers and administrators alike. More importantly, it also has a direct impact on inmates at prison facilities for *women*. This phenomenon is the pervasive tendency among correctional workers to *dislike* working with female offenders or to *avoid* working at women's prisons, and to view such duty as undesirable.

This dislike of female offenders appears to be very widespread in corrections and is well-known by almost all those who work in the field. As Pollack (1984) has noted, "There is informal agreement among correctional personnel that female offenders are somehow 'harder to work with' than male offenders" (p. 84). One has only to ask correctional officers whether they *prefer* working with male or female offenders. Spontaneously, most correctional officers (both male and female) tend to state a clear preference for working with *male* offenders.

Logically, this preference might seem somewhat counter-intuitive. After all, male inmates are much more likely than female inmates to be housed in very large facilities where supervision is somewhat more difficult, and male inmates are also more likely to physically attack and injure correctional staff. A layperson might well expect that correctional staff would prefer to work in smaller facilities with inmates who are unlikely to physically harm them. However, all the available evidence suggests that the opposite is true.

The layperson might also expect that such preference for working with male inmates would be wide-spread only among *male* correctional officers, given the macho-oriented nature of our culture in general and criminal justice professions in particular. A layperson might easily assume that at least *female* correctional officers would prefer working with female inmates, either for ideological reasons or because of a desire for less physically risky work. Again, however, this does not seem to be true. With a few notable exceptions discussed below, most female correctional officers also seem to express a clear preference for working with male inmates instead of female inmates. For the purposes of this discussion, this widespread phenomenon is referred to as the *male inmate preference.*

As far as can be determined, this male inmate preference is found among both male and female correctional officers, among both high and low ranking officers, among officers working at both male and female inmate facilities, and among officers in all regions of the country. It appears among both those correctional personnel working in prisons and those in community corrections. Baines and Alder (1996) also found it among juvenile justice practitioners who almost completely agreed that girls are more difficult to work with. When this sort of male bias is expressed, it usually seems to be articulated *immediately*, seeming to require little or no thought on the part of respondents. Indeed, a question about their working preferences usually elicits from correctional staffers a prompt, strong, even passionate response, such as the quotation which opened this chapter. Laughter and boisterous exclamations about their working experiences often result, along with unsolicited explanations for their preferences in the form of horror stories.

In fact, often the only correctional staff who do *not* seem to express the male inmate preference, at least in my experience, are long-time female staff members working at female-only correctional facilities. Such staff are often women who began their careers before institutional staffs were gender-integrated, and many have spent their entire careers working at institutions for female offenders. In general, their preference for working with *female* inmates seems to arise from long and successful experience in working with female offenders. However, some also express a strong ideological commitment to working with women offenders. This ideological commitment among the older, long-time female staffers is sometimes feminist in nature but it can also be religious. It should be noted that some *younger* correctional female staff members at female facilities (as well as a few *male* staffers) also express such an ideological commitment to working with female offenders. But outside of these comparatively few ideologically-committed or long-time women's prison staff members, my experience is that most other correctional personnel clearly express the male inmate preference—even though they will often simultaneously agree that male inmates are more likely to represent a hazard to their own personal safety.

The fact that the male inmate preference has not been well researched scientifically does *not* mean that it represents a new phenomenon. Observations about the comparatively greater difficulty of working with female inmates appear in literature dating back at least to the mid-nineteenth century. For example, Pollack (1986) cites one prison matron's description of female inmates in the 1860s:

It is a harder task to manage female prisoners than male. . . . They are more impulsive, more individual, more unreasonable and excitable than men; will not act in concert, and cannot be disciplined in masses. Each wants personal and peculiar treatment, so that the duties fall much more heavily on the matrons than on the warders; matrons having thus to deal with units, not aggregates, and having to adapt themselves to each individual case, instead of simply obeying certain fixed laws and making others obey them, as in the prison for males. (Pollack, 1986, quoting a prison matron in the memoire *Female Life in Prison*, published 1862)

Somewhat more recently Charles Turnbo, who served as the warden of the female prison at Pleasanton, California from the late 1970s to the early 1980s, recalled that when he was made the warden in 1978 he "received as many condolences as congratulations" (Turnbo, 1993, p. 13). He was also subjected to hearing the war stories of other colleagues who had pulled duty in women's facilities, since "many wardens want nothing to do with an all-female prison population" (Turnbo, 1993, p. 13). By way of explanation, Turnbo quoted Heffernan (1978) in observing that "Women are seen as a persistent and continuing problem in corrections for two reasons: one, their small numbers, and two, their perceived nature" (Heffernan, 1978, cited in Turnbo, 1993, p. 13).

By far the most extensive scientific research on this phenomenon to date has been done by Pollack (1984, 1986). Her research on correctional officers' attitudes revealed that what is referred to as the male inmate preference is a real component of what she calls the prevailing modern "CO culture." Two thirds (68%) of her sample of 45 experienced correctional officers who had worked in both male and female facilities stated preferences for working with male inmates, and two-thirds (67%) also agreed that female inmates were harder to supervise. Interestingly, female correctional officers generally expressed a *stronger* preference for working with male inmates than did male correctional officers (f = 72%, m = 66%) and were *more* likely than their male colleagues to agree that women inmates were more difficult to manage (f = 83%, m = 55%) (Pollack, 1986).

However, male and female correctional officers may not always have the same reasons for holding the same preference. As shown on Table 1, Pollack (1986) found that the reasons given by male officers for a male inmate preference included perceived difficulties in supervising the opposite sex and fear of being framed for rape. Male officers also perceived the

---

TABLE 1   Reasons Given by Correctional Officers for the Male Inmate Preference

Reasons given by male officers for preferring to work with male inmates included:
1. Difficulties in supervising the opposite sex and fear of being framed for rape.
2. The need to modify their behavior toward women inmates (e.g., curb their speech, be careful about the use of force).

Reasons given by female officers for preferring to work with male inmates included:
1. Male inmates were seen as more likely to treat women officers with respect.
2. Male inmates were seen as appreciating them as women, which made the job more enjoyable.

Reasons given by both male and female officers for the male inmate preference included:
1. Women inmates are more demanding.
2. Women inmates complain more.
3. Women inmates are more likely to refuse orders.

Source: Pollack (1986).

need to modify their normal behavior when working with women inmates (e.g., curbing their speech, being careful about the use of force). By contrast, the reasons given by female officers for a male inmate preference included perceptions that male inmates were more likely to treat women officers with respect and that male inmates seemed to appreciate them as women, which made the job more enjoyable. In short, male correctional officers were likely to perceive more potential penalties for working with female inmates, while female correctional officers saw more rewards in working with male inmates. Interestingly, however, reasons given by *both* male and female officers for disdaining work with female inmates included perceptions that women inmates are more demanding and tended to complain more than male inmates, and that women inmates are more likely to refuse orders.

Pollack (1986) also found that there were a few correctional officers in her sample who preferred to work with women inmates, even though they agreed that women inmates were more difficult to supervise. These officers indicated that they enjoyed the challenge of trying to deal with the demands and problems of female inmates. These atypical correctional officers also stated that they enjoyed the "variety, unpredictability, and constant turmoil that was likely to be present in settings for women" (Pollack, 1986, p. 99). Normally, qualities such as "constant turmoil" are *not* listed as desirable job attributes!

As part of her research, Pollack (1984, 1986) explored correctional officers' views of male and female inmates by giving officers lists of adjectives which they could apply to different types of inmates. As Table 2 shows, Pollack found that some adjectives were applied frequently to *both* male and female inmates. Thus, both male and female prisoners were seen as being defensive, distrustful, and manipulative (1986).

However, female inmates specifically were characterized as emotional, temperamental, moody, manipulative, quarrelsome, demanding, changeable, complaining, argumentative, excitable, immature, and noisy. By comparison, choosing from this same list of adjectives, *male* inmates were characterized by correctional officers as active, defensive, boastful, aggressive, and manipulative. Pollack noted that "only three adjectives for males were agreed upon by more than 60 percent of the officers, whereas 60 percent or more officers agreed on twelve adjectives for females" (1986, pp. 34–35). This greater consensus among the correctional officers about which adjective labels to apply to female inmates

> raises the possibility that officers possess a stereotype of females. It is not unusual to obtain a high rate of agreement among those who possess a common stereotype of a group; likewise, one is less likely to get consensus on a description of any group for which a stereotype is not operating, since people interact and perceive each other differently. (Pollack, 1986, p. 35)

Ultimately, Pollack found three "themes" emerging from the adjective descriptions of female inmates selected by correctional officers. As shown on Table 3, the first theme was "*defiance*," which involved selecting descriptions of women inmates as being likely to oppose the officers in various ways. This included descriptions of women inmates as being argumentative, less likely to follow rules, demanding, and harder to handle. In the closed world of the prison, *defiant* inmates are uniformly disliked by correctional officers, whose jobs often hinge on the degree to which they are able to manage inmates smoothly.

The second theme Pollack (1986) found emerging from the adjectives correctional officers chose to describe female offenders was "*open display of emotion*." This

---

TABLE 2   Adjectives Used by Correctional Officers to Describe Female and Male Inmates

Some adjectives were applied frequently to both male and female inmates:
   Manipulative (65%)
   Defensive (54.5%)
   Distrustful (50%)
But female inmates were also characterized as:
   Emotional (83%)
   Temperamental (76%)
   Moody (74%)
   Manipulative (71%)
   Quarrelsome (64%)
   Demanding (69%)
   Changeable (67%)
   Complaining (82%)
   Argumentative (69%)
   Excitable (64%)
   Immature (62%)
   Noisy (64%)
By comparison, male inmates were characterized as:
   Active (64%)
   Defensive (60%)
   Manipulative (60%)
   Boastful (57%)
   Aggressive (55%)

Source: Pollack (1986).

TABLE 3   Themes in the Description of Female Inmates by Correctional Officers

---

1. *Defiance:* descriptions of the women as opposing the officers, which included women inmates described as being: argumentative; less likely to follow rules; demanding; harder to handle; questioning rules; more troublesome; more complaining; confronting verbally; more critical; less respectful; and harder to reason with.

2. *Open display of emotion:* descriptions of women inmates as expressing more feelings; being louder/noisier; screaming/hollering more; having a greater tendency to cry; having spur-of-the-moment outbreaks; fighting spontaneously and easily; being ready to explode; being crybabies; being explosive; losing their tempers easily.

3. *Gratification seeking:* described women as needing and wanting more from their environment; needing/wanting both material and personal commodities such as attention, friendship, or sympathy; wanting things with little or no patience; being emotionally demanding, less independent, more childish; having critical demands; and having a greater need for friends.

Source: Pollack (1986).

involved characterizations of women inmates as expressing more feeling, being louder and noisier, having a greater tendency to cry, erupting in spur-of-the-moment outbreaks, fighting spontaneously and easily, and losing their tempers easily. Clearly, such boisterous displays are viewed by correctional officers as management problems, particularly when the emotional outburst of one inmate might provoke emotional displays among others.

The third theme characterizing female offenders in the eyes of correctional officers, according to Pollack (1986), was that female inmates were seen as "gratification seeking." This described women inmates as needing and wanting both material and personal commodities such as attention, friendship, or sympathy more than males, and wanting things immediately with little or no patience or willingness to wait. Such impatient and demanding inmates are, once again, viewed by correctional officers as "management problems," who tend to create a major fuss over minor problems and who, therefore, make supervision more difficult. Overall, Pollack (1986) found that there was strong agreement among her respondents that men and women inmates required different styles of supervision (91%), and that there could be situations where they as correctional officers needed to respond to men and women in different fashions (73%).

Interestingly, when asked to account for why these perceived differences between male and female inmates exist, Pollack (1984, 1986) found that correctional officers referred to general "sex differences (whether biological or socialization) rather than institutional factors" (1986, p. 116). In other words, women *inmates* and women *in general* were seen as being similar.

> The inmates' behavior, in other words, is taken for granted, and the officers see themselves as doing their best within the confines of that assumption. Attempts to change behavior by changing procedures, policies, or other situational components are unlikely to be viewed as effective since it is assumed that the behavior is not situationally induced. We could, therefore, expect the officers to view inmate-generated problems with exasperated resignation, which indeed, appears to be their attitude. (Pollack, 1986, p. 116)

In short, correctional officers did not think there was anything they could do about the greater difficulty posed by female inmates because it was a product of nature. Women inmates were just being *women*.

Pollack's reports on correctional officers' different attitudes toward male and female inmates are by far the most scientific analysis of a sentiment which both experienced correctional workers and outside observers readily assert runs throughout the field. This tendency to view female inmates as more difficult to manage leads to the perpetuation of what is referred to as the male inmate preference.

PERCEPTIONS VERSUS REAL DIFFERENCES

The question which follows is whether there are *real* differences between male and female inmates in terms of supervision and management requirements, or whether correctional officers are merely articulating unfounded prejudices and stereotypes. As it turns out, there is a considerable literature on the differences between men and women in captivity.

Not the least of these differences, of course, is that by yearend 2008 men continued to out-number women in state and federal prisons by 14 to 1 (Sabol, West, & Cooper, 2009). Be-yond that, however, there are at least three dimensions of difference between male and female prison inmates.

The first dimension of difference between male and female inmates is their *demographic profiles*. The demographic characteristics of women who are in prison are different in some important ways from those of males who are in prison. First, African-Americans are clearly over-represented in American prisons in general. While there are several reports of larger per-centages of African Americans among women in prison than among men (Binkley-Jackson, Carter, & Rolison, 1993; Goetting & Howsen, 1983; Rafter, 1985; Sarri, 1987), this appears to be true only in a dozen states as of 2004. In most states, there is a somewhat lower proportion of African American and other minority women than men (ACA, 2005). Overall, women in-mates have tended to be *slightly older* as a group than male inmates. Women inmates have also tended to be *slightly better educated* than their male counterparts—though this is not saying much, since both male and female inmates tend to be less academically skilled when tested than their respective completed years of formal education would suggest.

The vast majority of women in prison are mothers. Women inmates are highly likely to have minor children *in the home* prior to imprisonment and have usually been the pri-mary caregivers for their dependent children, which is much less true of male inmates with dependent children (Glaze & Maruschak, 2008; Koban, 1983). Compared to male inmates, female inmates are imprisoned more often for economic and drug-related crimes than vio-lent or assaultive crimes (Greenfeld & Snell, 1999; James, 2004). Women inmates are less likely to have been *legitimately* employed compared to their male counterparts, despite the fact that they were often the sole support for their minor children. Of those women who were legally employed prior to prison, most were at very low-level jobs at low pay; two-thirds had never held a job paying more than $6.50 an hour (Greenfeld & Snell, 1999).

The majority (60–80%) of women in state prisons have *problems with substance abuse* (Center for Substance Abuse Treatment, 1997; Mumola & Karberg, 2006). Women prisoners have been shown to have a higher likelihood of drug addiction/abuse than males, especially addiction to heroin, cocaine, and other intravenous drugs. Women are also more likely than men to have used methamphetamine in the month prior to their arrest (Mumola & Karberg, 2006). In the light of this, it is perhaps not so surprising to find out that a higher percentage of female inmates are *known HIV positive* than of male inmates (Maruschak, 2009). Women prisoners also have *many other physical health problems*, more than male prisoners (Maruschak, 2008). It has been gauged that up to a third of incarcerated women go on sick call each day compared to 10 percent or less or incarcerated men (Bloom, Owen, & Covington, 2003).

Also, women prisoners have been found to have high levels of sexual and/or physical abuse as either children or adults, or both; usually these are much higher levels than even the high levels sometimes reported for male prison inmates (ACA, 1990; Arnold, 1990; Carlen, 1983; Chesney-Lind & Rodriguez, 1983; Fletcher et al., 1993; Gilfus, 1992; Immarigeon 1987a, 1987b; Sargent et al., 1993). Thus, in 2002 over half of all women jail inmates said they had been physically or sexually abused, compared to only about 13% of males in jail (James, 2004). And imprisoned women had tripled the likelihood of reporting an abuse history than were male prisoners (Harlow, 1999). With this history, it is perhaps not surprising to learn that women in prison are also highly likely to have had prior experience with the mental health care system. Women prison inmates have a higher likelihood of mental disorder than women in the outside world (Bureau of Justice Statistics, 2001), or of men in prison (James & Glaze, 2006).

In short, a national profile of women offenders reveals that they are:

- Disproportionately women of color.
- Mostly in their early to mid-30s.
- Most likely to have been convicted of a drug-related offense.
- From fragmented families that include other family members who also have been involved with the criminal justice system.
- Survivors of physical and/or sexual abuse as children and adults.
- Individuals with significant substance abuse problems.
- Individuals with multiple physical and mental health problems.
- Unmarried mothers of minor children.
- Individuals with a high school or general equivalent diploma (GED) but limited vocational training and sporadic work histories. (Bloom et al., 2003, p. 8)

In addition to such differences in their demographic profiles, a second dimension of difference between male and female inmates is that they have quite dissimilar *needs during incarceration*. Some differences between the sexes are obvious and expected. For example, women have needs for gynecologically-related goods and services, such as menstrual supplies, annual gynecological check-ups, prenatal care for those who are pregnant, and postnatal care and counseling for those who give birth in prison. Only recently have prison systems begun to acknowledge that such prenatal and postnatal care and counseling needs to be both of the *normal* variety, which might be given to any woman before and after giving birth, and somewhat *specialized* care, given to women with greater needs. Such specialized care is needed partly because of the large proportion of prison pregnancies which are considered to be "high-risk" in nature. That is, women who are pregnant in prison are more like than those in the general population to have been in ill health previously, to have received little prior prenatal care, and to suffer from a variety of chronic conditions which increase risk during pregnancy or afterward (Acoco, 1998; Resnick & Shaw, 1980; Ross & Fabiano, 1986). However, specialized care is also required because following a prison birth there is (in all but a few women's prisons) an inevitable "loss" of the newborn, who will be immediately taken away from the mother and placed outside the prison with foster caregivers. Though the child lives, its physical loss immediately following birth may be experienced as almost "death-like" by the imprisoned mother. Special health care, both physical and mental, is required under such considerations. Male inmates, obviously, do not require such services.

Also among the obvious and expected differences between the sexes in needs during incarceration are that women inmates need different sorts of routine health and beauty aids, and different types of clothing. Women prisoners also express a much higher need for privacy than do male inmates. Furthermore, women generally need a different kind of diet, with fewer calories and carbohydrates overall and more of certain vitamins and minerals than men require. Ironically, the growing trend over the past several decades to standardize treatment of male and female inmates has reduced or eliminated some of the individualized food service, clothing options, and commissary health and beauty choices which used to be accorded to women in smaller female facilities.

Less obviously, it is only recently that have we begun to realize that women inmates need specialized counseling for sexual and/or physical abuse which most received as children and/or adults. Perhaps it is not surprising that two-thirds (68%) of the women in state prisons who were designated as having mental health problems also reported physical or sexual abuse histories (James & Glaze, 2006). Indeed, women are more likely than men to be in prison precisely for killing an adult abuser, particularly a spouse, lover, or other family member. They are also somewhat more likely to be imprisoned for having killed their own children—though many women who kill their own children explain their actions as a form of "mercy" killing in the face of what they saw as intolerable conditions (Totman, 1978). Also, because they were often the primary caregivers to their minor children prior to their imprisonment, women inmates seem to need more help than do male inmates in dealing with the separation from their children, which many view as the harshest single aspect of being imprisoned. There is now considerable evidence that for all these reasons women inmates need more counseling and psychiatric services overall than do male inmates. Certainly women inmates receive far more psychotropic drugs than do male inmates.

In part because of all these unique stressors, women inmates seem to need different kinds of supervision techniques from correctional officers. Because so many women inmates have an abusive history, correctional staff may unwittingly trigger "flashbacks" of painful past abuses if they utilize the common in-your-face confrontational approach often favored for handling male inmates. Male correctional staff may be more likely to run into this problem, since women inmates are likely to have been abused primarily by the males in their lives. But it should be noted that even female staff can employ confrontational supervisory tactics which may backfire with female offenders.

In discussing these first two dimensions of difference between male and female inmates, demographic profile differences and different needs during incarceration, it is noteworthy that we have NOT made any references to the third dimension, *differences in personality*. This is important because we have already seen that there are big differences in the ways staff *perceive* the personalities and behaviors of incarcerated men and women in general. As it turns out, there is evidence to suggest that some of these perceived differences are real. For example, some researchers (Joesting, Jones, & Joesting, 1975; McKerracher, Street, & Segal, 1966) have found women prisoners are more likely than male prisoners to engage in what is usually called "acting out" behaviors (e.g., extremely emotional outbursts). A higher level of emotionality is, indeed, a consistent theme among writers describing women prisoners, including higher levels of emotional attachment *between* female inmates than is usually found between male inmates (Giallombardo, 1966; Lekkerkerker, 1931; Ward & Kassebaum, 1965). This higher level of emotionality is perceived by correctional officers as problematic because "emotions displayed by the inmates may translate into hostility toward the officer . . ." (Pollack, 1984).

It seems clear that there are many *real* differences between male and female offenders in prison which could translate into differences in required management and supervisory approaches. If we add the third dimension, differences in personality, it would seem that not only must the overall management of an institution be revised in certain significant ways to accommodate female offenders, but the day-to-day business of direct inmate supervision might need to be altered significantly in order for things to go as smoothly as possible.

SHOULD INMATE DIFFERENCES LEAD TO SPECIALIZED STAFF TRAINING?

By 2004 there were 198 state prison facilities in the United States which housed adult female offenders only, plus another 156 state cogender facilities housing both male and female adult inmates. Such facilities include not only traditional prisons but also detention centers, diagnostic and reception centers, community residential facilities, pre-release and work/study release centers, medical facilities, mental health or substance abuse centers, geriatric facilities, and boot camps. In addition, there were 420 public and private facilities for female juvenile offenders, and another 422 cogender facilities housing both male and female juveniles. At least five female-only institutions are run by the Federal Bureau of Prisons. In short, at least 1196 correctional facilities in the United States house female inmates (ACA, 2005). This is a remarkable expansion of women's prisons if you consider that in 1996 there were only 68 female-only and 97 cogender correctional facilities in the United States (ACA, 1998). Of particular note is the spectacular increase in privately contracted facilities, particularly in the area of youth services and juvenile justice, a majority of which appear to be cogender.

While men still vastly outnumber women behind bars in the United States, the *number* of women incarcerated by the states and the federal government has increased at a much faster rate than did the number of men since the 1980s. This has resulted in most states now having record-high numbers of women prisoners. Prior to 1980, most states had only one separate women's prison facility—and some states did not even have that, continuing instead to house women in small separate units within larger men's prisons or in coeducational facilities, or even sending them to women's prisons in adjoining states. A very few states still do not have a completely separate female-only adult institution (e.g., Alaska, Maine, New Mexico, and Utah), but due to the huge population growth of prisoners in the 1980s and 1990s, many states have now opened *multiple* women's institutions. By yearend 2008 there were over 114,800 women in state and federal prisons, with an average annual increase of 3.0 percent between 2000 and 2007 (compared to 1.9% for men) (Sabol, West, & Cooper, 2009). Indeed, by 2004 at least 21 states had two or more women's prisons, of which three states had at least five female-only institutions. Most female-only adult correctional facilities today house hundreds of inmates each, though in 2004 the numbers ranged from as few as 128 in Maine to multiple thousands in California (ACA, 2005).

Most states added to their correctional workforce exponentially in the 1980s in the effort to keep pace with burgeoning prison populations, and thousands of correctional staff are now employed by these women's institutions and coeducational facilities. Add to this the correctional officers in the thousands of jails, prerelease centers, work release centers, and other facilities around the nation which house one or more women detainees, and the numbers of correctional officers affected by the management differences required for female versus male inmates becomes enormous.

Furthermore, the inmate population boom of the 1980s led to some remarkable and dramatic facilities changes. In some states, within the span of just a few years, facilities changed from housing male inmates only to housing co-correctional inmate populations, to then housing females only as inmate populations grew or shifted. This meant that correctional officers who were experienced in working with male inmates have sometimes found themselves suddenly supervising female offenders with little advanced preparation.

Given all the differences between male and female inmates noted above, we might expect that correctional systems would be concerned about providing specialized preparation to those correctional staff members assigned to work with female offenders. However, there seems to be little evidence of specialized and targeted training for correctional staff assigned to female facilities. In a survey of correctional officer education and training conducted in the 2002, Corrections Compendium found that all but five responding states indicated that they trained new officers on issues related to special inmate populations, though it is not clear what that included. Only 10 states reported specific training on sexual harassment or across-gender supervision, while only two reported training officers on working with female inmates (Anonymous, February 2003). The American Correctional Association recognized the need for specialized training the mid-1980s when it noted that the "requirements and opportunities for staff development often overlook the needs of administration and staff for professional, on-going training in managing the female offender" (ACA, 1986, p. 29). Modern researchers on women in prison, likewise, have also noted the lack of specialized training for staff in women's prisons:

> Typically, state correctional systems have moved from an approach that isolates and differentiates the women's institution to an approach that alleges that all inmates and all prisons are the same in terms of rule, supplies, assignments and other factors. This latter approach is no more helpful than the benign neglect that previously characterized the central office's attention to facilities for women; women's prisons obviously have unique needs, different from men's institutions. (Pollack-Byrne, 1990, p. 115)

Of course, the counter-argument to the claim that specialized training is needed for staff working in women's prisons is that regular correctional training is sufficient. That is, if the routine training given to new correctional officers includes training for the different supervisory requirements of female versus male inmates, then no specialized training would be needed for those assigned to women's institutions.

THE CONTENT OF ROUTINE CORRECTIONAL TRAINING

The idea of requiring any training *at all* for correctional officers to prepare them for their duties is not a very old one. The first correctional training school was begun in New York in 1930 by the Federal Bureau of Prisons (Schade, 1986). Both prior to and after that, the states apparently hired correctional officers directly into their jobs, with little or no formal training of any kind except that received on the job. For example, the warden of Sing Sing Prison in New York from 1921–1941, Lewis Lawes, reported that when he began his career as a guard in 1905 at Clinton Prison, he was given a tour of the facility along with a pair of sneakers (in order to patrol quietly) and a large baton for protection. After this preparation, he went on duty alone (Olsen, 2005). His was not an unusual experience. Official reviewers and reform-minded critics at the time often complained about the quality of the correctional staff, but they usually recommended remedies in the form of taking more care about *who* was hired—rather than expressing concern about what preparation was given to that individual *after* hiring.

Thus, for example, shortly after the Civil War, prison reformers Wines and Dwight (1867) set forth guidelines for the hiring of prison officers, in which they asserted that:

> Prison officers should be men of strict and uniform sobriety. . . . They should be men of mild temper, quiet manners, and pure conversation. . . . They should be men of decision and energy. . . . They should be men of humane and benevolent feelings . . . They should be men having a sincere interest in those placed under their care . . . They should be men of high moral principle, and distinguished by habits of industry, order and cleanliness. . . . They should be men possessing a knowledge of human nature in its various aspects and relations. . . . They should be men of sterling and incorruptible honesty. . . . They should be men of experience. . . . They must be men of a just and steadfast purpose, free from prejudice and partiality. . . . They should be men of untiring vigilance. . . . They should have a liking for the occupation in which they are employed. . . . Finally, prison officers should be men duly impressed with religious principles; men who fear God, and are in the habit, as the expression of that reverence, of attending the services of some religious body (Wines and Dwight, 1867, pp. 120–122)

It is only after this long recitation about what kind of *men* corrections should seek to hire that Wines and Dwight provide a brief paragraph on *female* officers, about whom they recommend:

> The qualifications of female officers are, in many respects, the same as those of males. It is especially important, however, that female officers should be distinguished for modesty of demeanor, and the exercise of domestic virtues, and that they should possess that intimate knowledge of household employment, which will enable them to teach the ignorant and neglected female prisoners how to economize her means, so as to guard her from the temptations caused by waste and extravagance. (Wines and Dwight, 1867, pp. 123–24)

These are certainly descriptions of outstanding prospective employees. Such exemplary persons, both then and now, might possibly be attracted to high-paying, high-prestige jobs. But what was the likelihood that corrections was able to attract large numbers of such inherently good and skilled workers in the 1800s—or could even do so now? Modern writers Hawkins and Alpert (1989) have provided a much more brutally frank description of a modern correctional officer's job:

> A candid job description for a correctional officer position would read something like this: Excellent employment opportunity for men and women who are willing to work eight-hour shifts at varying times (early morning, afternoon, and late nights) on a rotating basis. Applicants must enforce numerous rules with few guidelines. They must be willing to risk physical harm, psychological harassment, and endure the threat of inmate law suits, which could involve civil liability. They must be willing to spend eight hours each day among people who do not like them. They will not be allowed to fraternize with these people, but are expected to control as well as help them. Applicants must accept that they have little or no input into the rules they will be asked to enforce, nor will they be privy to the policy rationale for these rules. They should realize that management will probably not listen to their complaints. Work superiors, located in a military chain of command, are likely to have a great deal of time invested in organizational rules and therefore will resist employee innovations. The person at the top of the chain of command is likely to be a political appointment, but applicants are not

allowed to engage in political activity. Promotion is infrequent and opportunities for advancement in the organization are very limited. All applicants are considered untrustworthy: frequent questioning and searches of private possessions are designed to reduce corruption. Applicants must give up some civil rights for employment to continue. Women and minority groups are encouraged to apply, but will be discriminated against once on the job. (Hawkins and Alpert, 1989, pp. 338–339)

This "job description" of a correctional officer is exaggerated, of course, but there is some evidence that persons who seek correctional employment are entering into an employment area which does *not* have much inherent attractiveness. For example, Smith (1974, cited in Farmer, 1977) found that the social position of the correctional officer had very little prestige compared with other occupations or careers. This low prestige may be not so much a reflection of the low pay and minimal qualifications which corrections work has traditionally involved as it is a reflection of the *object* of that work: prison inmates. Jacobs and Retsky observed that the job of a prison guard is not entirely unlike other guard jobs, except that bank guards and Secret Security Agents derive some measure of esteem from the objects they guard, while "close contacts with convicted felons seems morally profaning for the (prison) guard (p. 10)" (Cited in Farmer, 1977, p. 238).

There is ample evidence that the commitment to the job at the lower levels of correctional work is not generally very great and that the field suffers from relatively high turnover rates (Patenaude, 2001; Workforce Associates, Inc., 2004). This may be because of the lower prestige of the field and its less desirable working conditions. But it also may be because there is some evidence that a significant proportion of persons who enter correctional work do so out of *economic necessity* (Shannon, 1987; Crouch & Alpert, 1980); in other words, most people do not enter correctional work out of a zeal to work with prisoners. Interestingly, the degree to which economic necessity plays a role in correctional recruitment may vary somewhat by sex. In at least one study, a much larger proportion of women indicated that they had sought correctional employment because they were interested in human service work (f = 55%, m = 14%) whereas males more frequently indicated that they took the job because there was not alternative work available to them (m = 14%, f = 3%) (Jurik & Halemba, 1984). Overall, however, it may be concluded that the dedication of correctional officers to their work varies greatly, and that there is little internal incentive to seek more difficult or challenging posts, such as assignment to women's prisons.

There has been little analysis of the training afforded to staff working in women's prisons. In 1993, pre-service correctional training in the United States varied from a minimum of two weeks (in Louisiana, North Dakota, and Wyoming) to a maximum of 16 weeks (only in Michigan), with the average being about five and a half weeks (for 48 states which reported plus the Federal Bureau of Prisons) (Maquire & Pastore, 1994). What is the content of that training? Wicks (1980) noted several decades ago that the emphasis was increasingly on *standardizing* correctional training in the U.S., so that there could be some assurance that all correctional officers have received basic training in certain skills and knowledge areas which are consistent with state policies and procedures. Shaver (1993) observed that training in Oklahoma, for example, consisted of four weeks of intensive, centralized group training of new recruits, followed by another three to five days of in-house training and orientation once new correctional officers arrived at their actual work site. However, little of this training is directly related to their new positions.

Rather, the training focuses on the policies, rules, regulations, and values of the correctional agency (Shaver, 1993, p. 122). More recently, Collins (2002) noted that basic correctional officer training usually includes course work in the areas of professionalism, legal issues, communication skills, searches, contraband, crime scene preservation, firearms, use of force, and defensive tactics (p. 16).

There is no reason to assume that these reports are incorrect. When asked about the content of the training they had been given, Shannon's correctional officer respondents indicated that the training they most frequently received had to do with firearms training, housing and body searches, contraband hunting, report writing, rules and regulations of the institution, self-defense training, key and tool control, riot control tactics, and CPR certification (Shannon, 1987, p. 174). In general, Shannon notes that:

> The officer's formal training consists primarily of instruction in the skills and mechanics of security procedures and the handling of inmates to maintain order and prevent trouble. The real learning (training) occurs on the job under inmate testing and manipulation attempts. (Shannon, 1987, p. 173)

Apparently not much has changed in this regard since 1980. A *Corrections Compendium* survey of correctional officer education and training in 2002 found that departments were very consistent in defining the most important elements of training. The top dozen most frequent components were: report writing, self-defense, inmate manipulation, communications, crisis management, ethics, first aid, inmate classification, use of force, CPR, fire/safety, and security devices. As shown on Table 4, nowhere on the list of thirty subjects most likely to be required in basic training is a specialized component on working with female inmates (Anonymous, 2003).

Of course, training does not end at the correctional academy. It is after formal preservice training that the new correctional officer learns about and enters into the "officer subculture," which may well train the recruit somewhat differently than did the academy. For example, while the academy trains rookies in approved ways to handle inmates, the officer subculture "encourages officers to use intimidating behavior to establish authority over inmates" (Shannon, 1987, p. 173). It also provides working definitions of kinds of inmates the new correctional officer can expect to confront, and anecdotal evidence of what techniques work best with different kinds of inmates.

In short, while most academy training today still seems to focus on mechanical skills and operational procedures, the real "wisdom" about inmate handling comes from on-the-job inculcation into an officer subculture which may emphasize stereotypes and extreme examples. It is perhaps not at all surprising that such training leaves most correctional officers ill-prepared to deal with the unique needs and demands of working with female offenders in custody.

THE NEED FOR SPECIALIZED TRAINING FOR STAFF WORKING WITH FEMALE OFFENDERS

So far, we have seen that there are a variety of factors which combine to produce the widespread presence of the male inmate preference among correctional officers: the perceptions of and stereotypes about female inmates which are conveyed in the correctional

---

TABLE 4   Correctional Training Component Percentages

Percentages represent the number of correctional departments (of 46 states and 4 Canadian provinces responding) which required each component as part of basic training.

100%	Inmate Manipulation	93%	Suicide Prevention
100%	Report Writing	91%	Inmate Gangs
100%	Self-Defense	91%	Race Relations
98%	Communications	91%	Stress Reduction
98%	Crisis Management	89%	Substance Abuse
98%	Ethics	89%	Inmate Management
98%	First Aid	89%	Special Populations
98%	Inmate Classification	89%	Transportation
98%	Use of Force	87%	Firearms
96%	CPR	87%	Chemical Agents
96%	Fire Safety	85%	Inmate Programs
96%	Security Devices	83%	Inmate Mental Health
93%	Communicable Diseases	78%	Administration
93%	Hostages	78%	Inmate Health Care

Revised from: Correctional officer education and training. (February 2003). *Corrections Compendium, 28*(2), p. 11.

officer subculture; the very real supervisory differences posed by the needs of female inmates compared to their male counterparts; and the limited and largely operations-oriented training given to officer recruits. All these conspire to virtually insure that most correctional officers are somewhat biased against, and certainly unskilled in dealing with, female offenders in custody.

Little wonder, then, that so many correctional officers report unsatisfactory experiences in working with female offenders or—in the absence of any actual experience in female prisons—much anticipatory prejudice against such assignments. Little wonder, additionally, that women inmates continue to be viewed as more difficult to manage, since little (if any) routine training is aimed at helping correctional officers understand their female inmate charges or what supervisory techniques might be more effective with this population. Not surprising, then, that a recent study of correctional staff attitudes a year after first being employed found that officers working in female-only institutions were particularly *un*sympathetic to differential treatment of females. These officers tended to view the approaches toward female inmates as more lenient than standard practice and evidence of double standards rather than gender-appropriate management. Obviously, an understanding of departmental rationales for different policies and practices in female facilities seemed lacking (Young & Antonio, 2009, p. 13).

Under these circumstances it is little wonder that charges of sexual harassment and inappropriate behavior from correctional officers toward inmates emerged in the 1990s as one of the more problematic features of managing female institutions. Many state correctional systems have found themselves facing such charges—either in the media or in the courtroom—from individual inmates, interest groups representing inmates, or the federal government. As Wells (2008) has noted, those organizations not currently involved in failure to train—or similar litigation should take a lesson from those that are: such litigation is becoming increasingly common and more expensive in the justice and safety field (p. 116). In fact, concerns about sexual misconduct in prisons led the government to adopt new requirements to prevent such abuse. The *Prison Rape Elimination Act* (PREA) of 2003 was enacted by Congress to address such concerns and applies to all private and public facilities housing adult or juvenile offenders, as well as to community-based agencies (National Institute of Justice, 2010). To the degree that this law makes it obligatory to train staff to prevent sexual misconduct against prisoners, it must be regarded as a step forward. But such training, not focused on women inmates, also does not substitute for specialized training about the needs of female prisoners and how best to manage them.

To make matters worse, the U.S. economic crisis and its resulting budgetary impact on correctional departments means that many states have actually *reduced* training requirements. With staff turnover still a major problem in corrections, trying to balance the financial cost of losing staff to the cost of training new staff has become increasingly problematic. As one training leader in Ohio has noted, such costs become more evident within agency budgets when one realizes the need to constantly recruit, assess, and train replacements for staff who leave (Reveal, 2009, p. 40).

Suffice it to say that confronting the problem of male inmate preference and all that it means *should* become a high priority of all correctional systems housing female offenders. The costs of defending the system against lawsuits and media reports are high. But there is little evidence that, absent media attacks or lawsuits, most correctional systems are taking preventative measures by providing appropriate specialized training to their correctional staff members in women's institutions. Though the costs of such specialized training would be comparatively modest, it appears that most correctional leaders still regard the male inmate preference as the norm, or an anecdotal curiosity with little effect on daily operations. Since their systems are always populated predominantly by male inmates, the fact that correctional officers overwhelmingly prefer duty with male inmates does not seem to be a problem. Those comparatively few correctional officers assigned to women's institutions, and their discontent with such duty, seems like a small problem in an ocean of difficulties facing the modern correctional administrator.

The result of all these pressures is that those correctional staff members who are assigned to women's prisons continue to work with inmates about whom they hold highly negative perceptions and for whose management they have never been properly trained. If nothing else, it is these correctional officers and the female inmates they supervise who are the losers.

REFERENCES

Acoco, L. (1998). Defusing the time bomb: Understanding and meeting the growing health care needs of incarcerating women in America. *Crime and Delinquency, 44*(1), 49–70.

American Correctional Association (ACA). (1986). *Public policy for corrections: A handbook for decision makers.* Author.

American Correctional Association (ACA). (1990). *The female offender: What does the future hold?* Arlington, VA: Kirby Lithographic Company.

AMERICAN CORRECTIONAL ASSOCIATION (ACA). (1998). *Directory: Juvenile and adult correctional departments, institutions, agencies and paroling authorities, United States and Canada, 1997.* College Park, MD: American Correctional Association.

AMERICAN CORRECTIONAL ASSOCIATION (ACA). (2005). *Directory: Juvenile and adult correctional departments, institutions, agencies and paroling authorities, United States and Canada, 2004.* College Park, MD: American Correctional Association.

ANONYMOUS. (2003, February). Correctional officer education and training. *Corrections Compendium, 28*(2), 11–17.

ARNOLD, R. (1990). Processes of victimization and criminalization of black women. *Social Justice, 17*(3), 153–166.

BAINES, M., & ALDER, C. (1996). Are girls more difficult to work with? Youth workers perspectives in juvenile justice and related areas. *Crime & Delinquency, 42*(3), 467–485.

BINKLEY-JACKSON, D., CARTER, V. L., & ROLISON, G. L. (1993). African-American Women in Prison. In Fletcher, et al. (eds) *Women prisoners: A forgotten population* (pp. 65–74). Westport, CT: Praeger.

BLOOM, B., OWEN, B., & COVINGTON, S. (2003, June). *Gender-responsive strategies: Research, practice, and guiding principles for women offenders.* NIC 018017. National Institute of Corrections. U.S. Department of Justice.

BUREAU OF JUSTICE STATISTICS. (2001). *Mental health treatment in state prisons, 2000.* Washington, DC: Department of Justice.

CARLEN, P. (1983). *Women's imprisonment: A study in social control.* London: Routledge and Kegan Paul.

CENTER FOR SUBSTANCE ABUSE TREATMENT. (1997). *Substance abuse treatment for incarcerated offenders: Guide to promising practices.* Rockville, MD: U.S. Department of Health and Human Services.

CHESNEY-LIND, M., & RODRIGUEZ, N. (1983). Women under lock and key. *Prison Journal, 63*(2), 47–65.

COLLINS, M. (2002, Aug.). Traditional warrior ethics in modern correctional training. *Corrections Today, 64*(5), 16–20.

CROUCH, B., & ALPERT, G. (1980). An exploration of the prison guards attitudes toward correctional components. *International Journal of Offender Therapy.*

FARMER, R. E. (1977). Cynicism: a factor in corrections work. *Journal of Criminal Justice, 5,* 237–246.

FLETCHER, B. R., SHAVER L. D., & MOON D. G. (1993), *Women prisoners: A forgotten population.* Westport, CN: Praeger.

GIALLOMBARDO, R. (1966). *Society of women: A study of a women's prison.* New York: John Wiley and Sons, Inc.

GILFUS, M. E. (1992). From victims to survivors to offenders: Women's routes of entry and immersion into street crime. *Women and Criminal Justice, 4*(1), 63–90.

GLAZE, L. E., & MARUSCHAK, L. M. (2008, August). *Parents in prison and their minor children.* Bureau of Justice Statistics Special Report. NCJ 222984. Washington, DC: USGPO.

GOETTING, A., & HOWSEN, R. M. (1983). Women in prison: A profile. *The Prison Journal, 63*(2), 27–46.

GREENFELD, L. A., & SNELL, T. L. (1999). *Women offenders.* Bureau of Justice Statistics Special Reports. NCJ 175688. Washington, DC: U.S. Department of Justice.

HARLOW, C. W. (1999). *Prior abuse reported by inmates and probationers.* Bureau of Justice Statistics Selected Findings, NCJ 172879. Washington, DC: Government Printing Office.

HAWKINS, R., & ALPERT, G. P. (1989). *American prison systems: Punishment and justice.* Englewood Cliffs, NJ: Prentice Hall.

HEFFERNAN, E. (1978). Female corrections—History and analysis. Paper presented at the Confinement of Female Offenders Conference. Lexington, Kentucky. Cited in Turnbo (1993).

IMMARIGEON, R. (1987a). Women in prison. *Journal of the National Prison Project, 11,* 1–5.

IMMARIGEON, R. (1987b). Few diversion programs are offered female offenders. *Journal of the National Prison Project, 12,* 9–11.

JACOBS, J., & Retsky, H. (1975). Prison Guard. *Urban Life, 4*, 5–29.

JAMES, D. J. (2004, July). *Profile of jail inmates, 2002*. Bureau of Justice Statistics Special Report, NCJ201932. Washington DC: US Government Printing Office.

JAMES, D. J., & GLAZE, L. E. (2006, September). *Mental health problems of prison and jail inmates*. Bureau of Justice Statistics Special Report, NCJ213600. Washington DC: US Government Printing Office.

JOESTING, J, JONES, N., & JOESTING, R. (1975). Male and female prison inmates' differences on MMPI scales and revised beta I.Q. *Psychological Reports, 37*, 471–474.

JURIK, N., & HALEMBA, G. J. (1984, Autumn). Gender, working conditions and job satisfaction of women in non-traditional occupations: Female correctional officers in men's prisons. *The Sociological Quarterly, 25*, 55–556.

KOBAN, L. (1983). Parent in prison: A comparative analysis of the effects of incarceration on the families of men and women. *Research in Law, Deviance and Social Control, 5*, 171–183.

LEKKERKERKER, E. (1931). *Reformatories for women in the United States*. J. B. Wolters' Groningen-The Hague: Batavia.

MAQUIRE, K., & PASTORE, A. L. (eds.). (1994). *Sourcebook of criminal justice statistics: 1996*, U.S. Department of Justice, Bureau of Justice Statistics. Washington, D.C.: USGPO.

MAQUIRE, K., & PASTORE, A. L. (eds.). (1994) *Sourcebook of criminal justice statistics: 1993*, U.S. Department of Justice, Bureau of Justice Statistics. Washington, D.C.: USGPO.

MARUSCHAK, L. (2008). *Medical problems of prisoners*. Bureau of Justice Statistics. NCJ 221740. Retrieved on January 30, 2010 from http://bjs.ojp.gov

MARUSCHAK, L. (2009, December). *HIV in prisons and jails, 2007–08*. Bureau of Justice Statistics Bulletin, NCJ 228307. Washington, DC: U.S. Government Printing Office.

MCKERRACHER, D. W. STREET, D. R. K., & SEGAL, L. S. (1966). A comparison of the behavior problems presented by male and female subnormal offenders. *British Journal of Psychiatry, 112*, 891–899.

MUMOLA, C. J., & KARBERG, J. C. (2006, October). *Drug use and dependence, state and federal prisoners, 2004*. Bureau of Justice Statistics Special Report. NCJ 213530. Revised 1/19/07. Washington, DC: USGPO.

NATIONAL INSTITUTE OF CORRECTIONS. (2010). *PREA—Offender sexual abuse*. Retrieved on February 12, 2010 from www.nicic.org/prea

OLSEN, B. E. (2005, December). From A guard @school to training school: New Yorks evolution. *Corrections Today, 67*(7), 68–71.

PATENAUDE, A. L. (2001). Analysis of issues affecting correctional officer retention within the Arkansas Department of Correction. *Corrections Management Quarterly, 5*(2), 49–67.

POLLACK, J. M. (1984). Women will be women: Correctional officers' perceptions of the emotionality of women inmates. *The Prison Journal, 64*(1), 84–91.

POLLACK, J. M. (1986). *Sex and supervision: Guarding male and female inmates*. New York: Greenwood Press.

POLLACK-BYRNE, J. M. (1990). *Women, prison and crime*. Pacific Grove, CA: Brooks/Cole Publishing Co.

PRISON MATRON. (1862). *Female life in prison*. NY: Hurst & Blackett. Cited in Pollack (1986).

RAFTER, N. H. (1985). *Partial justice: Women in state prisons, 1800-1935*. Boston: Northeastern University Press.

RESNICK, J., & SHAW, N. (1980). Prisoners of their sex: Health problems of incarcerated women. In I.P. Robbins (ed.) *Prisoners' Rights Sourcebook* (pp. 319-413). New York: Clark Boardman.

REVEAL, R. L. (2009, April). Structured on-the-job training addresses turnover in Ohio. *Corrections Today, 71*(2), 38–40.

ROSS, R. R., & FABIANO, E. A. (1986). *Female offenders: Correctional afterthoughts*. Jefferson, NC: McFarland.

SABOL, W. J., WEST, H. C., & COOPER, M. (2009, December). *Prisoners in 2008*. Bureau of Justice Statistics Bulletin. NCJ 228417. Washington, DC: USGPO.

SARRI, R. (1987). Unequal protection under the law: Women and the criminal justice system. In J. Figueira-McDonough and R. Sarri (eds.). *The trapped woman: Catch-22 in deviance and control* (pp. 55–64). Newbury Park, CA: Sage.

SARGENT, E., MARCUS-MENDOZA, S., & YU, CHONG HO. (1993). Abuse and the women prisoner. In Fletcher, et al (eds). *Women prisoners: A forgotten population* (pp. 55–64). Westport. CT: Praeger.

SCHADE, T. (1986). Prison officer training in the United States: The legacy of Jess O. Stutsman. *Federal Probation, 50*(4), 40–46.

SHANNON, M. J. (1987). Officer training: Is enough being done? *Corrections Today, 49*(April), 172–175.

SHAVER, L. D. (1993). The relationship between language culture and recidivism among women offenders. In B. R. Fletcher, L. D. Shaver and D. G. Moon, *Women prisoners: A forgotten population*. Westport, CN: Praeger.

SMITH, W. (1974). Some selective factors in the retention of prison guards. Unpublished masters thesis written in 1963 and cited in E. Johnson, *Crime, corrections and society*. Homewood, IL: Dorsey Press. Cited in Farmer (1977).

TOTMAN, J. (1978). *The murderess: A psychosocial study of criminal homicide*. San Francisco, CA: R&E Research Associates, Inc.

TURNBO, C. (1993). Differences that make a difference: Managing a women's correctional institution. In American Correctional Association, *Female offenders: Meeting the needs of an neglected population* (pp. 12–16). American Correctional Association.

WARD, D. A., & KASSEBAUM, G. G. (1965). *Women's prison: Sex and social structure*. Chicago: Aldine.

WELLS, J. B. (2008, October). How rigorous should your training evaluation be? *Corrections Today, 70*(5), pp. 116–118.

WICKS, R. J. (1980). *Guard! Society's professional prisoner*. Houston: Guf Publishing Co.

WINES, E. C., & DWIGHT T. W. (1867). *Report on the prisons and reformatories of the United States and Canada*. Albany: Van Benthuysen and Sons Steam Printing House. Reprinted by AMS Press Inc., New York, 1973.

WORKFORCE ASSOCIATES, INC. (2004). *A 21st century workforce for Americas correctional profession*. A study commissioned by the American Correctional Association. Retrieved on February, 10, 2010 at www.aca.org/Library/1020181

YOUNG, J. L., & ANTONIO, M. E. (2009). Perceptions of leniency and support for inmate rehabilitation. *Corrections Compendium*, Fall, 9–17.

36

Women in the Legal Profession

Challenges for the 21st Century

Jody Clay-Warner, Jennifer McMahon-Howard, and Katie James

The 20th century saw women making significant advances in the legal profession. They entered the profession in record numbers, leading some to conclude that the law is a profession in which gender equality has been attained. In order to investigate this claim, we review recent studies that examine women's current position in the profession, paying particular attention to those that examine the ways in which race and parenthood impact women's opportunities. Evidence indicates that while women have made great strides, gender inequity remains. In particular, women face significant wage and partnership gaps, and these gaps are particularly salient for women of color. Additionally, women confront a substantial professional penalty for motherhood. As a result, a decade into the 21st century, women continue to face challenges in the legal profession.

The appointment of Sonia Sotomayor to the U.S. Supreme Court in August 2009 marked an important achievement for women in the legal profession. As Sotomayor is the third female justice and the first Hispanic justice, her seating is a victory in the long battle for equality in the legal profession fought by both women and racial/ethnic minorities. There is no question that women have made significant advances in the legal profession since the American Bar Association admitted its first female members in 1918 (Feinman, 1986). Consistent with the history of other elite professions, however, once women were admitted to practice they experienced decades of documented discrimination in hiring, salary, and promotion, and this discrimination was amplified for women of color (Epstein, 1993). In the 21st century, women are now visible and vocal members of the legal profession and have reached near parity with men in admissions to law school (Glater, 2001). In fact, scholars now talk of the "feminization" of the profession and ask what effect this large influx of women will have on the practice of law itself (Menkel-Meadow, 1988; Chiu and Leicht, 1999). Research reveals, however, that despite significant change in the legal profession, the structure and culture of the profession continues to present women with unique challenges in their efforts to advance.

In attempting to understand the barriers that women attorneys now face, we focus here on the effects of motherhood and racial discrimination on women's advancement. We begin by reviewing women's recent experiences in the legal profession more generally by examining the gendered wage gap and barriers to partnership. We then highlight the roles that race and parenthood play in differentially shaping women's experiences as legal professionals. We conclude by suggesting ways that the legal profession could reduce gender and racial discrimination as well as policies it could enact to achieve work-family balance.

GENDER DISCRIMINATION AND JOB SATISFACTION: THE PARADOX OF THE CONTENTED FEMALE LAWYER

Though gender differences in salary today are certainly smaller than they were in the past, men's earnings continue to outpace those of women. According to 2008 data from the Bureau of Labor Statistics, the weekly median earnings of women lawyers is 80 percent that of men lawyers. Part of this salary variation is due to the "partnership" gap that continues to affect female attorneys. As late as 2007, only 18 percent of partners in large law firms were women (National Association for Law Placement, 2007). The gap is particularly large for minority women. The National Association for Law Placement (2009b) reports that only 2 percent of partners working in firms listed in the Association's Directory were women of color. To examine this partnership gap, Noonan, Corcoran, and Courant (2008) recently compared the outcomes of two cohorts from the University of Michigan Law School. They found that among those who stayed at firms long enough to make partner, men's probability of attaining partnership was 13 percentage points higher than that of women in both the early and late cohorts, even when controlling for credentials, career plans, and work activities.

Women in the legal profession also continue to report high rates of discrimination. Noonan, Corcoran, and Courant (2008) found that 90 percent of women in both of the University of Michigan cohorts that they studied reported experiencing either a little or a lot of sex discrimination between five and 15 years after graduation, with about half reporting that they were discriminated against in some way by attorneys in their employing firm. The American Bar Association's Commission on Women in the Profession (2006b) reveals staggering rates of discrimination faced by women of color in the legal profession. Specifically, almost half of women of color in private law firms reported subjection to demeaning comments and harassment, and 62 percent felt excluded from formal and informal networking opportunities. Almost half of women of color reported that they were overlooked in the assignment of desirable work opportunities, while almost a third stated that they received at least one unfair performance evaluation. In all of the situations considered above, white men lawyers report very low levels of these forms of discrimination.

Women of color in law firms face additional obstacles such as invisibility, the need to prove themselves, and misidentification (Garcia-Lopez, 2008; Blair-Loy and DeHart, 2003; Multicultural Women Attorneys Network, 1998). These are all factors that once posed major barriers for white women's advancement in the legal profession (Epstein, 1995) and also shaped the legal careers of women of color (Simpson, 1996). Recent research focusing on Hispanic women demonstrates the pervasiveness of these issues.

Garcia-Lopez (2008) finds in her study of Chicano women attorneys that they feel invisible and that when they attempt to make their concerns known, they are often blamed for being "trouble-makers" (Garcia-Lopez, 2008). They also often report that their colleagues attribute their success to affirmative action, leaving women of color feeling as though they must constantly prove their worth. Garcia-Lopez (2008) finds that Chicana lawyers often report being misidentified for translators or janitorial staff. She also argues that these misidentifications are a mechanism through which white lawyers heighten boundaries between themselves and lawyers of color, rather than mere "confusions."

In response to discrimination and inhospitable work environments, some women leave firms before partnership decisions are made, as they perceive the barriers to be too great to overcome (Epstein et al., 1995). In fact, women of color have a nearly 100 percent attrition rate from the law firms in which they work after eight years (Commission on Women in the Profession, 2006b). Both white and non-white women who leave private practice firms often retreat either into government work or into the less stressful world of in-house counsel (see Hull and Nelson 2000). These sectors are generally considered to be less prestigious than are private firms, and salary levels are certainly lower. As Hull and Nelson (2000) find, the segregation of women into these lower paying areas of practice is only partly a result of personal preference. They suggest that the constraints law firms place on employees disproportionately affect women, further contributing to the exodus of women from private firms. As Epstein et al. (1995) note, one of the most significant ways in which this problem manifests itself is in the perceived inability of women to combine motherhood with an elite legal career.

Despite greater levels of salary discrimination, sexual harassment, and barriers to partnership and promotion, women lawyers report similar levels of overall job satisfaction as men (Chambers, 1989; Dinovitzer et al., 2004; Kay et al., 2004b; Mattesich and Heilman, 1990; Heinz et al., 1999). While there are some areas of their jobs in which women lawyers have lower levels of satisfaction, such as job setting and advancement (Commission on Women in the Profession, 2006a; Dinovitzer et al., 2004; Kay et al., 2004a, 2006; Wallace, 2004), most women lawyers report that they are highly satisfied in their jobs. Considering the barriers that women face in the legal profession, this is an interesting paradox that is evident across many professions, and is what Crosby (1982) terms, "the paradox of the contented female worker." Still, this paradox is particularly interesting in the case of women lawyers considering these women are trained to be contentious (Mueller and Wallace, 1996; Hull, 1999). Although women lawyers report similar levels of job satisfaction as men, they are significantly more likely than men to experience feelings of depression and despondency. Specifically, women's concerns about the consequences of children on their occupational mobility in the practice of law increase their feelings of depression. These findings lead Hagan and Kay (2007) to suggest that women "are more likely to internalize feelings of despondency deriving from their work than they are to externalize these feelings through expressions of job dissatisfaction" (p. 69).

CAREER AND MOTHERHOOD

It is widely recognized that child and family responsibilities differentially affect male and female attorneys (Blodgett, 1988; Coltrane, 2004; Epstein et al., 1995; Foster, 1995; French, 2000). Addressing these differential effects, Foster (1995) describes the dominant, one-dimensional paradigm of the legal profession as conflicting with the multi-dimensional requirements of the family. The legal profession demands complete devotion and commitment to an uninterrupted career (Foster, 1995; French, 2000; Korzec, 1997). Given that law practice has been based on male norms and "patterned around the traditional male life cycle" (Korzec, 1997, p. 140), the current standards of success in the legal profession are more attainable for male attorneys than for female attorneys who feel that they must also meet conventional standards of success in the family (Rhode, 2001).

According to the traditional standards of the legal profession, to be a successful attorney one must work long hours both during the week and on the weekends (Foster, 1995). Indeed, there is a premium put on maximizing billable hours and "face-time" or time spent in the office (Reichman and Sterling, 2001). The National Association for Law Placement (2009a) reports that the average number of billable hours worked in 2007 was 1,838 and that over 85 percent of law firms require lawyers to bill a minimum of 1,800 hours per year. In order to accomplish this number of billable hours, most attorneys must work far more than the traditional 40 hours per week. Indeed, the average attorney worked more than 2000 hours in 2007. Additionally, a successful attorney must be constantly available to clients, be willing to come into the office or go out of town on short notice, and be available for business and social outings to generate clients (Foster, 1995).

With such standards, the demands of the legal profession often conflict with the demands of children and the family. Given that the legal profession is based upon male norms, it comes as no surprise that women may find it difficult to achieve work-family balance. Due to the premium placed on time spent at the office, high billable hours, and round-the-clock availability, women attorneys with children are often at a disadvantage (Reichman and Sterling, 2001). Even if women attorneys are willing and able to put their work responsibilities ahead of their family and childcare responsibilities, their colleagues often "assume that they will not be available or *should not* be available" (Reichman and Sterling, 2001, p. 951).

Although male attorneys express dissatisfaction with not having enough time to spend with their families, significantly more married male attorneys compared to married female attorneys have a stay-at-home spouse to take care of home and childcare responsibilities, while most married female attorneys have a spouse who also has a demanding full-time career (Rhode, 2001; Hersch, 2003). As a result, female attorneys with children must constantly struggle between being a dedicated lawyer and being a devoted mother (Rhode, 2001). Cunningham (2001) explains the "double-bind" for a female attorney with children— she is either viewed as an uncommitted lawyer or an uncommitted mother—"if she is a good lawyer, she must be a bad mother, or vice versa. She can only be a successful lawyer at the expense of her children, and she is often seen as failing on both fronts" (p. 997).

Interestingly, though, research finds that there are no between-gender differences in productivity, despite the fact that fathers report more work demands than mothers, while mothers report more family demands than fathers (Wallace, 2008; Young and Wallace, 2009). There are, however, within-gender differences in productivity. Overall, mothers of school-aged children are less productive than non-mothers. Conversely, fathers of preschool-aged children are *more* productive than non-fathers (Wallace and Young, 2008). These findings suggest that children may be advantageous to male lawyers, though they may disadvantage women, who are typically the primary caregiver. Nonetheless, research finds that mothers who practice law report higher levels of job commitment than do fathers who practice law (Wallace, 2008).

Due to the difficulties and/or negative effects of trying to balance work and child-care obligations, deciding when (or if) to have children is often a very difficult decision for female attorneys (Epstein et al., 1995). The issue is even more complicated when women are on the partnership track. Partnership decisions are typically made seven to ten years after an attorney has been working at a law firm, which for many women also happens to encompass the prime childbearing years. Female attorneys who wish to have children are, as one female attorney explained in an interview with Nancy Blodgett (1988), "caught between the brass ring and the biological clock" (p. 58).

Indeed, there are risks associated with any choice that a female attorney may make regarding motherhood. Women who decide to have children prior to partnership may be viewed as less committed to the firm, a perception that may adversely affect partnership decisions (Coltrane, 2004; Cunningham, 2001). Such women may also need to work part-time or on an alternative work schedule, which may remove the women from the partner-ship track altogether (French, 2000). On the other hand, while choosing to delay or forgo motherhood allows female attorneys to devote more time toward making partner, French (2000) points out that firms may still deny these women partnerships because it is often assumed that women will have a child shortly after making partner. Thus, it is not neces-sarily the choice that a woman makes regarding whether or when to become a mother that adversely affects her becoming a partner. Instead, women lawyers are disadvantaged because society tends to view all women as either mothers or potential mothers (Smart, 1995). This results in statistical discrimination, which occurs when the future productivity of a particular worker is assessed in terms of the perceived average future productivity of others who are like the worker in question (Arrow, 1972; Phelps, 1972).

When women do choose motherhood and take time off to care for children, they may pay an additional penalty. In a study of graduates from the University of Michigan Law School, Noonan and Corcoran (2004) found that taking time out from work for childcare responsibilities decreases a lawyer's chance of making partner and decreases their earnings if they do become partner. For men, a one-year family leave reduced the probability of making partner from .58 to .00 and working part-time for forty-two months reduced the probability from .58 to .39. For women, their chances of becoming a partner dropped from .35 to .22 for taking a one-year leave for childcare purposes and from .35 to .28 if they worked part-time for forty-two months. Although the effects of taking a leave and working part-time appear to be more severe for male attorneys, it is important to note that very few men actually take a leave or work part-time. In fact, in Noonan and Corcoran's (2004) study, only 1 percent of the male attorneys with chil-dren had taken childcare leave compared to 42 percent of the female attorneys with children. Similarly, just 1 percent of the fathers had worked part-time compared to 47 percent of the mothers.

Noonan and Corcoran (2004) point out that their results do not suggest that there is a direct penalty for motherhood. In fact, they find that having children does not reduce women's likelihood of making partner when controlling for other factors, such as experi-ence and leave-taking. Their results indicate, though, that it is taking time off from work to care for children, and not simply having children, that negatively affects women's chances for partnership, as well as their earnings. Given limited options for childcare, however, having children often requires women to take leave, which translates into an indirect penalty for motherhood.

ACHIEVING EQUALITY

The question remains as to if and/or how female attorneys will be able to achieve equality in the legal profession. Most researchers recognize that there must be a change in the law firm culture before this can be achieved (Cunningham, 2001; Foster, 1995; French, 2000; Korzec, 1997; Reichman & Sterling, 2001; Rhode, 2001). French (2000) proposes that time will correct the problem. He argues that as older cohorts of male partners age out of the profession, they will be replaced by younger cohorts that include an increasing number of women. As a result, there will be more women on partnership committees and subsequently more females promoted to partner. Even if these younger cohorts include only a small number of women, according to French (2000), younger male attorneys will have been more exposed to female attorneys in law school and while practicing law. As a result, this younger cohort of males will be more sensitive to the needs of female attorneys.

Reichman and Sterling (2001), however, criticized this attrition hypothesis because it fails to take into account the fact that many women are choosing to leave law firms prior to making partner. Indeed, with large numbers of women leaving before making partner, partnership committees will continue to be dominated by men. Also, many of the women who have made partner have assimilated to the one-dimensional paradigm of the law firm, thus perpetuating the existing norms of the law firm culture (Foster, 1995). As Reichman and Sterling (2001) state, "women will not rise in substantial percentages to partners in law firm practice until law firms recognize the gendered nature of these organizations and provide avenues for women to accumulate the professional assets necessary to advance" (p. 962).

According to Cunningham (2001), changing the law firm culture is going to take the efforts of both male and female attorneys advocating for a more realistic work-family balance. As long as only female attorneys are offered and/or utilize part-time or alternative schedules as a mechanism for balancing the demands of the firm and their children, female attorneys will continue to be marginalized in the legal profession (Cunningham, 2001; Rhode, 2001). Instead of waiting until the older male attorneys age out of the profession, Cunningham (2001) believes that the senior partners need to be convinced that adopting more family-friendly policies for both males and females would serve the firm's economic interests. Specifically, Cunningham (2001) points to the increasing dissatisfaction with the current legal culture and the increasing desire among younger cohorts, both male and female, to achieve work-family balance. In competing with other firms for the most talented lawyers, the firms with the most family-friendly policies are going to benefit the most. Also, addressing the high rate of attrition, Cunningham (2001) states, "if law firms wish to acquire and retain talented lawyers in the emerging economy, they must look for ways such as modified work schedules to lure lawyers in and keep them from leaving" (p. 1003). Cunningham (2001) adds that job satisfaction can increase productivity, and he points to research indicating that many part-time attorneys work more efficiently than full-time attorneys.

Recognizing that women of color face a double-burden, the American Bar Association's Commission on Women in the Profession (2008) suggests several strategies that law firms can implement in order to reduce racial discrimination. First, the commission suggests that firms should maintain outreach programs to women of color in recruitment efforts. Second, firms must develop unbiased measurement tools to evaluate the progress of their lawyers. Third, firms need to be cognizant of the exclusion of women of color from formal and informal networking opportunities, and they should develop networking activities and mentoring programs that are inclusive of all of their lawyers. Fourth, in situations where attorneys are evaluated, firms should train the evaluators to do so in an unbiased manner. Finally, the Commission advises firms to create diversity committees in which firm leaders are active participants.

Ultimately, changing the culture of the legal profession requires that law firms adopt gender- and race-neutral policies and practices (Commission on Women in the Profession (ABA), 2008; Cunningham, 2001; Korzec, 1997; Rhode, 2001). Such policies should allow both male and female attorneys to take a family leave without penalty (Cunningham, 2001; Reichman & Sterling, 2001). Also, researchers stress the importance of law firms allowing attorneys to utilize alternative work arrangements (which allow for flexible work schedules and part-time hours) while on the partnership track (Cunningham, 2001; Foster, 1995; Korzec, 1997; Reichman & Sterling, 2001). Furthermore, calls for changes in the law firm culture have included recommendations for eliminating the emphasis on billable hours (Cunningham, 2001; Foster, 1995; Rhode, 2001). In fact, researchers (Cunningham, 2001; Foster, 1995) point out that focusing on billable hours as a measure of success actually discourages efficiency, causes burnout, lowers the quality of work, and may cause the firm to lose clients. Alternative billing methods, such as value billing or a fixed fee, would take the emphasis off of time and place it on the quality of service provided, thus encouraging efficiency and increasing opportunities for work-family balance (Korzec, 1997). According to Foster (1995), changing the culture of the legal profession is key to accommodating multi-dimensional attorneys. Furthermore, these changes will help to break down the separate spheres ideology and stereotypes regarding the different roles for men and women (Cunningham, 2001; Rhode, 2001).

CONCLUSION

Historically, women have faced discrimination in the legal profession,[1] and even today a salary gap continues to exist. Nonetheless, women have made impressive advances, largely owing to the tremendous expansion of the legal profession in the last two decades. Currently, 31 percent of attorneys practicing in the United States are female (Commission on Women in the Profession, 2009), and women now comprise 47 percent of students awarded law degrees in this country (Commission on Women in the Profession, 2009). At the beginning of the last decade, the Bureau of Labor Statistics (2000) predicted that growth within the profession would slow at least through 2008 and that competition for jobs would increase substantially. Indeed, the number of women in the profession declined 3 percent since 2003, though the number of women awarded law degrees remained relatively stable during this time (Bureau of Labor Statistics, 2008). Thus, despite women's advancement in the legal profession in the past two decades, there is a substantial risk that women's gains will be lost due to changes in the labor market.

Challenges remain for women entering the legal profession in the 21st century. The challenges that women attorneys face today, however, are different from those they faced decades years ago when law school either placed quotas on women admission, or refused to admit them at all. Today's challenges involve changing the culture of the legal profession to allow more women to pursue both partnerships and parenthood. It also involves confronting the discrimination that women of color continue to face. Meeting these challenges will help to create a legal profession that more accurately reflects the demographics of the United States, which may lead to greater levels of equality across societal domains.

REFERENCES

ARROW, K. 1972. The theory of discrimination. In O. Ashenfelter & A. Rees (Eds.), *Discrimination in Labor Markets*. Princeton, NJ: Princeton University Press.

BLAIR-LOY, MARY, & GRETCHEN DeHART. 2003. "Family and Career Trajectories Among African American Female Attorneys." *Journal of Family Issues* 24.7:903–33.

BLODGETT, NANCY. 1988. "Whatever Happened to the Class of '81?" *American Bar Association Journal* June 1, 1988, 56–60.

BUREAU OF LABOR STATISTICS. 2000. *Occupational Outlook Handbook 2000–01* (Bulletin 2520). Washington, DC: U.S. Government Printing Office.

BUREAU OF LABOR STATISTICS. 2008. *Current Population Survey*. Washington, DC: U.S. Government Printing Office.

CHAMBERS, DAVID. 1989. "Accommodation and Satisfaction: Women and Men Lawyers and the Balance of Work and Family." *Law and Social Inquiry* 14:251–87.

CHIU, CHARLOTTE, & KEVIN T. LEICHT. 1999. "When Does Feminization Increase Equality? The Case of Lawyers." *Law & Society Review* 33:557–83.

COLTRANE, SCOTT. 2004. "Elite Careers and Family Commitment: It's (Still) About Gender." *The Annals of the American Academy of Political and Social Science* 596:214–220.

COMMISSION ON WOMEN IN THE PROFESSION (American Bar Association). 2006a. *Charting Our Progress: The Status of Women in the Profession Today*. Chicago: American Bar Association.

——. 2006b. *Visible Invisibility: Women of Color in Law Firms*. Chicago: American Bar Association.

——. 2008. *From Visible Invisibility to Visibly Successful: Success Strategies for Law Firms and Women of Color in Law Firms*. Chicago: American Bar Association.

—— (2009). *A current glance at women in the law*. Chicago: American Bar Association.

CROSBY, FAYE. 1982. *Relative Deprivation and Working Women*. New York: Oxford University Press.

CUNNINGHAM, KEITH. 2001. "Father Time: Flexible Work Arrangements and the Law Firm's Failure of the Family." *Stanford Law Review* 53:967–1008.

DINOVITZER, RONIT, et al. 2004. *After the JD: First Results of a National Study of Legal Careers*. The National Association for Law Placement Foundation for Law Career Research and Education and the American Bar Foundation 1, 2.

EPSTEIN, CYNTHIA FUCHS. 1993. *Women in Law* (2nd edition). New York: Basic Books.

EPSTEIN, CYNTHIA FUCHS, ROBERT SAUTE, BONNIE OGLENSKY, & MARTHA GEVER. 1995. "Glass Ceilings and Open Doors: Women's Advancement in the Legal Profession." *Fordham Law Review* 64:291–449.

FEINMAN, CLARICE. 1986. *Women in the Criminal Justice System* (2nd edition). New York: Praeger.

FOSTER, ELIZABETH. 1995. "The Glass Ceiling in the Legal Profession: Why Do Law Firms Still Have So Few Female Partners?" *UCLA Law Review* 42:1631–1688.

FRENCH, STEVE. 2000. "Of Problems, Pitfalls and Possibilities: A Comprehensive Look at Female Attorneys and Law Firm Partnership." *Women's Rights Law Reporter* 21:189–216.

GARCIA-LOPEZ, GLADYS. 2008. "'Nunca Te Toman en Cuenta [They Never Take You into Account]': The Challenges of Inclusion and Strategies for Success of Chicana Attorneys." *Gender and Society* 22.5:590–612.

GLATER, JONATHAN D. March 26, 2001. "Women Are Close to Being Majority of Law Students." *New York Times*.

HAGAN, JOHN, & FIONA KAY. 2007. "Even Lawyers Get the Blues: Gender, Depression, and Job Satisfaction in Legal Practice." *Law and Society Review* 41.1:51–78.

HEINZ, JOHN P., et al. 1999. "Lawyers and Their Discontents: Findings from a Survey of the Chicago Bar," *Indiana Law Journal* 74:735–57.

HERSCH, JONI. 2003. "The New Labor Market for Lawyers: Will Female Lawyers Still Earn Less?" *Cardozo Women's Law Journal* 10:1–59.

HULL, KATHLEEN. 1999. "The Paradox of the Contented Female Lawyer." *Law and Society Review* 33:687–702.

HULL, KATHLEEN E., & ROBERT L. NELSON. 2000. "Assimilation, Choice, or Constraint? Testing Theories of Gender Differences in the Careers of Lawyers." *Social Forces* 79:229–264.

KAY, FIONA M. et al. 2004a. *Turning Points and Transitions: A Longitudinal Study of Ontario Lawyers from 1975 to 2002*. Report Submitted to the Law Society of Upper Canada. Toronto, ON: The Law Society of Upper Canada.

—— 2004b. *Contemporary Lawyers: Diversity and Change in Ontario's Legal Profession*. Report Submitted to the Law Society of Upper Canada. Toronto, ON: The Law Society of Upper Canada.

—— 2006. "Growing Diversity and Emergent Change: Gender and Ethnicity in the Legal Profession." pp. 203–236 in *Calling for Change: Women, Law and the Legal Profession*, edited by Elizabeth A. Sheehy and Sheila McIntyre. Ottawa: University of Ottawa Press.

KORZEC, REBECCA. 1997. "Working on the 'Mommy-Track': Motherhood and Women Lawyers." *Hastings Women's Law Journal* 8:117–140.

MATTESSICH, PAUL, & CHERYL HEILMAN. 1990. "The Career Paths of Minnesota Law School Graduates: Does Gender Make a Difference?" *Law and Inequality* 9:59–114.

MENKEL-MEADOW, CARRIE. 1988. "The Feminization of the Legal Profession: The Comparative Sociology of Women Lawyers." pp. 196–255 in *Lawyers in Society* (vol. 3), edited by R. Abel and P. Lewis. Berkeley: University of California Press.

MUELLER, CHARLES W., & JEAN E. WALLACE. 1996. "Justice and the Paradox of the Contented Female Worker." *Social Psychological Quarterly* 59.4:338–49.

MULTICULTURAL WOMEN ATTORNEYS NETWORK, THE FEDERAL BAR ASSOCIATION, AND THE NATIVE AMERICAN BAR ASSOCIATION. 1998. "The Burdens of Both, The Privileges of Neither: A Report on the Experiences of Native American Women Lawyers."

NATIONAL ASSOCIATION FOR LAW PLACEMENT. (2007). "Minority Women Still Underrepresented in Law Firm Partnership Ranks – Change in Diversity of Law Firm Leadership Very Slow Overall." Washington, DC: National Association for Law Placement.

——2009a. "How Much Do Associates Work?" Washington, DC: National Association for Law Placement.

——2009b. "Women and Minorities in Law Firms by Race and Ethnicity." Washington, DC: National Association for Law Placement.

NOONAN, MARY, & MARY E. CORCORAN. 2004. "The Mommy Track and Partnership: Temporary Delay or Dead End?" *The Annals of the American Academy of Political and Social Science* 596:130–150.

NOONAN, MARY, CORCORAN, MARY E., & PAUL N. COURANT. 2008. "Is the Partnership Gap Closing for Women? Cohort Differences in the Sex Gap in Partnership Chances." *Social Science Research* 37:156–179.

PHELPS, E. S. 1972. "The Statistical Theory of Racism and Sexism." *American Economic Review* 62:659–666.

REICHMAN, NANCY, & JOYCE S. STERLING. 2001. "Recasting the Brass Ring: Deconstructing and Reconstructing Workplace Opportunities for Women Lawyers." *Capital University Law Review* 29:923–977.

RHODE, DEBORAH. 2001. "Balanced Lives: Changing the Culture of Legal Practice." A report by the American Bar Association's Commission on Women in the Profession. Washington, DC: American Bar Association.

SCHWARTZ, FELICE. 1989. "Executives and Organizations: Management Women and the New Facts of Life." *Harvard Business Review* 67:65–76.

SIMPSON, GWYNED. 1996. "The Plexiglass Ceiling: The Careers of Black Women Lawyers." *Career Development Quarterly* 45:173–188.

SMART, CAROL. 1995. *Law, Crime, and Sexuality*. London: Sage.

WALLACE, JEAN. 2004. *Juggling It All: A Study of Lawyers' Work, Home, and Family Demands and Coping Strategies*. Newtown, PA: Law School Admission Council.

———. 2008. "Parenthood and Commitment to the Legal Profession: Are Mothers Less Committed than Fathers?" *Journal of Family and Economic Issues* 29: 478–495.

WALLACE, JEAN E., & MARISA C. YOUNG. 2008. "Parenthood and Productivity: A Study of Demands, Resources, and Family-Friendly Firms." *Journal of Vocational Behavior* 72:110–122.

YOUNG, MARISA C., & JEAN E. WALLACE. 2009. "Family Responsibilities, Productivity, and Earnings: A Study of Gender Differences among Canadian Lawyers." *Journal of Family and Economic Issues* 30:305–319.

ENDNOTE

1. See Bradwell v Illinois 1872 "Man is or should be women's protector. The paramount destiny and mission of woman are to fulfill the noble and benign offices of wife and mother. This is the law of the Creator.

BIOGRAPHICAL STATEMENTS

JODY CLAY-WARNER is an Associate Professor of Sociology at the University of Georgia.

JENNIFER MCMAHON-HOWARD is an Assistant Professor of Criminal Justice at Kennesaw State University.

KATIE JAMES is a doctoral student in the Department of Sociology at the University of Georgia.

SECTION VI

A Note on Women and Terrorism

37

Women's Attitudes toward the Threat of Terror

Ramona Brockett, Jonathan C. Odo, and Peter C. Ezekwenna

The fear of terrorism is a reality that had not been a part of the social landscape in America until September 11, 2001. America was victimized. Even further, America waged a "war on terror" in response to this victimization against those in the Middle East and others around the world who despise the philosophy and way of life that America calls "freedom." Having done so, this has given rise to a social problem and new form of violence in America—terrorism. While victimization and threat are not new criminological phenomena for people in America, especially women who have suffered domestic abuse and rape, the fear or threat of terrorism presents yet another crease in the analysis of victimization that affects the coping mechanisms of those who have historically been victims.

The four major objectives of this chapter are (1) to measure the fear of the threat of terrorism and its impact on American women who have traditionally suffered violence and domestic abuse; (2) to analyze whether the threat of terrorism has had more or less of an effect on American women who have chronically suffered from the victimization of violence and domestic abuse—as opposed to those who have not had a history of domestic abuse or violence; (3) to establish an understanding of the reaction of those women who have been victimized through domestic abuse or violence; and (4) to distinguish the reasoning behind difference in the reactions of these women to the threat of terrorism brought on by the acts of 9/11.

DOMESTIC ABUSE AND PATRIARCHAL TERRORISM

Analyzing the impact of the threat of global terrorism on women in America who have suffered domestic abuse must include an analysis of "terrorism" and its impact on victims of violence. In 1995, Johnson defined two types of domestic abuse and violence while using data from the 1985 Second National Family Violence Survey—couple violence and patriarchal terrorism. According to Johnson, "couple violence" is common among both men and women. He found that this type of domestic violence does not occur frequently. In fact, his findings concluded that this type of domestic abuse is illusive in that there is not a pattern of escalation; further, it tends not to be physically injurious (Johnson, 1995).

Johnson's second finding of "patriarchal terrorism" differs from the first. This is the first instance where he uses the term *terrorism* to define a violent domestic occurrence. Here, this type of violence, or domestic terrorism, is perpetrated by men toward women escalating over time in both frequency and severity. This violence is not only physical, but, through the use of control, it includes threats, isolation, and economic subordination (p. 284). Further, the roots or historical aspect of this violence comes from a Western family tradition that is rooted in patriarchy, where the home is dominated by the male.

Carlson, in 1997, similarly describes woman abuse as patriarchal terrorism as defined by Johnson. That definition includes patterns of behavior that involve physical, emotional, psychological, verbal, and sexual abuse for the purpose of controlling and demeaning a woman (Carlson, 1997). The definition in itself is synonymous with the act of terrorism. Emotionally, the result of this type of terrorism perpetrated against women produces specific cognitive and behavioral responses that include anger, anxiety, fear, low self-esteem, depression, risk of suicide, confusion, feelings of being overwhelmed, memory loss, poor concentration, suspicion, paranoia, and the recurring trauma of abuse and avoidance of the emotions associated with it (Dutton-Douglas & Dionne, 1991). Further, this type of abuse, albeit terrorism, causes a condition known as posttraumatic stress disorder (Thomas, 2003). Dissociation is a resulting symptom associated with domestic violence and, as a contributing result of posttraumatic stress disorder, it allows the battered woman to separate from her emotional, mental, and physical self (Abel, 2001). In essence, this type of abuse causes the woman to separate from her emotions in order to cope with the trauma. Hence, the definition of patriarchal terrorism and the resulting psychological disorders that affect the victims' cognitive and behavioral patterns of reaction lay the groundwork for understanding the post-9/11 effect global terrorism may have in the lives of those American women who have historically, albeit chronically, suffered domestic abuse.

Similarly, the effects of global terrorism have been found to have a similar effect on the psychological and cognitive behaviors of women in America (Thomas, 2003). In a study conducted by Thomas measuring the reactions of "midlife women" to the 9/11 tragedy, she found that four to six months after 9/11, 61 percent of the women in the study were still distressed, exhibiting symptoms of fear, sadness, anger, powerlessness, distrust, and vigilance (p. 853). Further, in the aftermath it was found that there was an increased incidence of posttraumatic stress disorder, depression, stress-related physical illness, generalized anxiety disorder, and an unfamiliar sense of vulnerability regarding the safety of the home (Pyszczynski, Solomon, & Greenberg, 2003). The theoretical framework upon which these studies of women's stress were premised included terror management theory. Terror management theory, which was formulated in 1984, posits that events that produce acute awareness of death will cause humans to buffer existential anxiety through proximal and distal defenses due to death anxiety brought about by terrorist threat (Thomas, 2003). Theoretically, this seems to explain the similarity in the cognitive reactions of women who have been abused by their spouses and those who react to the potential threat of terror. Actually, both forms of "terrorism" bring about the same result—fear, anxiety, and helplessness. This further aids in explaining the benign reaction to the threat of global terrorism brought on by the events of 9/11 by women who have suffered abuse in the home.

Women who have historically suffered chronic domestic abuse reacted differently to the fear of terrorism than and those who have not. While a comparison of abuse suffered by those women who are victimized in their homes and those who suffer from the threat of victimization as a result of the actions perpetrated against the United States after the 9/11 attacks may seem spurious, the fear of threat is strikingly similar. Further, knowing and understanding the abused woman's fear of post-9/11 global terrorism must be understood within the context of paternal terrorism. The woman who has been abused in the home reacts differently to the threat of 9/11 terror than the woman who has never suffered abuse. Further, because the same mechanisms for coping with abuse occur within the domestic sphere of patriarchal terrorism as occur in the global sphere of post-9/11 terrorism, the similarities between them are characterized by the cognitive reaction of the women as victims of these types of violence.

In the studies conducted by researchers, findings show that earlier life trauma heightens susceptibility to posttraumatic stress disorder when these victims are exposed to subsequent trauma (Brewin, Andrews, & Valentiner, 2000). Further, researchers found that women who had suffered previous trauma and violence in their lives had a "tempered" response to the 9/11 tragedy (Thomas, 2003). Several factors influence this tempered reaction including cultural background, age, economic circumstances, sexual orientation, experiences in the victim's family of origin, and the victim's level of intelligence (Carlson, 1997). The abused woman reacts to the stress of the violence actually occurring in the home as well as the anticipated stress (Mitchell & Hodson, 1983). In fact, women who had backgrounds of previous trauma and violence felt as though these experiences helped them cope with the trauma of the 9/11 incidents because they are familiar with the trauma associated with terrorism in domestic violence.

On the other hand, researchers found that women who had never suffered domestic violence or patriarchal terrorism had a hard time coping with the anticipated threat of another post-9/11 attack. In fact, in the Thomas study (2003) the findings showed an increased incidence of posttraumatic stress disorder, generalized anxiety disorder, fear, sadness, anger, distrust, and other psychopathology among women who had not previously been abused. This finding is relevant as women who had never suffered abuse react to the potential threat of a post-9/11 terrorism attack in the same way the abused woman reacts to the threat of patriarchal terrorism in the home. In fact, it has been found that the abused woman reacts to the stress of the violence actually occurring in the home as well as the anticipated stress associated with the possibility of its reoccurrence (Mitchell & Hodson, 1983). What emerges from these findings is the difference between those who have traditionally suffered terrorism in the form of domestic violence, and those whose experience with terrorism came about as a result of the 9/11 events. While women who have suffered violence in the home react to the threat of post-9/11 terror as survivors of domestic violence, women who have never suffered patriarchal terrorism react to the threat of post-9/11 terror similarly to those women who react toward those who perpetrate patriarchal terrorism in the home.

TERRORISM AND THE OPPRESSION OF WOMEN

One common theme within patriarchal terrorism and the threat of post-9/11 terrorist threat is the effect it has on the oppression of women. Patriarchal terrorism is based in the Western philosophy of patriarchy, with the cornerstone of its philosophy lying in the oppression or secondary citizenship of women (Johnson, 1995). The result is the justification of the act of violence in the home because that sphere is controlled by the man through subjugation of the woman. Further, in patriarchal terrorism through emotional, physical, and economic oppression the woman is victimized and rendered helpless through the act of domestic violence. The result is a feeling of fear, lack of control, helplessness, and hopelessness on the part of the victim who, in the case of patriarchal terrorism, is the woman. The resulting fear comes from the basis of the justification of oppression as the woman's classification is that of a secondary citizen who neither has power, legitimacy, or authenticity within the framework of the home or society.

Interestingly, in an article written by Dr. Karla Cunningham comparing cross-regional trends in terrorism, and specifically in female terrorism, something very similar to patriarchal terrorism happens with women in these societies. Cunningham notes terrorist organizations who are practicing global terrorism tend to come from societies where the women are oppressed and treated as secondary citizens (2003, p. 172). She notes that similar to the Ku Klux Klan (KKK) and the Third Reich, terrorist networks like Al-Qaeda tend to be male dominated and discriminatory toward women. Although the terrorist organization may use women to carry out its terrorist acts, these women who are used as suicide bombers are invisible within the terrorist organizations, and their roles deeply embedded within the constructs of their social networks make them marginally important (Cunningham, 2003). When these organizations use women to carry out their terrorist regimens, these women's participation is less authentic and less legitimate because they are politically peripheralized due to their status as women (p. 175). Further, their status as women prevents them from having a voice subjecting them to doing what they are told and renders them inconsequential and unimportant. The consequences of the terrorist actions they are forced to participate in may result in death, and because of their status that result is again of no importance. This, in itself, is a form of violence similar to domestic violence or patriarchal terrorism because the use of women for such acts (i.e., suicide bombers) represents violence perpetrated toward women; they are merely being used as a tool to promote the terrorist mission.

A comparison of patriarchal terrorism and global terrorism or terrorist threat provides an interesting comparison of similarities between the actors—the perpetrator and the victim. As illustrated by the definition of patriarchal terrorism, oppression and victimization are the cornerstone of male domination and violence toward the female victim. Further, Western patriarchal philosophy is embedded within the operationalization of the terrorism resulting in fear. Women—who are considered secondary citizens and ancillary because they are not seen as an authentic part of legitimate society rendering them helpless, hopeless, and unimportant—allow the resulting domestic violence to occur. Terrorist networks similar to Al-Qaeda, which have threatened the United States since the 9/11 tragedy—view the roles of women in society similarly, using their women in violent, destructive, and life-threatening ways to promote their networks of terror.

The purpose of this chapter is to analyze the reaction of American women who suffer from domestic violence, or patriarchal terrorism to the perceived threat of post-9/11 terrorism. As we see from a review of the literature and an analysis of theoretical perspectives, it appears American women who have suffered trauma, violence, or domestic violence have a benign reaction to the threat of terrorism. Further, those who have never suffered trauma prior to 9/11 suffer the same symptoms as those women who have experienced domestic violence or patriarchal terrorism. What becomes more interesting and even complex is that women who fear the threat of potential post-9/11 terrorism experience a cognitive response to trauma similar to those victims of domestic violence.

AMERICA'S ASSAULT ON DOMESTIC VIOLENCE VERSUS ITS WAR ON TERROR

It is apparent from the literature that patriarchal terrorism and the threat of terrorism evoke the same cognitive response by American women. In order to rescue women who experience trauma either by the hand of a patriarchal terrorist or the threat of a post-9/11 global terrorist attack, there must be significant intervention tools in place to prevent the violence from continuing to occur, ultimately providing an intervention for the victim. With regard to the nation's "assault on domestic violence," a combination of external and internal factors such as policing strategies along with mental health services have been employed to address this assault (Hamilton & Coates, 1993). The message to the victim and the perpetrator is that the impact of the violence does not end when the victim leaves the relationship; instead, as this trauma impacts society at large it must be addressed as a major public and mental health problem. Similarly, the war on terror must be approached in terms of intervention.

Prior to the early 1990s, domestic violence left untreated resulted in police visiting the domicile of the assault and walking away, often leaving the perpetrator and victim in the same home with deadly results (Neilsen, Endo, & Ellington, 1992). Analysis of intervention strategies led to an assault on domestic violence, which promotes coping and stress mechanisms that help promote not only the protection of the victim, but also cognitive strategies to move beyond violence and toward safety. This intervention strategy promotes cooperation with police, health care workers, and mental health professionals.

Similarly, with regard to the war on terror, Sarbin (2003) notes that successful suppression of terrorism requires continuous, patient, undramatic civilian work and cooperation with other countries including coordination within American government for "a systematic approach addressing what to do before, during and after a potential terrorist attack" (p. 153). Sarbin points specifically to the 1993 terrorist plot to bomb the New York Lincoln and Holland tunnels, along with their attempt to destroy 11 American passenger planes in Asia in 1995 (p. 154). Therefore, intervention strategies have been successful in thwarting terrorism both in domestic violence, or patriarchal terrorism, and global terrorism. These types of strategies can ultimately serve as successful coping tools and mechanisms for American women who experience trauma resulting from terrorism.

The next portion of this chapter will analyze the results of a survey taken of women on the East Coast and their response to the threat of terrorism. This analysis seeks to establish the validity of the literature and its significance for women's cognitive response to patriarchal terrorism and the threat of global terrorism, determining whether American women who have previously experienced trauma and domestic violence have a benign response to the threat of terror post-9/11.

METHODOLOGY

Data for this study was analyzed by the second and third authors. The data were taken from a 23-item administered survey created to measure American women's perception of the threat of a post-9/11 terrorist attack on the United States. The measuring instrument was given to a random sample of women at various locations on the East Coast who were asked to complete the questionnaire.

Of all the participants, 11 percent were Caucasoid, 86 percent were Negroid, and, "other" represented the remaining 3 percent. The age of respondents varied from 17 to 60. Most of the participants were single (89 percent), while the married (10 percent), and divorced (2 percent), made up the rest of the participants. When asked if they feel safe since 9/11, the categories and percentages of response included: "no" (68 percent), "somewhat" (31 percent), and "yes" (2 percent). Of the participants, 81 percent were not victims of domestic violence, while 18 percent were victims of domestic violence. When measuring violence, in general, the question "Have you been a victim of violence in general?" received a response of "no" (55 percent) and "yes" (44 percent).

Next, in order to determine whether women who had experienced domestic violence felt safe, or less safe since the attacks on 9/11, 53 percent of the women who were victims of domestic violence expressed that they felt "less safe," while 15 percent of these same women indicated that they felt "safe." Those women who were victims of violence in general responded that they felt "less safe" (35 percent) and that they felt "safe," (32 percent) since the attacks.

In order to determine whether women who had not experienced domestic violence felt "safe," or "less safe," since the attacks on 9/11, the data indicated 50 percent of the women who were not victims of domestic violence expressed feeling "less safe," whereas 27.4 percent of these same women indicated feeling "safe." Those women who were not victims of violence in general responded by indicating that 36 percent of them felt "less safe," and 12 percent of these same women felt "safe" since the 9/11 attacks. Finally, when all of these women—those who suffered violence and domestic abuse along with those who did not—were asked, "Do you think America will suffer another terrorist attack?" 86 percent responded "yes" and 11 percent responded "no."

DISCUSSION

Overall, results from the data gave a sense of insecurity among the subjects that participated in the study. The 9/11 terrorist attack on America has undermined a great feeling of safety and confidence in their environment. Further, it is clear that indications from the literature correspond with the survey. Women who have not experienced domestic abuse and violence tend to react to the threat of terrorism differently than those who have experienced patriarchal terrorism and violence. While these surveys seem to indicate that women regardless of their experience with domestic abuse and violence seem to feel less safe since the 9/11 attacks, their feeling of safety seems to vary. For instance, those who never suffered domestic violence had a greater feeling of safety than those who were abused. Further, those women who suffered a form of violence felt safer than those who had not suffered violence. Hence, these findings would indicate that the experience of violence determines the extent to which the American woman may cognitively experience the threat of a post-9/11 attack. This may influence her ability to cope.

CONCLUSION

America is a nation whose experience with terrorism coming from outside its borders is limited. In fact, as seen by the literature, the experience of terrorism has been through domestic violence in the form of paternal terrorism. Terrorism is violence, and the data seem to indicate that those American women who experienced violence may experience the threat of a post-9/11 terrorist attack differently than those who have not experienced violence. As the literature indicates, their cognitive ability to cope is vastly different than those women who have not had the same experiences with violence.

REFERENCES

ABEL, E. M. (2001, December). Comparing the social service utilization, exposure to violence, and trauma symptomology of domestic violence female "victims" and female batterers. *Journal of Family Violence, 16*(4), 401–420.

BREWIN, C. R., ANDREWS, B., & VALENTINER, J. D. (2000). Meta-analysis of risk factors for posttraumatic stress disorder in trauma exposed adults. *Journal of Consulting and Clinical Psychology, 68*(5), 748–766.

CARLSON, B. E. (1997). A stress and coping approach to intervention with abused women. *Family Relations, 46*(3), 291–299.

CUNNINGHAM, K. J. (2003). Cross-regional trends in female terrorism. *Studies in Conflict & Terrorism, 26*, 171–195.

DUTTON-DOUGLAS, M. A., & DIONNE, D. (1991). Counseling and shelter services for battered women. In M. Steinman (Ed.), *Woman battering: Policy responses* (pp. 113–130). Cincinnati, OH: Anderson.

HAMILTON, B., & COATES, J. (1993). Perceived helpfulness and use of professional services by abused women. *Journal of Family Violence, 8*, 313–324.

JOHNSON, M. P. (1995). Patriarchal terrorism and common couple violence: Two forms of violence against women. *Journal of Marriage and Family, 7*, 283–294.

MITCHELL, R. E., & HODSON, C. A. (1983). Coping with domestic violence: Social support and psychological health among battered women. *American Journal of Community Psychology, 11*, 629–654.

NEILSEN, J. M., ENDO, R. K., & ELLINGTON, B. L. (1992). Social isolation and wife abuse: A research report. In E. C. Viano (Ed.), *Intimate violence: Interdisciplinary perspectives* (pp. 49–59). Washington, DC: Hemisphere.

PYSZCZYNSKI, T., SOLOMON, S., & GREENBERG, J. (2003). In the wake of 9/11: The psychology of terror. Washington, DC: American Psychological Association.

SARBIN, T. R. (2003). The metaphor-to-myth transformation with special reference to the "war terrorism." *Peace and Conflict: Journal of Peace Psychology, 9*(2), 149–157.

THOMAS, S. P. (2003). None of us will ever be the same again. Reactions of America women to 9/11. *Health Care for Women International, 24*, 853–867.

Conclusions

Looking to the Future

Roslyn Muraskin

According to Catherine MacKinnon, "[e]quality in human societies is commonly affirmed but rarely practiced. As a principle, it can be fiercely loved, passionately sought, highly vaunted, sentimentally assumed, complacently taken for granted, and legally guaranteed. Its open detractors are few. Yet despite general consensus on equality as a value, no society is organized on equality principles. Few lives are lived in equality, even in democracies. As a fact, social equality is hard to find anywhere" (2001, p. 2).

Then how do we conclude? Women are committing crimes at a higher rate than ever before. Have we failed to remember the women? Are women not deserving of the same rights and privileges as men?

According to the *Universal Declaration of Human Rights* (1948):

Article 1. All human beings are born free and equal in dignity and rights. They are endowed with reason and conscience and should act toward one another in a spirit of brotherhood.

Article 6. Everyone has the right to recognition everywhere as a person before the law.

This Declaration of Human Rights is a document of international rights and is a component of international law. But are all human beings born free and equal? "Sex equality is often guaranteed by law, including where sex inequality is pervasive in society. More imagined than real in life, sex equality guarantees vary dramatically, its observance ranging from obvious to anathema. Around the world and throughout history, in settings from the institutional to the intimate, sex equality remains more promise than fact" (MacKinnon, p. 3).

In the words of Justice Ruth Bader Ginsburg, "[t]he classification man/dependent woman is the prototypical sex line in the law and has all the earmarks of self-fulfilling prophecy." That discrimination against women is a long tradition is an understatement.

Words are more than a collective art; they are simultaneously a collective cage. Unconscious and unquestioned obedience to established meanings bind humankind with steel bands to both the good and bad of yesterday. Law is called upon to serve goals other than predictability and certainty, which logic being what it is, walk backwards. The paramount obligation of law is to secure, to make safe, equal rights and justice under the law. This is the daunting task of the remarkably few words which comprise the United States Constitution. (Thomas, 1991, p. xx)

We have come a long way since the days of Rousseau[1] (1906), when he wrote that "[t]he whole education of women ought to be relative to men. To please them, to be useful to them, to make themselves loved and honored by them, to educate them when young, to care for them when grown, to counsel them, to console them, and to make his life sweet and agreeable to them—these are the duties at all times, and what should be taught to them [*women*]from their infancy."

Even a longer way back since Napoleon Bonaparte spoke, "nature intended women to be our slaves; . . . they are our property, we are not theirs. They belong to us, just as a tree that bears fruit belongs to a gardener. . . . Women are nothing but machines for producing children."

And from Lord Chesterfield, "women, then, are only children of larger growth: they have an entertaining tattle, and sometimes wit; but for solid, reasoning good sense, I never knew in my life one that had it or who reasoned or acted consequentially for four and twenty hours together."

In the words of Aristotle, "we may thus conclude that it is a general law that there should be naturally ruling elements and elements naturally ruled . . . the rule of the freeman over the slave is one kind of rule; that of the male over the female another . . . the slave is entirely without the faculty of deliberation; the female indeed possesses it, but in a form which remains inconclusive." Remember that the word *man* meant human being; the males appropriated it.

As we have learned throughout this work, women have had to struggle to be considered persons under the law and to be afforded the same opportunities as men before the law. The struggle continues. Men may have been considered to be the protectors of women, but in the world we live today, every woman and man deserves to be given the same opportunity to succeed. The criminal justice system has an obligation to treat both genders on a par with each other. There is no room for disparate treatment. History has taught us that women have suffered as much and perhaps more than men. As confirmed in the Declaration of Seneca Falls in 1848, "[T]he history of mankind is a history of repeated injuries and usurpations on the part of man toward woman, having in direct object the establishment of an absolute tyranny over her."

The Fourteenth Amendment to the Constitution of the United States declares that "no state . . . shall . . . deny to any person within its jurisdiction the equal protection of the laws." That amendment is to be applied equally to women and men. Hopefully in today's world we no longer adhere to the tenets of the words of Justice Brenner as he delivered the majority opinion in the 1908 case of *Muller v. Oregon:*

That woman's physical structure and the performance of maternal functions place her at a advantage in the struggle for subsistence is obvious. This is especially true when the bu of motherhood are upon her. . . .

---

[1]These following quotes can be found referenced in a work by Barbara Sinclair Deckard, *The Women's Move* published in 1979.

[H]istory discloses the fact that woman has always been dependent upon man. He established his control at the outset by superior physical strength, and the control in various forms. . . . She is properly placed in a class by herself, and that legislation designed for her protection may be sustained, even when like legislation is not necessary for men, and could not be sustained.

Admittedly, laws can discriminate, but such discrimination becomes unconstitutional when it is judged to be arbitrary and serves no legitimate purpose. *Frontiero v. Richardson* (1973) needed one more vote to declare that *sex was a suspect classification*, although it did concede that differential treatment accorded men and women serves no practical purpose. Today, the attitude of the criminal justice system seems to have changed. We recognize that women are victims of crime and that they, too, perpetuate crime. We also recognize that equal treatment is demanded and is an absolute necessity. Having moved from traditional homebound social roles into positions of power and influence, women have become more assertive and aggressive while capable of competing with men in all realms of life. As noted throughout this work, litigation, changes in law, and constitutional amendments have held the U.S. criminal justice system to task in demanding that women are properly defined as people and are deserving of all the rights and privileges of men. Doing otherwise would make our system of law a public disgrace.

From cases of domestic violence, where traditionally the abuser was taken for a walk around the block, to today when there are mandatory and pro-arrest policies, to maternal drug use during pregnancy and the complex legal and ethical questions that pit the rights of pregnant women against those of the fetus (rights that are nonexistent under *Roe*), to the systematic white racism that exists in the United States with regard to executed black women, to woman serial killers, to the impact of gender decisions with regard to young girls, to female involvement in acts of terrorism, and to cases of rape that are treated differently from any other crime, we find ourselves overwhelmed with women's rights and factors of privacy.

In the words of MacKinnon (2001), "[u]nless something is done, even if recent rates of measurable progress for elite women continue, no American now alive will live in a society of sex equality nor will their children or their children's children" (p. 2). MacKinnon continues: "More imagined than in real life, sex equality in law tends to be more formal or hypothetical than substantive and delivered. In legal application, the meaningfulness of sex equality guarantees varies dramatically, its observance ranging from obvious to anathema. Around the world and throughout history, in settings from the institutional to the intimate, sex equality remains more promise than fact" (p. 3).

In the words of philosopher Richard Rorty (as noted in this text), to be a woman "is not yet the name of a way of being human" (Person, 1992). "His formulation at once recognizes that woman's lives would not be 'human' by the standard set by men, and that women's reality has not been reflected in the standard for what 'human' is. It invites redefinition of the human standard in the image of women's realities and unrealized possibilities, as well as proposes change in women's situation to meet the existing standard of a 'human' life. Can one challenge the validity of a standard and assert a right to the benefits of its application at the same time? Are women 'human'?" (MacKinnon, p. 3).

Although litigation provides an opportunity for all persons to have a role in altering their conditions of life, a judicial opinion requiring such comprehensive changes does not necessarily bring about such change. We have found that litigation is a catalyst for change rather than an automatic mechanism for ending the wrongs found. We know that within the criminal law, litigation indicates that disparate treatment of any kind is not permissible absent meaningful and objective justification. From Lombroso to the present, "criminological thought has been wrought with the sexism inherent in assuming that there exist two distinct classes of women—those on pedestals and those in the gutter" (Muraskin, 1989).

Throughout history, we have lived with a double standard. Disparate treatment can no longer exist, for it is all about women and men—justice and fairness. And we must never forget the ladies, for OR ELSE WE WILL HAVE *WOMEN AND JUSTICE: IS IT A CRIME?*

REFERENCES

DECKARD, B. S. (1979). *The women's movement: Political, socioeconomic, and psychological issues* (2nd ed.). New York: Harper & Row.

MACKINNON, C. A. (2001). *Sex equality.* New York: Foundation Press.

MURASKIN, R. (1989). Disparity of correctional treatment: Development of a measurement instrument. Unpublished doctoral dissertation. City University of New York.

PERSON, G. B. (ed.). (1992). Feminism and pragmatism. *Tanner Lectures of Human Values,* 1(7).

ROUSSEAU, J. J. (1906). *Emile, or a treatise on education.* (W. H. Payne, ed.) As found in Cynthia Ozick, "Women and Creativity" in Vivian Gornick and Barbara Moran, eds., *Women in Sexist Society.* New York: Signet 1971.

THOMAS, C. S. (1991). *Sex discrimination in a nutshell* (2nd ed.). St. Paul, MN: West.

UNITED NATIONS. (1948, December 10). *Universal declaration of human rights.* Adopted and proclaimed by General Assembly Resolution 217 A (111).

CASES

FRONTIERO v. RICHARDSON, 411 U.S. 677 (1973).

MULLER v. OREGON, 208 U.S. 412 (1908).

Index